St. Martin's Paperbacks Titles
by Gerry Spence

FROM FREEDOM TO SLAVERY
OF MURDER AND MADNESS

Available in hardcover from St. Martin's
Press

HOW TO ARGUE AND WIN EVERY TIME

GERRY SPENCE

OF MURDER AND MADNESS

St. Martin's Paperbacks

OF MURDER AND MADNESS

Copyright © 1983 by Gerry Spence.

Cover photograph by Garth Dowling/Jackson Hole News.

Library of Congress Catalog Card Number: 82-45968

ISBN: 0-312-95687-8

Printed in the United States of America

Doubleday hardcover edition/October 1983
St. Martin's Paperbacks edition/October 1995

10 9 8 7 6 5 4 3 2 1

To my angel mother

AUTHOR'S NOTE

The story of Joe Esquibel is based on voluminous trial transcripts, court documents, files, Carbon County welfare and Wyoming State Hospital records received as exhibits in the trials, investigative reports, and my own more than seven years of personal experience with Joe, his mother and family, and the numerous witnesses in the case. In several instances the names of certain persons have been changed to protect their identity when it was believed desirable.

The characters Mona Lee Murphy, as Sharon Esquibel's mother, and Harvey Watkins, as assistant director of the Carbon County Welfare Department, are purely fictional, and all dialogue attributable to them as well as the story of their lives as portrayed in the book are also fictional, and are not intended to resemble any person, living or dead. These two characters were invented for dramatic purposes and for the economy of telling the story since there were numerous caseworkers and welfare personnel involved in the lives of the Esquibels over the more than two decades covered by this book. However, Sharon Esquibel's mother actually worked for many years as a secretary at the Carbon County Welfare Department and was a good and respected citizen in the town of Rawlins, Wyoming. She was involved from time to time with the Esquibel family and was a close friend of numerous caseworkers and office personnel who dealt with the Esquibel family over the years, and she witnessed Sharon's death at the hands of Joe Esquibel in the welfare office when Joe shot Sharon in the presence of several witnesses mentioned in the book. The testimony of Sharon's mother and references by other witnesses to her have been attributed to the fictional character, Mona Lee Murphy, and surnames and other facts have been changed wherever necessary to accommodate this fiction.

The substance of all trial testimony attributed to Sharon's mother is true, as is all other trial testimony.

I have struggled with how to deal with the problem of cultural labeling. The words "Chicano" and "Hispanic," which have wide acceptance today, were not in common usage in Wyoming when this story took place, and even today in Rawlins, Wyoming, there is no consensus among Spanish-speaking people of Mexican origin as to the noun of choice, some still preferring "Spanish" or "Mexican-American" to "Hispanic" or "Chicano." It was my decision to use the words in common usage at the time hoping that this decision will not be interpreted as insensitivity on my part.

1

JOE ESQUIBEL looked acceptable in his coffin, considering it was lined in baby blue satin and was too small. I hadn't gone to the funeral, but Pam told me about it later. She was a narrow-hipped, broad-shouldered, flat-bellied woman with brown hair and blue eyes who usually looked tired. She wore an old-fashioned navy blue dress she borrowed from her own mother. The dress was too long, and she admitted she looked like hell in it, but then nobody is supposed to look good at funerals, except the corpse. Everyone, everything, every flower and bug and bird has its time, and the funeral is the time for the corpse. She said the main point of contention she had with Agneda, the mother, was the suit he wore. Pam said he looked awful. She said she told Agneda, "It's an old man's suit, and Joe is not an old man." But Pam was his last woman.

"He look good," Agneda answered, and then Pam told me she felt helpless, and had these crazy fantasies about snatching the body, and running off with it to bury him right. She felt a frenzy coming over her. But she tried to be patient with Agneda, the mother, and there was Elma, the sister, and the others standing farther back beside the mortician. Pam wanted to scream out, "He's my man," but she said she knew Agneda would only say something like, "He no is your man. You no marry him." Pam said she knew she had no rights. Love creates no rights.

"Mother, I brought along Joe's nice brown suit, the

one he wore through the trials. He always looked so nice in his brown suit. Here," Pam said, handing Agneda the brown paper bag containing the suit. But, no, she said, Agneda turned away and wouldn't reach for the sack.

"You keep," Agneda said, and then Elma, the sister, a couple of years older than Joe but not much larger than a ten-year-old, came up to Pam and touched her on the hand. Elma had large eyes, which were red and swollen from having wept a long time. People usually commented that Elma had a face like a madonna; it was Elma who had really been the mother to Joe Esquibel. Elma took Pam's hand into her own, and she held it for a while. Finally she said, "Mama bought that suit this mornin' for Joe, and she say it looks like the suits them bankers wear, and she say Joe is as good as them bankers."

The suit on the body was navy blue, with narrow pin stripes, three-pieced, and the hands were crossed and nicely relaxed. He had what looked to be a sapphire ring on his left ring finger. The face was waxen and more yellow than brown, as if the mortician had tried to make the corpse look like a white person. He had jet black hair in a neat crew cut, and one would have to say his features were more regular than anything else. One could tell he had been handsome all right, not like someone well bred, but a more primitive sort of good looks, and he had a small grin on his face—a "shit-eatin' " grin someone later called it. The mortician and the family talked about money. "How much is for the place to put him?" Agneda asked, and her voice was loud enough, but lifeless.

"Oh, you mean the lot?"

"Yeah, the lot," Agneda said.

"That lot is in one of the best parts of the cemetery, and it goes for the standard price of two hundred and twenty-five dollars, same to you as to the president of the bank, Mrs. Esquibel," the black-suited mortician said.

"They don' bury no bank presidents in that part," Elma said in a kind way, speaking mostly to her mother and not meaning to contradict the mortician.

"We want that other lot," Agneda said.

"Oh," the mortician said, "you mean the one down

here in the low side of the cemetery?" He pointed a white, stubby finger to a plat pinned up on the wall. "Well," he said, "that lot is quite a bit cheaper." And then Elma looked up at the man, and in her quiet way Elma said, "We are poor people."

"We are no poor people," Agneda said, and she spoke with a firm voice that sounded like it came from a one-noted flute.

"That lot is a hundred twenty-five," the mortician said. "Standard price."

"Oh." Agneda looked as if she suddenly understood and approved. "And how much for the rock?"

"You mean the headstone?" the mortician asked. "Well, I can give you . . ."

"We are poor people," Elma said.

"Well, a nice stone with his name and the dates and all, well, a hundred twenty-five, too."

"And for the diggin'?" Agneda asked, but her eyes were not like her voice. People said that Agneda Esquibel was in her eyes.

"The whole thing, Mrs. Esquibel, the casket, the lot, the stone, all services—seven hundred dollars. Everything right. Everything okay, you understand?" He patted her lightly on the back and flicked her a smile. "However, I would recommend the other casket. It's a little longer, a little more roomy one would say."

"Is okay," Agneda gestured toward the body.

"She like the blue one," Elma said.

The next morning they buried Joe Esquibel in the low part of the cemetery in Rawlins, Wyoming. I didn't hear about Joe's death until two days later.

I had been hiding out at the ranch trying to get a little rest from my clients, who sometimes ate me alive, and who also kept me eating, when Raymond Whitaker, a brother of the bar, called. The last time he called like this out of the blue, I was writing some poem about hollyhocks, and I was leaning over the deck railing of my little ranch cabin staring down into the clear mountain water which rippled and gurgled by. I tossed a sliver of firewood into the creek, and watched it float on down out of sight, and I felt at peace, because it was hard to be any other way in the presence of the North Fork of the Wind River.

"Gerald," Ray Whitaker said in what sounded like a happy voice, and he always called me "Gerald," like my mother called my father, but everybody else, including my mother and my father, called me Gerry. And so, I called Ray Whitaker "Raymond." "Gerald, what are you doing?"

"I'm writing a poem about being God to the meadow grasses."

"Gerald. You will never be a poet—a great lawyer, yes, but never a poet."

I ignored Raymond Whitaker. "It is a poem about the deistic powers of a man over the helpless grass—about a man who takes over for God by irrigation, by digging this ditch and turning the water on the thirsty meadow. God has been a little derelict here recently, Raymond. Things are too dry." I paused. It was time to let Raymond Whitaker tell me why he was calling, but he was silent. Not like him to be silent, and when he said nothing back, I grew uncomfortable and I began again.

"But God is just getting old," I said. "He's been around a long time—through eons of time, and He's getting a little senile. Can't keep His attention where it belongs. Lets things get dry up here, and then dumps all the water where nobody needs it, and it causes floods. He's a pain in the ass."

"Who is?" Raymond asked as if he hadn't been listening.

"God is," I said. "Hard to manage like any forgetful old man."

"Yeah," Raymond said back, and he cleared his voice and I could tell he was about ready to say whatever it was he had on his mind. "Well, speaking of God and His erratic behavior—I wondered if you'd heard about Joe Esquibel?"

"No," I said. "What about Joe this time?"

"He's dead," Raymond said, just like that. "Buried him a couple a days ago in Rawlins. I didn't go to the funeral or send flowers. Wasn't anything in the paper." And then we talked about Joe being dead for a short time, and Raymond Whitaker hung up before we hardly talked at all. I felt defeated and wasted, and I felt afraid.

I went back out on the deck and I looked down into the innocent water flowing by, lapping and laughing down to the sea. It was the same, seven years ago, when I received the first call from Raymond Whitaker. Then he was cute and contentious and he began as he always did.

"Gerald!"

I stopped him. "Raymond, why did you call? I have been looking at hollyhocks, tall and pink, like gangly choir girls, and I am writing a poem."

"Gerald, you will never be a poet. How will you ever amount to a damn as a lawyer in Riverton, Wyoming? I have called to plague your poor parochial mind with the thought that you are wasting your life."

"Yeah," I said. "What are you doing with yours this afternoon?"

"Well," Raymond Whitaker said. "At least they can never say that I closed down the Little Yellow House." It didn't take much for Raymond Whitaker to get started on the Little Yellow House. "That was an ugly economic sanction to take against the town of Riverton—a serious social crime. Now everybody has to drive a hundred twenty miles to Casper to fornicate at Fifi's." He liked the sound of his words and he let out a little laugh. "But Fifi loves you for it, Gerald. Are you trying any lawsuits? We should try one together some time."

"Sure," I said, not really meaning it.

"Oh yes," Whitaker went on, amusing himself and getting into it now. "Not just any case—not a case of murder with even the slightest defense, but a case of murder totally without redemption—a hopeless case."

"A hopeless case," I echoed.

"Yes. Yes—we will combine our illustrious skills, our supreme beauty as the state's greatest trial lawyers, and we shall show the world the most impossible case of the most guilty, the most desolate and depraved killer, and we will win it together."

"Yes," I said, egging him on a little. I liked to listen to Raymond Whitaker when he got fired up like that.

"He will be a killer who is so obviously guilty that the public will demand that he be hauled away without even a trial," Whitaker went on. "Guilty without grace—a crime so horrendous, so plain, so unimaginative, so sordid and disgusting that there could be nothing left to say in the killer's favor—nothing," he said.

"Absolutely nothing," I echoed.

"And you and I will hold up the system so it can see itself—its own filthy blemishes and its ugly fat wrinkles. We shall . . ."

"We shall take the case, twist it, form it, mold it into that infamous surgical tool and do a proctological examination of the very system itself," I said, mocking Whitaker's style.

"Yes, yes," Whitaker said. "We shall do just that!"

"Why?" I asked.

"Why?" Whitaker seemed shocked. "Why? We will do that to amuse ourselves, of course."

"Yes, of course," I said.

"Come see me some time, Gerald. We will go visit Fifi and her girls. Fifi is always up for visiting celebrities." He hung up the phone. Then he called me a couple of weeks later—wanted to talk about a new case, about a killer named Joe Esquibel, charged with murder, an indefensible case, Raymond Whitaker said.

2

I PACKED my easel, my paints, a fresh canvas and a bucket of brushes into the back of the plum convertible, and in the good morning light of early summer, I headed out across 120 miles of prairie to Wyoming's largest town, Casper, the home of the celebrated lawyer, Raymond B. Whitaker, and of Fifi. I passed through the irrigated fields, by the yellow sunflowers blooming along the road's edge and by the purple alfalfa fields, which were also in full bloom. It was still morning as I drove into Shoshoni, and its streets were empty. The town was a dumpy little place of a couple of hundred souls, good souls, hanging on forlornly. I drove past the Shoshoni bus stop, which used to be a whorehouse, too, before I closed it along with the Little Yellow House. I got no thanks for any of my crusades, not even from the preachers. Now the wisdom of the county was that the womenfolk would be raped by the fuckin' Mexican sheepherders, who came to town with crazy hard-ons, like boars, they said. Mexicans screw anything, you know. Screw like animals. Screw sheep and dogs, and little girls, and Spence will have to carry the responsibility for it on his own shoulders.

The bus stop was an old gray stucco one-story affair and a "Closed" sign hung from the door. "Bus Stop Café" had been painted across the broken glass. Inside, I could see the chairs stacked on top of the tables. Before the whorehouse was closed, the madam, an efficient woman, had her girls waiting tables when the bus came through. Nothing else to do. It was the day's only business, and Christ, that Spence even shut down the bus stop. The madam was a crusty old one, all right, who had her friends. She'd been there a long time, since I was in diapers, she said.

"Well, I know you've been here a long time, Beulah," I said. "But you're gonna have to close 'er down."

"Well, how come, honey?" she asked, and I said, "Just because—because it's against the law. It's that simple," and finally she said, "Ah, go fuck yourself, kid." Then, realizing what she'd said and not wanting to make trouble, she suddenly softened her eyes, like some women can, and she leaned over. "You got a problem, kid?"

"Yeah," I answered, looking hard into her soft eyes, and then she leaned way over to whisper to me.

"Well, honey, why don't we go upstairs and see if we can take care of your little problem?" It made me angry that this madam in a run-down old whorehouse in Shoshoni, Wyoming, could make me stutter and turn red, and I got up to leave.

"Whatsa matter, honey?" she asked, her rough voice coming out nice and sweet, and then she wiggled her shoulders a little and it made the rest of her wiggle all the way down, and I just got the hell out of there.

The next week I invited the mayor of Shoshoni over to the house for a little barbecue in the backyard and told him I had a list of the license numbers of every car that had been parked at or near the Bus Stop Café past midnight for the last three months. I said I sure intended to subpoena every last car owner to testify before a grand jury—and, of course, I'd have to subpoena the mayor, too, because I told him his car was on the list—unless, that is, the mayor wanted to close the place down himself. The mayor looked at me pitifully, a little pale, and he said his car was in his wife's name, and surely I wasn't serious, and I said I was damn well serious.

"What possible harm, Gerry?" he said. "What harm? Them girls go to the doctor every week. Certified clean." He was pleading.

"I know," I said.

"And the sheepherders gotta . . ."

"I know," I interrupted.

"Well, then," he said, as if that settled it.

"Clean isn't the issue, mayor. And sheepherders aren't the issue either. You're missin' the point. The point is that prostitution is against the law," I said, trying not to sound too self-righteous, but feeling that way anyway. I dropped a thick file in front of me on the table, as thick as my thumb, and gave it a little pat. It was just a pile of magazines I'd stuck in the file for effect. "It's all in there," I said. "I'll be back up to Shoshoni in a week," and I gave the mayor my hard look. I never did see the madam again, maybe she went to Thermopolis or Rock Springs or some place where the prosecutor was a reasonable man, and one of the girls went straight. Opened up a laundry in Riverton.

I drove the remaining hundred miles to Casper across the barren prairies, past herds of grazing antelope, past brave little roadstops that waited, nothing much going on, except the gas sign swinging in the wind. I drove past rattlesnakes and prairie dogs and red-tailed hawks that ate the dead rabbits flattened into hair-cakes on the highway by the speeding cars, which were crazy to cross these desolate places and get on with their commerce. I drove into the oil capital of Wyoming. First there was the gasoline refinery, and the industrial section of town devoted to the oil industry, certain warehouses and busy-looking places with stacks of iron and big trucks parked around. It was a place of progress and prosperity. Downtown there were several larger buildings five stories or taller. One was a bank and three were hotels all across from each other on opposite corners, the Gladstone, the Henning, and the Townsend. Major oil companies had their offices in Casper and there was a big stone courthouse where Raymond B. Whitaker himself had been the prosecuting attorney during my own term of office as prosecutor in Riverton. Now he was in private practice up the street a little ways from the courthouse next to the VFW Club. I pulled the convertible to the curb and left the keys in the car. I skipped the parking meter, pushed open the door to the building, and walked past Raymond B. Whitaker's secretary, who paid no attention to me anyway. I opened his office door and I caught him sitting behind his desk drinking his morning coffee with a sort of vacant look in his eyes. His expression didn't change as he saw me walk in. It was as if I'd been there all along.

"Here I am," I said. Whitaker had the face of a Boston terrier—a small nose that refused to hold his glasses up, a protruding lower jaw, and a crooked smile, which usually expressed a sardonic amusement at the stupidity of his fellow man. "I have come to visit Fifi," I announced solemnly.

"At ten o'clock in the morning?" he asked incredulously. "That's indecent."

"Let's go." I walked over to his desk and grabbed him by the arm.

"They shoot people down on the Sand Bar in the daytime," Whitaker said, but he got up anyway and followed me out, ignoring his secretary, who ignored him back.

The old Sand Bar section of Casper was a handful of little shanty houses, mostly converted to cafés and "clubs," as they called them, after-hours joints that sold bad whiskey and offered a variety of girls. The Van Rooms, an old two-story frame affair, was the largest, and it was also the best known. It was obviously falling apart and looked like it needed a man around the place. Raymond Whitaker and I walked onto the sagging old wooden porch and rang the doorbell. A pale blonde opened the door slightly, surveyed us suspiciously, and said Fifi wasn't home. She stood with her face sticking halfway out the door and the sun made her eyes squint and she looked silly and half sick, like the wilted sunflowers in the heat of the midmorning, blinking against the light. Suddenly she recognized Whitaker, and then she quickly opened the door. Whitaker spoke to her like an old army buddy he hadn't seen since Anzio.

"Georgia, Georgia baby, you are a raving beauty this morning. Meet my friend, Gerald Spence, scourge of Fremont County. When the ladies of the night dream their dreams in Fremont County they are nightmares of Gerald Spence, and this is he, the one and only, the man himself, who closed down the Little Yellow House and who comes here to do business with you, instead."

I leaned up against the entryway wall and Whitaker continued his speech. The place was dark and dreary as dark places are in the sober light of day. Whitaker looked around. "This is a nasty time of day," he continued. "Don't be so standoffish, Georgia. Don't be such a prude, darling. It is not immoral for you to be friendly in the daytime. Give us a drink, Georgia. It is totally acceptable for a man to have a drink of good whiskey before noon. Ask my friend Gerald here." Georgia left and brought us each back a coffee cup with straight whiskey. Then she sat down. Whitaker turned to me with that grin. "They serve you whiskey in a cup, in case the po-lice come. But it's really just part of the experience at Fifi's. Drink up, Gerald," he said.

Georgia lit a cigarette. She looked at me absently. "What brings you to Casper?" Then she looked at me as if she were merely surveying one more potato in the bin.

"I came to immortalize you," I said in the best style of Raymond Whitaker.

"Don't give me that shit," she said, and blew smoke up past her nose toward the black ceiling. I thought her being so unfriendly like that was just her way of trying for sophistication.

"I want to paint you," I said. "I brought my paints along." I felt like a boy with his box of crayons in his pocket.

"Jesus Christ, I've heard everything now," she said with a heavy laugh. "You get all kinds of weirdos in this business," she said, looking at Whitaker and then back at me. "No offense," she said.

"Picasso painted the women of . . ."

"Shit, you ain't Picasso, honey. I ain't blind. I ain't drunk neither. Want another one?" I handed her my empty cup.

"Offer her some compensation," Whitaker said over the top of his glasses like a father to a son. The blond woman returned with more whiskey. She was wearing black leotards and a low-cut black blouse out of which parts of her hung somewhat like inverted pears. Her hair looked like the straw from a frayed mat and her lips were as red as a rose.

"I have to paint you." I handed the lady a couple of twenties. She took the bills, stuffed them away, and put on a mock pose that looked like Marilyn Monroe. "How do you want me?"

"Could you, you know, take the clothes off?" I asked sheepishly.

"Yes, by all means, the clothes off," Whitaker said, peering at her over his glasses like a professor suddenly coming alive.

"Are you kidding?" Georgia asked. "What do you think I am? This has gone far enough." You could tell it was Georgia's final word. "If you want to come to the room with me, honey, that's one thing. Taking my clothes off for some weirdo to paint—that's something else again. A workin' girl's got her pride," she said.

"Sorry. Okay," I said. I set up the easel and poured some turpentine for a quick sketch. She sat down on an old wooden café chair. She did have Marilyn Monroe in mind. She wet her red lips and opened her mouth.

"How's this?" she asked as she threw her head back and crossed her legs.

"That's fine," I said.

"That is absolutely superb," Whitaker said.

The turpentine made the place smell better. I sketched with quick dripping undisciplined strokes. The brush could go as it pleased—could go as I went. I outlined her body sitting stiff and straight like a tree bearing irrelevant fruit. Her face was pale as parchment, and that peroxide hair—I thought there was something inherently evil about peroxiding the hair. I painted it orange instead, and as I painted Whitaker watched. The painting made him quiet and you could hear the strokes of the bristle brush against the canvas. After a while I leaned back and measured the leg of the woman against the handle of the brush and I said, "Well, Raymond, tell me about your murder case," and that's all it took, like unleashing the hounds.

"Well, this Mexican shot his white ex-wife between the eyes," he began with an ominous sound in his voice.

"That's nice," I said, stroking the canvas.

"No. No, he shot her in the presence of a bunch of witnesses, eight of them—in broad daylight in the welfare office in Rawlins—and one of the witnesses was a deputy sheriff who had his gun drawn, and this dumb bastard shot her anyway just to prove that he intended to kill her, I guess, just to establish that it was premeditated murder. There are no defenses, Gerald, believe me. It's a hopeless case, and I love it, Gerald, love it. And we shall take this case for this poor miserable impecunious bastard and we shall prove to the world how gloriously incompetent and helpless the system really is, and how undeniably beautiful Gerald and Raymond are. We shall save this poor bastard—save him! Don't you think that will be amusing?"

"What about justice?" I asked, and then I wished I hadn't asked Raymond Whitaker that.

"What do you mean, *'What about justice?'* What is justice? It's justice just to break the afternoon's boredom."

"Of course," I said.

"It'll be fun."

"Yeah," I said, and then you could hear the bristles of my brush against the canvas again. I put more orange on the hair. Peroxide hair said a lot about the person, my mother said, about not being natural like God made us, but I thought it just made the hair feel dry and crumbly, like straw, not good to touch, and it always made shivers go up my spine. It reminded me of when I was a kid and ol' Calsey took me up to his favorite whorehouse, home, he called it, the Rawlins Rooms. It was a Saturday night when we'd come to town off the old Lembke and Hermberg Ranch—north of Medicine Bow. Most of the ranch hands had gone off to war. I was probably fourteen, doing a man's job in the hayfield. At first I drove the scatter rake behind a team of old plugs, which is a kid's job, but later I cut hay with a pair of broncs on the mow-ing machine, which wasn't a kid's job.

I climbed up the long set of narrow squeaking stairs behind ol' Calsey to this place he called home. When we got to the top he pushed a buzzer, and a black woman came to the door, brushed aside the curtains, saw it was ol' Calsey all right, and let us in without a word. Calsey stomped into the waiting room like he owned the place, took a seat in an overstuffed chair with cotton coming out of the arms, and I sat down on the folding chair beside him, the kind of wooden chairs they had in the church basement for the covered dish suppers. This was just what a kid ought to do, ol' Calsey said. The idea was education—a kid should learn about women right—not mess around with some little skinny-ass preacher's daughter who'd claim you got her pregnant or give you a dose of clap. The girls up here treated a man like a man oughta be treated, no bullshit or tears, no wantin' to get married, or any of that, and they were safe. A good workin' girl is plum safe—takes care of herself—it's her workin' tools, Calsey said—wouldn't mess with a guy who's got the crud. That's more than those preachers' daughters could say. I thought there wasn't any reason for Calsey to lie to me. He was an old man already, about forty-five, too old for the war. He was gray-headed, with one cocked eye that always looked up like it was praying or something, and he had brown teeth on the bottom that stuck out over his top teeth. Calsey was a mean-looking bastard, barrel-chested with skinny bowed legs like the legs of a billy goat. He looked like a pirate, but he wore laced cowboy boots with little flappy doodads, down where the tongue of the boot started, and the boot had round toes and an underslung curved heel. He wore a black cowboy hat, Levi overalls, we called them, a riding denim you had to buy two sizes too large because they shrank when they were washed, and a Levi denim jacket with copper-colored Levi buttons. He wore a black neck-erchief around his neck like a dirty bandage, and always the dirty long underwear, summer and winter, which showed through his open shirt collar. He usually smelled pretty good right after a bath in the creek, which he took before he came to town on a Saturday evening.

Calsey didn't have any more use for preachers than for preachers' daughters. He said he trusted the madams in the whorehouses a helluva lot more than any damn preacher. He'd cash his check in the saloon and after a couple of what he called boilermakers (whiskey with a beer chaser), he'd deliver what was left over to the madam upstairs, and she'd give him the balance when he got ready to go back to the ranch Sunday evening, which usually wasn't much—maybe enough to buy a case of Bull Durham, from which he rolled rotten-looking cigarettes—he could roll one with one hand on a galloping horse in a windstorm he said—and he usually had enough to buy the current issue of *True Detective,* and a pint of Seagram's 7. Calsey and I slept in the same bunkhouse— an old man too old to go to war and a kid too young. Calsey was a stacker.

Usually some little kid drove the team that pushed the hay up the old pine pole stacker until the hay came flying over the top down to Calsey, who stayed at the edge of the stack out of the way of the flying hay watching for snakes. But when the hay settled and the dust cleared, he moved in and forked the hay out to the edges—built it straight up on the sides and "let the middle take care of itself," he said. It was hard work. Sometimes when I was far enough ahead with the mowing I'd get up on the stack and help him. A man could bust his gut shoving and lifting that hay around all day, and when a man came down at night his face was as black as the railroad men's, from hay dust. Then Calsey'd pull out his pint of Seagram's 7 from under his mattress, and take a couple of shots straight out of the bottle. But when ol' Calsey got drunk he was a mean son-of-a-bitch. Even he admitted it. I kept away from him as best I could, like a half-grown pup keeps back from an old mean dog.

Up in the whorehouse this peroxide blonde had come into the parlor. I didn't know what to say or do. I didn't know what was going to happen next, but ol' Calsey said, "This here is a good girl, Gerry. She'll treat you right."

Then he winked at the blonde with his old cocked eye and grinned a big wet smile, and there was Bull Durham juice in the corner of his mouth and you could see every one of his brown lowers. Suddenly he just got up and walked out of the room and left me standing there with her, and then as soon as ol' Calsey was out of sight she motioned for me to follow, which I did like a stray pup with no place to go—followed her down a long narrow hall into a little room where she closed the door behind us. God, I was alone with her.

There was a chipped white enamel washbasin on the dresser, and the place smelled like a hospital, Lysol and all, with some loud-smelling perfume on top of it. There was an old faded pink chenille bedspread on the single-sized bed—like a cot—which sagged a little in the middle. The blonde motioned for me to sit down on the bed and then she sat down beside me. The woman wore a bright red, Christmas-red, satin blouse. That's all I can remember about her, except for her high heels and her ruby red lipstick, which made her mouth look wet and slippery. She had a gravelly voice, like you hear on women who are getting close to Calsey's age—after they drink too much whiskey and smoke too many cigarettes —at least that's what Grandpa Spence used to say. She lit up a Raleigh. Her lips wrinkled around the butt of the cigarette as she puffed, and then she pulled it out of her mouth, leaving a perfect red lip print. She looked over at me and blew smoke in my face. She wanted to look at it, she said.

And I said, Oh no. She wasn't going to do any such damn thing of the kind, at all, to which she said she damn sure was going to have a look at it if we were going to do any business together. She'd seen enough of those damn dumb kids who didn't care where they stuck their dicks, and she wasn't going to have any drip-dicks screwing her, so she was going to have a look at it. She reached down to unbutton my overalls and I jerked back and crossed my legs. I could feel my face turning red. I wanted to run out, but it would be worse facing ol' Calsey later if I did. Then she looked up at me and saw the expression on my face and started to laugh, and she got to laughing harder and harder, and slapped her leg, and finally she was laughing so hard she started to cough, and then she hacked away for a while—couldn't stop hacking—probably the cigarettes, like Grandpa Spence said. Finally when she had laughed enough she sat back up, hitched up her brassiere straps, thumb-at-a-strap-at-a-time, rearranged both breasts with the cups of her hands until they were sticking out as straight as guns, and she kind of massaged her breasts, both at the same time, one hand on each, with her eyes still on me, curiously, humorously, and then she got down to business. "Come on, kid. You ain't the only trick I got tonight," she said.

This time she got very serious—very businesslike. It wasn't anything more than showing your ID, I thought. I was scared. I didn't watch, but I could tell she was inspecting it carefully, all over, like my mother did once when I was a very small boy, and she said it would be five dollars, and I paid her—just like that. Before I knew what was happening I was in the stream of things, like floating down the river in a canoe, and once you're in the flow you just sort of move on with what's happening. It's just a process, I reasoned, like everything else in life, and I shut my eyes and I thanked God for my power to reason, and all, and then suddenly the canoe floated over the waterfall.

Ol' Calsey had been drinking boilermakers, and he was drinking them as fast as he could, getting drunker by the minute. He was sitting in the overstuffed chair again when I got back.

"That didn't take you long, kid," he said, tossing down a straight shot. "A girl don't have to work very hard on your kind." He was laughing and belching. His voice was raspy like the peroxide blonde's, and he was beginning to stink of old booze. I felt dirty, guilty. I could see my mother's face.

"How was it?" He laughed again, cackling. Pretty soon the peroxide blonde came back and she began to cackle, too. "Ya ain't got much stayin' power, do ya, kid?" Ol' Calsey cackled again, and slapped his leg and then hers, and his old cocked eye was lookin' up to the pink roses on the ceiling. I left Calsey up there. He didn't want to leave. It was like home to him, he said. I walked out into the black Rawlins summer night. I could hear the puffing of the steam engines across the way and the smack and rattle of the railroad cars colliding together like giant steel animals in some feral coupling of their own.

"Let's take a break," I said to my peroxide blond model, who unfolded her legs, came out of her pose, and left Marilyn Monroe behind.

"It's totally indefensible," Raymond finally said again out of the blue, still thinking about his murder case while he watched me paint. "Worst case of murder I ever heard of . . ."

"I'm not intrigued by totally indefensible murder cases," I said.

"Ah, but this case." Whitaker looked at the ceiling with ecstasy in his eyes. "This case is a crime spawned out of the very bowels of Rawlins, Wyoming."

"Why did this Mexican kill his ex-wife?" I asked.

"Killed her because he wanted to," Whitaker said. "Just because he wanted to. It's beautiful! And we'll represent him for the same simple reason, because we want to." He looked up at the dark ceiling of the whorehouse as if he were looking out into the universe. "It will be a great case—of men who will epitomize the ultimate truth, of . . ."

"Is there any budget?" I asked.

"Do you mean, is there any money?" He said the word as if it were dirty. "Of course, there is no money." And then he went right on with it. "This Esquibel is a handsome bastard and the women all love him. Big for a Mexican—six feet tall, Gerald, almost as tall as you, and he's kicked the shit out of everybody in Rawlins. The town's stud, and he's beautiful." Then he stopped. "But he's dumb as a rock. Claims he doesn't remember shooting his ex-wife. What a defense, Gerald! 'I don't remember, ladies and gentlemen of the jury, whether I shot my wife or not—can't say one way or the other,' ha, ha," Raymond laughed, " 'and I therefore ask you to turn me loose. I won't do it again!' That's the defense!" He laughed again and then the peroxide blonde came back and took up her pose without saying a word to either of us. I began to paint, but this time Whitaker kept on talking.

"He had a bunch of kids with this white woman, Gerald. The kids were there when he killed her. Well, Gerald, go see our client. I made them give him a haircut. I told him we'll take the case. Gerald! Do you hear me?"

I kept on painting.

"Well, it isn't far from the county jail in Rawlins, Wyoming, to the gas chamber—gas chamber's just up the street a little way, you know. I saw the warden the other day—says he's getting the old chamber all primed up for Esquibel. The people in Rawlins can't wait. This guy Esquibel has been a pain in the ass to the whole town for years—knocked up all the girls, the pretty ones twice, they claim, and they're scared as hell of him—but now they've got him. The warden said he'd drop the cyanide pill on the bastard himself—personally! Said it wouldn't bother him a bit. I told the fucker he'd never drop the pill on anybody—that he'd have to beat Raymond Whitaker and Gerald L. Spence first. So what do you think of that, my fine feathered friend? What, Gerald, speak to me?"

"Well, I hate the goddamn gas chamber," I said, still painting.

"There is a necessity to hate in any great legal drama. Hate is the mother of pride, the seed of honor, perhaps the source of all justice! And, if we win, Fifi will be proud of us. Go to Rawlins and see him, Gerald. Go see our client. He's in a cage—like they cage a mad dog." I was through with the painting.

"This is a good woman," Whitaker said when he saw I was getting ready to leave. He gave the peroxide blonde his warmest smile. "She'll treat ya right, Gerald," and the blonde turned her wet smile on me.

"I have no doubt, Raymond," I said.

"Well, that settles it then," Raymond said, sounding happy, and he presented the blonde to me with a grand flourish of his hand. "Have fun," he said. I could see ol' Calsey in my mind's eye, and maybe that's why I heard myself suddenly say, "Well, I'm going to Rawlins." Whitaker looked surprised. "Gotta go see our client, Raymond," and I walked out the door of Fifi's, and that's more or less how I got involved in Joe Esquibel's murder trial.

3

JOE ESQUIBEL was six feet tall and in his early twenties, with broad shoulders and young skin yellowing in the dankness of the Carbon County Jail at Rawlins. He wore his hair in a crew cut, like a petty officer in World War II. His features were even, slightly oriental, and for a Mexican I thought he was too tall, too muscular. His face was boyish with a child's short nose. There was a tattoo of some kind on his arm. I wondered if he were demented— something in his eyes—or if he were just confused and afraid? I sensed the animal in him. It showed in his mouth and at the edges of his teeth. Perhaps it was only because he was caged.

The jailer closed the steel door behind me with the startling sound of steel on steel and whistled back down the corridor of the cellblock. I stood in the little cell alone with this man feeling anxious and tight. "I'm Gerry Spence," I said, extending my hand. He didn't look at me. He said nothing. He barely extended his own, which was soft, not a workingman's hand at all—damp, boneless, a hand too small for a man of his frame. It was hard to believe he was a barroom fighter.

"I'll be working with Mr. Whitaker in your defense, Joe. I've come to talk to you about your case."

"Yeah, I've heard of you, Mr. Spence," he said, and his accent was Mexican all right, and his voice was high, a little pinched, and soft. He spoke from the top of his throat. He wore a clean white T-shirt, blue jeans, and a pair of black navy-issue round-toed oxfords. I wanted to wipe off the sweat from his hand on my pants, but I wanted him to like me, or at least to trust me. I felt trapped with this man with whom I wished to be friendly, but over whom I needed to take command.

"I'm sorry to meet you under these circumstances," I said. It was meaningless. "I need to get to know you, to understand your case. It doesn't make any difference to me whether you killed your wife or not. What's important to me is that you tell me what you actually know and what you really remember. Do you understand?"

There was no expression on his face. None. Even his mouth was straight and hardly moved when he spoke, like a man who was afraid to move his lips for fear of tasting something vile. The voice was level and empty. His eyes looked sleepy. How could he be sleepy in the middle of the morning in the Carbon County Jail talking to me?

"I didn't kill her," he said simply.

"Of course you killed her, Joe. Seven or eight people saw you, including a deputy sheriff. But it doesn't make any difference to me, Joe, whether you killed her or not. I'm here to defend you. That's my job."

"I don't believe I done it, Mr. Spence." His politeness seemed unforced. Now he looked down at the freshly scrubbed concrete. It smelled of some disinfectant. "I don't remember nothing about it."

"What is the last thing you do remember, Joe?" He shook his bowed head slowly and his eyes were on his hands. I noted three or four scars on the top of his skull showing through his fresh crew cut. I waited for his answer and the silence grew uncomfortable. He only kept shaking his head, saying nothing, and looking at his hands, turning them over slowly and looking at them on both sides as if he were seeing them for the first time.

"I can't remember nothing," he said finally.

I was feeling stronger. "But, of course, you remember something, Joe. Of course, you remember. What's the last thing you can remember? Think."

There was another long silence, and now the man was

utterly still, as if he were sitting there dead. Only once was there the slightest movement of the mouth. I began to pace up and down the nine-foot cell, three paces to the right, three to the left, three to the right, and finally he said, "The last thing I remember is driving around in my car." The voice was the same. No affect, the psychologists called it. "I had a few beers. I don't remember what time it was."

"I need to know all about you, and what happened. You have to see me like a doctor. I'm going to try to cure you in a way. If I don't know what's wrong with you—if I don't know what the symptoms are, I can't treat you. You understand?"

"I didn't kill her, Mr. Spence," he said in a heavy Mexican accent. "I couldn't have. I wouldn't have done no such thing. They are just saying that about me. They always say things like that about me. I never killed nobody in my life." He spoke in short sentences, like a third-grade boy writing an essay about himself. He used to sweep the streets, he said. He put the gravel on the streets and once in a while he drove the gravel truck. His boss would speak good about him. He don't cause no trouble. And he don't remember being in the welfare office—don't remember getting the gun—don't remember shooting his ex-wife in the head. He don't remember nothin', didn't shoot her. The man made no mention of any sorrow over the death of his ex-wife, whom he said he loved. They were still, flat-sounding words. He didn't say he missed her. He showed no remorse. No tears. No anguish—not even dismay. He was flat with no feeling.

"I gotta get out of here, Mr. Spence," he finally said. "I can't stand bein' in jail. Drives me crazy." For the first time since I'd been in his cell he looked at me. But his eyes were still vacant. "I always go crazy in jail. Ask the sheriff—he knows me. He knows I go crazy."

Only his words spoke of the animal panic of his having been captured. I saw no panic on his face, not even a frown, but I thought I knew something of the feeling of bears in the bear cage and monkeys in the monkey cage, and all the cages had wet cement floors freshly hosed down. I remembered the cages at the zoo as a child, and I felt trapped with this man. I wanted out. When I left he would hate me because I was free, and as I left he might lose control and suddenly I would hear his wild high scream, and I would try not to run down the hallway between the cells. I reverted to logic. Logic is supposedly an antidote against fear. He had been there for many days and had never screamed once.

Dumb as a rock, Whitaker said. Yet he told this non-story about not remembering anything awfully well. Perhaps he even believed it now, as some of my own stories have long ago grown into the truth. Maybe the truth had been smashed from his memory by the shock of seeing the blood spurt out of the little bullet hole in her head, by seeing life and death cross each other in her eyes, by seeing her crash to the floor, by hearing the screaming people, and seeing his own horror reflected in their faces, but I thought I would like him better if he would simply say he remembered it all right, but he couldn't talk about it because it was too painful.

Maybe he just didn't trust me, or maybe, having killed the woman intentionally, evilly, and with premeditation, he was now coolly trying to hide behind this crude assertion that he couldn't remember. Not remembering is no defense, but Joe Esquibel couldn't know that. Perhaps Whitaker was right. Maybe it was the story of one who was obviously guilty but too dull to think up any better defense. Could be that his actual memory of what he had done was too horrible. He must have remembered fetching the gun. But I could force the truth from him because he'd believe that unless he told me he'd go to the gas chamber, and he'd be afraid of the gas chamber and because of that fear I'd have power over him.

"You could be looking at the gas chamber, Joe, unless you tell me the truth in every detail. I've represented many a defendant in criminal cases, and when they tell me the truth I can save 'em. It's like a doctor asking the patient what's wrong and the patient says he's got a headache when he's got a bellyache instead. Patient'll probably die of appendicitis, Joe, or he'll die when the doctor

operates on his head instead of his belly, you understand? You've gotta tell me the truth, in every detail."
But he just looked down at his shoes.

I had no rapport with the man. Probably thought I was
another gringo bastard he couldn't trust. He told me
nothing more. He didn't spin some schizophrenic tale
upon which a defense of insanity could be based, nor did
he claim it was an accident when he pulled the trigger,
just trying to scare her and the gun went off or something. All he said was he didn't remember. That's all.

Raymond Whitaker was right. It was an indefensible
case. Maybe he could remember simple things.

"Where did you live, Joe?"

"With my mother."

"What is your mother's name?"

"Agneda," he said.

"How did your mother make a living?"

"She was on welfare."

"Welfare?"

"Yeah," he answered absently. Welfare. They keep
records. It was a place to start.

I needed out of there. I hollered for the jailer.

"Mr. Jailer," I sounded out good and clear. "Hey, Mr.
Jailer," cheerfully, nonchalantly, as if I were calling my
wife from the kitchen. I was grateful when the deputy
came promptly, swinging his ring of keys from leg to leg.
He opened the cell with a courteous smile, and I walked
out with a certain air of importance, of confidence, and I
made a joke with the jailer in passing which I have forgotten. I decided that as long as I was in Rawlins anyway I'd
go see Oscar Hall, who'd be prosecuting the case. I'd ask
him for the welfare records.

Oscar Hall, the prosecutor, was a sheep rancher's son,
like many of the second generation Rawlins citizens who
lived up on the hill. "Snob Hill," Oscar called it. He'd
struggled against being a rancher like a woolly-worm
fighting out of a cocoon, yet at the bottom of Oscar Hall
he was a rancher. He lost his father at thirteen, saw him
die in front of his eyes, pinned under a truck, out in the
damned prairie. His father said, "Oscar, you better start

bein' a man right now, because in the mornin' I ain't gonna be here, and you'll be takin' over," and Oscar couldn't get his father out, and he cried for his father not to die, and prayed, but the prayers of thirteen-year-olds out on the lonesome prairies of Wyoming are never heard, and at thirteen Oscar became responsible for himself, his mother, and the rest of the kids. Then the war came, and Oscar stayed home from the war to run the ranch. His youngest brother went, and when the war was over it was the brother's turn to run the ranch. Oscar went to law school, and after he finished he came back to Rawlins again and lived in the old family home, slept in the same room he was born in, and took over the ranch once more from his brother, who'd had enough. Oscar ran it as best he could. That's what he really wanted to do, always wanted, but those were tough times in the ranching business, and the old outfits were breaking up, the grass was gone. Oscar practiced law, ran for county attorney, and was reelected every four years. The salary helped. And Oscar hung on—hung on to the ranch, and although Oscar Hall finally got the ranch mortgage paid off so that he owned the ranch, nevertheless everybody knew the land owned him.

Oscar and I were friends. We had been drawn together mostly because we were different from the others. There was nothing fancy about Oscar Hall, no pedigree, no experience in long, languishing days in the sun at the country club by the pool, tennis in the afternoon, no private schools or fast cars. He knew nothing of large cities. He was unsophisticated, tough, thickly built and solid, a little fat, like a breeding bull in good shape. He wore flappy pants that wouldn't stay up and an old suit jacket that looked like he wore it the last time he sheared sheep. His tie got twisted as ties always do on a man who fights them, and his shirt collar was usually unbuttoned at the throat under the tie, complying with the dress code of the court in substance, if not in spirit.

I liked Oscar Hall because he was real. His thick blond hair stuck up in unlikely places and he didn't give a damn, and his big brown round-toed shoes were scuffed.

He was who he was. He had fought the battle of trying to change over the years and he had tired of it, and of trying to escape Rawlins, Wyoming, and finally he had resigned himself to himself, a rancher's son, now a public servant doing his job as the county prosecutor, as best he could. He was a better lawyer than he knew. The people never really appreciated Oscar Hall, nor did Oscar, I thought. He saw himself the way everyone else did—a plain honest man who had always been there, working away. Oscar looked like he was glad to see me, but when I told him I'd decided to represent Joe Esquibel he looked dumbfounded.

"What in the world for, Gerry?" he asked. "What's in it for you?"

"I don't know," I said, and I didn't.

"He can't afford you, and he isn't worth savin'. I've known him all his life. World would be a hell of a lot better off without him." That's how Oscar saw things, and saw himself for that matter. He was either adding to or taking away from a better world. "Now ya gotta tell me why you're in this case of all cases," Oscar said.

"I don't know," I said again. Then I added, "That's the truth." Oscar gave me a look like he didn't believe me and didn't understand what had come over his old friend who had never lied to him before. Then I asked Oscar to get me the welfare records, and Oscar said he'd do just that. We were entitled to them, but he knew the Welfare Department would squawk like a pig stuck in the gate if he gave anything to us. Everybody wanted Esquibel in the gas chamber. He'd killed Sharon Esquibel, a white woman, the daughter of Mona Lee Murphy, a social worker, killed her right in the welfare office in front of everybody, splattered her blood all over the place, and they wanted this Mexican bastard dead like a herd of sheep longs for the blood of the marauding coyote. But Oscar Hall said he was going to get the welfare records for his own use, and he'd make me a complete copy. Oscar Hall was a man of his word.

Then Raymond Whitaker asked the law school to assign a couple of their best kids to help us in the investiga-

tion, and they did, a couple of high and mighty wild-eyed
eager young cocks, strutting and feeling big in such an
important case. They had notebooks in hand, and carried
briefcases, and looked gawky and smart, and they were
packed full of propositions of law and fancy legal talk,
and they marched out into the little town of Rawlins,
Wyoming, to discover the seeds of the crime. They found
Agneda Esquibel, Joe's mother, in a second-floor Front
Street hotel down by the railroad tracks in Rawlins, Wyoming. The Rawlins folks called the place the Rawlins
Rooms.

4

RAWLINS, WYOMING, was a small squalid town stuck out alone on the high desolate plains of southern Wyoming. It looked like it had been blown there by the incessant winds, and had gotten caught, house after house, in that one stark place. The town sheltered, more or less, four or five thousand souls who huddled tightly together inside the city limits as if there were no room at all in the vast uninhabited expanses that surrounded the town in all directions, the closest neighbors being Rock Springs, then 110 road miles to the west, and Laramie, 120 miles to the east. All were water stops along the Union Pacific Railroad for the old steam engines, and division points, as they called them, where the trainmen ended their trip, and rode another train back home again, back home to Rawlins, Wyoming.

The wind never gave up. Never.

General George Rawlins, Chief of Staff to Ulysses S. Grant, came through the area in 1867 with the government surveyors laying out the railroad. It was a hot summer day, and the wind was blowing, and the horses, and the men, and especially the general needed water, and when the men found the spring there they named it in honor of the general himself, Rawlins Springs, and that made the general happy.

A couple of years later hordes of Chinese workmen were imported to build the Union Pacific Railroad across the full length of the territory, east to west, along the southern part of Wyoming from Cheyenne to Evanston, across the high desolate plains where there were no mountains to cut through, and nothing to stop the wind. But when the railroad got to Rawlins Springs they had to cut the railroad bed down through a high rock bluff. The cut was made by tough men driving teams of horses pulling fresnos, and then the railroad was built on west, and in the winter the wind blew the snow off the tracks. There wasn't a tree in sight, not for as far as a man could see in any direction, only sagebrush and native grasses, and gullies cut by sudden summer gully washers. It was the easiest place to build a railroad, but a hard place for man and beast to live.

The workingmen camped at Rawlins Springs near the water. At first they lived in tents, and later they built a shack or two, and somebody put up a saloon and a general store and the shacks and saloons stayed on at Rawlins Springs after the railroad was built because the trains stopped there for water, there and farther west at Rock Springs. And still later at the turn of the century the sheepmen came, the English and Irish and Danes and Scotsmen and even some Swedes, and they built homes at Rawlins Springs, and they also built up great herds of sheep, which roamed over millions of acres of free government range and ate the knee-high grass and salt sage and grew fat. The sheep ranchers took up the land of the homesteaders, which controlled the water, the springs, the trickling creeks. Then sheepmen bought out or ate out the homesteaders, and the sheepmen's flocks devoured the rich native grasses, year after year, and the sheepmen built better and bigger homes higher up on the hill north of Rawlins Springs, and the ranchers built corrals and shipping pens at Rawlins, and they shipped their lambs and their wool to market on the Union Pacific Railroad. In tough winters they shipped in native grass hay for the sheep from Saratoga, on the same said Union Pacific.

The ranchers needed sheepherders and they imported them on the railroad, from New Mexico, Mora and Taos, and from Las Vegas, New Mexico, the toughest town on earth. Some of the Mexican sheepherders, who for the most part couldn't speak English, brought their families to Rawlins and put them in one-room shacks, which they built on the south side of the railroad tracks. They put the women and kids in dugouts and lean-tos covered with tar paper, and later some of the shacks were covered with cardboard boxes opened up and nailed over old boards to keep out the relentless Rawlins wind. On the north side of the tracks the sheepmen who lived up on the hill looked down on the Mexicans as they were called, Spanish as they wished to be called. The sons of the Mexicans became the section hands for the railroad and repaired the tracks for the U.P. and some of the sons and daughters of the Mexicans became dishwashers and maids and laborers for the sons of the ranchers, for the elite of Rawlins—for N. R. Greenfield, and for the Gus Larsons and the Gus Strandbergs, and for the Stratton brothers, Abe and Tony and Joe and Ike, and for the McKays and the Johnsons and the Vivions, and for the Rasmussens, who were sheep ranchers first but who also ran the furniture store and the funeral home. Oscar Hall's father, an old country Swede named Holquist, renamed Hall for short, went to work for old man Rasmussen as an undertaker at seventeen, and later on he started a little ranch of his own.

The railroad put in switchyards at Rawlins, and the white railroad men also lived on the north side, below the ranchers, but on the north side, nonetheless. Rawlins was a tough frontier town.

Early on they say Rawlins had the choice of getting either the state's only university or the penitentiary, and the Rawlins fathers chose the latter. Rawlins was a man's town. No place for pansy-ass professors and sweety-pie little college boys with beanies on their heads. The men of Rawlins were hard-bitten, no-nonsense men, and they wanted the penitentiary—straight business, better business than letting the town get taken over by the silly-headed liberal intellectuals who could ruin a good place to live. They put the penitentiary at a place of esteem, across from the town's only mansion built up high on the hill by old man Ferris himself, the copper king of the Ferris-Haggerty copper mine.

The U.P. put its depot at the corner of Fourth and Front streets. It was a liver-red one-story building with a fancy little white Victorian scroll around the edge of the roof, which looked like an old picture frame peaked up in the middle with a kind of curlicue fancy knob at the center of the roof. The sign at each end of the depot read, "Rawlins, Elevation 6,750."

Before the war the whorehouses were all on the south side—out in front of Mexican town—two or three blocks of shacks of various sizes, one two-story affair, all in a line so close to the railroad tracks a switchman riding by on the caboose of a train could toss a clod over and hit any one of the places. But when the Second World War came along and the troop trains were passing through Rawlins, stopping for water, and for new crews, well, it was just good business to let the houses move over on the north side, on North Front Street, down next to the depot.

Get a quickie at Rawlins, boys. Treat a fellow right at Rawlins. Good saloons, pool halls, and the whorehouses are upstairs. Place for a quick drink and a quick piece, gamble a little if ya got time, play some cards, low ball, play a little pool, have some fun in good old Rawlins, Wyoming. Yeah, man!

Take a look at 'er. Jesus Christ, this is a hell hole—looky—ain't a tree in sight for a hundert miles 'cept right here in town, and ain't many here. Look at 'er, boys. This here is Rawlins, Wyoming! Jesus Christ. Look at the wind blowin', and paper and garbage flyin' every which way, little whirligig winds blowin' them cinders! Get me out a here! Get me a drink, boys. A drink—little shot and a beer chaser, and then up to the whorehouse. Five dollars for a quick time. Ten dollars French. Who wants French anyways? Some fuckin' pervert. Some queer bastard. Gimme 'nother shot and we'll go on up to the Annex Hotel. Walk on up there, boys.

In the early days the Annex Hotel used to be a fancy place. The Odd Fellows and the Elks held their meetings upstairs, walked around and through the chairs, and said their secret prayers. Whorehouse now.

And next door to the west was the pawnshop, with a lot of pistols and guns of every kind and character stuck in the window—a pistol was always good for a buck at a pawnshop. The Paris Rooms was upstairs. Best whorehouse in town, best girls, youngest and prettiest, not all wore out. High price, all right—twenty dollars short time.

But a man should go first class when he buys a piece of ass. Ha. Let's have another 'fore we go. Les go now. Ain't got much time. Man can get a drink up there fer a dollar.

Farther west along Front Street, heading toward the depot, was the pool hall, and then the famous King Fong Café, one of several Chinese cafés run by the sons of some Chinese who had come to build the railroad fifty years earlier. The King Fong stayed open all night. The wind blew the cinders from the coal-burning railroad engines into the faces of the railroad men coming and going to work, and the men, with their eyes almost squinted shut, ducked into the King Fong for coffee. Gimme a cup a java. Gimme one of them chop sueys, too. Pork or beef? Pork. And the King Fong Café also caught the drunks who came wobbling and belching and bellowing out of the bars sometime before dawn, and the café caught the sheepherders and railroaders and soldiers staggering down out of the whorehouses.

West of the King Fong was the Senate Tavern, run by a fellow named Schumann, a nationally ranked heavyweight boxer. The men came into his bar just to look at him, and to talk fight, and to talk tough. Then came the Tivoli Bar and the Silver Dollar and the New Palace, which was across from the depot, and then the Sportsmen's Pool Hall and Cigar Store. Up Fourth Street were four or five more saloons, including the Silver Spur on the east side of Fourth and the Western Bar on the west side, and upstairs next to the Silver Spur was the Alcova Rooms, a low class place. Across the street was the Midway Bar, which the townspeople called Sloan's Gymnasium, a place run by Jim Sloan, which was so rough there were damn near around-the-clock fights, and upstairs was another whorehouse, the Midway Rooms, which catered to the gamblers.

If you were back at the depot and went west again, there was the Luxus Café, reputed one of the finest eating places in the state, where most of the railroaders and the town's businessmen hung out, and then Gid's Liquor Store, run by a former tie hack, and the Green Mill Bar, and another pool hall and a Mexican place called Patsy's Café. Then came the Wyoming Bar, where the sheepherders drank and fought, and above the Wyoming Bar the Cozy Rooms, another fancy whorehouse owned by the same man who ran the Paris, and then the Club Bar, an exclusive Mexican hangout. The Olsen Rooms, a run-of-the-mill whorehouse, was upstairs and across the street, on Fifth and Front, was the Rawlins Rooms, home to ol' Calsey.

The sheep ranchers' sons lost their virginity at about halfway through high school to the same women who serviced the servicemen and the trainmen and the sheepherders, probably at one of the cheapest whorehouses, and ol' Calsey used to say the bankers came up to the cheap whorehouses too, but they were the kind who claimed they just slipped up for a nightcap. Once ol' Calsey told me that one of the girls came stomping out into the whorehouse lobby hollering for the madam at the top of her lungs so everybody could hear her good and clear. "Mr. Arnold P. Smothers wants a rubber," and she sounded real disgusted and snotty-like, Calsey said, and everybody in the whorehouse laughed because one a them goddamn bankers thought he was too good to "ride 'er bareback" is how ol' Calsey put it.

Some Rawlins people proudly said there were more shootings and stabbings and fistfights in those few blocks in Rawlins, Wyoming, than in any place in the good old U.S. of A. But one street north of Front Street, Cedar Street they called it, there was a hardware store, a J. C. Penney's, a clothing store, and a Woolworth's, just like in any nice little town, and right there on the main street was the United Presbyterian church with a big sign in front in black and white that read, "Love One Another." The Catholic church was farther north and higher up.

At night in the railroad yards at Rawlins, there was the sound of steam switch engines working in the dark. There was a single bright beam at the front of the train, and red and green lights on the caboose, and there were other moving lights from the swinging lanterns of the switch-men, but except for that, the yards were dark.

The sounds were of switchmen yelling to other train-men in high strained voices, and laughing or cursing, cursing just to be cursing in the dark. And the sounds were of the incessant puffing of the switch engines, the puffs growing closer and closer together, faster and faster, until they puffed out in one final heart attack of puffs, and they were of the occasional high rolling whine of a fast-approaching train, maybe the *City of San Francisco,* its whistles crying, wailing, woefully, the train speeding by with lighted windows and fancy people peer-ing out, streamliner people blazing by, and the train hardly slowed for Rawlins, Wyoming. And the sounds were of fast freights and troop trains carrying tanks and men to war, pulling into Rawlins for water and a new crew. Then it was quiet again except for the distant little dinging of bells on the lumbering, panting switch engines and the smashing of the freight cars, making echoes up and down the tracks, car to car, rattling against each other the full distance of the yards like distant thunder from the barren prairies beyond, and then the sighing of the switch engines as they let out excess steam like exas-perated old men, noises to the ears of strangers in the town, but to those who lived up on the hill in Rawlins, they claimed it was a quiet town.

Back in the dark part of the railroad yards, on the siding, were usually a couple of empty boxcars waiting to be switched onto the makeup tracks, to join some train in a day or two for the West Coast. The doors on the empty cars were open, and up close it was easy to see that the floor of the boxcar came chest-high to a big man. Some claimed Agneda Esquibel carried on with the railroad men down in the switchyards at night in the boxcars. Said she was a boxcar woman. A trainman would have to boost her with a good shove, foot in hand, up into the empty car.

A distant yard light shone on the face of the kid sitting in the corner of the boxcar, fat-faced little bastard, big brown eyes as wide as dollars, scared, shining in the dark, his black hair stubbing out all over, making him look like a little animal who needed to have his hair licked down smooth. Kid looked crazy. But he was mostly dirty and afraid of the dark. The light shining into the boxcar occasionally caught the naked white ass of a man ascending, and there were the noises, like animals fighting, panting noises, and the groans of animals struggling. The trainman gave the woman a dollar. Enough for a boxcar woman.

The welfare records said the boy's name was Joe, Little Joe his mother called him. The kid didn't want to stay at home with the old man dying of cancer, the kid's father's father, skinny and stinking of the disease that filled the little shack full of the smell of the old man. The place was already full of kids, and when Agneda tried to leave, Little Joe made a hell of a ruckus, tough little bastard, brown as a bean, strong, big for his age, and he tried to follow his mother until she had to either let him go along or beat him half to death. He was three years old, maybe a little older, couldn't tell his age from the welfare records, but Agneda said the welfare records were all wrong anyway.

The white men in the boxcars all looked alike to Little Joe, men with faces black from railroad soot, and they had white asses that pounded on top of his mother, who was a little bit of a thing, pounded the breath out of her, white asses up and down, leaving her groaning and gasping in the railroad cars. Once one of the men gave Little Joe a quarter, but Little Joe didn't remember his face.

Then after the trainman left, his mother got down to the ground by herself and Little Joe jumped into her arms, and she gave him a quick hug before she put him down. She smelled of the man, and on the way back to the shack she squeezed Little Joe's hand in the dark and then hollered at the passing switchman, "Hey, buddy, you wanna have a leetle fun over in the boxcar?"

"Ah, go fuck yourself, you fuckin' Mexican whore," he shouted back, and then he whistled some tune in the dark, a nonchalant tune like his world would never end, and rode the train on by.

"Go fuck yersef, you no good fuckin' draft-dodger," she shouted back in her high shrill voice. Then Agneda and Little Joe walked hand in hand across the yards toward the shack on the other side of the tracks.

But Agneda said she never did any of that. "Them records is wrong," she said. "I take care of my kids. Dario, my ol' man, he tol' that stuff on me to the welfare."

The welfare records showed that Agneda Esquibel was born on May 15, 1923, in San Pablo, New Mexico, as Agneda Montoya. She was educated to the fifth grade. She claimed she only went through the first. She married Dario Esquibel on January 9, 1939, in Las Vegas, New Mexico. "Dario, he was my first man," she said, and in 1941 they moved to Rawlins, Wyoming. Dario came to herd sheep.

Agneda Esquibel was a small woman who had six living children. There was something still of her early good looks. You could see it in the angular face, at the high cheekbones that other women wished for, and at the small hard nose of the ancient Aztec. She had a full mouth, and strong teeth, but her sturdy body had started to broaden, and already her brown skin was beginning to crack and check at the edges of the eyes, and the same was happening at the corners of her mouth. But Agneda Esquibel was mostly in her eyes, a fierce little woman whose eyes could magically soften, just for an instant, as if the lioness inside were giving away to the greater power of the turtle dove.

The welfare records said Dario Esquibel, the father, was born August 16, 1918, in San Jeronimo, New Mexico. He was a small man with a tight, wiry body, like a skinny fighting cock. He had a sharp Mexican beak between

fierce black eyes that were too close together, and a few
scraggly miscellaneous hairs on his chin, like an adolescent boy. He spoke in a high, crying, Mexican accent—
had these six children to support. The welfare had
opened a file on him long before his divorce from
Agneda—when he'd asked the welfare to help with his
father, Fidelan Esquibel. The old man was suffering from
cancer—not operable the doctor said—gone too far, and
he had no one to care for him in New Mexico. Vicente
Pacheco, director of the San Miguel County Welfare Department in Las Vegas, New Mexico, wrote Louis Groh,
director of the Carbon County Welfare Department in
Rawlins, saying that the old man's welfare check from
New Mexico, $19.50 per month, would be stopped be-
cause the old man had left the state. But when Dario
tried to reason with the welfare man, saying that his father was too sick to live in New Mexico alone, and was
dying, and that he himself was out of work, the welfare
man said, "There is no reasoning with rules. You do not
reason with rules."

Dario had been herding sheep north of Medicine Bow,
and he got drunk only when he came to town, once every
couple of months. They said he was a good herder. But
hard times came for the sheepmen; the Bureau of Land
Management cut the land up into allotments, and the
Australian and South American lambs and wool made
hard competition, and the tall, rich grass and salt sage of
the old days were gone. The ranchers cut the herds, and
the welfare records said Dario was laid off. Then he'd
gone to work for the U.P. Railroad, $1.03 an hour on the
track gang, but he'd been laid off there, too. He was out
of work and there were Dario and the wife, and the old
man dying, and six kids, all living in the shack on the
south side of Rawlins in Mexican town. Dario built the
shack. He was proud of that. One room. But when all
the kids were hungry, and there was no work, he finally
went to the welfare. They gave Dario a B.D.O., whatever
that is. It was good at Ferguson's Grocery for what was
supposed to be two weeks' groceries—thirty-two dollars
was what it was.

In the last few years there had been trouble between Dario and Agneda. She wanted to be out, away from the kids. They drove her crazy, and some said she'd actually gone crazy, cooped up in one room, but the Welfare Department records didn't report that. Mexicans were used to living in shacks. They lived in cardboard crates across the border, whole towns of people living in nothing more than cardboard. But when Dario brought the old man to the Esquibel shack that had been the last straw for Agneda because the old man took a whole bed. For the love of Christ, there were nine of them now in one room, counting the new baby.

Sometimes Agneda went over to her sister's place, Patsy's Café, down on North Front Street. It was a cheap dump with a dance floor and some small tables crowded over in the corner with checkered red and white oilcloth table covers. The Mexicans came mostly at night, usually after hours, after the gringo bars had closed. And Patsy served her customers drinks, without a license, of course. They played the jukebox and danced and fought—fought each other, cut one another up with their switchblades, and sometimes stabbed each other as if a Mexican were the mortal enemy of a Mexican, and they sliced and hacked away at one another's poor, brown, skinny bodies to cut out their rage and empty places. Sometimes they fought over some woman, and out of cut veins, as in any letting, came the hated blood of the enemy, of a town of whites, of the rich and powerful, the blood of the people who claimed to have morals and who prayed and sang carols to each other on Christmas about love and who lived on the other side of town. And out of the veins of stuck Mexicans came the blood of those who passed judgment on them, pointing long white fingers at them. The white people needed the poor, for without the poor there could be no charities, no graciousness, and the white people could not achieve the kingdom of God without godly compassion for the poor. And without the Mexicans there would be no one to herd the sheep or wash the dishes or repair the tracks for the Union Pacific. And as the knives in the brown bloody hands slashed out and as the Mexicans dissected each other, the blood of a system spilled on the floor, a system that sneered and shunned and disdained and detested the Mexicans. Out flowed the blood of the police—brutalizing and battering and beating the brown people to keep them in their place, in shacks on the south side. But such self-slaughter was better than nothing; better to butcher each other than weep and rage silently in some empty corner alone.

Agneda went to Patsy's Café because there was also excitement there, men and women laughing and dancing and fighting and bleeding, and puking from bad whiskey, all of which the townsfolk allowed since it was only the Mexicans opening up each other's bellies—only Mexican guts, only the unclean entrails and the brown blood spilled and dumped on the dirty floor of a dirty shack. It was all right. They needed their place and they should stay in their place. Let them have it. Let them fight.

At Patsy's Café Agneda was beautiful, for she rose above the squealing and tugging of a den of pups. Here she was like a bitch coyote out on the prairies, running and attacking the sheep, the lambs, in some mindless, breathless bloody struggle that affirmed that she, Agneda Esquibel, was alive, and that the six pups were not sucking on dead tits. Death is important only to vouch for life.

Finally Dario got a job herding sheep again, and sometimes he was gone for more than two months at a time, away from the kids and the dying old man and the high screeching voice of Agneda, screeching all day and all night, trapped in the shack with the kids. Dario had gone back to the mountains, to fill his ears with the peaceful baaing of innocent sheep and the sound of tumbling clear water, and to fill his eyes with the sight of lush, flower-covered meadows owned by the United States Government where the rich men leased the government's best pastures. But when he returned he found the old man almost dead and the children sick and listless around the place. They were hungry and dirty, he thought, too hungry. They were like lambs, which take any tit once their mothers are dead. And Agneda was down at Patsy's Café again.

He went to Patsy's and hollered to Patsy, Where's Agneda, but the jukebox was too high and the laughing and screaming and pounding on the poor floorboards were too loud, and the sweaty Mexican bodies were jumping like jumping beans, like crazy savages, wild with the music and the beat of the drums, and he couldn't find his wife. He pushed his way across the dance floor a little at a time and finally there she was, in the corner, rubbing bellies with some young Mexican stud who stood there with lusty drunken eyes and a wet mouth, and he looked strong as a young bull, but Dario stepped in between them and jerked Agneda away.

"This here is my woman," Dario said. They stood there facing each other, this young stud staring at this older skinny husband with eyes sucked in so close to his nose—the two glaring like animals, sizing each other up. Then the stud reached fast into his pocket, never taking his eyes from Dario, and his knife flashed, switchblade, and Dario stood frozen. To run?

But what is a man?

And what is a man without pride? Dario stood straight and stiff, ready to be punctured, and the stud jabbed the knife out into the air between them. Then suddenly Agneda threw her arms around the young man, and held him close to her with both hands behind his head, and she kissed him hard on his wet mouth.

"Come on, honey, les you and me dance," she said, pulling him away, and Dario stood there like a silly scarecrow, still in his sheepherder's dirty clothes and his old beat-up straw hat, until finally the bouncer came for him, pulled him aside, and then shoved him, stiff-legged, out the door. Dario hollered, "That there is my woman," but Agneda was not to be owned by no damn sheepherder, she said, and she and Dario fought about it later. They fought like that almost every time he came home from the mountains. Then one day she divorced him. Got Bob Bates, the lawyer, and Dario was ordered to pay sixty-five dollars a month support, the divorce decree said, and that was more than Dario could pay, and so he had quit the sheep and gone back to the railroad as an extra on the track gang.

Agneda never said much against Dario. She told the welfare lady Dario said bad things about her mother, who lived behind them in another shack on the same lot. She defended her mother. After all, she was her mother, but some said that Agneda had gone plain crazy in that one room with seven other souls.

The old man had been near death for many days. His hair stuck out so that his head looked like a dirty white sea urchin, and his face was dead gray, bone gray, undistinguishable from any old dead man's face. Once he whispered something in Spanish to Agneda, and the words stuck in his throat. He tried to clear them, hacking away weakly at the words he tried to whisper. His eyes were open, sightless, like the eyes on the chicken heads lying out in the yard, half eaten by the dogs. Finally, Agneda heard him say his feet were still cold. He always complained of cold feet. He used to whisper that a proud man should not die with cold feet, and Agneda dumped everything on his feet she could find—old towels, a couple of gunnysacks—she even took a blanket off the kids' bed, folded it in fours to put over his feet, and slipped a pair of her own stockings on his old bony feet. It made no difference. Nothing kept them warm. And the children were cold, too. Everybody was cold in Rawlins, Wyoming.

The doctor, old McNamara, wouldn't come to the shack. He said he couldn't help the old man anyway—belly cancer, probably too many hot peppers, he laughed, and slapped Agneda on the back lightly as if to make her forget, to accept this thing like a good sport. The old man was Dario's father, not hers, but she had even offered to give the doctor ten dollars if he would come see him. She would get the money, she had said determinedly, and her voice had gotten high and taken on the scolding, pleading tones of some Mexican women.

"Save your money, Agneda. Money won't do any good." And the doctor had patted her on the back again and reminded her that she already owed him ten dollars from her last miscarriage and that she should pay that if she wanted to pay something. "But money won't do the old man any good. . . . One thing at a time, Agneda," he had said kindly.

She took Communion, prayed for the old man, prayed as hard as she knew how, but he had died and had never stopped begging for warm feet. The cold feet had helped keep his mind off the pain of his old rotting body. Agneda told the priest that she was a bad woman. If she had paid the doctor he could have saved the old man. She wept silently at this confession.

The welfare refused to bury him because he had a piece of property in New Mexico that the department appraised for a thousand dollars. Dario and the other brothers and sisters thought that the family should keep the property for hard times that might come, and they all promised to pay Rasmussen's Mortuary, but they never did.

Little Joe and the other children had gone to the funeral at the big Catholic church on the north side, and they saw the priest in black, and heard the magic words and the ringing of the bell, and they saw the smoke and the sprinkling of holy water, and they saw their mother weeping. She cried while the priest was there with long sad sobs that sounded like the wild dogs they heard at night behind the shack, and she cried so long it frightened Little Joe. Then they all went home and the kids fought over the old man's bed.

5

WHEN I got back to Riverton I took the painting of the peroxide blonde up to my studio behind the house and stacked it face to the wall with the others. I had painted the body naked, gray, like death, like dead flesh sitting up straight with the legs crossed, the excessive breasts hanging dead and empty, and the woman's hands were firmly grasping a can of Budweiser beer, and part of the red label showed through; for a face there were only the sunken orbs, and, of course, the orange hair. I called it "Nude with Orange Hair."

Then I went into the house to face Anna, the mother of my four children. She stood at the stove, not speaking. Cleo, my secretary, had told Anna she didn't know where I was. Hadn't come in that morning, hadn't called, and then there had been nothing else for Anna to do but put the kids to bed and wait, like a mother does for her teenage child. She used to say she fought terrible fantasies when I didn't come home. The crazies, I called them. She said she saw a tangled plum-colored convertible before her eyes as she stared in the dark and saw the bloody corpse of her drunken husband, who had died ignobly on some desolate part of the highway at night, and she saw the images, over and over, from which there was no escape, until the dawn came, and the sun frightened the demons away. Among the sane, demons are not comfortable in the daylight.

This time Anna hadn't called the police or the highway

patrol because she said all the thanks she ever got for her worry was humiliation, and me waltzing in like some sweet smartass, acting like she should have known all along that I was okay. And what should I say now? She wasn't speaking. Just standing at the stove like I wasn't there, but waiting for me to say something. I felt guilty. What should I say? I've been to a whorehouse party, honey, to paint. If Picasso can paint the ladies of Avignon, I can paint a girl from Fifi's, and what about Marcel Duchamp, who painted "Nude Descending a Staircase"? If he had had to explain to his wife what he was doing watching some silly nude walk down the stairs, we would have been deprived of one of the great touchstones in art history. Then Katy, my youngest, my five-year-old little blond nymph, came running, patter, patter, fast, and hollering, "Daddy." She threw her arms around me and I picked her up and hugged her and she held on. Anna turned around and was looking at me, cold and fierce as a Norseman, and she turned back to the stove again, and I thought, To hell with it. I walked up and gave her a little kiss on the neck, ducked quick, and ran out the back door, and then went down to my office where I could feel like a big shot again.

"Cleo," I hollered as I came in the front door, not even saying hello. "Cleo. I have an important letter to give you —maybe the most important letter of my life." No need to make an explanation to a secretary. She wasn't my mother, either, this angel-faced Mexican. Didn't want to be called Chicano or Hispanic or Mexican-American or anything like that. She was a Mexican, she insisted proudly, this Cleo Arguello.

"Cleo." I was still hollering. "This is a letter to the *American Bar Association Journal.*" I tossed my coat on the couch and sat down at the round oak table I used as a desk. I leaned back in my old captain's chair, put my feet up on the table, and began to dictate.

" 'Best Trial Lawyer in America Needs Work.' That's it. That simple. Put my name and phone number down."

"You don't need work," Cleo said. "You need to work. Look at that pile over there."

"Got a new murder case, Cleo," I said. "Mexican fella. Killed his white wife." Cleo's eyes were suddenly sad and serious.

"Why did he do it?" she asked.

"Because he wanted to," I flipped back, and she didn't know what to say, and then the first of my five o'clock friends began coming in like they did about this time every night, a couple of lawyers, and my old hunting partner, Sam, tall and lean as a bean growing in the shade, and Jim from the radio station, who had a head as large as a pumpkin, which sat on a small soft frame. He liked to argue about the meaning of life because he needed to know, and I would say the meaning was this—pooof—just this, and I would snap my fingers, and say, "pooof"— that was the meaning of life. The women came, too, usually a couple of secretaries, and Sam's bookkeeper, and they came because Riverton was a lonely place and they were lonely, and the women had long-past bright eyes, coming as they did at the bottom of the day.

We drank a man's whiskey, Old Cabin Still, and I read them my poem about the hollyhocks, and I sometimes felt trapped in Riverton, Wyoming, and we talked about that, too. I said we all made our own traps, all of us, and we could also get out of them ourselves, but I didn't know how to get out of mine and sometimes I wanted to go someplace and be somebody. Then I could hear old Calsey saying that at the Saturday night dance a cowboy who wasn't drunk wasn't nobody and wasn't no place, and at that point my five o'clock friends and I had another Old Cabin Still. "Do you see that tomato plant over there next to the window?" I asked. They all looked and nodded. "I brought the damn thing inside to save it from the frost. Do you see it blooming? It won't stop. It's like some insatiable nymphomaniac, that tomato plant, but it never bears fruit. It just blooms on, this empty-wombed weed, and the blossoms wilt, unfertilized, barren of bees, and the plant's poor pollen falls to this cold floor, and at night the janitor sweeps it away because it blooms alone." And I told them that sometimes at night, after the janitor had left, I sat alone with the tomato plant, and I wept for the barren plant, but mostly for me.

One day Raymond Whitaker called to say that Sheriff Chuck Ogburn wouldn't talk to our law school investigators. "It's a conspiracy of silence, Gerald," he said. "And it's the same with all the witnesses at the welfare office, too. They won't give us the time of day. They're closed up tight," Whitaker said.

There had been a preliminary hearing. Oscar Hall presented the evidence, a mere formality to show there was sufficient evidence to hold Joe Esquibel for trial without bail on a charge of murder in the first degree. The deputy sheriff was the chief witness, and testified he'd been called by the welfare office to come quick, that Joe Esquibel was there with a gun, and yes, the deputy testified he recognized Joe Esquibel, that was the man all right, the one sitting over there in the white T-shirt and jeans next to Mr. Whitaker, same man as was standing there that day, October 17, 1966, with a gun when he, the deputy, got to the welfare office. This Joe Esquibel fellow was threatening his ex-wife, Sharon Murphy Esquibel, and all the others there in the welfare office—had 'em all lined up. The deputy said he ran into the office with his own gun drawn and about that time this fellow, the same one sitting over there, and he pointed to Joe Esquibel again, well, he was holding the gun up to his ex-wife's head and before the deputy could do anything this fellow pulled the trigger. Sharon fell to the floor and then this fella Esquibel fell right down after her, like an echo of death, and he began thrashing around, crazy-like, like a damn chicken with his head cut off, talking to himself, "Joe, Joe, why did you do it?" The deputy had handcuffed him, dragged him bodily out of the building, and literally shoved him into the sheriff's car. Esquibel kicked around in the front seat for a while before they got him to the county jail.

The preliminary hearing took half an hour or so, enough to establish the intent to kill and the premeditation necessary for first degree murder. It would be a death penalty case. Probably the warden already had some poor inmates fixing and shining up the old gas chamber. It's a public asset, the warden had said, and public assets should be used for the benefit of the people.

On November 14, 1966, Judge Glen Stanton presided at the arraignment of Joe Esquibel in district court. The judge was a white-haired, ruddy-faced, robust, solid man who reminded me a little of my grandfather Spence, but his eyes weren't as sparkly or as pale blue, or his smile as quick and broad.

"This is a charge of first degree murder," the judge said solemnly. "Has the defendant read the information?" It was another formality.

"Yes, Your Honor. We have been supplied a copy of the information by Mr. Hall and we have read the same," Whitaker said. He looked over his glasses, and his jaw stuck out from long years of leading with his chin.

Judge Stanton droned on in response, as if he were reciting a ritual at an Elks meeting, "The defendant, being represented by counsel, and being fully advised of his rights, and the defendant having waived the reading of the information—is the defendant now ready to plead?"

"Yes, Your Honor," Whitaker said.

"To this information, how does the defendant plead?"

"To the information the defendant pleads 'not guilty,' 'not triable by reason of present insanity,' and 'not guilty by reason of insanity at the time of the commission of the offense,' " Whitaker said. Judge Stanton mumbled on automatically. "The clerk will endorse the pleas on the information."

Under the law, clearly stated in black and white, Joe Esquibel, having entered a plea of insanity, must now be sent to the state hospital at Evanston so that doctors could "study the mental condition of the said Joe Esquibel as it existed on or about the seventeenth day of October 1966, the date of the alleged offense, and to further study the ability of Joe Esquibel to stand trial."

Was he insane? An insane man didn't look as afraid as Joe Esquibel looked when they led him away. Raymond Whitaker and I knew the process. After Esquibel was transported to Evanston they would deposit him in the maximum security ward at the state hospital and then the men of medicine would poke and probe and feel around with silly questions, and they would write a large-worded long report, and we already knew the report would be that Joe Esquibel was sane then and now. He was an evil man, and evil men should not escape the gas chamber. Killers must be killed. Killers cannot avoid punishment by claiming they're insane. Killers never are insane. Never.

"He could be crawling on his fucking hands and knees and foaming at the mouth and chewing the table legs and they'd find him sane," Whitaker whispered.

I wanted to leave the courthouse before they led Joe away, but I saw the big deputy give the chain on his cuffs a little jerk, and Joe jumped obediently to his feet like a stiff-legged goat on a leash. I shook Joe's hand. It was wet. I felt a slight shiver in his body.

"When can I get out, Mr. Spence?" he asked in his high soft voice. "I go crazy in this place. Ask the sheriff. He'll tell you. I go crazy."

"Pretty soon, Joe," was all I could say. Then I hurried away to gather up my papers so I didn't have to watch him follow the deputy out.

"Hey, Spence," another deputy from the sheriff's office hollered at the door as I walked away. "Hey, Spence, come 'ere." He was as skinny and tight as a dried cowhide on a post. "There's some bettin' goin' on. Wanna make a little wager on this one?" His teeth were brown, and his grin repulsed me. I didn't answer and started to leave again, but he moved in front of the door.

"How come you shysters are all like that? Not a decent one among ya. How can you stand there in front of that judge with a straight face and claim he's not guilty? Eight people saw that greaser shoot his old lady." He laughed an empty laugh and reached in his pocket for his can of Skoal. "They oughta gas all you bastards along with your clients. Hard to tell which is worse."

"Fuck you," I said, and pushed on by him, catching up with Whitaker.

"Christ, Raymond, we could just as easily resurrect the dead as defend this guy."

"Well, it's a wonderful case, Gerald," Whitaker said. "A wonderful case," and we walked out of the Carbon County Courthouse into a clear, crisp, late fall day.

"It's just salesmanship," Whitaker said as we walked along. "Winning jury trials is just plain and simple salesmanship, and you're good at selling." He seemed happy. I couldn't understand why. Good at selling, he had said. Selling is a big thing. The world turns on selling, my mother used to say. A good salesman can make a living any time, like my mother's brothers who sold cars and were wealthy men, but preaching is God's work, and preaching is selling, too—selling God's word to the people. My mother had told me that a boy should learn how to sell—walk right up and offer what you have, and ask the people to buy. Selling is mostly asking, she'd said. "Ask and ye shall receive." She used to talk to me like that very quietly.

When I was a kid I sold flowers from our garden— sweetpeas, two bouquets for a quarter. My mother took asparagus ferns and made up the bouquets, and then I sold them.

"This is Gerry Spence," I said in my ten-year-old's voice over the telephone. "Would you like to buy some sweetpeas?" They hung up.

"No," my mother said. "You need to make them actually see the sweetpeas over the phone. Say, 'I have some very nice fresh sweetpeas—they are very pretty, all colors —very good smelling. I could deliver them to you, two bouquets for a quarter. Should I come right on down with them?'" And I had practiced. I was a quick learner, my mother said—a smart young man, and she expected great things from me. Someday I would be a great man doing God's work. I thought I would probably be a chemist, like my father, and a great hunter. I would be a great man like him, not like some sissy-ass preacher.

My mother had me get out the telephone book and call all the cafés and all of the hotels in town. A lady answering the phone at the Rex Rooms said she'd take some. I walked a mile or more down the streets of Sheridan in the hot summer with the sweetpeas done up by my mother in wet newspapers. As I went past the open barroom doors on Main Street, I could smell the hot musky odor of men and malt, the aroma of booze, and I heard the sounds of drunken laughter, and I knew the fearsome specter of drunken men, maybe women, witch women, cackling and haggling, hanging over the bars with evil men on one of God's bright summer days. An Indian squaw sat on the sidewalk outside a bar and as I walked by she grunted, "Kid." As I passed, I saw an Indian stagger out of the barroom door glassy-eyed, with a bright red nose, and I hurried on by and held my breath like my mother had told me to so as not to breathe in the awful smell of booze. Booze—it was made by the devil himself and one should never even smell of the devil.

Two doors down was the entrance to the Rex Rooms. I walked up the narrow wooden steps to the top where there was a doorbell. A white lady with hair as black as an Indian's came to the door. She wore a black silk flowered bathrobe and high-heeled slippers. I thought she looked good.

"Come in, son," she said. "You've got the flowers for Mazie?" She patted me on the head and stooped down to look me in the eye. I could see parts of her sticking out from under the silk robe, and I tried not to look, but I got all light-headed. I remember how she smelled, better than flowers, better than the lilacs in the spring, better than roses even. Better than the sweetpeas I handed her.

"Hey, Mazie," another woman coming toward us in a fancy bathrobe yelled down the hall. She was smoking a cigarette. I thought about what Grandpa Spence said. Bad women smoke cigarettes.

"What do we have here, Mazie?" The bad woman smoking the cigarette stooped down and looked at me, too. "What is this here—a towel boy?" she laughed.

"What's a towel boy?" I said to the woman.

"A towel boy carries towels to the ladies." Mazie laughed. And then the two women looked at each other and laughed together. The bad woman gave me a kiss on the neck. She was blond, with a lot of rouge on. I could feel my face getting red, and my knees began to wiggle, and I just stood there and the women laughed some more. Finally Mazie gave me the quarter and I started to leave.

"Thank you," I said. "I hope you like the sweetpeas." And then I didn't know why I asked, but I did. "What do the ladies need towels for?"

And the two women looked at each other again and they broke out in loud laughter. As I walked down the stairs the bad lady called out, "Good-bye. Good-bye, sweetpea." And I could hear them laughing even after I turned back down Main Street and headed for home.

The main streets of all small Wyoming towns are pretty much alike, I thought, and as we walked along in the good sunshine of Rawlins, Wyoming, Raymond Whitaker said, "I love this case like I've never loved any case before. I love it because it is symbolic of man's poor plight on this earth." The wind was blowing.

"How's that?" I asked absently.

"We are all helplessly condemned to death," he said. "Like they say, none of us ever escape this earth alive. None of us." Whitaker didn't often philosophize, I thought. "But Joe—Joe will be given a reprieve—by us—by you, Gerald. You will save him in this case. You will save him through salesmanship."

6

THINGS WERE better for Little Joe in the summer after the old man's death. He and Timato, his older brother, played marbles in the dirt all day and ran fast as rabbits in the dust. They were good boys, doing what their mother said, getting the bean money by gathering up the Coca-Cola bottles and old beer bottles along the road, which they traded at the store. Doesn't take much money for beans. Sometimes they stole milk from the door of the gringo houses across the tracks early on a summer's morning, when the sky was just turning light gray at four o'clock, and the boys were following quietly blocks behind the milk truck, and the summer dew was cold on the grass and made their bare feet wet. They walked on the black pavement. It was still warm from yesterday's sun. The fat cops were having coffee at Adam's Restaurant. The boys never went back to the same neighborhood twice in a month. Agneda said, "White people don' miss no couple quarts of milk. Don' hurt 'em none, and they don' put no little Mexican kids in jail for stealing milk. And run down the alley. Don' run to this house, ya hear? You run behin' the other houses because if the cops come to this house they will steal you kids."

Agneda was gone almost every night and the children stayed home together. Elma, the oldest girl, born just eleven months after Timato in the same year, was a good little mother and Little Joe held onto her now like he used to hold onto Agneda. When he did that to Agneda, she would scream, "I wheep you good if you don' let loose," and she would jerk free of him, but when the whipping did no good, sometimes she had to take him along. But this summer he stayed home with Elma and held onto her. In Rawlins, Wyoming, they say summertime is best for Mexicans.

After the divorce, Dario didn't come to the shack very often, and when the children asked where Dario was, Agneda said he had gone away. He is good for nothing, she said. Drinks too much whiskey, and don't give nothin' for them kids. She told that to Ramon, who was always at the house these days. All he wants to do is to fuck me like a dog and eat beans and drink whiskey. Ramon sat in Dario's chair, and his shoulders stuck out on both sides like a bear's and also his potbelly stuck out in front. Ramon was younger than Dario. Agneda was tired of old men—good for nothin' old men, she said. Sure, Dario could work hard. Never missed a day's work. So what, she said. He don' bring nothing home—just a hard cock, and when he was drinking he beat her up sometimes.

She had won Ramon in a fight at Patsy's Café. Ramon had come into the place proud and horny as a boar, and the men knew him—were afraid of him because he'd been in the penitentiary for killing a man, and although he was not much taller than the other men he was twice their size across the chest. The men drank to Ramon—to his happy days, to his good health—and Agneda had asked him if he wanted to have some fun, and then she'd asked him to buy her a drink and had rubbed her big breasts across his back and made him turn around, and then some fucking Mexican whore had thrown her arms around Ramon and kissed him, and Agneda had grabbed the bitch by the hair and pulled her off him. They fought and the men had yelled, clapping their hands and hollering, whistling and whooping while the two women pulled one another's hair and rolled on the floor. Agneda was smaller, but quicker, and she got up again, fast, and kicked the woman in the head, twice, smashed her nose out flat by stomping on it with her high heel, and when the woman's eyes started to bulge and stare and the blood came out of her mouth somebody pulled Agneda off the woman, and Ramon picked Agneda up and held her up in the air as the winner, and she dangled there, her feet kicking back and forth like a little child's. She had won him, and she took him home with her that night, and when Dario came in, he said to visit the children, he saw Ramon and then he didn't say anything at all. His small eyes were dark and sad. He looked over at Little Joe and that's when he hugged Little Joe and left, and Little Joe didn't see Dario for the rest of the summer. The welfare records just said, "The department knows that Agneda is 'running around' and not so long ago was involved in a barroom brawl with another welfare mother over some young fellow recently released from the penitentiary."

Ramon came at night and when the lights were out Little Joe heard them and knew what the noises were that kept him awake and made him look in the dark, and when he looked he saw the white asses of the railroad men pounding, and what he saw in the dark made him feel crazy. Ramon slept at other places, too, and Little Joe didn't see much of him.

This Ramon had a black '37 Ford car, a coupe, with baby booties dangling down from the mirror. It had what they called straight pipes that foretold the car's coming a half mile away, and it had a tall radio aerial from which a big brownish fox's tail hung and bounced and billowed in the breeze. It was a hell of a car Timato told Little Joe, and Ramon took Agneda in the car to the dance at Elk Mountain, forty-two miles away. The dance floor was built on old car springs and when the music got loud and the dancers got wild, the whole place rocked and reeled in rhythm. Ramon was a Mexican, all right, and they didn't allow Mexicans at the Elk Mountain dance, but they never gave Ramon any trouble. He was a proud man.

Once the sheriff tried to question Agneda about the fight she had at the barroom over Ramon. The sheriff had come to the shack and beat on the door, but Agneda never let him in. She told the kids that the sheriff wanted to steal them. Later the sheriff found her at Patsy's Café, and then she said, "I no understand English." But all the facts about the fight ended up in the welfare report anyway, along with information about this new man in the house, Ramon, a known felon who had been convicted of murder. The report stated that his presence provided a negative experience for the children, especially since they loved their father, Dario Esquibel. Little Joe, especially, missed his father. The report concluded by saying that since the old man, Dario's father, had expired and providing for his care was why the file had been opened in the first place, the file was ordered closed.

As for me, about then I'd been slappin' horses on the butts all summer on the Lembke and Hermberg sheep ranch north and east of Rawlins, but I wasn't any more bother to the old horses than the horseflies, big as dimes. I'd give slap after slap with the lines and holler a loud "geed-up"—and the old horses would finally break into a slow lazy trot, swish their tails in protest to the leather on their backs, and barely shake their heads from side to side in rhythm with their slow gait.

One morning I was driving the dilapidated old scatter rake over the dry hayfields. The rake rattled and wobbled along, with me sitting up high on the iron seat, which was riveted to a spring steel arm, and I braced myself against the buck and the bounce caused by the crooked iron wheels, wheels almost taller than I, and the rake staggered drunkenly down the wind rows picking up the hay left behind by the horse-drawn sweeps. By midmorning it was hot, the breeze off loafing in some other county—too hot for even the hayfield mosquitoes, which retreated to the cooler side-field bogs. Once in a while a field mouse scurried in the dust out of the way of the horses, and on the edge of the field, sitting in the top of tall willows, were a couple of young magpies, in their formal black and white, using up their energy in the midday heat squawking noisily at the rake as it rattled by. I slapped the horses on the butts with the lines, but after a step or two of trotting, the old horses fell back to their same slow walk, knowing that their rumps would outlast my arms, and the sun grew hotter, and the horses walked slower, and pretty soon even the magpies were quiet. A man gets thirsty. They gave ol' Calsey a jug of cold spring water covered with burlap—he kept it under the stack on the shady side—but nobody gave a shit for the scatter raker, just a green-ass kid anyway. I slapped the old horses again, but their heads just bobbed up and down as if they were counting their slow steps with their noses, step at a time, counting across the field and back again, and across and back once more. The old horses were wet with sweat, foaming at their flanks and their necks and shoulders. There wasn't any damn shade.

I could see there was a spring over by a set of green willows growing at the edge of the field. The red-winged blackbirds in the swamp grass sung at each other, cutting out their territories with their strange "sca-wings." It was the same song, generation after generation, with which they fought their wars. A pity we had not learned their weapons. Yet there had never been a red-winged blackbird who could break away with some new glorious warble. It was always the same, "sca-wing." I pulled the team over close to the cutbank so as to reach the water's edge without having to let loose of the lines, and then the whole damn bank let loose, caved in with me. I gave a surprised holler and went rolling down into the spring with a splash, and the lines jerked the horses as I fell, and they bolted, pulling the lines right out of my hand. I scrambled up the bank dripping wet. "Whoa, whoa," I cried in my boy's soprano, but the old team was running now at full gallop, and the rake behind them was bouncing four or five feet off the ground every time it hit a little bump, like there was a crazy driver behind, and the more the rake bounced and rattled the faster the old team ran. They ran to the far edge of the field, and when they were about to the fence they turned sharply in the other direction, and then they galloped at full speed, around and around the field, a wheel popping off the old rake here, and another there, and the old team ran until they were exhausted and had to stop. Then they just stood there panting, their sides heaving, their poor bodies quivering with fear. They were frothing wet all over, and the rake was a scatter rake, all right, scattered all over eighty acres —nothing left, wheels gone, the teeth mostly broken, and those not broken were bent until they were useless.

I didn't know what to do. A man who lets his team run away is a jerk. Finally I unhitched the team from the rake and walked the horses back to the ranch yard. Nobody said anything to me. Nobody even talked to me at supper. I didn't ask anybody to pass the catsup or the Kool-Aid or nothing. I was afraid they'd say something to me. When I was in bed that night in the bunkhouse ol' Calsey blew out the lantern with one big vile puff, and then he said, "Good night, jerk." I pretended I was already asleep.

The next night was Saturday. Ol' Calsey said he was going to the dance at Elk Mountain, name band, big time. The people came down from Laramie, even from Cheyenne, 100 miles away, to hear the band—hell of a time in Elk Mountain, ol' Calsey said. All the ranch girls, the cooks, the sweet señoritas, he said with a toothy grin, all of 'em comin' to town. "Ya wanna go? I got the yeller pickup," he said.

Elk Mountain sat at the foot of a high lone humpbacked mountain with the same name that was separated from the rest of the Laramie Range by a space that looked like the gap in ol' Calsey's mouth where a couple of teeth had been knocked out. It was a high green timber-covered mountain mostly famous for having reached up and plucked down an airliner some years before. The town had a general store and a filling station, a post office, and one of the ranches had its headquarters there. The rancher's big barn sat right next to the highway that went through town. It had a huge hayloft full of last year's hay where the cowboys took their girls at night, and across the highway was the bar with a parking lot and the dance hall. It was dark by the time we got there.

The place was already stomping and there were drunk cowboys everywhere. I walked around looking at the people in the dance hall. There were some pretty girls my age sitting together next to the wall. I didn't want to talk much. I thought about going over and asking the one with the big tits to dance, but I knew once she heard my soprano voice she wouldn't have anything to do with me —with my pimples and all. The only place anybody liked that awful voice was in the Methodist church choir, and there I was a star of sorts. At least that's how I saw it. So I just stood there looking at the girls. The light wasn't too good on my side of the dance hall, and I pulled my straw cowboy hat down over my eyes a little, looking tough, and the girls saw me and just giggled and grinned back. I wished to Christ I didn't sing soprano in the Methodist church choir. I hated the Methodist church with its fat-ass sissy preacher, whose cheeks were soft and hung down on both sides of his nose like an old lady's tits, but I still said my prayers every night—The Lord's Prayer, and Now-I-Lay-Me. It wasn't that I was so religious. I had questioned God, and all—took Him right to the mat, like they say. Jim Brown, my friend, said there wasn't any God. But I knew somehow that that wasn't right. There was a God, all right, but He was a lot different from the one the fat-ass preacher talked about. How could God love a sissy? My dad invited the preacher on a hunting trip with us once, and my dad shot an antelope. A fellow gets his hands bloody gutting a critter out, and when it came time to eat the sandwiches Mom had fixed us, peanut butter and lettuce sandwiches, well, my dad never gave it a second's thought—just started to eat with his bloody hands leaving red bloody fingerprints on the white bread, and the damn preacher got sick!

I figured if ol' Calsey had had a little religion he would have been just about right for a man. I could see ol' Calsey stomping out on the dance floor with his crooked legs, dragging some potbellied scraggly camp cook with kinky brown hair around with him. They were both sweating and laughing, the ugliest pair I ever saw in my life. They looked more like they were wrestling than dancing.

After a while I walked over to the saloon, and I couldn't help but think of Mother. Knowing her son was

even near such a place would have hurt her worse than
stabbing her in the heart, but a fellow has to leave his
mother sometimes and live his own life. She wouldn't
know anyway, and I'd never even tasted whiskey or beer
or anything else for that matter, and I hadn't ever
smoked a cigarette.

The bar had fresh sawdust on the floor, ankle-deep. It
was a noisy, crazy place. People acted like they were in an
asylum—wild-eyed and slobbery—hanging on each
other, putting their faces into each other's faces, nose to
nose, and as close as that, hollering, and laughing, and
the men threw their arms around each other, too, in
some kind of friendship that grew out of this insanity of
alcohol, and they shook each other into recognizing
through it all that this was life, this was it—the Saturday
night dance at Elk Mountain. Some of the women sat in
pairs along the bar. A cowboy and a young woman came
toward the bar door from the direction of the barn.

"Brush off my back," she said. "Get that hay and stuff
off my back!" She turned to the young cowboy. He
stopped and looked at her with a grin, doing nothing, just
standing there, teasing. "Come on," she pressed, "brush
me off before we go in." They weren't paying attention to
a gawking kid and everybody was swatting mosquitoes
now, drinking and laughing and swatting. "Come on!"
she said again.

"Ah, hell," the cowboy said back. "Everybody knows
what we been doin' up there anyways." He pushed
through the barroom door, almost knocked me over
when he went by. Left her standing there, and then ol'
Calsey came along and I was glad to see him. Needing a
drink, he said, bad, because he wanted to be somebody
on a Saturday night at the Elk Mountain dance. "I'm
needin' a drink, jerk," he said in his cracky voice. I didn't
say anything back. You don't say anything to Calsey when
he's had a drink or two.

There was this thick Mexican at the bar, short but as
broad as a boulder, with his arm around a small Mexican
woman who looked worn out from having kids, but her
brown skin bulged at the breasts, stuck straight out from

inside a good uplift bra, good cleavage at her age they
would have said. Ol' Calsey saw her, knew her.

"Hey, sweetheart," he yelled across the noise. "Hey,
you, Nellie, sweetheart," he yelled. "Remember me?"
You could tell she knew him right off. "Come on over
here and I'll buy you a goddamned drink," he hollered to
her. She started toward ol' Calsey, but the thick Mexican
held her back. "You're my woman," he said. Then he
turned to Calsey and hollered across the room. "This
here woman is drinking with me," the Mexican said, but
you could hardly hear him over all the screaming and
laughing. Ol' Calsey started over to him through the
crowd. "You fucking wetbacks ain't even suppose to be in
here," ol' Calsey yelled. Then he grabbed the woman's
wrist and pulled her to him. And fast as a striking rattler,
the blade flashed in the hand of the Mexican and stuck
clear to the hilt in ol' Calsey. Calsey didn't even blink,
like he didn't feel it at all. The knife struck him just above
the waist and off-center a little, sticking easy into the soft
liver. The blood spurted out. Then there were two more
quick, bloody thrusts and this time the Mexican hit a rib
and ol' Calsey felt it and he got pale and his knees wobbled. The Mexican grabbed the woman called Nellie and
ran out the bar door. Somebody hollered, "That goddamn Mexican stabbed a man." But nobody went after
him that I could see. The hollering stopped, and also the
laughing. They crowded around poor Calsey, who was
sitting on the floor, gasping, pink foam coming out of his
mouth, and his old cocked eye looking up like he was
praying. Somebody said to lay him down, but ol' Calsey
wanted to sit. They crowded in close to him. "I'll get you
to a doctor," I said. Calsey looked up, and his eyes were
starting to glaze over as he looked at me. "I have been
kilt over nothing but a Mexican whore," he gurgled in his
blood.

"You gotta take him to Rawlins," somebody said. A
couple of guys pulled him up and helped haul him by
armpits and legs to the yellow pickup truck. I sat with ol'
Calsey in the back, holding his head on my lap all the way
to the hospital. I didn't know who was driving. Some half-

drunk cowboy, I suppose. Calsey kept breathing foam
and gasping, and once I could hear him rumble, "You
ain't no jerk, kid."

He was in the hospital fourteen days. Then he went to
live with his sister for a while to get back his strength—in
St. Louis, I think.

7

THE LEGISLATURE put the insane asylum, as we called it, as far from the state capital as possible. The capital, Cheyenne, is in the southeastern corner of the state, while the state asylum is in the far southwestern corner, near the town of Evanston. They even built the hospital away from the town, put it up on a desolate hill surrounded by land that looked like Siberia must look. The mountains surrounding the place were rugged and windswept, and hard and barren, and the hills near the town grew sparse brown grass and sagebrush, and in the winter the wind blew the cursed snow out of Utah and left it drifted and crusted, and it was to this high, stark place that the people of Wyoming sent their forlorn and rejected. The hospital was a lonely cluster of old brick buildings without style or grace, put up in an efficient, businesslike manner by resourceful men over a half century ago, a place to imprison the unloved and the abandoned, and those who fought their demons in the daylight. Joe Esquibel entered the Wyoming State Hospital in chains. Two deputies delivered him.

The records did not show whether or not he appeared frightened, but he was promptly placed in the maximum security ward in Sublette Hall, at the end of a long, bleak passageway that is divided by what the prisoners, both sane and insane, called the "Golden Gate," prison bars that reached from the floor to the ceiling. Behind the bars were small iron cages for the maximum security patients. There was the "dry side" and the "wet side," the difference being a toilet on the wet side. They put Joe Esquibel on the dry side. All the cells had cement floors with a barren cotton-filled pad, no sheets, no blankets and some of the prisoners were naked, and some claimed they were cold, but then they also claimed they were insane. They locked Joe Esquibel in the cell next to Jason. Jason screamed constantly and spoke no words.

In the sixties it had become fashionable in Wyoming to send young marijuana smokers to Evanston for a ten- to thirty-day "visit," to assist them in understanding the evils of their ways. They locked the young men up in the maximum security ward behind the bars of the Golden Gate in a cell next to Jason, "that crazy nigger who screams all day and all night," and as one of the sheriffs told me, "It don't take long to get the message across to them kids. That Jason is a damn good teacher."

Joe Esquibel would be seen by the forensic psychiatrist, a physician trained in both law and psychiatry, a sort of wedding of the professions, so that if the two were at odds they might accommodate each other in court through the testimony of the forensic psychiatrist.

Each year in Wyoming there are scores of prisoners accused of serious crimes who have no better defense than to claim they are insane, poor devils. They would prefer offering up any other defense, such as proving their innocence or using an alibi defense or even self-defense—any defense known to man except insanity—but there are those cases to which there is no defense at all, and so they finally had no choice except to plead insane. Some say those who are really insane, those who suffer and retch in the agony of their hallucinations, cannot recognize their own insanity, and that only the sane are sane enough to claim insanity.

After the arraignment Raymond Whitaker and I were sitting in the Adam's Restaurant having one last cup of coffee before we parted and headed for home. I was gazing out the window, and suddenly there was the sheriff's car, a couple of deputies in front and poor Joe in the back, still in chains.

"Jesus, look at that!" I said. "They aren't wasting any time getting old Joe off to Evanston." Whitaker looked out the café window. "There goes an insane man," Whitaker said with a sardonic grin on his face, and then he let out a short laugh.

"What's insanity?" I asked, and the waitress poured another cup and acted like she wasn't interested.

"Insanity is what the law says it is," Whitaker said, "and since the laws are different in different states, it depends on what state you're in as to whether you're insane or not." He laughed again. "I'm insane in Utah, but sane in Wyoming."

"Insanity is like a cancer in the belly. You either have it or you don't," I said.

"That's it! That's it, Gerald!" Raymond screamed out, and the waitress hurried back to the table acting like she thought we'd called her. "That's it. You are a genius, Gerald. You have just discovered a cure for cancer. We will create a new discipline in medicine known as forensic surgery! And then we will call the forensic surgeon as a witness, and the forensic surgeon will deny we have cancer, and we will be cured." We both thought that was funny, and we emptied our cups and refused more when the waitress came back one last time. Then we said goodbye, and Raymond left for Casper. I asked the waitress when she got off. She wouldn't say. Nothing else to do except to drive back home, home to good old Riverton.

The staff at the hospital had a routine to handle the likes of Joe Esquibel, who claimed insanity. A whole cadre of physicians and specialists would examine him, a psychiatrist or two, a neurologist, a couple of psychologists, a social worker, and a criminologist, all would ask him questions and record his answers and make their reports, and then they would read each other's reports, and have a meeting, called "staff," and they would come to a consensus, as in any democracy, and they would agree on a diagnosis. Whether a person was sane or insane was a matter of majority rule. Then the reports of the hospital staff were filed away, and what Joe Esquibel said to them was carefully recorded for possible use against him later on at the trial, the Fifth Amendment notwithstanding. Other citizens can claim the protection of the Fifth Amendment against self-incrimination. It is a part of our Bill of Rights, you know. We've done away with those old medieval tortures in this county—can't stretch a man on the stretching rack or pry off his fingernails anymore to get his confession. But the man who pleads insanity will have to answer questions for the staff, and his answers are recorded, and the state will probably use his answers against him at the trial.

On December 15, just eighteen days after Joe Esquibel entered the Wyoming State Hospital at Evanston, he was returned to Sheriff Ogburn at Rawlins, and, of course, the staff had agreed that Joe Esquibel was quite sane. The judge had ordered that they observe Joe for not less than thirty days, but eighteen days was enough. They were convinced—seen enough of him. The judge would understand. The hospital was an efficient, busy place. Dr. William Karn, the superintendent, wrote his report to the judge twelve days early, saying that the staff had gathered Joe's complete social history and they had performed physical, psychiatric, psychological, and neurological examinations of the man and a battery of laboratory and clinical tests as well. Joe's claim that he couldn't remember was merely a clumsy, primitive lie. It was obvious he wasn't some alcoholic suffering a blackout of memory, and he had no physical injury to his brain, and there was no evidence of epilepsy, which sometimes blocks out memory during seizures. He was sane enough all right. How could one conclude otherwise? He was simply a man without a conscience, a man who felt no remorse. Their report said that all his life "he has been on the 'wrong side of the tracks' socially, morally, emotionally, and intellectually, a man who simply 'acts out' whenever he is angry, except this time he acted out with a gun."

Dr. Karn's letter to the judge said it might seem strange that Joe Esquibel chose to act out in the presence of so many witnesses, but it was simply a case of his not caring about the consequences of his behavior, and he wasn't suffering from what the law calls "irresistible impulse" either. Dr. Karn handled that one easily. "I would say," he wrote, "that Joe Esquibel chose not to resist the impulse . . . he did have a choice, and he chose to shoot his former wife rather than not shoot her," and then he closed the door on the defense of "irresistible impulse" once and for all, saying, "the concept of 'irresistible impulse' is not compatible with his personality makeup." He was diagnosed as "a passive aggressive personality, aggressive type," and he was neither medically nor legally insane. He knew the nature, the quality, and possible consequences of his act. He knew the difference between right and wrong, which was the legal test, and he knew that what he was doing was wrong, and he was presently sane. He could aid in the preparation of his own defense, which is the test as to whether or not he could stand trial, and the report concluded, "there is no medical or psychiatric reason why he should not be tried for the offense for which he is presently charged.

On May 12, 1967, Oscar Hall filed suit on behalf of the state asking the court to declare Joe Esquibel presently sane and able to stand trial. In response, I subpoenaed Dr. Karn for his deposition, and ten days later the doctor appeared in the court as ordered.

The courtroom was empty except for the participants in the depositions, which, besides the doctor, included the court reporter, Oscar Hall, and me. Dr. Karn sat easily by, waiting for the proceedings to get underway. He was just forty, with black wavy hair, quiet eyes, and he looked out over the courtroom like a man seeing a field of lilies. He smoked his pipe with gentle, occasional puffs and absently and peacefully watched the smoke rise. He had largish features. Maybe the nose was a little round, but his skin was pink and healthy-looking and he was a handsome man, even more pleasant-looking than handsome, I thought. He reminded me of someone I couldn't identify right then, but the jury would trust him. I cleared my throat to begin, and he looked over at me forgivingly. I felt anxious. I attacked. "You had an hour and a half conference with Joe?" I asked.

"Yes."

"Well, where are the notes of that conference?"

"I no longer have them."

"You destroyed them? . . . What did you say at this interview and what response did the defendant make?"

"I can't give it to you verbatim . . ." he said quietly. "The purpose of the evaluation was to get to know him." He puffed lazily away on his pipe.

"I didn't ask you the *purpose,* I asked you what he said." I was trying to push him to the edge early, but if the doctor perceived that, he gave no visible sign.

"I don't remember what he said," he continued, after thinking a little while.

"And so, as a matter of fact, you destroyed the original clinical record of the examination you made, which is the basis for your conclusions in this case, isn't that true?"

"I no longer have those notes."

"The answer to my question is simply 'yes,' isn't it?"

"That's right," he said, still puffing away.

He said he remembered that Joe was brought into his office—his hands behind him locked to his belt in handcuffs. The handcuffs were removed, but a guard stayed in the room, watching, and then Joe was cuffed up again and the guard took him away. But the doctor recalled that Joe was malingering, nice word for lying, when Joe said he couldn't remember. The doctor could tell he was lying from his sweating and the flushing of his skin, and other signs over which he said Joe had no conscious control. Joe remembered much more than he was willing to admit, the doctor said solemnly, pleasantly.

"What about being dragged in there like an animal? Wouldn't that cause flushing and sweating?"

"Well . . ." The doctor didn't remember and the doctor also didn't remember the details of Joe's education, nor that he was first married at sixteen, nor to whom. He didn't remember whether Joe claimed Sharon was seeing other men. Didn't ask. And he couldn't recall what the problems were in Joe's first marriage, and he made mistakes in his answers about the number of children Joe and Sharon had had, small details, certainly, "But wouldn't it be helpful to Joe if you remembered?

Wouldn't you please try, Dr. Karn?" I asked, and then Dr. Karn insisted he himself wasn't malingering about his own memory, and he still puffed quietly at his pipe, unperturbed. I wondered if his hands were sweating. Suddenly I reached mine out to him. He looked at it and then at me quizzically. I held it there looking him steadily in the eye. Finally, as if to satisfy me, he took my hand and shook it, like a father patronizing a child in some silly game. His hand was wet.

"Your hand is wet, Doctor."

"Yes, I know," he said. "Hot pipe." Then he smiled nicely, and went on puffing. I thought I observed a transient flushing, a pinking of the area above his cheeks below the temples.

"Have you undergone psychoanalysis yourself?"

"No."

"But undergoing psychoanalysis is a prerequisite for men who themselves wish to practice psychoanalysis, isn't that true?"

"Yes."

"But you haven't been interested in psychoanalysis, have you?"

"No."

"How big was this woman Joe Esquibel shot?"

The doctor put his pipe in his pocket and returned my gaze more intently now. He hesitated a minute. "I actually don't know," he said.

"You don't know?" I asked incredulously. "She was considerably smaller than Joe, wasn't she?"

"Yes," he said.

"And what kind of a personality would see a small, frail woman as 'powerful,' as someone who could 'manipulate him' as you have reported to the court?" But now he was comfortable again.

"It wouldn't fall into any particular category," he said. "It would be the personality trait of an individual who perhaps had been markedly influenced in his developmental years by females . . ."

"Your psychologist reported Joe's basic defense was

repression. You didn't tell the court that in your report, did you?"

"I didn't think it would be particularly meaningful to the court."

"What is repression?"

"It's a mental process by which we regulate our unconscious mind against things we don't want to see," he said.

"We kinda close our minds to hurtful things, isn't that right?"

"That's true."

"And amnesia is sometimes a form of repression, isn't that true?"

"In the broadest sense, yes."

"And didn't this man claim he couldn't remember?"

"Yes."

"And when your own psychologist finds there is repression, he is telling about a subconscious defense?" I underlined the word "subconscious" with my voice.

"Everyone has repression."

"Yes, I know," I came back quickly, slapping the psychologist's report on the table. "But everyone doesn't have amnesia, does he?"

"That's true."

"And you didn't tell the court that this man's basic defense mechanism was repression, did you?"

"No," he answered in a friendly way, but his eyes were no longer soft and he seemed alert now to all of the irrelevant movements around him, the paper shuffling, the court reporter filling his machine with a long ream of paper upon which the proceedings would be recorded. Dr. Karn had come to the edge with me, but he held back, insisting that Joe Esquibel simply didn't want to remember. We all have repression, the doctor said. We all have it; and then we took an adjournment of the deposition for the evening.

The next morning I sat down in the same empty courtroom looking at this man whom we called, respectfully, Dr. Karn. I looked over at him. I slapped my hand flat on the table, hard. The doctor jumped. Then he quickly relaxed into his classical clinical look, a sort of uninterested inquiry as to what this man across from him was about.

"I want you to wake up, Doctor."

"I am awake," he said pleasantly, smiling an amused smile.

"I am trying to find out what you really know about Joe Esquibel."

"I have written my report," he said.

"Yes," I said, "and your report admits he saw women as powerful and manipulative." I started there again.

"Yes," the doctor said. "I think his development is compatible with a person who has a very unhappy, and I would say, a traumatic childhood."

"That means in common English that he was hurt emotionally as a child?"

"Yes, as a small child he grew up with impressions which are still pretty indelible in his mind—that women can be powerful, can be domineering, dominating, controlling, manipulative . . ." He ran out of adjectives.

"Would this affect his judgment and feeling with respect to all women?"

"It tends to generalize, yes," he said.

"And the fact that he was neglected by his mother as a child . . . would that reinforce his fear of women?"

"Fear, surely . . . hatred."

"And this kind of treatment by a mother can result in the mental illness of the child, isn't that true?"

"It certainly can," the doctor said pleasantly.

"What has been your experience with mothers who have had numerous illicit lovers, especially in the presence of their young and impressionable children . . . very young and very impressionable?"

"It would have a deleterious effect . . . possibly resenting her . . . even hating her," he said again.

"Are you aware of the fact that Mrs. Esquibel had numerous boyfriends?"

He stopped to think a minute. He was sitting on the edge of his chair now, his hands bracing the seat and his knuckles white. "No, sir," he said finally.

"Weren't you aware of these findings by your own people in your own file, and I quote, 'Many of these male companions have spent the night with her in their home. He, Joe, states this upsets him very much and makes him very angry at her, and he feels like striking out at her.'"

"He is referring to his mother, yes," the doctor said matter-of-factly, as if he knew all along.

"Wouldn't this pattern of striking out at his mother who had hurt him later be duplicated by his striking out at his own wife?"

"I think it is very compatible with that type of dynamic, yes."

"His own wife, who had also been out with men after they were married in much the same way that his mother had behaved—would this all be a kind of pattern in his life, in his background?"

"Yes, that would be true. Now, he never told me about this himself," he added hurriedly, knowing there was nothing of that kind in his report to the court.

"Do you see a parallel between Joe Esquibel's hatred of his mother for having affairs with other men, men who stayed all night, and Joe Esquibel's hatred of his wife for also having affairs with other men?"

"Surely, I see a parallel."

"What does all this mean to a lay person?"

"Simply that if you have a negative experience and it is repeated a second time, or third time, or fourth time, it's ingrained upon you more indelibly."

"And you are liable to react as you have in the past?"

"Maybe so."

"Impulsively?"

The doctor heard the word "impulsively." He knew I was moving toward the defense of "irresistible impulse," and he sat closer to the edge of his chair and leaned toward me, and we were like two men ready to engage each other in wrestling, but his voice was soft. "I wouldn't say he would likely react impulsively, but certainly aggressively."

"So the very mother whom he sometimes hated, who

was promiscuous, was the very kind of woman he would choose for his own mate, isn't that true?"

"That very frequently happens."

"And whom he would likewise, subconsciously, hate?"

"Hate, or abuse, or perhaps even try to reform."

"Did you note that your social worker says that the patient also stated his wife reminded him very much of his mother?"

"Yes, he says that."

"What insidious implications are involved in that statement, if any?" I waved the paper at him. The doctor sat back a little, but his voice was still calm. And now he reached into his pocket, withdrew his pipe, filled it carefully, packed it with his thumb around the edges, and lit it. Finally he answered.

"It would be entirely theoretical."

"This is all theoretical, isn't it?"

"Yes."

"Tell me what your theory is in that regard."

"This, again, would be the desire to possess his mother, which can be on an entirely unconscious level."

"By possess, you mean to have sexual relations with her?"

"Physically, yes."

"In other words, it would be a means by which he could obtain the love from his mother that he hadn't had?"

"Vicariously."

"Vicariously?"

"Through his wife," he said. He watched the smoke rise quietly in the empty courtroom, looked back down at me, gave me a nice little smile, and then waited for the next question.

"And that causes stress, doesn't it, Doctor?"

"Yes."

"It is the kind of stress that could—excuse the term, Doctor—I don't wish to engage in any semantics with you, but to use the language in its most typical general sense—that is the kind of stress which could be deemed an 'irresistible impulse'?"

"It's possible," he said softly, and smiled again at me. I

led him now where I wished him to be, like a fresh-broken horse on the end of a hard halter rope.

"And Joe Esquibel was dependent on his wife, wasn't he?"

"Dependent, yes."

"As he was on his mother—as a child, for all things, including love?"

"Surely," he admitted matter-of-factly.

"And when what he needed was taken from him, he might well respond as a child responds, isn't that true?"

"That's true."

"And in your business you often see crimes of violence committed against another, with no showing of remorse, because the person feels his act was justified, isn't that true?"

"Surely."

"And this is often seen in psychotic individuals?"

"Yes."

"Often you see psychotic individuals believing they have been called upon from some other source of authority to murder, isn't that true? That it's their duty to kill?"

"Yes."

"That's typical of a schizophrenic, isn't it?"

"Yes, surely."

"And you found in this case that Joe Esquibel had no real remorse after the killing?"

"That's true."

"Can you also explain his lack of remorse because of his hatred for his mother?"

"It's possible, on an unconscious level."

"This is kind of a schizophrenic approach, isn't it, if you wanted to give it a tab?"

"Yes, very informally."

"It's certainly a manifestation of a psychotic response to the situation, isn't that true?"

"Could be, sure."

The doctor had that pleasant smile on his face again.

"Is there any hope of changing this kind of personality structure?" I asked.

"In our experience, very little." And there was that smile, that kind, sweet smile again, and I smiled back.

"That's all the questions I have right now, Doctor," I said.

8

HARVEY WATKINS was the assistant director of the
Carbon County Welfare Department although he'd been
in the Rawlins office five years before Louis Groh had
come to take over the directorship. Politics, you know,
even in the Welfare Department. But Harvey Watkins
was a dedicated welfare worker, a man Louis Groh could
count on—took responsibility on his shoulders, like the
department was really his to run and the people in Mexican town, in fact, his subjects.

At the same time the records revealed that a certain
caseworker named Mona Lee Murphy, along with Watkins himself, had been making a routine visit of welfare
clients on the south side of Rawlins, down in Mexican
town, as people called it, when the chief of police and an
officer named Gould happened by, just patrolling in the
chief's car. I suppose the chief had recognized Watkins
standing there in Mexican town with the snow blowing
around his white-stockinged ankles so that it was hard to
tell what was snow and what were ankles. Watkins stood
there on skinny, stork legs with black rubbers over his
shoes, and a small tweed hat pulled down on his head as
if to try to get ears and all inside. The chief pulled up next
to the curb, and Watkins nodded, looking down at the
chief in the car. He always looked down from his six feet
five inches—sighted down his long nose through old wire-
rimmed spectacles, which usually sat in about the middle
of the nose, slightly askew to the right. He was huddled

inside an ill-matching tweed topcoat with the thin coat collar up, and a red bow tie protruded in the front, also slightly askew to the right.

Mrs. Mona Lee Murphy, trim and proper, stood erect and shivering beside Harvey Watkins on nicely stockinged calves, which were half covered by a shin-length skirt, just in style at the time. She was a honey-haired woman, early thirties, not long out of college, a married woman, with a single child, a little girl, and a colorless husband who switched on the railroad. Except for her red earmuffs, which covered her perfectly ordinary ears, she seemed, after all, as plain as potatoes.

"What's up, chief?" Watkins said in his most friendly manner.

"Why don't you folks jump in?" the chief asked through a little crack in the window. "It's warm in here. I want to show you something." Watkins folded up his stilt legs and crawled in behind the red earmuffed woman in the back seat.

"This is Mona Lee Murphy," Watkins said. "Mrs. Murphy," he said with emphasis on the missus to the chief, and then he laughed a little.

"Hi there, cutie," the chief said. "Let's all go down here to 218 West Center. A Mexican whore with six kids lives there. Been gettin' complaints on 'er for a long time. It's a boar's nest, they say."

"No, a whore's nest," said Watkins, and he laughed at his own joke with a couple of groans, slapped a bony leg, and looked over at Mrs. Mona Lee Murphy, to whom he gave the slightest elbow in the rib. "Isn't that right, Mona Lee?" The red earmuffed lady smiled sweetly, and the police car spun forward in the snow.

"I want you to see it yourself," the chief said. "This is in your department." The chief looked at Mexican town as they drove through. "They oughta take a bulldozer and clear this whole mess up—I used to run a cat myself. I could clean this son-of-a-bitch up in two hours—put it in one pile—fifty shacks an hour," he laughed. "Light one match to the son-of-a-bitch and Rawlins would look a hundred percent better." The chief stopped the car in front of a tar-paper shack with a shed roof—a one-room affair. The tar paper was covered with chicken wire, waiting for the stuccoer.

"Let's go in," the chief said.

"You got a warrant, or something?" Watkins asked.

"Don't need no warrant in Mexican town," the chief said.

The four people made a fresh trail across the morning's clean unmarked snow to the front door of the shack. The chief knocked. No answer. He knocked once more, looked over and up at Watkins, who shrugged his shoulders, and then the chief pressed his own heavy shoulder against the door. The door flew open like the flap on a cardboard box and the chief stepped in and looked around in the dark room.

"The kids are all home," he shouted out the open door. "Your mama here, kid?" the chief asked a ten-year-old boy who didn't answer. The boy ran to hide under the single bed in the corner.

"Hey, kid." The chief started in pursuit out of habit, like a cop, like any dog after any rabbit when it runs, but then he stopped short when a little girl with wide eyes and matted, tangled black hair, a couple of years older than the boy, but smaller, stepped in front of him.

"His name is Little Joe," she said. "What you fuckers want?" She was a tiny thing, like a six-year-old, and she had an angel face.

"Jesus, look at this dump," the chief said, ignoring the little girl and surveying the dark room. "That Esquibel woman lives here. Where's your mama, kid?" the chief said to the girl. The girl picked up the baby, also a girl, already half her size, from the floor—bare-bottomed—in a dirty wet undershirt, nose running to her chin, dull-eyed, her black hair matted like a black lamb fresh from the thistle patch.

"There used to be nine in this one room," the chief said.

"Grandpa died," the girl holding the bare-bottomed baby said.

"Where's your mother, child?" Mona Lee Murphy asked sweetly.

"She's workin'," the girl said. She looked scared.

"Where does she work?" Mrs. Murphy had a notebook and pencil out. The baby made a noise, like a whimper from a pup, and the little girl began to bounce the child, her head flopping aimlessly around as if its neck had been sprung, and the eyes of the baby were wide open, staring, dark, and dull as the dirt floor.

"God, it's cold in here," Watkins said, shaking his shoulders, and looking down his long nose through his spectacles to the girl with the baby.

"You fuckers come to turn off the gas? It's already off," the girl said matter-of-factly. "You come to steal us?"

"What's your name, child?" Mona Lee Murphy asked, pencil poised. She reached out to pat the girl's head, then thought better of it, and drew back her hand. "What's your name?"

"We got a new bed," the girl said, still bouncing the baby. "See!" She pointed to a rusty spring cot sitting in the corner with an old army blanket bunched up in the middle. Next to the bed was an accumulation of dirty clothes, mostly women's clothes and underthings, wet matted diapers, a man's blue denim shirt, various rags, and next to the pile of clothes in the middle of the room was an old Monkey-Ward tub-and-wringer washing machine. There were a few wooden chairs, four by actual count, not enough for the whole family to sit down at once. There was a small, wooden straight-legged table and on the table was an empty bottle of catsup. The room also held various other children, including a boy, maybe twelve, named Timato. He appeared to be the eldest.

Timato's hair was long and straight and hung past his shoulders like an Indian's, and unlike the rest of the fat-faced, skinny, half-starved, naked children, Timato's face was bony and hard. Only his eyes and his soft mouth belonged to a child. There was a younger little boy with a protruding belly, naked from the waist down, who jumped up suddenly from behind the cot, maybe six, and in the far corner of the room was a little girl, probably four, it was hard to tell. The little girl stood barefooted, holding onto a dirty rag doll. Mona Lee Murphy walked toward the little boy, who scampered back behind the bed again.

"That child is not circumcised," Mrs. Murphy declared, and made a note. "And it smells in here."

"They teach you that in college?" Watkins asked with a long-nosed sneer. "I'll give you college girls a little lesson. You want to know about people? Well, dealing with people is our business. Gotta get to know 'em—really know 'em—well, just go look in their cupboard. People are what they eat," he said, as if the saying were original with him. "The cupboard'll tell you the whole story." He grinned again, and you couldn't help but wonder if he was putting on a show for the chief. Then he slapped his skinny leg and grabbed ahold of Mrs. Murphy by her nicely formed arm, as nicely formed as her leg, and he said good-naturedly, "Come here. Take a look." He opened up the single cupboard on the wall, which was a box with an old bath towel nailed up at the top for a cover. "Now take some notes," he commanded. "One half loaf of old bread, white. One can condensed milk. Here's half a cup of uncooked beans and some flour, maybe half a pound. That's it. That tells it all," he said. Mrs. Murphy was writing.

"Where does your mother work?" Mrs. Murphy asked the little girl again.

"I don' know, but she's workin'."

"When will she be home?"

"Maybe tomorrow," she said.

"I'll tell you where she's working," the chief said, giving Mrs. Murphy a knowing wink. "She's workin' up at the Rawlins Rooms—works in the boxcars in the summertime with the railroad men and in the Rawlins Rooms when it gets cold."

"Let's go," Watkins said. "I've seen all I need to see. Seen one, seen 'em all. The kids are dirty—like their parents. You can't change 'em—can't do a damn thing with 'em. Makes a fella sick. But you're better leavin' 'em alone, I say. They've come this far alone, no help, nobody's dead. They're not on our rolls anymore. The father was once, before the old man died. But they're gettin' by now. They can live damn near forever on a few beans and a little flour. But if you get 'em on the rolls, get 'em used to fancy food, well, later it's like tryin' to get 'em off dope. You don't know 'em like I do."

The chief and Officer Gould followed Watkins out, and nobody said anything back to Watkins. Finally Mrs. Mona Lee Murphy closed the door. Her face was tight and pale, and plain.

"They'll freeze to death," Mona Lee Murphy said.

"Nah," Watkins said. "They won't freeze. Those kids are tough. They're used to it. My kids would freeze—your kids would freeze, but not them. They're like little animals, believe me. Never seen a pup freeze yet." He laughed a little bit and looked down his straight nose at everybody sitting in the car.

"I think they should have an emergency order of food and we should get the heat turned on," Mrs. Murphy said.

"You're making a mistake," the assistant director said. "I've been in this game a long time. We got budgets, you know, and you can't go feed every wetback you meet on the street. Spoils 'em. Once they get on the dole, well, you never get 'em off, I'm tellin' ya."

"I'm going to report this case to the county attorney," the chief said. "They ought to take those kids away from that woman."

"Nobody wants 'em," the assistant director said. "Let us off here." The police car pulled up alongside Watkins' old Pontiac station wagon. Harvey Watkins got out, gave the chief a little salute, and promised his department would make a report right away.

"Thanks," the chief said, and gave Mona Lee Murphy a smile and a wink, but she looked like she didn't see it.

Mrs. Murphy filed her report saying she had gone back to the Esquibel shack on Saturday. It was her day off, but good works are not bound by a five-day week. The Rawlins wind was still blowing snow and railroad cinders, and the gas was still shut off in the shack. The report said that the caseworker, Mrs. Murphy, had returned to find Mrs. Esquibel at home. No, no, Mrs. Murphy had insisted to Mrs. Esquibel. She was not from the funeral home to collect for the old man's funeral. Mrs. Murphy was from the Welfare Department.

"No spick English," Mrs. Esquibel said through the closed door, and she wouldn't let Mrs. Murphy in. So Mrs. Murphy had gone to Mrs. Leyba's house next door for help, and the two women had gone back to Mrs. Esquibel's and pounded on the door some more. "Agneda, Agneda," Mrs. Leyba shouted, "let us in." And Mrs. Leyba said something to Agneda in Spanish. "This woman wants to help you." She spoke something in Spanish and knocked on the door some more, and pretty soon the door opened a crack.

"Esta hermana buena," Mrs. Leyba said, and Agneda said something back. "No, no," Mrs. Leyba said. Then she turned to the welfare lady. "She thinks you wan' to collect some money, but I tell her you wan' to help." Pretty soon the door opened and the two women went in.

"This woman wants to help you," Mrs. Leyba said again. Then she said it in Spanish once more. "She said she don't wan' no help," Mrs. Leyba translated. "She say you let the old man die. She say you no take him to the doctors. She say all you do is cause trouble. You don' do no good. She don' wan' no help. She don' wan' no trouble. She don' wan' you to stick your nose into nothin'. She don' wan' you to take her kids. She don' wan' you aroun'," she said. Then Mrs. Murphy took out her notebook and began to write. "Ask her who takes care of the children while she works." The two Mexican women spoke in Spanish for a while.

"She said she don' wan' you asking no questions neither. She don' need nothin'. She says she has a baby-sitter —pays the baby-sitter twenty dollars a month—that's a lot of money—twenty dollars for a baby-sitter! I never seen no baby-sitter here," Mrs. Leyba said, with a surprised look on her face.

"I fuckin' do have a baby-sitter," Mrs. Esquibel blurted

out in good English, followed by a barrage of cursing in Spanish. Then Mrs. Leyba turned to Mrs. Murphy and said, "She says to get out of her house. She does too have a baby-sitter."

"Tell her if she will ride uptown with me to the store I'll give her an emergency order for ten days' of groceries—about thirty-five dollars' worth. All she has to do is come uptown with me. Where does she buy her groceries?"

"She says she buys 'em at the Sel-Right." The little kids were hanging onto Mrs. Esquibel and Little Joe shoved the smallest boy away. He had his mother's leg to himself.

"Shoo—" Mrs. Esquibel said, and gave a quick slap at the kids, who scattered like chickens.

"She says she's goin' downtown anyways and she will ride with you."

The welfare records said, "Mrs. Esquibel took the groceries but refused to answer any further questions. She was questioned in detail about who her baby-sitter was, but she could not name the person. She does not speak English very well, and is confused on the birth dates of her children. In many cases she had no record of their birth. She was given a ten days food order in the amount of thirty-five dollars and eighty-three cents, and she was again cautioned about failing to feed the children, and she was told she must keep enough groceries in the house so that the children would have enough to eat." It was a complete report, duly filed in the office of the Carbon County Welfare Department, and a copy was sent to the chief of police.

After Mrs. Esquibel came back with the bags of groceries, she suddenly turned to Elma. "Elma," she screamed at the twelve-year-old, "I tol' you not to let them gringos in the house." She spoke in rapid bursts. "They steal Mexican kids. You wan' that they steal you and your brothers and sisters? I gotta work. I canno' watch you all the time. I should wheep you good." She grabbed a handful of Elma's matted hair—shook her and slapped her face with one quick whop of the hand. Then quickly she grabbed the child up and held her to her large bosoms and kissed her over and over before Elma could cry. "I get the gas turned on tomorrow." Then she let the child go.

"Elma, you gonna do the wash or not?" Agneda said to the little girl, as if nothing had happened.

"We ain't got no soap, Mama."

"I get soap tomorrow," Agneda said.

"You gonna help me, Mama?" Elma asked.

"Little Joe help you. Little Joe, you help your sister carry the water over from Grandma's, you hear? Go on now—Little Joe. Let loose. I can't stan' you goddamned kids hangin' on me all the time like goddamn pups. It drive me crazy." She pushed Little Joe away. "You're nothin' but goddamn pups."

But the boy, ten, the largest of the children, a head taller than Elma, really too tall to hold onto his mother's short leg, clung there anyway.

"I don' like it when you go, Mama," Little Joe said.

"You suppose to be in school," she scolded. "Why you no go to school? I gotta work. I canno' be here all the time fussin' with you pups."

"I ain't got no clothes," Little Joe said. "I don' wanna go to school."

"I get you some clothes tomorrow," Agneda said.

"I don' wan' no clothes," Little Joe said. "I wan' you . . ."

"You help your sister do the wash," Agneda interrupted. "You hear? You do a ten-bucket wash. I get the gas on tomorrow. You heat up the buckets—all ten—on the stove. Be careful. You know how, Little Joe."

Little Joe didn't say anything. Then the woman pulled away from the boy and walked over to the small mirror hanging above the washbasin. She peered in—took off the old black navy pea coat she wore to keep warm in the house, looked carefully, adjusted the straps of the brassiere, and pulled a lipstick out of a small bag she carried with her everywhere. She put the lipstick on. It was bright red. She started to run a rat-tailed comb through her kinky hair, a bad home permanent, and then gave up, sticking the comb and lipstick back in the bag. She rearranged her flowered low-cut jersey dress around her short hips, put her black navy pea coat back on, and tied a black scarf over her head.

"Where you goin'?" Little Joe cried, his eyes big as quarters. The other children came running, grabbing her, holding on. The baby started to cry. The mother picked up the baby.

"Elma, why you no clean up the baby?"

"I ain't got no more diapers," Elma said.

"I get the soap in the mornin'," Agneda said again. "Elma, you feed the baby." She pushed the baby over to Elma, shook off the children, and pushed open the door. Little Joe chased after her.

"Where you goin', Mama? Mama!"

"Your mama gotta go to work, Little Joe." She stooped down and kissed the boy. Then she picked Joe up and hugged him until he couldn't breathe, and he started to cry but no sounds came.

"You don' cry!" she screamed. "You don' cry! You're a big boy—you're the man!"

"Timato's the man," Little Joe sobbed.

"Timato's sick. His chest hurts," Agneda said.

"Timato's always sick," Little Joe sobbed.

"Bad heart, Timato. I take Timato to the doctor tomorrow. You are the man, Little Joe—you're the big man." She gave him a final shake loose, and walked off down the street.

The chief of police said he had no other choice but to file against the Esquibel woman with the county attorney —what with the complaints he was getting and all. Got three calls just last week alone—seven for the month. Nobody gave his name, because nobody wanted trouble, not with Agneda Esquibel. She was as likely to stick you with a butcher knife or cut your tires or hit you in the back of the head with a rock as she was to say good morning. Nobody fooled with her. But letting kids freeze to death—letting them starve right in front of your eyes with a file full of complaints was another thing. The chief said he would have arrested her on the spot if he had his way. But what was he to do with six kids? Didn't have facilities for them in the city jail, and besides it was the county's problem. They lived in the city, all right, but the city had no welfare program and taking kids away from their mother was the job of the District Court of Carbon County. That much was clear.

And so the chief skimmed the report from the Welfare Department and told the dispatcher that at his first break he should stick the report in an envelope and send it on to the county attorney. He'd call the county attorney himself. The county attorney was a dedicated man, a serious man from a good old-time Rawlins family, and he would take care of the matter. Besides, the chief had seen the Esquibel woman headed up the steps of the Rawlins Rooms the night following his visit to the Esquibel shack, and enough was enough. No other way to stop this Esquibel woman, he argued, and like Harvey Watkins said, once a whore, always a whore. He'd found that out too, and he also found out that once you got a file set up in the welfare office, then things took place automatically, like follow-ups and audits by the state office wondering why there were no follow-ups, and reports that went to budgeting, and reports that made up the yearly statistics, and case study reports, and state case load reports, and case evaluation reports, so that once the first report was filed, well, it was like tossing a stick in the river. It just kept on a-goin'.

But the chief thought he should make one more call— she had nice legs. A man should give a woman credit where she's got it coming, and the plain lookers are the kind who will fool you the most sometimes—never can tell about the plain lookers. He called the welfare office.

"You wrote a dandy report, darlin'," he said in a real friendly voice.

"Thank you," Mrs. Murphy said. "But I have to get some more information—birth dates, proof of eligibility, all that sort of thing. I'll be going over to see Mrs. Esquibel again. Do you want my follow-up report?"

"I'll come by and pick you up—take you over there."

"I can't find the woman in the daytime," Mona said,

"and when I drove by the other night the house was dark."

"They probably got the electricity shut off now," the chief said. "The kids were probably in bed. You have to find the mother at work. I'll come by and take you up to the Rawlins Rooms. Ever been in a whorehouse?" The chief laughed. He could just see Mona Lee Murphy's face growing red, blushing like a schoolgirl. She was a schoolgirl. Those are the kind, sometimes. Her face would be as red as her red earmuffs. Strange woman. Serious. Why they teach them all that social stuff in college was more than the chief knew. Finally Mona Lee Murphy answered, no, she had never been in such a place.

"I'll come by and get you at nine tonight. That ought to be about right. Things usually don't get hopping in the Rawlins Rooms until after the bars close. Maybe I'll buy you a drink." Later the chief picked up Mona Lee Murphy at the welfare office. She was all bundled up against the cold, and she looked ridiculous, still with the red earmuffs and bobby socks over her hose—in saddle shoes, they called them, white, round-toed, red rubber-soled flat shoes with brown leather middles, stylish in high school ten years earlier. She dressed for the occasion like a person would dress for a hike in the country. The chief was out of uniform, off duty, he said.

They climbed up the narrow wooden steps at the front of the Rawlins Rooms—up into that place of "carnal copulation" as the chief liked to call it. There must have been thirty steps up, at least, and as they climbed the chief felt a need to explain to Mrs. Murphy. He grabbed hold of her arm to reassure her and then stopped halfway up to catch his breath.

"These houses of prostitution are illegal," he declared.

"I thought so," Mrs. Murphy said plainly.

"But we let 'em stay open—got a lot of sheepherders around, toughs and the like. Close up the houses and we'll get a lot a rapes. It is a choice, ya know, in law enforcement—which is worse, the rapes or the prostitutes? But the town folks are behind us. It's a kinda rape control if you wanta know the truth."

"Oh," Mrs. Murphy said. The chief, his name was Renford, or something close, just stood there talking and holding onto Mrs. Murphy's arm. "The girls get inspected by the doctor every week."

"Really?" Mrs. Murphy asked.

"Of course. We make 'em put up a certificate. Try to run the thing right. And every Monday morning each girl pays a fine to the city. Helps the city budget a little. Good business. Everybody wins. The money's strictly accounted for," the chief added.

"Oh," Mrs. Murphy said again. At the top of the stairs was a door. There was a window in the door with a heavy curtain over it. The chief pushed a little black button and they could hear the long buzz inside. Shortly a black woman appeared—silently, without expression, she let the chief and Mrs. Murphy in. An old peroxide blonde in a red blouse and with ruby-red lips greeted the chief with a formal handshake. To what great honor did she owe this visit from the chief she asked, to which the chief replied it was strictly business, just helping Mrs. Murphy of the welfare, who wanted to see Agneda.

"We ain't got no Agneda here, honey," the peroxide blonde said to the chief.

"Come on, Maybelle. I know better. I seen her here a dozen times—the Mexican with the big tits." The chief turned quickly to Mrs. Murphy. " 'Scuse me," he said. "Sometimes a man gets to talkin' a little plain." Then he turned back to the madam. "She's the little Mexican with the big bosoms—got six kids for Christ's sake. You must be hard up for girls. The kids are frozen and all." Then the chief got stern, and his voice dropped about an octave. "You go get her, Maybelle," he said. "Now."

"Oh, Nellie? You mean Nellie Montoya? Okay. Hold on a minute," and in a little while the blonde came back. "She don't want to talk to you, chief. I can't make her talk to you, ya know." The chief burst forward—pushed past the blonde, and headed to the kitchen, which was behind the waiting room. He knew his way around. Three other women in scanty blouses and long tight skirts were in the kitchen. Agneda Esquibel was there. She still had on the flowered jersey dress. She looked pretty good in it.

"Miz Esquibel—you stay there." The chief turned to the other three. "Get your asses out of here," he said. Then the madam came in.

"A drink?" she asked.

"Pour us all a drink. Pour Nellie here a drink, too," he said to the madam. "And pour Mrs. Murphy one. We are gonna have us a little talk." The blonde took out four white coffee mugs, one with a broken handle, which she set in front of herself. Then she took a bottle of Seagram's 7 down from the cupboard and poured about a shot in each of the cups.

"I really don't drink, thank you," Mrs. Murphy said.

"Everybody drinks up here," the chief said. "It is part of doin' business in a whorehouse, ain't that so, Maybelle?" He laughed and winked at everybody.

"You know it, chief," Maybelle smiled back, and she hitched up her bra strap. They all sat down at the table, which was covered with a red-flowered tablecloth. The wooden chairs were brightly painted, one red, one light blue, two yellow.

"They drink out of coffee cups in case there's a raid, ain't that right?" he laughed. The madam didn't answer. "Everything in a whorehouse is illegal. They got no license to sell booze here. They got no license to sell nothin'. They just give their customers a drink—ain't that right?" The chief laughed again. "Maybelle makes more money up here sellin' this whiskey in these coffee cups than she does off of them girls. You can always get a drink of whiskey from Maybelle here anytime of the day or night, that is if ya got a dollar. Course, they rob ya," the chief said, in a friendly conversational way. "A dollar for a fifty-cent shot, but you can always get a drink. That's what counts." The chief laughed once more to let everybody know it was all right. "Well, here ya are," the chief said to Mrs. Murphy, "right in the middle of a whorehouse. Ya can see how the other half lives now. That's something they didn't teach ya in school, I bet. Well, go to it," he said to Mrs. Murphy. Then he turned to

Agneda. "You talk to her, now, Miz Esquibel. You talk if you know what's good for ya." Agneda looked down. Then suddenly she emptied her cup.

"I no spick English," she said.

9

MRS. MURPHY filed another report in the welfare office, which said she had persuaded Mrs. Esquibel to come in to talk over a proposed budget so the welfare could give her more money for food. The report said Mrs. Esquibel did come in and the budget was as follows: "Food for a month, $107.50; clothing, $37; household supplies, $4.25; additional allowance, $18.75. This totals $167.50. This amount, less the $65 a month which Agneda Esquibel stated her husband, Dario, was to send her for support of the children under the divorce decree leaves a balance of $102.50." That was the end of Mrs. Murphy's report. But Harvey Watkins wouldn't approve it. "What about the money she's makin' at the Rawlins Rooms?" he asked, jabbing a long finger at Mrs. Murphy's report. "You know damn well she's makin' money up there," Watkins said.

"Well, we can't count that," Mona Lee Murphy said quietly, "because if we count that money she'll be over the budget and we won't be able to help her at all, and she'll just have to stay up there and work." But Harvey Watkins wouldn't hear of overlooking any collateral sources. It was in the regulations. You deduct all collateral sources, and the department was responsible for the taxpayers' money, all of it, and then Harvey Watkins took Mrs. Murphy's report and finished it up himself. He put down that Agneda was earning $150 a month from the Rawlins Café. You couldn't say she was earning $150 a month in a whorehouse, but you had to account for the money, and $150 was an estimate anyway. Probably made more than that, but you figured $5.00 a go, $2.00 for the house and $3.00 for the girl, and just two goes a night for five nights a week, two days off, that was $120 right there. And you gotta figure she probably averaged another half a go each night, and that was another $30, so $150 a month was a fair estimate. After you subtracted $20 a month for the baby-sitter, that left Mrs. Esquibel making $37.50 over the budget.

Harry Watkins ended the financial section of the report with the conclusion that since there was no deficiency Mrs. Esquibel should receive no allowance from the welfare.

"What about paying the city something every week?" Mona Lee asked.

"What do you know about that?" Watkins demanded, looking down his long nose with a surprised look on his face.

"I just know," she said.

"Well, I don't know," he said, and then Watkins wrote in the report that while Mrs. Esquibel was in the office the assistant director cautioned her against going to work without having a baby-sitter.

"This woman," the report said, "is known by several aliases, including 'Nellie Montoya.' Mrs. Esquibel was not a bit cooperative in either of her interviews with the caseworker. Mrs. Esquibel did say, however, that she had a miscarriage about ten days before and that Doctor McNamara had been the attending physician. Again she was cautioned about working in the Rawlins Rooms or any other rooming house and participating in prostitution."

Mrs. Murphy complained to the assistant director about reporting that Mrs. Esquibel's income came from working at the Rawlins Café. How in the name of reason could the assistant director count Agneda's earnings from prostitution in making up her budget? Wasn't that condoning prostitution, or something? Mrs. Murphy argued. Wasn't it making it impossible for her to quit? But

Harvey Watkins laughed. "They didn't teach you anything in school," he said. "Regardless of where it comes
from, $150 a month is $150 a month," he said. "That
should be obvious—even to a full-fledged social worker
with a fancy degree. You can't change people. You can't
buy good morals. You can't make good mothers out of
whores. Once a whore, always a whore. The best thing to
do is to keep 'em off the rolls. We have our budgets, you
seem to forget. We are not Santa Claus. The state office
is on our ass all the time . . ."

"What about the children?" Mrs. Murphy asked.

"They'll be all right," Harvey Watkins said. "Believe
me, they'll be all right."

On March 26 the county attorney signed a complaint
against Mrs. Esquibel for child neglect and a warrant was
issued. The chief went to the Esquibel home to carry out
the command of the law. When he got there things were
better, he had to admit. The heat was on. The dirty laundry had been washed. The kids looked better, too, but
none were in school. Anyway, it was his job to serve the
warrant, that's all. He didn't necessarily want to, he said,
but then he asked for this job as chief of police, and there
wasn't any reason to put the dirty work on one of his
other officers. He brought along Officer Gould again. He
knocked on the door of the shack. Mrs. Esquibel was in
bed. It was ten o'clock in the morning, for Christ's sake.
He punched open the door with his shoulder. Agneda sat
up in bed with nothing on but her bra and panties, her
pale yellow body looking weak and anemic—sick, like a
plucked chicken or something—didn't look good to the
chief at all.

"What do you fuckers want?" Agneda asked, peering
at them through blurred eyes.

"Get dressed," the chief said. "You're goin' with us."

"I don' spick English," she said.

"Get yer clothes on," the chief said.

The woman huddled down inside the bed covers again
—pulled them up over her head—and the kids ran for
her bed, Little Joe first, and they crawled up and held
onto the covers that hid their mother, and the children

covered her like nursing puppies, whimpering, and their frightened brown eyes lighted up the place, blinding bright brown eyes staring out with animal fear at the chief.

The chief walked over, pulled a yellow arm out from under the covers, and jerked Agneda to the floor. Her bosoms were still pointing straight out of her big uplift brassiere, and her stomach was sagging, folded, skin over skin from the many pregnancies, six of which had produced these children and all of which had left her belly striped with white stretch marks, crossing her yellow belly with the jagged design of a brood woman. She stood there, small legs holding it all up, but solid legs, one would have to say, and strong wide feet. She began to shake, grabbed at the covers, and once more pulled them around her like an Indian blanket.

"Get dressed," the chief commanded again.

"What you wan'?" she asked.

"I got a warrant for child neglect," the chief said. "You're goin' ta go down to the station with me." Little Joe grabbed her leg and began to whimper. The baby was crying. Elma held onto the baby, and the youngest boy, six, began to cry.

"Stop these fuckin' kids from cryin'," the chief hollered. "I can't stand kids cryin'. Get dressed or I'll take you down this way."

Agneda grabbed her jersey dress off the chair and quickly slipped it over her head. The chief was pulling her out the door—no coat, but she was able to slip on her shoes without stockings—and then she balked, her feet skidding. "Come on, bitch," the chief hollered, tugging at the woman, and Officer Gould grabbed the old navy pea jacket off the chair, tossed it over her head, and gave her a shove out the door.

"You dirty bastar's," she hollered. "My kids! I no do nothin'. You dirty bastar's," she screamed. And then suddenly from behind the washing machine or someplace came a wild-eyed Mexican boy—his mouth open in a silent scream—and the butcher knife was flashing.

"Watch out, chief," Officer Gould hollered. The chief

stepped aside like a less-than-average boxer, grabbed Little Joe's arm, and swung the kid around.

"You little Mexican bastard," he said, snapping the boy's arm just once so that the knife fell to the floor. He gave the kid a push, and Little Joe went rolling, picked himself up halfway across the room on the last roll, and then charged back again—mouth still open, the cry frozen in his throat—coming at the officer, arms flying, legs kicking. "My mama"—he finally got it out—"my mama." The chief was still holding onto Agneda with one hand. "Hold that kid till I get her in the car," the chief hollered to Officer Gould. "See, it's in 'em—in the blood. The kid starts knifing at ten years of age. He'll be a killer by the time he's twenty." He threw the woman in the back seat and crawled in beside her. Then he pushed her over into the corner of the car, pushed her until his own body was flat against her big breasts and then he looked down at her, looked at the cleavage and patted her lightly on the wet forehead teasing, cooing, "Now are ya gonna be a good baby—or do you want daddy to put the cuffs on ya?"

"Go fuck yoursef," Agneda said, kicking.

Then the chief hollered again to Officer Gould. "I'll hold her while you put the cuffs on 'er," and the chief pushed up against her closer, until his mouth was almost on top of hers. "Careful, now, she's a mama—that's it," and Officer Gould pulled her arms behind her and snapped the cuffs shut. Then the chief backed off her and pointed to Gould. "Don't forget to have me write up that kid," the chief said. "He's a natural with the knife. Just as well make a record on the little bastard now. We'll need it sometime."

After the chief hauled Agneda away, Elma just stood there, not crying anymore, but the baby was crying in Elma's arms. Then Timato came silently out from under the bed. He sat down on top of it, but he didn't cry either. He was too big to cry.

"I gon' kill him," Little Joe sobbed.

"I gon' kill him, too," Timato said. "I kill him first."

"The fuckers," said Elma, bouncing the crying baby.

"They stole Mama." The younger children were crying also. "It was my fault," Elma said finally, in her soft little voice. "My fault. I should never let them gringos in. They come and stole Mama. They gon' steal us too," Elma said.

In the police car the officer told Agneda to quit her kicking. He tried to explain to her it would be easier on her.

"You gonna send me to Canyon City? I don' do nothin'," she said. They drove along silently for a while and then Agneda screamed out again, "You fuckers gonna send me to Canyon City?" she asked. They didn't answer.

Canyon City was the women's penitentiary in Colorado and since Wyoming had no women's penitentiary of its own, the state had a contract with Colorado to handle Wyoming's women criminals, but there was a woman's cell in the Carbon County Jail. Agneda had been there before—twice. She always told the truth. That was the problem. She didn't have no head for makin' up no stories, she said.

"How do you plead?" the judge had always asked Agneda before.

"I don' spick English," she had always replied before, standing there in some wrinkled dress.

"How do you plead?" the judge had asked again, patiently.

"Sure, I done it," she'd finally say. She always looked pitiful just standing there, looking down at her feet, but her eyes were dry and hard as black beach pebbles. Once before she wore a pair of black rubber galoshes on her feet and an old ragged bright pink coat. Looked like a frozen flamingo. They gave her thirty days each time, and each time the sheriff let her out in ten days—his trustee he said. The sheriff was a good man. She got along good at the sheriff's place. She wasn't no dumb Mexican bitch.

When they took Agneda before, the children cried, and the welfare finally had to call Dario to come over. Four days later Dario had shown up with this fat woman named Helena. Little Joe didn't like the fat woman. He wouldn't help her. She wasn't his mama.

"You are not my mama," Little Joe said. "I don' have to mind you." He said it in good Spanish, cursed her in good Spanish too, and when she tried to catch him, he and Timato ran under the bed. She was too fat to stoop down to get them. Sometimes she swiped at them with the broom handle under the bed, but it didn't hurt. They called her "Fat Goat." She ate all the beans. Fat Goat refused to feed Little Joe because he wouldn't help her, damn near starved him to death, but he still wouldn't mind her. She wasn't his mama. Fat Goat took away his shoes, too, and Little Joe had to walk barefoot on the dirt floor, and when he had had enough, Little Joe walked out barefooted in the snow looking for his papa. He walked down the tracks he knew so well, stepping from wooden tie to tie under the steel rails, trying to walk on the ties that had no snow on them. He trekked across the railroad yards until he finally found his papa working with the other men on the tracks. Little Joe was nearly frozen to death. His feet were past blue, white and frozen. He grabbed his papa's leg and cried and then somebody at the welfare heard about that too, and got after Dario— told him that he should feed the children better and that if he didn't take care of them, they would be taken away from him and sent off to an orphanage.

"What can a man do?" Dario had said respectfully to the welfare lady. "What can a man do? I left the fat woman plenty of money for beans. A man has to work," he said. But the welfare lady had written a careful report that time. She knew for a fact that Dario got drunk every night. You can't hide things like that in a town like Rawlins, population four or five thousand, and everybody soon knew about the kid walking barefoot in the snow and his drunken father, Dario.

"I keep him at home. I wheep him good," Dario promised. And then later on Dario looked at Little Joe with sad eyes, and his voice was high and quiet. "Little Joe," he whispered. "I love you. I love you more than the Fat Goat." And he pulled at the bottom of the little boy's ear and kissed him, and then Dario walked out into the dark, and left Little Joe. After that, the fat lady didn't stay very long. She went back to New Mexico where Dario had gotten her in the first place.

But this time the prosecuting attorney filed a direct information against Agneda Esquibel. Child neglect, high misdemeanor, up to a year in the county jail and a thousand-dollar fine. That was the place for her, the county jail. But Mrs. Mona Lee Murphy thought otherwise, and before court convened she took up the argument on behalf of Agneda Esquibel with the county attorney right there in the courtroom. "If you'd like my opinion," and she knew he didn't, "it is the county who is contributing to the neglect of the children. I'll tell you how you cure child neglect," she said sarcastically. "You cure child neglect by starving the kids and taking the mother away from the children, by leaving them orphans." But her point wasn't well taken. The county attorney said, what the county does, it does under the law. What the mother does, she does against the law. "You can't get confused with nice social ideas. The law is no place for college philosophy," the county attorney said. "The law is the law." Then the district judge took the bench and spoke very carefully. "Does this woman have an attorney, counsel?" the judge asked. The court reporter took it all down, as the judge dictated into the record.

"No."

"Do you want a lawyer, Mrs. Esquibel?" the judge asked.

"I no spick English," Agneda said.

"I see," the judge said.

"She speaks English when she wants to," the prosecutor said. "She is a street-wise lady, Your Honor. She's been here before. Several times!"

"I see." His Honor frowned. "Why were you here before? I can't recall and I don't have the record in front of me."

"I no spick the English," Agneda said, standing there with her breasts pushing straight out against her tight jersey flowered dress.

"It was . . ." the prosecutor said.

"Well, never mind," the judge interrupted the prosecutor as if at least to protect the record. "Let's put it down on the record as, 'Not Guilty.' That's fair. Call your first witness, counsel."

The prosecutor put Mrs. Murphy on the stand. He introduced her well-written reports typed in black and white, which told of the deplorable conditions in the home—no food, no clothes, filth, children not in school, mother working in the Rawlins Rooms—it was that clear.

"But I'd like to say something," Mrs. Murphy said when the county attorney had finished his questioning.

"What would you like to say?" the judge said with his eyebrows raised up very high and a surprised look on his face.

"Well, I think we could work with this woman. We could set up a budget . . ."

"The time for working with this woman has long since passed, Mrs. Murphy," the judge interrupted, and then smiled down with his nicest smile, his eyes kind. "Life is mostly timing. There is a time for everything. There is, my dear, a time for compassion, for mercy. But that time is past. Off the record," the judge said to the court reporter, who was still taking everything down. "I've seen a lot of these Mexicans come and go. A little jail time will help her, give her time to get her head screwed back on straight. We're still off the record," he said to the reporter again, and the reporter obediently stopped his fingers. "I've found a little jail time usually helps these Mexicans, Mrs. Murphy," the judge said. "In the long run the merciful thing to do is give her a little time to think it over. These Mexicans are basically pretty much alike."

"Well, Your Honor," Mona Lee Murphy said in a most reverent voice, "we're all pretty much alike."

"Well, Mrs. Murphy, I'm not here to debate with you." The judge sat up straight, raised his eyebrows, and dropped both corners of his mouth. "But, surely you recognize that there is a difference in different, ah—shall we say, breeds of the same species. Take the dog for in-

stance . . ." Suddenly the judge turned to Agneda as if
he had decided against the argument.

"On the record. Do you have anything to say, Mrs.
Esquibel?"

But Mona Lee Murphy answered the judge first, as if
everyone were merely having a nice dinner conversation.
"Why, you're quite right, Your Honor." The judge
looked surprised at her agreeing with him. "These people
are all pretty much alike." Then she stood up and looked
the judge in the eye, and in a voice as nice as a Sunday
school teacher's, she said, "These people are all dead
poor. And how can you compare them to dogs?"

The judge turned to the reporter with a cold angry
sound in his voice. "Off the record again. A spaniel isn't
the same as a Doberman pinscher, and you don't treat
them the same or train them the same." The judge
looked away as if that settled it.

"We're not training animals," Mona Lee said. "If we
were we wouldn't need judges. We'd need animal train-
ers. And you don't train a dog by locking him up." She
was nice. She was infuriating.

The judge looked over at the reporter whose fingers
were flying. "I told you, off the record," he shouted. The
reporter's fingers dutifully stopped. The judge turned to
Mrs. Esquibel, who looked up at him with a defiant face,
and the same stony eyes. "Do you have anything to say?"

"I no spick English. You no fuckin' good," she said.

The judge glanced at the reporter, who was patiently
standing by. "That's on the record," he hollered. "That's
on the record!" Then he glanced down at the little
woman standing on firm feet below him. "Your sentence
will be eight to ten months in the county jail and five
hundred dollars' fine, the fine to be suspended on your
good behavior in the county jail. Draw up the papers, Mr.
Prosecutor."

"My kids . . ." Agneda started in her high voice.

"Mr. Esquibel has been called in," the prosecutor
quickly interrupted. "He's the father."

"No! No!" Agneda screamed. "Dario, he drink too
much. He no good for them kids."

"Mr. Sheriff," the judge said to the sheriff, who had been sitting in the rear of the courtroom waiting for the return of his prisoner. "You may take custody of your prisoner." The sheriff came up from the back. The sheriff was a tall dark wiry man. Looked like an old-time gun-fighter. But he had a kind face and a gentle demeanor, which could probably turn to fury in a second's notice. Tough man, they said. Ran a good jail, no escapes, no nonsense. The voters liked him. Kept things in order. People in their places.

"Come on, Nellie," the sheriff said. "Let's go home."

The county attorney had already called Dario and told him Agneda was in jail again. Dario should do something with the children—right away. It was his duty, you know, as a father. "Yes," Dario said in his small high voice. He would do something.

10

I WAS walking down the streets of Laramie, Wyoming, fifteen years old. I walked with a good high bounce, kind of a gorky walk I called it. Fella needed something good about himself even if it was just a gorky walk. I had pimples.

In those days everybody knew what caused pimples. My father talked to me about it, man to man, and finally he put it plainly enough. It was "adolescent sexual excitement" that caused pimples. Threw the whole hormonal system out of balance, and he should know about scientific things like that. He was a chemist. He never said whether he had pimples at my age, and I never asked. I knew he didn't anyway. He was my father. And I also knew that both he and my mother knew what I was doing. She never said anything about it, but she gave me a Boy Scout manual and there was a place in the back which she had clearly marked with a little bookmark. It was a discussion about "self-abuse," as the Boy Scout manual called it, and my father went on to say that that sort of thing was a well-known cause for pimples. "I'll leave it at that," he said.

I thought it was cruel that I should bear such marks of guilt naked on my face for everyone to see. How could a merciful and loving God render such misery and humiliation upon one of His children? As I walked down the street I thought I could tell which people knew what I was doing and which didn't. Little kids didn't—little girls didn't—a few of the older girls didn't but they were mostly fat or ugly themselves. The old ladies didn't—but all the men and the beautiful women knew. I could tell by the way they looked at me. It was cruel, like in Hawthorne's *Scarlet Letter* in American literature. "Imagine the poor woman," Mrs. Trautewig, my teacher, said. "Imagine her shame being condemned to walk in public with the scarlet letter *A* on her breast!" But no one seemed concerned about God's greater cruelty against adolescent boys, against me, marking me with scarlet pimples.

There wasn't much use in my trying to keep down my interest in sex. I was a bad case. Worst I'd ever heard of. Started when I was just four years old. I remember clearly the day. I felt it first lying on the floor looking up the skirt of the baby-sitter, and then I felt it again when I was five and I'd been taking my nap, and I woke up early and my mother was gone someplace and I started crying and hollering for my mama, and I ran outside still crying and hollering as loud as I could and pretty soon the big fat lady next door came over and took my hand and led me back into the house, and she sat down on our big overstuffed chair and put me on her lap, and I could see both of her huge breasts, all the way down, and even though I was sobbing I could feel it then, and I felt it again when I was eight with my piano teacher, Helen Bird. I used to like to watch her walk. She was tall and blond and I thought she was beautiful, and sometimes I couldn't help but see down her front, too, when she leaned over and marked the piano music at the lesson—couldn't help but see, and she smelled good and I had thoughts, and then I felt guilty because my mother said bad thoughts were as bad as the bad deeds themselves, well, almost as bad. And once I had thought about how it would be to see Helen Bird's whole body naked, but that was too raw, too frightening for an eight-year-old to think about very long. Helen Bird didn't really have a whole naked body. Only my mother had a whole naked body. She used to say there was no false modesty in our home. She undressed as she pleased, as often as not in front of me. She said a boy should know what a woman looked like from the beginning so as not to get the wrong impression about women. The body of a loved one is God's work. The body is holy—to be kept clean and upright and healthy. That's why it was a sin to smoke and to drink. Someday I would marry, and then my wife's body would be no strange thing to me, she said. But I told my mother I would never marry—never leave her, and besides she was the only naked woman in the world I ever really knew about.

I usually did what my mother said. It wasn't that I was such a good boy—but not to mind one's mother was a sin. Not one of the big ten, but a sin was a sin. Murder was a sin, cheating, taking the Lord's name in vain was a sin, stealing—those were the big sins—sex before marriage was sinful, probably one of the big ten, too. But big or little, sin was all alike. It got mixed up and ran together— the big sins and the smaller sins, and if I sinned she knew. If she didn't know about my sex feelings, well, God knew, and I had a hunch they got together sometimes behind my back.

Once Mrs. Taylor caught Buddy, her son, and me out behind the Taylor house in the garage with some girls. "I'll show you mine," I said, "if you'll show us yours." And we made a bargain and the girls peed in a milk bottle and I peed in front of them on the dirt garage floor, and I felt excited—more excited and wild than I had ever felt before, even a little crazy, I thought. Maybe I was going crazy. Then Mrs. Taylor came walking right into the garage, and there I was with my thing out with the two neighbor girls and I didn't know what to say. I knew she would tell my mother. What shame! What horrid shame! My mother might never forgive me, and it would be like stabbing her in the heart. Maybe I'd never be her son any more, and things between my mother and me would never be the same again. But I was a quick thinker even then, they said. I could think on my feet.

"Well, we shouldn't be doing this, I guess. I'm sure glad you came along, Mrs. Taylor," I said, as I buttoned up my pants. "I don't know what would have happened if you hadn't come along." I smiled weakly at Mrs. Taylor and she just looked back, shocked and pale. She was a chubby, big-bosomed woman. Buddy called her his "nice, fat, juicy mama." She had a pretty face—a classic nose, and I thought, Oh, God, she'll tell my mother. Oh, God. Then I said, "Well, you won't have to go and tell my mother." I was talking very calmly. "I'll go over and tell her myself . . . I'm going right now, Mrs. Taylor, and I'll tell her—you hear? Thank you. Thank you." And I ran across the street, and my mother was fixing up the Easter egg coloring. I didn't want to color Easter eggs. I was sick and hot, and afraid, and crazy, and excited. Girls actually peed in a bottle! God knew it—knew what my mother didn't know yet. I wasn't going to tell her. Never. But she and God would probably get together anyway later on.

The Boy Scout manual said a boy should take "a cold hip bath," which should prove to be a help when a boy was inclined to engage in "self-abuse." I thought about sitting in a cold tub of water. The manual was probably written by a preacher. Ol' Calsey had the best idea, but sometimes I felt ashamed and guilty about what I'd done when Calsey took me to the Rawlins whorehouse.

I was gorking along. I could match my walk against any in Laramie. I passed by the Cathedral Home. It was an orphanage in Laramie, one of the city's beautiful stone buildings, and I loved it. I stopped a minute to consider the structure. The architecture seemed Continental to me, and I thought it was built by some church much more powerful than our Methodist church, which was constructed of plain red brick. This Cathedral Home came out of another age, a society I didn't understand, out of places covered with ivy, where there were wise-looking men and beautiful women. Those who built this orphanage must be very rich and very powerful. Must be rich orphans, I thought. Maybe someday I would know rich and powerful people too.

There was a strange-looking mixture of children behind the stately black iron-spear fence. These must be the orphans, I thought. They ought to be happy enough. They probably once had important parents. One was a little fat-faced blond kid, maybe a bishop's illegitimate kid—probably some damn preacher who didn't take his goddamned cold hip bath and got some choir girl in trouble, in the name of God. The kid pushed his fat little face in between the black iron spears of the fence and peered at me with big sober blue eyes. I said, "Hi," and he said nothing. The kid obviously didn't know my secret. I gorked on by, fought the blowing cinders in the stubborn Laramie wind, which, except for a few nice days in the fall, never rested. Laramie was a rude place to live. Step out and the wind slapped railroad cinders in your eyes, or smashed snow and sleet square in your face. I walked past a Mexican kid who was also looking through the fence. He looked sad. Not much hair on his head for a Mexican, I thought.

I worked for Herwitz Brothers—swept the jewelry store—never swept it right, not once; polished the glass cases—never perfectly, not once; washed the windows—left streaks; brushed the cinders from the sidewalk into the gutter; unpacked new shipments of merchandise, and generally did poorly all the things they would have otherwise done properly themselves but for their generosity in having made a job for a poor boy—twenty-five cents an hour—good wages in those days. The boys calling the train crews made fifty cents an hour. But their fathers were railroaders.

I never did go out for sports. That made it even worse. It was one thing to be a pimple-faced kid, but not to redeem oneself by being a respectable athlete in at least one sport made me nobody. I could sing. But that was nothing. At fifteen I still had my soprano voice. I imitated Bing Crosby's trills, in soprano. It was just as well. He couldn't have imitated me. I sang in some of the school programs and my folks still had me in the church choir, and I sang for a couple of weddings. Christ, I even took typing with a class full of girls because my father thought a boy ought to know how to type.

My father had been a good light-heavyweight boxer in college, and he'd fought well in some "smokers" as they called them in those days, and a father's son should be a

good boxer too. He spent hours teaching me—the left jab
—jab, straight from the shoulder where the power is, the
right cross, the combinations, over and over. He put up a
heavy bag in the basement when I was ten, and after a
while I got good. When the high school put on a boxing
tournament there was no escaping it. I should box. I
could at least do that much to redeem myself.

I was big for my age. At fifteen I was larger than most
eighteen-year-olds. But I still had baby fat and those
damned pimples, and that goddamn soprano voice and
no pubes—not a single one—just a little bald white affair
down there while all the rest of the kids were popping out
hair all over, and carrying around fire hoses, and everything. I was ashamed to undress in the locker room.
Someone would point—"Hey, what's that thing? Looks
like a drowned fish worm." Somebody else would say,
"Yeah, but a guy couldn't catch much of a fish with bait
like that," and everybody would laugh, and everybody
knew I couldn't fight.

But I fought a couple of big heavyweights, and to everybody's surprise, including mine, I won. I never really
hurt anybody—but then my good gorky bounce and my
jab worked out pretty well in the ring. I was a fancy Dan,
and I was going to fight for the high school heavyweight
championship at fifteen. My father came to watch,
proudly, even wrapped my hands for me before the fight
so that the fist would be solid—a man could hurt his
hands if they weren't wrapped right, he said.

When the time came I got into the ring with a big
freckle-faced Swede who looked like Joe Palooka and
had a head about the size of a baseball and a neck like a
country stump. I gave him my fancy footwork and my
good left jab but it didn't matter. I tied him up in clinches
to keep him from hurting me, but he hurt me anyway. I
was out on my feet from the middle of the first round on,
I guess, because I don't remember what happened after
that. They said it was pitiful. I finished the fight, but my
father didn't say anything when I got home—and he's
never mentioned it to this day.

Then "L. V." Wyatt, as we called him, a little 125-

pound skinny kid, and a friend of mine, said he didn't like the way I'd been treated in the fight at all. "That was no way for a man to treat you," he said to me. "He shoulda either knocked ya out or let ya go. He shouldn'a punished you like that, Gerry. It was humiliatin'." He said he figured on doing something about it immediately. Then he walked up to the new heavyweight champion, with me in tow, and started then and there in the locker room to right the wrong.

"You think you're tough, don't ya?" L.V. said to the new heavyweight champ.

"Nah," the new champ said, smelling something coming. L.V. pushed him in the chest.

"Whyn't you try me?" L.V. said—grinning wickedly, pushing again.

"Nah, I ain't got nothing against you," the new champ said.

"Well, try this 'un then," L.V. said, and hit the new champ square in the mouth with a good right. The champ fell back over one of the benches onto the cold concrete floor, and then the coach came in and that was all there was to it. L.V. didn't avenge me in the slightest. Just made it painfully clear that at fifteen, gorky walk and all, heavyweight or not, pimples and all, I couldn't even whip the man a 125-pounder just busted flat.

I walked on past the orphans at the Cathedral Home. They were lucky, I thought. They didn't have fathers who thought they should fight or mothers who knew God. They lived in this beautiful stone building while I lived in a stucco house, a made-over place that everybody knew had once been a chicken house to start with—remodeled and added to, but it had been a chicken house once all the same, and besides that, during the next summer I worked for that rancher who headquartered there at Elk Mountain, and I had had a *second* runaway out in his hayfield, and I was, truly, a bottom-line, genuine, honest-to-God jerk.

11

DARIO WENT to the shack as soon as the county attorney called him. The county attorney had told Dario he should send the children to the Cathedral Home in Laramie. Good place, the county attorney said. But Dario shrugged his skinny shoulders and wiped his face with an old red cotton bandanna like he was getting ready to do something bigger than he was ready to do. He wiped his eyes with the bandanna, as if to get a clear picture of what this was all about, and then he wiped the corners of his mouth, and then he wadded the bandanna up again and stuck it back in his pocket, and he put on his old straw cowboy hat, and hiked up his floppy overalls, which hung loose around his skinny legs like they were dressing up a scarecrow, and then Dario stuck both hands in his overall pockets and closed his eyes and tried to figure out what to do this time. He didn't want to send his kids to no orphanage.

"Good place, Dario," the county attorney repeated. But Dario didn't know, and so he went to see the kids. The kids had been wandering around aimlessly in the shack, but now that they saw Dario standing there in the light of the doorway they all ran to him. They loved him. That much he knew.

"Papa, Papa," the words of his children.

"Papa, Papa," of the baby, echoing the words of his children. They grabbed their father, mobbed him, hung to him, and cried and laughed, and he cried, too, and he stooped down and held onto all of them, gathering them into his arms and holding them until he was about smothered, and they were about smothered, too.

"You've been gone a long time, Papa," Elma finally said when they got untangled.

"I know," he said quietly. "I been herding the sheep."

"Them fuckers stole Mama again," Elma said.

"I tried to kill him," Little Joe said proudly. "I took the butcher knife. I almost kill him."

"You are a tough guy," Dario said. "You are my tough guy." He stooped and picked up the child again. The boy looked lovingly and proudly at his father and then hugged him. His father put him down.

"What you got to eat?" he asked Elma.

"Nothing," Elma said. "Grandma brought some beans last night."

"I'll fix that," Dario said, starting for the door. "I'll fix that."

"Don' go," Little Joe cried, running out after his papa.

"I gotta go to the store," Dario said. "Gotta get some groceries."

"I don' wan' no groceries," Little Joe said, still holding onto Dario's hand. "I don' wan' no groceries. Don' go. Maybe you don' come back again if you go." But Dario left and he did come back again and in the morning he went to the Welfare Department to have a talk with Mrs. Murphy. He should get someone to come and live in the house with the children, Mrs. Murphy said, and Dario talked about getting the fat woman again, old Fat Goat. Surely she would come, and Mrs. Murphy said the welfare would pay for Fat Goat to come to Rawlins from New Mexico, but when they called the woman she refused, gave no real excuse. Only said there were no "sanitary facilities." She was used to sanitary facilities, she said, and it was impossible to care for the children anyway, and that left Dario no choice. He could either send the children to the Cathedral Home in Laramie or to St. Joseph's Orphanage at Torrington—it was his choice, Mrs. Murphy said.

It was a hard decision for Dario, so hard that Mona

Lee mentioned it in her report. "Mr. Esquibel is having a little difficulty in understanding the situation." He was having trouble going home to the kids. They cried and hung onto him when he left. It made him sad to come to the shack—sad to stay—and it hurt him to leave. Little Joe, especially, begged Dario to take him with him, and cried for his mama. Mona Lee told Dario the children had to be seen by the doctor—they had to have a clean bill of health before they could go to this Cathedral Home.

"That is a good place for the children, Dario," she said. "Laramie is on the railroad, and if you go to work on the section again, you can get a pass, and go down and see the children sometimes. But the children have to have a clean bill of health first."

"The children are not sick," Dario said. "Why they have to see the doctor?"

"Because the Cathedral Home wants a medical certification of their health before the home will take them."

"I don' understand," Dario said. "The kids are no sick, 'cept Timato has a sore chest, bad heart maybe. But I don' think so."

"It is like the sheep," Mona Lee said. "You know, before you can ship the sheep to market they have to be inspected—do they have any disease?—are they healthy sheep? The inspector gives a clean bill of health, or something, and then they can ship the sheep. These children will be with other children. Do you understand?"

"Oh," Dario said. But finally Mona Lee had to come with the car and she helped Dario load the children up, and together they took them all off to Dr. McNamara's. A nurse filled out the papers.

Timato and Little Joe vowed a holy vow over the heart of the sacred Mother Mary that no one would steal them again, not them or any of them. Little Joe said he would kill the gringos first—this time for sure. He had the butcher knife, carried it with him all day around the shack, and he put it down only occasionally, even took it with him to the outhouse behind the shack. And Timato had a switchblade of his own. He stole it from Ramon when Ramon lay with his mother drunk in the shack. It was all right. Timato hadn't really stolen it. It had fallen out of Ramon's pocket while he slept on the bed, and the bed belonged to the children. It was pay for the bed. Timato had thought of it that way, and then Timato had picked it up and quickly hidden it in the bottom of a cracker box in the cupboard until the man had left. Timato would help Little Joe kill the gringos if they tried to steal the kids—swore to it over the heart of the sacred mother.

"We could go rob the bank and get some money and get Mama back," Timato said.

"Yeah," Little Joe said, and they stayed up half the night making plans. The next day Father Meyer came to the shack to visit. He had never been there before, and the children didn't know him and Elma wouldn't let him in.

"You come to steal us," she screamed. "I no open the door." But the father talked to the children through the door, told them he knew their mother, that she confessed her sins to him, and that he had come to bless the children. "Let me in and I will bless you." Finally Elma let him in, and sure enough, the father blessed the children and left. The next day Mrs. Mona Lee Murphy got a call from one of her informants, a client living close by, who had seen Father Meyer go into the shack, and so Mona Lee called the father immediately. No, he was not duplicating the services of the welfare he assured her, absolutely not. The church had no intention of interceding in any way—that was beyond its jurisdiction, and Mrs. Murphy could rest assured that no one was trying to interfere with the department's jurisdiction over the children at all. Please rest assured, he said again. However, in view of the fact that the children were Catholic, the father thought they should be sent to St. Joseph's Orphanage. It was a fine place for Catholic children. He requested a short summary of the case and guaranteed his total cooperation.

Mrs. Murphy found a place for the two youngest girls in a foster home, but when she came with the foster parents to pick up the children, Elma would not open the door again and Mrs. Murphy had to call the chief and, of course, the chief came out to the place and pushed the door in with his shoulder and they took the two little girls. The chief disarmed Little Joe right away, took the butcher knife from him as easy as pie. Little Joe had put up quite a fuss, but Timato, seeing that it was useless, kept his switchblade out of sight in his pocket. No use losing a good switchblade, he thought, but later on Little Joe wouldn't speak to Timato.

"Why you don' speak to your brother?" Elma finally asked like a good mother. "You want me to whip you?"

"He let them fuckers steal the little kids," Little Joe said. "He promised. He'll go to hell," Little Joe said loudly, so that Timato could hear. "He will go to hell for letting them gringos steal the little kids."

"You give up too easy," Timato said. "You give up and they took your butcher knife. I couldn' fight 'em alone. We could go get a gun."

"Where?" Little Joe asked.

"We could go bust in the pawnshop. I seen them guns in the window." And they talked half the night making plans.

Dario wouldn't go with Mona Lee Murphy to get the kids. "I can no go," he said.

"Well, the children will wonder where you are," she said, looking sad, fixing her eyes on Dario's, and waiting for him to answer. But Dario didn't answer. Finally Mona Lee said, "Well, Dario. I'll go get the children and take them to Laramie. I'll tell the children you couldn't come and that you'll see them soon, and . . ." But Dario just walked off, rubbing his face with his red bandanna.

The next morning Mona Lee Murphy called the chief again, and then she and Harvey Watkins met the chief and Officer Gould and the four of them descended upon the Esquibel shack. They had made their plan of attack in advance.

"Gould, you take the back door," the chief said. "I'll hit the front, and then I'll pick the kids up, one at a time, and load them in the car. Mona Lee, you and Harvey here keep 'em in the car, once I get 'em to you." It was a simple plan, and it worked. But when the chief pushed in the front door, Timato didn't even pull his knife, nor did they run for cover under the bed. They just stood there, blank-faced, dull-eyed, like dumb little Mexicans, the chief said later. And then the chief told them to get into the car, and they did, and they said nothing—hardly mumbled, like coyote pups who can smell the death of their mother from across the valley. The mother is the heart of the child, and the coyote pups, smelling the dead mother, curl up quietly, usually without a whimper, and begin to die.

"How come the kids didn't cause no trouble this time, chief?" Gould asked.

"They learned their lesson. These Mexicans ain't so dumb in some ways. I suppose I taught 'em something or other," the chief said, proudly. "Need to start on 'em young though."

Then Mona Lee Murphy said, "Well, we'll drive them straight to the Cathedral Home." She waved good-bye to the chief and with the last of the Esquibel kids safely loaded in the back of Harvey Watkins' old Pontiac station wagon the expedition headed down Highway 30 for Laramie.

"Well," Mrs. Murphy said to the children as she turned around to speak to them. "Well, this will be a nice trip. This will be a lot of fun!"

The children looked back blankly.

"Your father couldn't come," she said. "Well," Mrs. Murphy tried again, "do you know where we are going?"

The children didn't respond—not at all. No nodding, no frowns, no consternation or wonderment on their faces—no tears. Only empty eyes.

"Well," Mrs. Murphy said, "we are going to a nice place in Laramie, Wyoming. Do any of you know where Laramie is?"

Nothing.

"Well," she said again. "The place looks like a castle. It *is* a castle. You are going to a castle where there are a lot of other little children. Isn't that going to be fun?"

Nothing.

"They have everything there that children could possibly need," she said. She reached over and patted Little Joe on his hand. "How do you feel about that?" She looked the boy in the eyes. He pulled his hand back and looked down. Mrs. Murphy turned to Harvey Watkins. "One needs to help the children get their feelings out," she said. "It will be better if they could just get their feelings out." Then she spoke to Little Joe.

"What do you want, Little Joe? What is it you want?" Her face was kind and open—plain to be sure, but nice— a nice face for children to look at. "Cat got your tongue, Little Joe?" she smiled.

Nothing.

The car sped along Highway 30—across barren sagebrush-covered plains. There was the pale blue sky and there was the dull prairie, a sickly gray with a subtle hint of green beneath, only enough to show that there was life still hanging to the edges of the shallow roots of grasses, to tender plants and tiny prairie leaves, small things lost to the eye in this empty place.

"Elma, what is it that you kids want?" Mrs. Murphy said again. Mrs. Murphy looked over at the assistant director, knowingly.

"Little Joe wants his mama," Elma said finally. Then the children said nothing more. Mrs. Murphy talked about her own child, her own Sharon, about two years older than Little Joe. She was a pretty little blond girl, Mrs. Murphy said. All you could do was to raise them right and hope for the best. Sharon was such a darling child, precocious, smarter than the other children in her class. She was a regular little mother already. Probably got it from her, from Mona Lee Murphy, the big mother from welfare. She laughed. It was probably in the blood, the way the Murphys were, all natural mothers you know, probably what led Mona Lee into "the helping business" as she liked to call it, being a mother to everybody, and now all these little Mexican kids. Weren't they really quite darling? Her own Sharon would love them so . . . she feels sorry for the Mexican children. She tells me about them. Sorry at her age! Imagine what kind of a welfare lady she'll be when she's twenty! And Mona Lee had laughed.

It was hard to be a mother. It was hard to have a family these days—ah, the family, she said. It's hard when a person has to work—hard on a mother, and on the children, too. Mrs. Murphy had done all the talking—Watkins the driving, the looking, and the children sat silently and sullenly in the back seat.

"Don't you care about where you're going, Elma?" Mrs. Murphy finally said to the child.

"No," Elma said.

"It's sad, in a way." Mrs. Murphy turned back to Watkins, with compassion warm and heavy in her voice. "I wish I could help them. I wish you could see my Sharon." She touched Watkins lightly on the arm.

"I wish I could too. I wish I could help you," Watkins said to Mona Lee. He reached a helpful hand over toward her, hesitated with it in mid-air a moment, like a bird suddenly confused in its flight. Then he let it fall, half the weight of gravity, on Mona Lee Murphy's thigh, kindly on her thigh, with a reassuring little pat, friend to friend.

"You've been very helpful," Mona Lee said to him. "That's what's important in life—to help people. That's why I went to school. I need to be helpful. You understand that, I know," she said, and he left his hand there. The warmth of her thigh leaked through.

"I'd like to get to know you better," Watkins said. "People who work together should know each other better—we should get closer. We would do a better job."

"Yes," Mona Lee Murphy said thoughtfully.

"And," Watkins said, looking over to her and down his nose to the plain face below him, "I have felt a wonderful warmth from you whenever I am around you—you do so much for people. You have so much to offer," he said.

"Oh, thank you," she said. They drove silently for a while, Watkins with his left hand carelessly caressing the wheel, his right still touching Mrs. Murphy lightly. She moved just perceptibly, as if to shift her weight a trace toward him. Then Watkins looked at her again, and she at him, and they were two people looking at each other who wanted to help. "Damn," he said, and now he leaned over to whisper, and Mona Lee Murphy leaned over to catch his words. "Damn," he said again, "I wish we didn't have a carload of kids."

"We have the whole trip back," Mona Lee Murphy said, reassuringly. Then she touched his hand, which rested on her thigh, touched it lightly, grabbed a big finger, and held onto it, like a friend.

They processed the four Esquibel children at the Cathedral Home in the regular course of business. Mrs. Murphy delivered a bill of health for each of the children and took a written receipt for their safe delivery, and then she and Harvey Watkins returned to Rawlins the same afternoon without undue delay.

Mrs. Kelly of the Cathedral Home was only slightly disturbed about this new lot. She knew what to do. Their hair was so matted it couldn't be combed and they were dirty and half-naked. "You'd think they could have cleaned them up first," she said to the night lady. She sent a report to the welfare, which was filed along with all of the other reports, and it said that there were lice in the children's hair and that, therefore, for sanitary reasons, they had to shave the head of each of the Esquibel children, boys and girls alike. Not one of them cried or protested. They were very cooperative children, the report said. However, they seemed to be dull, far below the average of the other children of the same age at the home, but that was just an initial impression. Perhaps there would be time later on to do some testing. The children were issued clothes from the storeroom, used clothing gathered up by the several charities in the area, and they were given new shoes. Then they separated the boys from Elma, and the littlest boy cried first. His head was shiny and white, and when they sent Elma to the girls' quarters, Little Joe, with his own head also bald, looked at Elma and he cried, too, half from the fright of being left alone for the first time without mother or sister, and half from seeing her, a strange haunting little creature with a smooth egg head and wide eyes, and Timato looked strange, too, half demented with his shiny, freshly shaved, bald head—but Timato only stared straight ahead. His waxen face and eyes looked like they held the lost spirits of the ancient Aztecs, home at last in this frozen-faced Mexican boy, who, with the rest of the children, stood on display in the processing room of the Cathedral Home.

Later on Little Joe looked at himself in the mirror in the boys' bathroom.

"You look like a jailbird," an older kid said, pissing and laughing. Little Joe looked in the mirror. He looked like a jailbird. He was a jailbird. "Hey, you some kind of a jailbird?" The kid pushed Little Joe.

"I ain't no jailbird," Little Joe said.

"What you do?" the big kid asked. "You musta done somethin' or they wouldn't shave your head." Little Joe said nothing, and started out the door. But the big kid stepped in front of him. "What did ya do? You musta done somethin'," he said as he pushed Little Joe again.

"I didn't do nothin'."

"Did you kill somebody?" the big kid asked.

"I never," Little Joe said.

"You musta killed somebody. You're a jailbird. Hey, Albert, this here new kid killed somebody. He's a jailbird! Look!"

"Who'd ya kill?" Albert asked.

"I killed the fucker from the welfare," Little Joe said.

"Oh," the big kid said.

"Oh," Albert said.

And still later it was reported that the Esquibel children were ostracized by the other children at the home because of their shaved heads. Elma said their shaved heads had nothing to do with it. It was only that the others were white—gringos. "The gringos don' like us," she said, "none of 'em like us." And Elma said that one of the older gringo kids had told her it was the first time he'd ever seen the home do something right. They should shave the heads of all greasers everywhere. That's what they ought to do, just shave their fuckin' greasy heads.

12

I WANTED out of the Esquibel case, but Raymond Whitaker didn't understand. He still thought it was the greatest case in the history of American jurisprudence, as he put it. I thought we were wasting ourselves defending Joe, and maybe we were being cruel to him. After all, let's be honest about it, I told Whitaker. We got into the case in the first place just to amuse ourselves, and it isn't amusing any more.

"Suppose we convince the jury he's insane and can't stand trial for murder," I said. "What have we really done?"

"Why, we've won, Gerald," he said, flipping me that sardonic smile of his.

"Won what?" I said. "We've won the right to send Joe back to Sublette Hall to hear Jason scream all day. And all night," I added.

"Well, Gerald, that's better than listening to the little plunk of the cyanide pill hitting the acid pan in the gas chamber," Raymond said.

"I don't know," I said. "Think about it. Jason is screaming all day and all night until one day you begin to scream yourself, and your screaming is uncontrollable, day after day, and then one day you begin ripping off your clothes, like Jason. You've become a caged beast, and you've awakened terrorized by these strange things which men call clothes which are choking you, and you rip them off, and scream." I stopped a minute. Whitaker was silent, and the smile had left his face. He looked sad. "And then they leave you naked in the dry side because they say you rip off your clothing, and you gather calluses on your body like a red-butted baboon in the zoo."

"Well, that's just your nightmare, Gerald," Raymond said.

I started up again. "And the fucking psychiatrists will write up reports—publish a paper—and they'll probably see the similarity in the screaming of Jason and the screaming of Joe, and they'll probably give the malady a new name—the Sublette Syndrome or something."

"You *are* having nightmares," Whitaker said. "And in the daytime, too."

"Well, that's just if we win. But someday we'll lose, and a jury will say he can stand trial, and when he's tried for murder we'll have no defense. That could be ten years from now. Then they'll send him to the gas chamber anyway. It's a goddamned waste," I said.

"Well, maybe we should call up Oscar Hall and tell him he can have Joe—tell him we'll change his plea and they can gas him."

"Sometimes I think we shouldn't be messing around in something like this. It's too big to mess around in. Maybe we're dealing with forces we don't understand. Maybe we weren't even meant to understand them."

Whitaker didn't seem to hear. "Did you ever see a man die in the gas chamber?" he asked.

"No," I said. I should have said something else.

"Well, Gerald, first they take the defendant into the gas chamber and they strap old Joe in the chair, see, and then somebody probably prays over him, and then they all get the hell out of there—all except for Joe, of course, and they shut the chamber up with a little wheel, a little whirlimagig and . . ."

"Yes, but . . ."

"And then when everybody's ready, the warden, or somebody, pulls this little gadget which lets the cyanide pill drop into the pan of sulphuric acid—it's a crude affair —and when the pill hits the acid, then the gas comes boiling up out of the pan."

"Come on, Raymond," I said. "Those are your night-mares. Not mine."

"Gerald," he continued in the same voice, without the slightest smile on his face, and his eyes were bright and fierce, or frightened, I couldn't tell which, as if he actually saw the whole thing. "Joe Esquibel will hold onto the arms of the chair and he will either rip off the arms of the chair or his fingers, and he will hold his breath until his eyes pop out, like fish eyes. Did you ever gouge out the eyes of a trout for bait when you were a kid?"

"Raymond, for Christ's sake . . ."

"Just watch Joe's eyes and you'll know when he finally takes the first gasp of gas. It's a dirty irony, Gerald, my boy, that we must breathe to live, but that Joe, in the gas chamber, must finally breathe to die. It will be a happy time in Rawlins. There will be great rejoicing among the people. There will probably even be dancing in the streets. They might sell programs to the affair. Maybe there will be a band, and maybe even a beacon—yes, a six-foot beacon that will flood up the sky from horizon to horizon."

"Raymond, you've lost your mind. You really have been having nightmares . . ."

"No doubt of it, Gerald—it'll be a fine time when they execute Joe Esquibel. There'll be a few women who weep, Front Street hags, I suppose, and they'll drink a drink to Joe Esquibel. 'Remember old Joe,' they'll say. 'Remember when he was in here and kicked the shit out of half the bar one night and then, for kicks, screwed the banker's daughter on top of it—just for good measure?' "

I gave up interrupting him. He was raging on in this silly soliloquy, and I felt sick and tired. I had a bellyful, like an old horse about to founder. I held my breath.

"They claim that the witnesses at the execution won't have to hear his screaming if he chooses to gasp and scream. The chamber is nearly soundproof, and it's been fully tested. They'll have the windows washed clean so that Joe'll be clearly visible to all the witnesses of justice who have gathered together, like friends at a wedding, and they will officially observe the whole affair, and it will all be recorded, officially . . ."

I let out my breath and gasped a fresh, clean breath of good Wyoming air. "I have this fear," Whitaker continued. "I'm afraid he'll stand there quivering all over when his time comes and the tears will be running down his face, and he'll still be trying to convince us he doesn't remember killing his ex-wife. I'm afraid he can't understand that his not remembering is no legal defense at all. I've tried to explain to Joe that we just can't have killers running around claiming they don't remember. God, Gerald, this ghastly chamber is so stark and unpleasant a place to die!"

"I know," I said.

"This Joe Esquibel is merely an uneducated Spanish-American of low intelligence. How can he appreciate the niceties of the system—this great system which has survived for centuries. I've tried to tell him, and I'll tell him once more as he stands there shaking all over—tell him for the last time. 'Unless the facts of your case fit correctly into the nice legal boxes of our system, you cannot be declared legally insane. Joe, the test of sanity has nothing to do with not remembering.' But he'll never understand. I suppose he'll finally stop shaking and start laughing." Whitaker laughed his sardonic laugh again.

"Why would Joe laugh?" I asked.

"He would laugh because it all sounds stupid to him. What does Joe Esquibel know about our system of precedent, of *stare decisis?* God, the lawyers and the judges speak of it with such reverence! They worship *stare decisis.* What's happened in the past dictates the future. *Stare decisis!* It's only an excuse to foist past misery on men all over again. It's like riding down the road backward. We can see where we've been, and therefore we claim we should know where we're going. But what does Joe know about such things?" he said.

"Come on, Raymond." I tried to sound kind.

"Gerald, Joe is still laughing. He is actually standing there laughing, giggling, even drooling out of the corners of his mouth." And I began to share Raymond's night-

mare. Didn't mean to. I could see it. "And I have told Joe
to stop laughing. I have told him that it is embarrassing
me . . . that this is a serious and solemn occasion. I've
explained to him that he should be comforted in knowing
that we have stuck by him to the last moment—that we
never deserted him—never deserted him once, neither
you nor I, Gerald. He could've been represented by some
rascal of the bar who would have left him halfway
through the case."

What could I say? I said nothing.

"But I don't think Joe will thank us," he said. "He's
really too frightened, and his legs are giving out on him
and his eyes are growing glassy and are rolling around in
his head. I'll be grateful if he doesn't scream."

"For Christ's sake, Raymond, stop!" I said.

"No, Gerald, I don't believe he'll scream at all. I think,
instead, he will finally be like a little puppy taken from his
mother and left cold and alone and shivering in a strange,
blinding world. The lights are so bright in the gas chamber, Gerald. Maybe we will have to hold Joe up, you on
one side and me on the other."

"God Almighty, Raymond . . . !"

"Well, Gerald, it's only a nightmare, I know. We'll
never be able to get the governor to commute his sentence. We'll never be able to even find the governor. He'll
be out someplace cutting a ribbon, or kissing Miss Wyoming, and he wouldn't take a call from the likes of us
anyway."

"I suppose not," I said.

"But, Gerald, the death penalty is such a wonderful
teacher! It'll teach old Joe a lesson for sure. He'll learn a
deep and abiding lesson from it all. The next time, yes,
the next time, Gerald, he'll remember, won't he?"

"I suppose so," I said flatly.

"When have they set the trial, Gerald?" he asked.

"It isn't set yet, Raymond," I said.

"Let me know when it's set," he said.

"Yeah," I said, and later on the judge set the trial for
November 6, 1967, and then I began studying the welfare
records in earnest, day after day and deep into the night,

because the only weapon we had was knowing what the
state didn't know. If the lawyer can only understand his
client, maybe he has a chance to make the jury understand him, too, and maybe he can save him. I thought if
only one person can understand me then neither of us is
any longer alone on the face of this lonely earth. I di-
gested the records. I committed them to memory. In the
records lay the power to save Joe Esquibel.

In May, Dario took the 4:10 A.M. train from Rawlins to
visit Little Joe and the others at the Cathedral Home.
Two hours and twenty minutes later the train arrived in
Laramie, at 6:32, to be exact, and by the time Dario
walked up the street a half mile to the Cathedral Home,
it was a little before seven, ordinarily a good time of
morning in May, in Laramie, Wyoming. At an elevation
of over seven thousand feet on a clear day in May things
are bright blue and crisp. The lambing would be mostly
done, Dario thought, and it was time to dock the lambs,
cut the tails, cut the nuts with what they called the cas-
trating blade of a man's pocketknife. The sharp blade
sliced off the top of the lamb's bag, the lamb being held
there by a couple of big boys. The slippery nuts were
squeezed out by fingers sure as a surgeon's, by Mexican
fingers, and then the man, as if to kiss the lamb, reached
down with his mouth and without love or hate took hold
of the warm, slippery testicles with his teeth, because they
were too slippery for the fingers, and with the testicles
firmly behind the teeth the man pulled back and out until
the testicle came out, cord and all. A man needed to get
all of the cord otherwise the wether wouldn't be quite a
wether, but would be a proud wether, a troublemaker in
the sheep herd in the late summer when there was no
time in the rich mountain meadow grasses for wethers to
lose weight pretending they were rams, riding the ewes,
and making a damn nuisance of themselves. Ordinarily it
would be a good time of the year with the snow still on
the higher peaks of the Snowy Range Mountains, and as
he rode along in the chair car Dario had noticed that
there was snow on top of Elk Mountain. The prairies

were green, but not for long, to be sure, but green now, and there was the sound of birds, sounds he recognized, not by name, but the way a man recognizes the bleat of a certain black ewe from all of the others in the herd.

Dario's steps were not so fast and sure as he walked up the street toward the Cathedral Home, up toward the dreaded place where his children were kept. It wouldn't be a time of joy, this time of seeing the children, because the early joy would turn to sorrow too quickly when he must leave again, and then he would hear the dreadful wailing of his children. It wasn't that fathers did not love their children—that was not the reason he hadn't visited them for these weeks. It was not that he wished the faces of his children out of his mind, but it was the nightmares of the father, and sometimes in his dreams Dario could see the torture of his own children, and the children were crying and screaming, being docked along with the lambs, the knife cutting his own babies, not the sheep, and the babies crying, "Papa, Papa"—and "Papa." Children have such power over fathers, these helpless babes who are weaker still than the lambs. Children have such power, Dario thought. They can do such things to a man, these babies who start out no bigger than worms, who grow out of pussy as fast as ragweed. It is a mean trap that's laid for a man because a man knows he's got to stick it, has to stick it like any man, and out of it—out of a minute, less sometimes, not even a good minute's time sometimes, these babies come to live for seventy years or more—out of a single hot minute or less, come these baby faces with little hands and with mouths to feed and cry, and they grow, anywhere, everywhere, like weeds, and the babies learn to say the word "Papa." It is a magic word that babies know. And the word made Dario want to run, and when he heard the word sometimes he wished to cut out his own nuts, to become nothing but a fat, woolly wether, a nutless lamb, to go to market. It would be easier to be cleanly butchered with the wethers than to face the babies crying, "Papa."

Dario had tried to forget the children, but when he closed his eyes he could hear the words, "Papa, Papa," and sometimes the words in the bad dreams caused him to bolt upright in bed, and he heard himself groan out loud. Next week he would see the children as soon as he had some money—next payday, for sure. And then another week had passed, and finally the third, and he could put it off no longer. He should go back to herding sheep. A hundred dollars a month was a good wage for a man plus the sheep wagon to sleep in, and they furnished the food and Dario butchered a mutton once in a while. They never missed a mutton. And there was peace. No drinkin', no bars, no pussy and trouble, no fightin', no gringos, just peace and clear creeks to water the sheep and for a man to drink from and a hundred dollars a month. Good time of year to go back. He'd heard of the Lembke and Hermberg Ranch out of Medicine Bow. Big ranch. Ten, fifteen bands of sheep they said, and they were putting on herders. He would find out. Have his friend Manny call for him. Manny was good on the phone.

Dario knocked on the iron knocker on the front door of the Cathedral Home. It was a big door with wrought-iron hinges, a proper door for such a building. Maybe it was a good place. He banged on the door again. No answer. Then he walked around the back and listened, and around the other corner of the building he could hear kitchen noises. He knocked on the door nearest the noises. An old woman with dough on her hands came to the door and whispered to him. "What chew want?" she said.

"I come to see my kids," Dario said loudly.

"Nobody's up yet," the woman said. "You are too early. Come back later."

"I come a long ways on the train, from Rawlins already," Dario said.

"Oh," the woman said. "Well, come on in then." The woman pointed to a door. "Go sit out there." Dario walked through the high-ceilinged hall into a large room that looked like a mess hall to him. There were long tables covered with white oilcloths. Dario sat down. The room seemed dark and dead. Then he began to whistle.

Where were the babies? Where were the babies? What would Little Joe say to him? Maybe they would be mad at him for having let them go.

"Hey, lady," Dario said. She didn't hear him. "Hey, lady," Dario hollered louder. There were only the busy kitchen noises. "Hey, lady!" He listened again and then a big woman appeared at the opposite door of the dining room, from behind Dario, a gray-headed woman with broad shoulders and huge tits and wide straight legs and a fierce face of fifty. "You stop that yelling, do you hear," the woman yelled herself. "Who in the world are you anyway?"

"My name is Dario. I come to see my kids."

"Dario who?"

"Dario Esquibel."

"Oh," Mrs. Kelly said. "You are the father of these Esquibel children. Well," she said. "You should call before you come. This is hardly the time of day for a visit. Well, you're here. Come with me."

Dario followed the slap-slap of the woman's big slippers down the hall to her desk. Then Mrs. Kelly sat down and busied herself in a box of cards while Dario stood there. Finally the woman said, "Let's see. They are Timato, Donna, Joe—"

"No," Dario interrupted. "It's no Donna. Donna is no here. Donna is in Rawlins."

"Well, don't tell me what children are here and what aren't," the woman said. "It is right here on the card. We have Donna, the oldest."

"Donna, she is no the oldest," Dario said.

"Well, Mr. Esquibel!" Mrs. Kelly said. She put the card back and then looked over her glasses at Dario.

"I come to see my kids."

"Wait here," the woman said. Dario waited a long time in the dark hallway. He had not waited any place for so long since he waited for Little Joe to be born. Then it was all night. Agneda had a bad time because Little Joe was a big baby. The others had come like slick worms, but not Little Joe. Then as Dario peered down the dark hallway he could barely make out the form of a child approaching and finally Dario could see it was Little Joe who came walking, softly, carefully, toward him, looking, looking, and when he saw his father his eyes grew bright as silver dollars and Little Joe hollered, "Papa, Papa," and Little Joe went running into his father's arms. He hung on and started to cry, "Papa, Papa, Papa," and Dario swooped him up. "I knew you'd come. I tol' 'em you'd come and kill 'em for stealing us." He looked his father straight in the eyes, and his eyes were full of baby's tears. "They steal us, Papa," Little Joe said. "Are you gonna take us home?" Then Timato came quickly down the hall and when Timato saw his father he said nothing. He came a few steps closer and stopped, his eyes down. "How you doin', Timato?" his father said, but Timato didn't answer. Then the baby boy came. "Papa, Papa." The baby ran to his father and grabbed Dario's hard leg, a leg like a crooked stake, and held onto him.

"Papa, Papa," cried Elma. "We knowed you'd come. I told the boys you'd come. They no think you gonna come. But I know you gonna come," she said proudly. "You gonna take us home. We gotta get out of here, Papa. They hate us here." She started to sob. "They cut off all our hair—see?" She ran her little hands over the stubs less than half an inch high. "They call us jailbirds. They put Little Joe in a closet. He hit a fuckin' gringo."

"I hit 'em with a bottle," Little Joe said. "I hit 'em hard."

"Broke his head—made it bleed," Elma said. "He was bigger'n Little Joe, a white guy. Called Little Joe a 'fuckin' Spick'—a 'fuckin' jailbird Spick.' They all call us jailbird Spicks," she said, and her eyes were big and bright. But you could tell, even with the hair cut off, that she was a little girl. Anybody could see that. "They put Little Joe in a closet all day."

"It was dark in there," Little Joe said. "You gonna take us home right now?" Dario hugged the children, and then they walked out in the yard. "We ain't s'posed to go outside the yard without gettin' permission from Mrs. Kelly. We wan' to go with you," Little Joe said, and then later in the morning Dario went back inside because Mrs. Kelly said she wanted to talk to Dario.

"That there is Elma, not Donna," Dario said.

"Oh," Mrs. Kelly said. "There must be some mistake. The welfare must have given us the wrong name. We have called her Donna since she's been here, and she's answered to that name and hasn't said a word, Mr. Esquibel. The children are very sullen, I would say. Timato, the oldest boy," she said, as if Dario didn't know the names of any of his other children either, "well, he is simply morose, hangs around, says nothing, does nothing, doesn't even speak to his own brothers and sister. Seems despondent. Perhaps, yes, of course." She was reading more on the cards now. "He can't even read and he is already twelve years old. He's not even at the first grade level." She read some more. It was all there on the card. "Timato is a dull child to start with—but how dull he is we really don't know. Tests should be made of this child." She picked up another card. "It says here that Joe is ten years of age, that he has already been in the first grade twice, and that he didn't start the first grade until he was over eight years old. Must not be very bright either." She looked over at Dario, who sat there staring down the hallway. "You haven't understood a word I've said. It's little wonder that they're slow," she said, half under her breath. "That child, Timato, the oldest, looks like you."

"Yeah, he do," Dario said proudly. "Timato, he is a good boy."

Mrs. Kelly scolded Dario, saying that the children still didn't have enough clothes and that she had taken the children with the clear understanding that Dario was to pay fifty dollars a month to the Carbon County Welfare to help defray expenses, which he had failed to do so far. "The first payment was due on the arrival of the children. You are already three weeks in arrears."

"I pay next payday, for sure," Dario said.

Still later Dario went back out into the yard to see the children again and to say good-bye. He gave them each a dollar, but the children said they didn't want the dollar. They wanted Papa, and they cried and held onto him, all of them except Timato. Dario made no attempt to break loose. He just stood there at the gate, the children crying and hanging onto him, and he touched their heads and looked up into the blue May sky, and felt his own tears, felt his own weak legs wet from the slobbering, crying mouths of his babies, and he wished to die, to place the long blade of his pocketknife into his breast, to feel it reach deep into his very heart, and to cut his heart, to feel the real blood of his veins, to know the real pain of his flesh, once and for all, and to have it over with. He stood looking at the sky a long time with the babies hanging onto him. Finally they cried themselves out, and the children stood silently together at the black iron gate watching Dario walk slowly down the street toward the railroad track.

Later Mrs. Kelly wrote a letter to the Carbon County Welfare in Rawlins demanding that the father's visits to the children cease. This is a "must" she wrote, because he disturbs the children too much. The father has very little to offer the children, and he gives them money for candy, which they eat all at once and get sick. His influence on the children is a negative factor, Mrs. Kelly wrote. The children would be much easier to manage, easier to process and institutionalize, without the disturbing influence of the father. Her studies revealed that orphans are always better children to work with than children whose parents continue to intercede in one way or another.

The night after Dario left the night lady found Little Joe walking in his sleep. He came down from the third floor, naked as a jaybird, walking along, his eyes wide open. The night lady grabbed the naked child, lifted him up to her, and went back up the stairs with him. She told Mrs. Kelly about it the next morning.

"I suppose he cried for his father?" Mrs. Kelly said.

"No," the night lady said. "No, he didn't cry for his father. He held onto me, and was sobbing, 'Mama, Mama, Mama,' in his sleep."

"I thought it would be his father," Mrs. Kelly said.

"No," the night lady said. "Children never cry for their fathers at night—none of the children I've ever been with over the years ever cry for their fathers at night. At night they cry for their mothers."

"You can't generalize like that," Mrs. Kelly said. "There is no empirical evidence whatsoever from any of the studies I've reviewed to that effect at all."

"I only know what I know," the night lady said.

The children had no summer underwear the welfare records said, but Dario had also promised to get them underwear, next payday, for sure. Summer underwear is important. "Can I take off my long underwear this mornin', Mom?" I used to ask every spring.

"Not today," my mother would say in a nice way that seemed a little distant. "Maybe next week." But next week never seemed to come. Days are long to a boy waiting for springtime in Wyoming so he can take off his long winter underwear.

"Can I take 'em off today, Mom?" and she would finally say yes. "I can?" I'd ask in disbelief.

"Yes," she'd say again.

"I can! Oh, boy! It's spring!" I could take 'em off, shed my hide, like every animal in the spring sheds its old coat, and I could put on my BVD's. It's not springtime even when the shooting stars are out, light purple with pointed yellow noses. It's not springtime even when the yellow waxy buttercups begin their blooming along the old creek bank. It is springtime only when a boy can get out of his long winter underwear—then; and when he awakens one morning to the thunder of thousands of tiny feet crossing the old wooden Fifth Street Bridge, and above the din he hears the holler of the Mexican herders on their horses.

"Haw there, haw, haw." And there was the bleating of a thousand head of sheep, maybe more, and their lambs, lost from their mothers, the ewes bawling for their lambs, and the lambs crying back. I bounded out of bed at the sound, slipped on my pants, no shoes, and ran the three blocks down the gravel road to the Fifth Street Bridge, and I found this Mexican herder riding on his horse at the edge of the flock and hollering, "Haw, haw," and swinging a gunnysack up and down to scare the sheep along. A black ewe wore a bell that made little dings as she ran—"counter sheep" they called them, one every hundred or so.

"Hey, mister, got any bums?" The Mexican herder paid no attention to me. "Haw, haw," he hollered, swinging his sack out at the sheep.

"Hey, mister." I ran alongside his horse looking up. He had to stop swinging to keep from hitting me with the sack. "Got any bums?" He was a fierce, skinny-looking man with the bones of his face sticking out against his hide, and his eyes were flashing, sparkly black eyes as mean as a rooster, and he had big, white, bony teeth.

"Geet, keed," he yelled, and his old white big-footed horse moved slowly through the sheep, which parted for the horse and rider like water around a river rock. It was noisy, and I was hollering to the herder as loud as I could, and the sheep were baaing and bleating, and the ground was covered with their little round turds, like brown peas, and it was dusty, and there was this little lamb with a long tail who had missed the docking. It was tired already. Anybody could see that. It didn't baa . . . hardly walked, its head down, pushed forward mostly by the other sheep, which scattered ahead as the herd moved up Fifth Street Hill toward the green summer pastures of the Big Horns.

"Hey, mister," I hollered, still in the way of the Mexican herder. "Can I have this bum?" I looked up, blue eyes looking up into those mean black eyes, and I pointed to the lamb, which was hardly walking now.

"Take that fuckin' lamb, keed," the Mexican said with a flip of his sack. I ran for the lamb and grabbed it up, woolly and warm against my summer underwear, and when I looked back I thought I saw a little smile on the mean face of the herder.

I took care of my lamb all summer, fed it from a bottle four times a day, taught it to lead on a rope, and took it on hikes with me up the draw, and I named it "Cousin." I don't know why.

"Hey, Cousin," I'd call, and the lamb would come, suck my fingers, suck the bottle, suck and wag its long tail happily, and follow me. I gathered what is called lamb's-quarter, wild spinach, on the creek bank for my mother in a Pay-and-Save brown paper grocery sack. The lamb ate the tender lamb's-quarter, too. Then one day in the fall after I had gone back to school the lamb disappeared. It was only after we had eaten that good sweet meat, fresh in the early fall, before Dad brought home the wild-tasting antelope and deer that I realized what had happened to my lamb, to Cousin.

"Why?" I cried. "Why!" I stomped and rolled on the floor, sobbing, and pounded the oak floors with my fists, and then I rolled and cried some more. "Why?"

"It has to be that way, Gerry," my mother said softly. "Lambs grow up to be eaten!"

13

AGNEDA ESQUIBEL, trustee at the Carbon County Jail, seemed happy for a guilty woman. Just watching her it was hard to tell that the state had treated her badly. Mona Lee Murphy always argued her case, but most people thought this Murphy woman leaned a little too far to the left, especially for a place like Rawlins, Wyoming. This Murphy woman said, for instance, that most people don't commit crimes, that the state commits them first against its own people. She said she could prove it in the Esquibel case. Mrs. Esquibel wasn't guilty of any crime at all, she said.

"Well, what about prostitution and child neglect for starters?" one of the other caseworkers asked as Mona Lee Murphy held forth one afternoon during a coffee break.

"She didn't commit the crime of child neglect and prostitution first," Mrs. Murphy argued. "Agneda Esquibel became a prostitute in order to feed her children. The first crime was committed by the state, which failed to provide one of its own, a helpless woman, and her children with the bare necessities. All creatures have certain natural rights," she argued, but they barely listened to her at the afternoon coffee break. They were polite all right, these fellow workers, but they hardly heard her at all when she said the least of the natural rights of all people is to have enough food and to have adequate shelter for simple survival. "It was the state's failure, the state's crime," she said, her voice growing strong and authoritative. "It is a crime for any government to permit such huge wealth to be deposited into the hands of a few and to permit its less fortunate citizens to starve. It was the government which permitted this—and the economic system that encouraged it," she said. And she drank her coffee out of a cup that had her name on it, which she held onto now with her little finger extended, just so. "The state committed the first crime, all right. It was the crime of letting its citizens go hungry."

"How can the state commit crimes?" one of the other workers said. "The state doesn't commit crimes—people commit crimes."

"The guilt lies on all of us," Mona Lee Murphy argued, looking very serious. "And then the state committed its second crime against the Esquibels when it took away those children from their mother, and vice versa. You see," she said, "it is a crime to abandon one's children, so to punish a woman who abandons her children, we take the woman from her children. The state itself committed the crime of child neglect by taking the mother from her babies," Mona Lee Murphy said.

"Well, you can't leave a woman like her with those kids," someone said; then somebody else said she thought that what Mona Lee Murphy said was so much B.S., if Mona Lee didn't mind her saying so, and besides, you could have given her a thousand dollars a month and she still wouldn't have stayed at home. No, Mona Lee Murphy said. Yes, the other caseworker said.

"Well, we will never know about that," Mona Lee said. "I tried to talk to the judge—but you know judges. They have no social understanding." Then someone blurted it out—it just came out. Later the person wished she'd never said it: "At least judges aren't pinko commies."

"What is that supposed to mean?" Mona Lee Murphy turned now in sudden anger. "I'm no communist. I'm as patriotic as anybody. I just have a sense of social responsibility." Then she quieted down right away, and put a smile back on her plain face. They were poorly educated, she thought, even if they had degrees.

"This is a free country," another caseworker said. "Every person has the right to do the best he can and the government should stay out. This is a free country," the caseworker said again to emphasize the point.

"Babies are free to starve?" Mona Lee Murphy asked. She thought of Agneda Esquibel, and for a moment her heart reached out for the poor woman. Then she took the cup with her name on it over to the sink, rinsed it, and turned it upside down to dry.

But Agneda Esquibel had never wept a tear in the Carbon County Jail. Why weep? She was no dumb Mexican, as they say. She knew the lay of the land, and made her own accommodations with the sheriff, who was a fair man. Women shouldn't be locked in little cement cells, the sheriff said. That's no place for a woman. A woman's place is in the home, and so he made Agneda Esquibel his trustee and put her in his house, to clean and scrub and help the missus, as he called his wife. His wife needed help feeding the prisoners and all, and as a matter of fact the sheriff liked Agneda, a lot. A little work never hurt a woman, nor a man for that matter.

This was a time of peace for Agneda, a time without the crying and tugging of the pups, an almost magical time when all the pups had been weaned at once, taken by some master hand from her den, whimpering and whining, yes. But it was not her fault. This hand had come like the owner's hand into the brood bitch's pen, and the puppies were weaned and sold, and the place cleaned up for another litter. She had enough to eat. There was always plenty of boiled antelope, confiscated by the game wardens from poachers and furnished to the sheriff by his game warden friends, and there was usually some beans.

The sheriff told Agneda the children were at the Cathedral Home, a good place, that Cathedral Home—the kids would be all right. Sometimes he had her clean his office and then, with the door closed for privacy, they talked a little. The sheriff liked to talk to her, but the sheriff was a private man.

The sheriff looked over at this woman standing there

unself-consciously in front of him in his office. "They say Dario is fixin' the place up," the sheriff had said to Agneda. "He's adding another room."

"Dario's a good man," she said. "I should no have left him." She just stood there in the sheriff's plain office.

"How come you left him?" the sheriff asked—a social man, this sheriff. People said he was hard, but there was a soft part that only a few who were close to him knew about. There is always a soft part inside every powerful man. If not there would be no reason for all that power on the outside to protect the soft inside. The sheriff looked at this woman standing there. It was a moment when nothing should happen, when Agneda should just stand there.

"How come you left Dario?" the sheriff asked again. "How come you left him if he was such a good man?"

"I don't know how to spick it in English," she said.

"You *no comprende,* huh?" the sheriff laughed. "Well, he must not 'a been too bad. Ya had six kids by him," the sheriff said with an accusing look on his face. He put his feet up on the desk and leaned back to seem casual. He was not a man to get excited easily. Everybody knew that. Agneda looked away—out into the bright blue morning with the cars passing lazily by in the street as if the drivers were sleep-driving. There were the sounds of birds going about their business feeding their young, which filled up the nest with mouths, only mouths, always open, squawking, no matter how much or how often they were fed, the mouths always open and always squawking. It is the way of baby birds.

Agneda had no desire to leave the sheriff's home. She was the sheriff's trustee, humbly, helplessly, standing there. She was in the power of the state. The power was too big for her. She had given in. Outside the sheriff's door was the sound of the lonely dispatcher's voice and the crack and pop of the radio with broken shattered words, which would be lost in the eternal static of space. It was a lazy time in the sheriff's office. Nothing happens on a sunny summer morning in the office of the sheriff of Carbon County, Wyoming.

"Well, Nellie," the sheriff finally said. "I think there's something wrong with Dario you don't want to tell me." He laughed, and swung his feet off the desk.

"I gotta go," she said suddenly. "I gotta go clean the house for the missus."

The welfare records said, "It was learned today that Dario Esquibel and Felipa Espinosa are getting married. Mrs. Espinosa is an ADC mother (Aid to Dependent Children) with four children of her own. This worker called at the Espinosa home." It was a place down the street from the Esquibel shack. Not so different from the Esquibel shack, in fact.

Harvey Watkins and Mona Lee Murphy found Felipa at her home and Dario was there, and Watkins, finding that Dario and Felipa Espinosa had already gotten married, exploded, saying, "How come? How the hell can you do something like that without even talking to me about it? Christ Almighty, you got six kids and she's got four—ten kids on welfare. All you do is do the fucking and let us pay the bills!"

Dario didn't answer for a long time. He just stared back at Watkins with fiery black eyes, and his mouth looked like it was sewn shut, and his lips pulled against each other. Finally Dario said, "I know what I need. A man don't need much—something to eat, a roof over his head, and a good woman." His words were soft, sounded sure, as if they were wise words which had come down from some mountaintop, but Harvey Watkins didn't hear them that way.

"Goddamn it, that's all well and good," Watkins said, like a father speaking to a mere child, "well and good, Dario." Then there didn't seem anything else for Watkins to say.

"Me and Felipa here is in love," Dario said innocently, sincerely. Felipa sat saying nothing, looking down.

"Is that right?" Watkins said in mock surprise. "In love! Christ! How can anybody be in love with ten kids!"

"Well, we are in love," Felipa whispered finally. She was a younger woman than Dario, slender—there was a thin, haunted look in her face. She said the words bashfully, like a little girl confessing something nasty.

"Oh, great," Watkins said. "There ain't any regulations in my books about love. There ain't any 'aid to dependent lovers,'" he said, with his sarcasm coming into final bloom.

"We can make it somehow," Dario said. "We can make it."

"Sure," Watkins said. "I know what you Mexies make," he exploded again. "We all know what you make—kids!" And then Watkins burst out of the screen door dragging Mona Lee Murphy by the arm, letting the door slam behind them.

Mona Lee tried to calm Watkins down. She touched him lightly on the arm and then held onto it. He was a practical man—trained and hired to solve problems in the most practical way, but Lord knows that was almost impossible in the Welfare Department. There were more reports than anything else, more papers, more people shuffling the goddamned papers than anything else.

Watkins turned to Mona Lee Murphy. "Look at us," he said. "If it weren't for your kid and your old man I'd run off with you probably. We ought to do it anyway. Let the fucking welfare take care of us for a change." They separated to get into Watkins' car, and all Mona Lee Murphy did was laugh lightly back, in her way, and her laugh touched Watkins and made him feel something, actually feel it, like something coming alive, like sunshine on a frozen field, and then she sat next to Watkins in the car looking proud.

"Well, we do what we have to do," Watkins said to Mona Lee. "We can't run off. We have responsibilities. A man has to take his love where he can find it. It's that simple. There's no other answer—take it where you can find it or don't take it at all," he said, driving away.

"I'll take it," she teased lightly, and squeezed him and then squeezed him again.

"Goddamn it," Watkins hollered, and rolled the car sharply to the curb, and there in the broad daylight in front of the cars lazying down the Rawlins streets, in front of the people walking by, in front of Mona Lee Murphy, her plain face sparkling, her quite ordinary mouth open and wet, he threw his arms around her, like a scarecrow's arms grabbing and flapping into the wind, and he put his mouth, open and hot, on hers, and after a while she pulled loose.

"A man needs a good woman," she breathed. "Dario knows," and then she laughed in her way again. "That's what a man needs," she said, and she gave Harvey Watkins another little squeeze with her hand.

When Dario visited the children the last time at the Cathedral Home, Elma had begged him to take her and the other children to see their mother. "Little Joe is screamin' all the time at night and he's havin' crazy dreams, and he's wakin' everybody up," she said. "And the night lady says we should go see our mama. She says it will help Timato, too. He don't talk to nobody yet—not even to us. He don' talk at all—just walks around like he's crazy or somethin'."

"You kids should forget 'er," Dario said. "Mrs. Kelly won't let me take you kids anyways, and this place is like a prison," Dario said, looking around him. "I get ya out of here," he promised suddenly. "I get ya out of here."

"Ya ain't got no place to put us, Papa," Elma said. But when Dario left he called Mona Lee Murphy and told her what the night lady said, and Mona Lee called Mrs. Kelly, and the conversation hadn't been friendly at all, Mrs. Kelly saying she considered it the worst kind of interference, and she wasn't going to stand for it, and that Mrs. Murphy could come and take the children—permanently. They were nothing but trouble and had been from the start, from the first day they came. But Mona Lee knew about people, and so she heard Mrs. Kelly out, kindly, without any reply, just a "Yes—yes, I know," and a "Yes, yes, I suppose it has been awfully hard," and answers like that, so that when all of Mrs. Kelly's anger was expelled there would be nothing left for her to do but agree.

The next weekend Mrs. Murphy and Harvey Watkins

drove to Laramie in the old Pontiac station wagon and got the kids. They were people working to help other people, on a Saturday, out of their own good hearts, and when they finally got back to Rawlins it was late in the afternoon. Mona Lee had the children get out of the car and line up on the sidewalk at the front lawn of the courthouse and the children stood there, bashfully, looking down, all dressed in their Sunday clothes that Dario had bought so they could go to church, and new shoes that the welfare had bought. Mona Lee had it arranged so that Agneda would come out the front door of the courthouse, not the jail, and then there Agneda was, coming down the same steps that important ladies came down every day, and she walked very stately on the sidewalk toward the children, who looked at her like she was an apparition, and she looked at them as if she were, and they did not know what to do or say. As she walked toward the children there was no expression on her face and her head wobbled slightly from side to side, like the head of some bride who was trying too hard to take the right size steps in the wedding march.

Then Little Joe broke like a wild lamb from the herd and went running to his mama. "Mama," he cried. And Agneda grabbed the boy, big as he was for his ten years, and held him up, little as she was, held him to her bosom and Agneda Esquibel started sobbing, loudly, and the sound of her voice was a strange sound Little Joe had never heard from his mother before, like she had been hurt, hit hard inside or something, and it frightened him and he cried louder, "Mama, Mama," as if to drown out her noise. Then he held onto Agneda and the other children ran to her, all holding onto her, weeping, and finally, Agneda looked up and there stood Dario, too, his little eyes, which were always too close to his nose, looking sad. Nobody said anything. The silence made everybody feel naked, and finally Agneda shook herself straight, and she raised her Aztec face up, and after a while she said, quietly to Dario, "You're a good man, Dario." Dario said nothing, standing there alone with the children still hanging onto her. "I hear you got married," she said, speaking to him in Spanish. And Dario nodded his head. "I hear you married that Felipa Espinosa," she said. Then she turned away from Dario and said, "You are too good a man for me, Dario." One could hardly hear her voice, and Dario, who maybe heard it and maybe not, said nothing.

I asked Cleo to take the welfare records, back them with white cardboard, and make exhibits of them for court, and then I numbered the exhibits, and stacked them up in a neat pile on my desk. I leaned back in the old oak captain's chair and looked at my grandma Spence's ivy growing up the window's edge that separated my office from the walled patio outside. The ivy clung to the rough cedar walls of my office like a child to its mother, and I wondered what was going to happen to me. I wondered if I was going to grow old and die in Riverton, Wyoming. "You will be a great man someday," my mother had said when we were sitting together on the train and she was reading me a story out of the *Upper Room* about Abraham Lincoln. "And he was a great man, too," she said. "He did God's work in his own way. He freed the slaves." We were rattling and clicking along on the train headed for Grandpa's during the summer vacation, and the train was flicking by the Wyoming prairies, by the forgotten places, by Claremont, Wyoming, and the train clattered and jiggled on by Upton, Wyoming—"Best Town on Earth" the sign said. Best Town on Earth, with its dry summer winds blowing the land dead and brown. I didn't believe the sign. I thought Sheridan, where we lived, with Little Goose Creek close by, was the best town on earth, and we went through Edgemont, South Dakota, and then into Alliance, Nebraska, deep in the night, a time of night I never knew except when we were at Alliance, Nebraska at two o'clock in the morning. We changed trains there for Grandpa's and we waited on a hard oak bench with a high straight back for the Denver train, and in the morning you could see the Mexicans working on the track gang, standing aside as our train crept up to a siding to let a roaring freight flash by. I waved at the Mexicans, but they never waved back. I had only seen a few—weren't any at J. S. Taylor School—not even one at that plain school sitting there on the poor side of town—down on West Seventh Street and Main, where I lived in an old non-fancy, non-frilly part of town, down where the white working people lived, the railroaders, the butcher, and the policeman.

The Mexican men working on the tracks leaned on their picks and bars and watched our train pass by with tired, hard looks on their faces. They were skinny men, and they had a sidecar, they called it, a little wagon affair with small train wheels, and they pumped a handle on the wagon up and down, moving the little wagon wherever they wanted to go. They were definitely not a friendly people, I thought, but they were doing the work of slaves, my mother said.

"You wouldn't be friendly or happy either if you were a slave," she said softly.

A black porter in a white cotton coat came through. "Sandwiches—cold drinks. Sandwiches—cold drinks," he cried, as he walked down the aisle toward the place where my mother and I sat.

"Can I have a pop, Mom?"

"No," my mother said. "But you can have a milk with your lunch." She got down the brown paper sack containing her own peanut butter and lettuce sandwiches, lettuce fresh from the garden but wilted and soft as wet gauze now, and cold deer meat sandwiches with salad dressing and also with wilted lettuce. I took the peanut butter. I didn't like cold deer meat. The cold fat stuck to the roof of my mouth.

"A milk, please," my mother said pleasantly, with a nice smile on her face.

"Yes, ma'am, yes, ma'am," the black porter, very black, said, flashing white teeth, and he held out the half pint bottle of milk to me from a metal rack in which he carried all the bottles—pop and milk and all. The black hand was light brown inside—almost yellow—it looked funny. I didn't know whether to touch it or not. But my mother patted me. I took the milk from his hand. "Ten cents, ma'am," the porter said.

My mother reached into her purse and handed the dime to the porter. It was a lot of money, for just milk, I thought. And when I finished drinking it I would have nothing to show for it. But it was pasteurized milk my mother said. The milk tasted different, good—better than raw cow's milk—better than our goat's milk, which tasted weedy a lot of times, too rich and too musky. My mother saw me staring at the porter.

"Don't stare at people, Gerry," she whispered. "It hurts their feelings for you to stare at them. They were freed by Lincoln. They are not slaves any more like they used to be. There are no slaves in America. This is a free country—and Lincoln made this country free." I loved Lincoln. I felt sorry for the porter.

"Was he really a slave?" I whispered to my mother.

"No," she whispered back. "But maybe his grandfather was. Your grandfathers were never slaves." Then she whispered, "And someday you will be a great man, too." I wondered how she knew, and what it would be like to be a great man. I wouldn't eat cold deer meat sandwiches with cold deer fat that stuck to the roof of my mouth if I were president, that was for sure.

We had a five- or six-hour layover at Denver, four hours to see the big city, the tall buildings, and to walk through the stores. I wore my cowboy hat, of course, and people smiled at me as I walked by, and I liked that. We carried the suitcase. It cost ten cents to check it. Ten cents was a lot of money to give for nothing—not a single thing to show for it afterward. A person should have something to show for his money.

We stopped at Woolworth's, and it had an escalator. I made my mother wait while I rode it up and down twice, and then I ran over to the toy counter where there were huge bags of marbles in bright orange net sacks, and stone marbles called agates, shooters, which cost a quarter. But you could get a whole bag of glass marbles for seven cents. I never could afford an agate, I thought. I shot with steelies, got them free down at the Sheridan

Iron Works from the men in the shop. The men called them ball bearings . . . and then I lost my mother in the dime store. I looked up and she was gone. She had disappeared. Maybe God came and took her, and left me alone! My throat almost clamped shut. I cried out, "Mom, Mom!" I started to run. "Mother!" I couldn't see over the aisles. I ran frantically up one aisle and down the next. "Mother, Mother!" I screamed as loud as I could scream. A lady stopped and said, "What's the matter, son?"

"I lost my mother!" I screamed, running by. I was alone in this horrible place. It must be hell. Alone with horrid faces which looked at me blankly as I ran by. I screamed louder, "Mother!" But the people in the aisles paid no attention, and fat ladies and small children like me just walked calmly by as if nothing were happening to me, and some saw me, and some even smiled. It was hell.

And then from somewhere, like magic, my mother came—she suddenly appeared, from where I did not know. God had given her back to me, and she had a nice smile on her face, like the Virgin Mary, and I knew her secret—knew that she and God were all tied up somehow. Even Grandma Spence had admitted it to me. Once Grandma Spence said she wished she could be as near an angel as my mother—my angel mother. And now my mother didn't even mention that God had taken her from me. I grabbed her hand and magical things happened again. The people in the aisles became alive and real. I could even smell them—nice people, friendly, and the city became an exciting place once more, full of wonderful things. It was not hell at all, and as I walked by people smiled at me again and said, "Hiya, cowboy," and my mother gave me a little squeeze with her hand that said mighty and marvelous things to me. That was all. I would never leave my mother again. Never. When I grew up I would even marry her.

Grandpa Spence's farm was up a canyon behind the red hogback where the mountains opened up and gave way to some little pastures and one nice hill, on the top of which Grandpa and Grandma had built their house. An apple orchard surrounded it. Grandpa Spence had a calf, and he had put it in a little pen in the barn by itself. I crawled over the pen and there I was alone with the calf, with Grandpa watching, a big grin on his face, big enough to show almost all his false teeth with the brown clay-colored false gums. He put his teeth in a glass at night.

At first the calf paid no attention to me. When I patted it on the head it shook its head, like my touch was from flies or something. But when I touched its wet nose, wet and slimy like a trout's skin fresh out of the water, the calf grabbed at my finger. I thought it would bite it off for sure, and I jerked it back. But Grandpa Spence only laughed and his eyes sparkled like Santa Claus's. Maybe he was Santa Claus, I thought. Yes, Grandpa Spence was Santa Claus, only he was disguised as a farmer.

"The calf won't hurt you. It only wants to suck your fingers," Grandpa said.

"Suck my fingers! Why?" I asked like I always asked.

"Because," Grandpa said. "Because he misses his mother."

"Why can't he have his mother?" I asked.

"Because," Grandpa Spence said, "because if I leave him with his mother he'll drink all of her milk and there won't be any left for you and me and Grandma." He grinned a big grin at me but I didn't think it was funny, and I didn't think Grandpa did either because his pale old blue eyes were sad and kind. Then he sat down on his old one-legged milk stool and put his head up next to the cow and began to milk the cow and the calf bawled for his mother, but the cow said nothing back. She had a mouthful of sweet-smelling grain, oats, I think, and she chewed and looked back once in a while at Grandpa with bulging eyes as Grandpa squeezed her teats and the warm milk made music on the bottom of the pail. I let the calf suck my fingers. Poor calf, I thought. And then Grandpa filled a tin cup full of milk and handed it to me—fresh and warm and foaming. It smelled good, and it tasted good, but I felt guilty. I felt like a thief. The milk belonged to the calf. And I wanted the calf to be with its mother.

* * *

The welfare records said that on November 20, Dario Esquibel came to the office to talk to the worker. He stated that he and his new wife had had a bad quarrel and that he had returned to his own home a couple of days previously, that he suspected that his new wife had been seeing someone else. However, he had not been certain until the night before his visit to the office. He said he returned to the home to pick up some clothing for the children and found her in bed with another man and that he did not know exactly what he would do about the situation; however, he was not going to support Mrs. Espinosa any longer. "The worker and director suggested that possibly Mr. Esquibel should get in touch with an attorney so that the situation could be settled at once. Regarding the payment for the care of the children at the Cathedral Home, Mr. Esquibel stated that he would pay the amount he owes after the next railroad payday, for sure," and Dario went to see an attorney named Robert Bates, the record said.

Dario worked on the addition to the shack every night after he got home from the track gang. I supposed it helped pass the time. The shack was empty, and it was not a house to be empty. It wouldn't have been so bad except summer nights in Rawlins did not come until an hour past bedtime. Then gradually, finally, it grew dark, and he would be tired from the long day's labor and would sleep. The framing of the new room had gone on easily. He got the materials from the junk man, as he was called. You could get anything you wanted from the junk man. Once Dario even got a pup from the junk man, a good pup, worked naturally with the sheep, but he had long ears like a bloodhound. Dario owed for the lumber, but he would pay, next payday, and everybody knew he was an honest Mexican.

The floors in the new room would be dirt. Nothing wrong with that. That should be made clear. Agneda had been on dirt floors right here in this house from the time they were married. She was born on dirt floors. They get hard, and can be swept like any floor, not shiny, not

fancy, but don't forget that dirt is warm. In the winter a
home with dirt floors is a warm place to be, and the floor
gets little cracks, like pores in an old man's skin, and the
warmth from the center of the earth comes up to you.
Dirt is the skin of the earth, Dario said. There is nothing
wrong with being next to the skin of the earth.

He did not have the addition done on time as he had
promised Mrs. Murphy. He swore he would have it done
when they let Agneda go. Then they could bring the kids
home, too, and everybody would hold onto each other
and cry for a while, and be happy together again, the kids
and their mama and papa. And Agneda would have
learned that jail is no place for a mother to be, and that it
is all right to be a mother, a good mother—that good dirt
floors, and kids, and beans on the stove are what is good,
and Dario would forgive her for her bein' crazy with
those men because everybody knew she was crazy, and
she would never be crazy no more. He laid the hammer
down to survey his work, and roll a cigarette, and it was
just when he was rolling the cigarette that Mrs. Murphy
came to the door. It was open and she said hello, and
walked on in like she owned the place. She looked over
his work but didn't say much, just that Agneda would be
home tomorrow, and when Dario had asked how come,
how come so early, she just shrugged her shoulders. She
only knew what she was told—parole, or good time, or
something. The sheriff was turning Agneda loose.

"That Agneda, she always knows how to get her way,"
Dario said.

"Well, she says she will be a good mother. She deserves
a chance," Mona Lee said. "Will you give her another
chance, too?"

"Well," Dario said, "I gotta see how the woman is. A
person don' learn nothin' in jail. I know that."

"But you will . . ."

"Well, miss, I will see," Dario said abruptly.

"I told them you would. . . . I promised them you
would give her another chance. You're a good influence,
I think. I promised for you." Mona Lee Murphy reached

out to touch him and almost did. Then she drew her hand back. "I promised for you."

Dario looked down. It was a compliment to him, a good influence, she said. He felt a little pain of pride, up high over the right of the center of his chest. He didn't say anything, but picked up the hammer, and then he looked at Mona Lee Murphy with his sad Mexican eyes, dark as a dark bird's eyes.

"I don' have this place finished," he said.

"I know," Mona Lee said. "But you'll make out," and she touched Dario on the sleeve . . . just touched the edge of the sleeve, like a shy person who is being very brave.

About ten o'clock the next morning the sheriff drove up in front of the Esquibel shack and Agneda got out, a small bundle of things in her hand, the same dress, now months older, faded further, her long hair hanging straight down the back in a ponytail. She looked pretty good, Dario thought. He did not run to her, nor her to him. She just walked up like she was coming home from the grocery store, or something, and she said, "Hello," barely, him standing in the door and stepping aside for her to walk in, and then he followed her.

"I don' get the room finished," he said.

"I got out early," she said, letting the bundle fall on the table. "I go get me a job," she said, tossing her head back as if to put the ponytail in place.

"I'm workin' on the gang now," Dario said.

"Where you stayin'?"

"Here."

"They're bringin' the kids in the mornin'," she said.

"I know," Dario said.

"I s'pose they'll be growed up," she said. "They probably won't know me." Dario got a bottle out of the cupboard. He poured a big drink into two glasses—straight whiskey is real, a man can count on that. The world gets crazy and sometimes is not real. But straight whiskey is real. He handed a glass to Agneda.

"Here's to you," he said.

He drank half the whiskey in one swallow, and held his

face straight against it. Finally he said, "I could go back up to the sheep camp with Manny. They want me back up there."

She said nothing. He wanted her to say something. It was not like this when he was alone pounding on the frame of the house at night. Then she had said something back, like, "Don' go," and there was a special look in her face, and then they came together and made love again, as they used to, and she was wild with passion like only she of all women was, and they were in each other's arms afterward and it would be all right again. He would forgive her.

"I could go up there with Manny," Dario said again. "I make good money. They need 'nother herder." He waited for her to say something—to give the look. "If I could go up there, there would be one more bed for the kids. I could come down and fix the other roof this fall." He waited for her to say something. "Well," he said, and poured another drink for the two of them, "here's to you, Agneda." Then they drank in silence.

"How was it at the sheriff's?" he said finally. "You wasn't in jail."

"It was okay," she said flatly, like beans without salt.

"I could go up to the sheep camp . . ."

"Yeah," she said. Dario poured another drink apiece, and later he reached over to touch her on the hand, like old times, but she got up and went out back, and was gone a long time, and when she did come back she seemed drunk. She lay down on the bed.

"You want to do somethin'?" Dario said. But she didn't answer, and he drank some more whiskey— straight from the bottle—and then left for Manny's.

Mona Lee Murphy and Harvey Watkins brought the kids home that next morning. They swarmed all over Agneda, and they did not let her go for a long time. Finally she had to go out back. They didn't follow her there. It was the one place. Then the sheriff came, same car, about the same time as yesterday. Little Joe saw the sheriff's car first.

"Them bastar's are here," he cried, running for his

mother. "Them bastar's!" He pointed to the door and started to sob quick jerky sobs. The other children ran to their mother also.

"What do you wan'?" Agneda said to the sheriff, who stood at the door with a faint smile on his face.

"Well, Nellie, that's no way to treat an old friend." The sheriff took off his cowboy hat and came inside the door and sat right down in the chair by the table. "I got some news, Nellie," he said.

"What news?"

"Well, Dario was killed last night." Nobody said anything back.

Finally Agneda said, "I don' believe it," and the children were hanging onto her, hanging, four white-faced brown babies.

"Well, it's true, Nellie. He was driving—him and Manny. Both killed. Head on. Couldn't tell who was driving at first—so bad. Couldn't even recognize 'em. I know you didn't have nothin' for Dario no more, but as soon as I got the news I thought I'd better come over and tell ya. My job, ya know." Agneda just looked at him for a minute with blank eyes, blank as dead silence, and then Little Joe started to sob again, and Elma started to sob after him, and Agneda just looked out the little square window, and patted Little Joe, absently, once or twice on the head, and she stared out the window until the sheriff got up to leave.

"I don' believe it," she said, as if to stop the sheriff from going.

"Well, you don't have to believe it if you don't want to, Nellie," and then he started out the door.

"Take us there," Agneda said suddenly.

"Where?"

"Take us to the place where Dario was killed."

The sheriff said no, he couldn't, and Agneda insisted, and they argued about it for a long time, back and forth, and Agneda got loud, and she seemed hysterical, and was screaming and sobbing, mostly in Spanish, in agony, and then the sheriff finally agreed, and he loaded the whole bunch of them into his car, on top of each other, packed up nearly to the ceiling, and he drove them all to the spot, twenty-seven miles east of Rawlins, on U.S. Highway 30.

There was nothing there at the spot except sagebrush on both sides of the road and long rolling hills covered with short grass, fescue grass, good nourishment for the sheep, and it even made cattle fat, if there was enough of it and enough water. And there was dirt between the clumps of fescue grass, plain dirt with nothing growing, and there were harvester ant hills, three feet across, which killed twenty square feet of earth, or more, around the anthill, and there were high clouds, rolling and billowing up in the blue sky, like giant white geysers. The sun was hot on the pavement. When they got out the sheriff directed the traffic and while he did so he pointed to the place with his back to it.

"It's there where that blood is," he said. There was brown dried blood, a place so big—maybe three feet across, not round or square. Agneda walked over to it, her head bowed. The children held onto her, and Little Joe's eyes were wide.

"This is the blood of your father," she said. The children said nothing. She started to weep so one could barely hear her. "I am a bad woman," she said, and she sobbed softly in the sunshine. Little Joe looked at the blood of his father—brown like a Mexican, not red, and that was all that was left of his papa. He did not understand the feeling. It was a feeling like having lost part of himself, and of being afraid, and it was then that something happened to his heart.

14

WHEN I was sixteen I thought mothers were a pain in the ass. One morning, my father was watching me come down the stairs. I can see him now, as plain as if it had happened ten minutes ago. He looked at me solemnly, coldly.

"You ought to be real proud of yourself," he said. I felt guilty already. "Your mother has been awake all night crying over you."

"Why?" I asked. "Why for Christ's sake?"

"Well, right there's an example of it, takin' the Lord's name in vain, and she just found out you've been smoking, too, and she knows some other things."

"What other things, for Christ . . . ?" I followed my father out to the kitchen where he was starting the Sunday breakfast. He made good pancakes.

"Well, she told me that last Sunday she drove the car to church with the little kids. You were still up in bed sleeping—too tired from whoring around all night to get up and go to church." My father always called being with the girls "whoring around." "You know it isn't a very big thing to do for your mother—to go to church one hour just once in a while—to give her an hour once a week sometimes—especially after all she does for you." He dumped in some flour and baking soda without measuring it. I just stood there. What was I supposed to say? Then he dumped in a cup of milk and some sugar and continued. "Anyway, you had the car out the night before." He turned to look me in the eye. It is a terrible thing when your father turns like that and looks you in the eye. "I don't understand why you can't be a little careful . . . just a little. Your mother let the kids off in front of the church and parked the car, and there sticking to the back seat window of the car was a used rubber you threw out—just stuck wet up against the window where God and everybody else could see it. People were all watching her, she told me. Embarrassed her almost to death. She didn't know what to do—to pull it off while everybody was watching or to leave it there. Mrs. Howe pointed at it, I guess, and she hollered, 'What's that, Esther?' "—that was my mother's name—"And your mother just looked. Couldn't say anything. Everybody else was lookin' and snickerin', she said."

"Jesus Christ!" I said.

"Well, I'll say no more," my father said, "except your mother always thought her firstborn should be given to God. Now you and I know how religious she is. But you gotta accept people the way they are. Don't try to change 'em, just accept 'em, includin' your mother. Ya gotta accept her. I mean, she is your mother."

I know my father didn't go along too much with all of her churchy ways. He had his own religion. Used to argue it with the preacher. You could go to church outdoors, my father said, and since God made the outdoors it was a more godly place to worship. And there was something godly, too, in holding onto the end of a good fly rod—better than sitting in some stuffy church bored almost to death listening to a poor preacher making a bad sermon, and an off-key choir trying to sing. My father said he'd rather listen to the birds and the sound of the creek. That was a lot better music.

God made the outdoor church while man made this miserable brick monstrosity, he said. And it was all right to skip church on Sunday during hunting season since a person only has Sundays off to go hunting during the big game season—for antelope in the early fall, and then for elk and deer later on. God made only so many Sundays during a year. And it was godly, totally godly, to fill a trout basket full of rainbows or brooks, or bring home a fat dry cow elk to feed the family. Besides, my parents always tithed—even with the wild meat. A lot more than ten percent went to the poor, I knew that, to the neighbors who were not good hunters like him, to the tie hacks down at work, and the poor widow up the street, and to some of the people on relief in those late depression days when I was a child. And in the summer my mother seemed to think the outdoor church was all right, too.

She loved the outdoors. Sometimes she would just sit under a pine tree and sew or crochet, and sometimes she and I walked together down by the creek while my father was fishing in places I couldn't tag along. She told me the names of the wildflowers, like they were my friends, like I should know them by their first names, like a fellow should know everybody he likes by their first names, and late in the summer the whole family picked chokecherries after the day's fishing, and wild currants and gooseberries, which my mother mixed with crabapple juice for jelly. My mother never admitted that the outdoor church was as good as the Methodist Episcopal church. She never could make herself believe one could be happy and still be totally holy, but she was happy out there. She had a peaceful look on her face and her eyes were soft. And she mostly gave in to my father about church in the summer. I never heard them fight. A few "discussions," but they never argued or fought. People who argued in front of the kids were not good parents, my mother said.

My mother was the president of the Women's Christian Temperance Union, the good old WCTU. They held meetings each week all year, and I could remember one particular Sunday in the summer when I was just a boy, and my father agreed to put on a demonstration, a scientific demonstration about alcohol for the whole Sunday school, all the classes at once—it was part of his bargain with my mother, kinda like a tithing of a good Sunday's fishing, to go to church with her at least once in the summer. The preacher turned the pulpit over to my father, and there he was, up there all alone where the preacher usually was! I couldn't wait to see what my father would do! I wondered how it would feel to be up there all alone.

"Now, this is pure alcohol," my father said to the room full of kids and Sunday school teachers, and the ladies from the WCTU. I sat with the other kids away from my mother. "Now this is just like the alcohol in whiskey, but in its purest form. See, it's clear." My father held up a test tube full of alcohol, clear as water. He smelled it. I thought he shouldn't. "Now," he went on, "here is an egg." He cracked the egg on the preacher's podium, and grinned a little bit, embarrassed, I thought. Probably believed this was all a little silly, but he was doing it for my mother. "Now, I'm going to put this egg in this glass sauce dish so everybody can see it, and I'm going to pour the alcohol over this raw egg." He did it. "Now watch the egg." I watched—it was turning white, like it was being poached, or something. "See there. I just cooked the egg with this alcohol. Now," my father said, "that is what happens to your body when you put alcohol in it—more or less," he added. "It attacks the living tissue—it is a poison. It is found in beer and wine and whiskey of all kinds and other drinks." He was a man of few words. He stepped down. But then a lady from the WCTU got up and said it was against the will of God for us to let alcohol touch our lips—it was a sin. She knew. It led to murder and other horrible crimes. She said she had studied the effects of alcohol on people. It was all in the book she held there in her hand for us to see—a thick impressive-looking book which she said was the authority on the subject. People ended up in the penitentiary on account of alcohol. No doubt. She had the statistics and everything—right there in the book. Alcohol is a curse—a curse above all curses, and God would be angry with any little Christian boy or girl like us who ever drank it—ever, even one drop. A drop is a sin—and a sin is a sin. We all knew that.

Later that same Sunday we separated again, and went to our own classes, and ladies from the WCTU came around to each class with "pledge papers," which they read to us. The papers said we promised, took an oath before the Lord, Jesus Christ, that no matter how we were tempted by the devil, no matter how or when, we would never, never, touch a drop of alcohol. Never. Before Jesus Christ. Signed—I signed it Gerald Leonard Spence. Everybody signed, right down to the last dumb kid. No holdouts. Holdouts were on the devil's side, on the side of hell. Nobody wanted to be part of the devil. Then my mother and father and I drove to the Castle Hamburger Stand in our old Model A, got six nickel hamburgers with everything on them, mustard, dill pickles, and onions, and there was still plenty of time to get in a good afternoon's fishing up Little Goose Canyon.

Now, at sixteen, I had to contend with my mother and this goddamned rubber stuck on the back seat window of the family car, and my father's speech—he usually didn't make speeches to me, but he was now, a father to a son. He dripped three nice little round puddles of dough onto the griddle, and then continued.

"It might not seem fair to you, son, but your mother doesn't ask much of you. And just a little discretion is all I ask. To her, whorin' and smokin' are sins, and her son is sinnin'—makes her feel like a failure, you carryin' on and all the rest. She was crying last night—couldn't stop. Cried all night. She says she has failed as a mother and that she has failed God, broke her promises to God and all. You know how she is, and your mother is not one to break her promises." My father gave the cakes an easy flip. "She always had great hopes for you—used to hold you up to everybody as something special—especially after Little Peggy died." He was silent for a moment. I could see them lowering the casket of my little sister into the ground, dead from meningitis. Little Peggy was just two. I was over four. After she was gone I felt alone—afraid.

My father was a country boy who got through college by just plain hard work. He left the little farm of his parents where Grandpa Spence labored on a few acres with a couple of mules, and milk cows, near Fort Collins, Colorado, back of Horsetooth Mountain. And my father had also left his mother, a little bony, worrying woman, skinny and flitty as a bird, with legs like a sparrow, left home at the bidding of his parents to better himself by education. He got a degree in chemistry at Colorado A & M, where he met my mother, and after he graduated he worked as a chemist for the railroad at a tie-treating plant at Galesburg, Illinois, where Little Peggy died. They moved out of Galesburg right away because my mother couldn't bear being there after Little Peggy's death. The best job my father could get in those deep depression days was a job as a laborer at the Johns-Manville plant in Lompoc, California, and after that he got a job at Sheridan as a chemist with the tie-treating plant for the CB&Q Railroad, and we lived there until 1941 when the war came, and the tie plant was threatened with closing. My father moved us to Laramie where he also worked as a chemist at the Sponge Iron Plant. They were trying to make iron for the war out of low grade ore that was plentiful in the mountains near Laramie.

"After Little Peggy died your mother told me that God saved you for a special reason." My father continued his speech, still making his Sunday morning pancakes. "You could have died from the meningitis, too, you know—same as Little Peggy. But you were spared. Your mother made promises to God about you, you know."

"Jesus Christ," I said. "How can she go around promising me away like that?" That wasn't right, I thought. "That isn't right," I said out loud. "What right has she got to do that?" My father flipped another cake over, very precisely, and then looked me in the eye again.

"She's got the right, Gerry. She's your mother."

"Jesus Christ," I said again.

Mothers! What power they have! A magical power that one takes for granted, like the flow of the river down and the rising up of the sun and early robins in the springtime. The power of mothers is part of nature. I was never concerned about what God thought of me. His judgments were never as important as the judgments of my mother. To be rejected by one's own mother would be the worst of all condemnations.

My mother was born Esther Sophie Pfleeger, in Parkstone County, Minnesota, on August 24, 1901. She was the eldest daughter and the second child of Leonard and Barbara Pfleeger, German immigrants, who had come to this country a decade before. Leonard Pfleeger had dodged the Kaiser's draft, used to brag about that. Wanted nothing to do with the Kaiser, he said. In the old country he was slated to be a teacher because he was a bright student, but he wanted to be a farmer, and so he got to America somehow about 1890, worked like a slave, fared like a slave, and in about five years saved enough to return to Germany for his mother and two sisters. He met Barbara Lang, my grandmother, on his passage back. They were married and settled in Zion, Illinois, in the midst of a religious group who called themselves Christian Zionists, a professed Christian order with emphasis on the wisdom of the Old Testament and on Jewish biblical law.

But Leonard Pfleeger used to laugh at the Zionists. They said you could hear his thunderous voice roaring in laughter across eighty acres of good Illinois farmland. He laughed until he was sick, they said. When the Zionists went up on Peachtree Hill to meet the Lord, this time for sure, and to be swallowed up into heaven, this time without fail, for eternity, praise the Lord, well, they locked the doors of their houses, like good responsible people would—just in case the whole thing didn't come off.

But one day Leonard Pfleeger's soul was opened—by God knows what or why. His laughter ceased across the eighty. He was a mortal man. He had seen the truth, and he would bring his life into order, as ordered by the Lord. There was no fanfare about it at all, no witnesses, really, except Barbara, his wife. But he never spoke to Barbara about it beforehand, never looked into her dark, sad eyes and asked if he should. He only picked up the rifle one day and walked out into the pigpen and shot every pig, the sows, the boars, more pigs than Grandma had chickens altogether, he used to brag, and he shot the nutless shoats, and the little piggies by the scores, killed them all. And with a team of horses he hauled them away, one and sometimes three or four at a time, hauled them off into the draw and dumped their fresh, meaty bodies over the side to rot—better the carcasses than his soul in hell.

"Pigs don't chew their cuds. The meat is unclean. It will not be eaten. It is unclean, do you hear?" he had bellowed. "It causes sickness and disease and is the flesh of the devil put here to tempt the Lord's people," he screamed. "So it says in the Good Book, and it is I, Leonard Pfleeger, who has heard the word of the Lord," and then he had gone with the rest of them up to Peachtree Hill to meet his Maker, and Grandma, with dark eyes and the quiet sad face, locked the door when they left.

Later Barbara and Leonard Pfleeger walked down Peachtree Hill and unlocked the door and a year or so later, in 1907, they packed up all of their possessions in three or four railroad cars, the cows, the chickens, the horses and plows and harrows, the seed drills, the furniture—everything—down to the dogs and cats, like Noah in the ark, and then they loaded the children and themselves. The railroad company took them to Colorado, and dumped them off to homestead—there on the Colorado plains at Limon Junction, where one railroad track from Colorado Springs and one from Denver met. Grandpa was an American citizen. Nobody spoke German in his house anymore. Not his wife, not his children, not even his German neighbors.

Grandpa Pfleeger was a big-boned man with hands like a huge old cedar tree, gnarled and rough, the fingers twisted every which way from having been broken and bent at his work. In 1917 the Kaiser was at war with the world, and Leonard Pfleeger, too old now for the American draft, was nevertheless a loyal American. He was at the bank one day to deposit his bean checks. They say one of his neighbors was there buying a Liberty bond. Of course, the neighbor said, Pfleeger, the German, would buy no Liberty bonds. Then the story went that Leonard Pfleeger walked over to the man, grabbed him by the overall straps, and lifted him almost a foot off the floor before he set him down. "I'll match you bond for bond for bond." Of course it was a duel. Leonard Pfleeger bought bonds until his bean checks were gone and then he started signing notes to the banker for more bonds. So did his neighbor, and they bought bonds and signed notes until the banker wouldn't lend any more money to Leonard Pfleeger's neighbor. Later on in the early thirties, in the time of the dust bowls and the jackrabbits, in the heavy depression days when the farmers gasped for one more breath in those eastern Colorado winds, when man and beast dried up together, when their very souls became parched and cracked, and the trees stood dead from the drought, Leonard Pfleeger bought out that neighbor, gave him honest-to-God American cash, not much, but it was cash. Leonard Pfleeger bought the other farms around him, too, with cash, like every good American entrepreneur should. My middle name was Leonard, after my grandfather.

Grandpa Pfleeger's farm was a frightening hostile place, like a desert, like a place God forgot. The head of last year's calf, taken from the calf to be vealed, lay behind the barn, and the crows ate the calf's eyes, and the rats the lips, and then the rats got caught in the traps inside the barn, and in the field behind the barn a dead dog's carcass rotted in the sun, shot for killing lambs, and Grandpa Pfleeger cut the nuts from the calves and threw them to the chickens, and the chickens pecked and tugged and fought over the flesh, and the tails were burned from the lambs and thrown to the dogs, which, at the price of their lives, were required to distinguish between a live tail and a dead one. Death and farming are partners.

The dust blew up to the top of the fence posts, and later on in the dust bowl days there were no birds left, not even the crows, and the only flowers were Grandma's moss roses, which grew along both sides of a little ten-foot-long cement sidewalk, and which she watered every day with the rinse water from the dishes—yellow and pink moss roses in this forgotten place.

Then one day the clouds gathered, and the folks were afraid to say that maybe it would rain for fear that the very suggestion of rain might make it go away. But the clouds continued to gather, and the sky grew black as night, and there was excitement in the air. My mother called me in and whispered that maybe it was going to rain. Maybe, God willing.

"We need the rain so badly," she said. "Pray to God for rain. Grandpa and Grandma need the rain for the beans and the wheat. The land is so dry, so you pray, too. God can hear you, Gerry," she said. I didn't want to go in. I pulled away from my mother's hand, and sat down under the eaves. I pouted, but I prayed, and then the thunder came, and the lightning, and I watched it, wide-eyed, sitting there under the eaves, and I felt the power of it all, the power of prayer, my power—at ten years of age. It was wonderful. "Make it rain, dear God, and make it rain harder and harder," I prayed. And it did. It started to pour, and the water came running down off the eaves and onto my head, and I loved it—sat there, the stream of water running down my face and soaking me to the hide. My uncle Clarence, big, with brown eyes like my grandma Pfleeger, came running into the house. He stopped. "Come on in, kid," he said to me. "You'll get wet."

"I'm already wet," I said. "I like it here." My mother came to the door.

"Come on in, Gerry," she said. "You'll get wet."

"I don't want to come in," I said. "I like it." I was shivering. "It's hot," I said. The cold water falling on my head felt hot. "It's hot, it's hot." I felt the power!

"This kid is really dumb." My uncle Clarence laughed a laugh like Grandpa Pfleeger's. "He's really dumb. Ain't got enough sense to come in out of the rain."

That night at supper by the light of the kerosene lamps we all gave thanks to the Lord for the rain. I heard the sweet sounds of my grandma Pfleeger's voice praying softly in her broken English, thanking the Lord. My mother quietly reached over and took my hand, and I could feel the hardness of her hand along the edges from her work. She squeezed my hand and I could feel it touch me in the heart. Everybody prayed around the table, thanking God. But nobody bothered to thank me.

15

ONE NIGHT I had a nightmare of my own. I dreamed
Joe Esquibel was walking down the long hall to the gas
chamber through a crowd that separated as his little en-
tourage passed by like a group leading the heavyweight
champion of the world slowly toward the ring. The spectators were peering and gawking, clucking softly. Joe
walked on by me behind the priest. Didn't look. I reached
out for his hand, but he didn't stop his slow, plodding
pace. The warden was leading the procession, and behind
the warden came the priest in a long, black robe with a
Bible in his hand. Looked like a judge, I thought. They
moved forward in small steps, foot after foot. Suddenly I
hollered, "Joe!" But he didn't look up. "Joe," I hollered
again. Maybe he didn't hear me. I pushed my way up and
grabbed at his hand, and the hand was limp. The hand
was wet. I dropped it like something dead. "I need to talk
to you, Joe," I screamed, and pushed through the crowd
after him. "I did my best. God, please, believe me! I did
my best! Hey, Joe! Jesus, what did you want me to do?
Buy a witness—buy a juror? What more could I have
done?" But then a guard stepped in front of me, and the
procession moved on. I hollered to Joe once more. "I'm
sorry I took your case just for the hell of it, Joe." And
that's all I could say. But he didn't acknowledge that he
heard me; never turned around; his head never moved.
Then there was the sound of iron on iron, like the sound
of the freight cars smashing into each other down on the

makeup tracks, and I knew they had shut the door of the gas chamber, and I woke up in a sweat, whining. I felt crazy. The next morning I called Raymond Whitaker from the office.

"The sons-of-bitches have all the evidence," I said to Whitaker, "all the experts. They have all the cards. Dr. Karn'll win this case for the state by just looking at the jury—just looking." Karn had those soft eyes, kind like a saint, no smile on his face, but a pleasant mouth that naturally turned up a little, and he would speak to the jury like Perry Como sings Christmas carols, and the jurors would love him back. Karn would say, "Oh, he's quite sane, all right. There's no doubt he knows the nature and consequences of his act, and he can aid in his own defense if he wants to. That's the test." He would even look a little sad when he said it, and the jury would feel sad, too, but probably on edge in having had a hand in killing a man—for justice's sake, of course. But they would believe Dr. Karn because they wanted to believe him, and the jury would say Joe was sane. Yes, he was sane, and a sane man must be punished for his crimes. The jury would know that the accused always pleads insanity when he doesn't have any other defense. Catch some bastard red-handed doing his dirty killin' and the law gives him one last loophole—insanity! And every one of the bastards will try to crawl through it. Some red-faced bulldozer operator on the jury would probably say, "Jesus, it's disgusting. Oughta take the bastard out and hang 'em then and there when there ain't no doubt and everybody and his dog watched it, seen 'em do it with their own eyes. No question. What the hell is all the fuss about?" "Bunch a shysters makin' a buck," another juror would say. "That's what it's about. Now he claims he's insane!" Then the jury would remember what Dr. Karn had said and how sad he looked. Well, the doctor ought to know. He's a doctor ain't he, and besides a man don't need a fancy-ass psychiatrist to tell him he was sane. Got the gun, didn't he? Chased her into the welfare office, didn't he? Stood there arguing with everybody, sane as hell, and then just shot her. Done everythin' a sane man

does and now he says he's insane! Just a bunch a bullshit.
Besides them Mexicans is all alike, can't trust any of 'em.
And then one of the jurors would remember that Joe
Esquibel pulled a knife on the chief of police when he
was damn near a baby. It was all there in black and white
in the chief's own records. They're born that way. Then
somebody would say, but the white woman had it coming,
in a way of thinkin'. Got her just dues for marryin' one of
them greasers, but a course, that don't give nobody an
excuse to kill 'er and then try ta get away with it by
claimin' insanity.

And about then a soft-eyed lady, probably a schoolteacher, would say in a tiny voice, a voice so quiet that
everybody had to really listen carefully, that she thought
that anybody who kills is insane. A man has to be insane
to do a thing like that. And so if this man killed and was
insane, as she was sure he was, then anybody could get
off, anybody could kill and nobody would be safe. The
whole jury would have nodded in agreement. They
wouldn't be out very long, and when they came in with
their verdict I'd know what it was even before the foreman read it, because they wouldn't look at me—wouldn't
look at Joe—but they'd look over to the prosecutor's
table, very sternly, some looking sad and haggard from
the weight of the decision they had made, but their bodies would lean toward the prosecutor and the red-faced
bulldozer operator would probably be the foreman.

"God, Raymond, we need a psychiatrist of our own—
somebody who will testify that Joe *is* insane. There's got
to be somebody out there who could say that."

"Psychiatrists are a dime a dozen, Gerald," he said.

"I only need one," I said. "Just one."

"No budget, don't forget that. Poor men don't have
psychiatrists. Psychiatrists are for the rich, for the wives
of corporate presidents."

"Well, sure," I said. "But what's that got to do with Joe
Esquibel?"

"Don't be so impertinent, my friend Gerald," he said.
"Psychiatrists are for the rich, and the rich hate Mexi-

cans. Therefore psychiatrists hate Mexicans, don't you understand? It's that simple. Simple logic."

"It is not that simple," I said. "It's not logic."

"It is simpler even than that," he argued. "Psychiatrists do not give care to the poor, and they feel guilty about that. People hate people who make them feel guilty. Not a single Mexican in the whole town of Rawlins ever knew a psychiatrist. Psychiatrists are for the rich, I tell you, and the prosecuting attorney is elected by the rich, not by a bunch of Mexicans over in Mexican town in Rawlins, Wyoming, and the judges are appointed by the power structure—by the rich. The president of the First National Bank can call up the judge any day he wants and have a good talk with him, but if Mrs. Esquibel calls him up, he'd probably throw her in jail for trying to tamper with justice. The judge'll listen to Mrs. Murphy at the Welfare Department—drink coffee with her, pat her on the shoulder, tell her he's sorry. 'I'm sorry,' he'll say, 'sorry about your daughter. We'll do what we can. Isn't much. Law can't do much with people like that Esquibel. But we'll do what we can.' Can't you hear him saying that, Gerald?"

"Christ, Raymond, all I want is a psychiatrist for our side of the case."

"I'll petition the court," he said, and hung up.

Judge Stanton ordered that the state provide five hundred dollars for the mental examination of the defendant by a psychiatrist of our choice. The state was fair. Some psychiatrist in Denver was recommended to me by another defense lawyer, said if we had any case at all he'd help us, and I was unable to find anybody else anyway, not for five hundred dollars—five hours' work.

Then they hauled Joe down to this fellow—kept him in chains all the way, Joe said. I hoped it would be a good trip for him—just to get out of the jail for a couple of days, but the doctor completed the examination the same day, and they headed back to Rawlins with Joe still in chains. We got the report from the psychiatrist two weeks later. Joe was only troubled, the report said, but "He has been a social deviate all of his life." I called up Whitaker.

What should we do now? There it was again in another goddamned report—the moral judgments of the men of medicine on their fellow man.

"Christ, Raymond," I said. "How can psychiatry be a science? It's like asking a doctor to diagnose your bellyache. The doctor says 'You are a social deviate, or you wouldn't have a bellyache.'"

"Does that surprise you, Gerald?" Raymond asked.

"Well, yes, frankly, it does. Do you know what he says? He says, and I quote, 'The killing was merely an extension of that deviant conduct, a hostile act against not only his ex-wife, but society as well.' Ain't that a hell of a way to earn five hundred dollars?"

It was probably all true.

"Well, what else could the doctor do?" Raymond said. "If he found Joe sane he'd have to testify, and you'd put him through a day, maybe two, of bullshit in the courtroom. He'd get cut up and who'd pay him for that? He's got no stake in this Mexican deviate who killed to get even with the system."

"Well, what are we going to do?"

"You will make a great closing argument which will put Clarence Darrow to shame. You will be beautiful and Mrs. Esquibel will cry—in Mexican, of course. The jury will love you, and her, and justice will prevail!" Then he was silent for a moment and when I didn't answer, he said, "I'll petition the court for another psychiatrist—for another five hundred dollars," and he did. Raymond Whitaker actually talked the judge into another examination on the grounds that the state had a couple of psychiatrists and a psychologist and a neurologist and social workers—a whole army of professionals against one little hungry incompetent Denver shrink. Certainly due process required that the defendant have at least one more pitiful five-hundred-dollar examination—all for the sake of justice. "I'll never ask for another penny, Judge, but you need to make the record at least look fair. The law is of no value, justice or not, without the *appearance* of justice," Raymond argued, and so they took Joe Esquibel down to Denver again, in the same set of chains, to another psychiatrist.

This time I chose the psychiatrist. I knew the man. I chose one who thought everybody was crazy. Once after my mother's death when I was depressed and feeling unloved because I was unloved, because I was so unlovable, and I was so unlovable because I was feeling so rotten, so guilty, which made me feel depressed, I made the mistake of saying I thought that dying wasn't such a big fucking deal after all. I felt worthless and nasty. I said if there'd been a mess like that in the front yard Anna would have made me clean it up and haul it away, and if there was an ugly glob like that on one of my paintings I would have painted over it. I was feeling like that and talking that way and Anna thought I should see a shrink, and I didn't give a shit one way or the other. And so I went to see this old boy, chubby-cheeked little devil with a big reputation, in Denver, professor and all, still practicing at seventy. He sat in a wonderful walnut-paneled office with thick leather chairs, and he looked like one of the seven dwarfs with a little red nose and glasses, and I could hardly see him in that dim room of his, looked like he was hiding back there, and he said I should get tested. Tested? Yes, psychological testing. Important. Get the psychological facts so that he could make a proper diagnosis. "You must know, Mr. Spence, that you can't advise your client without the facts, and that's what we need here, the psychological facts."

He had his own psychologist—big-titted woman I remember, who wore a very tight sweater—and she took me into a bright little closet, with an orange-colored round table that took up the whole space, and she sat down next to me and I couldn't keep my eyes off of her. She wanted to know how I felt. I was fine. I was no longer depressed. Felt good, I told her. Felt good. Then she showed me some inkblots on a card. What did I see? I turned to her and I said, well, did she really want to know the truth? And she said yes, that she really did want to know the truth—wanted to know it more than anything in the world. She looked at me and she licked her big mouth like she was hungry, and she said the testing was very important, and that it wouldn't work unless I told her exactly what the truth was. Then I said, well, all right —that I didn't always feel this way, but that right then I felt a certain way. And she held up the inkblot again, and leaned over close to me, holding the card for me to see, and she said just to tell her exactly what I saw, and I told her I didn't see much except an inkblot but that at that moment, that very goddamned moment, I was feeling something. Something was coming over me, and coming clearly to my mind's eye, and she wanted to know very much what it was. Very much. The truth. It was all in the testing. And then I said all I could see was tits—big beautiful white luscious tits with pretty pink nipples, and then she held up the next card and leaned over close to me again and asked me what I saw there and I said, well, it might seem strange to her, but I saw the same damn thing as before. Wonderful delicious tits, except these were swaying in the breeze, like coconuts up in palm trees, and she said, oh.

Later on the doctor made an appointment for me at a private hospital. Said I should go there right away. I would be all right as soon as I took a series of shock treatments. Needed them. And what was shock treatment? I asked, and he said it was treatment done with electricity. Like in the electric chair? I asked, and he said, not exactly, but I was obviously suffering from a psychotic episode and that if I didn't act now I would likely be a danger to myself and others, probably commit suicide, and I certainly needed treatment. He said the tests of his psychologist were evidence of severe disorientation. He had a serious talk with Anna alone, and after I left he wrote a long letter and warned us both that unless I submitted to therapy immediately he was washing his hands of any responsibility, not only for the quality of my life, but for my very life itself. It was urgent and dangerous to let another day go by without treatment.

"I'm crazy," I said to Anna, but no, she wouldn't even give me that much. She even wanted to argue about that.

"You're not crazy," she said. "You may be a little nuts, but you're not crazy."

"How do you know so goddamned much?" I said. "I suppose you know more than the shrink."

"Well, I just know certain things," she said.

And I said, "It was your idea to go to this goddamn shrink in the first place, and now you don't believe him. What you're really doing is driving me crazy. I'm going to be one hundred percent looney one way or the other, either on account of this goddamned shrink or on account of you."

But she held firm, wouldn't budge, wouldn't sign any papers, she just knew, and pretty soon I got mad, and that got me over the depression, and I knew Anna was right, so I thought for sure that this same certain doctor would find Joe Esquibel insane all right. But this same certain doctor happened to be a friend of our first psychiatrist, colleagues, you know, and he had made a casual call to our first psychiatrist—just a way of confirming his own independent findings, and the second report was a carbon copy of the first. Joe was sane and he killed because he was a social deviate.

"Well, that's it," I said to Whitaker over the phone. "That's justice!"

"Now, Gerald," Whitaker said. "We have accomplished a great deal. Think of it! Think of this bargain! Why, for only a thousand dollars the appearance of justice has been preserved, and the psychiatrists got fair pay and Joe had two nice trips, and we, Gerald, can never be criticized. We left no stone unturned. Not one. We asked for not one but two independent psychiatric evaluations. What else can they expect of us except, of course, your great final argument?"

"Yeah," I said, "it'll have to be a great one, all right. Wonder what kind of a psychiatrist we could hire for fifty thousand dollars?" I asked.

"A good one," Raymond said. "We could hire two good ones, twenty-five thousand dollars apiece. They would put Joe in a nice hospital for three weeks and run a lot of nice tests and nice nurses would make nice notes . . ."

"Yeah," I said.

"And they would x-ray his head."

"Yeah."

"And run an EEG, and call in a neurologist."

"Yeah."

"And run a battery of psychological tests, ten or twelve of them."

"Yeah."

"And for twenty-five thousand dollars there would be a report as thick as the Chicago phone book, and a history that would cover his life from the time that he wet his first diaper right up to the present time, not a breath left out."

"Yeah, that's important," I said.

"For ten thousand dollars we could get a Harvard professor, or one from Stanford, maybe, one on the President's committee for this and that, and he would be a member of the International Society of Psychiatry, or whatever the hell the big big shots belong to, and he would have written twenty-five articles on passive-aggressive conduct, and we could probably even hire the professor who taught Karn for five thousand dollars, and the professor would say that poor old Bill Karn didn't understand, and I could hear you say in court, 'Well, Doctor, maybe Bill Karn skipped that class,' and the professor would just smile, and the jury would smile back, and there it would be . . . You wouldn't even have to make a great closing argument. Money is justice," Whitaker said.

"Got five grand?" I asked, but Whitaker didn't answer, and then he wanted to tell me about the prosecutor's latest attempt to close down Fifi's in Casper.

I went back to the welfare records. Only place left. And I sent the law school kids out to ask more questions, like talking to Mona Lee Murphy and Harvey Watkins personally, but Mona Lee Murphy was never in, and Harvey Watkins said he wouldn't talk to us. No way, he said. He hoped they hung the son-of-a-bitch twice, didn't have a damn thing to say to anybody who was working on the Esquibel case, and particularly not a bunch of silly-assed kids. The new director, Luke Massingill, who had replaced Louis Groh, said no one in his department was authorized to give information on the case either, except to the prosecuting attorney, of course. The law students made their reports the way their professors showed them, used fancy language in a stilted formal style, and the reports were neatly typed and bound together, and they had nice margins, and they were put under a green-colored cellophane cover and submitted to me.

The welfare records showed that Agneda Esquibel had come into the welfare office and stated that she was about five months' pregnant again. Mona Lee Murphy tried to understand the woman, but how does one really understand? She had argued it with Harvey Watkins many times before and part of the argument was there in the welfare records themselves. "Man is basically good, Harvey," Mona Lee started out as usual, "and therefore every person always tries to do the best they can. It's that simple, Harvey."

"Man is *not* basically good," Harvey Watkins always argued back. "Man is an animal. Man can always do better if he's made to. Otherwise, he won't. But you're good," he laughed, and then he would whisper something in her ear when nobody in the office was watching like, "You are really good. But man isn't worth a shit. I only like the animal in you." And then he would try to look serious and go on working at the day's correspondence.

Agneda Esquibel and Mona Lee Murphy sat looking at each other across the small plain gray desk. The women's faces were sad, one white and ordinary and unwrinkled, and the other brown with heavy leathery lines and high cheekbones, older. Agneda looked down at the tops of her own brown hands and the bottom of her hands touched her belly.

"How did this happen, Mrs. Esquibel?" Mona Lee Murphy began with a sympathetic sound in her voice.

"It don' make no difference," Agneda whispered, still looking at her hands.

"Well, I have to make up a report," Mrs. Murphy said in a kind way again. "Who was it, Mrs. Esquibel?"

"I was gonna marry him," Agneda finally said.

"What is his name? He may be a source of collateral funds."

"You put him in jail," Agneda said.

"Well, he does have a duty to support the child, don't you think?" She was being as understanding as she could.

"And if he no pay, you put him in jail," Agneda said again. "You put Dario in jail that time, don' forget that."

"Yes," Mrs. Murphy said. "I don't like that either. But it's policy here—if the collateral source does not respond to his legal obligation, then it becomes a matter for the county attorney. I don't really approve of the policy myself, but policy is policy. I just work here, Mrs. Esquibel. You know that."

"You made me sign the papers against Dario that time, or no money," Mrs. Esquibel said. "Then they put Dario in jail. You remember that."

The women sat across from each other silently for a long time. Finally Agneda said in a whisper, "The kids are hungry. I no can work no more. I been sick."

"I'm sorry to hear that," Mrs. Murphy said, and then Mona Lee Murphy said nothing further. Finally Mrs. Esquibel looked up, but there was no sadness in her eyes. "Narcisco Flores. He no live here. He is from New Mexico and he died."

And Mona Lee Murphy said, "You have never lied to me, Agneda."

But Agneda said, "He died." She sat there saying nothing more, hands still folded against her belly, looking down, immobile.

Waiting.

Waiting.

Then Mrs. Murphy opened up her desk drawer, as easy as that, and wrote up a pink medical form for Dr. McNamara, and she made a special emergency requisition for groceries because she knew that the children were hungry. And in less than a month the hospital informed the welfare office that Agneda Esquibel, also known as Nellie Montoya, had given birth to a baby boy. It weighed two pounds, seven ounces, and the report said the baby passed away.

Later Mrs. Murphy went to see Agneda, and she reported that the home was in very poor condition, and still later in the same year the hospital called the welfare to state that "Mrs. Montoya had entered the hospital again and the department, wishing to know the nature of Mrs. Montoya's illness, was informed that she had an abortion, evidently performed by herself." The welfare record said she was dismissed four days later, and after that Mrs. Murphy had visited Agneda Esquibel again in regard to the report of the school nurse, who complained to the Welfare Department that Joe had been absent twenty-eight and a half days, Elma twenty-six days, and Timato forty. The report said that Joe and several of the other children were in need of "immediate attention for malnutrition as well as immediate attention on skin, scalp and throat," and that "all of the above children are in need of dental care." Mrs. Murphy reported that Joe looked sort of mangy and gray, had scabby patches on his head, and his face was blotted with light gray spots. Joe said his throat was sore, and Mona Lee Murphy said his eyes looked dull as dirt. And Timato was not going to school at all. Instead she reported he was simply roaming the streets.

Mrs. Esquibel said that she herself was not running around. "No, I am not doin' nothin'. I ain't going nowhere. I no do that no more." But Mrs. Murphy knew better, she reported. The attitude of Mrs. Esquibel was that she was taking care of her children and if the court didn't believe her, well, the court could take the kids. "That court can have them kids," she said. And, it didn't seem to make any difference to Agneda whether or not they returned her to Canyon City to the women's penitentiary or not. Mona Lee Murphy had even warned her about that. "Who cares? I no care no more," she said. "You no make me a-scared no more."

And Mona Lee Murphy said, "We're getting calls ev-

ery day, Agneda. The people say you're not taking care of
your children properly, leaving them alone, and . . ."

"Them people don' know nothin'," Agneda said.
"Them people don' take care a their own kids. Them
people should mind their own business."

"Well, these people know the county attorney and
they're calling him, too, Agneda, and we have to do
something. You should understand that," Mona Lee said
with a serious look on her face, looking straight into the
fiery eyes of Agneda Esquibel. "You need to understand
this clearly now, no mistake about it, so you don't claim
later on you weren't fairly warned." But Mona Lee Murphy's voice was kindly sounding.

"I don' know the county attorney," Agneda said.
"Them peoples know 'em." And then she wouldn't look
at Mona Lee any longer, and she would say nothing further, and that was the end of it. Later on the county
attorney did ask the welfare for a full report on the Esquibel family, suggesting that it might be necessary to
take the children from Agneda permanently, and Mona
Lee went to see Agneda to warn her again. The house
was still in a mess and the kids were still running around,
not in school, and Agneda was in bed, claiming she still
didn't feel well.

"I no feel good. Sick. I no can do nothin'." And her
face was pale, like all the blood had been drained out of
her.

"Well, we have to do something here, Agneda. We
can't just go on like this. You have to understand I have
my job to do, and I have to write up a report. You can
understand that." But Agneda would not even say she
understood. She just said she was sick. Had a miscarriage, and Mona Lee Murphy did report that Mrs. Esquibel appeared as if she hadn't regained her health after
her last miscarriage, but all in all it would have to be
viewed as a negative report. The truth is the truth.

Later Harvey Watkins himself had gone over to see
Mrs. Esquibel about the Social Security payments from
Dario's death. A collateral source, you know. Have to
report all collateral sources. He made Mrs. Esquibel

promise to contact his office if and when she received the money. He was required to account for it. But Agneda failed to contact Harvey Watkins when she got the $1,015 lump-sum benefit, and later Harvey Watkins reported that when he visited her to talk about this money Agneda Esquibel became "very haughty" and stated that she and Timato, her fifteen-year-old son, had gone to Casper and they had purchased an old Mercury automobile for $800, and she said the money was for the kids and that the kids wanted the car, and she also bought a washing machine.

"How can you spend money on a car when your children are hungry and half-naked?" Watkins had asked incredulously. "How? How for Christ's sake, Agneda?" She didn't answer.

"How!"

She didn't answer again. Finally she said, "I don' have to talk."

"Yes, you have to talk to me. I feed you and those kids out of our budget, and the minute you get a little money you go out and spend it on a goddamned old junk heap of a car which has probably already fallen apart, and I'll tell you one thing. We're not buying gas for that goddamned car, and we're not paying money to fix the damn thing up either. And that's why you're going to talk to me about spending that money!" But she didn't talk to him, and later when Watkins said he was going to take the car out and sell it to get some of the money back as a collateral source, she told Harvey Watkins he was not going to sell it. "It is the kids' car. They wan' a car like them other kids."

"You can't even drive it," Watkins said.

"Timato, he drive," she said.

"He's not old enough to drive. Doesn't have a license for Christ on a crutch," Watkins shouted, his arm flailing at the air, and Agneda backed up, and the kids held onto her, especially Little Joe, and Elma was busy doing the dishes and pretended not to hear, and Timato sat over in the corner and didn't say anything, just looked at the man like a young curious chicken, like a baby rooster looks, and he tipped his head one way and listened, and then the other, and then his eyes got as hard as marbles and he stared straight at the crazy Watkins. Crazy as hell.

"You no holler," Agneda hollered. "You go fuck yoursef. I don' need you bastar's." About then Timato got up, and his hand went in his pocket where Agneda knew he kept his knife, but she waved Timato back. "I git the Social Security—$169. I don' need no welfare no more and you can take my name off them"—she didn't know what to call it or how to say it—"off them papers and stuff. I git that money from Dario being dead now, that Social Security, and I gonna spend it like I wan', like I please. You bastar's no bother me no more—no more," she screamed. "Shoo," she screamed again at Watkins, like she was chasing an old rooster out of the house. "Shoo. You go," she said. "You git!" And then Watkins put on his funny hat in a huff and wrapped his red muffler around his long protruding neck, and he stomped out of the place.

The death benefit was $28.20 per child, Watkins wrote in the welfare records. "Her case will be terminated as soon as it can be verified she is receiving that sum." And in a couple of days the Social Security people confirmed the payment, and a copy of the letter from Social Security was sent to the county attorney and to the judge, and two days later, just two days, there was an order from the judge placing all of the children under the jurisdiction of the juvenile court, but placing the children in the actual physical custody of the Carbon County Welfare Department, and ordering Agneda to pay all the money she got from Social Security to the Welfare Department. It was that simple. Now she had neither the money nor the children, and the judge sentenced Agneda to three months in the county jail for child neglect. It was all done for the welfare of the children, of course, and perhaps Agneda Esquibel would learn her lesson, too. Time to get her head screwed on right.

"The system works wonders," Mona Lee said sarcastically when she read the court's order. "Just wonders! It does such miracles when it comes to protecting its own money," but Harvey Watkins said nothing. This woman took certain liberties with him, he thought, like her constant haranguing and her endless pontificating about her old-line pinko social theories, but that was the price a man has to pay when he has "dipped his pen in the company ink." "Don't dip your pen in the company ink" was always his motto at the office, his own policy, and he himself had violated it, and this was a good example of the validity of his policy against "intra-office copulation," as he liked to call it, and he raised his eyebrows and smirked.

The chief and Officer Gould came first for Agneda, jerked her out of bed in the morning like before, but this time she didn't resist. She slipped on her dress and shoes and walked right out and got into the car by herself, and left without saying anything, not even good-bye to the kids, and the kids didn't cry anymore either and didn't say a thing, didn't even hide under the bed when the chief burst through the front door. They only watched with frightened eyes, and Joe and Timato stood together over in the far corner where it was the darkest. After the chief left with Agneda, Harvey Watkins and Mona Lee Murphy came for the children and took all but Timato to the Patrick home, a foster home, until things could be arranged for the children on a permanent basis.

But Timato would not go. He said he'd rather go to jail than to go to any damned foster home. He wanted to be with his mother, he said. Both Watkins and Mrs. Murphy tried to reason with Timato, but he stood there in the corner alone, defiant, and when they started to get close to him he pulled his knife, and he stood there with his knife flashing, looking back and forth between Watkins and Mrs. Murphy. His hair had grown past his shoulders, and some said he looked wild and demented. It was before the days of the hippies, and Timato was a strange wild sight, all right. He looked as if the blood of his Indian forebears had suddenly burst through and taken him over, possessed him as a true Aztec during this time of his childish terrors.

"Timmy," Mona Lee said. "Come on, Timmy. We'll go to a nice place together." Timato said nothing. Just stood his ground with the knife, looking beady-eyed, fierce, looking like Dario, looking so much like Dario it was frightening, Mona Lee said later, and so they had to call the chief and his officer back.

"Come on, boy," the chief said when he came. "Give me the knife." But no. Timato flashed the knife back and forth between the officers, the knife handle in the palm of his hand and his fist closed shut around it the way a good knife fighter holds his weapon. "Come on, boy," the chief said, and he and the officer moved in closer, and Timato made more menacing gestures with the knife, slashing the air ahead of him. Harvey Watkins stood back and said nothing. Everybody has his job.

"Timmy," Mona Lee pleaded. "I'm your friend, aren't I? I've always been your friend."

"You ain't no fren'," Timato finally said, keeping his eyes on the chief and punching the air. "You steal Mama, and you steal us kids all the time."

"Give us the knife, son," the chief said again.

"I ain't gonna," Timato said in his little voice.

"Come on, son," the other officer said, still pushing forward with the chief, and the boy was now tight up against the wall in the corner, and then the officer just jabbed his nightstick out fast, right into Timato's skinny belly, and Timato's eyes popped out, almost out of their sockets, and the knife fell from Timato's hand and he doubled over like he was broken in two. Then the officers took Timato to jail. He would have to stay there until the welfare completed its reports. That much was clear the chief said.

"Did you see his eyes?" the officer laughed to the chief on the way to the station. "Damn near popped 'em eyes clean out of his skull—little greaser bastard. All of them Mexies is handy as hell with a sticker. And what's a man s'posed to do when they pull on ya like that? A kid can kill ya just as fast as a man—faster. Got them fast kid reflexes—like fuckin' around with a rattler."

There were those who offered to take the children. The Vena Montoyas, for instance, offered to take them, and Virginia Trujillo offered to take Elma. "Give that kid to me," she said, "I will take care of her," simple, just like that, and then C. T. Gonzales asked for all the children. But the welfare sent the people to the county attorney because the welfare didn't have jurisdiction over the kids any longer, since the children were in the custody of the juvenile court. The people went to the county attorney to offer to take the kids, but the county attorney said he'd have to get the Welfare Department to investigate the peoples' homes before he could do anything. Jake Montoya, an uncle, had driven all the way from Casper to Rawlins in order to talk to the Welfare Department about Timato. Always liked the boy, he said, and the boy liked him. He could give Timato a good home, and after all he was employed—had a job as a carpenter, had five kids of his own, he said, and he knew how to take care of kids and he would make room for Timato. But Mona Lee Murphy had to be fair. She tried to explain to Jake Montoya that Timato was a very defiant boy, very resentful of discipline of any kind. He'd never been reprimanded by his mother for any of his many misdeeds, she told him, and it is, after all, the mother who makes the difference in the way children grow up. She knew from her experience with her own child, Sharon, who was about the same age as Timato, and she was no trouble at all. "Girls is no trouble," Jake Montoya said. "Boys is somethin' else again." But Mona Lee Murphy didn't agree with Jake Montoya about that.

Mona Lee had tried to get the children back in the Cathedral Home in Laramie. But Mrs. Kelly said the father, Dario, was too much trouble, and when Mona Lee Murphy pointed out, kindly, of course, that Dario was dead and would therefore cause no more trouble, Mrs. Kelly hadn't even said she was sorry to hear of Dario's death. She said, well, it made no difference really. The oldest boy, whatever his name was, was a sullen child and caused the other children to be despondent and hard to manage.

"He was the rotten apple in the barrel and besides, he was demented," she said, "and belonged in the children's home at Lander."

And Mona Lee Murphy said, "Well, Mrs. Kelly, I have a full report on Timato made by Lillian Portenier, the psychologist from the University of Wyoming who lives right there in your own hometown of Laramie. You might check with Dr. Portenier herself. She thought Timato was a normal boy and in good health except for needing dental work and that there was nothing mentally wrong with him at all."

Then Mrs. Kelly said, "I don't put much stock in psychologists or psychiatrists, whichever is which. I can never keep them straight."

"Well, Timato has missed a lot of school because they thought for a long time he had a bad heart but it turned out to be an anemic condition and he got considerably behind on account of that. The poor boy quit school. He was fourteen and only in the fifth grade," and Mona Lee Murphy pleaded Timato's case with the facts, with fervor, like a good trial lawyer, but Mrs. Kelly won. She had learned long ago there is a certain grace in being able to say no. She said she didn't want Timato or any of the other kids under any circumstances, and that was that, and so Mona Lee had gone to Father Meyer, who in turn had contacted St. Joseph's Orphanage, where he very frankly thought the children should have been all along, and then Father Meyer came over and blessed the children again before they left Rawlins.

The orphanage in Torrington said that Timato and Elma were too old. Timato was still in jail. He wouldn't eat. Wouldn't talk. Just sulked, like Mrs. Kelly said, but finally the welfare people got Timato released to go to his uncle Ralph Montoya, who lived close by and who promised the county attorney and the court that he would keep tabs on Timato, real close tabs, and besides, he said, he lived right down the street and the welfare could check anytime they so pleased. Anytime.

Timato had refused to cut his hair, and a Dr. Herrold, a psychiatrist with the Department of Public Health, had examined Timato, and Dr. Herrold thought "the control and occupational training at the State Reformatory at Worland would be salutary," and the principal of Pershing School told the welfare that frankly he had adverse feelings, is how he put it, about Timato. He said, "I have been observing him very closely because I feel Timato may be a sex pervert. Just look at his long hair style, and when I've seen him, he's continually primping and he prefers to be with the girls rather than with the other kids during recess," and the principal added, "and to be honest with you, I'm afraid he'll take out his anger on the younger children." They wouldn't take Timato in the Casper Orphanage either because they'd heard that he was a sex problem or something, liked to be with the girls, this fifteen-year-old. One of Timato's teachers reported that "Timmy's withdrawal into a fantasy is probably his most serious problem and has undoubtedly led to a distortion of his perception of reality. For this reason, he is potentially dangerous since he appears to look upon his environment as threatening." The welfare records said the department agreed with that evaluation, and so they left Timato with his uncle, Ralph Montoya.

As for Elma, well, they finally did leave her on a temporary basis with Virginia Trujillo, but Elma soon became sullen, too, and she often burst into tears like any little mother might who had her children taken from her. After all she had been the mother, and she was "unhappy" is what the record said, "and she misses her brothers and sisters."

Then one day Harvey Watkins and Mona Lee Murphy gathered up the remaining children from the Patrick foster home for the long drive to St. Joseph's Orphanage at Torrington. When they arrived they quickly deposited the children in the front office, and as soon as they had received receipts for the children, they left before there was time for much of a scene. Then they took the long drive home again, and later, as they traveled along the dark highway without speaking, each with separate thoughts, Harvey Watkins suddenly broke the silence by saying something which Mona Lee Murphy thought was terribly irrelevant. . . . He said, "Once a whore, always a whore."

"How can you say such a thing, Harvey?" she said

quickly. "Isn't there any salvation for mankind? If there is no salvation for Agneda Esquibel, there is none for any of us either."

"You can save me again," Harvey Watkins said, looking extra serious the way he did when he was being funny, and he reached out and just touched Mona Lee Murphy, as he did at such times, touched her in the dark, lightly.

But Mona Lee ignored his hand and said, "If man is born in sin, and can never be saved, if 'once a whore, always a whore' is the state of the human condition, then we are working here at the welfare office for nothing."

He touched her again, lightly.

"Tell me," he said, touching once more.

"I will tell you," she said with determination. "I will tell you." And then there was this nice country road off to the north, and the headlights picked up the wild yellow sunflowers with the dark brown centers which were blooming along the edge of the road and Mona Lee Murphy had changed the subject by saying that the sunflowers were pretty at night in the headlights. They turned up the road and she didn't ask him where they were going. She just touched his hand gently, and then there was a wide spot by the side of the road where they parked. With the headlights off, the crickets began singing sweet sounds at each other among the sunflowers and under the tall yellow clover, and the male crickets fiddled their songs and the females threw cricketing sounds back, strumming the cricket mating songs in the dark, and once in a while the darkness along the road was broken by the headlights of some rattling old country truck and the noise silenced the crickets for a moment, and then they began their singing again.

"You can save me, darling," Harvey Watkins said again with a little song in the night.

"Oh, Harvey," she sang back.

"The Esquibel woman just likes to do it. Likes to do it with white men, like an animal," he breathed.

"Oh, God, Harvey," she breathed back at his touching.

"Likes to do it and do it," he sang.

"Oh, God, Harvey," she sang back.

"It's that she is an animal. . . . We are all animals."

"Yes," she whispered. "Yes, I know. Yes. Yes." She answered even though he hadn't said anything more.

"And you can save me, baby, if you have to save somebody." An old car rattled by, and they paid no attention to it.

"I will," she said. "Oh, I will," she whispered.

"And you can save me right now," he breathed.

"I am saving you."

"Yes, you are," he whispered, touching more.

"Yes, I am," she whispered, touching back. Touching.

"We are all animals," Watkins said out loud in the dark, and his loud voice made the crickets stop their singing for a moment.

"Yes. Oh, God, yes," Mona Lee said out loud, and then the crickets began to sing again. After a while Harvey Watkins started the car up and they drove along silently toward home. A long time passed. Finally Mona said, "Agneda Esquibel is saved." Watkins didn't answer. "She is absolutely saved. She does it for the right reasons and therefore she is saved. We do it for the wrong ones."

"Is it right to be a whore?" Watkins asked, driving down the road, the bright headlights illuminating the side of the road, but they were past the sunflowers now and there was only the tall summer grass turning brown.

"No, it's not all right to be a whore," she said, "but it's all right to feed your children."

"Is what we do wrong?" he asked, but she didn't answer him, and the station wagon bumbled and bounced down the road on bad shock absorbers and the car swerved wildly at the curves because it was empty in back and long, and it rattled into the night, down the vacant road and across the dark Wyoming prairies on the slow trip home, and the trip became longer because their passions had been emptied.

After a while Mona Lee Murphy began talking about Sharon, her little blond girl with the bright blue eyes, blue as bluebells, with the darling little square face like a Dutch girl, who was quick as a bug, and Mona Lee Murphy said it was society's fault that children grew up to be

criminals. Watkins didn't want to hear it, but it was the
price he had to pay. Children are helpless. Children are
economic victims, she said, crippled by poverty, crippled
by a class system as surely as if they had caught something as bad as polio. Poverty was just as devastating to a
child as polio ever was, she said. You could actually see
the devastation of polio in the shriveled limbs of the
children but how could you see a disease of the soul?
Poverty and degradation and disgrace crippled the souls
of children. Poverty, she said, took away the right of a
child to feel good about himself. The miles dragged on,
and Harvey Watkins drove along in silence, not wanting
to engage this woman, just wanting peace. But she kept
on. A child has the natural right, the inherent God-given
right, to feel good about himself or herself because every
child is perfect, and when we destroy that sense of selfworth with poverty we have destroyed the child, destroyed it with poverty. But Harvey Watkins just drove
on.

"If it wasn't for poverty, these children would grow up
as straight and strong and happy as my own Sharon," she
said, "as bright as a dollar. Her teacher says she is especially gifted, but I know it is only that we provide a home
for her where there is plenty of security, and love. She is
an only child, but she knows we love each other."

"How does she know you love each other?" Watkins
finally asked.

"She knows. Children know such things."

"Then what are we doing here, tonight, together like
this?" Watkins asked. He turned on the radio, and the
static and the sound of faint stations filled the car, and
then he found a loud station playing some wild music,
and he began keeping time on the steering wheel, and
once in a while he would dim the lights for an approaching car like a good citizen.

"Well," Mona Lee Murphy said, "what we do tonight
doesn't make any difference to a child who doesn't know.
It hurts no one. We do it for us."

"But don't you think children know things like that?"

he asked, talking in a strange high voice as if he knew something she didn't know.

"Of course they don't know such things," she said.

"Do you love your husband?" Watkins asked abruptly. She didn't like it when he changed the subject like that.

"Of course I love him," she said.

"Do you love me?"

"Oh, Harvey!" she said. And they drove along in the night, and later on they stopped for a hamburger and coffee, and then Watkins parked the car along another country road, but there were no crickets out in the prairies. Finally Mona Lee said, "It isn't that I don't love you," as if she hadn't waited for an hour to answer his question.

"Well, what is it?" Harvey Watkins asked as he touched her once more.

"Well," she laughed, "it's just that I need to save you again," and she laughed a little impish laugh from deep down in her throat, which he actually loved, and it excited Watkins, and he readily agreed she really should save him once more, but afterward he said that all her talk about poverty and social classes and crime coming out of poverty, well, that was just so much commie horseshit. He just had to say that before the trip was over.

He said, "Look at the Esquibel woman—she really didn't want her kids—practically gave them to us— seemed glad to get rid of 'em. We got plenty of poor people on the rolls who want their kids. It isn't poverty."

"It is surrender, Harvey. Surrender. There is a time when people have to give up," she said.

"Crime doesn't come from poverty. Crime comes from bad people," Watkins said. "There's plenty of poor people who aren't criminals."

"When I was a little girl I found a skinny little kitten, one of those little striped yellow ones, you know?" she asked.

"Yeah," he said.

"This little kitten was so weak it could hardly walk. It actually fell over when it took a step—fell over to one side—and then it would struggle back to its feet, and it would take a step, and it would fall over to the other side. It was so weak! Harvey, are you listening? It was so hungry. It just happened by our back door, and so I took the little kitten in and fed it. We thought it was lost from its mother because it cried out, and meowed so loudly, so pitifully, crying for its mother. I didn't know a kitten so weak could cry so loudly. We put it out on the back porch where its mother could hear it—the mother couldn't really be very far away, we thought. We propped open the back door with a shoe so the mother could come and get her baby, left milk for the kitten, and all night we could hear the kitten crying, and it made us want to cry, and we hoped that the mother would come. So in the morning we rushed out to the porch to see if the mama had taken her kitten back, and guess what we found when we got to the back porch, Harvey?"

"What?" he asked, dimming his lights way ahead of the other car.

"Well, there were six other little starving kittens there in the morning—all colors. The mother left them there with the first one. They were all so weak that hardly any of them could walk."

"Yeah," Watkins said.

"The mother didn't take her kitten back. She brought us the others to feed instead. It took me a month to find a home for all of them, Harvey."

"That proves my point," Watkins said. "Get them on the dole, a cat's kittens or a mother's kids, and you can't get 'em off."

"No," Mona Lee Murphy said. "It shows that a mother, even a cat, is willing to give up her young in order to save them. Aren't mothers great?" Mona Lee Murphy asked lightly with a little trill in her voice.

Harvey Watkins didn't answer but from that day on, when talking to Mona Lee Murphy about a budget for a client, he called the food allowance cat food.

The records revealed that Agneda was in jail for a couple of months again, and when she got out she had gone to see attorney Bob Bates. C. L. Bates was his real name and the law school boys had talked to attorney

Bates. Bates said Agneda came in, promising to pay him.
She always promised to pay him, he said, and she actually
did pay him if she had the money. One time she walked
clear across town and waited out in his office for an hour
to see him and all she wanted to do was pay him five
dollars. He said, "You must help people like that." She
wanted him to help her get her children back.

"You got a bad record, Nellie," Bates told her.

"I know," she said, and she looked down at her feet,
and she didn't seem proud anymore. Bates said she
seemed so humble, and then he said, "I told her she had
to convince the authorities she had changed, had to get a
good home for the kids, a good house, you know, something that would impress the welfare, and keep it spic and
span, etc., etc. She seemed to understand, and then she
left, and I didn't see her for about six months. Then one
day she came back and gave me another five dollars, said
she had the home like I told her, and everything. Then I
said, 'Well, Nellie, let's go impress the hell out of the
welfare.' So I called up old Watkins, who I knew personally, and I said, 'Harvey, let's you and me go have a little
look at Nellie's new home,' and he said, 'What?' and I
said, 'I want to meet you at Nellie's new home,' just like
that. I gave him the address, and told him to meet me
there in half an hour, and when Nellie and I got there
Harvey was already there with Mrs. Murphy, lady from
the welfare you know, and they started looking over the
home, five rooms with a bath, living room, dining room,
which could be used for sleeping some kids, and she already had a double bed set up in the dining room, and
the two bedrooms had double beds. Everything neat. Everything nice. I don't know where she got all the furniture, but you know Nellie. If she gets her mind set on
something, well, she gets it done one way or another,"
and Bob Bates laughed his little laugh. He had chipmunk
cheeks that looked like they were full of nuts on both
sides. He said the kitchen in the new house was large
enough to accommodate all the members of the family
without crowding them, and there were enough chairs for
everybody to sit down at once, and the home was very

clean, very clean he repeated. This impressed the hell out of Harvey Watkins, who looked at Mona Lee Murphy, and Watkins then made a big point out of the fact that people can do better if they really want to. This change in Agneda's life proves that people can do better. "And Nellie was so proud of her new home and yet she was so humble," Bates said.

Watkins made a record of his visit and reported that "Mrs. Esquibel seemed very desirous of having her children returned to her and she said, 'I have learned my lesson.' She says she will be a good mother to her children and that she will use all the Social Security benefits to take care of her family properly." Moreover the report said that "our department has not received any adverse reports during the past six months on Mrs. Esquibel's behavior and as far as is known she is not frequenting the bars, bringing men in her home at all hours and it appears she has made an honest attempt to change her way of living. She is also aware that if the children are returned to her and if she is again charged with child neglect she would never again be given another chance." Then Harvey Watkins had written the judge and had said that "as a result of my investigation I find her behavior satisfactory and feel the court would be justified in returning the children to this home." A copy of the letter went to Bob Bates, of course, and then, just like that, the court ordered the children's return, and Mona Lee Murphy wrote a letter to Father Morgan at St. Joseph's Orphanage thanking him for his "fine service" and sent him a copy of the court's order, and it was all as simple as that. The children were home again with Agneda and the welfare records also stated that after Timato was returned to his mother the change in him was simply miraculous. He immediately became a well-behaved boy, and he cut his hair right away.

The law school students found out that this had all come about because Agneda had married again, a Mexican-American fellow who worked on the track gang. He had promised Agneda that he would help her get her kids back, and he got Agneda the house, actually rented it for her. But now that the kids were all home again, well, there had been trouble between Joe and this new husband. Shortly after Agneda's marriage the welfare reports said that Joe had robbed some old man, and Joe had been taken into juvenile court. The judge was the same one who presided over the district court, the same one who had rendered all of the decisions involving the various members of the Esquibel family, who had sent Agneda to jail, and ordered the children taken from Agneda from time to time. He was the same judge who earlier had granted Agneda her divorce from Dario, and who had once found Dario guilty of criminal non-support. The judge, from Laramie, now presided over the juvenile court of Carbon County as well, and he ordered a full report from the Welfare Department on Joe Esquibel.

Mona Lee Murphy went to see Agneda about this most recent matter involving Joe, but Agneda would tell her nothing, would sign nothing. She said she didn't even know where her son was, and that if Joe had got himself into trouble he'd have to get himself out of trouble, too, and that's all she would say. When Mona Lee went back a second time, Agneda wouldn't even answer the door, and when Mona Lee tried to contact Joe through his friends she was also unsuccessful. So she filed the best report she could—poor grades, Joe in the first grade three years, absent nineteen days, tardy twelve, I.Q. 67, a teacher reporting, "Joe craves success and security and seldom can have either. Needs to be handled with a firm hand."

Reading was his greatest handicap. Made his tests show poorly. He was sullen if disciplined. That sullenness was genetic, Harvey Watkins said, and finally Joe's behavior got so bad he was expelled. This was all in the welfare records. Mona Lee's report said Joe had been accused of shoplifting, and of breaking windows and busting toilets in some vacant house, and of abusing some other boy, a white boy. There were several such accusations, as a matter of fact. And they also accused him of stealing a bicycle. But these were only accusations. No charges had been filed against him, and he had no convictions. But

Mona Lee Murphy put all the accusations in black and
white in her report to the juvenile court because she
wanted to make a complete report. She knew nothing of
the rules of evidence, and besides, the strict rules of evidence didn't apply in the juvenile court. It was just an
informal proceeding more or less for the benefit of the
child, you know. In due time the juvenile court placed
Joe Esquibel on probation for two years, released him to
his mother, but put him under the control and supervision of the Welfare Department.

One day when Timato was sixteen, this Mexican guy
shot him. He shot him in the chest, and he fell dead at
Joe's feet, red blood gushing out into the dirt, soaking
into the ground making brown mud, out behind Patsy's
Café. There hadn't been much of a fight. The guy was
drunk. Called Timato some bad names. Timato's hair was
slicked back, all right, like Rudolph Valentino or somebody, but with a pompadour in front, and he wore a fake
gold chain down the side of his peg-legged pants, and
Timato was, in fact, a skinny little sixteen-year-old Rawlins, Wyoming, zoot-suiter. He looked even more like
Dario, pretty in his young way, and Joe loved him, followed him everywhere those days, and although Joe was
actually quite a bit bigger than Timato, larger bones and
taller, Timato was the boss. He had hair on his balls.

"Someday you'll get hair on your balls, Joe," Timato
said, and laughed his high squeaky laugh. "Come on," he
said, "let's go to the dance"—the Saturday dance at
Patsy's—"and fuck them girls." Then they had gone to
Patsy's and this Mexican called Timato nothing but a
zoot-suitin' little prick and they had gone outside. There
wasn't anything else for Timato to say.

"Come on outside, then," Timato said, timidly.

"Sure, I'll come outside," the Mexican said. "I'm
gonna stuff your fucking greasy head up your ass—that's
what I'm gonna do," and another Mexican laughed, and
said, "Come on, Timato," and held open the door for
Timato and there wasn't anything else for Timato to do
except go.

"Why don' you guys go over to the Wyoming Bar?"

Timato added in his small high timid voice. They were all
standing behind the café, Joe next to Timato, and there
were a lot of people gathered around eagerly waiting for
it to happen.

"We go where we want. I come here to fuck your
women," the fat one laughed. He stood a foot above
Timato, and his arms were as big as Timato's waist.

"I ain't got no woman," Timato said.

"I can see why," the fat guy said with a sneer and a
laugh. "No woman would want a little skinny piece of shit
like you."

Then Timato jumped him. He had the switchblade in
his hand—the one he had taken from Ramon—and the
crowd let out a hiss—and then the big one pulled a gun
out of his pocket and shot Timato, and Timato fell over
in the dirt, and folded up funny, and he kicked there in
the dirt for a few minutes, like he was still running. Nobody said anything, and Joe looked down and saw Timato
kicking, and he saw the blood running out of Timato's
body, and then Joe ran at the fat guy, and the guy shot
Joe, too. Joe could feel it in his arm, and then somebody
screamed to Joe, "Run, run, Joe," and somebody pushed
Joe away from the crowd, pushed him forward until he
almost fell, and they hollered, "Run, run, Joe," and he
began to run, and he could see Timato's legs running,
too, thrashing at the air as Timato lay in the dirt, and
blood flowing out, and then Joe stumbled and fell and
that was the last Joe remembered until he woke up in the
hospital. Agneda was there.

"You gonna be okay, Joe," she said. He looked around
in that clean white place and felt suddenly dirty.

"Where's Timato?" Joe asked.

"Timato's dead," Agneda said without a tear, from a
frozen face. Joe looked back up to the white ceiling. "Timato's dead," she spoke quietly again of her firstborn.
And when she said it again, that was when Joe knew
something had happened to him. Something in his heart.

After Timato's death Joe just ran wild. He was picked
up in Colorado with some toughs, white men, and there
were charges about ransacking cars both in Colorado and

in Rawlins, and finally Mona Lee Murphy had to make another report to the juvenile court, which started by repeating all the prior accusations of thefts and break-ins, and the like, and ended by saying, "Because Joe's home environment is obviously not conducive to his training, it would not be well for him to remain there longer, and since Joe threatens he will run away if he is placed elsewhere, a foster home will not profit him." Mona Lee Murphy asked that her department be relieved of further responsibility in supervising Joe because, "Joe is not complying with the terms of his probation." And so the judge sent Joe Esquibel to the Boys' Reformatory at Worland. The judge said he had no choice.

16

IN THE WINTER, still at sixteen, I left home. Had to get the hell out, I said. I can't even remember whether I kissed my mother good-bye. I had enough credits to graduate from Laramie High. No use staying on another day, I argued. They could send me my diploma in the spring when the rest of my class graduated.

I took out the Monkey Ward catalogue one Sunday morning. I refused to go to church and then my mother asked only one question. "Gerry, why have you given up God?" She looked at me a long time with her sad blue eyes, and a lock of her hair hung strangely out of place for Sunday morning, and her red dress was smoothed down nicely over her corset, and she stood there straight, with plain black shoes and her glasses, rimless and square-edged, made her eyes a little sharper than they really were, because when she took them off her eyes were sadder and softer. I never answered her. I just looked back into the Monkey Ward catalogue, and she stood there a little while longer, and then she left. I considered the items, the Victor traps—different sizes for beaver and mink, for the arctic fox of Alaska—and there were bedrolls, and boots, and a special heavy coat with a fur hood. It was all there in the catalogue, and I added up the total cost after the family had left for Sunday school, my little brother and sister, Tom and Barbara, ten and twelve years younger, not old enough to know better, and my father in his old blue suit with his goddamn white stockings showing at the bottom of his pants cuffs, and the pants always too short. His collar was wrinkled and his tie seemed always crooked. My mother didn't straighten it any more. I can't remember now what the total cost of the equipment was, but it would take all the money I had saved, dollar at a time, for sixteen fucking years, to buy all this stuff and go to Alaska. I could talk Jim Brown into going, and we could become trappers, make it big in furs and pay my money back to the Federal Savings and Loan, which had kept it all this time like it belonged to them. They paid only pennies interest.

"See, you have got interest, Gerry," my mother said once. "See here . . . it's right in the book. Money grows." The interest wouldn't buy a friggin' Popsicle, I thought. I decided to go to San Diego where Jim Brown was. I'd hitchhike. I had told both my father and mother the day before at supper, but my mother had said nothing, just looked a little sadder, but said nothing, and my father, who always said I should grow up to be independent, had said nothing.

"I'm gonna hitchhike out and see Jim Brown," I announced again at supper the next night, as if I had never said it before, and again they said nothing. "I ain't gonna wait around all winter to graduate. Got enough credits already." My father and mother just looked at each other, just a quick glance between bites, and then they went on eating. No protest—couldn't tell whether they wanted me to go or whether my leaving hurt them so much they couldn't talk about it. They probably didn't want to fight with me, didn't want a scene. Peaceful people, but I said the hell with it. It was time to get the hell out.

The next morning my father drove me out on U.S. Highway 30, headed for Rawlins. "Be careful. Call home," he said. "Write," he said, "and be careful." I didn't kiss him. A man kisses his father only when he's a little boy, or when he's a man and his father has grown old and decrepit. I just waved good-bye and then in almost the same motion I thumbed at the first car that passed while my father was still parked there in the old black '37 Ford. He saw me thumb, and looked down, and then I thumbed again, standing big and sure, and then he made a U-turn across the highway and I watched the old Ford drive away, the fenders flapping in the wind, ridiculously, like tin wings, and I could hear the rattle of that old rattletrap for six blocks or more. It was a piece of junk, and as I watched the old Ford bounce down the street, my father at the wheel, and I was no longer able to see the back of his head and finally no longer able to see the old car, something happened to me. I could feel it, in the chest, tight, like being sad, but not really being sad.

I stood there thinking of my father and that car, both back on top of the Big Horns. A man can't put a sixty horsepower Ford on the top of the Big Horns without a little damage, my father had said once, grinning like he was apologizing. He had a reputation for being able to put a car damn near any place a man could walk. How the hell did a damn car get up there? the horseback hunters would marvel. Jesus, he musta flew it up here, but my father got it there, forward a little and backward, little at a time—move a log here and some rocks there, and get it running up backward as far up as it would go and then forward and backward and forward, like making a figure U up the mountainside until he was close enough to where he'd killed the elk to get it out, all the meat, right down to the brains and liver and the bloody empty heart. Mountain driving and elk hunting are sister arts, I thought.

Pretty soon somebody picked me up. I was stamping up and down, running in place to keep warm, and they must have felt sorry. It took four days to go across the country to San Diego. I don't remember the trip now. It has faded into scores of trips to there and elsewhere, and the faces that were sharp then and in focus right down to the roots of the whiskers and to the special design of blood vessels on a whiskey nose have been lost in the years, faded into each other like old watercolors on paper.

I stayed the first night in San Diego at the Brown School for Boys, or a place by some such name where Jim had gone because his sister who cared for him after the death of both of his parents thought that was a good place for a boy to be. The school and Jim Brown weren't related at all. He sneaked me into his room, and then we had eaten together in the dining room, and I felt proud about being his guest, different from the rest, glad of it. They wore uniforms, like little soldiers, some pimple-faced soldiers, and some were soldiers with high boys' voices and chubby cheeks. We walked downtown that day, Jim and I, to send a telegram to my father and mother that I was all right.

I can remember the air. It was warm and the palm trees were blowing gently—imagine, in the middle of the winter—and it was glorious, like a balmy heaven. Who could believe it? But I didn't say anything about my feeling to Jim Brown. If I had said, "Oh, God, just feel this place, just look at it—it's beautiful!" he would have looked at me like I was crazy, mushy on the edges. I still had that special kind of gorky walk, that was good, but you couldn't help but notice that Jim Brown walked funny, like a man swaggering into the Malamute Saloon, or something. He liked to read the poems of Robert Service, about tough men in the North, and when I got there he was in his uniform all right, and somebody called out across the street, "Hey, Brown, what color is shit?"

The first night we went to Tijuana. I remember how crossing the border, suddenly it was dark, even right there on the town's main street. They had electricity all right, but what lights there were on the street leaked out from inside the buildings. The honky-tonks and cafés were mostly dark on the outside and up the street there was a little place on the sidewalk where a mariachi band played and sang and tried to send their voices over the noise of drunken sailors in white who walked together in little groups, laughing and shouting. Jim and I stepped aside for the sailors. They were older, been to war. Men already. Most of 'em shaved. There was a string of Christmas tree lights around the place where the mariachis played.

"We should join the Merchant Marine," I said to Jim.

"A guy can get in and out whenever he damn pleases, and a guy can see the world."

"Yeah, man," is all Jim Brown said.

And then a little Mexican my age came up. "Hey, buddy, you wanna have a good time?"

"What do ya mean?" I said.

"Hey, come on, buddy. You wanna girl?" I looked at Jim. He shrugged his shoulders and grinned, big. His front teeth pointed in and his gums showed when he grinned like that.

"Hey, buddy, gimme a dollar. I show you where to have a good time."

I gave the kid a dollar and we followed him down a dark dirt street where four or five skinny dogs were panting in the night's heat, trying to mount a bitch lying dead, freshly run over and bleeding into the road, the blood making mud. I watched carefully where we were going— two blocks this way—one over, and besides I could get back by the sound of the mariachis playing, clearly, sweetly, and I could still hear the shouts and laughter of the sailors coming out of the bars behind me. I felt in love, in love with this good life, with my feet in the dust, and following this boy, skinny like the dogs, bare-chested, brown, through this Mexican town, shacks on both sides, nothing but shacks, like cardboard boxes, and my heart beating with adventure. I was scared, too. I gave Jim a nudge with my elbow, and winked, but he was intent on the skinny kid ahead, and pretty soon we were there.

"Here," he said. "Have fun. It cost ya three bucks for a short time," he said, and left in the night. In front of us were a dozen or more sailors lined up in a row in front of a little shack like they were waiting for mess, and there was a single light hanging down from the ceiling inside the shack. I got in line with Jim, and we just stood there for a long time not talking, and then pretty soon some other sailors got in line behind us. We were the only ones not in uniform, probably thought we were a bunch of draft-dodgers, but we were as loyal as they were, and we were all in this together, waiting there to take our turn with some Mexican whore. There was a lot of whooping and laughing when somebody would come out, and a sailor would holler, "Hey, how was it?" And the guy coming out would holler "It was too damn good for you, buddy," and everybody would laugh again, and then pretty soon we were up there. The guy in front of me pushed the door of the shack open a little with his foot and I could see a sailor there in the room. The light was on and it was as bright as day inside and the sailor was between the short brown legs of the woman, and his bare ass was pumping away, and she had one foot on the bed and she held the other foot up a little higher, a little off the covers, and the foot dangled in the air, relaxed, waved up and down with his pumping like a hand waving good-bye and her short toes were gray and calloused from walking barefoot in the dirt. I said to Jim, "Come on, let's go." And Jim said, "Well, ain't ya gonna go? You're next." I said, "No, I musta left my money in my other pants," and Jim said well he'd loan me three bucks, and I said no, and he said I was chicken, and I said I'd wait for him and he said he never had any intention of goin' in there in the first place. Later we went to San Pedro and signed on as messmen on the S.S. *Roanoke,* a Texas company tanker, an old coal burner, converted to oil, and nobody knew where the hell she was really going—maybe to Russia—maybe we would be sunk and drowned in the ocean before we reached seventeen.

It was a big secret where the old ship *Roanoke* was really sailing. It said on the trip board she was headed for Port Arthur, Texas, wherever that was, but Jim Brown and I both knew that was just a modern-day shanghai, putting it up there on the board that the ship was sailing one place and then, once the old ship was past the three-mile limit with a good crew of men, they would send her off to Russia for sure. They said there were still German subs out there that hadn't surrendered yet—fanatics who were torpedoing American tankers. The war was over all right, but not for some Nazi sub captains. The S.S. *Roanoke* was an ugly old thing, red, white, and black with the paint peeling on her old black hull and a scummy-looking waterline all around her. No decent crewman would board her in the first place, and since no ships would really be going to a place called Port Arthur, Texas, it must be obvious to any logical mind that this old tub, little loss if she were sunk, was really headed for Russia. They would probably fill her up with gasoline because the Russians were desperate for it with the war just over. So the sixty-four-dollar question would finally be whether any respectable submarine would bother wasting one of its last precious remaining torpedoes on such an old derelict as the S.S. *Roanoke*. There has always been an advantage in being old and decrepit and ugly. Anyway, nobody fooled Jim Brown and me. We figured we were brighter than most, and anyway, it was the only ship we could get on. We had no seniority, no status with the Texas company, nor with anybody else for that matter.

They assigned Jim to the officers' mess and me to the crew's. Officers always got the first choice. I think they took Jim because he was a good-looking kid and he didn't have any pimples and his voice had already pretty much changed. The crew got what was left. They were an unholy conglomerate of men and boys, of Mexican zoot-suiters and street bums and a few old company hands to run them around—non-union, they said proudly. We are non-union!

"The rest of the ships in this country are run by them communist cocksuckers," the steward said, but not the Texas company ships. The steward had a crooked mouth and front teeth like a muskrat's and his thin lips furled and unfurled as he talked. He had a big belly, which he always covered with a clean white T-shirt, and his eyes looked like they were spit-out watermelon seeds. "Now, you take the crew's order for breakfast, give 'em what they want, 'eggs over easy and a side a ham, stack a cakes,' you understand, whatever. You give a man a good breakfast, good coffee, wash out this urn with soda every mornin', understand? I can tell if you don't—taste it right away. And if I catch you not washing out that urn I'll stick your head down the goddamn thing and clean it out with your ears—want it cleaned every morning—every morning—so's a man can have a good cup of coffee, and then you clean this mess hall, you understand, scrub these benches. Want that wood shiny white. Don't matter that them oilers and wipers come in here and grease 'em up again. That is their privilege. This is their mess hall. It takes a little scrubbin' to get the grease out of that raw wood, but scrub them benches every day and you can keep up with it, and mop the floor, polish the brass, wash them portholes—wash 'em every day. Don't want no salt spray grayin' up the portholes. Man needs to look out while he's eatin'. Man needs a clean place to eat. Keep 'em happy and you don't need no unions run by a bunch a commie cocksuckers," he said. It was simple. "Ship out under the NMU and you'll find out. They don't get fresh coffee for breakfast, and the cooks are just a bunch of goddamn Baltimore niggers." I understood. I kept the mess hall spotless. The galley was run by an old Mexican, skinny as an alley dog with a little potbelly and spindly legs and feet that always pointed straight out, one to the port and one to the starboard, and he tried to comb his hair straight back, but it stood up, straggly hair like the hair on the back of some mad mangy dog. And the cook wore thick silver-rimmed round glasses, which were always dirty with grease spatters. Nobody could understand the cook when he talked and he was a temperamental bastard to boot. Sometimes he wouldn't speak to us at all. But I struggled, listening carefully to learn his brand of English so as to communicate with the man, and finally he appreciated my trying, and he accepted me, like a son, he said.

One night after supper he called me out to the galley. "Babe," he called me like I was a little boy. "Babe," he said again confidentially when I came over. "The steward —he is no fucking man." The steward was the cook's boss, too. I didn't say anything. The cook's eyes were beady and bright, and his hair was standing straight up as usual. It was a time of secrets between friends, a time for sharing the souls. "Babe, the steward, he's 'fraid to fuck." He laughed a high laugh and shook his head from side to side. . . . " 'Fraid to fuck. Can you geet it?"

"No," I said seriously, and I shook my head, too, in disbelief.

"He think he geet the clap." He laughed some more. I felt ashamed for the steward. He was not a man—afraid to fuck? I shook my head in disbelief.

"We go to the whorehouse in Galveston last treep, and the son-a-bitch would no fuck. They showed him the paper."

"What paper?" I asked.

"You know, babe, the paper—on the wall—that says them girls is okay," he said. "Sees the doctor and all, no got the clap."

"Yeah," I said.

"Yeah," he said. "Them girls see the doctor every week for the clap. The steward he seen the doctor paper—says okay and everythin'—and still he no fuck." We both shook our heads in disbelief.

"Here, babe, have a cup of coffee." He poured me a cup out of my own freshly scrubbed urn and he sucked on the rim of the hot cup with his wet, yellow lips. "You make good coffee, babe," he said, tipping his cup to me and giving me a kind look. My heart swelled with pride. My mother would have been proud—toasted by the cook. I loved him. He was wise. We were friends. "I fucked them girls," he said, and pointed his finger to his chest proudly.

"Yeah," I said.

"I get the clap," he laughed. God, I thought he was brave—he got the clap—not afraid of the clap, probably not afraid of anything.

"The clap more better than a cold." I didn't understand. "Kill the clap more easy than a cold. The nose, she run. The peter, he run—but the peter he no cough with the clap," he laughed. He thought it was a great joke. I laughed too.

"A coughin' peter," I laughed again.

"A coughin' peter," the cook repeated, and we were hysterical, friends together, drinking my coffee, and laughing and slapping our legs.

"One good shot of penicillum gets her, gets the clap,

and no more drippin' peter. But she no fix a cold, and a man he no die of a drippin' peter." He blew on his coffee. "The steward—he ain't no man." Then he turned to me with one more secret. "The girls in Galveston give you a better go than Port Arthur. I show you," he said. "I show you when we get there, babe."

"Yeah," I said like a man, "you damn right. We really going to Port Arthur?"

"Yeah," the cook said. But I knew better.

It was a romantic, peaceful time. The sea was calm, like glass, and the flying fish came sailing out over the water, gliding gracefully, and then like the end of some inglorious life they splashed with a common plunk back into the sea, and the porpoises played at the bow of the ship, and the seagulls followed, and the blue sky descended into the blue ocean with hardly a line between— seven miles out, somebody said. That's how far a man can see the horizon—seven miles, and since I knew nothing, whatever anybody said was knowledge. I didn't think Jim Brown learned anything. He read books.

Just as I expected, we went through the Panama Canal. We were on our way to Russia! It was hard for me to believe. On the way to Russia! And what I saw at the Panama Canal—the lush land, islands covered with trees, jungles, beautiful and deep green and steamy. I was a boy from the prairies, from long, open spaces with the gray sagebrush, where a man on a clear day could see fifty miles, eighty, maybe.

The place was populated with countless little brown skinny people, almost naked, some barefoot, some wearing sandals, usually pants, naked above the waist or with nothing but a light shirt with short sleeves and the buttons usually ripped off. They talked Spanish. I couldn't catch a word. They looked like happy people—laughed a lot—looked like Wyoming Mexicans in the summertime to me. The place made me feel like I was in a womb, warm and sexy, in a hot, wet womb, and I thought about getting off the ship, learning the language of the people —living there, exploring the jungles and burying myself in the gay señoritas, but we were going to Russia. But nobody got off a ship going through the Panama Canal. In about a week I woke up one morning to find the ship in port. I was surprised. I soon discovered it was Port Arthur, Texas, all right, and like the cook said, the girls were better in Galveston than in Port Arthur. Measurably better.

Jim Brown and I sailed on a couple of different ships together. I can't remember their names now. I still thought they were ships headed for Russia. Needed to go to Russia for some reason. Maybe it was just so a fella could say he'd been overseas. Overseas! But you could never tell which ships were really going. We joined the National Maritime Union, the NMU. We thought they were probably a bunch of commies all right, and the cooks were bad—bad food and bad coffee. Nobody bothered to wash the coffee urn. It was probably in the union contract not to have to wash the goddamn coffee urn every morning. I shipped on as an ordinary seaman to get out of the mess hall.

An ordinary seaman is about as low as you can get. Yet I stood watch at the lovely, lonely times of night on the bow of the ship with the stars in the black sky above the black sea so bright a man could never tell which were stars and which were the lights of some distant vessel. Sometimes I got confused and rang the bell—one bell for a light on the port side and two for the starboard—but it was usually just a big star on the horizon. The bow of the ship cut through the sea making low, slushy sounds as if both the ship and the sea were alive, and the wake of the ship stirred up the phosphorus, which sparkled like fireflies in the wet grass, and the ship's bow plowed quietly through the night sea, lapping and laughing to me, and I thought up poems in the dark about old seamen and about love. I turned seventeen. I made speeches to the sea, and talked to the porpoises out loud. Nobody could hear me anyway, but I thought the porpoises heard me and cared and understood what there was to understand, and I thought I was on the edge of discovering some immense universal secret about the meaning of life, but I never learned the secret, and there in that blackness which reached from me out to infinite places was a simple Wyoming boy not even knowing the right questions to ask. I felt religious standing there with my hands on the wet iron of the bow and the warm sea breezes on my head. My heart was open. If there were a God, surely He would make Himself known to me here, I thought. I lifted my hands from the ship's bow, and like a boy riding a bicycle without hands, I moved up and down with the movement of the ship through the black night with my arms outstretched, my chest uncovered, and my heart open and ready, and I said out loud, "Good God, come into me. Come into me! Give me the answers! I am your child, and I am entitled to know." And I waited, and then I counted a hundred movements of the bow of the ship up and down with me balancing there and my heart aching to embrace the spirit and my ears straining to hear the slightest response, and every nerve of my body poised to catch the most subtle signal, but there were only the silly songs of the sea, merry, carefree, saying its nothings, blabbering, wave after wave like some mindless child gurgling against the bow of the ship.

"Speak to me!" I hollered. "Speak to me!" I hollered again, and pounded my fists down on the rough, paint-peeled bow. "Speak to me," I said finally in a whisper, and then I said nothing more because I did not have the power or the right to demand that the universe divulge its secrets to me.

But I learned one thing, and that is that monkey pee is strong stuff. I learned that because one of the wipers, a crazy kind of kid, brought a wild monkey on board. He wasn't supposed to. And the monkey got away and sat on top of the main mast, a beast as frenzied and fierce as any on earth, screaming and scolding the crew, and laughing monkey laughs up there where no one could reach him. But at night he would slip down, rob the garbage, and piss on the canvas lifeboat covers, and the monkey pee ate a hole right through the canvas, which we, the ordinary seamen, had to patch. Monkey pee is potent. You didn't learn things like that from the books Jim Brown was reading, books about lawyers and poems by Robert Service, and things like that.

We sailed to Aruba, where the girls sat on the bar naked and went with you in a cab to the beach. The cabbies called it "beachy-beachy," and the people in control cut the island in two with a high fence with barbed wire at the top so that the sailors had to stay on the same side with the beachy-beachy girls and the native workers. The cabbies drove the sailors to the "beachy-beachy," stopped the cab close to the water, which lapped up on the clean sand like on clean white sheets, and left little foamy spots that soaked down quickly, and the cabbies pulled out a grass mat from their cab trunks, and then they turned their backs, looked out into the warm black balmy night, out to where the sea and the sky met, and the truth was there on the grass mat. They were only girls, but they looked old with early potbellies that came from poor diets and they had bad brown teeth. They tried to look their young ages by using lipstick and makeup that made their brown skin appear unhealthy, and they tried to cover up their hollow eye sockets with powder, and some put a fresh flower in their hair. Their feet were bare and wide and hard. They were just poor tired girls, some maybe only fifteen, the oldest no more than nineteen, shipped in by the dozen by white slavers from Venezuela, for use.

"I'm gonna fuck me a company man's daughter," the wiper said, and drank up. "I'm gonna climb the fence and get me one a them pink-ass company girls. Ain't gonna fuck any of them Mexican whores," he said. "Clap traps," he said.

"Them ain't Mexicans," the boiler said.

"They all look the same ta me," the wiper said, "I'm gonna get me one of them company men's daughters instead. I'm yearnin' for white ass again," he said, and everybody laughed.

"If ya don't do no better in gettin' a company girl than ya do catchin' that monkey, ya ain't gonna get much," somebody else said. "Better try catchin' the monkey and fuckin' it instead," and everybody laughed again. "You'll get the clap off'n them company women faster than off one of them beachy-beachy girls," the oiler said.

And then we sailed other ships to other ports—up the quiet old muddy Mississippi past the whorehouses of New Orleans and up the coast to Philadelphia and back again to Tampico, Mexico, where the women were like the beachy-beachy girls, always bad-toothed, sad-faced, potbellied, dull-eyed women sitting in the doorways around the town square, and Jim Brown and I walked, looking, looking, on those warm happy evenings an hour past suppertime, strolling along looking for a girl with bright eyes, like picking through old peaches at the market.

Then we sailed to New York on a ship I knew was headed for Russia. Everybody said so. Even the bos'n's mate. He'd just got back from Russia on this very ship, a tanker, disguised like a liberty ship with artificial booms on the deck and all, and even with the war officially over she still had a gun crew from the U.S. Navy to operate the deck guns. The lazy bastards didn't do a thing all day —just rode around, sunned themselves, and ate. Didn't even polish their own guns. Since torpedoes were too dear to be wasted on a regular old liberty ship, the subs would surface and shell the defenseless ship with their deck gun, and the idea was that this old liberty ship would fire back like in the olden days, ship guns against ship guns. But this old liberty tanker, with all its artificial getup, its false masts and booms, would have fooled anybody until you stepped right up on her and saw her hull was full of oil tanks. The bos'n said the Russians unloaded the ship at night from a barge, using women, big, husky, broad-shouldered thick-legged women, "Russkys," he called them. "I'd rather fuck a good friendly bitch dog any day than one of them Russky women," he said. "Had hair an inch thick on their legs and it hung down under their arms like a billy goat's, and they stunk," he said. "You could smell 'em coming a city block." But the liberty tanker only shipped to Baltimore, a little, old, local, embarrassing load, to Baltimore, and then back to New York Harbor again.

We never did get to Russia and it was getting around fall and time to go back to school, time to start amounting to something, by education, as my father said. We hitchhiked home, old Jim and I, but we hadn't figured on it—going to take the train, like folks, we decided. We were standing in the center of Grand Central Station, in that huge palace of a place, with marble tile, a place so big you could hold a quarterhorse race inside, and the ceiling, like the dome of a cathedral, was tall enough for a Piper Cub to take off, I thought, and the station was crowded with people, running every which way, in a hurry, hustling, jumping, not looking at each other, always looking past each other, going in all directions, crazy, hardly a peaceful place for a country boy. A fella could get panicked in a place like this except it would be hard to tell in which direction to run. So Jim and I were standing there kinda lost and dumb, and this guy with slick hair and a mustache, like David Niven, and a whiny little voice came up to us and said right out, without ever having met us or a damn thing, if we didn't look like a couple of guys needing a ride, and where were we going, and sure, he had been in Wyoming once, across Highway 30, past Rawlins and Rock Springs and Evanston, he remembered, and it was a hell of a place to be *from,* and he laughed, saying he himself was driving his Buick convertible to Los Angeles, and would we like a ride because he was looking for company, and we said sure.

The Buick convertible was flying along the Pennsylvania Turnpike, where the pavement was wider than any road I'd ever seen. We were all cozied down inside with the top up—Jim in the front seat and me alone in the back seat. It was a sleepy day, raining a little, and the monotonous green trees, more green trees than in the whole state of Wyoming, were blurring by, when suddenly I heard Jim Brown say, "Let me out of this son-of-a-bitch. Let me out!" I could tell he meant it. But the driver didn't say anything back, and the car went on silently, and pretty soon old Jim said, "You gonna stop this son-of-a-bitch and let me out or not?" And the man still didn't say anything.

I says, "What's the matter, Jim?" and Jim says, "This son-of-a-bitch is a little off." And I says, "What's the matter?" And he says, "This son-of-a-bitch better let us out of here, that's all I gotta say about it," and the guy stopped the car and we got out. I thought that that was one time having pimples paid off.

When I got home things were messed up. The folks were selling out, moving to Bolivia, South America, for Christ's sake. It was a bad combination, the exploring blood of my father and my mother wanting to do missionary work with the poor Indians there. Probably felt she had to make it up to God for failing to give her firstborn to Him, like she promised. My father got a job in the tin mines as a chemical engineer, signed a three-year contract, and now my folks were ready to drag off my little sister and brother, Barbara and Tom, up into those Andes Mountains to a little village fourteen thousand feet above sea level called Catavi, at the Patino Mine. But there was nothing for me to do there, no schools, nothing, they said. But maybe seeing I was coming back home to go to school and would be living with them, they realized they couldn't bear all those years ahead cooped up with this wild-eyed heathen child of theirs who must have grown nothing but a brown burr for a soul, and who had come screeching out of his mother's womb only to make trouble for them and all the rest of the world, forever. I was too much for those quiet, peaceful, God-fearing folk, I thought.

"You'll be all right," my mother said, with quiet eyes, and God still on her face. "You go to church, go to school, and we'll be back in three years—it'll be a short three years, and then we'll all be together again." She still looked sad.

"One thing I always taught you," my father said, "and that's how to be independent, how to do things on your own. You've already been around the world yourself. You'll be all right here," he said, as if to reassure himself, not me.

"Yeah," I said, and then my father went out the door.

"And we're not leaving you," my mother said softly,

still standing by the door sadly. "Don't think we're leaving you."

"I don't think that," I said.

"You are a man, now. You don't really need us anymore," she said. Then she left, too, and I said, "Yeah," and my heart felt empty with hurt places around the edges, and I wasn't going to cry—to cry out for my mama like a baby, and for Daddy. A man can't do that anymore. No man can. I would be my own father and my own mother. "Well," I said, as I followed them out the door, "I hope you have a damned good time, and that you dig up a lot of tin at the tin mine or whatever you're gonna do, and write often. Doesn't cost much to write," I said, like they used to say to me, and I stood, tall and skinny, trying to look tough, and I swaggered on the bus after them as my family was boarding, and I kissed my little sister and brother good-bye, like trying to kiss a handful of pet coons, and I kissed my angel mother good-bye, and my throat clogged up and it got to aching and feeling so tight I couldn't say a word, and then I walked off the bus, and down the street, and around the corner, and lit me a Chesterfield cigarette, and blew the smoke out into the rainy night and I said to myself out loud in the dark on the street, "Well, Gerry, here you are. For Christ's sake, who needs a mother?" Every damn calf gets weaned. I walked down the wet main street of Laramie, past the store buildings, past the jewelry store where I had worked. The streets were empty except for the rain, which quieted down the blowing cinders from the trains, and all I heard in the streets was the sound of the steel taps on my leather heels on the concrete.

Slap.

- Slap.

I still had my good gorky walk. I was alone, but I was all right, independent, like my father said, and I could take care of myself. I never said that. He said it, but in my heart I didn't believe it. I would never be weaned. I knew I could never live without them. I would never be a man. Even when I am as old and craggy as some twisted cedar standing alone on a high desolate hill, having outlived all of the other cedars, even after I have withstood the storms and the gouging glaciers of the ages, and after my soul has finally been dissipated across the universe, whatever is left of me will still be crying for her. Mother!

Where are you?

Why am I left alone?

Even the earth has its mother sun, which shines on it every day, and the old cedar has its roots in the mother soil. But I was wandering alone over those desolate places, in the rain in the bleak, black empty night of Laramie, Wyoming.

Slap.

Slap.

Once beneath that pavement the Indians raised hides over teepee poles like raising a new womb in memory of Mother, and down on Front Street next to the tracks lonely men were crying in the night, drinking, and I looked, and I tried to bring up her angel face, but I could not see my mother. There was only the rain falling, and if one listened, the puffing of switch engines down in the railroad yards.

Jim Brown and I took a basement apartment together in Laramie, and we both enrolled at the University of Wyoming. Freshmen. I waited anxiously for some fraternity to ask me to join—to rush me as they called it. They never did. I didn't play football and I didn't have money. I wasn't a scholar. My father hadn't been in a fraternity, and nobody knew my father's name right off either. Never heard of G. M. Spence, the chemist. I didn't have a great personality. Didn't know how to socialize, never did. I wasn't a good guy. I had pimples. I wasn't a vet. The returning vets on the GI Bill were the heroes. The fraternities vied for them and they smoked cigarettes in class, drank booze down at the Cowboy Bar, told war stories, and took the pretty girls, the ones with the big stuff, the good legs, and the long hair and the little wiggly asses and the high noses, the sorority girls, clean and fresh like cherry blossoms, and if you didn't have a fraternity pin to pin one of them, a fellow didn't amount to a damn. How can a man be worth a damn if he can't pin his woman? I mean it's like you have nothing to give, like being a eu-nuch, more or less, and if you weren't a fraternity man, then at least you should have been a veteran, and if you weren't a veteran, you should have been overseas at least —to Russia, or someplace. "Was you in the service? Been overseas?" Probably some draft-dodger, maybe one of those who pleaded family hardship—only person to sup-port a poor old helpless mother, or you have flat feet or a murmur in your heart, or maybe the piles or a split dink, or something. Any way you cut it, if you weren't in the service you were a worthless bastard, one of them sneak-ing son-of-a-bitches who stayed home while the real men of the country were out fighting the war, giving of their lives, wounded, bleeding, like my uncle Fred, who left his leg blown to hell all over the Anzio beachhead, while you were safe at home fucking the girl friends of the boys who were giving their lives for their country. That's who you probably were, or maybe some fucking commie.

Well, Jim Brown and I acted like we didn't care. It didn't do any good to explain that we were too young to go to war, and that the war was over, because nobody wants a couple of young smart alecks around and no girl wants a fuzzy-balled kid when she can have a man who fought for his country, somebody on the GI Bill with a regular monthly income, and a car. Jim Brown and I were definitely not in the running, but Jim said he didn't give a shit.

Jim and I played poker at Hick's Poker House, down-stairs at 210 Front Street. There was a good whorehouse upstairs that catered to the college boys. The railroad men came to Hick's for an honest game, and the house took its cut, bought a round of drinks now and then, and kept things friendly, lent a little money when railroad men's checks were gone and furnished a new deck of cards to a player who claimed the old deck was cold. Give me a fresh deck—and they only played low ball draw poker and straight five-card stud. Jim and I played good poker at sea, and I sent the money home for school, but now we walked from Fourteenth Street to Front Street with a hundred dollars in our pockets to play cards at Hick's. Give me a hundred in chips. We sat down, sneaked a look at the cards, eased out the cards, card at a time, easy, easy, as if to see the whole hand at once would be bad luck, and we kept poker faces, absolutely, but nobody looked at my face. The good players all looked at their hands, at the pot, at the cards on the table, but never at me, and they didn't talk to each other, except to mumble the number of cards that they wanted to draw, and it was just a round of bad luck, Jim said. That's the way luck was. It would be all right the next night. But hard luck set in, and the house always bought a drink when we left, a hundred gone, and pretty soon it was all gone, all of it from the savings account, the fifty cents at a time I collected for a night's rent on my room from the summer tourists in Sheridan, the same fifty cents I earned ironing the sheets and sleeping in the tent in the summertime, and the dollar for each birthday from Grandma Pfleeger, that goddamned dollar that I couldn't even spend, not any of it. "Put it away for your education," my mother had said. Well, I lost it on some sixty-four. Sixty-four is a good hand. Man should bet on it, but there was a wheel across the table, ace, two, three, four, five—a damned wheel in the hands of a professor. The fella taught speech at the university but he acted more like a mathematician. Never could give a speech himself. Never taught me a thing either, except a sixty-four doesn't win. The houseman pushed the pot to him, past the hands of the brakemen who had their money in it, too, past a couple of other toughs sitting there, and I was cleaned out, finally, after a couple of months of playing, a couple of months of bad draws and bad luck, of sixty-fours always at the wrong time. God was getting even, and my mother was crying in my ear, and all of the money was gone, and I told Jim Brown one night I was thinking seriously of suicide, thinking seriously of the unforgivable sin, suicide. I'm man enough to do it, don't think I ain't, I said. What was there in life anyway? What was life's goddamned meaning? There was just me and Jim and Hick's Poker House and school, and the vets smoking Camels in class and the pretty-ass girls not speaking, and there was this English Lit class with this queer little dink of an English professor who said I wasn't smart enough to get an A, and he was probably right, and I said, "Fuck this," and fuck the Spanish class that I couldn't pass—also too dumb—and fuck geology, and if a man had to go through this humiliation, dig through this ton of crap in order to be a lawyer, well, fuck it—and fuck life. Fuck it all. Suicide. But my mother said that suicide was something that God couldn't forgive. Well, fuck that, too. Murder, she said, even murder . . . if you ask for forgiveness and truly repent, you will be forgiven, but to murder oneself can never be forgiven. It's logical, can't you see? You can't ask forgiveness after you're dead. Anyone can understand that. My grandma Pfleeger's brother had taken his own life. Drank a whole damn bottle of Black Leaf 40, which they used to kill potato bugs. Nothing but solid nicotine, my father said. Terrible way to go. They found him in the barn all twisted up. But my mother spoke to me confidentially about it once so I would understand, and the tears came to her eyes. But Jim Brown only laughed when I talked of suicide—never said, "Sorry you lost, pal"—just laughed. "Don't worry, kid," he said. "You win some and you lose some." But Jim lost, too, and then he went back to sea, and I wondered how he could go without me. I was alone.

I got a job as a night bellhop at the Connor Hotel. There wasn't much of a check-in between eight and one o'clock in the morning. I was there mostly to mop the tile floor in the lobby, clean the ashtrays, dust. That was the night bellman's job, fifty cents an hour, and tips. The salesmen always tipped a quarter, fifty cents if they didn't know where the whorehouse was and you told them. I stayed in school, met this older woman, a non-sorority girl with thick lips and pimples. I knew her kind. She was hot like me, a tough woman, loud talker, laughed a lot, and made me feel small, and she had calves on her like a hurdler, and then there were a couple of others, I think, but I can't remember. Once in a while I got in a nooky

pool up in the whorehouse at 210 Front Street, or up at
100 Grand, where the girls were even better. Five fellows
put up a dollar apiece, and the madam cut the cards, and
the high card won, and the winner got the girl for a short
time, for five bucks. I won—once.

Finally I went to work as a switchman on the Union
Pacific Railroad, down on the tracks, across from the
whorehouses on Front Street, across from Hick's Poker
House, switching at night, there in the cold, black railroad yards which were kept in working order by the Mexican track gangs who labored away with shovels and picks
and sledges, worked with their brown, skinny backs and
with dull eyes. At night I helped make up the trains,
working with the switch engines. I was captured in that
dark and lonely place called "the yards," where men
whistled in the dark, and there was the sound of steel
sucking steel, of the railroad cars smashing one against
the other, and there was the dob-dob-dob of the steel
wheels of the cars passing over rails that weighed 130
pounds a yard and were thirty-nine feet long, thirty-nine
feet between each dob-dob, and I held onto the ladder
with one hand and one foot, and the rest of me, like any
good switchman, was hanging out with my lantern in my
hand, and I rode out past the switch blocks, and swooped
down to the ground a little ahead of the car so as not to
fall when I hit the ground, and then I threw the switch
and signaled with the lantern, and the train came back
now onto the new track, and I grabbed the last car again,
and up ahead was only the panting engine in the lonely
night and the tough, motherless men cursing out into the
dark, and then the sun came up over a field of boxcars,
and I walked up Ivinson Avenue toward the university
carrying my lantern after a night's work. The college boys
were getting up, peering out of second-story bedroom
windows with bleary eyes and yawning, up for their eight
o'clock, and I walked to mine, the soot of the railroad on
my face and my lantern still in my hand. I pulled my blue
denim cap down to my ears and I said, fuck 'em, and I set
the lantern down by my desk in the classroom there in

Fundamentals of Philosophy and I said, teach me. Teach me, if you can.

Then that spring I met this bright bluebell of a girl named Anna.

17

I STOOD with the jailer at the far end of the cellblock. The door opened with barely a sound. Joe Esquibel didn't look up. Watch any man alone in a prison cell. He leans up against the cold cement wall, his head tilted back, his eyes looking straight out as if he can see beyond the walls. His muscles fall down off the bones. His hands occasionally twitch, accustomed to years of grasping tools of labor, and his whole body longs for activity, and becomes slowly, corpuscle after corpuscle, mad. His breathing is too fast, slightly irregular, and he coughs at nothing. He cannot sing out because a song is rotten in jail. No whistle for the same reason. No speaking out loud to one's self, which is a sign that brings on panic, which says the brain cells have finally surrendered, too, and next there will be scream after unanswered scream. And so the prisoner coughs. The cough is an acceptable sound, and the belly tightens up and falls back loose again. The eyes are dead holes. The bars are too close to his face and cast a shadow on the right side. His nose is dry. It cracks inside. He can feel the beat of his heart—he counts the beats sometimes since there is nothing else to count—and his fingernails have been chewed halfway to the quick. After a while, he will move over to the steel bunk absently, as if he had been there all along, and he will sit on the striped mattress, dirty, sheetless, with old stains in irregular shapes, and there are stains on stains,

stains of what one would not wish to identify nor to say. The man looks at the colorless concrete at his feet.

I followed along with the jailer to Joe Esquibel's cell and now Joe raised his head, saw us coming, and watched us. The jailer opened up Joe's cell and locked me in with him. Then he left, swinging his keys from side to side, from thigh to thigh, humming a little tune I did not recognize.

"Hi, Joe," I said. "How ya doin'?"

"Ya gotta get me out of here, Mr. Spence. I been here a long time already, three months," he said. "I go crazy in jail. Ask anybody."

"You've been here longer than that. You've been here five months."

"Oh," he said. He turned away and walked over to the corner. Two steps. Then he leaned back onto the cold cement with his head tilted up. His eyes were empty and looked past me.

"Your trial's coming up in three weeks," I said.

"Oh," he said again without interest.

"You can wait that long, can't you, after all this time? And then if we win, you'll be out of here—out of here at least!" I added with a cheerful sound.

"Where will they send me?"

"Back to Evanston."

"I don' wanna go back to Evanston, Mr. Spence. Them people is crazy there, and I'm goin' crazy here. Ya gotta believe me, Mr. Spence." Joe's voice was hollow like his eyes, and his once boyish face seemed flat now, flat as a board, flat also like the eyes, and his cheeks were drawn tightly against the bone. His mouth hardly moved when he spoke, and I noticed his hand twitched, but he didn't notice it.

"I can't stand being in Evanston," he said again, as if I hadn't heard him. "All them people is crazy, screamin' and hollerin' and everythin'. Can't sleep at night."

He walked over to the corner of the cell to the single steel cot, sat down on the dirty mattress, and looked at his feet with the dead eyes. I sat down beside him.

"What was it like being a Mexican-American boy

growing up in a place like Rawlins, Wyoming, Joe?" I began. He didn't answer. He looked at his feet. "Well, I'm trying to get a sense of it. I'm strugglin' to get to know you. Maybe you could tell me just a few things about the Cathedral Home at Laramie for starters." He watched his feet.

"Do you remember?"

No answer.

"Well, Joe, do you remember your father? Let's start there."

No answer.

"Do you remember going to the place on the highway where your father was killed?" Maybe I could jog one specific traumatic memory, and then it would all come rushing out. But there was no answer. I looked at him. His face was immobile. He was hardly breathing.

"Do you remember hitting the boy with the bottle who called you a jailbird spick at the Cathedral Home? I read about that in the welfare records." He didn't move.

"Do you remember them shaving your head? Joe, I don't mean to pry into painful places, but we have to start talking about this sometime . . . we're going to go to trial! Do you understand? You probably don't believe it. Probably thought the time for trial would never come. But we're going to trial in three weeks!"

He made no sound. No movement. I tried again.

"What happened to you after they brought you back from the Cathedral Home?"

He didn't say a word. It was as if he didn't hear me. I repeated my question. No answer.

"Do you remember going to Torrington?"

"Mrs. Murphy," he said suddenly.

"Who is she?"

"Sharon's mother."

"What do you remember of her?"

"They was laughin'."

"Who was laughing, Joe?"

"Sharon's mother and ol' Watkins."

"What were they laughing about?"

"I don't know."

"What do you think?"

"Laughing at us," he said in the same voice, and the colorless light from the single fluorescent tube in the center of the cellblock made his flesh look dead.

"Maybe they were just having a good time, a joke between them, or something," I said.

He didn't answer.

"Did you like St. Joseph's at Torrington?"

"It was okay," he said.

"Why did you like it?"

"Father Morgan liked me."

"How do you know he liked you, Joe?"

"He told me I was tough." The hand farthest from me came up to explain something but it fell down helplessly again and crossed over his other hand on his lap, limp and lifeless.

"Did he ever give you a hug?"

"What?" He looked up blankly.

"Did he ever give you a hug?"

He didn't answer for a long time. Finally he answered, "No."

"It must have been hard on you to be away from your mother, Joe," I said.

He shrugged his shoulders as if he didn't know. Then he said, "I missed Elma."

"How come Elma?"

"They wouldn't let her come. Too old."

"What happened to Elma?"

He shrugged his shoulders. Didn't know.

"Do you remember coming home after Torrington?"

"Yeah."

"What do you remember?"

"Timato was home. He was glad to see me. He wouldn't go no place without me. Me and him was close. We was always together," he said. His voice was higher now but still flat.

"You must have loved Timato a lot—been through a lot of things together," I said quietly, and I gave him a quick pat on his thigh.

He didn't answer. He looked down at his feet. Then finally he said, "Me and him was close."

"What did you do when you got home from Torrington?"

"Stole some stuff, took some stuff from some old white guy. Give it to my mother. . . . Stole some stuff outa some cars, too," he said suddenly. "Them white guys stole it. I was with 'em."

"Where?"

"Colorado, and I give some of the stuff to my mother," he said again, as if that explained it.

"Why did you give it to her?"

"Don't know. She needed the money," he finally added.

"Where did your mother get her money? Musta been a pretty short item," I said.

No answer. Finally he said, "We was on welfare." There was a slight tightening in the tone of his voice.

"Did your mother have any other source of income?" I asked matter-of-factly, as if filling in some form.

No answer. I let the silence fill the cell, and after a while I caught my ears straining for a sound. There was not a stir, not a fly buzzing, not even the hum of the fluorescent light on the ceiling—no traffic noise outside, only silence. I tried to adjust to it, to get comfortable with it. Then suddenly he broke the silence.

"She done what she done," he said.

"You must have felt guilty sometimes about your mom," I said. "Sometimes a fellow feels like it's his fault," I said quietly. "I know."

"It wasn't nobody's fault," he said. Then he added, "They didn't catch them white guys."

"How much did you take from the old man?"

"Forty dollars and some dimes."

"And what happened after you stole the stuff out of the cars?"

"Sent me to Worland."

I had to pump for it, word after word. He was only fourteen when the judge sent him to Worland, and there for the first time in his life he had been all alone. No

mother. Where was his mother? Timato dead. No little
mother, Elma, no brothers and sisters, and the father,
dead, and he was afraid, and the bigger boys beat up the
little boys, including Joe, beat him until he couldn't
stand, and once they actually held him down and pissed
on him and laughed, and when he got up he began to
fight. He didn't know he could fight like that, a fighting to
the death, and he hurt them big guys, he said, and they
were afraid of him because they knew they would have to
kill him, and they were afraid to kill him. By the time he
got out he knew how to fight and was not afraid of any
man, because a man would have to kill him with an ax.

His mother was the one who got him out of Worland.
The welfare records said she came to the office sick, and
that a Dr. Baker called saying her diagnosis was pregnancy, bleeding and cramps, and that when he examined
her there was no heart tone in the baby. She had never
felt any life, and the doctor told her she would probably
miscarry again. Then about 4:30 P.M. she passed a "glob"
and nearly bled to death, and later the doctor found a
large abscess, which he thought had brought on the miscarriage. The records said that Dr. Baker had talked a
few minutes to Mrs. Esquibel and "she stated she had
been pregnant fifteen times, had six children living and
she had had five miscarriages, one each year for the last
five years. She told the doctor she might have had a couple of abortions but didn't know for sure." Dr. Baker said
she told him her brother would take care of the bill.

There was a letter in the files from the superintendent
of the Boys' Reformatory at Worland to the state probation and parole officer that said, "Mrs. Esquibel would
like to have Joe returned to her home in the very near
future to act more or less as a baby-sitter for the other
children while she undergoes surgery. Would you please
evaluate the situation." And the parole people recommended that Joe be sent home, but when the superintendent at the Boys' Reformatory asked Joe if he wanted to
go home, Joe said, "It don't make no difference to me
one way or the other." The boy seemed sullen.

Then out of the clear I asked Joe, "Joe, do you recall

being with your mother down on the railroad tracks in the boxcars when you were a tiny little boy?"

There was no answer.

"Do you remember the white men there?" There was the slightest sound. I wasn't sure, something like a whine that had gotten free of him, against his will. I changed the subject as if it weren't important.

"Tell me about Sharon, about your wife." At first he didn't answer, and then after a long while he looked up at me, and for the first time he held me with his dark eyes, and they had become alive now, and wet.

"I loved her, Mr. Spence. I didn't kill her," he said. "You know that." His voice seemed sweet and soft.

"What was she like?"

"Blond."

"Yes," I said, "I know, but could you tell me about her?"

"She knew everthing," Joe said. "She was smarter 'n me. Knew everbody. Knew how to get everthing she wanted. She got stuff for me. Give me stuff. She was smart."

"How did you meet her?"

"Me and a friend of mine was just walkin' along. She come up in her car, her and this other girl, and asked us if we wanted a ride. She was older 'n me."

"I know," I said.

"She had some beer. We just got ta goin' together. She come got me at the house."

"What did she look like?"

"Pretty." The sweet voice. Not hollow any longer.

"I know," I said, "but what did she look like, Joe?"

He thought for quite a while. "She had long fingers."

"What did her face look like? Do you remember her face?"

"I don' know," he said. "I can't remember." He looked out past me and the shadow of the bars crossed his forehead.

"Can you see her face?" He didn't answer. "Can you see her eyes?"

He didn't answer.

"What color were her eyes?"

"Blue."

"Think a minute, Joe. Can you see her in your mind's eye?"

He said nothing. Suddenly he got up and began to pace, like the clock pendulum moving two steps to the north and two to the south. But it was not north or south. There was no sun. There were no windows. It was right and left or left and right, depending from which side one observed the pacing.

"Were you happy together?"

There was the long silence again that was as much a part of Joe Esquibel's presence as his words. Finally he said, "Yeah, we was happy."

"Joe, I know this might hurt you, but we need to talk about it. My law students say Sharon had been with some other men. Did you know anything about that?"

The silence set in again like concrete on concrete, but I had no need to test his will. He stopped his pacing and sat down on the iron bunk, and his head fell down again, and finally I broke the silence myself.

"Well, Joe, you need to tell your lawyer everything because your lawyer needs to know. I need to know."

But he said nothing at all. After a while I called for the jailer, loudly through that silent place, and my own voice startled me and sounded strange and irreverent, and then the jailer came, this time whistling, still slapping his keys on one leg and then the other. He opened the cell and let me out. I followed him and as I was about to leave the cellblock I heard a high, choked, gasping sound, like a rabbit trapped in its own hole, and I thought the rabbit belonged to me, and I wanted to free it.

18

BY THE TIME Joe came home from the reformatory, Agneda had moved the whole family back to her one-room shack, and the room Dario had once started was still just a skeleton, like Dario now. Elma was gone. Married a guy named Frank Fisher, and Joe missed her.

"We'll always stick together, Joe, no matter what," Elma said once.

"Yeah, Elma," he said very softly. He could talk to Elma. "You and me, we'll stick together."

"The rest of them kids is too little to know. They don' understan'," Elma said, looking into Joe's eyes. And her eyes were big and soft and wet, doe eyes, Joe used to call them, and she had that sweet face that didn't tell what Elma had already seen, and Joe wanted to have her stop looking at him so dearly like that. She never yelled at him, and her voice was soft, unlike his mother's, and he wanted to hold her close just to stop her looking at him like that, and then he did, grabbed her, and squeezed her so close to him it was hard for her to breathe, and then Elma smiled up at him again with those eyes, and she kissed him on the cheek, and there was love between them, but Joe couldn't say out loud to her that he loved her maybe even more than his mother; but with his mother it was different.

Mothers have mother power over sons, all mothers over all sons. It comes out of the blood of the mother. It is in the son's blood, and it is a magic power that goes to the soul of the son, which the son knows but does not understand. In the son there is a longing for mother, for her muggy presence, her breasts, her blessing, for the very moisture of her breath breathing on the son, for the smell of her, of mother, which is her separate smell, and although the son loves his mother as he breathes and as his heart beats, yet she is not of this world. Like the beginning cell she is bewitched, and the mothers suck up their young again and own the souls of their sons, and therefore Joe Esquibel could not love his mother like he loved Elma. He had sworn he would never leave Elma. But now that he had come home from the reformatory Elma was gone, and with Agneda going to the hospital for an operation, there wasn't anybody left to take care of the kids except Joe.

He was already a tall, well-muscled boy, and a fighter, and although Dario had from time to time denied certain of Agneda's pregnancies, "I was herdin' them sheep, I no was even there," he had said, nevertheless, that sinewy little fighting rooster of a man had never denied having fathered Joe. He had been proud of this boy, and at sixteen it would have been this larger son already looking down on the father, but it is the way of sons to exceed their fathers. Now that Joe was home he didn't know which he hated worse, the reformatory or this being a mother.

Joe came home on the Greyhound bus, and walked to the shack carrying a few things in a cardboard box under his arm, and when he opened the door of the shack and walked in, Agneda didn't kiss him or hug him or hold onto him at all. She acted like he had never even been gone, like he had just come in that afternoon off the street. She said, "You take care of them kids," like she was talking to a good goat herder. Joe thought she looked bad, pale and droopy-eyed, and he couldn't tell whether she didn't want to talk or was too sick, but she had gone right away to the hospital for woman trouble, she called it, and Joe was still at the shack when she came home in about a week. The little kids were well tended, and the house clean, and things scrubbed and put away, and the little ones had their hair combed and wore clean clothes. He'd done a good wash, and Joe himself, who wore his hair in a crew cut now, could have passed inspection in the marines.

"Joe was a good boy," Agneda told our law school student investigators. "He take care of them kids good. He was all I had. He was a man already, but I could no keep him at home. He was like his old man—liked to go and go, and drink that whiskey like a man already, and I try to stop him, but he say he is a man, and I no can stop him, and he chase after them women. No," she corrected herself. "He no chase after them women. They chase him, come to the house all the time. Pick him up. He don' have no car, and they was hollerin' at him on the street all the time. Crazy about him." She seemed proud. "And he could whip them white guys. This guy come to the house for money all the time. Insurance. Says I owe him three dollars. Three dollars every week. Come every week— says I owe him and I say, 'shoo—geet out,' and Joe, he's only sixteen, and he walks up to this white guy, bigger'n him, a man, ya know, tough guy, ya know, and Joe he no says nothin', hit him, three, four times, kick him a little, and that's all. They come get this white guy and take him to the hospital. I have Mrs. Leyba next door call. She always call for me. Joe, he take care of me. He was all I had. Good boy. Used to say, 'Mama, I love ya and I take care of ya, and ya be okay now that I'm home. Ya need stuff, ya say, and I get, ya understan'? Ya be okay now,' he says."

But Agneda said that the women kept coming and there was this Louisa, an older girl, a year or so older, maybe, a skinny little girl who didn't look as old as Joe. Agneda didn't know what Joe saw in this girl who would bend in two if you put anything on her, but she and Joe were out together all the time, and when Agneda was gone, well, the two of them were in the house, doing what, she didn't know. Nice girl, this Louisa. Never sassed Agneda. Agneda had tried to keep her away from Joe. "Shoo—get home, girl," she said, but the girl just looked sad and hung onto Joe and Joe was good to her.

She didn't have no place to go, Agneda said, so Agneda finally kept her, and then the girl got pregnant.

" 'You should not marry this girl,' I tell Joe, once. 'She is too young, and you is too young.' "

"Who will take care of the baby?" Joe asked.

"That is for the welfare," Agneda said.

"Oh," Joe said. And then he and Louisa went up to see Mona Lee Murphy and she wasn't there, and Harvey Watkins, the assistant director, said that Joe had committed a crime. Rape, he said.

"I didn't rape her," Joe said.

"He didn't rape me," Louisa said, looking down, being afraid, and holding onto Joe.

"It's rape under the law, statutory rape, when you have carnal knowledge of a female child under the age of eighteen," Watkins said, but Joe didn't understand the words.

"I didn't rape her," Joe said. "She's almost eighteen anyways."

"I can't give you any assistance unless you file a complaint against him," Watkins said to Louisa as if Joe weren't there. "It's the policy of this office." Joe looked at Watkins blankly, just sat there, a sixteen-year-old with this little skinny chicken of a girl holding onto him, shivering, her eyes wide open and afraid, and Joe was afraid, too. Didn't rape nobody. Didn't know what to say himself, and there was nobody to speak for him. He would hit Watkins square in the mouth, and again in the belly, and again in the mouth, and then in the mouth, and in the mouth once more until Watkins' teeth would be hanging loose and would be flapping from his gums and Joe's knuckles would be raw and bleeding, and then he would pick Watkins up off the floor and hit him three or four more times. Watkins was taller than Joe by almost a head, but he had arms like a crane's legs, and his elbows were knobby. Joe would hit him while he still had his glasses on, drive the glasses through the silly nose. Suddenly Joe started to get to his feet, and Louisa, shivering on his arm, felt it, knew it, had seen it twice before and knew that when Joe fought, there was no stopping him until the other guy was gone. They would have to kill him with an ax, he said, and she had warned him about that. "Joe," she had said very softly in a timid little voice. "You will kill somebody someday, and then they will send you up to the pen." She held onto him with both of her arms and maybe she tipped the scales against it by hanging on. Well, Joe did not get up.

"Come on, le's go," Louisa said, and then Joe did get up, with Louisa still hanging on with both hands.

"You can't go around getting little girls pregnant and expect us to take care of 'em," Watkins said.

"Come on," Louisa said to Joe, pulling hard again.

"She's older 'n me," Joe said. "I never raped her."

"Come on, Joe," Louisa said.

"Why don't you go home to your folks, girl?" Watkins asked. "One baby more or less never seems to make any difference over there." He motioned with his long crane-legged arm in the direction of the tracks, and his elbow joints were bigger than his arms sticking out of his short shirt sleeves, and he got up in a way that told Joe and Louisa it was time for them to leave. Louisa still hung onto Joe's arm with both arms and all her weight and then Joe started to pull away from her. She threw herself around Joe and started to cry and held onto him tightly, and Watkins left the room. And that's why Joe Esquibel didn't hit Watkins right there in the Carbon County Welfare Department. At sixteen he was a man, they said, not afraid of anybody.

After Joe and Louisa left the welfare they walked back across the tracks toward the Esquibel shack, and Louisa's hanging onto him made it awkward walking, but they stayed in step as they crossed over the rails, step over rails, rail on rail, step over rails, rail on rail, and around the boxcars toward the Esquibel shack.

"We could go to New Mexico, and have the baby," Louisa said halfway across the railroad yards. "It's warm in New Mexico."

"How we gonna get there?" Joe asked.

"We can hitch."

"Yeah," Joe said. "How we gonna eat?"

"We could make it." Suddenly Joe turned around in

the other direction, swinging Louisa with him. "Le's go," he said, and she held onto him, and they walked back in the direction from which they had come, back across the rails, rail on rail, and then across the streets of the little town, on the white side of town, past the stores, up the main street to the edge of town which was also the highway, and then they walked about a mile and stopped on the side of the road, and there they stood, these two Mexican kids, Louisa holding onto Joe as if she thought he would fly away, and Joe standing there, looking fierce and proud and straight, the cars passing by, people in the cars not looking, like they weren't even standing there. Once a pickup truck went by with a dog in the back, and the dog barked at them, and when no cars stopped and it was dark and they were hungry, Joe finally said, "Okay, le's go home."

They walked back across the tracks, rail on rail, and finally they got to the shack, which was lit by a single light from the ceiling, and it seemed warm, and there were the smells of home, the smell of kids, and beans, and there were the noises of home, and Agneda, the mother, was screeching at the kids, and there was the sound of a little radio in the corner that played music one couldn't hear very well through all the static, and Joe was the man there.

"He was my beeg man," Agneda said proudly.

Joe finally found work washing dishes at a Chinese café on Front Street. They said he was a good dishwasher, came promptly every day for about three weeks until he got into a fistfight with some white guy he'd had trouble with before, and the white guy was a good customer, which made it worse, they said. Not over much of anything. Nobody could remember anymore what it was about. They went out in the alley and the guy got hurt in the fight, and before the police could get there Joe ran down the alley and never came back for his pay or anything.

"Couldn't keep track a Joe no more—didn't even try," Agneda said. "He was a man, ya know. Sometimes he gets work and sometimes no. Too young they say to him.

He goes lookin' all the time anyways, and always fightin'. 'You got experience?' and he say, 'No.' Joe he no talk much anyways. They say, 'You got experience?' and sometimes he just leave and don' answer, and then them white guys' kids gets them jobs. He don' even know how to herd sheep like Dario. Don' know nothin', but he was a big boy, a man—sixteen then."

In December of 1960 Louisa had her baby at the Esquibel place. Agneda helped. She knew about such things. It was a healthy little boy. Louisa wanted to call him Joe, after his father. "Little Joe" they called him now, but after the baby was born, there was trouble. Too many in the shack and Louisa would sit in the corner and cry to herself, Agneda said. Joe was out running around, and Louisa and her baby were crying at the same time. "Drive me crazy, and I feel sorry for her. I tell her, 'Look all the kids I got. You only got one, an' I ain't got no man neither and you got Joe,' but she just keep on a-cryin'. She was just a baby herself. Sometimes I hold her on my lap and rock her till she quit cryin'. One time I keep the baby for her and Joe when they go off to New Mexico to get married, but when they come back it's the same thing all over again, and then one day when I was gone and Joe was gone, she left. I don' know where she went. Just left, like that. Left the baby, too. He was a fat little bugger, I gotta say that. Looked like Joe. Big boy. She took good care of that baby. I gotta say that."

This Anna Fidelia Wilson, at the university, this blond, blue-eyed, bluebell of a girl, told me one day she loved me. She had asked me to play tennis with her. People who play tennis come from different places than I, out of social clubs, with pretty white shorts and cute little white tennies on their feet, and they seemed as tender as tulips, but they also seemed powerful to me. They had money, and things, cars and good clothes, and knew people I never dreamed of knowing, and they knew how to act around other people, to make nice conversations about nothing, social graces, as they say, "the upper crust" my father called them. Anna Wilson was from the upper crust. I didn't know how to play tennis. She borrowed a racquet for me and I swung at the ball viciously, and missed, and she laughed at me, but she laughed like she liked me, like I amused her, and finally I dropped the racquet, jumped over the net, and grabbed her and kissed her, which stopped the laughing. And it wasn't very long before she was saying that she loved me and I was saying I loved her back, and to this day, I don't know how that happens. This love thing comes out of a certain opening up of the hearts of young people who haven't had much experience with such hearts and who worry about what to say and how to say it, and I got caught in my own sputters trying to explain how I felt, strange feelings, and Anna Wilson laughed, and sputtered back, mocking me, and then I laughed too, and kissed her again to stop her. I couldn't believe she loved me.

But, she said it was the way I said things, and the way I was so wild—"so spontaneous," were the words she used —and how I walked. It was that good walk, maybe, but she said she couldn't really explain it, didn't have the words for it. You don't need words, I said, and finally she said, well, it was just the way I was, that's all, and she knew she loved me. When I got around her and got near her big breasts, which hollered out of her tight sweaters, and when I got the smell of her in my nose and touched her, I felt fierce and wild, but I held all that back, and covered the feelings with deep dignified sounds in my voice, stilted words that came out like a movie star's, like Clark Gable, maybe, suave, and all.

Anna lived at Hoyt Hall. There were hours to keep at the place, and she'd get points if she got in after nine on the week nights, and it didn't take many points to get "campused," campused to the goddamn girls' dorm at the University of Wyoming. We stood at the door, holding onto each other, pulling apart for the girls coming in and out, and then holding onto each other again, our bodies close, with thick winter coats between us. We buried ourselves in each other, like mating grasshoppers. I felt parts of my own heart I had never felt before, and she told me things about me I never realized, like how I had this beautiful deep voice, she said, and maybe I should be an opera singer instead of a lawyer. I did take voice lessons from Mr. Gunn at the university. My voice had changed. Baritone. Maybe even a bass, and I practiced the scales and learned to sing from the diaphragm, to let it come booming out of the chest through a loose and happy throat. And Anna said I was kind and good, which I really hadn't known before, that I was capable of love, and that I was very strong, very independent, a man already at eighteen, and although I didn't shave, I never told her so.

I've tried to remember how she looked. She had long fingers. I remember her long fingers playing on the piano like the piano keys were playing them. I'd recognize her hands anywhere, out of ten thousand pairs of hands, and she was blond. But how do you describe such a woman? She had a smile that made her face look crisp and clean, and her lips were not too thin, but thin, and dimples in square cheeks, one on each side, which her mother said were put there by an angel, and on top of her blue eyes were those heavy eyelids, "fat eyelids" she called them. Gave her an interesting blue-eyed oriental look, and she had freckles, and she was tall and big-hipped. I liked that. Some fellows wanted those little swivel-assed girls, but I used to laugh and say, "How do ya get any action from a little, swivel-assed girl?" She wore her skirt above her knees about three inches, just right for the times, and had beautiful clothes, and those big breasts, and she was a sorority girl. A so-roar-it-y girl! Kappa Kappa Gamma, whatever the hell that was supposed to mean, but she didn't live in the sorority house because she was a freshman and freshmen lived in the dorms.

The Kappa house was a big, white brick affair with green shutters, impressive as hell, built by the rich for upper-crust daughters, I thought, and it had a huge concert piano in the living room, which Anna would play, and I would stand above her reading the words and singing, "On the Road to Mandalay," practicing for my voice lessons, and some of the girls in the house would stop to listen for a minute, and sometimes applaud before they went wherever Kappa girls went. Anna said she was proud of me and showed me off to her sisters in the sorority, and I told Anna I didn't have a pin to pin her. I did think that the Sigma Nu's were interested in me, but I wasn't interested in them, I told her. Maybe she knew that wasn't true, but she never said so.

"Are you an Independent?" she asked when I first met her.

"No," I said. "I'm not a goddamned Independent. I am independent of the Independents. I am my own self," and Anna said that was what she loved about me.

Her upper-crust parents were very rich, of course. Anna's mother came to pick her up for the weekend once in a new Oldsmobile, and I went home with them to Cheyenne. Mr. Wilson, "H.R." they called him, was a big, sharp-nosed man, built like an egg, heavy oval body and soft hands and a high, strained voice, a strong man with the right amount of gentleness about him, who ran a heavy equipment business, sold big road graders and such things. He had a practical kind of wisdom that made me like to be with him. And he could listen. I knew he understood me. Mr. Wilson was a wise man who cared about me, and he became my friend.

Anna was born in Jackson, Mississippi. She had been adopted, she said, and she told me her mother used to warn her when she was a little girl about being good—if it hadn't been for her mother she'd still be in an orphanage, her mother used to say. Maybelle was her mother's name. She was a good-looking woman, and would have been a beauty in her day; she still was, I thought, built trimmer than Anna, tall, and graceful, but she came from poor places and never had much of a chance at an education, hadn't needed one anyway. She hollered, and she butchered the king's English, didn't give a damn, and she let out a loud laugh and cussed a lot with harmless little cuss words like "hell" and "my God," which my mother never would have said, and she nagged at H.R., and she wore too much makeup, blinked and winked big blue eyes at me and at all the men, and liked to flirt, a little, harmless fun, anybody could tell that, and she tinted her hair

henna red. Lord knows, she put so much Maybelline on
her eyes it was a wonder she could lift her poor lids up at
all. She wore wonderful fur coats and could walk like a
New York model, and she'd twirl the coat around just
showing off. Usually she was fun to be with, lively, glam-
orous, neurotic, and moody as hell, and I thought she got
along pretty well with the upper crust for a poor woman.
My mother only had two pairs of dress shoes, one for
summer and one for winter, but Maybelle had a closet
bulging with new shoes. Mrs. Wilson kept an immaculate
house, a lot neater than my own mother used to keep,
and her house smelled good, never smelled of fresh
canned corn or relish cooking on the stove. Her house
smelled of her own perfume, and of fancy-smelling guest
soaps in the bathroom. The house was in the old rich
section of Cheyenne and had thick, wall-to-wall carpeting
like I'd never seen in a house before—everything expensive, store-made drapes, pictures with mats and fine
frames, varnished woodwork, and a forced-air furnace.

Anna yelled back at her mother whenever she felt like
it, and her mother yelled at H.R., and H.R. didn't say
much of anything at all to either of them. He was too
good a man to get involved in petty personal things, I
thought, too wise. Maybelle was a lot younger than H.R.,
and she was outrageous at times and didn't make sense.
She would laugh at illogical things, and torment poor
H.R. with a diatribe of irrelevancies that were often so
unique I thought they acquired the stature of art. Usually
H.R. seemed amused and he was patient with Maybelle
and Anna, but sometimes I'd see a flash of hurt in his
eyes when Maybelle had cut too deep, reaching down
sometimes to the gonads. But Maybelle could also make
a man feel big, and she said she liked me, called me son,
and bragged about me—going to be a lawyer, she'd tell
her friends in front of me, "And he's going to be an opera
singer, too." God, I had never felt it before like I felt it
with Anna. To be shown the good parts of yourself by
someone you love is such ecstasy. It is falling in love.

I was no longer a skinny, poor, pimple-faced jerk. I was
a man and a poet. I wrote poems to Anna and she heard

my poems and they excited her, she said. Love before
Anna had been a sort of religious experience for me, but
my love for Anna transcended mere religion. Before,
with Virginia, when I was twelve, maybe thirteen, and
Virginia was sixteen, and I was a freshman and she was
the president of her junior class, well, she loved me, too,
she said. I wrote her name, and mine, on the frost of the
window at her front door, and in the springtime on one of
those exquisite warm days when I was already in my summer underwear, we climbed up the hillside of the city
park and we lay down with each other under the blooming chokecherry bushes, which smelled like love—and I
knew there were delicious forbidden succulent places
there, but I loved her too much, far too much to do
anything. I was innocent and so was she for that matter,
and love was exciting. Yet it was beautiful and religious.
But I loved Anna too much not to. It was a love beyond
holy love, but it was a holy love, and we made promises to
each other, over and over, the same promises, like some
church liturgy, I admit.

"I love you."

"Yes, I love you, too."

"We will be together forever."

"Forever, darling."

"And we will never leave each other, ever."

"No, and, oh, I love you."

"And, sugar, I will always call you sugar."

"And I will always be your sugar."

Oh, God, it hurt! It was so sweet it ached. At eighteen
my heart felt like a chicken gizzard cut open and peeled
back.

I decided to study in Mexico in the summer. I would be a
writer. My folks dug up the money and sent it from Bolivia. An artist must have his patrons. It was all right for
an artist not to work in the summertime. Everybody knew
that the art movement was in Mexico, not Paris—besides
Mexico was closer. I hitched a ride as far as El Paso, and
then I got on a bus full of Mexican peasants who brought
along their kids and chickens in crates and their dogs and

all their other earthly goods, stacked inside the bus to the ceiling, and finally I got to Mexico City. But I couldn't concentrate. I was sick without Anna, and I couldn't sleep, and I felt like I couldn't breathe because she had my breath. I wrote her poetry every day and when I couldn't bear it any longer after hardly more than a week, I caught the next bus back, and she came to meet me, and we held onto each other and kissed and cried and I was happy again. Then I went to work in the hayfields near Cheyenne at the old Fred Boice ranch, near my sugar.

I liked putting up hay with horses, and men who worked horses were happy men. You could tell.

Some ranchers had turned to tractors. A man can put up a lot of hay with a tractor, but tractors are not alive and a tractor is no company for a man, and they spew out their hatred of the land, exploding inside themselves, ripping up their own innards, and the land as well, and they fill the land with noise and gas, and after a few years they cover the land with their iron corpses, and because the tractor has never been alive in the first place, it won't die, and the tractor parts lie out in the sun year after year, the big wheels, the solid steel chassis with the rusty motor mounted on top, and the abandoned rusty combines and the monstrous old galvanized iron threshing machines look like prehistoric beasts lying out there in some prehistoric graveyard where the dead will not die. And the rancher who uses tractors gets so he never sees his own junkyard anymore, or the weeks which are all that grow up around the junk, and he never sees the oil-covered ground around the junk, which will grow nothing at all, and mostly, when the rancher lays his own head down to die and they have finally carried him off somewhere to give him up to the good earth, his junkyard lives on to mark what remains of his dreams and what is left of his sweat, and the junkyard is usually all that is left of his profit, and it is a part of the soul of the man who used tractors.

Old Fred Boice used horses to put up hay, and he usually put the young strong half-broke broncs on the mowing machines. Good place for a team of broncs. The work of the mower, the horsepower required to pull the machine through all its gears and to activate the high-speed sickle back and forth through the thick grass, makes a heavy pull for the horses, and it's enough all right to make a couple of smart-aleck broncs get serious about their work.

My first day on the job I was given a team of young broncs, Pete and Hefty were their names, which I managed to get hitched up, but with the cutter bar up and the mower out of gear a mowing machine pulls as light as a chariot, and it was a couple of miles from the barn to the hayfield, down a rutty wagon track. I was afraid the team would get away acting up like they were, wanting to run with the mower out of gear hardly taxing the team at all.

Every good team likes to trot, like boys jogging down the street together with the boundless energy of boys. Pete got to trotting faster than Hefty, and then Hefty wanted to trot faster still, and their necks bowed and pretty and their tails were up, and as they trotted faster and faster on a gallop's edge, their necks swayed back and forth and their tails switched. I held my breath because if they broke into a gallop, it would be another runaway. Pete on the left was nipping Hefty on the neck, who humped up and bucked and kicked up his hind legs, half in protest, and half in spirit. I pulled the team in, but they didn't want to be pulled in, and finally I had all my weight on the lines, my feet braced on the axle housing, and my whole body leaning back, pulling harder, as far back as I could, pulling harder yet, but the team conspired against me and fought the pressure back, pulled their heads aside to avoid my harsh tugging on the lines and fought the bit. They wanted to run.

"Damn you. Whoa. Whoa," I hollered, and pulled back even harder, as hard as I could pull, but the team headed down the old rutted road faster still and the old mower was bouncing and clattering and rattling, and I was scared. I couldn't hold them, and then suddenly, thank God, there was the gate, and Pete and Hefty just pulled up short and stopped and waited for me to open it for them, like I was their servant, not the other way around.

"Sons-of-bitches," I said out loud—funny thing for a kid to call a couple of horses, but it sounded tough. Horses aren't supposed to know how afraid a kid can be trying to become a man. I walked back and let down the cutting bar and threw the old mower in gear. That would spoil their fun. Then I opened up the gate.

The horses wondered why I'd turned into such a spoil sport, interfering with a good run in the best part of the day, the sun just up, when it was still cool and crisp and the grass was bent and wet with heavy dew and the red-winged blackbirds were singing away in the cattails along the edge of the irrigation ditch like they owned the world. Now with the mower in gear it was a tough enough pull and the horses put their heads down to go to work, to tug against the pressure at their shoulders, laboring in unison, so that the work between them was smoother and easier. I apologized, talking out loud to a couple of beasts.

"Well," I said. "Well, you sons-a-bitches will know next time to slow down when I holler whoa. Sorry," I said. It's important to speak to living things. It's not hard to talk to horses. But a tractor? How can a man talk to a god-damned tractor?

There is a relationship between living things on this earth, and there is a contract between man and other beasts. There'd been a bargain struck between a man and his horse, especially in Wyoming where the winters can be long and the wind so cold and raw it can raise a blister on your hide, and a hungry horse can freeze standing in his tracks. The bargain is for the beast to work every other day for two months and then to run practically free with the rest of the hay horses for the rest of the year, and there is no old age, no getting sick and weak and hanging on and dying, no heart attacks, no cancer, and no fear of what's going to happen after death. One day when the joints of old bones are a little too stiff to work, and the teeth too smooth to cut a good mouthful of hay, and the ribs are sprung, well, then the old rancher, stiff and rib sprung himself and feeling like a worn-out old hay horse, loads the old horse into the truck, and with a tear behind his eye which never gets all the way out, the old rancher drives the truck to the sale barn. Dog food. The horse doesn't know. It is a great gift to a good faithful horse, the gift of innocence and a healthy life which is mostly free. I drove down the road with the cutter bar in gear clacking and cutting away at thin air and I wondered who was really intelligent, man or beast.

One time I said to ol' Calsey, "Horses never kill each other. They're smarter 'n us." Ol' Calsey never said anything. Just took another long pull out of his half pint of Seagram's 7.

I said, "Horses only work a few days a year. We work all the time all our lives, and we're scared to die."

"That's right, kid. But they ain't got whiskey. That's on account a we're smarter 'n them."

"Yeah," I remembered saying. A fellow never wanted to argue with ol' Calsey when he was drinking, and now a couple of years later I was mowing hay all week waiting for Saturday night to come so I could be with my sugar.

There was something of the same power of my mother in this woman Anna, but they were different. My mother never raised her voice, and when she laughed she acted like she wasn't sure it was all right and let it out in tiny sucking sounds, but Anna was different. She was wild like me, smiling and cooing one minute and the next, screaming, raging, loving, and she opened up my very being and all of me poured out. But there was the mother in that woman, the universal mother.

We spent almost all our time together and I got bad grades, no time for school, only for Anna, and Anna was having grade trouble, too. She was on probation at the Kappa house and when her parents finally had enough, they sent her off to the Barnes Business School in Denver. Maybe she could at least be a secretary, and maybe this whole love thing would blow over, but it didn't blow over. Anna grew pale and thin and didn't eat in order to save up her food allowance to come see me, and she

pined away for me, and her grades weren't much better at
the Barnes Business School in Denver either.

On my birthday, January 8, I hitched a ride home from
town on the back of this motorcycle. The roads were icy
and I balanced on the seat behind the driver sort of holding on with one hand and holding a bottle of birthday
wine in the other. Suddenly at the corner of Seventeenth
Street, where I was getting off anyway, the cycle slipped,
and I went flying down into the curb against my left knee,
and the bottle of wine broke, splattering all over, and I
suppose the people passing by thought I was drunk, lying
there groaning, with the wine flowing over the street. The
guy on the motorcycle left me there. I don't remember
why. Maybe he asked if I was okay and I said yes, in the
night, or something. After a while I got up on one leg
somehow, but it was too painful to walk or even hop, and
I crawled up over the curb and across the sidewalk
through the snow on my hands and one knee, and down
the steep steps into my basement apartment. I had a
broken leg all right, femur, they called it, at the knee
joint, and I was in the hospital with a cast up to my hip.

Anna came to see me, and later her mother took care
of me. I couldn't go to school, didn't have a car, and I
could barely get around on my crutches. Anna's mother
became my mother and she nursed me and took my pants
off at night and helped me into bed. Then one night on a
weekend Anna's parents found us stretched out together
on the couch in the front room—oh, the horror of it!
They pretended not to see, but almost immediately the
idea of these two nineteen-year-old babies getting married didn't seem so unthinkable anymore, and I was a
man and independent, wasn't I? Everybody said so, and I
had made promises, promised my life to Anna, even
promised the hereafter to her, forever. And I thought we
should do it, too. We should get married.

I dropped out of school and went to work for a seismo-
graph company. My leg was fresh out of the cast, and I
went hopping and limping over the frozen ground, jug
hustling, they called it. I carried out the long strings of
instruments that picked up the sound of the seismic ex-

plosion that was set off in the earth, and these "jugs" picked up the sounds and transmitted them to an instrument that recorded them so the people in the oil company could map the underground structures looking for oil. Then I was a driller's helper drilling holes into the ground in which the charge of dynamite was packed and then exploded. Later still I became a shooter's helper too, and quit smoking—too dangerous around the dynamite—so we all chewed plug tobacco instead, and I called Anna almost every night, and wrote her every day, and saved her letters and numbered them as if they were holy and I thought of her when the seismic explosion came shooting out of the hole, shooting upward, high into the Wyoming winter sky. I was working outside of Evanston, Wyoming, a town known only for the insane asylum, and if a man looked he could see the crazy house where they put the nut-os, there in those stern, red brick buildings with the steam floating up from a hundred little stacks in the frozen heights of a Wyoming morning with the temperature about twenty-five below zero.

There were plans for a big wedding made mostly by Anna and her mother. I would sing. Why should I let anyone else sing to my bride? I practiced the song driving down the highway in the water truck that furnished the water for the drilling rigs. I was bouncing along singing deep out of my diaphragm, "Because you come to me with naught save la-of." I could hardly hear the sound of my voice above the roar of the engine in the old truck, but I could feel the love in my throat as I sang. And then the June wedding came. Who has the right to question the course of things with such huge energies? It was a big wedding. And I sang the wedding solo from the church balcony, as planned, in a good, deep baritone that cracked once or twice when my throat got tight, and then after the song I hurried down and waited at the altar for Anna. The place was full of her friends, and her parents' friends, and I can't remember anybody on the groom's side of the church. I kept my promises to Anna Wilson. Like my mother, I am a keeper of promises.

19

SOMEONE HAD clipped the newspaper story of the shooting from the Rawlins *Daily Times*. The story included a picture of Sharon Esquibel. She was blond all right, with her hair in the style of the sixties, high school picture, no doubt. Her eyes were wide apart, and she had a nice forehead, a square baby face, actually looked like a child, but she was older than Joe by two years. By the time of the killing she and Joe had had three beautiful children. The children were motherless and, with Joe in jail, fatherless. They were living with Mrs. Mona Lee Murphy, their grandmother.

People in a town like Rawlins, Wyoming, liked to talk, about all there was to do, and that included the city fathers, the mayor, who everybody said was just a professional glad-hander, and the chief of police, of course, and the bank's lawyer, with bushy red eyebrows and an imposing bald head who didn't say much and smiled a knowing smile like Calvin Coolidge, and the president of the bank himself, with his tight little potbelly on a skinny frail frame and a face like an ax, and the retired sheep rancher who was on the bank's board of directors, and also on the city council, and who was the largest single depositor in the bank, only one bank in town, who looked old and chronically hungry, and made a person wonder how he survived so long in this desolate place with such an empty belly. And also among the city fathers was the congenial manager of the power company and also the

manager of the local credit bureau, the latter devoting
major chunks of his life collecting the unpaid bills of the
former, and the Ford dealer, who wore a white ten-gallon
hat, even at the coffee table, and who sold a lot of used
cars to the Rawlins Mexican-Americans. The city fathers
met at Adam's Restaurant at ten o'clock in the morning
and three in the afternoon—coffee time. Time to talk.

That Sharon was one of them women who liked her
men, wild as a March hare, I hear. My kid used to date
'er. Told me all about it. Ha. Ha. But ya know kids these
days. Hey, Daisy, ya got any of them fresh doughnuts?
And then somebody said, well, I'd like to know what that
spick has. She sure must a liked it. Sure must a liked
them chili beans. Ha. Ha. And then somebody tried to
change the subject by saying that the Outlaws, that was
the Rawlins High School football team, didn't do so good
again last Saturday. Laramie beat the hell out of 'em.
May have to change coaches again, and somebody else
said that's cause you guys never give anybody a friggen
chance. Takes time to build somethin' up, and then somebody else who had never said much at all and who just
sort of sat over in the far corner kind of brooding, said,
well, they ought to take that Mexican cocksucker out and
shoot 'em, and especially that one—ain't hardly one of
them bastards worth savin'. And then he looked right at
the chief and said, and I s'pose the law'll just give 'em a
sweet little pat on the ass and a kiss on the cheek. Gimme
another cup of coffee, Daisy. And the chief said, it ain't
up ta me, ya know. If I had my way, I'd put 'em in the gas
chamber myself. That's what it's for. Pass the sugar over
here will ya, Jonesy? I worked them Mex's a lot a years,
and ya gotta come down hard on 'em. That's all they
understand. There was a little silent space at the coffee
table when nobody said anything, and then, like there'd
been no space at all, the laughter and the talk started up
again, and somebody was saying he sure felt sorry for the
girl's mother.

The law student investigators talked to a lot of people
about Sharon Esquibel, and there's no doubt she did

seem just plain addicted to Joe. In the early days before she got pregnant the first time, she called Joe her "gorgeous animal," and then Sharon had been sure to add that he was such a little boy, such a fragile little boy. "He has the softest hands!" she told her girl friend, and the two of them talked about love, Rawlins girls dragging Main as they called it, driving up and down Cedar Street in Sharon's car, talking and driving and honking, and waving and hollering out the windows to other kids in passing cars that were also dragging Main. Sharon's girl friend thought she understood what it was about Joe. She tried to say it. "It's the way he talks to you—doesn't say much—and it's the way he looks at you when he's talking," and Sharon nodded yes, and the two of them laughed and shared breathless secret things into the night.

"I love him," Sharon said, "but sometimes he's so crude—like a beast." And then they had looked at each other again and repeated in unison, "He's a beast."

"But I know how to control that beast," Sharon said.

"Yes, I'll bet you do. Oh yes, I bet you do!" the girl friend said, and she giggled.

"I really do know what to do with him."

"But what do your folks think?"

"They don't think."

"They don't?" the girl friend asked, puzzled for the moment.

"No. They just think they think."

"That's good," the other girl said. "That's really good. They just think they think," and the girls giggled together again.

"My mother thinks it's horrible, just plain horrible about me and Joe. She raises all kinds of hell. But I tell her I have to live my own life. 'It's my life, Mother,' I tell her. She thinks she's going to run my life for me, but she's not," Sharon said. "Wants me to marry Hal Johnson or somebody. Says, 'Marry somebody like Hal Johnson, not some uneducated Mexican who'll just get you into trouble,' she says. Hal Johnson! Can you imagine! I dated him once. Wears boxer shorts. Looks so silly, spindly little white legs and glasses, and skinny little arms. God, I'd just die if I had to marry him, and he's such a bore!"

"Bankers are bores. All bankers are bores. But they have money."

"Hal Johnson doesn't have any money. I make as much as a secretary at the bank as he does as assistant—whatever he's assistant at. Went with him to Las Vegas once. Ended up asking me to pay part of the hotel bill."

"But he has a future at the bank," the girl friend said.

"Well, the bank can have him," Sharon said. "When I'm with him nothing happens. It is like being full but being empty," she laughed a vacant half-disgusted laugh, "if you know what I mean."

"Being full but being empty! That's good," the other girl said. "I wish I knew what it was like, like with you and Joe."

"Well, I'll tell you what it's like," Sharon said with her eyes dreamy and distant. "It's like swallowing your whole self all at once, and you all of a sudden die, and then you come alive again as a new soft person—like coming alive again as a baby, soft and happy," she said.

"Oh," the other girl said.

"And it's like getting all mixed into the other person, too, so you are one person."

"Oh," the girl friend said, almost in a whisper.

"But he is like a little boy sometimes, and he gets down on himself and feeling bad and then he gets drunk." When they got to the end of Cedar Street they turned around and drove back again. Back and forth they drove. That was the way in those days, dragging Main, just dragging Main.

"What's he doing now?"

"Nothing. Living off of me mostly," Sharon said, and snickered a little as if it wasn't really funny. "It isn't that he's lazy. But nobody hires Mexicans. Mexicans are as good as other people, I say, and he's a whole lot better," she said, making the word go a long ways—stringing it out, like stretching taffy, "a wh-oo-le lot better," she said again, "and when he gets drunk he fights. He is tough like a tiger. I call him my tiger. He is my tiger. I own my own pet tiger. Nobody else in Rawlins owns a pet tiger," she said. "Nobody even looks at me when I'm with him. I'll tell you that much. Afraid to. I can get some guy to come on to me and Joe'll kill him right there, with his bare hands. Did it one night with Ernie, and Ernie isn't any slouch. Joe knocked him out and was kickin' him. It was terrible. I finally had to lay down across Ernie to stop him," Sharon said excitedly.

"Yeah, and what about Billy Seymore. I seen you out with him the other night."

"Yeah. Joe saw us, too. It was awful. Joe chased us. I knew if he caught us he'd kill us both." She looked afraid now even though her mouth stayed smiling. She had learned to do that somehow, and her mouth stayed smiling when she was angry, too. It was confusing. Couldn't tell for sure how Sharon really was, but sometimes you could see it around the eyes and the way the jaw was set behind the smiling mouth. Pretty mouth. "He was coming after us and we ran for the car, and him behind us—got to the car just in time, locked the doors and took off, and he was beating on the windshield with his bare fists before I could get the car started and we got away. He was crazy—just a madman—can't tell you how scared I was—cut his fists up and was screamin', and I panicked, didn't know what to do, and I almost ran over him before I could get the car out of there. Billy Seymore was white as a ghost, too. Took him home and he locks himself up in his apartment, and I went up to the folks' and we locked all the doors, and pretty soon Joe came like I knew he would, and he knocks and hollers, but I wouldn't talk to him, and then he calls me on the phone."

"Yeah?" The girl friend wasn't smiling anymore, or giggling.

"And he's begging me and wants to see me, and says he can't live without me, and I says, 'No, you'll beat me up,' and he promises he won't, and I says that he beat me up before, and he says no—promises he won't if I'll just come back, and finally he gets to cryin', and says he's going to kill himself, and then I didn't know what to do anymore, so I went on back to my apartment and let him in. He was moonin' around, cryin' and all, and his fists were cut up, and he looked so pitiful."

"How come you'd go out with Billy in the first place?" the girl friend asked. "He ain't nothin'. Thinks he is tough. You ought to hear him on that radio show of his. You hear him? Gossips worse than my mother and cracks jokes that aren't funny. Disc jockeys don't make anything either."

"Nobody makes nothin' around here," Sharon said. "My mother says you have to pick a bright one, marry him, and put him through school. Make yourself your own doctor, or lawyer. That's what she says, but Joe can't ever be a doctor or a lawyer. Don't know what I'm gonna do with him." Then she laughed. "I know some things I'm gonna do with him. Oh, yeah!" she said, and raised her eyebrows and nodded her head up and down. And they both giggled like girls. "He can hardly read." Then she was quiet for just a second. "But he *is* a man."

The half-painted car ahead laid down fresh rubber, its rear end sticking up high like a silly bug ready to be bred. "Cop'll nab him," Sharon said. "When he's out I sit up and wait till he gets home, and sometimes he's drunk and mean when he comes home, and I have to humor him, baby him, and sometimes he gets to crying and says nobody wants him and that he's no good—keeps saying that over and over, that he's no good, and I tell him, no, he is good, and he says he doesn't have any work and he shouldn't be taking money off of me and he has this terrible inferiority complex, and he's scared to death I'm going to leave him. I can make him do anything. All I have to do is pretend like I'm going to leave him and he'll do anything—I mean anything. He's my pet tiger."

"It must be nice," the other girl said, waving at the blond kid in the '52 Ford. "Hey, Georgie, whatcha doin'?" she hollered. "Hey, you're slicker'n ape shit," he hollered back, and that's all the time there was as the cars met and passed.

"Joe says I'm all he has. Says I'm the only one who makes him feel big, and I says, 'Well, Joe, you are big. Look how big you are. And strong. And you're beautiful.

You're as beautiful inside, too.' And then he says I am the only one who makes him feel like he is as good as other men, and I tell him he is a whole lot better, which I shouldn't have said, comparing him to other men, you know, 'cause it gets him all riled up again, and he asks, like who do I mean?"

"You shouldn't say he is a whole lot better. He probably takes it wrong," the other girl said.

"Well, anyway, he hangs onto me all the time till sometimes I think I'll go crazy. He can't do anything for himself. Can't even write a check. Wants me to buy his clothes. Thinks he doesn't look right if I don't buy his clothes and tell him what to wear. Practically dress him. But he's like a big gorgeous tiger, and inside he's just a kitten."

"Do you really think you love him, Sharon, or is it just infatuation, I mean . . ."

"Of course I love him," Sharon said. "But sometimes I feel like he is going to smother me. That's all. When he's home he just sits there watching me. Watches me for hours! Can't even go to the store without him, he's so scared I'm going to leave him, and pretty soon I want to scream, and I got to get out, and so when Billy Seymore saw me that day and Joe was on the night shift working at the city, street cleaning, terrible job—street cleaning—and Joe was sleeping, well, I just slipped out to have a Coke. Just a Coke is all, and Billy was there and says, 'What ya doin'?' and I said, 'Nothing,' and you know how things go like that, and he comes on strong, like he's on the radio or somethin'. I just had to get out. But you can't do anything in a town like this. Everybody knows your business. I shoulda known better."

"Is Billy a good time?" the girl friend asked, sort of out of breath, and then hollering, "Hi!" to a passing carload of kids.

"Yeah," she said, like she meant no. "Yeah, but he isn't like Joe, you know. I told Joe I didn't do nothing."

"He'd think you did even if you didn't. You just as well have the game as the name," the girl friend said, saying a saying she had heard before.

But Sharon didn't say anything back, and in a little while she went on. "He's worse than he ever was. I can't even look out the window and he wants to know who I'm looking at. And if some guy says hello to me he wants to know if I've ever done it with him. 'Ever do it with him?' he says, and I say, 'No, Joe, I never did it with him.' " And then the girls both laughed again. "God! And my mother's on me, too. Can't even go home any more. Raises hell, screams and hollers about me gettin' pregnant by a Mexican. God! You'd think I was sleeping with a nigger, or something. She acts like he's worse than a nigger!"

"Hi, again, Georgie," the girl friend hollered to the blond boy in the '52 Ford. "Hi, sugar tit," he hollered back. "Georgie's cute," the girl friend said.

"Yeah," Sharon said, "I hear he made Valerie walk down off of the hill 'cause she wouldn't put out . . . That time I went to Las Vegas with Hal Johnson I had to call the sheriff when I got back—Joe blacked both my eyes, beat me up," she said, and the other girl didn't laugh. "Oh," is all she said. "You're supposed to get married," Sharon said. "Everybody thinks it's terrible to live with somebody you're not married to. But I couldn't marry Joe anyway. He's married to Louisa. Had Joe's baby, and she stays at home with Joe's mother all the time with the baby. Never leaves. She and Joe weren't even married when she had his baby and it made me feel so sorry for that poor girl stayin' home with Joe's baby and not even being married. He just leaves her there all the time—like she's dumped there, and then he goes off with me and it makes me feel ashamed. It wasn't my fault she had a baby and had to stay home with Mrs. Esquibel and the other kids. But, God! Imagine! And I got to feeling so bad about it I told Joe I was going to leave him if he didn't at least marry the girl for the baby's sake— give the baby a name, I told him. 'At least do that.' I had to practically make 'em do it. God, it was weird, me livin' with Joe and getting those two married. I sent 'em off for the wedding to New Mexico where her folks live. Could at least get married out of town. So now I can't marry Joe even if I want to. He's already married. It would be bigamy," she laughed again.

"Bigamy!" they both said and laughed together, but it didn't seem funny.

"You could get 'em a divorce, now," the girl friend suggested, but Sharon didn't know if she wanted to marry him anyway. Sure she loved him all right, but it was hard enough living with him. She could at least kick him out if she wanted. The deputy would always come over and take care of things for her, the deputy being the good friend of the family that he was. Later that night the girl friend got into Georgie's '52 Ford, and that's the last she saw of Sharon for a while.

Harvey Watkins used to tell Mona Lee Murphy that she had done everything but give Sharon a frontal lobotomy. You can't physically tie her down, and you can't give her a brain transplant either, he would say. All parents can do is worry a lot, hurt a lot, be patient, and trust that what they put into the kid will come out all right, and it usually does, he would say to Mona Lee, trying to reassure her, but Mona Lee couldn't help but get preachy. She didn't want to be that way. She knew it would just cause her and her daughter to grow farther apart, but she couldn't help herself, and her voice would get high and loud and sort of sing-songy shrill. "How would you like to get pregnant by a Mexican? How would you like to have a bunch of Mexican kids?" And then she and Sharon would have a terrible fight, and finally after one of those fights Mona Lee Murphy had decided she just had to stop it once and for all before Sharon did get pregnant. If Sharon got pregnant and Mona Lee hadn't done everything she could to prevent it, then the blame would rest on her, she thought. She was still the mother. And so she filed criminal charges against both Joe and Sharon for what the law called "unlawful cohabitation." She argued to Harvey Watkins that it was better to make a petty criminal of her daughter than to have a bunch of illegitimate grandkids.

"Imagine what hell it would be for everyone if that animal got her pregnant," Mona Lee said to Harvey.

Then the deputy came for Joe and Sharon, and hauled the two of them off to the Carbon County Jail, but the deputy was a friend of the family's, nice man, a man like a good loving uncle, and the deputy liked Mona Lee Murphy, and Sharon, too, for that matter. He and Mona Lee were fellow government employees, good citizens, servants of the people. They were like a little family in Rawlins, Wyoming, and they needed to cooperate, to help each other. The deputy felt sorry for Mona Lee Murphy. He thought she was basically a good woman, a little too far to the left, maybe, and she probably brought this trouble on herself with these liberal ideas of hers, but for his part he would have shot the fuckin' Mexican if he'd been messin' with his daughter. He'd known Sharon since she was a little towheaded blue-eyed baby with chubby legs, and, of course, he knew Joe—put Joe Esquibel in the same damned cell in the Carbon County Jail about twenty times, for fighting in the bars mostly, and a couple of times for beating up Sharon. The fuckin' Mex would beat up his daughter just once. And the deputy knew Mrs. Esquibel. Nellie. Good old Nellie. Good old Nellie, all right. There was a song the kids used to sing with a lot of verses about some drunken Swede and a whore named Nellie:

> My name is Yon Yonson.
> I come from Wisconsin.
> I earn a dollar a day.
> I go to see Nellie,
> And bounce on her belly.
> She takes my dollar away. Oh . . .

And as far as this Joe Esquibel was concerned—well what could you expect of a kid with a mother like that? The deputy was an understanding man. As for Sharon, he let her out of jail on her O.R., her "own recognizance," as they call it, her own bond. No money. Just took her promise to show up at the trial. Her promise was enough. After all, the purpose of bonding a defendant is to ensure the accused's presence at the trial. It is not the purpose of the law to keep people in jail awaiting trial. People in this country are presumed innocent until proven guilty, and therefore putting them in jail until the trial is putting innocent people in jail. That's easy to understand. The only time you put them in jail before a trial is if you're afraid they'll take off.

After Sharon got out of jail on her O.R. she promised her mother she'd leave Joe once and for all if only her mother would drop the charges and let Joe out, and finally after a couple of weeks Mona Lee thought Sharon had learned her lesson and Joe, too, and she got soft like she always did, and forgiving. She dropped the charges and the deputy let Joe out. Then the first damn thing Joe did was beat the hell out of Sharon over something, and Sharon had Joe thrown in jail again, thirty more days, and when he got out Joe and Sharon went right back at it again, so Mona Lee Murphy charged them a second time with illegal cohabitation, and the sheriff picked them up again. This time he left Sharon in jail overnight. Thought it might do her some good to spend at least one night in jail to think it over. In the morning the deputy let her out on her O.R.

"Why don't you let Joe out, too?" Sharon shouted at the deputy.

"He didn't put up any bond. And you shouldn't holler at your friends," the deputy said.

"Neither did I put up any bond," she shouted again, and her smile was actually gone this time, and her lower jaw was shaking.

"I know your mother. I've known you since you were a baby. You ain't going no place, Sharon," he said kindly, quietly.

"Neither is Joe. He's never been any other place but Rawlins in his life. You've known him since he was a baby, too. You've known his mother." She was still shouting and she started to sob.

"Now, Sharon, both Joe and his mother got criminal records. Crimin-al records," he said again. "Now you be reasonable," he said in a low voice, like a good old uncle.

"You can't let people out on their O.R.'s that's got criminal records."

"I have a criminal record, too," Sharon shouted back. "What about the last time Mother did this to us? Remember? I got a criminal record."

"Your mother had a right to put you two in jail."

"She had no damn right," Sharon screamed, striking the air with both fists at the same time, her whole body heaving, her breasts flailing, and her cheeks vibrating as she stomped her foot on the floor.

"You ain't married, Sharon," he said kindly. "Sleeping with Mexicans when you ain't married is 'illegal cohab' in anybody's book," he said very softly.

"What if I was sleeping with a white man?" She was hysterical. "What if I was sleeping with a fucking banker. Would it be illegal cohab then?" She screamed in his face, "Would it?" The deputy didn't answer. "Well, I confess it! Hear me? Get your goddamn steno in here. Get this confession down. I slept with that banker. Fucked the banker. Fucked Hal Johnson. You know him. You bastards kiss the bank's ass all the time. I fucked him for two solid weeks while Joe was in jail the last time! That's illegal cohab, you old rotten son-of-a-bitch. Now get that down. And Joe knew it, too."

"Shut up, Sharon," the old deputy said. "You're making a scene." But she went on screaming at the deputy, sobbing, the tears rolling down her face, and her fists were clenched and she was still stomping the floor to emphasize every word, and her breasts jiggled in her brassiere. A man couldn't help seeing that.

"I won't shut up. I don't know how Joe knew about me and Hal, but he kicked the hell out of me, and then I had to call you, and you threw him in jail for thirty days more. Now arrest me and go get Hal Johnson, too," she hissed, and then burst into more sobbing.

The old deputy walked over and, like a nice uncle, put his arm in a friendly way around Sharon, but she pulled back.

"Don't touch me, you filthy old bastard," she said. She was a big-breasted girl and trim, with that baby face. The deputy kept his distance now, and his cool. Then Sharon stopped her sobbing for a minute, and her face changed. The smile started to come back on her face a little and she looked at the old deputy in a different way. They were alone in the booking room, and she started to walk toward him, but he backed off a step or two. He kept his distance, and he just kept talking.

And then Sharon said, "I'm not leavin' until you let Joe out." She was speaking in a different voice, which was quiet and reasonable-sounding.

"I can't let Joe out," the deputy said, this good man, stern and serious. Patient. "I have to keep him here, that is unless your mother drops the charges. If she'll drop the charges, well, then I got no choice but to let him out. Go on home and talk to your mother, Sharon."

Finally Sharon put on her coat, and without saying anything more she drove to her mother's house, stormed through the door, called her mother a no-good bitch, and said other things that hurt Mona Lee. Later Sharon felt sorry for having said those terrible things, but she talked to her mother like daughters do to their mothers during those times of late adolescent madness, and she had cried some more and began throwing things, and her mother had to call the deputy again. But when the old deputy came he acted calm and talked low and quiet, and tried to be reasonable and to smooth things over, and he tried to talk sense into the girl.

"Make your mother just a simple little promise and she'll drop the charges on Joe and then I'll let Joe out," he said to Sharon almost in baby talk.

"What promise?" Sharon sobbed, sobbing and smiling again at the same time.

"Promise your mother you'll never live with him again."

"That same old promise. I can't," she sobbed again.

"Why?" her mother asked. "Why, Sharon? Why, for God's sake, can't you promise me that?"

"Because I'm pregnant," Sharon whispered.

"Oh, God!" Mona Lee Murphy gasped, and she sat down and pretty soon she began to cry, too, and there they were, those two women, mother and daughter, both crying, and the deputy sheriff just stood there, feeling helpless, not being able to say anything more. "Oh, God," Mona Lee Murphy whispered so softly one could hardly hear her now. "Oh, God, save me. Save me."

Sharon's girl friend told our investigators from the law school that Sharon's getting pregnant by Joe humiliated her something awful, and she didn't actually leave Joe until she was swollen up really big, and then she finally had to go home—no other place to go. She hung around the house and her mother seemed glad and was as sweet as pie to her. She had finally left Joe. At least that much good had been accomplished. Always some good comes out of everything bad Mona Lee Murphy used to say, but it was awful to see Sharon. She grieved for Joe, and he was running around again being crazy, chasing girls, like some damn stud horse, and it wasn't any fun seeing Sharon helpless, all puffed out and pregnant like that. Sharon said sometimes she wished she were dead, and that this was worse than being dead. She used to be so spunky, the girl friend said. "Spunky and tart and a wee bit smart," that's what Sharon used to say about herself with that little rhyme all the time, but getting pregnant just kicked it all out of her.

Then she had the baby, and it wasn't but a little while after that that she was right back running around with Joe all over again, and everybody thought her mother was going to die over it. But Sharon didn't seem to care. It was insane. She couldn't leave Joe alone. Didn't seem to learn a thing from getting pregnant the first time. "I don't know how that mother of hers took it," the girl friend said, but Sharon said, "He's my man. He's my tiger. He belongs to me." Sharon said she got her power back, and she could make him do whatever she wanted, and she seemed happy again. She was going to have her tiger and do what she wanted to with him, and it was nobody's fucking business, she didn't care what anybody thought, including her mother, especially her mother, she said, and then Sharon started thinking seriously about marrying Joe.

She went back to work and saved enough money to talk to old Bates, the lawyer, old Bob Bates, you know him. Kind of a half Chinaman-looking fellow, the girl friend said. But I think he's Irish. He is always taking those kind of cases. Smart old devil. If you ever get into trouble in Rawlins, well, go see him. Talks funny—funny sound in his voice, kinda like an Englishman without the English accent, like he was talking with his mouth full, or something. Sounds really funny. Sounds good in a way. Impressive. But anyway old Bates figured out a way to get the divorce even if they didn't know where Louisa was, but Sharon didn't have enough money to pay for the divorce in advance and Joe wasn't working. Just drinking and fighting. Couldn't keep a steady job. Extra for the city sometimes, and he wouldn't go to work on the section with the other Mexicans for some reason. Maybe they wouldn't have him there because they were afraid of him. I don't know. Beat the hell out of everybody all the time. Well, anyway the girl friend said Sharon paid something down on the divorce, but by the time she got enough money together to pay for it, Joe was in trouble again. Had him in jail this time over a little fourteen-year-old girl named Roberta Rodriguez. The Rodriguez girl claimed she was pregnant by him, too. God! It almost drove Mona Lee Murphy mad they say. Mona Lee started getting sick. Had an ulcer. Nervous aches and pains. Headaches. Hurt all over. Nothin' but worry over Sharon. You know how mothers are about their daughters—want them marrying somebody nice, somebody big in the town, or somebody who is going to be big someday—with a pretty wedding and all.

Mona Lee Murphy couldn't even say how she felt any more. She tried to talk it out with Harvey Watkins. He was the only person she could talk to. And sometimes he didn't understand her. Sometimes talking to Harvey Watkins was like talking to a stranger, and Mona Lee's husband, who worked at night on the railroad down on the switch tracks, had nothing to show for all those years except his seniority, which is half a gold watch. He seemed helpless as usual to come up with any kind of a

firm decision as to what should or shouldn't be done
about his daughter. It was his daughter, too, Mona Lee
kept reminding him. He should be decisive. One minute
he was decisive. He was mad and he hollered and
pounded his fist on the table, but Sharon paid absolutely
no attention to her father. Treated him just like her
mother did as a matter of fact. Daughters learn from
mothers. And then the next minute he would be crying,
actually sobbing, feeling guilty, saying it was all his fault
for having been such a poor father, and he admitted he
was weak, and he hated himself for it. But when it finally
came down to making a decision, he couldn't. Left it up
to Mona Lee. He was a blank, and, as a matter of fact, he
had always been a blank, she thought. Mona Lee never
did understand how she came to marry this man and to
stay with him all these years. It was her own inexperi-
enced passion at first, she thought, but it had soon
burned out like some tiny bonfire, and after Sharon had
been born, the passion was replaced by her devotion to
this darling daughter, who was sweeter and cuter than
Shirley Temple even, a little angel, and she gave the child
everything she had.

Mona Lee couldn't understand why this was happening
now in view of the fact that she'd been a good mother
and had given Sharon a loving home. She'd gone to the
school programs, smiled when she was supposed to smile,
acted charmed, made friends with the teachers, and
taken Sharon to Sunday school every Sunday. Every Sunday. It was the right thing to do—give the child a Christian exposure early. Children can make up their minds
for themselves later on when they're adults. It had
amused Mona Lee when Sharon was only in the third
grade and had come home from Sunday school saying
that the Mexicans in her school were just as good as
white people, and she was singing a song she had learned
in Sunday school which went,

> Red and yellow, black and white
> All are perfect in His sight,
> Jesus loves the little children of the world.

Sharon argued like a little Christian missionary that if Jesus loved the Mexicans, then everybody else should, too, and that pleased Mona Lee so much. She had been very proud of her daughter, and told the story to a lot of people, to Harvey Watkins, among them.

Mona Lee even worked with the PTA, although she thought it was an organization established to exploit parents, making them work against their own children. It was an anti-child organization, the purpose of which was to make children conform to the norm set by establishment teachers, who themselves had blindly sold out to a decadent system. It was an organization not to help children but to put pressure on them so that they would grow up being like all the others. The PTA was just a cog in the educational machinery. The function of the PTA was to help produce a product, namely children, who would fit into the system. But she joined the PTA and quietly took part in its programs so that Sharon would know her mother was like the others, so she wouldn't feel alienated from the rest of the children because of some rebellious woman the poor girl hadn't chosen for a mother.

Mona Lee had helped with Brownies and Job's Daughters, too, even though she secretly thought those organizations were similar to the PTA in that their principal function was to help little American girls grow up to become obedient housewives who would thereafter have sex with their husbands, and only their husbands, at the snap of their oppressive fingers, and as good wives they would joyfully have babies and raise the fighting men and the future consumers for the system with a patient and kindly smile on their wifely faces, and a halo of motherhood around their heads, and who, with their offspring, would experience the good American life by buying a new car every three years, a color TV and a dishwasher, and all the paraphernalia and products which were supposed to be bought in order to fulfill the American dream, which Mona Lee said was false and corrupt. Sometimes Harvey Watkins thought he would go insane listening to her leftist theories. But Mona Lee, despite the fact she had given the appearance of a very ordinary mother, knew she had had her influence on Sharon. She knew she had raised Sharon's level of consciousness far above that set for little girls by the PTA and Job's Daughters and Brownies.

Sharon had gone with the right crowd in high school, studied, no budding Phi Beta Kappa, or anything like that, but she had done pretty well. Anyway Mona Lee would rather have a good healthy girl than some maladjusted genius or a bookish little stay-at-home worm, and Sharon and Mona Lee had been able to talk frankly about boys, and love and marriage, and there had been no secrets between mother and daughter.

Then without notice, as if suddenly there had been a horrid macabre brain transplant, Sharon slid down into this frightening pit of psychosis, this "late adolescent psychosis," as Mona Lee called it, trying to give it a name so that she could understand it better. And there was something about this Mexican. Mona Lee wished she could kill him. No, she wished he were already dead. No, she wished he would leave and go someplace else. That was a better thought. No, she wished she could kill him. She might just as well admit it.

"Some kids get through their adolescence harder and later than others," Watkins told Mona Lee. "And some never get over it at all," he added. "Of course, I think Sharon will get over hers, don't misunderstand me. I've seen plenty of cases like hers—it's the Oedipus thing—the mother-daughter conflict—it's the way a daughter throws off the shackles of her mother and becomes her own person. Rebellion," he said. "These kids all rebel in one way or another. Have to. She takes this Mexican who has long-cocked every girl in town, and then she shoves him right up your ass, too."

"Oh, Harvey!" Mona Lee said. "You're so common."

"Sharon knows how you've despised those people," Watkins said.

"I haven't despised them, Harvey. You know that!" Mona Lee said. "Why in the world would you say that? If anybody in this world has cared about them, I have. I've loved them too much. That's the problem."

"You hate those Mexicans," he said. "You just make it look like you love them. You fuss around with them, dole out all this dough—move 'em here and move 'em there." His long arms with the bony elbows sticking out of short sleeves were flapping around while he talked and his tie waved back and forth, too. "You moved them whenever you wanted like you used to put your dolls on the shelf. You had power over those people. You used them."

"That isn't true, Harvey. I don't need power. I don't understand how you can say such a thing." She was on the edge of tears. "What do you know about anything? What do you know about feeling, about love?" But before she started to sob she stalked out of the coffee room, and then Watkins followed her into her office, leaving the door open behind him, as usual, so that no one passing by would misunderstand their relationship.

"You need poor people. That's why you're in this helping business." He always called it "the helping business." "Without poor people you have no power," Watkins said.

"Why, that's—crap!" She finally got the word out.

"Without the poor, you're nothing," Watkins said.

"Why, that's crap, too," she said quickly, and she bared her white straight teeth, clenched them, and her plain face was tight with anger, and the anger stopped the tears.

"You couldn't stand it till you got your hooks in that Esquibel woman. And once you got her you never let her loose. Haven't let her go all these years. Couldn't let her go if you wanted to. You'd lose your power."

"Aren't you getting a little tired of playing psychiatrist?" she whispered through her teeth.

"If you loved them, you would have left them alone," Watkins persisted.

"Let them starve, I suppose—and freeze to death, like you wanted to do. I remember that," she said. "You would have let them freeze!"

"There were beans in the house, you remember that, too, and flour."

"The kids were cold," she said with sudden pity in her voice.

"The kids were all right. They were cold, but you needed them worse than they needed you."

"How can you say that?" she said, and now she sounded exasperated, and she still spoke in a whisper.

"You held those Esquibel people up to your daughter—I've heard you do it. 'Don't be like them—if you don't go to school, you'll grow up like those Esquibel kids. If you don't learn a profession, you'll be like Mrs. Esquibel—be a whore, have a bunch of kids with no father, no house—live in a shack—live on beans. You want to live on beans? Want to have dirt for floors—have to do it with the railroad men to make a living? Be a boxcar woman? Do you want that? And they do it like animals.' I remember hearing you say that. 'They do it like animals. Don't get mixed up with them. They do it like animals. Animals!' Don't you remember that?" Watkins asked.

"No."

"Do you and your husband do it like animals?" Harvey Watkins asked with a small sneer on his face and an eyebrow cocked.

"Don't be impertinent," she said. "Get the hell out of here. I have work to do."

"You didn't even sleep with your husband. You know that. You don't sleep with him now."

"I do," she said.

"You do not," he said, as if he were reading a plain script plainly, and Mona Lee Murphy just looked down, fumbled with the papers on her desk and acted like she was reading them. She said nothing. Harvey Watkins could get to a person, right to their bottom, and sometimes he wasn't kind. "I know your passion," Watkins said, starting it all over again.

"I gave my passion to you, Harvey," she said, putting the gentleness back in her voice.

"Yes," he said, as if he hadn't heard what she was really saying. "And Sharon knew."

"She knew nothing. She knows nothing," she protested suddenly in a loud voice.

"She does know, maybe not about us, but she knows there is nothing animal between you and him—nothing animal at home. No passion. No love. Death and marriage—who wants it?"

"You have it," she said.

"Yeah," Watkins said. "I have it." This time he looked away. "But who wants it?" Then he had reached over and grabbed her arm firmly, looked out the door to make sure no one was looking in, and leaned over to Mona Lee and his long nose with the glasses at the end was almost in her plain face, and he shook her arm just a little so that she had to look him in the eye. "And you told Sharon they were animals. She knows that animals are at least alive. Sharon knows how to punish you. The animal in her is her weapon." Mona Lee was silent, and Watkins was silent, and he let loose of Mona Lee's arm, and he began to think about Agneda Esquibel. Finally he said, "People need dignity, not money."

"It's not dignified to be a whore," Mona Lee Murphy said absently, almost automatically, starting the old argument again. "But I always believed Agneda Esquibel was a whore who did it for the right reasons."

"There's more dignity in selling your ass than begging for food," Watkins said, and the conversation had gone nowhere, as always.

"It's the system that's wrong, then," Mona Lee Murphy said. "People shouldn't have to be either hungry or whores. This is a lousy system and you know it, Harvey." It was easier to talk about the system. "How can the rich hoard it all so a poor woman like her has to either let her kids starve or sell her body to feed them?"

"Cut that shit," Watkins said. "I don't need any more of that commie shit."

"You never can face it, Harvey—never want to talk about it with me, or anybody, like you're afraid of it—like knowing the truth might hurt you. All welfare is is society's sick tribute to the poor. You know that. It's the token payment by the rich to the hungry so the rich can go on taking from the poor." She sounded like one of those raging radicals who preach on a street corner in big cities, Watkins thought, and when she was like this, the words came tumbling out of her lips and there was no stopping her. "Welfare is only a salve for the conscience of the rich—it's a gift out of guilt so they can look moral. They can't look moral when they wrest it from the poor and the weak and the helpless, and let them starve. So we have *welfare!*" She slammed her small soft fist down on the table, but there was hardly a sound from it. "We have welfare," she said again, and pounded her fist again, "and that makes it all right. Now they can go on stealing and grabbing from the poor, and we're nothing but their lackeys. They need you and me to dole it out, and, by God"— she hardly ever said by God—"and, by God, I'm going to give as much of it away as I can." There wasn't any reason to argue with the woman and so, as he always did at times like that, he got up and quietly left.

But later on that day Mona Lee Murphy talked to Harvey Watkins again. She waited until the office was empty, and she held back from the others who were leaving, and when Watkins himself was about to go she walked up to him, looked up again into his long face, which appeared like some face a careless sculptor had turned out before it was finished, and she said, "Harvey, help me think this through. Couldn't we make them get married?"

"Who? Joe and Sharon? What do you want to do that for? You can't make anybody do anything," he said kindly, looking back down at her while he wound a red woolen muffler around his long neck. "You're wanting to move your dollies around on the shelf again—have the dollies get married. Besides, you've been against them getting married all along. What's changed your mind?"

"Oh, God, Harvey," she had sobbed softly, numb and almost falling into his arms. "She's pregnant again." And then Mona Lee Murphy had cried a long time and Harvey Watkins had held her in his arms and felt ashamed that he had been so cruel to her, so dense and insensitive. He should have guessed something was wrong. He should have heard the hurt in her angry voice, and so now he waited patiently for the sobbing to stop. And suddenly Mona Lee Murphy did stop it, as if she had slammed a door on a bad scene, and she pulled herself away and brushed the wrinkles out of her blouse left there from his embrace.

"Well," she said, with her chin up and her eyes red and dabbed dry, "well, we'll just have to make the best of things." She was that kind of a woman—always had been. "But I think they'll have to get married this time."

"Leave things alone," Harvey Watkins said. "Let 'em work it out. You can't just keep moving these people around."

"Well, I have to save the babies," she said. "They need a name."

"You want them to have 'Esquibel' for a name, I suppose," he said.

"I have to save the babies."

"That isn't your job," Watkins said. "That's what God does, if you believe in God, and if you don't, that's what nature does. It's survival of the fittest out there."

"God. Oh, God, I can't stand to hear any more of that. It's so cruel. You couldn't talk that way if you had children." All of a sudden she knew she had hurt Harvey Watkins, and she knew it by the look on his face. He hadn't wanted children he said once, and he claimed even now he was glad he never had any. Mona Lee rushed to him and touched his arm, and looked up into his eyes, up along the long bridge of his nose, which hung down sadly, the glasses having slid almost to the end again. "Oh, Harvey, I'm sorry," she said. "Oh, Harvey, sometimes I wish I were a man. I wish I weren't a mother—that I didn't have any children at all. I wish I were like you. This is driving me mad," she said. "Children cause more pain than joy. You'll never know the pain of a mother," and then she walked away from him to get her coat.

Harvey Watkins didn't say anything. He didn't know what to say. Finally he said, "You lose sight of the overall plan of nature." He tried to say it gently, compassionately. His voice even cracked a little, but he didn't think he had let it crack on purpose. "If we fed all the starving people in India, they would just have more and more kids until there wouldn't even be room for anyone to stand. Then there would be disease and famine and war to kill off the excess. It's the way of nature. It may be cruel, but who said nature wasn't cruel?"

"Can't man rise above nature? Must he always just be an animal?" She put on her coat. "But one's own children—one's own grandchildren—it's the law of nature to protect your own, too, Harvey. That's the law of nature, too." Suddenly she said, "You're right, Harvey. I should've let the Esquibel kids starve." Then she put her hand to her mouth, too late. She had already said it. Oh, God, she had already said it! But her grandchildren were entitled to be something more than the illegitimate offspring of some Mexican stud horse. She had even said so to Sharon and then daughter and mother had fought again.

Sharon's first little girl was born in January and one month later this fourteen-year-old Mexican girl, Roberta Rodriguez, had filed charges against Joe—statutory rape —and now Sharon herself was pregnant again, a second time! Joe was in jail, and besides he was still married to Louisa, and they kept his child, Little Joe, at home, probably Mrs. Esquibel's idea to keep Joe out of trouble and to stop the prosecuting attorney from charging him with non-support or something.

"Fourteen years old!" Mona Lee Murphy exclaimed. "While he has my daughter pregnant the second time, he's out raping little fourteen-year-olds." She hadn't meant to scream the words. "What are we supposed to do, Harvey? The Rodriguez girl was in the other day and wants assistance. What are you going to do, Harvey?" Mona Lee was suddenly quiet and she fixed her tired eyes on Harvey Watkins.

"You know the policy," Harvey Watkins said.

"The policy," Mona Lee Murphy said back. She knew the policy all right. Harvey Watkins would take the girl over to the county attorney's office to sign a complaint against Joe Esquibel before Watkins would agree to give her assistance for her baby. You want money for the doctor? For the hospital—for the baby? You'll have to sign a complaint. It's policy here. And then they would throw Joe Esquibel in jail. That was the policy, all right.

"What if they send him to prison, Harvey? What will happen to Sharon and the babies?"

"Well, what are you asking me? Do you want me to make an exception for Joe Esquibel so he can go on screwing all the little fourteen-year-olds in this county, so we can have a new and bigger crop of bastard babies to feed each year? A policy is a policy or it isn't a policy at all."

"Oh, Harvey, do you really have to be that way?"

"Yes, I have to be that way, goddamn it," he shouted. "And I'm doing it for you. Somebody has to stop him. I'm doing it for you." He didn't sound like he was doing anything for anybody. He only sounded angry. "If I don't stop him he'll give you a half dozen more little bastard grandkids, and we'll end up feeding them, too."

"Oh, Harvey." She started to cry again. She couldn't stop herself. It was plain to see. "Oh, Harvey, what shall I do? I'm a mother. Can't you hear me?" She was weeping softly. "I'm a mother. She is my child. My baby." She was trying to cry like a lady, and Harvey Watkins' heart was touched again. It hurt him to see her hurt. She was a good woman, he thought, fuzzy-headed as she was about all her social theories, which had been pounded into her head at college when she was young and impressionable. There were too many commies in the colleges nowadays. The colleges in the country were run by the commies. But he loved her. He was sure of that even though he had always tried not to get involved, to remain professional. A man can't do his job if he gets involved, and a policy is a policy.

Harvey Watkins put his arms around Mona Lee Murphy and then kissed her wet cheek, and then he kissed her mouth, and she came up close to him and they felt each other's heat through their heavy coats, and then as if to lighten things up, just to show her his funny creative side, which she said she always loved, he unwound his red scarf, and he tied the two of them together with an overly serious look on his long sad face, and then with the red scarf tied around their waists as tightly as he could tie it, they began to move, their coats still between them, and

Mona Lee had quit her sobbing, and she breathed harder now with her mouth open and her eyes kind of glazed and half shut, and then the two of them struggled over to the light switch as if they were in a three-legged race. Harvey Watkins led the way and when they turned out the early evening lights in the welfare office it was dark, and Harvey Watkins locked the doors from the inside. He untied the scarf and took off her coat, and then his, and he laid Mona Lee Murphy down on his desk. Later on she told Harvey Watkins she couldn't have respected him if he hadn't gone on with the case against Joe Esquibel.

That same night Sharon came to her mother and begged her to go to Harvey and get the complaint against Joe dropped.

"Please, Mother," she begged. "I promise I'll never see him again. I'll do anything you want. Just go to Harvey Watkins and get Joe out of jail and get the complaint dropped—please, Mother. Please.

"Oh, please, Mother.

"Oh, please," softly, through tears.

"Oh, please."

But Mona Lee Murphy said she couldn't. It was office policy. And then Sharon finally stopped crying, and looked straight at her mother.

"Office policy, my ass. You could get Harvey Watkins to do anything you want," Sharon said.

"Why don't you leave Mr. Watkins out of this?"

"What's Harvey Watkins to you, Mother?" Sharon shouted. "What's he to you? Why don't you tell me?"

"Harvey Watkins is nothing to me," Mona Lee Murphy said in a very quiet voice. "Just leave him out of this."

"I don't believe he's nothing to you," Sharon said, "but I should—he's such an ugly silly bastard."

"Get out!" Mona Lee Murphy said. She said it in a whisper. "Get out!" she whispered again. And Sharon had gathered up her baby and had gone back out into the night holding the baby close to the other baby growing inside her. Then she drove her '53 Chevy down the dirt back streets of Rawlins to Agneda Esquibel's little shack across the tracks, and Agneda Esquibel let Sharon in, and she lived there with the brown faces, with the brown babies, and the brown tribal mother, all in that one room with the dirt floor, and she felt the warmth of the good earth coming up to her in the early winter.

20

THE ENDLESS silent sea was as clear and deep as a Wyoming sky, and on the silent bottom of the sea the silt and sand were slowly cemented together over a time so vast that the sea itself became equivalent to some mere salt droplet that had emerged from primeval pores, and then the drop dried up and the ocean floor became a prairie for farther than the eye could see, and the silt and sand became plain gray rock out of which men, of late, had fashioned a place to cage other men, a place they called the state penitentiary. The rock had been dug out of the innocent earth, fractured and shattered, chipped and hammered, contorted and cut and gouged into squares and sharp-edged shapes, which were stacked and recemented into a mostly square but irrelevant and ugly place on the peaceful plains. And later, man, finding it easier to make his own material than to rip and tear it from the virgin earth, had manufactured a plain yellow-gray brick, which he then also cemented together to make the Carbon County Courthouse at Rawlins, Wyoming.

Inside the courthouse after the passage of less than half a century, which is a time so short it is hardly measurable in the course of history, the stairs that lead to the courtroom above were already creaking, claiming to be old, and close by the courtroom were other important rooms that were used in the justice business—among them the judge's chambers, where the judges sat alone and pondered the nature of justice, the Clerk of Court's office, the jury room, and the rooms where books and records were kept—all of which had an official smell, like the smell of old paper and old men. The doors of the courtroom were open and there were different smells inside, of human bodies, of the faint odor of sweat oozing out of frightened pores—creating new salty droplets on the skin, which, in the judgment of the universe, were indistinguishable from other primeval oceans—and inside the courtroom there were the sounds of people, muffled monotonous sing-songy sounds of people engaged in their terrible work of banishment.

It is not easy to banish. Even the Indian chief held long powwows before he exiled a member of his tribe. He and the tribal family danced around the night's fire and counseled and sang, and listened to the woeful cries from the widow of the slain. And the children of the accused held back, wide-eyed and afraid, hanging together in a small cluster separate from the children of the slain, and the noises of the singing warriors and the sounds of the beating drums drove out the yapping and crying of the prairie wolf in the distance so that on such occasions one could not hear any of the night sounds, and the night snow, falling lightly into the black late fall forest, fell on the warriors' heads and made them wet so that they glistened in the firelight, and made the dancing ground sticky under the pounding feet. And the late fall snow foretold of the agony of banishment in winter, and finally the chief pronounced it, his eyes as bright as the fire, and his arm pointing straight to the tip of his finger. Banishment. Banishment from the tribe was the verdict, and the accused and his squaws and the children of the accused went out into the late fall without horses, or teepees, or bows, or arrows, and in years past some had chosen to die at the hands of the tribe rather than to be banished. It was better to die in honor than to live as the lowly "sheepeaters," to creep after the flocks of the Big Horns, to follow them so meekly with heads bowed so close to the ground that even a coyote following the buffalo herds in the winter to eat their dung, and hoping to eat their dead, was ashamed. The sheepeaters followed the sheep like docile helpless lambs, at a great distance at first, and gradually over a long time closer, until they were like the alpine raven, which lands among the sheep to peer and to peck, and then the banished were one day accepted again, not by man but by sheep. They became sheep, and they ate their own, stole a lamb or ate an old ram too stiff to find his way down the great rock walls that touch the sky in the back mountains, down from the lonely and haunted places that rise up, barren and empty. The sheep lived where the sharp rocks cut the feet of men and the wind cried endlessly without reason, where the clouds whirled by like the crazy twisting twirling ghosts of squaws and there were no trees—too high, no willows—too high, no paintbrush or lush and lazy flowers in the spring—because it was a place that was too high, and no wolves—because it was too high for even the father of the dog to live. There was only rock and space and sky, and the banished, crawling and shivering on the ground, holding back until one day they touched an old ewe and her lamb and they were accepted into the herd. But most of the banished died in the winter and were covered by snows deeper than a teepee.

In the Rawlins courtroom Joe Esquibel stood trial for rape. The undersounds were the heavy breathing of men and the whispering of the mothers. In the courtroom on the east side sat Agneda Esquibel, and the sisters of Joe Esquibel, and the husband of one of the sisters, and some children, along with the friends of Joe Esquibel, young bucks, tough and sinewy, their faces quick to smile and quick to sneer, and they sat restlessly, ready to spring up, ready to move, to move out of bodies accustomed to moving. But the young bucks held back. There was a railing that separated the spectators' seating from the court arena, the bar, they call it. Immediately behind the bar in the first row of seats sat this young white woman, the only white woman in the courtroom. She had a baby in her arms. She was pregnant. Her name was Sharon Murphy, and she was blond and scrubbed as a nun, blue-eyed, and she covered her pregnancy with a heavy black cloth coat with an artificial black fur collar and she whispered over the bar to Joe's attorney, Frank Bowron.

Across the way on the west side of the courtroom sat the family of Roberta Rodriguez, the complaining witness, who had just turned fifteen years old, the prosecutrix, as she is called in the law. She was a small girl, already two weeks past due with the baby she claimed was the child of Joe Esquibel. She was sitting next to her mother. It was a place of mothers, this courtroom, as are all courtrooms, and other places where humans fight for their lives. The mothers watch while their offspring are judged and in the judging the mothers are judged. Behind Roberta Rodriguez and her mother sat the father, seeming alone, and behind him were other brown faces, all on the west side of the courtroom, faces which held together on the side of the prosecutrix.

The judge came in. He was the Honorable Vernon Bentley, judge of the district court, and he lived in Laramie, but the town of Rawlins was in his district. He was a bald man with a remnant of blond hair on the sides of his temples, now seeming gray, and he had wide open blue eyes as if he had been frightened once and all but the eyes had recovered. But they were kind eyes, and he had a relaxed, easy smile, like Bing Crosby's, I always thought.

Joe's attorney, Frank Bowron, was a tall man, as tall as Harvey Watkins, taller maybe and better muscled. He was balder even than the judge himself, and had sharp features and big feet encased in plain-toed black shoes—nothing fancy about the man, a friendly man, and as soon as he opened his mouth one could tell he was intelligent, different from other men, and sensitive. "You can't tell much about a person by how he looks," my mother used to say, "but you'll know him the first time he opens his mouth." There is something about a sensitive man that comes out even when he tries to be professional. A lawyer is not supposed to show his feelings, because a courtroom is no place for feelings, they say.

Joe looked good. He had a new crisp crew cut, and wore a plain brown suit with a plain tie, and his cheeks were still a little chubby, making him look boyish, and his eyes were as bright as a wolf's dark eyes, and his tall, lean body was muscular and wound tight. He and Bowron whispered back and forth. Then the jury came in, all Rawlins people, all white, and Joe Esquibel and Frank Bowron stood up as the jury filed by them into the jury box. The jury was made up mostly of nondescript men and one or two plain-looking women, ordinary people who a person would pass every day on the street and never notice, a small, unremarkable mob one would say. But the prosecutor was a handsome man, Oscar Hall's predecessor, a young man named John Crow. He was also tall, not as tall as Frank Bowron, but dark with good skin, and even features.

Bowron was complaining to the court, as lawyers always do, but they use technical language so it does not sound like complaining, and if one listens, the lawyer talk sounds like a chant, like the singing of some ancient liturgy. Bowron was saying that the prosecution, the state of Wyoming, must "elect" as he called it. "Was the alleged act committed on the fifteenth or on the fourteenth of February? The state must elect." Then the state, through its handsome attorney, John Crow, had joined in the chanting and said, "Well, the state did not have to elect. The act was committed *on* or *about* the fifteenth." Then the court joined in the chanting and said that the defendant's objection was overruled and that the state's position was sustained, and that the state did not have to elect, and it was proper for the proceedings to continue. The prosecuting attorney had called the little Rodriguez girl to the stand.

It seemed almost obscene to watch her waddle to the witness chair, baby carrying baby, her stomach begging to be emptied of this child, so stretched past due, and she claimed that she was now fifteen but she had been only fourteen when it happened. She was one of twelve children, she said, in the small voice of a child with a Spanish accent in answer to the prosecution's questions. She said her father was not working. Made a person want to cry to hear her, and her stomach stuck out past her knees as she sat there, and she clamped her knees tightly together on the witness chair. Her mother worked at the City Steam Laundry. Roberta Rodriguez had had several dates with Joe Esquibel, she said, and then on February 14, Joe had picked her up on the corner near her home. That was because her folks didn't like him and wouldn't let him come to the house for her.

"Where did you go?" John Crow, the prosecutor, asked, a man speaking to a child, sweet-like, awfully kind and nice.

"We went riding around for a while and went and parked."

"Where did you park?"

"The Rawlins Hill, where you can see all the cars and the whole town."

"What happened then?"

"Well, we talked awhile, and then he asked me to give in to him," she said in her baby voice. "And I didn't at the time. I hesitated awhile and then I did."

"Now, Roberta, by 'give in,' what do you mean? Tell the jury."

"To have sexual intercourse," she said, this baby, with baby, sounding like she was reading from a sex education text. Joe whispered to Frank Bowron, his lawyer, and Bowron put his hand on Joe's knee to quiet him, and Sharon was leaning over, her blond hair looking out of place in this place of black-haired people, and her blue eyes looked worried and wild and strange in that room of black eyes, and she had her hands wrapped around her coat, holding it tightly to her own pregnant belly, holding onto her child, and whispering strongly to Frank Bowron, who tried to ignore her.

"Are you aware of what sexual intercourse is?"

"Yes," Roberta Rodriguez said. "It is when the man puts his male organ into the woman's female organ." She said it with big eyes at the prosecutor. Then she looked over to the jury quickly and down to her hands folded below her stomach.

"Did that occur?"

"Yes."

"And the defendant's male organ entered your female organ, is that correct?"

"Yes."

And there was the state's case, as easy as that, statutory rape, the felony that arises out of unlawful carnal knowledge of a female child under the age of eighteen. Rape, they call it, because by law an unmarried female child under eighteen is conclusively presumed, no exceptions, to be unable to consent, and sex without consent is rape. The logic is clear.

"I gave in to him the last part of January the first time," she said. "And he was drinking a little bit, and I thought I'd better give in to him or else he will hit me, because I had heard he had hit other girls so I gave in to him that night."

"Did you ever tell Joe Esquibel how old you were?"

"Yes. He asked me once. I told him I was fifteen, but that was before I was fifteen." And then she told the jury that Joe used rubbers before, but on the fourteenth of February he didn't. Then Frank Bowron cross-examined her. He stood there towering over that small pregnant sparrow and she became the jury's sparrow, and the judge's, and as it always is with the weak and helpless, she became the most powerful person in the courtroom. She said the assistant director of public welfare did not, absolutely did not, tell her she would get no help from the welfare unless she prosecuted Joe for rape. He never said anything to that effect at all. No. And, yes, she said to Frank Bowron weakly on cross-examination that she had been in the welfare office and she was getting the slips to go to a doctor from him, meaning Watkins, and the court sustained an objection to Bowron's question about the family receiving funds from public welfare for the support of other illegitimate children in the same home; and then the girl said no, again, that Watkins did not make her file charges of rape against Joe Esquibel.

"What he told me," Roberta said, "was I should tell Mr. Watkins who it was and maybe that way they could help me out." Then she had gone to the office of the county attorney in the company of Watkins and had signed a complaint against Joe, but she said she had not been influenced to sign a complaint at all.

She admitted to Bowron that when she was twelve she had made complaints to the sheriff about other men. "You named a number of people, didn't you?" Bowron asked. She was so young.

"Well, I just named two."

"Just two?"

"Well, before that I was scared, and I named two more before that, ahead of them first two."

"That makes four?"

"Yes."

"And no prosecution was ever made of any of these four men, was there?"

"No."

"Were those charges true? Had those people raped you?"

"Yes, they had."

"Had they?"

"Yes," she said.

And Joe Esquibel was whispering wildly to Bowron now, who came back to the table to hush him, and Sharon was leaning over the rail, and there were noises rising up out of the people in the courtroom, like a whole tribe holding back, and the judge called a recess. And at the recess Bowron had to tell Sharon that he, not she, was running the case—that he was the lawyer, not she. Then she said why didn't Bowron tell the jury that the girl was lying, and that it had already been proved that she had made false claims against four men, and that she was a wild one and had been sent off to Sheridan to the Girls' Reform School because of this whole thing when she was only twelve, and now the girl was trying to do the same thing to Joe. Why didn't Bowron tell that to the jury?

"You gotta stop her," Sharon had said. "I paid you. I scraped it together, to save Joe—not to hear that girl get up there and lie to that jury, and you have to do something."

Bowron had to get tough. He told her to sit down and be quiet. He was handling the case, and when Sharon did the talking Joe said nothing. Afterward, the testimony went on.

Roberta knew that it was on the fourteenth of February that she had given in to Joe because he didn't have any rubbers that night, is how she put it, and *"No, on the fifteenth of February she did not go out with him—not on that night."* And the only date she was sure she had sexual relations with Joe Esquibel was the *fourteenth,* and she was fourteen years old then and fifteen now.

Then she said "Sharon," and she looked over at Sharon sitting behind the bar on the edge of her seat. "Sharon, she wanted me to drop the charges, but I told her it would be up to the county attorney." And when she said that, Sharon leaned over again, frantically trying to get the attention of Frank Bowron, and he had to get up again and go talk to her quietly, to calm her down, and to warn her once more to contain herself, especially in front of the jury.

Then the swearing match began, as if out of some primitive place of the past, as if out of the very memory of man, recorded and programmed in every cell, the families in the tribes lining up. Roberta's mother—Mrs. Lupe Rodriguez—took the stand. The mother. Oh, the mother of twelve, whose words carried the weight of all of the babies of her womb, and no, she said, Joe Esquibel was not allowed at their house, and that's about all she could say, but in saying it she had blessed her baby and her baby's side of the case. Frank Bowron asked only if she had ever seen Joe Esquibel with her daughter, and she admitted she had not, and other than that there was no cross-examination by Bowron, not of a mother of twelve.

And then the sisters came in—first it was Maria Rodriguez, the eighteen-year-old sister, who had seen Roberta with Joe one night and had grabbed Roberta and said, "Let's go home," but Roberta had said, "No," and it was the *fourteenth for sure* because she was uptown to get a Valentine card for a guy she was going with. Then came another sister, Leila Sanchez, twenty, who double-dated with Tony Marquiz and Joe and Roberta, and she said that she and Roberta told each other everything and especially about when their periods were due, that they were just that way with each other. When Bowron asked on cross-examination, "Was it because you knew your sister was having sexual relationships with many men that you asked such things?" Leila Sanchez said, "No, sir." And then, subject to calling the doctor out of order later on, because the doctor was too busy to come to court when it was his turn to testify, the state rested its case. Easy cases, statutory rape.

It is clear that fourteen-year-old girls should be protected against the likes of Joe Esquibel. No one disputed that, and yet Frank Bowron thought Joe should be defended. It is the way the system works. Even the guilty should receive a defense in this system, but old men pass the sex laws. Wise old men who vote "Yea." Yea to the statutory rape law, which says that no matter what, even if the girl begs for it, cries for it—it makes no difference. What if the boy is only ten and the woman is one day short of her eighteenth birthday? What then? It makes no difference. It is statutory rape. But what if the woman helps the child get it in, just partway, quick like, "penetration," as the men of the law call it? Even if she helps the boy penetrate, well, it's rape nonetheless, statutory rape. But what if she puts a gun to the head of a man and says, "If you don't do it to me I'll kill you"—what then? Well, she is conclusively presumed by the lawmakers, out of the very wisdom of the ages, to be unable to consent. Rape is no defense for rape. Old men know about justice.

Old men in the legislature stand together away from the women, like a herd of useless old bulls shaded up in the breeding season, and the senators make private jokes among themselves in the latrine where great bills are finally settled, and one honorable senator from a county up north said, "The only reason there's a line like this in front of the pisser is that half these old bastards can't start, and the other half can't stop," and they all laughed. And the other senator, puffing his cigar and holding up his belly, said, "Yeah, I know what ya mean." There is camaraderie among senators. And then the one from up north spoke. "Well, like the fella says, 'I'm gettin' so old I

have to stand 'em on their heads and drop it in,' " and he
talked in a loud voice, and everybody laughed again, and
they forgot when they were boys, boiling hot boys who
suffered along in their insanity watching the young girls
with pretty tight little swinging asses, but old men know
about justice.

Frank Bowron called his first defense witness, Lupe
Rodriguez, the father of the girl herself.

"In your dealings with your daughter have you found
that she has always been truthful with you? Has she always told you the truth?"

"Not all the time, no."

"Did you, in January or February, see your daughter in
the downtown section of Rawlins?"

"Yes, lots of times."

"What would she be doing?"

"Walking the streets," he said in a thick accent from an
honest face. "That is all I can say." Then the handsome
Crow went after this father on cross-examination.

"Mr. Rodriguez, you have a lot of trouble around the
house, don't you?"

"Quite a bit, yes."

"You are involved in a divorce action, aren't you?"

"Yeah."

"One of the reasons is the fact that you use obscene
and vile language around your children, isn't it?"

"Yes, I do," he said, and his face was sad and he
seemed embarrassed to tell the truth.

"All right," the prosecutor said. "You call them dirty
names, don't you?"

"Yeah," he said, looking down, this father of twelve,
looking down at his own hands and not at his woman.

"Call your wife dirty names?"

"Once in a while."

"As a matter of fact, you don't like your children, do
you?"

He was still looking down, but his face was as easy to
read as a signboard with big print, and he looked hurt.
He loved his children, but he was trapped.

"Sometimes I don't and sometimes I do."

"Do you provide for them?"

The man hesitated. "Sometimes."

"Where do you work?"

"I don't work no place. Worked three weeks last time for the Water Department."

"Do you believe Roberta Rodriguez when she says she is pregnant by Joe Esquibel?" The prosecutor was asking for it.

"I don't believe it," he said.

"You don't believe that?" the prosecutor said in dismay.

"No."

"Why don't you believe that?" the prosecutor was shouting, asking for it again.

"Because the way she was going out all the time. I don't know who it could be—could be somebody else and blaming Joe."

"You talked this over with Joe, didn't you?" The prosecutor was still shouting.

"No."

"Did you talk to Joe's attorney about it?"

"No. Last night a little bit, yeah. Nothin' about Joe. Nothin' about Joe. . . . Everybody would honk. She would go out and say, 'I'll be right back.' How did I know?"

"Do you know that it wasn't Joe Esquibel?"

"No. I can't say it was Joe or who it was."

And now John Crow shouted again, saying this father had a lot of nerve coming into a courtroom claiming his daughter was a liar when he really didn't know, and Bowron objected that the statement of the prosecutor was argument. Attorneys aren't supposed to argue with the witnesses, and the judge sustained Bowron's objection.

Then the prosecutor, one could hardly blame him, I suppose, seething yet, asked for it once more. "Let me ask you again, why don't you believe your daughter?"

And again the poor father said it.

"Because lots of the time they lie too much. That is why."

And the prosecutor was shocked, as if he'd never heard the answer just a minute before, and he repeated the poor man's answer with a deep sarcasm in his voice, "Lots of times they lie too much?"

"Yeah, not only to me. They lied to my wife, too." He looked over at his woman now, but she wouldn't look back, and Roberta just sat by her mother, looking blankly at her father with her big black eyes, and then Frank Bowron called Agneda Esquibel to the stand.

She got up slowly from the opposite side of the courtroom from the Rodriguezes, and she walked solidly, heavy-footed, like a tired woman walking across the fields of her labor, and her face was naked, and you could see the fear there. The walls of this courtroom had witnessed the woe and the retching of this woman before, had soaked up her cries, and the cries of other mothers before her. Agneda Esquibel sat down in the witness chair, to swear for her children, in the way of mothers, and now the words of Agneda Esquibel came out in tiny choked-up sounds like mumblings out of some nightmare.

"Speak up," Bowron said. "How old is your son, Joe?"

"Twenty," she said down into her hands.

"Speak up."

"Twenty." One could hardly hear her. And the court said, "If you don't speak up, you won't be able to testify." He knew Agneda Esquibel. "You can talk louder than that, can't you?" the judge said in a loud and unfriendly voice.

"Yes," and she looked more frightened.

"Where were you on the fourteenth of February?"

"I was home."

"What were you doing?"

"I was making a party for my girl."

"What is the name of your girl?"

"Donna Esquibel."

"What was the date of her birth?"

"Fourteenth February." She couldn't remember who was there at the party. There were adults, children, maybe thirty or forty people, and they were there from seven in the evening until late that night.

"Was Joe there in your presence through the whole evening?" Bowron said.

"Yes," she said. Yes, the mother said for her son, and then the others on the west side of the courtroom joined in the swearing match. Gilbert Torrez, the owner of the Wyoming Bar on Front Street, was at the party. He knew it was the fourteenth. Checked his records and saw where he had hired old Archie to sit in for him while he went to Donna Esquibel's party, and Donna, Joe's little sister, testified it was her party. She was so bashful, only fifteen, too. Joe was there all night. Never left. And then Elma had testified, now Mrs. Frank Fisher, and she said that Joe was there all night except to go to the restroom, and Frank Fisher, her husband, said the same thing.

While he was testifying, Frank Fisher, twenty-four, said that when Roberta was twelve she had accused him of rape, and the sheriff had come for him and when Roberta admitted it wasn't him at all they had sent her to the girls' school at Sheridan. Then Nick Trujillo took the stand and said Roberta had also accused him of rape and the sheriff had come for him, too, but he took a lie detector test in Casper and passed it. And Leo Trujillo said he was twenty-three and had dated her, and he had never seen Joe and Roberta alone. He and Joe had picked her up sometimes, drove around a little, but just dropped her off and then they would go down and shoot a game of pool.

Lawrence Gonzales, sixteen, said he was at his cousin Donna's party and was playing the guitar for the party's music along with his dad, Casey Gonzales, who played the sax, and his other cousin, Ernie Montoya, who played the guitar. To his own knowledge Joe was there all the time. Finally, Frank Bowron called Joe himself.

Joe walked up to be sworn with tight steps, different from the way he usually walked, and he looked as solemn as a soldier. Sharon watched him go to the witness stand, her arms folded across the baby in her stomach, and she sat back as far as she could on the hard wooden courtroom bench. She looked over at the jury, and if they had looked back at her they could have seen the fear frozen on her face, and then Sharon looked over to Frank

Bowron, who was the most imposing man in the court, although he had this softness about him. Joe sat down on the witness chair, crossed his legs, and then uncrossed them as if he were uncomfortable. Bowron asked him only a few questions, got right to it, no warm-up at all. "Have you gone out with Roberta Rodriguez?"

"Well, I have took her riding around and that, but actually I have never really gone out with her." His voice was high like the sound of a man with hands on his throat.

"Have you ever had sexual intercourse with her?"

Joe didn't blink. "No, I haven't . . . we used to pick up them girls once in a while when she was walking around," and that was it—that was his testimony, nothing much more, two or three minutes, but it wasn't like that on cross-examination. The handsome county attorney asked Joe if he didn't offer to marry Roberta if she would just drop the charges, but Joe said no, that was his mother's idea. That's what his mother wanted. You know mothers. He had gone with his mother to see Roberta and his mother and Roberta had talked, but he didn't remember what they talked about.

"What did Roberta say, if anything?"

"Well, nothin'. She just talked. That was all. She didn't say much of anything that was important or anything like that."

"What did she say?" the prosecutor asked again, pushing Joe hard as he could.

"I don't remember what she said exactly," Joe said in an angry way. The pink came to his cheeks, and you could see the fight come on his face. He could probably have jumped down from the witness chair, and grabbed the prosecutor, but he was tied without ties to that chair. His knuckles pressed white. He had a short fuse, they said. Didn't take much with Joe Esquibel. "I ain't supposed to remember everything," he said finally, sarcastically, angrily, and the judge, sensing something coming, called him down for it. He called him "Mr. Witness."

"Mr. Witness, you are instructed not to argue with counsel in the manner in which you are." Judge Bentley sat straight and stiff and stern. And then the prosecutor kept at it. What did he remember that Roberta said, and Joe kept denying any memory, remembered nothing. Nothing.

"Did your mother ask Roberta to marry you?"

"I didn't hear her ask," Joe said, and that was the defense, that simple. Joe didn't do it ever, and he didn't do it on the fourteenth of February for sure, because he was not even with the girl that night and his whole family and all his friends had sworn to the alibi, and besides the girl had sworn falsely before about men and had been sent off to the Girls' Reform School at Sheridan and even her father knew that and freely admitted she was a liar, and Joe didn't remember any of the rest. Moreover, when the doctor finally took the stand, Dr. Charles Roland, he said she was a couple of weeks late already and it didn't look like she was going to deliver right away, maybe sometime in the next ten days, and barring complications, 97 percent of all females with the same last period date as claimed by Roberta would have delivered by now.

So with all that the prosecutor had to call Roberta back to the stand. Now she testified to a different date—the date was now Friday, the *fifteenth*. She remembered that because she was carrying her books home like she always did on Friday afternoon for her weekend study, and now she said she and Joe did it on both the fourteenth *and* the fifteenth although she previously said she didn't do it with Joe on the fifteenth at all, but had done it only on the fourteenth, and she said Joe admitted the baby was his, and he had asked her to marry him.

"Then I told him, Joe, I don't think it will work, and he says, 'Why couldn't we try it out?' and I says, 'No, I wouldn't like to try it out,' " and she said, "Well, all I wanted in the first place was my bills to be taken care of and my baby taken care of. Right then," she added, "when we was talkin' he admitted it was his baby, but I knew he wouldn't settle down."

On cross-examination Bowron called her attention to the fact that she previously swore she hadn't had sex with

Joe on the fifteenth, and now she said she did, after all
those people had come forward from the west side of the
courtroom to testify to Joe's alibi. But it made no difference. She had the power, this little bird, the power to
erase testimony, to rearrange the facts, the great power
that protects the meek, and which, as the prediction goes,
will cause them to inherit the earth. It was the time of the
meek, and there was nothing Frank Bowron could do
with this child with child. Even the judge said right in
front of the jury that he, the judge, didn't remember
Roberta's testimony as Frank Bowron now stated it on
cross-examination. And when the judge said that, the jury
relaxed and sat back, waiting patiently for the chance to
return their verdict.

Next John Crow called Maria, one of the Rodriguez
sisters, who came back up and testified under her same
oath that, yes, Joe admitted it was his baby, and Leona
Rodriguez came back to say that Joe had admitted the
same thing to her, and then Judge Bentley instructed the
jury that *on or about* the fourteenth was close enough.
The jury wasn't out for very long. Found Joe guilty and
Joe was sentenced to the penitentiary up on the hill for
one and a half to two years, to that penitentiary built of
the gray rock dug from the innocent earth by frightened
men. He would be banished.

The whole case so upset Frank Bowron that he ap-
pealed it to the Wyoming Supreme Court without fee—
just on his own, as sometimes good lawyers do—and later
the supreme court reversed the case, sent it back for a
new trial because they said Judge Bentley should have
required the state to select either the fourteenth or the
fifteenth as the date of the rape, especially after Joe had
stated in his alibi that it wasn't the fourteenth—unfair,
they said, to permit the prosecutrix to change her testimony. To hold otherwise would deprive the defendant of
his alibi defense, the supreme court said. But for reasons
never made public, the state never chose to retry Joe
Esquibel for the statutory rape of Roberta Rodriguez.

I looked at the welfare records concerning the matter.
Frank Bowron had never seen them during the trial, nor

had the jury, but it would have made no difference. The forsaken, feeble fallen sparrow has the power to change even the written word. The girl had come to the welfare office with her sister for help on August 30, 1963. The record read as follows:

"8-30-63, 1:00 P.M. Roberta and sister, Maria, called at the office this day. Assistant Director asked Roberta about her pregnancy and inquired as to who the father was. Roberta refused to answer and said she did not want to get anyone in trouble. Assistant Director informed Roberta that before we would give her any help we would have to know the father and what plans were being made by the proposed father for supporting the forthcoming child. Assistant Director informed Roberta that if she would not answer today she would have to come back at a later date." She wouldn't say who the father was at first, but the baby was blooming in her belly, I suppose, and finally she went back for the baby's sake. It is the way of mothers. The record said:

"9-5-63, Roberta and sister, Maria, again called at the office this day at which time Roberta informed Assistant Director that the father of this child was Joe Esquibel. Due to the age of Roberta, Assistant Director suggested she talk with the County Attorney. Assistant Director, Roberta and her sister, Maria, met with the Assistant County Attorney at which time a charge of statutory rape was drawn up against Mr. Esquibel. The charges were read by Roberta and the Assistant County Attorney explained these charges. Roberta was then asked to sign these in the presence of Mr. Castle, County Justice of the Peace, her sister, Maria, the County Attorney and the Assistant County Attorney. Roberta agreed to sign." That made an airtight record.

"9-6-63, Roberta and sister, Maria, again called at the office this day to talk to the Assistant Director in regard to what was going to happen. It is the Assistant Director's feeling that at this time Roberta would like to drop the charges against Mr. Esquibel and that she feels sorry for him. Director talked to Roberta about a great many things including the forthcoming birth of this child and what her plans were. Roberta also stated during the interview that she had been threatened by Mr. Esquibel's mother. Assistant Director informed her in the presence of another caseworker, Mr. Schwartz, that she should, if ever threatened again, immediately inform the County Attorney or the Assistant County Attorney."

"11-24-63, Hospital called stating Miss Rodriguez had been entered this day. Assistant Director stated our Department would be responsible for expenses."

"11-26-63, According to information from the hospital, Miss Rodriguez gave birth to a son on 11-26-63. She is going to keep her baby."

Then two years later one more entry appeared in the welfare records.

"4-23-65, On this day an office call from Mrs. Lupe Rodriguez, mother of Roberta, revealed that Roberta and her son, were again living in the Rodriguez house and had been for a month or so. Roberta is again pregnant reputedly by the same person who is the father of her son, namely, Joe Esquibel."

21

THE JAILER let me in the cellblock, humming an old-fashioned tune. Sounded like "The Missouri Waltz." I first heard it sitting on my father's lap, and he'd rock me and hum it, and later on I heard it at the dance at Elk Mountain when ol' Calsey was out there stomping away with some suffering scraggly ranch woman, and now I heard those sweet strains again, echoing back and forth out of tune off the cold concrete walls of the Carbon County Jail.

"How ya doin', Joe?" I asked. He was leaning up against the concrete corner of his cell.

"They gonna kill me," he said.

"You're lookin' a little thin," I said.

"Them guys put me on bread an' water. I don' eat it."

"How come they did that to ya?" I asked.

"Fer jest talkin'."

"Who did you talk to, Joe?"

"I jest talk to that girl over there in that other cell. This deputy tol' me I couldn't talk to no girl, and I says this is a free world, and I say I'll talk to anybody I want, and this guy say 'You talk to her and I'll fix yer ass,' and I say you come in here and I'll fix yer ass, and then he called me a fuckin' no-good spick bastard, and I been on bread and water ever since."

"How long?"

"Two weeks."

"The trial's next Monday."

"What day is this?" he asked. His eyes were dull as bread and sleepy-looking.

"This is Wednesday." He didn't seem interested. He wanted to talk about the girl across the way in the cell-block who was passing him notes now that they couldn't talk, and saying she loved him, and things like that.

"I'll make 'em feed you, Joe," I said.

"It don' make no difference," he said. "Food is shit. Antelope," he said. "Ever taste boiled antelope, Mr. Spence?"

"Yeah," I said. "The fat sticks to your mouth and it tastes worse than old jackrabbit meat. Never could see how people could eat antelope. My father says he likes it, but I never could figure out why. It's better when it's canned."

"Oh," he said. "They boil it here. Stinks up the whole place. Ya can smell it comin'," he said. Then he sat down on the dirty mattress again. A big long chocolate-colored bug crawled up the wall, looked to the right and stopped, and then to the left. The bug stopped again about even with Joe's eyes. The floor smelled of disinfectant and was still wet where Joe had mopped. "Joe mops it every day," the jailer told me. "Cleanest prisoner we ever had. Gotta say that much fer 'em!"

"Get that bug, Joe," I said as it started crawling toward the ceiling, and then Joe looked at the bug, but he turned his head back. The bug stopped. "Well," I said, "I need to know some more about you."

"Okay, Mr. Spence, but I don' remember nothin', ya know."

"I need to know some more about Sharon."

"I don' remember nothin'," he said again.

"Well, the boys at the law school dug up your record. You were charged with statutory rape by Roberta Rodriguez. Surely you remember that?" I said, wanting to get a foothold somewhere.

"Yeah," he said.

"What happened there?"

"Got her pregnant," he said. "But she still likes me," he added quickly.

"Well, why did she charge you with rape then?"

"Them peoples at the welfare," he said, as if I should be able to fill in the rest.

"Well, tell me about it, Joe. What happened?"

"They throwed me in jail. Sharon said her mother had that Roberta sign a complaint against me, and I tol' 'er if they send me to the pen, they'll kill me in the pen. They kill Mexicans there, Mr. Spence, and then Sharon got me out." He stopped and looked at the bug again, which hadn't moved. "I loved her an' everythin', but I couldn't stop her from runnin' roun' with them white guys." I could see the hurt in his eyes like you see it sometimes when a man is hit hard over the heart.

"But they say you beat her up, Joe," I said quietly, trying to be kind.

"Nah," he said. "Slapped her a couple a times." He looked up and his eyes were still sad, and he popped his hands listlessly together to illustrate the slapping and even that small noise echoed across the cellblock.

I pushed on. "They said she got black eyes from it, Joe."

"She throwed me in jail," Joe said.

"Did you hit her hard enough to black her eyes?"

"Hit her easy. Real easy, like this." He clapped his soft small hands together again, and the slap echoed, slap, slap. Slap, slap.

"How come you did that, Joe?" I persisted.

"We was fightin' over them white guys—called me a son-of-a-bitch and I hit her. Not hard. And then she calls me a no good Mexican bastar'. I never hit her hard. She had me throwed in jail. Sheriff come. Picked me up. Done it a hunnert times, and then she says she'd get me out, but I gotta promise her no more drinkin' and no more womans and the like a that, and no more slappin' and stuff, and I says, 'Okay,' and I says, 'No more of them white guys neither and no more running aroun' with the baby in the back seat, and them dirty diapers and stuff,' and she says, 'Okay,' and then it was okay for a while, but after a while she run off with some white guy agin, and when she come back we had this fight and she put me in jail agin."

"Did you hit her again?"

"I don' remember, but the sheriff took me to jail and I was there about a month and then she came and got me out agin." He looked up at the bug absently. "Put me in and got me out whenever she wanted to, and I says, 'You shouldn't treat me like no dog,' and she said she wouldn't do it no more, and then we went to my ma's place, and lived there for a while." I let him run with his thoughts. "She was good to my mother, helped her. Good to Little Joe, too, and then finally me and Sharon had them three kids." He stopped. I waited. "After them kids we got married." Waited some more. "I miss them kids." Then he wrinkled his brow as if he was thinking hard, trying to remember, and finally he said, "The last time she tried ta throw me in jail, I says to the sheriff, 'If you wanna throw me in jail ya gotta shoot me in the back, cuz I ain't goin'.' An' I just walked away an' he never did shoot me, an' he never throwed me in jail that time."

"But why did you go back to Sharon? You fought. She threw you in jail, Joe, but you kept going back to her, and she kept taking you back, too?"

"I don' know," he said, looking down, and then the bug ran off and he said softly, "She was my woman."

How could I stand a man who beat up his woman. And the jury would see him that way, too, a goddamned woman-beater. How could I defend a man who, like Dr. Karn said, settled all his problems with violence. Had three kids. Hadn't even bothered to marry her. There didn't seem to be much else to say for him, and one of those long silences set in, and I sat there on the dirty mattress next to him, and for some reason I was feeling dirty myself, and it was raining outside. I remembered I tried to see the face of his woman, Sharon Esquibel. I thought of a blond square-faced girl, but the face of Anna came to my mind's eye instead and she was scolding me. It was our honeymoon. I had borrowed Mr. Wilson's car. Anna didn't have any money, and I didn't either. June 20. A rainy day. We could camp out, I said to Anna. Didn't have any money for tents, either. We could sleep under the stars in my sheepherder's bedroll, but the rain poured down and there was lightning and thunder on top of the mountains, and fog, and the roads were muddy. No place to go, so we parked along the side of the road for a while with the windshield wipers on the De Soto scolding, monotonously, waiting there for the rain to stop, and after a while the fog raised a little, but it was still raining hard, and down the road a short distance I could see a cabin.

I drove the De Soto up the muddy trail to the cabin, spinning all the way, the mud flying, and when I stopped, we were stuck all right, and the damned cabin was locked. Finally we decided there was nothing else to do with the rain turning to snow—no place else to go, so I broke out a small pane of glass in the door window, and then I reached through and unlatched the door from the inside and we became burglars on our honeymoon. We built a fire. There was a feather tick on the bed. We put a couple of raw potatoes in the potbellied stove and we had some Hershey bars, which along with the burned potatoes was our wedding supper.

Then in the morning we were doing our first simple job together—making the bed, and Anna wanted the corners square.

"What difference does it make?" I said. "Jesus Christ, they weren't square when we came in here. The people won't care whether the corners are square or not."

"You always make the corners of the bed square," she said. "If anything's worth doing, it's worth doing well," she said, just like my mother. Jesus. "Like this." She showed me. "Make yours square. You *can* do it!" she said. "Everybody can make bed corners square."

"How do you make a feather tick square? A feather tick is not square and a feather tick isn't round. A feather tick is a feather tick."

"You are bull-headed. I've known that all along," she said, pointing one of her long fingers at me, her chin jutting out, the dimples gone, the eyes fiery. "Make it square," she hollered across the bed.

"The hell with you," I hollered back, and I walked

away from the corner, leaving it unmade. Bullshit, I thought. She wasn't going to suck me up, head first, and turn me into some wounded whelp—sniveling and soaked. She walked over to the corner and started to make it herself.

"You son-of-a-bitch," she hissed between tight lips, and pushed me out of the way. I slapped her with my open hand before I knew what I'd done. Just once. God Almighty! How could I have done that? I felt sick. I was a woman-beater, and on the first day of our marriage, too! Jesus God Almighty! She looked at me with horror on her face. Just looked. Said nothing. And then I tried to justify it. It was a terrible crime, and terrible crimes have to be justified.

"You talk to me like a man and I'll treat you like one!" I hollered louder than a man should holler, hoping it would cover up what I'd done. And then Anna started to cry and I didn't feel like a man any more. I was an ugly little boy, ashamed and guilty, and I wanted to chop off my hand and give it to her, and then I cried and said, "I wish I hadn't," and we held onto each other, and both of us cried. I cried out of sorrow and mostly out of shame, and out of the pain of having hit this woman I loved, and we fought a lot in that marriage. Sometimes I thought she was trying to get me to hit her again. But I only cussed and made a lot of loud noise, and once I threw the typewriter through the front window, and sometimes when we really got in it, she would run into the bathroom and lock the door. Probably the only place she could get away from me, and I could hear her sobbing inside, and I'd feel dirty again, and worthless, and little Kippy would be crawling on the floor and slobbering, but when we fought, and I could never remember what it was over, little Kippy would stop crawling and just sit there with his eyes big, and even at that age he tried to act like he didn't hear us. "A husband and wife should never quarrel in front of the children," I could hear my mother say.

And Anna would still be weeping in the bathroom. Jesus Christ, I hated to hear it, and I thought she knew I hated it, and cried to punish me. Sometimes I'd walk out

and go downtown for a beer. Couldn't think. Probably
fail in law school—had straight A's after we were married, everybody investing in me like they did. Mr. Wilson
gave me the money he said he would have spent for
Anna's education. Anna had given up her own schooling,
her mother pointed out, her whole career, for Christ's
sake, for me. She was working at the university in the
P.E. Department as a secretary, and my own father was
still sending me fifty dollars a month. I had to succeed or
I would be cheating all those people. There was too much
invested in me by too many, but Anna and I were always
fighting, and it would be her fault if I failed, I said.

But after two or three hours things would change, magically, like the weather in Wyoming, like it is foggy and
dreary and raining and it will never be sunny again, and
we will be doomed to live in this horrid drizzle forever,
and then in ten minutes the sun peers through the eternal
drizzle, the distant mountains come into sight as if a great
stage has been set, and the curtain is lifted, a little at a
time, and there stand the majestic peaks in the distance,
and the sky gets deep blue, as blue again as eternity, and
it will never rain again, never again, and we would be
passionate and make love, and I would say I was sorry
and we would lie in each other's arms, and little Kippy
would crawl on the floor again and coo, and I would
laugh at him and he would laugh back. But pretty soon
the high Wyoming winds blew in another storm. It was
only the Wyoming weather, this marriage to Anna.

I was still afraid I would fail in law school, and I
couldn't understand how I kept getting the high marks all
the time, had the highest average in the class. Must be
something wrong. I was too slow in the intellectual stuff.
Never could logic-things-out, as they called it. Even that
goddamned little sweetpea of an English professor who
claimed he climbed the mountains at Vedauwoo said I
wasn't smart enough even to get an A in American Lit.
Those who really knew me knew I wasn't bright. But I
studied, sometimes twelve hours a day, and all weekend,
every spare minute, and I got the top marks. But I'd fail
the next quarter for sure. It'd catch up with me some-

where, sometime. But then I'd write a beautiful essay on my exams, write back in good lawyerese language the words of my professors, which I had laboriously noted in class, and then recopied and committed to memory, and I got those grades, beat the Phi Beta Kappa boys, beat the bearded vets with their hairy balls and purple hearts, and their war stories and their GI Bill. Never could talk to the vets anyway. Never got to Russia. I don't know how I was able to do it. I'd barely gotten through chemistry and physics in high school, which embarrassed my father, him being a chemist, but now I beat the engineers and the men of science, beat them in the law. Yet secretly I knew I was a fraud, knew it inside where the truth hangs out. The trick was never to let them find out. Now I had to face the truth again, this time with a man's life at stake.

I felt helpless. I could never save Joe Esquibel. He was condemned the moment he was born. Goddamn it!

"Joe, I'll make 'em give you something to eat," I said, and I got up off the dirty mattress. I hollered for the deputy and pretty soon he came down to get me, still humming "The Missouri Waltz." "I can't have you coming into court looking like a damn scarecrow."

I could never save him, and what would I be saving anyway if I did? Joe Esquibel never did a decent thing that I knew of in his life. All he had to show for it was a bunch of bastard kids, and I could hear my old friend Tom Fagan, the dean of the Wyoming criminal defense lawyers, saying, "Spence. You can never beat the big one —never beat the rap for murder one." He thought it was fate that intervened in some mystical way with its own punishment for murder, like the man Tom Fagan got acquitted once who was killed the next year in an automobile accident, or that other fellow who was let off by some jury and then drowned the next spring trying to save his own kids when their boat turned over in a stormy lake. He could cite a long list of examples to prove his point. "You can't beat the rap on the big one," Tom Fagan said, but then he kept on defending men charged with murder one.

What the hell was I doing in this case? The entire state

hospital staff and even our two defense psychiatrists were unanimous. Joe Esquibel was perfectly sane. How could I go into a court of law, as an honorable officer of the court, as all lawyers are, and argue with a straight face and a clear heart that Joe Esquibel was insane—"incapable of aiding in his own defense." When I got home I called Raymond Whitaker. It was only five days before the trial, which had been moved to Casper on our motion for change of venue.

"Raymond," I said. "What the hell are we into anyway? We haven't got a case! They're gonna find him sane and triable and then they'll try him for murder and they'll gas 'em for sure. What are we doin'?"

"Why, we're seeking justice, Gerald," Whitaker said.

"What's justice?" I asked the same old question, always asked it. Justice is when I win, I thought, and I wasn't going to get any justice.

"Maybe the jury will tell you what justice is," Raymond said. "Trust the jury."

"But the jury can never know him like I do. I know this guy. Been studying him almost a year now. I know more about him than he knows about himself." Then I said what I'd been thinking and never wanted to say. "Raymond, I think he's a lot like me."

"How?" Raymond asked, sounding surprised.

"Well, sometimes I feel like a Mexican. Part of me feels like I don't belong—and I want to belong. Makes me angry." Then suddenly I wished I hadn't said it.

"Well, well," Raymond said. "And what do you want to belong to—the Young Men's Literary Club in Cheyenne?"

"No," I said. "You know what I mean." And I knew he knew. Raymond was like Joe Esquibel, too, and he knew it. He didn't belong either, and he was angry, but he wouldn't admit it, wouldn't give anybody the satisfaction. Play life like a game—and take this case and shove it up the system's. "Well, tell it to the jury, Gerald," Raymond finally said. "Tell them he's like you. Trust the jury." And there was the same old bitter sarcasm in his voice.

"Okay," I said. "I'll trust 'em. I'll tell 'em. I'll tell the jury we don't have a case. I'll tell 'em, 'Take this fucking Mexican—take him, ladies and gentlemen! Take him! Send him off to the fucking gas chamber. He's sane. We don't have a fucking thing to say—not a fucking defense!' "

"How about a defense to fucking?" Whitaker said. Then he said with a nicer sound to his voice, "Just talk to the jury, Gerald. Just talk plain and sweet to them, like a good salesman. It's all salesmanship, Gerald. You're the best at selling juries of anybody I've ever seen." Trying to make me feel good, I thought. He was a friend. Ought to give the goddamned jury a couple of bouquets of sweetpeas and go home for all the good I'd do at trying to sell them Joe Esquibel's insanity. "Make a good final argument," Raymond said and hung up.

I looked out the window into the sad gray streets of Riverton, Wyoming. The people walked by seeing nothing. I could have run through the streets naked with my gonads painted purple—yellow even, purple and yellow —and half a pound of ostrich feathers stuck up my ass and no one would have lifted his eyes. I could cry out that I was alone, dying of loneliness, dying of an empty heart, and no one would have heard. The dead do not look up or hear, I thought, and here I was with Anna and the babies, four of them now, Kip, Kerry, Kent, and Katy, like a litter of pups, and the next litter would all start with L's, maybe. The L litter. Larry, Louise, Leonard, yes, Leonard for my grandpa Pfleeger, and Lois, and then there would be the M litter after that. No. I was only a child myself, back in the G litter. G for God, Gideon, Goliath, and Gerald. No. For Gerry, the gorky walking Gook, and, oh, God, the day was dark, and the clouds hung down and spit snow, and the wind was cold and rude, and the world was a hard place, and I was just a child hanging onto my own babies, a G baby with a K litter, and Anna could not hear me, tuned to her own places, whispering to the moon, and the moon heard her, and her answers to me were to questions I hadn't asked her, as if she spoke mostly in another language with only the words sounding the same, and we understood each other only in our fire and our fury.

"Cleo," I hollered, as she came in with that small peaceful smile on her face. "Cleo, for Christ's sake, bring me a Cabin Still."

"I have a letter from the American Bar Association," she said.

"What about?" I asked.

"About your ad, you know, 'Best trial lawyer in America needs work.' " She handed me the letter. It said that the American Bar Association could not run such an ad since it violated the Code of Ethics about self-aggrandizement. It's unethical to brag about yourself, or something, for Christ's sake. I forgot what section of the Code of Ethics. But it's also unethical to be alone in this world, in Riverton, Wyoming, in this isolated place, which was like living on some petty, pointless island, floating in an ocean of sagebrush. It is unethical to wish to be heard, and to want to grow, and to break out, and to wish to become what I was, whatever that was, which was more than someone defending a worthless Mexican just for the fun of it. It wasn't fun. Joe Esquibel and I were both in prison.

"Cleo," I said as she put the glass of whiskey in front of me. "Cleo, take off your clothes and hop up on this table. I'm going to make hot, passionate love to you."

"Oh, Gerald," she said kindly, forgiving me like a mother does a naughty child. How could one make love to his virgin mother? And later, she brought me another Cabin Still. Anna was angry with me when I came home, my eyes glassy, and a simpering smile on my face, late for supper, as usual, and the kids were in bed, and the supper cold on the table, and Anna raged at me again. Just part of our liturgy, of this marriage, I thought, and I raged back. And then little Katy, youngest of the litter, came running down the stairs, and crawled up on my lap, and I rocked her, and I cried, and she wanted to know in her innocent way why I was crying, and I didn't know what to say. I didn't know why. I held onto Katy and I rocked away and then I heard the judge say, Who stands for the defendant, Joe Esquibel?

I do. Gerry Spence. I would stand up.

Speak then.

I would speak, or could I speak in this fearful place, where nothing grows, where everything is dead, where the judge looked dead, looked down at me standing there trying to speak, looked down at me with dead eyes, wearing black, looked down ready to read the sentence of death, and I could feel my own heart beating, and my belly felt like it was being squeezed by a pair of belly-pliers, and my mind was tumbling with mad fragments of thought, and I was afraid. Could I say it right? Try Joe's case right? I wished to Christ Raymond Whitaker had never been born. I wished I had never agreed to this silly game. No, I wished I didn't care. Why should anybody care for this mad Mexican murderer? He was no tiger. He was a mangy alley cat. And I knew I had committed the unforgivable sin of a lawyer. I cared about my client. I cared about Joe Esquibel.

22

AT SEVEN O'CLOCK in the morning I carried a big cardboard box full of evidence and exhibits and files, my box, full of my preparations for the trial of Joe Esquibel, up the steps of the courthouse at Casper. It's important to walk into an empty courtroom and claim your table, the one closest to the jury—first come, first served, and if we're close to them maybe they'll feel closer to us, too. Don't separate me from my jury.

The door to the courtroom was open, but inside it was dark. I knew the place, like my bedroom, knew where the furniture was in this huge room with its high somber ceilings and blond wood-paneled wall. I walked down the center aisle past blond wooden pews on both sides, like walking down to the altar of a dark church, through the low swinging wooden gate, the bar, which separated the spectators from the members of the court, and the gate made the only sound in this hollow chamber as it flopped back in place on its springs. Flop, flop.

I set the box down on the table next to the jury, claimed the table by reason of prior possession, which is nine points of the law they say. The trial was set for ten o'clock. Justice cannot bear to see itself early in the morning.

I flipped on the light switch, and like magic there it was, this huge vault-shaped room with the air of a funeral parlor, and empty as an empty coffin. Nobody gave a damn about this Mexican in Casper, Wyoming, but they wanted his blood in Rawlins. Judge Stanton was a good judge, and thought like judges should think. If there was any question, it was settled in favor of the accused. He granted us a change of venue to Casper. Not many Mexicans in Casper. A few who lived with the whites, trying to be white, but I didn't trust them. Never trust a man who wants to be different from what he is. Doesn't like himself. How can he like you?

The first juror stuck his head in the room. This here the place? Yep. Make yourself at home. Come right on in and have a seat. You the lawyer? Yeah, sure am. I was on a jury once back in forty-six. Case about irrigation, or somethin'. You lawyers sure talk funny. Ha. Ha. Yeah, but I can't talk to you. The judge might think I was trying to influence you. Throw me in jail. Give him a smile so he at least knows you're friendly. Smiles say I like you. Smiles say it's okay. It doesn't hurt to put a smile on your face my mother said. So I can't talk to you, but I wish I could, and then other jurors came, strangers to each other sitting in different rows, and then one turned around and got to talking to the man behind him. You on jury duty? Yeah. How 'bout you? Yeah, me too. Had to leave a crew of men. Gotta get out of this goddamn jury duty. But a man better come to court when they call ya or they'll have ya throwed in jail I hear. Yeah. This here's my busy season. Got three jobs goin' at once. Can't paint in the winter, ya know. Make it now or don't make it at all. Only let the fancy-ass doctors off and the bankers. Ain't no bankers sitting on juries. Lotta women get on— better'n watchin' soap operas. Yeah. Ha. Ha. Two middle-aged housewives sat down beside each other. The room filled up with plain faces of plain people; a couple of businessmen in suits sat separately from the rest, and a young man in jeans and tennis shoes sat down up front. I liked the faces. Oh, the people lie a little once in a while —my alarm didn't go off, actually partying all night, but he'd worry himself sick about the parking meter, gotta go put a nickel in the parking meter—and they filled the room, begrudgingly, a man's duty as a citizen of the US of A.

I looked out on that room of a hundred faces, all pushed over on the right side of the courtroom by the clerk, my side, so there'd be room for whatever spectators wanted to come on the other side—keep the spectators and the prospective jurors separated so the jury don't get infected, don't want no spectator, member of the Esquibel family or somethin', talking to a prospective juror. Could cause a mistrial. Gotta be careful. And I couldn't see that the faces of those people were different from the faces I remembered seeing as a kid in the Methodist Episcopal church as a kid on a Sunday morning in Sheridan, Wyoming. People sorta dressed up, not accustomed to dressing up, surprised to see the old suit didn't fit quite right anymore—she's a little tight, yes sir, and they laughed, and there were the old narrow ties when wide ties were in style, or vice versa, I can't remember now, and the women sat with their coats on, when it wasn't chilly, and later they'd struggle to get out of their coats, and somebody next to them would help, friendly like, and they got to talkin', and the courtroom half full of prospective jurors got to be a noisy place.

Pretty soon our law students came in and took a seat on a bench on our side of the bar, up against the bar, and then Raymond Whitaker made his entrance, taking long swooping steps, a little snap-brimmed hat on his head sitting up a bit too high. He nodded to the folks as he walked down the aisle and somebody said, "Hear yer defendin' one a them murderers again." The people laughed and Raymond stopped, and the people's eyes were on him, and then the whole crowd quieted in unison, like suddenly crowds do, and in the momentary hush Raymond replied, and everybody could hear him. "I never defend murderers. I only defend those *wrongly accused* of murder by the state." And he grinned. And then somebody let out a ha, and the room was full again of the jabber and laughter of the prospective jurors.

Oscar Hall came in. He was in his same old brown, too loose suit, with a big flopping tie, like a flag hanging outside the coat, and the bottom part of the tie was inside out, and one of the points of his white shirt collar stuck out over his lapel. He wore a small-brimmed hat with the brim up all the way around. The hat sat up on the top of his head, two sizes too small. Oscar was friendly-looking, and smiled a wet smile as he walked down the aisle. The people would like Oscar Hall. Looked unfancy like them, and he acted a little self-conscious as he headed for the empty counsel table I had left him, his belly out, and pretty soon his shirt would start to bulge open in the front. I supposed that's why men wore vests, to cover their bellies sticking out, and then the three-piece suit got to be the style for skinny men, too, but Oscar said to hell with it. He didn't wear any three-piece suit. Two pieces to any suit was a plenty.

Raymond sat down beside me. "Good morning, Gerald," he said, and started to polish his glasses, and then a deputy came up to the table and asked if we wanted to see Joe Esquibel before the trial, and we did. He said, well, they had him out in an anteroom off the main hall and we could see him if we wanted, so Raymond and I followed the deputy to a small room, nothing more than a closet, really, and there he sat like a rabbit in a box trap, dark eyes afraid, sitting silently, stiff, ready to spring if the door were opened.

Joe wore a nice dark brown suit like young men wear in the J. C. Penney ads with a tie that matched perfectly with a neat machine-stitched fleur-de-lis just above the point, and his mother had bought him a new white shirt. His crew cut was trimmed even shorter, like a Marine fresh into boot camp. He looked at me but said nothing. Then he looked down and I could see the scars on the top of his head again clearly, slashed here and there without rhyme or reason, put there like a mad painter slashes white paint on a black canvas. Joe looked all right at first glance, but as I studied him I could tell there was something wrong. What I saw didn't hold together. He glanced up at me again, sorta sideways.

"Hi ya, Joe," I said. He nodded. Didn't say anything. Too afraid to speak. Too afraid of the fear to let any of it out, to hear the fear cracking in his voice, and his eyes were not the eyes of the man in the J. C. Penney dress suit at all. The skin around the sockets had yellowed, and as I looked into the eyes themselves, they looked like the eyes of the cottontail huddled back in between the logs of the old barn at Grandpa Spence's, crowded back in that little space, breathing hard, and gut-shot by a kid too young to know about killing small things.

"Joe," I said. "You ready?" He put those eyes on me. He nodded. "Now, Joe," I said, "I want you to do something for me. When you go into the courtroom, just look down at your feet. Don't look up. You understand?"

He nodded.

"Show me," I said.

He looked down.

"What are you looking at?" I asked.

"My shoes." His voice was flat.

"Where on your shoes?"

"Right here," he said, pointing to the bow on the laces.

"Look at that spot, do you hear?"

"Yeah."

"Don't ever talk to me in the courtroom," I said. "Don't ever look up during the trial. If you look up, you'll be looking at the door of the gas chamber. Do you understand?"

"Yeah."

"If they lie about you and you get mad and you look up, you'll be lookin' up to see them drag you into the gas chamber. You'll be dead. Do you understand?"

"Yeah."

"If you look up once, just once, you *are dead*. Do you understand, Joe?"

"Yeah."

"If you whisper, or grunt, or do anything but look at the bow on your shoes, you'll be dead. Understand?" He nodded.

"What are you going to look at?"

"My shoes," he said.

"What are you going to do if your neck gets tired?"

"Nothin'."

"Can you do it?"

"Yeah."

"If you ever look up, I'll leave you. I'll walk right out and Raymond here will walk out, too. Leave you alone in that damned courtroom by yourself. Do you understand?"

"Yeah." I knew the horror of being a child left alone in such a forest.

"That's crazy," Raymond said while Joe was still sitting there. "He'll look up, and then it'll all be over."

"He won't," I said.

"It's crazy," Raymond said again.

"I don't want the jury guessing about his insanity. I don't want them watching for every sign he might give. 'See,' they'd say, 'he whispered to his lawyer. He has to be sane to whisper. See, he's pissed off at what the sheriff said. See that! He was whispering like hell to his lawyers and raising all kinds of hell. He ain't crazy.' That's what they'll say," I said, "and they'll look for his reactions. They'll find him sane from just watching him."

"They'll get him if they think he's trying to fool 'em," Raymond said. "Sometimes jurors can forgive a man for his killing, but they never forgive a man for lying."

"He's not lying. He can do it."

"Do you really think he can follow your instructions, Gerald?"

"Yes, I do."

"Do you think his following his attorney's instructions will aid him in his defense?"

"Yes, of course," I said.

"Well, that's one test for sanity, isn't it—being able to follow the instructions of counsel—being able to thereby 'aid in his own defense'—that's how they say it."

"Yeah," I said.

"And so if he can follow your instructions he's sane."

"Well," I said. "What was it we agreed on?"

The deputy sheriff came, and then Joe got up and left with the deputy, and we followed.

"What?" Raymond asked, his face suddenly blank.

"You have a bad memory too. We agreed to take this man and show the system—with our brilliance—to beat the system."

"Gerald," Raymond said. "Good luck."

I was afraid.

And Joe was afraid. I knew his fear. But he looked down at his shoes, as he sat there between Raymond and me. There is no law against a fellow looking at his shoes.

"Everybody rise," the bailiff shouted, and the room roared with bodies getting up, and we stood up, too, but Joe sat at the counsel table looking at his feet, never moved, and then from the side of the room Judge Stanton walked on to the bench in half a waddle, fat as a friar, in his black robe and with ruddy cheeks, still looking like Grandpa Spence, and he said to please be seated and there was the roar again of the whole room sitting down in unison, and he announced the case: "State of Wyoming versus Joseph Esquibel." Was the state ready? Yes, the state was ready, Oscar said in a deep voice, sounding like Moses, and was the defense ready, and yes, the defense was ready, I said, standing up politely and saying it casually, quietly, with a solid sound to my voice, and if I had listened carefully through the ears of history carried in the genes of every one of my cells I could have heard the call of the king to battle, the call to the champions, the warriors to the pit, to the bloody pit.

"Well, here she goes," I whispered to Raymond. The clerk was spinning the jury canister, a large old tin cylinder about the size of a ten-gallon milk can, and the little slips with each juror's name would be bouncing around inside, like bingo-balls—the wheel of fate for the jurors, the wheel of fate for all, and the jurors were silent now, waiting to hear the name called out by the clerk. It was the skinny guy in the Levi's near the back who took long self-conscious steps to the jury box. He had a big grin on his face, and some of the jurors secretly wished it was them who had been called. The clerk stopped the spinning of the canister, reached in, picked out another slip, unfolded it, and called the name, and I wrote it on my jury chart. I watched each juror carefully as he or she walked to the jury box to take a seat. I watched the one going up there now, with a crew cut like Joe's. He had a solemn face, his step stiff and straight, like there was a brace from his head to his butt, and his knees almost locked as he walked. Must have been uncomfortable for him to live all these years in such tight places. People who live in boxes want everybody in boxes, and people loose and easy, free-walking and open, cannot endure boxes.

The clerk called another name, a frail nervous woman who looked here and looked there, taking little steps, ready to burst into flight at the drop of a finger. I wrote the word "bird" by her name, and then they called the old hard-faced charwoman, and the sweet pink-faced lady with the white hair, who looked like a waxed pink rose, and then they called a big man with a fierce scowl who walked like a hippo. Solid. His round-toed work shoes hit the floor of the courtroom heel first, then toe, flopping down with authority. Authority. Authority. And his stiff new bib overalls covered a big stomach that was also solid and didn't jiggle as he walked. The people who had been called to the jury box looked different sitting in the box. They all had their own kind of face masks on, and their hands were clasped nervously together. Some folded them across their chests, but all of them held onto themselves with their hands, holding their bodies tight and crossing their legs to protect themselves from who or what they did not know, against the feeling, against the fear of being a juror. Their faces were very serious now that they had been chosen, and some stole looks at me, and then Joe, who was still looking down, with the white scars showing clearly through his hair, and then the jurors would look at the prosecutor, trying to discover the secret of the case, trying not to look nervous themselves. After there were twelve in the jury box, the judge told the clerk to swear the jury, and they raised hands dutifully, and yes, each swore "to true answers make to the questions propounded them respecting their qualifications to sit in this case as a trial juror"—to true answers make to the questions propounded.

To tell the truth? To be interrogated in a public courtroom before the whole world by lawyers who use big words. To tell the truth. What will they ask? They ain't gettin' me offa this jury by trappin' me into somethin'.

I'm stayin' on . . . and I ain't prejudiced. A Mex was one of my best friends—good Mex, and I'll tell the friggin' lawyer so. Played basketball with the little son-of-a-bitch. Could dribble the ball like hell. The guy next to me wants off, says he'll piss the lawyers off so as they'll kick him off. Gonna tell 'em he read about the damn case in the newspaper and that he's already got his mind made up, but I ain't prejudiced. Grew up with them Mexies. Gotta be a little careful of 'em, watch 'em a little, like anybody I guess, and ya don't never want ta go drinkin' with a Mex because when they get to drinkin' they get crazy, and about half the time they'll try ta stick ya.

In the front row a plump old maid schoolteacher looked like she was going to faint she was so afraid. I felt sorry for her. She looked at Joe and looked away and then she looked worse, and I knew the judge would let her go. People with great compassion cannot sit on juries. People with great love who say, "I could never convict a man of murder—never take part in such a thing," are never chosen. The schoolteacher would be intelligent, and she took philosophy and sociology, and she would probably think things like it was society who failed Joe, and she would probably be excused by the judge because she would timidly admit that she would have difficulty following the court's instructions—goddamned bleeding heart. Oscar Hall would look for the bleeding hearts and if the judge didn't excuse them because they couldn't follow the court's instructions, well, then Oscar would get her off with a peremptory challenge—no goddamn bleeding hearts on his jury. If you can't follow the court's instructions or the law, well, you are lawless, an outlaw. It's that simple—an outlaw because you are a bleeding heart. And the court did excuse her. She couldn't say she'd follow the court's instructions until she heard what they were, she said.

I kept the charwoman with the deep, hard lines on her emaciated face. "She looks mean," John Ackerman, one of the law students, said. She was a widow. Lived alone in a little two-room apartment, but she had her job cleaning up the mess in the operating room at the hospital. What

do you do with the leg after you cut it off, Doctor? I hand
it to the nurse. That's all I know—hand it to her. The leg
off a big man is heavy—might weigh forty pounds and
what does the nurse do with it? She puts it in a pail, and
then the cleanup woman takes it to the garbage. The
cleanup woman mops the blood off the operating room
floor and disinfects with Lysol or something, but the doctors don't know her name. Martha Pittman. Never heard
of her. When she goes to bed alone at night, she's tired
and goes right to sleep, but about two o'clock in the
morning she gets restless, and out of habit she reaches
over for her husband, to the place where he used to lie,
warm and noisy and snoring and grunting and coughing
in his sleep, which had kept her awake for forty years—
well, his place is cold and empty, and when her hand
touches the cold sheet it frightens her and she wakes up
with a start. She forgets for a moment he is dead, and the
bed is empty on his side, cold and dead, and she is wide
awake, looking up at the ceiling, seeing his dead face in
the coffin, and she is alone and too afraid to cry out in the
dark, and no psychiatrist comes to hold her hand and to
hear her hollow old sobs in the night for a hundred dollars an hour.

"I know the woman," I whispered. "She's all right."

"How come ya took off the nice lady with the white
hair? Reminded me of my grandma," John Ackerman
said. I didn't know his grandma. But she was the one with
a face like a pink wax rose, and that was only the mask I
saw. A person couldn't tell what the mask covered—
other roses and lilies clear down to a lily soul, which
would never know Joe Esquibel anyway, or did the sweet
mask cover dark things, or maybe nothing at all? Maybe
it covered emptiness. I took her off, and I took off the
man who lived in a box, and the banker who would know
only that Mexicans wrote overdrafts and forged checks
and who was a practical man and knew the bastards were
crazy, crazy like a fox. And the bird, what about her?
Well, I left her on because she would never lead, only
follow, and fly away in the face of trouble but never cause
trouble, and I took off a red-faced rancher and another

rancher's wife, because they had stood there on those barren prairies of Wyoming and they knew what pain was, all right, and loneliness and lean years. They had stood up against nature, against raging winter winds when the sheep were crowded into a corner and smothered each other and then froze to death. They had survived the baking sun of the summer that had left the grass dead and the sheep thin, and their Mexican sheepherders were drunk most of the time and ate too many lambs, and everybody knew about the Mexican sheepherder and his pet ewe. God Almighty! You know about them! And the rancher and the other rancher's wife had survived, standing against the storms and the sun, and the joy they knew came up hard-bitten and pinched, a joy that said only that they had never given up, that they had played by the rules and won, and if they could win by hard work and courage then, by God, everybody else could too. A man is his own master. Reaps what he sows. They left their doors open at night and killed the golden eagle, which they claimed killed their lambs, and they killed coyotes with guns and poisoned bait and those animals that ate the poisoned coyote—the birds, a prairie dog—they were killed, too, and the animals that ate the poisoned birds and the prairie dogs died also, and the rancher poisoned prairie dogs with a special poison, and he poisoned the harvester ants because both the prairie dogs and ants ate the grass that belonged to the rancher and his sheep, and they shot wild horses on sight—too many of them, eat ya out of house and home—and a few ranchers, only a few, killed the antelope, and left them lie, got to keep 'em thinned down, ya know, and they do this killing not because they don't respect living things, but because they have the better right to survive, to exterminate the vermin and the competition that would otherwise exterminate them. Man is part of nature. There is no pity in nature. Pity is an unworthy emotion, and a man could respect a coyote more than Joe Esquibel, because a coyote does not kill its mate or starve its pups.

I kept the heavy man with the big feet and the fresh overalls. Didn't know why, just liked him—felt good with him, which is enough of a reason for me. We got a jury shortly after lunch.

"That's a good jury, Raymond," I said. He looked around the courtroom, which was empty now. No one else was interested in this trial, no newspapers, no curious housewives or bored retired men who had become court-watchers. It was just a trial of somebody sent up from Rawlins.

"Good jury," I said again.

"Yeah," Raymond said back. "There isn't one of them on the jury strong enough to hang 'em though. They've all been beaten up by the system already. Hall kicked off the strong ones, and you kicked off those ranchers."

"Well, I don't want 'em to hang anyway," I said. "I want 'em to find that Joe is insane—unanimous."

"Old Oscar Hall seems pretty happy with the jury," Whitaker said. He looked over at Oscar Hall, who had a happy look on his face.

"Well, maybe he doesn't know 'em like I do," I said.

"Everybody thinks he knows the jury," Whitaker said.

"Well, it's too late now," I said.

"Let 'er roll. Well, just let 'er roll, Gerald," and Raymond walked off. As he passed the deputy clerk he stopped, and she stopped, and he looked down his nose and over his glasses at her, and he said she was the most beautiful woman in Natrona County, maybe in the whole state of Wyoming, and he called her darling, and she blushed, and then they walked down the hall in opposite directions. At the recess Joe Esquibel, with his eyes still on his feet, walked down the same hall to the same little room where the deputy deposited him, and he sat there alone with the deputies just outside the door.

After the recess Oscar Hall made his opening statement in his deep Moses voice, sounding serious, solemn, respectable, reasonable. Joe Esquibel had killed his wife in cold blood and was perfectly sane then as he was now. Dr. Karn, superintendent of the state hospital, an outstanding psychiatrist, would testify that Joe Esquibel was plainly sane and triable, that the only claim to the contrary was that which the defendant made for himself.

"He claims he cannot remember; he claims he has amnesia," Oscar said with a slightly sick look of disbelief on his face, which stuck out over his crooked tie, and over his belly. "He claims he cannot remember pulling the trigger, nor can he even remember seeing his young, blond, beautiful wife fall dead to the floor with a bullet hole through her head. Those are his claims. But Dr. Karn, the superintendent at the hospital, who has examined him carefully, says his lack of memory is the result of malingering, that he is feigning his inability to remember.

"The evidence will show that Joe Esquibel killed his wife in cold blood and now wishes to escape a trial for murder by claiming he is not able to be tried, by claiming he is *insane!* It is only his claim," Oscar Hall shouted, pounding his fist on the lectern, "a claim this man has made in order that he may avoid the process of justice! There is not a single competent witness anywhere in the world who will testify that Joe Esquibel is insane. At the conclusion of the case we will ask you to find him presently sane and triable in order that justice may be done— without delay—now!" Justice.

The court called another recess. It had been a good opening statement and everything Oscar Hall said was true. We didn't have a witness who would testify that Joe was insane, and it was true we were trying to avoid a trial for murder. We had no goddamned defense. Should I just get up and admit it? Yes, ladies and gentlemen of the jury, what Oscar Hall says is true. Joe Esquibel is perfectly sane and all I'm trying to do is to keep him out of the gas chamber. I'd looked at the jury. Their eyes were cold, and their arms folded. They wouldn't be tricked or played with by some shyster representing a Mexican murderer, and there was that damned gnawing at my gut, that ugly, painful feeling that reminds me I'm just a coward standing in the courtroom, pretending not to be afraid, sounding confident, sounding powerful, looking bold and fearsome, as if I could rip off the heads of my opponents, but in my belly, in the wee bottom of my little belly, is a boy, still afraid, feeling alone, and not knowing whether what he has will be enough to win. Hoping. Only hoping. Did I prepare correctly? Overlook anything? Will I choke up? Will those silly brains settle down so I can start to think clearly—react calmly—God, will I make it through this trial, and my goddamned bladder is full—peed twice, for Christ's sake, in the last fifteen minutes. I walked up the aisle of the courtroom to go to the latrine again, and as I walked by the jurors I smiled nonchalantly like it was nothing more than business as usual—put a bored look on my face, and didn't hurry, but now my time had come, and now the fear was leaving a little as I opened up my notes. Thank God for that. In its place I could feel the anger slowly filling up my empty belly, and I loved my anger. It killed fear. It was easier to attack than to run. It felt better to be a lion, not a rabbit—oh, the pain of being a rabbit.

"Ladies and gentlemen—my dear friends," I began. "Once upon a time there was born a baby boy, a little Mexican-American boy as sweet and fat-cheeked and healthy both in mind and body as any baby anywhere. Except for a head full of black hair and slightly darker skin, he would have looked like your little boy, and like your little boy, he was born innocent, as innocent as a puppy.

"Now, take a puppy. When he comes up to you with his tail waggin' wantin' you to pick him up and love him, if you kick that innocent puppy instead, just kick him, and when that puppy wants to play you beat him instead, and when he's hungry you throw him out in the cold, without food, and when he wants to be warm and safe you let the vicious neighborhood dogs rip and tear at him, well, what about that puppy? How will that innocent puppy grow up? It wouldn't surprise you if he grew up to be a mad, vicious dog.

"Joe Esquibel never chose where he was to be born and never deserved to be hurt in those terrible ways. He was innocent. His baby mind couldn't understand why he was being teased and tormented and his little psyche tortured, and with the innocent wonder of a child he couldn't understand why his natural rights that even a puppy understands were taken from him, why as a member of this human species on the face of this earth, he was so despised when he was so innocent. He had only loved his mother, only loved his brothers and sisters. He had done no wrong, but he was so despised and he felt the horrid heat of hate against him—why did they stomp out the last tiny vestiges of selfworth from this child? What wrong had he committed? Why was he kicked and beaten and abused in both body and soul until one day the soul of this child cried out its last little sane whimper and gave itself to the madness of a man?"

There was nothing else to tell the jury except the truth —the facts, nothing else to do except to tell it to the jury like Raymond said. I recounted Joe's life in detail as we had discovered it, about the poverty and the hunger and cold, and about his mother. I looked over at Joe. He was looking down all right with only the flat top of his head showing. And then I told the jury about how they had taken his mother away from him, this criminal mother whose real crime was only her need to feed her children, and how she became a servant for the sheriff in jail and cleaned his house while her own children were sent off to an orphanage where the other children shied away from "those dirty Mexicans"—those lice-ridden children with a jailbird mother. He was only a little boy who wanted to do right by his mother, who loved her, but they took her away and then his father was killed, and then his beloved older brother was killed in front of his eyes, and they even tried to kill this boy, Joe Esquibel, too. And when he tried to save his mother from her pain and her shame and when he got money the only way left for him—by crime—a boy taking money from an old man to save his mother, then, of course, they took him away from his family and put him in a reformatory where he was beaten and exposed to so much fear for so long that he became fearless. He became a young mad dog.

"Ladies and gentlemen, my friends, it was this Welfare Department that took this child from his mother. The children were hungry and naked and cold and the answer was not the humane answer we would expect. The children were not given food and clothing and fuel and their mother. Instead their mother was taken from them and incarcerated. It is a crime, in Carbon County, Wyoming, to be hungry and cold. The crime is punishable by making innocent children orphans, by degrading and abusing innocent puppies until they have become mad vicious dogs.

"But that isn't all of the evidence. What about Sharon Murphy? What about this poor dead woman, shot by this mad Mexican sitting here?" I turned to look at Joe Esquibel, whose head was bowed. The jury looked too.

"Joe Esquibel belonged to her. He was her *thing*. She could control him, turn him off and on as she chose, manipulate him for her own pleasure, and they lived together whenever she wished. She held a magical power over Joe Esquibel. She was the most powerful woman he had ever known, even more powerful than his mother. When she was tired of him she kicked him out, like someone tired of petting a dog, and if he rose up in protest she called the sheriff. When he struck out at her she threw him in jail and Mona Lee Murphy, the woman who had taken this child from his mother and delivered him to the orphanage—Mona Lee Murphy, the mother of Sharon, Joe's ex-wife, well, this white mother with all of her power had him thrown in jail, too. His crime was he had become 'the thing' of her daughter.

"The evidence will show that when Joe was seventeen his skull was smashed in with a piece of pipe by some hidden assailant, and that he suffered a concussion. Now began a series of missing days for Joe Esquibel. There were times of violence and times of blackouts. There were fights in which Joe took on as many as five men at a time, and there were assault and battery charges, of course, and all the time Joe was living with Sharon, this powerful white woman, except when she threw him out, or threw him in jail."

I outlined the history of his head injuries, his blackouts, his strange behavior. It was all there in the medical records from the hospital and the doctor's office, I said. "Then one day, ladies and gentlemen, on one dark day, Joe Esquibel, in the grip of the blackest forces of life, forces over which he no longer had control, forces he cannot remember—well, those forces exploded and destroyed the woman he loved, his beloved wife," I whispered. "He cannot tell you about it because he cannot remember and he cannot remember because he is insane as he sits here, ladies and gentlemen, and out of this nightmare of human degradation comes this very real, very sane proposition: that Joe Esquibel received so many injuries to his mind, both emotional and physical, and he was so fully reduced to just a thing, a mere thing to be used by Sharon, more like an animal than a man— that one day his madness came busting out, came flooding out, and he sits here now, this mad man, unable to understand the nature of the charges being brought against him, and unable to aid in his own defense. It will be the burden of the state to prove that Joe Esquibel is sane—sane right now! They must prove it beyond a reasonable doubt. Well, we say the state will fail in their burden—fail in their case. We will ask you at the conclusion of the case to send Joe Esquibel back to the state hospital to be treated, for once, as a human being, to be cured, and then, one day, perhaps it will be fair for the state to try him for his crime. Then, one day, perhaps it will be fair for Joe Esquibel to defend himself, when he has regained his senses, and can aid us in his defense. Maybe that will be fair. We will ask you to be the first in this man's history to treat him fairly, to give him what we all expect and experience every day, and take for granted —fairness and justice. Just be fair. Return him to the state hospital for treatment—for humane treatment. That's all I ask. Thank you."

I looked at the jury and the jury looked back at me, with open faces. Their arms were unfolded now and some had puzzled looks on their faces, and one had his finger to his chin. They looked at Joe, and one looked down at his own feet, and the mouth of the charwoman in the back was straight and tight like a mother who had seen her child's horror, and I wondered if she had seen it through the eyes of Mona Lee Murphy or of Mrs. Esquibel. I walked back slowly to my chair and I reached over and patted Joe lightly on the leg. I could feel the warmth of his life there. His head never moved. His breathing was fast, a little irregular, and his hands were crossed at his legs, and I could see that his palms were wet with sweat.

23

"THE STATE will call its first witness," Judge Stanton said. He shut the file in front of him, and sat back in his big black chair, his face as expressionless as an onion, and he folded his hands in his lap, ready to do what judges must do, to listen. And listen. The clerk gave the oath to a nice little man named Chris Willis, the deputy sheriff. He was dressed neatly in a sheriff's uniform with a Carbon County patch on his arm, and he wore a pair of brown cowboy boots and his collar was open at the neck. His hair was clipped closely, and it was gray.

"Do you swear to tell the truth, the whole truth and nothing but the truth, so help you God?"

"I do."

Then Deputy Willis walked over to the witness chair and sat down, crossed his legs as most witnesses do, and held onto the arms of the chair as if it would otherwise get away from him. He waited for Oscar Hall's first question.

What had happened on October 17, 1966? Well, he received a call from Luke Massingill, then the director of the Carbon County Welfare Department. Come quick. Joe Esquibel is over here with a gun. When the deputy entered the welfare office with his own gun drawn, Joe Esquibel was backing out a door.

"What next, if anything, took place?" Hall asked, hanging onto the podium with his notes in front of him.

"About that time a shot was fired. Sharon Esquibel fell

to the floor. I had drawn my gun and I cocked it and pointed it at Joe Esquibel and told Joe to get back, at which time Joe had his gun at shoulder level, more or less, pointed down, and he did step back—he looked at me and stepped back and dropped his gun. Then he collapsed or fell to his knees, and then he got himself back up and sat in a chair that was directly behind him."

"Is there anything else you recall, Mr. Willis?" Oscar Hall asked.

"Joe looked at Sharon on the floor there and then he began sobbing, crying and sobbing, 'Joe, Joe, what have you done?' and all the time, or most of the time, his hands were over his eyes and he was in a hunched-over position, sitting down with his elbows on his knees."

"What next do you recall, Mr. Willis?"

"Then he more or less slid off the chair, and there was a chair opposite him on the other side of the corridor, and he more or less got over to it on his hands and knees. And he got up in that chair, still sobbing, attempted to get hold of the telephone, but one of the personnel at the welfare office, Marcella Redmond, got the phone away from him."

"Now you have testified, Mr. Willis, that he was sobbing. Now will you tell the jury just exactly what took place. That's something of an ambiguous term," Hall said.

"He was weeping, or appeared to be weeping, or more or less sobbing and crying, 'Joe, Joe, what have you done?' And while he was sitting in this chair Mrs. Mona Murphy ran up to him and beat on him with her closed fists, and I told Luke Massingill to get Mona Lee Murphy back away from him, and shortly after this I took Joe from the building. He was relaxed and acted like he couldn't walk on his feet and I more or less supported him and took him from the building and put him in the sheriff's car and handcuffed him. . . . I went around to the driver's side and got a pair of handcuffs out of a sack which we carry under the seats, and handcuffed Joe. Joe was not violently, but loosely, thrashing around, kicking and moving around in the car. I recall at the time, we have got a switch box for our red lights and things on the floor in the center of the front seat, and I was afraid he would kick those switches, but he subsided and sat there in the car while I took him to the office."

It sounded a little like an epileptic seizure or something, but Deputy Willis' testimony droned on past that into places Oscar Hall led him to show that Joe Esquibel acted naturally and normally. At the preliminary hearing Joe Esquibel said nothing, Willis said. He stood erect in court and held his head up, "like I would say a man should," didn't sit there with his head down like he was sitting now. In jail he was all right, too. He was one of the cleanest prisoners they had. He gave them no trouble, asked for a haircut at different times, which showed he was sane. And his mother came as did other members of his family. Willis didn't know who they were, but the sheriff required Joe Esquibel to speak to his family in English, even to his mother. Can't have prisoners speaking in a foreign language. Never know what they might be plotting. And they took him to Denver to be examined by a defense psychiatrist, and he acted normal then. Gave no trouble. Sat erect in the car. And Joe remembered once that he left some of his things in the sheriff's office, and Joe asked them to go back and get the stuff for him —so he was sane enough to do that—knew what was going on around him. He could understand ya. "Thank you, Mr. Willis," Oscar said, and then he turned to us and said, "You may examine."

Raymond Whitaker jumped up. He liked to cross-examine sheriffs. They were the natural enemy to Raymond Whitaker.

"Why didn't you shoot Joe Esquibel in the leg to stop the homicide?" Raymond Whitaker asked accusingly.

"Because I was packing a .357 magnum pistol and I knew the capabilities of my gun. The bullet would have ricocheted off the floor, possibly hitting someone else. I said, 'Joe, get back, get back, Joe.' Joe backed up a step or two and dropped his gun and fell to his knees. His legs were against the chair, then he worked himself back up into the chair."

"Now then, after this happened, do you recall some of the welfare employees yelling at you?"

"Yes, I do."

"What did they say to you?"

"They were screaming, 'Shoot him, shoot him. Kill him.' "

"That was, I remind you, *after* he had already dropped the gun?" Whitaker said, still sort of nasty-like.

"Yes."

"You had your gun on him?"

"Right."

"And he was on the floor, as a matter of fact, at that time?"

"He was either standing or going down to the floor about this time."

"And you felt, as a matter of fact, Officer, that it would be cold-blooded murder if you shot him then, isn't that true?"

"Yes."

Deputy Willis admitted that Joe Esquibel had been placed in solitary confinement in jail and fed bread and water because he had quarreled with another deputy who had forbidden Joe to talk to a white girl in the same cellblock, that they slid the food through a feeding hole called the "bean hole," and that there was no light in the cell. The window was even painted over to prevent the prisoner from looking down at the sidewalk. The deputy admitted all of that. Then Raymond Whitaker stalked back to the counsel table, looking angry, over his glasses, his lower jaw jutting out, and he said, "That's all, Officer Willis," in a way that meant that Officer Willis was nobody and had said nothing and that what he had said was disgusting anyway. That's what "That's all" meant.

"Call your next witness," Judge Stanton said, his head back and his eyes still fixed on the ceiling. It was Dr. Madison Thomas, a well-groomed neurologist from Salt Lake City. He wore a three-piece business suit and his shoes were black and freshly shined. He said there was no neurological evidence upon which to base a finding of insanity. He should know, he had been a member of the executive committee and vice-president of the American Epilepsy Federation, and now taught neurology at the University of Utah College of Medicine. He had tested Joe's arms and legs and eyes and reflexes. He stroked the bottom of his toes, gave him a subtraction test, tested his cranial nerves, had him make faces to show that his head and face nerves were intact. Joe told the doctor he had no memory of what happened, but that he remembered when he was younger he had struck his head when he fell once.

The doctor said Joe told him he had started to drink alcohol at the age of twelve and that he had several episodes while drinking when he couldn't remember the events of a whole evening—in other words a blackout—which was associated with the use of alcohol. He did not have any convulsive seizures. The doctor said he made a special note of that, and he looked at the x-rays of Esquibel's skull and found them normal. He gave him an EEG, which was normal, too, and he took a spinal tap. "The outstanding thing about it was that it had an appearance of being bloody." Then he took another spinal tap later to make sure that the blood was merely the result of the tapping procedure itself, and not an indication of an injury to the brain.

"The second tap was normal," he said. He hated to criticize his secretary, but, "it says here the tap was *fairly clear* fluid.' I am reasonably sure I meant 'entirely clear,' because I wrote in my handwriting 'clear' and underlined it." Joe did have a weak sense of smell but he had no definite neurological disorder.

Then Oscar Hall raised his eyebrow and moved a step or two toward the doctor and I knew the important question was coming.

"Doctor, what was your evaluation of this defendant's ability to make judgments?" He was really asking, can he aid in his own defense? Is he presently sane?

I jumped to my feet and turned to the judge, who saw my movement and came suddenly awake.

"Objection, Your Honor. There is no foundation for this question. There is no showing the doctor examined him to determine whether or not Joe Esquibel could make judgments or what kind of judgments he might make. May I *voir dire?*"

"You may *voir dire,* Mr. Spence."

"You didn't make any statement in your report to Dr. Karn about the defendant's ability to make judgments. That was an afterthought here, isn't that true?" I asked.

"The intent of my report to Dr. Karn—Dr. Karn knows that—"

"Just a minute," I interrupted. "I don't think you can testify as to what Dr. Karn knows."

"I felt it unnecessary to add specific statements . . ."

"Well, Doctor," I interrupted again. "Are you saying now that not only your secretary made a mistake in her typing but that you yourself didn't include everything in your report?" I raised my eyebrows and looked at the witness and then at the jury.

"No, no."

I had the report in my hand and walked over to the witness and handed it to him. "Read to the jury where you say something about Joe Esquibel's ability to make judgments." The doctor took the report in his hands, read it quickly and then pointed to some language.

"It showed that he was alert and cooperative. He showed no loss of memory, giving orientation date . . . serial sevens slowly, accurately, presidential recall was fair; these are things that . . ."

"Did it say anything about *judgment?*" I asked.

"I didn't specifically use the word 'judgment.' "

"As a matter of fact the serial sevens test doesn't have anything to do with judgments, does it?"

"No, not specifically. The orientation data I think does reflect his judgment, his description of his problem, his situation, being under charges and being concerned about his situation, it reflects some judgment about the situation."

"You didn't give him any specific test on judgment at the time, did you?"

"I did not do any extensive probing kind of an examination as a psychiatrist does."

"You didn't give him any specific test on judgment at that time, did you?" I asked again, holding him to the fire.

"No."

"And you made no specific finding about judgment evaluation, did you?"

"Except to the—you don't want me to say anything but yes or no—I made no specific statement."

"As a matter of fact, you talked about 'judgments' for the first time with Mr. Hall this morning, isn't that true?"

"I don't know that—" And Oscar Hall was on his feet objecting. It was improper *voir dire,* he said.

"I think I've asked enough questions to lay the foundation for my objection, Your Honor," I said. "I object to the testimony of the doctor on the grounds that he made no inquiry, no tests, upon which he could base a judgment of his own as to Joe Esquibel's ability to make judgments." And when the court asked Oscar Hall if he had anything to say, Oscar turned to the doctor and asked, "Is there a specific test, Doctor, for determining judgment?" And then he led the doctor, "Or is that the result of a combination of factors?"

"It's a combination of factors. I don't know of one specific test you can give for judgment," the doctor said in response to Oscar's cue.

"Thank you," Oscar said, and he sat down with a satisfied look on his face.

"Well, Doctor," I said. "There is a specific psychological test given to determine the ability of a patient to make judgments, isn't there?"

"I don't know if there is one that is universally accepted."

"I didn't ask you whether there was one *universally* accepted. Nothing is universally accepted. I asked you if there wasn't a specific psychological test for 'judgment.' "

"A collection of them," he said.

"Yes. Give the jury the names of a few of them, please, Doctor."

"Some of these are interpretations of things like proverbs, which, for an example . . ."

"Could you just give me the *names* of three or four of these tests? Just tell us the *names* of the tests, Doctor."

"Projection Interpretation is the first one that comes to my mind, asking what you would do in a given circumstance, that sort of thing. The ones that I am acquainted with are not too well standardized."

"And you didn't give any of these, did you?"

"I have no notes about it, and I can't certainly say that I did."

"Thank you, Doctor," I said, and I turned to the judge. "I renew my objection. There is no foundation. The doctor did nothing to test the judgment-making ability of this defendant."

The judge said to Oscar Hall, "Is there anything else, Mr. Hall?"

"No," Oscar Hall said, submitting it to the court for a ruling.

"The objection will be sustained. The doctor will not be permitted to give any opinion as to Mr. Esquibel's ability to make judgments." And Oscar Hall, having nothing left to ask, turned the witness over to me for my cross-examination. "Your witness," Oscar Hall said.

"How many times have you been called upon by the people at the hospital in Evanston to make examinations?" I asked.

"Let me see, that would average about ten or twelve or more per month."

"Yes, and do you get paid for that?"

"Yes."

"And are you getting paid for your presence here today?"

"I am going to send a bill for the time involved."

"Can you necessarily tell from an EEG whether a patient is insane or not?"

"No, not necessarily."

"There is no lack of independent neurologists in Wyoming who could have examined Mr. Esquibel, isn't that true?"

"Yes."

"Now you say your secretary made a mistake. You say

you said the fluid from the spine was 'entirely' clear but that your secretary wrote 'fairly clear.' "

"Yes."

"Was the report taken by dictation or by a voice recording?"

"A tape recorder."

"Well, the word 'entirely' and the word 'fairly' don't sound alike, do they?"

"No."

"And, as a matter of fact, wouldn't you rely more now on what your secretary transcribed than on your present memory?"

"I would rely on my original notes."

"Yes, where are your original notes?"

"I have the notes that I wrote on this chart, here, that's all." The doctor handed me a printed hospital chart.

"So you don't even have your original notes, do you, Doctor?"

"No, sir."

"What did you do with them? Destroy them?"

"I usually throw them away when I am dictating. Well, my original notes are not a complete record by any means."

"And then if things go wrong and you come into court you can tell the jury that the secretary made a mistake, isn't that right? In the meantime the original notes are gone. Did someone else see the spinal tap besides you?"

"I did the spinal puncture. I did not do the lab work."

"Oh, you didn't?"

"No, sir."

I pointed to the words on the lab report. "What do the words 'very finely cloudy' mean?"

"Just what it says, very finely cloudy."

"It doesn't mean, 'entirely clear,' does it?"

"No."

"And would you just put a circle around the words 'very finely cloudy' with a pen, please?" The doctor did and I asked the court permission to show it to the jury, which was granted. And the jurors themselves now looked at the words.

"Now, please tell me, was the second tap entirely clear or not?"

The doctor didn't answer. And I didn't force it.

"Do you know of any studies that show a correlation between blackouts from alcohol and brain damage?"

"Yes."

"Tell the jury about those studies."

"I am not sure I can quote any specific item in the literature, but it is understood that people with brain damage do tolerate alcohol less well than the average person."

"So a person with brain damage, Doctor, might black out with less alcohol than one with an undamaged brain, isn't that true?"

"He might have a period of amnesia, yes."

"And you didn't mention those studies in your report, did you, Doctor?"

"No."

"As a matter of fact, you found that the 'possibility of amnesia, and perhaps the crime itself, correlated with the effects of alcohol on Joe Esquibel,' isn't that right?"

"Yes."

"Now, Joe told you when you talked to him that he didn't remember any of the events from a point early in the evening before the shooting until after the shooting was over, isn't that true?"

"Yes, sir."

"And when one has an epileptic fit, the events that occur during the fit are not remembered, are they, Doctor?"

"That's true."

"And it's true that some epileptics are violent during an epileptic fit?"

"That is a rare occasion," the doctor said. He looked violent. His voice was tight. His eyes narrowed.

"But it's true, isn't it? Some epileptics are violent during a seizure."

"Yes."

"And it's also true that epilepsy is sometimes associated with brain damage?"

"Yes, sir."

"And one of the things you might see in an epileptic seizure is to see the victim collapse to his knees."

"Yes, sir."

"And you might see him crawl around on the floor, isn't that true?"

"You might."

"And afterwards, it's typical of epileptics that they are weak, isn't that true?"

"Some of them, yes."

"And you have seen epileptics who thrash about during a fit?"

"That is a convulsive pattern," he admitted, his eyes still narrow.

"Thrashing around in an automobile so that switches on the floor of the car might be bent from the thrashing is typical?"

"Yes."

"Do you know why the hospital requested the neurological study of Mr. Esquibel?"

"Yes. 'For court observation and bloody fluid.' "

"You weren't afraid of the defendant when you had his belt and cuffs off, were you?"

"No, sir."

"And you talked with him privately?"

"Yes."

"And he didn't seem like a vicious killer to you, did he?"

"No, sir."

"And you said you took some history from him while he was there. Did you take a history of him being hit over the head by someone who is a deputy sheriff at the Rawlins Sheriff's Office?"

"No."

"Did he give you a history of being hit over the head with a beer bottle?"

"No."

"Was any history given to you of his innumerable fights and many blows to his head?"

"No, sir."

"Did he give you a history of dizziness?"

"No, sir."

"Did he give you a history of other blackout spells?"

"No, sir."

"Did he tell you about the fractures to his skull that occurred on at least two different occasions?"

"No, sir."

"Or about being in the hospital after his skull was fractured."

"No."

"Now, if you asked him for a history of his head injuries and he gave you none, that would be some evidence of something being wrong with the patient, isn't that true?"

"Yes, sir."

I showed the doctor the records from the Rawlins Hospital of July 2, 1960, which noted a fractured skull in the right orbit. Behind the right orbit is the part of the brain that controls the memory, the doctor said. And smell. And he remembered that Joe showed a deficiency in his smell. And he admitted that x-rays do not rule out past fractures of the skull, and that the x-rays he took meant nothing so far as Joe's sanity or insanity was concerned. Joe could, he admitted, be a complete psychotic, a raving maniac, and have a normal skull x-ray.

"Yes," the doctor said, "epilepsy is a possibility here." Yes, the doctor admitted, amnesia can be associated with schizophrenia, and yes, amnesia can result from alcohol abuse. The normal pressure on a spinal tap is 100 mm and Joe's pressure was 165. An epileptic can have a normal EEG.

"So there is considerable doubt about whether Joe is an epileptic or not, based solely upon the EEG, isn't that true, Doctor?"

"The EEG won't settle that for certain, one way or the other," the doctor said.

"Yes, a normal EEG doesn't mean that he isn't insane, does it?"

"That's correct."

"But it is also correct that brain damage can cause insanity."

Yes, and the doctor admitted that brain damage can affect the memory, could explain why Joe had trouble keeping a job, could explain his irritability, and his quick temper. Temporal lobe seizures were a possibility in the case, too, and could occur in a person who had a long history of anti-social conduct. Moreover, the doctor admitted that where there is a doubt about brain damage a pneumoencephalogram is often taken, and none was taken here. And, finally there is always the importance of a good clinical history.

"And do you agree in this case the clinical history that you took was less than completely ideal?" I asked.

"I agree that there were additional facts that I did not get from him—that is correct."

"And therefore you are not suggesting he doesn't have temporal lobe seizures, are you?"

"There is no certainty that he doesn't." There is no certainty that he doesn't! And Joe's failure to have a sharp cutoff of memory at some special exact time argues against his having feigned amnesia because in true amnesia the place where the memory ends is fuzzy, and a person suffering from amnesia certainly cannot aid his attorney in his own defense. That's true, and amnesia was consistent with the evidence of brain damage in the case.

"Would you like some more facts, before you pass any further judgments on Joe Esquibel?"

"I think that would be ideal," the doctor said. "Yes." I looked at the jury. The jury looked back, passively. They looked sleepy. For Christ's sake, did they hear? The doctor wanted more facts. Did you hear that, jury?

"I have no further questions, Doctor," I said. "Thank you." I said it like I meant it, and I did mean it. I looked at Joe and he had his head tied to his shoelaces, and there was a vague smile on Whitaker's face and an expression in his eyes as if he had just seen the light, some glorious light in a distant sky.

"You may call your next witness," the judge said, as if

nothing had happened. "Let's move right along, here, gentlemen," he said.

The state called Deputy Frank MacDonald. He was a nice man with white hair and a lot of years, whom the jury would certainly believe. Old men don't lie. Too close to kingdom come, too close to meetin' their maker. The old man might be a little bit forgetful, but I'll tell ya one thing. He ain't no liar. He smiled at the jury, looked up at the judge with the same smile, and then he smiled at me, for Christ's sake. He testified he was in charge of the commissary at the jail. Sold the prisoners cigarettes and candy, at a little profit, probably, and he had once gone out to arrest Joe for an assault and battery against Sharon. And he said Joe had said simply, "Frank, I ain't going with you. Shoot me in the back, if you dare." Then Joe had walked off. And the next morning Sharon dropped the charges anyhow, Deputy MacDonald said. And he smiled. And the jury smiled back. And then he looked at me and smiled and I smiled back, too, and finally he got to what his testimony was all about, which was that Joe was able to make out his commissary slips for cigarettes and candy, actually knew how to make out the slips, the deputy emphasized, which proved he was sane. Then I smiled at the old man with my nicest smile and said, "No questions, Deputy." The deputy smiled back and nodded and thanked me and walked out of the room and then the state called Monty Moon.

Monty Moon was also a deputy sheriff. He was the one who had put Joe on bread and water because he wouldn't stop talking to the girl in the cell across the way. Talking to women across the way was against the rules. "No, the girl was not put on bread and water for having talked." And once he offered Joe a cigarette and Joe refused, saying he would smoke his own, and that proved he was sane. Joe was clean and neat, asked for a mop and broom and a dustpan every day to clean his cell, and Moon fed Joe beans and cereal and hot pancakes, meatloaf and liver. Didn't think Joe ever had any boiled antelope, although they did serve it once in a while, and he denied Joe Esquibel ever lost any weight in jail.

Oscar Hall's next witness was Joe Hay, the street superintendent for the city of Rawlins, who hired Joe in May for $1.96 an hour. He said Joe could drive a four-speed transmission truck with a two-speed axle and that he was dependable, took an interest in his work, and never failed to show up when he should. Seemed sane enough to him. He worked like other men worked, and he'd sure hire Joe again, he said, which was also to say that Mr. Hay wouldn't hire an insane person again.

The case was moving right along, and the judge was still looking up at the ceiling, and I started to look up at the ceiling, too. I looked over at Whitaker and he was looking up at the ceiling, and then they called Dr. Grady Browning.

This was a good-looking man, starting to gray, a stocky fellow, nice voice, and I thought probably that his female patients fell in love with him. I looked over at the women on the jury for clues, but they gave me none back—damned passive juries, never want to let anybody know what they're thinking. Dr. Browning was a clinical psychologist who said he had administered a battery of psychological tests to Joe at the state hospital at Evanston. He had tested Joe's intelligence, and he said Joe's low performance on his I.Q. tests was frequently seen in bilingual people. It was just a language problem. He admitted that the same low scores sometimes show up in cases of brain damage or epilepsy, and in psychopaths, and in persons who have character disorders and who are mentally deficient, but he said Joe's responses to the Rorschach ink blot tests were logical and normal for an individual who was socially, emotionally, and intellectually inadequate, as he called Joe.

Dr. Browning said the tests he gave showed that Joe Esquibel was hostile toward females, tended to see people as "insensitive things," and that Joe's basic defense process was repression, to forget. Joe had never learned to handle his emotions, was quick to anger. The tests the doctor gave for brain damage showed there was "a slight disturbance as to motor coordination, but insufficient to indicate significant neurological impairment." That meant he was hurt a little, but not enough to impress the doctor. There was no evidence of any confusion in Joe's thinking and he had concluded with a flourish, "that Joe Esquibel seemed to be in contact with reality at the time," and was therefore legally sane. Oscar Hall's shirt-tail had been blooming out in front, and he stuffed it back in his pants, buttoned his wrinkled brown jacket, said thank you to the doctor, looked over to me with another little smile, and sat down. "Your witness," he said.

Dr. Browning smirked at me, crossed his arms in front of him against the onslaught, and settled back in the chair. As he answered my first question, the sounds that came out of his mouth were different—louder, tighter, angry. I knew about that, anger, the secondary emotion, which replaces fear—it's easier to be angry than afraid, easier to attack than to run. I knew Dr. Grady Browning.

"Dr. Browning, it's true that the results of psychological testing depend in large measure on the tester?"

"Perhaps."

"Well, is that true or isn't it true?"

"Well, it is true in part."

"And it was you, Dr. Browning, who reported that Joe saw women as manipulative and powerful, wasn't it?"

"Yes."

"That could be a delusion, isn't that true?"

"Well . . ."

"A delusion is something that isn't so, but which the person believes to be so, isn't it?"

"Yes."

"And a delusion is a symptom of insanity, isn't it?"

"Well, sort of . . ."

"If somebody is delusional, that is, suffering from delusions, you would say that that is evidence of psychosis, isn't that true?"

"Yes."

"And psychosis is just a fancy word you use for insanity."

"Yes."

"And so when Joe Esquibel saw women to be powerful that could be evidence of his insanity, isn't that true?"

"Could be."

"Now, with respect to his mother—you did know of his mother's background in this case, didn't you?"

"Quite frankly, I don't recall it at this time."

I looked over at the jury. The jury looked back as innocent and blank as a herd of grazing goats. Goddamn it. Did you hear that? I began looking at each one of them separately as I asked the questions of the good doctor. "I heard you correctly, didn't I, Doctor, when you said just now that you didn't recall having known of the mother's background in this case?" I put the sound of incredulity in my voice.

"Yes," he said, as if it made no difference. I handed him Exhibit N, the report of the social worker at the state hospital who had also interviewed Joe Esquibel. The social worker had found that "this boy both loved and hated his mother."

"Would you think a little boy might hate his mother if he found her frequently with men who were not his father?"

"He might."

"Would that be a normal response for a little boy?"

"I would say it would be an expected response."

"And having learned that, might he later react the same way toward his wife?"

"He could."

"And could such early experiences lead to psychosis?"

"Well, anything is possible, Mr. Spence," he said as if to dismiss the question.

"Are you aware that Dr. Karn diagnosed Joe Esquibel as a psychopath?"

"No."

"You made no such diagnosis yourself, did you?"

"No."

"You and Dr. Karn didn't diagnose Joe Esquibel the same, then, did you?"

"Apparently not."

"Have you made any attempt, you and Dr. Karn, to settle your differences in this diagnosis?"

Oscar Hall interrupted. "I object. We don't know what a psychopath is to a doctor like Dr. Browning, and what a psychopath might be to a psychiatrist like Dr. Karn."

"Well, let's help Mr. Hall, Doctor. Give me a definition of psychopath."

"I can't give you a textbook definition because I am not a textbook." He was angry. He leaned forward and his eyes were hard.

"Well, you are a professor, too, aren't you? You do teach such things, don't you, Professor? What is a classic definition of a psychopath?"

"Can I give my own definition?"

"Don't you know the ordinary textbook definition?"

"Sir, I don't think I can give a classic definition from a psychiatric volume, no."

"Well, can you give a classic definition from a psychological volume—from any volume?"

Oscar Hall jumped to his feet, to protect his witness. "I demand that Mr. Spence treat this witness with respect, because he's a Ph.D. Let's not have these professional witnesses afraid to testify."

"I move for a mistrial, Your Honor," I said immediately. "Dismiss this case for the misconduct of Mr. Hall in making such remarks in front of this jury. An educated witness is entitled to no more consideration than any other witness. He either knows the answer to a question or he doesn't, and if he doesn't know, under his oath, he is required to say so, simply, like you and me, like anybody else."

Judge Stanton looked sleepily down from the bench. It wasn't that he was sleepy. It was only that he wanted to give the impression that nothing very serious was happening. "Your motion is overruled, Mr. Spence. Please proceed with your questioning."

"Mr. Hall suggested you might be afraid, Doctor. You aren't afraid, are you, Mr. Witness?"

"Not particularly," he said. He looked more fierce now. His eyes darted back and forth quickly, which gave the impression they were ablaze, and that he was ready to come down off the witness stand. His heavy neck was bowed forward and his arms were now holding on tightly to the arms of the chair. He looked ready for combat.

"You don't feel that I have abused you, do you, Doctor?" I was sweet.

"Not really."

"You diagnosed Joe Esquibel as 'an *inadequate personality*' while Dr. Karn diagnosed him as '*passive aggressive*' personality."

"Yes."

"That's a different diagnosis, isn't it?"

"Uh-huh."

"And you use the *same* diagnostic system in psychology and psychiatry, isn't that true?"

"Yes."

"That's true because the diagnosis comes from the same psychiatric manual that both professions use, isn't that also true?"

"Yes."

"And the code number for Dr. Karn's diagnosis is 51.5 and the code number for your diagnosis is 50.1, isn't that true?"

"That's what is says."

"And so have you decided when you and Dr. Karn will get together and come to some agreement on your diagnosis?"

Oscar Hall was on his feet. "Objection . . ."

"Sustained," Judge Stanton said.

"Well," I began anew. "If you and Dr. Karn can't agree on the diagnosis of this defendant, then how can you fairly expect a jury to come to a conclusion beyond a reasonable doubt?"

"Objection!" Oscar Hall said, and before he could finish his objection the court sustained him.

"No further questions," I said.

But Oscar Hall wasn't satisfied. It was war. "When you talked to Joe Esquibel in your office, Doctor, did he sit in a position like you see him now—with his head down, looking at his feet?"

"No," the doctor said firmly. "He was sitting across from me, looking up at me."

"That's all," Hall said and sat down, Dr. Browning's anger now clearly mirrored on his own face.

It was still war. "I have a question or two of my own now," I said to the doctor. "When you examined Joe Esquibel, you didn't examine him in the presence of twelve strangers, did you?"

"No."

"And when you were examining him, you didn't have the power to send him to the gas chamber, did you, Doctor?"

"I didn't have what?"

"You didn't have the power to make this poor man face the gas chamber, did you?"

"No."

"You were there alone, on a man-to-man basis, weren't you?"

"That's right."

"And you discovered that he wasn't afraid of other men, didn't you?"

"Oh, I don't know that I could make that kind of a statement."

"But you did discover that he was afraid of women and saw them as powerful and manipulative?"

"Yes."

"And there were no women in your office, were there?"

"That's right."

"And we have already discussed, you and I, the fact that his fear of women may be psychotic—that it's possibly evidence of insanity."

There was no answer. I looked over at two or three of the women on the jury. Took time to look at each of them individually.

"Did you feel as comfortable here on the witness stand today, yourself, as you did back in the confines of your own office?"

"No."

"And would you hold it against Joe Esquibel if he didn't either?"

"I haven't implied that I did."

"Thank you, Doctor. I have nothing further."

The court recessed for the evening. Raymond and I gathered up our things and headed for the Gladstone Hotel.

"A little libation for the gladiators at the Gladstone," Raymond said. John Ackerman and John Hursh, the law students, tagged along as we walked up the street to the corner. "Ah, the Happy-Rock Saloon," Whitaker said as he went in.

"The what?" I asked absently.

"Never mind, Gerald. The Gladstone. Ah, the Gladstone," he said as he held open the door. "Enter, oh, warrior," he said with a flourish. We sat down in the dark room and then a full-bloomed Mexican woman with nice legs sticking out of a very short skirt walked over to the table to take our orders.

"You defending Joe Esquibel?" she asked.

"Yes," I said.

"I love you," she said. "What'll you have?"

I looked at her. I thought I could love her back. "Cabin Still and a Coors." Then Whitaker ordered and the law students ordered and the Mexican waitress leaned over us with the drinks. We were all friends, close together at this table in this warm, dark place, safe for the moment, and I drank more Cabin Still and chased it down with beer like a man should.

"I got the doctor's ass, today," I said.

"You did that, Gerald," Whitaker said.

"And I got Browning's ass, too."

"Yes, yes, you did. You did, indeed," Whitaker said. "You were gorgeous."

"What's the jury doing?" I asked.

"Here's to the jury," Whitaker said, holding up his glass. "To that ineffable conglomerate of wisdom and caprice."

"Yes, here's to the jury," I said. "How are we doing with them?"

"Who knows, Gerald? Who can know a jury?" he said, looking off to the distance over the top of his glasses. "But this much I know. We are beautiful." And then we laughed and drank and I proclaimed my love for the bar waitress and she professed back to me, but she wouldn't run off with me. She said, "Oh, Mr. Spence!" just the way Cleo, my secretary, always did.

Sometime during the evening I staggered to the elevators and found my room in the old Happy-Rock Hotel. In my sleep my mother came to me. She had been gone for a long time. In my dream I didn't know where she had been or what she had been doing. How could she have left me? She was cold and distant. She didn't kiss me. She acted like she didn't love me.

The next morning was rainy and gloomy, and when I got to the courtroom Dr. Karn was sitting in the front row. No pipe. No smoking in the courtroom. He looked at me with the same pleasant face and quiet eyes and nodded hello. My belly started to churn. Could I do it? I had to do it. Maybe I would overdo it and the jury would love him. Be careful.

"Call Dr. Karn," Oscar Hall said as the first order of business of the morning, and I looked over at Joe sitting there, his eyes obediently fastened to his feet. I saw a little look of faint disdain on the face of Raymond Whitaker. The judge looked up at the ceiling. I leaned back in my chair, and I closed my eyes, and listened.

It was the reassuring voice of Dr. Karn. "Joe wasn't given to words," he was saying in response to Oscar's questions. I couldn't stand it. I opened my eyes and looked. Yes, there he was, with that kind look, and he was giving his answers directly to the jurors, as if he liked each and every one of them, talking to them, nicely, a little sad. Oh, God, they will love him. "He wasn't one given to words," the doctor repeated, looking down with just the right amount of self-consciousness, "but he seemed unwilling to explain the situation with which he had been charged. It wasn't that he couldn't. It was that he wouldn't explain it." Refused to. He was the typical passive-aggressive type personality. He had no lapse of memory before the shooting, and therefore one can safely conclude he had none, in fact, after the shooting. He simply didn't want to remember. "He refused to remember," the doctor said quietly, as if he were speaking about someone he cared for a great deal, and "he was properly oriented."

"Yes," Oscar Hall said. "Properly oriented. That means he knew where he was and what he was doing?"

"Yes."

"That means he was sane?" Hall continued.

"That's leading, Your Honor," I objected.

"Sustained," Judge Stanton said.

"Do you have an opinion, then, Dr. Karn, based upon reasonable medical psychiatric certainty, as to whether the defendant, Joe Esquibel, is triable now?"

"Yes," the doctor said. "I have an opinion."

"What is your opinion, Doctor?" he asked.

"I thought he was able to relate to me rather well and to the other staff members, too, and because of this ability I have no doubt he could relate to his own attorneys equally well. He can aid in his own defense. That is the test. He is presently quite triable. He is sane." He smiled at the jury apologetically, still a little sadly, and several of the jurors smiled back. My heart froze. Oh, God. There it was. How could I attack him? They loved him. If I attacked the man they loved, they would hate me. If I didn't, the trial for Joe Esquibel was over.

I looked at all the masks on all the faces in the courtroom. The judge's wooden face looked sleepy, and Joe's face was tied to his shoes, and Whitaker looked off into the distance like a just dead, sweet, pious monk, and the jurors' faces were blank, as barren as ground, and the sounds of the testimony had risen up in chanting native sounds, which filled this empty courtroom like sounds from some clearing in the tall pines that towered overhead, and the ground was packed from the pounding feet of the natives who danced around the accused who was huddled in the center of the dancers, his head bound between his legs with rawhide thongs, and the dancers wore brightly painted masks, some fierce, some silly, but they were all empty-faced masks, which rattled as the natives darted at each other, bird-witted, feather-headed, dipping and dancing around the accused, who sat there, one would say, passively. He is a passive-aggressive type —51.5.

"You say Joe Esquibel was putting on a false face for you, Doctor?" I began.

"I would say so," Dr. Karn said, with an almost imperceptible smile.

"That's how you saw it?"

"Yes, of course."

"Psychiatry isn't a science, it's an art, isn't that true?"

"Yes. A little of both, I would say."

"Like painting is a little of both science and art?"

"I suppose so."

"But the pictures that are painted by artists are as different as paintings by Picasso or by Russell."

The doctor only looked at me, kindly. No answer.

"All artists don't paint the same picture, do they?"

"Of course not," he said.

"And all psychiatrists wouldn't see Joe the same way, would they?"

"Possibly not."

"Yet you have testified to your conclusion to a *'reasonable psychiatric certainty,'* haven't you?"

"Yes, that's what I said."

"There is nothing certain in art, is there, Doctor?"

"I object. That's immaterial," Oscar Hall said fiercely.

"Sustained," the court said in a sleepy voice.

"Now, Doctor, in making your own diagnosis, you relied, to some extent, on Dr. Thomas' report, didn't you?"

"Well . . ."

"If Dr. Thomas had found that Joe Esquibel had brain damage, and that he was insane as a result of such brain damage, that would have influenced your thinking, isn't that true?"

"Yes, I suppose so."

"And Dr. Thomas has already told us he needed more

information—that he didn't have the facts about Joe's head injuries before he wrote up his report."

"Yes, I heard him say that."

"And a diagnosis is no better than the history that a doctor takes, isn't that true?"

"Yes."

"And if there is a defective history, isn't there also the likelihood of a defective diagnosis?"

"That's possible."

"Well, Doctor, it's more than *possible,* isn't it? You wouldn't put your name to a diagnosis if you knew the history was incomplete, would you?"

"No."

"But you did in this case, didn't you, Doctor?"

"I don't understand."

"Yes," I said. "You now know that part of your diagnosis was based upon the findings of Dr. Thomas, who himself had an incomplete history, isn't that true?"

"I know that now, yes."

"And you know that epilepsy can come from brain damage?"

"Yes."

"And you now know that Joe Esquibel may have had brain damage, isn't that true?"

"I don't know."

"You can't say one way or the other, can you?"

"No, sir."

"And, therefore, you can't testify to anything based on a *reasonable psychiatric certainty,* can you?"

"You haven't proved anything different to me, Mr. Spence."

"Doctor, the burden of proof rests with you, not with me. You can't testify to anything based on a reasonable psychiatric *certainty,* can you?"

"I think so," he said.

"You even made simple errors in the history that you did take, didn't you, Doctor? You reported to Judge Stanton, for instance, that 'the subject married a woman who had three children by a previous marriage.' That was wrong, wasn't it, Doctor? Those were his own children, weren't they?"

"Yes."

"And you made other errors in his history. You told the court he was employed principally as a truck driver. That was wrong, too, wasn't it?"

"Yes, I understand now that he drove trucks only occasionally. It doesn't seem important, however."

"No. What other errors did you make in your examination and diagnosis that *were unimportant*, Doctor?"

"I don't know of any."

"You relied on Sheriff Ogburn's report to you that Joe Esquibel, 'since the age of five has robbed, assaulted, and threatened numerous people.' You relied on that?"

"Yes."

"And if that were false you would be relying upon a false history, isn't that true?"

"Yes, if that were important."

"It was important enough for you to mention in your report to Judge Stanton, wasn't it?"

"Yes."

"But look here, Doctor, at Exhibit B-1, which is part of the welfare records of Carbon County. Read that portion of the exhibit to the jury, if you please."

"It says, 'the Esquibel children have never been in any trouble.' "

"And Joe was eleven on the date of that report, wasn't he?"

"Yes. I didn't have this to read at the time I made my report. I requested the welfare records. They were never sent to me."

Oscar Hall jumped up holding the welfare records out and with a sweeping wave of his hand, he said, "If the court please, we offer into evidence at this time, the complete voluminous report of the Welfare Department."

"No objection," I said quickly before he changed his mind.

"They are received," Judge Stanton said.

"You never read these before, did you, Doctor?" I

lifted up the big volume of papers thick as the New York City telephone directory.

"No."

"You had no idea about the specific history of Joe Esquibel's life as recorded in these records?"

The doctor thumbed through the thick volume I handed him, then looked up, and in a pleasant voice he said, "No, Mr. Spence. I never had these."

"And it's also true that you knew nothing before the trial, of the error Dr. Thomas claims his secretary made about the bloody spinal tap, isn't that true?"

"I didn't know that."

"And you know that a bloody spinal tap could be caused by brain damage."

"That's one possibility."

"That possibility was never ruled out, was it, Dr. Karn?"

"Well, I don't think it was very likely. It could have been from the tap itself."

"Yes, Doctor, but you are testifying here to a medical and psychiatric *certainty,* and you can't testify to any *certainty* until you rule out the possibility that the bloody tap may have come from brain damage, isn't that true?"

"If you say so."

"That's true, isn't it?" I pushed.

"Yes, I think so."

"Thank you, Doctor. But you failed to tell the court in your report that Joe suffered some lack of motor coordination, didn't you?"

"Well . . ."

"And a problem with motor coordination is consistent with brain damage, isn't it?"

"Could be."

"It's *consistent* with brain damage, isn't it?" I demanded.

"Yes."

"And, Doctor, you said in your report that 'longitudinally, Joe has been on the wrong side of the tracks, socially, morally, emotionally, and intellectually.' You said that, didn't you?"

"Yes."

"That means he didn't get what the folks on the right side of the tracks got, isn't that true?"

"That's what I meant."

"It means he didn't get the basic things he needed for normal development, isn't that true? He didn't get what he needed, did he?"

"Needed for what, Mr. Spence?"

"He didn't get what he needed in order to grow up in a healthy fashion, mentally, morally, and emotionally. Isn't that true?"

"Yes."

"And that deprivation in itself can lead to psychosis, can't it?"

"Yes, it's possible."

"You knew about Joe's blackouts?"

"I had heard about them."

"You must not have thought they were very important."

"Well . . ."

"You never told the judge about them in your report to him."

"No, I didn't."

"But you know that blackouts can be caused by brain damage, don't you?"

"Sometimes, under certain circumstances."

"And, Doctor, you admit, don't you, that you destroyed your notes?"

"I didn't destroy them, as such."

"Where are they, then?"

"I don't have them. I threw them away. I didn't need them anymore—just penciled notes, you know."

"You can't tell me, then, exactly what was on them, can you?"

"No."

"You have neither those notes nor an exact memory now, do you?"

"No."

"Did you know that Joe lost forty pounds in jail?"

"No."

"Can severe and sudden weight loss affect a person's mental capacity?"

"It's been reported."

"Now, Doctor"—I picked up a textbook from my table —"you admit that an 'epileptic can exhibit furors during which he may commit a serious offense, usually highly aggressive in type.' " The doctor watched my reading.

"Yes."

Then, quietly and slowly, I said, "You know, Doctor, the question in this case is one of 'reasonable doubt.' The question is whether there is *reasonable doubt* as to Joe Esquibel's present sanity. You understand that?"

"I've been told that, yes, sir."

"And the test of his present sanity, his so-called 'triability,' is whether he can assist his attorneys in his defense in any meaningful way. Isn't that true?"

"Yes."

"And wouldn't it be fair to say that Joe was unable to assist you adequately and intelligently in securing his social and medical history?"

"Well . . ."

"Most of the information on his history you got for the first time during this trial. Isn't that true?"

"Some of it, yes."

"Surely you did your job adequately—surely you tried to get that information from Joe?"

"Yes, I did."

"And you must now admit that he couldn't give you all of the information that you needed."

"Well, he was not as fully adequate in giving me the information as he might have been."

"Don't you think that he would have the same trouble in aiding his own attorneys in preparing his defense?"

"He might be impaired," Dr. Karn said.

"Thank you, Doctor. I have nothing further," I said.

At the evening recess I followed the deputy who was cuffed to Joe down to the small room where the deputy unlocked the cuffs. "Don't take long," the deputy said. "I get off at five. It's ten past now. Gotta put him to bed 'fore I can go home."

"Okay, Sheriff," I said.

Joe stood there, still looking down, and when the deputy closed the door, I said, "We're doing great." Joe kept looking down. I gave him a friendly push. "The sheriff's gone, you can look up now, Joe." Then Joe looked up and blinked his eyes as if he were looking into the light for the first time.

"How do you think we're doing, Joe?"

He just blinked his eyes back at me, like there was something in them. I shook him a little by the arm. He was nearly as tall as I, and as thin as he was, still heavily muscled, and I could feel a strength a man does not feel through neat business suits. "What do you think, Joe?"

He looked at me nervously, as if I were speaking a strange language to him. "How's the neck, Joe?" I laughed a little. "Gettin' stiff?"

He nodded, and reached up to the back of his head. "Them guys is gonna kill me."

"Who, Joe?"

"Them white guys. I gotta get out of here, Mr. Spence."

"You'll be okay. Don't panic now, for Christ's sake. We about got 'er made." I grabbed both of his arms but he was stiff as a mummy. "What's the matter, Joe?" He looked at me for a minute and then looked down at his feet to which his eyes seemed more accustomed.

"Look here, Joe," I said, giving him another little reassuring shake. "It's gonna be okay." He looked up, his forehead wrinkled in a quizzical look. His mouth hung loose on his face, and there was mostly the wounded Aztec there, the Indian, and I thought he looked like a young warrior about to face his time. Maybe the fear had lain too heavy and too long on him, and had paralyzed his tongue, maybe numbed his brain.

"Don't be afraid, Joe," I said. "We're gonna be okay."

"I ain't afraid of them white guys," he said suddenly. "I could whip them white guys easy."

"For God's sake, Joe, don't cause any problem."

"I gotta get out of here, Mr. Spence. I go crazy in jail."

"I know," I said. "Just hang on. We're gonna be all

right. Okay, Joe? Okay?" I shook him again, easy, friendly-like.

"I ain't afraid of them white guys," he said.

"I know, Joe."

"That sheriff says we are lying to the jury and that the jury knows that we are lying and he laughs at me. He says that jury is going to get me."

"They got to get me first, Joe. We're in this together. Don't talk to the fucking deputy."

"He takes my clothes away from me when he puts me in jail at night. Says he ain't gonna bring me my clothes in the morning, and he laughs at me."

"Well, fuck him," I said. "He'll bring you your clothes, all right. Need anything? Need cigarettes?"

"I ain't afraid of them guys, Mr. Spence."

"I know, Joe," I said. "I know you aren't afraid." I opened the door and nodded to the deputy, who was standing down the hall a little ways, and he came back with a tough walk.

"You take good care of my friend," I said.

"I'll take good care of him," he said with a smirk.

"And don't give him any shit about his clothes or anything else, do you understand?" I looked hard at him.

"Can't he take a joke?" he said.

"You treat him right, do you understand?" I put my hand on Joe's shoulder and whispered in his ear. "Don't talk to the son-of-a-bitch, Joe." And then I said out loud, "Have a good night, Joe." I heard the cuffs click on the wrists of my client and I saw the two of them walking down the long hallway toward the jail.

That night I promised the Mexican barmaid at the Happy-Rock that I would love her forever. "I love Joe Esquibel," she said.

"All women love Joe Esquibel," Raymond said.

"God, he's a beautiful animal," she said.

"But I have a beautiful mind, and I love you and I want to show you the animal in me," I said. She leaned over with the drinks. And she leaned over further and wiped the table, and I started to kiss her on her open front and then she slapped me in the face with the wet bar rag and laughed, and Whitaker laughed, and the law school boys laughed, and we drank up and toasted Dr. Karn.

"Here's to our best witness, Gerald," Raymond said.

"It wasn't his idea to be our witness," John Ackerman said.

"Yeah, John," I said. "He didn't intend it that way. Hey, Kewpie doll. I love you." She pretended not to hear. "Bring us another round," but she heard the drink order all right and came bouncing back to our table with full glasses.

The courtroom had been empty after the first day. Even the prospective jurors who had not been chosen had left. I have spent a lifetime toiling in important cases in empty courtrooms, and the next morning the courtroom was still empty. Sheriff Ogburn walked up like a man in command, the state's first witness of the day. He was big and good-looking, like a movie star, better-looking than Burt Lancaster, and he took the stand confidently, crossed his legs and smiled over at the prosecutor, Oscar Hall.

"Well, Sheriff," Oscar Hall began. "What kind of a jail do you run there in Rawlins?" he asked.

"We run a good jail, Mr. Hall, you know that. It's checked once a year by the Federal Bureau of Prisons. The jail has always passed inspection. It's properly equipped. My wife cooks the food."

"I suppose she's a good cook, isn't she, Sheriff?" Oscar asked.

"You damn right," he said. He looked up at the judge apologetically and said, "Excuse me, Your Honor." A couple of the jurors snickered. "She orders food every week, and the prisoners are fed twice a day. Bread and water is only used to discipline."

"How much are you allowed a day to feed a prisoner?"

"A dollar and a half a day is the allowance by the county. And the diet is approved by a doctor in Rawlins. The doctor also treats the sick prisoners."

"And so was Joe Esquibel treated all right in your jail?" Oscar Hall asked.

"You bet."

"No further questions," Oscar Hall said.

I walked up to the podium, some papers in my hands. Suddenly I looked up at the sheriff, caught him eye to eye and held him there. The silence in the courtroom was uncomfortable. He stared back. His face began to redden. I held him there longer, and then suddenly I said in a hostile voice, "You didn't know Joe Esquibel when he was five years old, did you, Sheriff?"

"Not when he was five." His voice was hostile back.

"But you wrote Dr. Karn a letter that said, 'Since the age of five he has robbed, assaulted, and threatened numerous people . . .' That wasn't the truth, was it?" I asked.

"That was his past record, before I was elected. They are all on file. I sent the records to the state hospital."

"Well, let's see if you sent everything to the state hospital." I threw Dr. Karn's records to him. They slid across his lap and onto the floor. I picked them up and handed them back. "Excuse me, Sheriff," I said. "Now show us where Dr. Karn received from you *any* evidence that Joe Esquibel has robbed and assaulted numerous people since he was five years of age."

"It ain't there."

"Who did he rob?"

"Well, check the police records."

"*Who?* I am asking you. *Who* did he rob at five years of age?" I was shouting at the sheriff and the sheriff was not accustomed to having men shout at him.

"His playmates."

"You're guessing, aren't you? You really don't know anything about what Joe Esquibel did when he was five. What you put down here was simply some kind of careless hearsay, isn't that true?"

"Hearsay is right," he shouted.

"It was *careless* hearsay, wasn't it?"

"That's right," he shouted, "but that's for Dr. Karn's information."

"And it was careless hearsay in a case where Joe Esquibel's life was at stake, wasn't it, Sheriff?"

"I wouldn't know."

"You knew he was charged with first degree murder, didn't you?"

"That's right."

"And so you knew his life was at stake, didn't you?" I was pointing my finger at him now, shaking it.

"Not necessarily," he said, and his face got redder and his neck seemed to swell.

"And it was the same kind of carelessness that was also evidenced in the way you treated your prisoners, isn't that true?"

"No."

"And sometimes you feed your prisoners antelope meat, don't you, boiled antelope meat that your wife cooks up good?"

"I buy an antelope carcass once in a while from the Game and Fish Commission for a dollar or two a carcass. Mostly confiscated game. The prisoners eat beans most of the time. That don't hurt Joe Esquibel none," he said.

"And Joe didn't eat any of the bread or water for the days that he was on it, did he?"

"I don't know."

"And the reason you finally put him back on some food was that you had to give him something to eat or he would have starved to death, isn't that true?"

"No, sir."

"And he lost forty pounds in your jail, didn't he?"

"No."

"Didn't you say to somebody in this case that 'we finally got that goddamned Mexican'?" I turned my back on him. He hollered his answer through me. "No." I whirled back with my finger pointing at him again and I shouted, "You never said that to anybody?"

"No! You produce him!" he shouted back, and the judge hit his gavel on the bench.

"That will be enough of that, gentlemen," His Honor said.

"That's all," I said, and walked to the table.

"The state rests," Oscar Hall said quietly.

"Call your first witness, Mr. Spence," Judge Stanton said.

"We have one witness. Call John Hursh." He was one of the young law students who had worked on the case. He was slender, but even so, his jacket was too tight. His blond head was already balding but his face was open and clean-shaven and his eyes were as blue and innocent as a baby's. He walked with a young swagger up to the clerk, was sworn, and took the stand.

"You know the sheriff, Mr. Hursh?"

"Yes, sir."

"How did you meet him?"

"I went to the sheriff's office to interview Deputy Sheriff Willis about what he saw when Joe Esquibel shot his wife."

"Did you talk to Mr. Willis?"

"No, sir."

"Why not?"

"Because Deputy Willis said I had to talk to his boss, Sheriff Ogburn, before he would talk to me."

"Did you ask the sheriff for permission to talk with Deputy Willis?"

"Yes, sir."

"Did the sheriff allow the interview?"

"No, sir. He did not."

"And did you have any conversation with Sheriff Ogburn with respect to the defendant, Joe Esquibel?"

"Yes, sir, I did."

"Did he say anything to you about Joe Esquibel at that time and place?"

"He told us he would not allow his deputies to speak to us and that 'he had that goddamned Mexican.' "

"I have no further questions of the witness, Your Honor. We have no other witnesses. The defense rests."

The next morning it was Judge Stanton's time to tell the jury the law. Lawyers say juries don't pay any attention to what judges say the law is, don't understand it and do what they damn well please, but the judge didn't act like he believed that, and I don't believe it either—seen too many jurors hung up on an instruction, always asking for clarification from the judge, and I've seen men and women turn the poor and the needy away and dismiss the injured and the maimed not because they wanted to, not because there was no compassion in their hearts, but because they thought they were following the law. They were sworn to follow the law, you know. Have to follow the law.

Judge Stanton was as solemn as the Lord, and now from the bench there was fire in his blue eyes as he read the jury his instructions. He said the jury alone should determine the credibility of the witness, that is, who is and who is not telling the truth, and he told the jury they could believe the experts or not. It was up to them. And he told them what the test for present insanity was. Did Joe Esquibel know what was going on? Could he help his attorney in his defense if he had a defense, and the state of Wyoming had the burden of proving that Joe Esquibel was sane beyond a reasonable doubt. Then Judge Stanton turned to Oscar Hall. "You may make your closing argument," he said, and now in anticipation of Oscar's final argument the judge leaned back and began looking at the ceiling once more.

Oscar Hall got up, shuffled his notes, cleared his throat, glanced at the jury with a quick smile, and told the jury that it was time to stop all this killing in the streets. "Violent crime is on an upswing in this country. We have to bring crime to a screeching halt," he said. "A screeching halt. We've got to stop people who know enough to get a gun, load it, chase their wives into the welfare office, argue and holler and threaten and raise hell, and then shoot their wives right between the eyes, and after they've done all that claim that they didn't know any better—claim that they are insane. We've got to stop these kind of people," he said angrily, hitting the podium with his fist. It was disgusting, he said. "Joe Esquibel knows how to get what he wants, and if he can't get it, well, he just beats the hell out of somebody or kills them. That's all. That's his way. Thumbs his nose at the law. Thumbs his nose at us. Always has. Dr. Karn has said so. Everybody says so. And the defendant just sat there with his head down all during the trial—who's he think he's fooling—me? You? Ha! The minute a verdict is in finding him insane, he'll look up and laugh in your face, that's what he'll do, laugh till he's sick. It's a big charade—you know what's real when you see it. You know as well as I. Enough is enough. Enough is enough, I tell you," Oscar Hall was saying. "To kill, and then to claim you don't remember, and to try to make fools of all of us!" Oscar Hall was outraged, to be made a fool of! "We brought the best men in the state to you and they told you. I've told you. Your common sense has told you. Now you tell us in your verdict. Thank you."

Raymond Whitaker leaned over across Joe Esquibel, whose eyes were still tied to his feet, and whispered to me, "Be beautiful, Gerald." I nodded back and got up. I didn't feel beautiful, I felt excited, full, and I felt about to burst. I felt like all my colors were running together, the red and green, for Christ's sake, and my colors would get muddy. I felt angry. I could feel my rage rolling up inside, but I knew underneath I was afraid.

"Ladies and gentlemen of the jury," I said. "Here we are together." It sounded pleasant enough. I smiled. Nobody smiled back. "We've come here to find the truth. We're not here to hate nor to avenge nor to be angry and outraged like Mr. Hall," I said softly, looking in the kindest way over to Oscar. "But we are here to find the truth. That's what you swore to do when you raised your hands. And when I raised my hand and took my oath as an attorney I swore to do the same as an officer of this court—I swore to aid you in the discovery of the truth.

"Now it's Oscar Hall's duty to prove the truth to you beyond a reasonable doubt. Do you know what the truth is? Think a minute. What is the truth in this case?" I let a curtain of silence fall around the jury, then I lifted it again.

"I am not one to play games. I didn't come here to try to hide the facts from you and then argue that the state, that Oscar Hall, failed to prove the truth beyond a reasonable doubt. You know what I did. We have been together in this thing from the start. I have tried to find out the truth. I tried to ask the questions you would have asked if you had been permitted to ask questions, and when we search for the truth we can't take things on their face. We have to look at the facts, turn them over, understand, and understand, and understand so well, understand so down deep and well, that the truth comes crying out.

"But I think we have discovered the truth in this case. The truth is that nobody knows the present mental condition of Joe Esquibel and that isn't because these are incompetent doctors, or bad men, these doctors, these men of great knowledge who have come here to testify. But I'll tell you one thing. If you and I did our job like they did theirs, they'd run us off the job." I looked over to the man with the fresh-pressed overalls, who sat with his arms folded over his belly. I thought he was closing me out. "I'll tell you something else. If you went out with the company bulldozer to build a road and messed around a little on the surface—pushed a little dirt here and covered a little over there, and never made a good clear straight cut for a road, and then you called that mess a road, well, they'd run you off the job. Calling a mess a road doesn't make it a road. It's just a bunch of dirt pushed here and there. The boss wouldn't accept that. They'd fire you if you did your job like the doctors did their job here. They had the same simple responsibility as you and I—to do their job right. And they can't come to us after they pushed a little of Joe Esquibel's dirt here, and covered some of it up there, and say they have a straight clean road to the truth. We've discovered the truth here, all right, you and I. We've discovered that they didn't do their job.

"Was there brain damage? Dr. Browning found evidence of brain damage. Did it cause epilepsy? Dr. Thomas didn't know, didn't have enough information, admits they didn't have enough facts to say. Dr. Karn, well, he doesn't know either. Was it epilepsy? Could be. Was it schizophrenia caused by his traumatic childhood as shown by those voluminous welfare records that Dr. Karn never read? Could be. Was it amnesia caused by brain damage of some kind? Could be. Was Joe Esquibel so destroyed as a little boy, his mind so ripped and torn and bruised and beaten that he became a mad dog, insane—unable to understand—unable to aid in his own defense—unable to help us? Well, it could be.

"Well, is it black or is it white? Could be either. Who knows?

"Now, I'm not asking you to turn Joe Esquibel loose. Let's be truthful. I am asking you to make these fellas do their job right. I'm asking you to send him back to those doctors with a clear message that they make this road right, open it up, take off the layers of dirt, a layer at a time, like a road should be built. Make us a road! I want a good workman-like road, straight as a string, an honest-to-God road to the truth! I want you to return Joe Esquibel to the state hospital with your verdict. And when you have done that, well, we will have found the truth in this case. Thank you, ladies and gentlemen." I walked back to my seat, and Raymond Whitaker smiled a proud smile and the law students sitting inside the bar of the courtroom close together smiled. And after the jury left we gathered up our things.

"Let's leave this garbage here," Raymond said.

"I can't."

"Why not, Gerald?"

"Because if the jury comes in with a verdict against us I won't be able to gather this stuff up. I'll want to run. I think I'd run all the way back to Riverton, run into the bedroom and jump into the bed and cover up my head and never come out again, and I'd have left the papers and files behind. Let's get 'em gathered up now," I said.

"You aren't going to have to run," John Ackerman said.

"Thanks," I said.

"How are you feelin'?" John Hursh asked.

"I'm feeling tight as a knot."

"Gerald, Gerald," Raymond said, folding a file and stuffing it carelessly into a briefcase with the papers hanging out all over. "Gerald, that is the wrong simile for a country boy. The correct way to say that is, 'Tight as a bull's ass in fly-time.' "

"Yeah," I said, "thanks." I paced up and down the

courtroom—across the little open space between the jury box and the podium. Paced. Paced like Joe Esquibel had paced in his own small cage in the Carbon County Jail.

"Where's Joe?" I asked suddenly.

"Goddamn, I don't know," John Ackerman said.

"I don't know where he is," John Hursh said.

"They must have taken him away already. I didn't see them take him. I never said good-bye," I said.

"He never said anything to us."

"They must have just taken him off," I said. "Just led him off, and he followed them like a dog on a leash."

"I'll bet he's going crazy waiting," John Ackerman said. "I'll bet he's going crazy waiting alone back in that hole."

"Christ Almighty, I know how he feels," I said.

"I'll bet he's just crazy back there," John Ackerman said again, as if he too had discovered the truth, the deep, clear truth. He got up and started out the courtroom door as if to find Joe, and then on second thought he turned back.

"If he isn't crazy now, he'll be crazy by the time this is over," John Hursh said softly.

"Well," Raymond said, "he's safe."

"Safe from what?" somebody asked. But nobody answered.

"Let's go get a little toddy for the body," Raymond Whitaker said after all the papers were gathered up and the briefcases closed and snapped tight.

"I'm afraid to leave," I said.

"We'll tell the clerk where we are," Whitaker said.

"I'm afraid if I leave it'll change the good vibrations or something," I said.

"Don't be silly, Gerald. What you need is a little libation. You deserve it. You were beautiful today, just like I said you'd be."

"If I leave, the jury will know it and hold it against us."

"They won't, Gerald. They're in the jury room."

"Jurors know things like that. They sense it. They have feelers out all over them like a caterpillar. If I leave they'll know it."

"Come on, Gerald." He started out the door. I held back.

"They might want the judge to clarify an instruction."

"Oh, come off it, Gerald." The law students were at the door and Whitaker was following. I stood there alone. And when Raymond got to the door he hollered, "Are you coming, Gerald?"

"I'm too tired," I said. I sat down.

"We'll carry you then," he said.

"Go carry him," he said to the two Johns, and they walked back toward me once more with little grins on their faces.

"What do you think they thought of my cross-examination of Karn?" I hollered over to Raymond at the door.

"Who knows? I thought it was great, but I'm not a juror. No respectable jury would have the likes of me on it," Whitaker said. "Come on."

"What did you think of Oscar's closing?" I asked John Ackerman.

"Well, I thought it was all he could say."

"I know," I said. "But did the jury believe him?"

"No," John Ackerman said. I knew he was humoring me.

"Don't humor me," I said, sitting back in my chair with my eyes closed trying to relax.

"I'm not humoring you, Mr. Spence," he said.

"Don't be impertinent," I said. He didn't say anything back. Finally I jumped up and looked Raymond Whitaker straight in the eye. "What's the jury going to do—what do you really think?"

"I don't know, Gerald," he said softly. "I wish I knew. I've been at this place a hundred times. It's the worst time for a lawyer. Any time is better than this."

"I know," I said. "I catch myself talking to God. And I don't talk to God. I catch myself promising I won't try another case. And I won't do whatever it is I'm doing bad anymore. I'll quit whoring around. Quit drinking. Go to church. Whatever I'm supposed to do—even quit lawyering if only He'll let me win this one. Made that promise before. Now I keep thinking it's going to catch up with me on this one. He's going to get me now."

"I know," Raymond said. Then he turned to the boys. "If you boys were smart you'd stay out of this business. This is no place for smart boys." And about then the clerk came in. I saw her coming.

"God, maybe we have a verdict already."

"The jury's got a verdict," the clerk said matter-of-factly, pleasantly.

"A verdict!" I said. "What the hell does it mean, a verdict so soon."

"It means they didn't hang, Gerald," Raymond said ominously.

"Yeah," I said.

"I told you there wasn't one of them that had the stuff to hang a jury," he said with a serious look on his face.

"God Almighty!" I said. "Maybe they found in our favor. They couldn't just turn him to the dogs in half an hour. They'd have to at least wait a decent time to do that," I said. But nobody said anything.

I paced back and forth. I was glad we had all the files and papers packed.

"Where's Oscar?" I asked.

"They called him."

"I wish to Christ he would get here."

"He's here, already," somebody said. I looked over and there was Oscar, his face pale and serious.

"Didn't take 'em long for that, Gerry," Oscar said to me. We were still friends. I still liked Oscar Hall, respected him.

"You did a good job, Oscar," I said, and shook his hand. "I better tell you that now than later. I might not be able to talk later on." I tried to laugh.

"Yeah," Oscar said. He tried to laugh too. "You did good too."

"Thanks," I said.

"Where's Joe? The jury won't come in until they bring Joe in first. Somebody get him?" I asked.

"They got to get him dressed," Oscar said. "They took his suit."

"Oh, for Christ's sake," I said.

And now the bailiff came in, the keeper of the jury, and now the clerk sat down at her little desk, and now the court reporter came in and sat down at his desk across from the clerk with his steno machine in front of him, and pretty soon, it was a long time, they brought Joe in. He walked over, locked to the deputy sheriff.

"How you doing, Joe?"

He didn't answer.

"It's going to be okay, Joe," I said. "They treat you okay?"

He didn't answer, just looked down now at his feet. But from the side I could see his eyes, bright as a new bullet, shooting down to the floor. He was too afraid to speak. The bailiff hit the gavel and the judge walked into the courtroom, which was empty of spectators. Not even a single reporter was there. Nobody cared. Joe sat there while the rest of us stood up at the bailiff's admonition, "Please rise."

I looked up again and there Agneda Esquibel sat, her face as blank as stone, and then the door opened and the jury filed in, one after another, filling the back row first and then the front. I watched their faces for the signs, each of the faces. And one of them looked at me, the one next to the bulldozer operator, who held a piece of paper. The verdict was in his hand. They sat down. Another juror looked over at me, the charwoman with the mean face. Her face was still drawn and hard, but I thought she wanted to say something to me.

"Has the jury reached a verdict?" Judge Stanton asked in a sleepy voice.

The bulldozer operator jumped up. "We have, Your Honor."

The foreman handed the verdict to the clerk, and the clerk took the same to the judge. He opened the paper and read it carefully to himself. I watched his face for a sign. I could feel my heart. I thought it would stop. The judge didn't move a muscle in his face. His eyes were as blank as the walls. He handed the verdict back to the clerk, and the clerk stood up and began to read.

"State of Wyoming versus Joe Esquibel. Verdict. We, the jury, duly sworn and impaneled to try the above entitled case, do find the defendant 'not triable by reason of present insanity.' " She read the foreman's name. The clerk looked over at Joe but Joe still had his head down. He was insane. The jury had decreed it.

24

I WAITED for the jury to leave and for the judge to hit his gavel and declare the court in recess. Then Oscar Hall came up and shook my hand again, said I'd done a good job, and his face was drawn and his eyes looked hurt. Then he quickly left, and for a moment I wanted to run after him and tell him I felt sorry, that I knew how painful it was to lose, but I didn't know how to say it to him, and so I watched him walk out the door with heavy steps. Agneda was the last to leave. She came up quietly, and touched my hand, said nothing, kissed Joe, and then she walked quietly out of the courtroom, too. Joe was still sitting there, his head stiff, still tied to his laces.

"Joe, we won." He said nothing back, didn't move. "Joe, we won. Hear me?" I shook him by the shoulder a little. "Come on, Joe." He started to raise his head but he stopped, like a man afraid of what he might see. "You can look up, now." And then he looked up at me slowly again, but there was no relief on his face. He looked around the room, a little at a time, looking first out of the side of his eyes, and then back to me quickly as if he expected an attack, and then he fixed his eyes away from me and stared, a stuffed trophy ready to be hung on some wall.

"Joe, we won!"

"I gotta go," he said in a high anxious whisper without changing his stare.

"Where are you going?" I asked.

"I gotta get outa here, Mr. Spence."

"Well, they're gonna take you back to Evanston after a while," I said, trying to sound calm and matter-of-fact. "But it'll be better for you there, Joe."

"I can't go back," he said. "Them guys is crazy there." He started to get up, but the deputy, who had been standing outside of the courtroom door, moved in quickly. He walked up to Joe and then turned to me.

"Can I have your client now, Mr. Spence?" he asked with mock courtesy.

"I'm not through talking to him yet," I said.

"Well, make it snappy. I'm responsible for him. Gotta take his suit back, you know. Ha. Ha. Got our own kind of suit for this fella. Ha, ha," he said, walking away.

"Up yours," I said, and the deputy spun around and Joe jumped to his feet, his eyes alive.

"That's all right, Joe, I was just kidding," I said. I put my hand on his shoulder. "Can't you take a joke?" I said to the deputy. "Joe, I'll be down to see you—get you out of Johnson and Sublette. Trust me, Joe, it's gonna be better." I couldn't think of anything more to say. I wanted out of there too—couldn't stand being there another second—didn't think I could bear seeing the deputy snap the cuffs on Joe again and lead him down the hall like some animal. Winning the case was losing. Two other deputies stood at the door, young, tough-looking men with shiny badges and brown shirts and the emblem of the Natrona County Sheriff's Office on their shoulders.

"You treat him right," I said. "I'll see you, Joe. Just remember, we won." He didn't say good-bye and he didn't say thanks, and when the deputy pulled out the cuffs and told Joe to hold out his arms, I said to the law students, "Come on, boys, let's get the hell out of here." Raymond Whitaker had already left.

"It ain't gonna be that easy next time," John Ackerman said as we walked out. I didn't look back.

"You thought that was easy?"

"Looked easy to me," Ackerman said. "Next time they'll be laying for us, have it all set up, be ready for your questions, know all the questions and answers by heart, and they'll be prepared to the teeth—to the very goddamned teeth."

"I got a sign out on my little ranch at Hidden Valley. It's over the bridge. Ever been to my ranch at Hidden Valley on the reservation?"

"Nope," John Ackerman said as we walked out the front door of the courtroom into an early Casper afternoon. The wind was blowing. Always blew. Slapped a fellow in the face when he walked out the door. Didn't make any difference who you were. Rude wind. "What's on the sign?" Ackerman asked.

"Oh," I said. "Well, the sign over the bridge says, 'Don't Cross This Bridge Until You Get Here.'"

Ackerman laughed out of his belly. "That's a good sign," he said, "but I still think they're going to be ready for us the next time."

It was still early in the afternoon, and the action would be at the Gladstone. Raymond Whitaker was already there. Too early to drink hard liquor. Ordered it anyway. Deserved it. Celebrate. And the Mexican waitress leaned over us, administered to our needs, and reiterated that she loved Joe Esquibel more than anybody in the world, and she was happy that we won, and I kissed her again when she leaned over and everybody laughed and she laughed this time and didn't slap me with the bar rag because she said she was so happy Joe had won, and I asked her when she got off, and she said wouldn't I like to know, and I said I'd wait for her, and she said no, she had a boyfriend, and I said what difference did that make, and the senseless litany went on and on, drink after drink, into the night, and she said I was married anyway, and I said that that shouldn't be a problem between friends, and we drank some more and John Ackerman toasted the sign over my bridge and implored each and every one of us not to cross that bridge until we got to it, and when the Gladstone finally closed we all went down to Fifi's and drank until Fifi was tired of us, and cleared us out at six o'clock in the morning.

I don't remember the 120-mile drive home to good old

Riverton, Wyoming. I didn't go to the house, couldn't bear to face Anna, to answer the questions—or talk about the trial. Didn't want to talk. Half drunk still. Eight o'clock in the morning. The kids would be around getting ready for school, good housewife up with sparkly eyes making breakfast, cleaning things up, hustling, like she always did, doing things in a hurry, doing things right. I won. But I didn't want to explain how it was to win and win nothing, to be so beautiful, and to be nothing, not husband, or father, or good citizen, not even a great lawyer who had won. I parked the car down the block and walked up the ditch bank behind the house and sneaked in my studio, which was my place to paint, and brood, and escape. I crawled in under an old buffalo hide on a cot in the corner, and I could smell the good smell of turpentine and linseed oil and of leather and buffalo wool, and I pulled the robe up over my head and slept all day and I dreamed the fever dreams of all trial lawyers, of arguments to the jury, of speeches and objections, and of pounding fists on the judge's desk in chambers, and what I heard were the bits and fragments of the trial echoing over and back again in senseless repetition.

Judge Stanton's order said the murder case pending against Joe Esquibel would be continued indefinitely until the defendant was found to be sane and triable, and Joe Esquibel was committed to the Wyoming State Hospital until further order of the court. I demanded that the order also contain the language, "and that Joe Esquibel be cared for and treated at said hospital to the fullest extent of the facilities available therein, including complete medical and psychiatric care in accordance with the highest standards of the medical profession." That made me feel better, but I hadn't been back to the office very long before Cleo started a campaign for me to go see Joe.

"Don't forget Joe."

"I suppose you love him, too," I said back absently.

"Oh, Gerald," she said. "You have to go see him. You promised him. Remember?" She was such a little mother, that Cleo Arguello, soft and gentle like mothers should be. Ten years earlier I had represented her husband, Manuel, against the Ford Motor Company. Manuel and some others were riding in a new Ford automobile near Evanston going to work, and the next thing he knew he was lying across a barbed wire fence in the snow, paralyzed from the waist down. Couldn't remember anything else. Vince Vehar, my old lawyer friend in Evanston, helped me try the case. We said there was a defective rivet in the front wheel, and the rivet gave way. We showed the jury how the air came out of the rim of the front tire, causing the tubeless tire suddenly to go flat and sending the car into a ditch. Manuel was thrown out of the car. It was the largest verdict in the state's history. Cleo and Manuel had two darling brown-faced little daughters and the state had tried to rehabilitate Manuel into a watch repairman. The money we collected from Ford for Manuel was paid over to a trust we had established at a Casper bank to provide his family a comfortable sum each month, but over the years the dollars eroded away, and Cleo worked in my office. She labored there faithfully and mothered me, the mother of all of us, of Manuel and the darling little girls, and of Gerry Spence.

"You can't just leave Joe there and forget him," Cleo said. "You have to do something!" She thought I could do anything, but the best thing for me to do was to forget Joe Esquibel. We saved him from the gas chamber, cheated the state, and now his choice was clear. Be insane. Stay insane—or be gassed. Live with the raging wild-eyed lunatics, with the madmen whose brains were possessed by demons, live with those who screamed out of twisted and contorted and jumbled cells—live, caged with the crazy, and rage on out of your own madness or be gassed. "There isn't anything I can do, Cleo, for Christ's sake," I kept telling her. "Give me another Cabin Still."

Then one morning Cleo came to the office early and when I finally got there she was even more cheery than usual.

"Well, today you go to see Joe, Gerald. I checked your calendar for two days—nothing to do. Isn't that nice? I called the hospital. You can get there by three, if you hurry, and I made a reservation for you at the motel so you won't have to drive home at night, and Vince Vehar is taking you out to dinner." She walked up and gave me a little kiss on the cheek and handed me a sack.

"What the hell is this?"

"I made some cookies for you to eat on the trip. Fresh Mexican cookies," she laughed happily. "Come on," she said. "You gotta get started if you're going to get there by three. Give Joe my love."

Well, for Christ's sake! All I could do was go.

When I got to Evanston I met Dr. Imogene Fairchild right off. She was a large, solid woman in her late forties with thin muscular legs and a tough swagger. She had short frizzy hair, which was getting gray, and it was obvious she didn't give a damn about that or much of anything else. She was the kind of woman you could talk to.

"Son-of-a-bitch is crazy," she said first thing.

"Who?"

"Joe. Crazy as a pet coon," she said.

"You have to be kidding," I said as we walked across the hospital campus to Sublette Hall. She moved fast, and it strained me a little to keep up with her, stepped right out, lot of arm action, legs flying, talking, "Hi" to a passing trustee with a green card, "Hi" to some aide.

"He's been nuts from the day he got here," she said. "Told Karn, 'Spence is a better psychiatrist than you are.' Course, that doesn't say much for you," she laughed irreverently.

"Well, I don't understand, Doctor," I said.

"Jesus Christ," she said. "He's been in a catatonic trance practically from the day he walked in here. Doesn't know who he is or where he is. Karn didn't believe it either. Thought he was malingering."

"Thought he was what?"

"Karn thought he was faking it. But even Karn admits it now."

"Well, for Christ's sake," I said back. "How do you explain that? Maybe he just went batso here. Maybe you people drove him crazy."

"The jury was right and we were wrong, that's how I explain it. But that ain't nothing new," she said. "We guess wrong here more often than not. Any damned fool can guess right 50 percent of the time. You either are or you aren't nuts."

"Yeah," I laughed.

"Yeah," she said. "Hi there," she said to a passerby. "Alcoholic," she said. "Got a good alcoholic program here. Have to say that much. Give the devil his dues, but that's about it."

I followed her into Johnson Hall, up the dark stairs, past the guard, and into a big room. I saw a television blasting, and men were walking aimlessly around, not watching the television or talking to each other, some wearing pajamas and slippers, others dressed in denim pants and shirts. It was a strange assortment of blank faces. All their hair was cut short, and some of the hair, as short as it was, looked like it had been slept on for days, and they all walked slowly, going nowhere, just walking. I looked for Joe. Couldn't see him.

"Over there," she said, pointing to a big overstuffed chair with its back to us. I could see the back of his head. I recognized the scars. A boy about fourteen wearing a cowboy hat with a toy tin pistol in his hand came up to us. Click, click. He shot both Dr. Fairchild and me.

"Good way for him to release his hostilities," she said. "Kid's in here for killing his father. Boys will be boys," she laughed, and then the boy went on with his work and systematically shot everyone in the room, about twenty-five men, young and old, and nobody fell, nobody winced, nobody even looked up. They kept on walking. One man was walking backward. "Claims he doesn't care where he's going," she said. "Only wants to see where he's been. Smarter than most of us." I didn't want to go any closer to Joe—didn't want to look him in the face now that I was here. I wished I hadn't come. I wanted to thank Dr. Fairchild politely and just leave.

"Don't be surprised when you see Joe," she said.

"What's the matter?" I asked in a whisper.

"You'll see," she said, and I followed her over to the big chair in front of the TV.

"Joe," she said, stooping down in front of the figure slumped in the chair in pajamas. "Joe," she said. "Mr. Spence has come to see you." He looked past her to the blaring TV where there was some soap opera crying out.

"Doesn't recognize you," she said. For Christ's sake he hadn't even looked at me.

"Hi, Joe," I said. "I came to see you. How you doin', pal?" Then he looked up at me with empty eyes and said nothing, like looking at a post, didn't even blink, and then he looked back over to the TV set.

"He's not feeling very well, today," Dr. Fairchild said. "You can see that. How are you doing, Joe?" she said in a loud voice as if he were miles away. He made no response. "His mother comes to see him every weekend, and so does his sister, Elma, and her husband, Frank, but he doesn't recognize 'em either. Prognosis is guarded, Spence," she said in front of him as if he weren't there. "Try to keep him manageable, but there's nothing much there. Full-blown psychosis. All the classic signs and symptoms. Schizophrenia."

"What do you mean his prognosis is guarded?" I asked.

"That means it doesn't look too damned good. 'Once a schizophrenic always a schizophrenic,' they say. Once a skitz always a skitz," she repeated. "They slip in and out of psychosis, back and forth. But ya gotta keep 'em manageable. When he comes sliding out he could be wild as a peach orchard boar. Haven't seen it in him yet, but anything can happen. Could be sitting here on a time bomb, but right now he's pretty catatonic, as you can see." She reached down and patted Joe on the head. He didn't stir a muscle, and he looked like cold boned turkey.

"Well, good-bye, Joe," I said, talking to the wall. Joe said nothing back, and we left. We walked past a large screened porch. It was protected with heavy iron mesh, like the monkey house, and from the television room a hallway led to the maximum security cells where Joe had been locked up before. Sublette Hall, they called it, and even without listening, I could still hear Jason screaming.

"How's Jason?" I asked.

"Don't talk to me about Jason," Dr. Fairchild said disgustedly. "Shame. Damn shame," she said. "I had Jason out walking around, happy, playing catch with the ball and all. I can stop that screaming all right. Just treat him like a human being. Treat him like an animal and he acts like one. Treat a man like he's crazy—he acts crazy. No big deal, but you have to give him a little attention—little love. Everybody needs a little love, Spence," she said, but she sounded like she didn't need any, and I was following her again, her arms flying.

"What shall I do about Joe?" I asked.

"You're asking me, aren't you?"

"You're damned right," I said, trying to sound as tough as she sounded.

"Well, I'd do something to make 'em give him treatment. He just sits there. Vegetates. We got things we can do, but they're just holding him like you hold a mad dog. Can't do much for a skitz on a long-term basis, but we could do something. We got some programs, not much, but they're better than nothin'. You're the lawyer."

"Okay," I said. "But if you cure him, they'll gas him."

"Nice world, Spence. Crazy world," she said.

"Well, maybe it's worse being crazy than being dead."

"Ain't nothin' worse than dead," Dr. Fairchild said. I wanted to see Joe's records. "Why sure," she said, like passing the salt and pepper. I followed her into a records room. "Here, nobody but me would show you these." The admission note by Dr. Karn said Joe didn't know where he was when he came back to the hospital, couldn't remember being in the hospital before—didn't remember the trial, refused to communicate with the other patients, sat alone in his room for hours looking blankly at nothing, and Karn couldn't tell whether he was malingering.

Yet the medical staff at the hospital said Joe was sane before the trial, perfectly sane, and triable, and they said so to the jury under oath. But the jury didn't believe them, and now Joe was back in the very hospital that had previously discharged him as sane. That bothered Dr. Karn, the admission note said, and he had called Attorney General James Barrett to ask what should be done. How could a jury make a medical finding? And how should the hospital view Joe Esquibel—as a "subject" or as a "patient"? As a patient, Jim Barrett told him—treat him as you would any patient. And so Dr. Karn asked that other doctors see Joe in consultation.

Dr. Thomas, the neurologist, examined Joe again. Ringing in both ears. Can't smell faint peppermint smell, and Dr. Thomas' report said, "On occasion Joe would put his elbows on the table to talk with me in an almost serious confidential manner, trying to explain things that seemed to be puzzling him, such as voices."

Ah, the voices.

Dr. Thomas said Joe was still hallucinating four months after his return to the hospital. Hallucinating in April. It was Thomas' opinion that Joe had been sane when the staffers first saw him, but then Joe had gone to jail to await trial—and there in the Rawlins jail he must have become schizophrenic. His sitting mute in court— his head down—looking at his feet was consistent with such a scenario, Thomas wrote. What the hospital was witnessing was a reappearing schizophrenic episode.

Dr. Jack Tedro, the forensic psychiatrist, also wrote his report, saying that he had examined Joe on March 15, 1967, and despite the fact that Joe knew he was accused of killing his wife, Joe thought she was still living at home and that God was speaking to him, telling him to pray.

The voices.

He didn't know the month, Tedro reported, and thought he only had one son, but he didn't know how old the son was—"gets hostile when we asked things he can't remember, and he dreams about his older brother, Timato, and seems restless in the interview, keeps looking around the room, and he is wide-eyed."

And then Betty Cluff, the social worker at the hospital, examined Joe, too. She thought Joe was probably medically insane, all right, psychotic, she called it, and he needed psychiatric treatment on a one-to-one basis with a psychiatrist rather than group therapy. But Dr. Karn, even in face of her report, placed Joe in group therapy, where he failed to respond, "and looked blank like 'what's happening to me?'" Later Owen Kennedy, Acting Director of Psychological Services, reported that the patient attended six group therapy sessions, was uncooperative, wouldn't respond even to direct questions, but seemed acutely aware of what was going on. "It is suspected that the role he is playing is mainly for the therapist's sake and he probably won't benefit from the group experience."

Robert Ashpole, a consultant in criminology, reported that "he definitely did not appear to be capable of comprehending the nature of the alleged act or cooperating in his own defense." In April, Dr. Tedro saw Joe again and reported that the patient was still hallucinatory, still wide-eyed.

Hallucinating in April—and as for me, well, I had met this dark-haired woman in Jackson Hole. Imaging Crow, I called her. She looked Indian but with snapping blue eyes, sometimes purple. It was the mere passing of passions between two people, I thought. I met her when she was skiing with her husband, and later I saw her in Casper, but each time I felt something, like the magical force that makes a daffodil pop out of the cold dead ground in the early spring. She and her husband had two boys.

It was insane for the two of us to speak to each other like that, and yet we were drawn together, and the point was simple: Should we give in to the passion, and I said yes, of course, and let the passion roll, and she had not even had time to really say, except to make some passing protest before she was swept up in the torrent too. But we made a desperate agreement. No falling in love. This coming together was bad enough. We were two people who did not understand what passion is to love, like trying to separate the fragrance from the flower, and we were afraid of love, but not of passion. We would not, no, never, fall in love. But to taste passion is the choice of the species, and it has been from the beginning—to taste of the apple, to do that forbidden thing when people have made other promises. No one would say it was right, but you can understand people giving in to it, breathlessly, and the heart beating so loudly one cannot hear the smaller sense of the mind. I would have gambled my soul, copulated with her in the leopard's cage, made love to her in any corner of St. Peter's cathedral—in the Smithsonian behind the exhibit of the Neanderthal man. In April 1967, Joe Esquibel had heard the voices and I had awakened in the night with Imaging Crow beside me, laughing at this poem about "an untoothed crow."

> An untoothed crow came Imaging around,
> And mocked right up to mockery town.
> Said he, some think I'm just a clown
> But to me, I'm just a drowned dog,
> And that's what I've maintained, all a-log.

I laughed hilariously at the poem I dreamed, and Imaging Crow woke up at my laughing, wide-eyed, not able for a minute to determine where she was, then finding herself in the dark, in this bed, in this April storm, in this motel with the creek gurgling by like some lunatic singing an indistinguishable tuneless song, this madman naked in bed beside her laughing, calling her Imaging Crow, which was not her name at all. She turned on the lights and her eyes were large and purple.

"You are Imaging Crow," I said, still laughing. "I have named you."

"Are you insane?" she asked.

"No. No." I laughed. I kissed her, and then I said, "I think I love you." Love is the sole cure for insanity.

We vowed there would be no falling in love.

"No falling in love," I had said when we first met.

"No falling in love," she repeated. "I've had enough of that." She'd already divorced her husband once and then remarried him in a panicked struggle for the children, for stability, for decency, for a good life, and she had settled down to being an interior decorator, and a mother, and she had had enough of this, and she couldn't understand what she was doing there with me. It was insane. But at least there would be no love.

Before all that I'd run into her having lunch at the Henning Hotel, and I stopped at her table and I said hello, and I also said, "Come see me in court, I want to impress you," but she laughed me off. Later I looked up from my cross-examination of the plaintiff, during that brief moment when I could see I had finished him off like the matador with his sword through the head of the bull, and there she was, sitting alone in the courtroom. I excused the plaintiff from the witness stand and he limped over to his seat and sat down silently, stiff with pain. The jury would never believe him, not after such a cross-examination, I thought, and the insurance man, in his dignified three-piece suit, pin-striped, and white-shirted, and with shiny black shoes, a shiny face, and a sick sweet smile, his hair black and shiny too, sat also incognito in the courtroom like some innocent well-dressed spectator, and nodded slightly to me, his eyes happy. I had saved the case for his company. He'd write up a good report on me—good attorney, this Spence. Saved the company a hundred thousand dollars, at least. And now at the recess I walked over to Imaging.

"Did I impress you?" I asked.

"You made a fool of that poor injured man," she said.

"That's the object of the game," I laughed. "That's why the insurance companies hire me." I was proud of my success as a trial lawyer. I'd been a poor boy who had struggled and made it, finally, made it the hard way, taken the little cases to start with, tried everything I could get my hands on. Then I tried more cases yet as a prosecutor when Raymond Whitaker and I developed a rapport, grew close out of the feelings of lonely men who fought for justice, or who thought we fought for justice, and we also thought we were the best prosecutors in the state. I'd never lost a case as a prosecutor, and Raymond Whitaker had prosecuted some famous murder cases. We were the best, we thought. But the proof was in the pudding. When an insurance company actually came to me and asked me to defend in one of its major trials, me,

Gerry Spence, representing one of the largest insurance companies in the world, well, that was success! That was proof! I was a trial lawyer! I won my first case for the company, and then I won all of the cases they sent me, and I began to kill in the courtroom for the sheer joy of it, like a renegade coyote kills in a herd of helpless sheep, leaving them ripped and bleeding on the ground, and eating only the bag off one lactating ewe for the luxury of sheep's milk.

I was speaking to Imaging Crow. "I'm sorry I didn't impress you." I reached over to pull her close to me in the courtroom with the passion plainly on my face. She pulled back. "You didn't need to make him look like a liar. It's bad enough that's he's hurt."

"Well, we'll see what the jury believes," I said. And I laughed again, and pulled her to me. But recess was over and the jury came in, and later the jury returned a verdict for me, all right, and I had killed once more. After the verdict was in, I looked up and Imaging Crow was gone. I started calling her on the telephone. She was home. I begged. I cried. I want to come over. I gotta see you. She hung up on me. And I called again and finally I was knocking on her front door in the night.

"For God's sake. What are you doing here?" she asked.

"I'm here to make love to you."

"Be quiet, you'll wake the whole neighborhood up," she scolded.

"Let me in, or I'll scream." I was laughing, and then she opened the door and I kissed her before the door was even closed, and after that we had come together for brief times and then one night, in April, in a snowstorm, in this plain motel with the creek singing silly songs outside, I had awakened next to her laughing again and I named her Imaging Crow.

I wrote her poems, and we walked out of the motel backward in the snow so that in my paranoia if they, whoever "they" were, came to find us, there would only be our tracks in the snow going in, and none coming out, only one set of tracks because I told her to step where I stepped, and when they broke in the door they would find no sign of us and it would be like magic. No one walks backward in the snow, and we had laughed and eaten fresh strawberries, Imaging Crow and I, and we were not in love, absolutely not, and would not fall in love. Never.

Only hallucinating in April.

Then Cleo had sent me off to see Joe Esquibel at the hospital and I was glad I'd escaped such madness. I handed the records back to Dr. Imogene Fairchild. The last entry of Jack Tedro, the psychiatrist, was that Joe's hallucinations in April had intensified.

When I got back to the office I dictated a letter to Cleo for Dr. Karn, which talked of the rights of human beings to receive treatment, of constitutional rights, and, in this civilized society, not just to be warehoused. We have closed up the snake pits. We have put out the fires under the witches. We have sung rock and roll and embarked on journeys on LSD that broke the boundaries of the universe, and we have peered into the faces of the witches, and then, seeing that they were real, we melted them down, and stood in color breezes cooling our faces, and then we marched and chanted, and cried out of our insanity in the sixties and dropped napalm bombs on little children and left the bodies burned and bloated, and we defoliated the countryside. We were angry even at the leaves.

We killed the flowers.

We hated the lily. It was a time of madness and madness is contagious. We are especially vulnerable in April.

I had done my job, hadn't I? I drove to Evanston, ate Cleo's cookies, saw Joe, talked to the doctor, read the charts, inspected the premises, found this Joe Esquibel in a cream-colored hole, heard the crazy sounds emanating from the hole, and crazy sounds of fake weeping from the television in a room where there was no weeping, only listless legs and faded faces and dead eyes, where the only human sounds were the click-click of a drooling fourteen-year-old cowboy killing everyone with his toy gun, and the sounds of Jason screaming. It was a place where humans were stacked to deteriorate and die. I wrote my letter to Dr. Karn reminding him of the court's order that Joe be treated "to the fullest extent of the facilities available therein including complete medical and psychiatric care in accordance with the highest standards of the medical profession." And I reminded Karn that just storing Joe was hardly meeting that standard. I registered the letter because people pay more attention to registered letters, and I had done my duty, hadn't I? What more could I do?

"You tell me, Cleo, what more can I do?" I demanded as I finished my dictation. Cleo didn't answer. She looked sad and her lower lip stuck out. "What more can I do?" I insisted.

"I don't know, Gerald," she said, but she sounded like she did think there was something more I could do. She sounded like mothers always sound. Maybe God was getting even with me, I thought, for monkeying around with His people, with His system, using poor Joe Esquibel just to show off our alleged brilliance. Well, now what do you think? You thought you pulled a fast one on the jury, didn't you? Played this game of yours. Well, take a look. Look at Joe! What do you think now? You told the jury he was insane and they believed you. Now he is insane! Tell me, what do you make of that? Couldn't answer the question. Instead I tried to forget Joe Esquibel, and I called Imaging Crow.

25

IT WAS CLEO who always brought the matter of Joe Esquibel up again, like something smoldering which finally flames to the surface. She blurted it out. "Joe is trapped. It's worse than being an animal, Gerald. An animal doesn't have a soul. An animal doesn't know, but Joe knows." She was standing in the office doorway with her angelic mouth forming the words. "Joe is trapped in Evanston. Can't you do something?"

I was trapped sitting in this pleasant cage surrounded by vines I'd grown from slips from my grandma's ivy, and the ivy clung to the rough cedar walls of my office. I sat at a round table, like King Arthur's, but I was alone. "We're all trapped," I said.

"We are not trapped," she said softly, but I knew she was trapped in her marriage with Manuel, who was trapped in a useless body cut in two at the waist, and she had these two little darling daughters, and there was no way out for her, but she didn't think she was trapped. She loved Manuel. Love springs traps.

"I'm trapped," I said.

"Oh, you are not trapped," she said with kind impatience. "You have everything. You are healthy. You have a wonderful family and you . . ."

"Jesus Christ, stop it," I hollered. I got up and poured my own whiskey. It was all right. Close to 5—4:30 P.M.—close enough.

"You could leave Riverton, you know," she said thoughtfully.

"Yeah? Where would I go? I've been fifteen years getting this practice on its feet. Where could I go now? Take Anna and all the kids, too, I suppose. Take my trap with me. Go to Cody? Go to Sheridan? How about Sheridan, Wyoming? Always wanted to go back to good old Sheridan. We could all starve to death in Sheridan, Wyoming, and in the springtime I could go pick flowers up Little Goose Canyon," and my eyes filled with tears. I hated that.

"You do feel trapped, then," she said sadly. She came over and touched my shoulder gently, and then my face, and her fingers were damp and soft and warm.

"Fuck it," I said. "The trap is in the head."

"You could go to New York," she said, "and be a big lawyer in New York," and then she thought for a long time, just touching my cheek lightly, absently, and suddenly she said, "I know some people in Roswell, New Mexico. That's a good town, they say. You could go to Roswell, New Mexico, or to any place."

"Roswell, New Mexico, is full of goddamned Mexicans," I said.

"So is New York. Mexicans are everywhere," she said proudly.

"I'm trapped with you goddamned Mexicans." I emptied my glass.

"If you were in New York, how would you get out? There are millions of people trapped in New York who can't get out. New York is a very big trap."

"I was in New York once and got out. Hitched a ride out. But I can't get out of Riverton. I should put all the kids, the dog, and the wife on the highway, and we'll hold up a sign. 'Roswell, New Mexico,' the sign will say."

"Your family doesn't trap you," she said. "A family is what life's about. If you had no family you'd really be trapped." Jesus, I loved this wonderful woman who was not trapped.

"But Joe is trapped," she said. "If he stays in Evanston he will never be able to live his life."

"He doesn't even know where he is, Cleo. How can he be trapped if he doesn't know it?"

"I know it. And his mother and sister know it, and you know it. So he is trapped."

"And so we are all trapped," I said. "Come over here and give me a big wet Mexican kiss."

"Oh, Gerald!" she said, and then she went back out to her office and pretty soon I heard her pounding her typewriter. I left before the evening drinking crowd got me in my office, and I drove home to my studio. I took up a brush and dabbed it in the wet red paint, and I smashed the brush, the helpless innocent brush, against the canvas, and the brush left a bloody slash against the perfect white, and then came another stroke of red and turpentine and the red paint faded in, washed, and I washed black into red, and a face appeared and it spoke to me. I felt mad. It was a mother's face, yellow around the edges of mother-eyes, which were hardly discernible, and the eyes could not see but were staring. There was no blue on the canvas, no love, and I was alone, still crying for my mother, and she answered, but in no way that I could hear—no words—just a mother presence, and I painted furiously on. Speak. Speak again. It was a large canvas in the silent studio and as I listened there was only the noise of my brush hitting the cloth, without rhythm, a beating, like a heart beating.

As I painted I could see Anna at nineteen. But I couldn't see me. I could see her looking as if she were ready to burst with the baby in that early fall.

My mother had come back from Bolivia after having been gone those three years. I had taken on this wife in her absence, without her permission, but she and my father had written saying, "You are so young, but you must do what you need to do. You have grown up and you are independent." As I painted I could see my mother again. I was holding her in my arms and I was tall and young, a little pimply-faced still, but strong. I held her and she was strangely still. I kissed her, but she was cold, as if she had lost herself while she was gone, and I looked into her eyes for the look of my mother, for the look of her eyes when we were picking the wild blue crocus in the early summer up Little Goose Canyon, but her eyes were empty.

"Mother, I missed you." It seemed as if she couldn't answer. She smiled an empty smile, and her black hair had become gray at the edges and she looked like a woman painted by an artist who couldn't get the life into the eyes, and I painted furiously on, not knowing what I was painting, but there was yellow on the edges and the hollow sockets.

"Mother. This is your new daughter, Anna," I said.

"Oh," she said back, as if she had drifted off someplace for a second. "How do you do." Anna had embraced her and called her mother.

"Look. Look!" I said, gesturing at my smiling blond bride. "You are going to be a grandmother! A grandmother! Think of it!"

"That will be nice," she said, like a tree speaking, and the painting took on the awful face of a witch, and the face could have spoken in the silence if I could have only heard it. Finally I glossed over the painting with a correct mix of varnish and linseed as if to preserve it, and I set the canvas face to the wall, to weep the glazes, and to dry.

I was insane. The organism knows itself.

In May of 1967, I went to the National Training Laboratories in Bethel, Maine, a small town with quaint little antique houses, and the sound of the birds was as different as the sound of foreign people. It was a national meeting place for ambulatory schizophrenics, I thought, for smiling social psychotics who claimed they were quite sane and only wanted to know more about themselves. "Sensitivity training" it was called—to be sensitive to one's own feelings. I claimed I was sane, just trying to grow. They said at the National Training Laboratories that it was all right to feel. I knew that. Don't speak out of the head, they said. Say how you feel! Can you feel how that other man sitting over there in your group feels? It is training, not therapy. You have to learn about yourself, your wonderful self. There was love there. We were not insane, and I had not wanted to talk about my mother.

Then a gentle woman with anguished eyes began to weep through her smile and she said she needed someone to hear her finally say she was not guilty. She was not guilty! At fourteen her father had accused her, but the man who had come to visit the family had never even touched her, and she had not been able to convince her father otherwise, who must have needed to believe it, and then the father died, and that unfinished business had lain rotting in her heart for all of these years, and she was weeping it out. I was inside her very hide. I could feel her sorrow, and I began to weep with her. No. You do not feel *her* sorrow. You cannot feel *her* sorrow. You can only feel your own grief, the trainer said. Why are you weeping? What is your grief? I couldn't speak. I could only cry.

"Jesus Christ," I finally sobbed. "Jesus Christ." There was love there. There were others who cared. I could see it on their faces, see it through their own anguish. "My mother," I said. It came bursting out. "My angel mother. She had barely gotten home, hardly back yet from Bolivia." I couldn't say it through the weeping. I was truly insane. I didn't care. The pain of retching was less than the powerful need to get it out, and our trainer, as they called her, an older woman with gray hair and soft pale eyes and a body like a high mountain willow, touched my shoulder, and now it came heaving out. My mother. My angel mother, just a short while after she met Anna, and we had just turned twenty—she got up in the middle of the night, out at Grandpa Spence's, and she went out into that good orchard and lay down in an empty irrigation ditch, and she put my father's old hunting rifle, the old .30–.40 Krag, in her mouth, and she blew the back of her head out, before she had seen her first grandchild, without even saying good-bye.

It was because of me.

No, it was because of her. "Can't you hear her? Can't you hear her voice now?" the trainer asked. The trainer put a watch on the floor. "This watch is your mother.

Speak to her," the trainer said, and I heard myself speaking.

"Mother. Why did you leave me?"

"What does your mother say?" the trainer asked.

"I didn't leave you. I had to go." The voice of Mother came from my own mouth.

"Why did you have to go? You never told me. Never said good-bye," I said.

"I left you because I couldn't stand the pain," I heard my own voice say in reply.

"Pain? Was the pain over me? Did I make your life so painful you couldn't bear it any longer?" I gasped through the weeping.

"No. You were not my pain. My pain was my own pain. You are my son. I love you." I spoke from my heart, out of my own knowledge—words that I knew to be true but that I had never heard before, and I felt the demons beginning to leave. After a while I stopped weeping and I felt purged, clean and new. And I also knew I loved Imaging Crow.

After my mother was buried, I studied with a mad frenzy to finish my first year in law school. And, although three years later I graduated at the top of my class, I flunked the bar—the first honor graduate in the history of the University of Wyoming to fail. I was devastated. I hung onto Anna. At twenty-three the truth was finally out. I was a fraud, and Anna and my little boy Kip would know, and the second baby, which Anna was carrying, little Kerry, would be born to such a father, and although I took the bar again, I took it without further study, reluctantly, without any zest for it, dreading the pain of failure a second time, but I took it because I owed it to Anna and her parents and my father and my dead mother— owed it to all of those who believed in me, too, and whom I had defrauded. I wasn't worthy of being a lawyer. No intellectual capacity, you know, but a man who nevertheless had somehow been able to fool the professors for three years. But one couldn't fool the examiners. They were real lawyers.

Then one day the results came in the mail. I passed the

bar. Must have fooled the examiners, too, this time. The chairman of the examining committee called me on the phone—best damned test he had ever read, damned proud to have me as a new member. Ha. Ha. Well, son, good luck. But there were no jobs anyway. Finally I moved to Riverton, Wyoming, population six or seven thousand, because it was close to the mountains and because a lawyer by the name of Franklin B. Sheldon said he'd pay me two hundred dollars a month, and then very soon he was appointed district judge and I was left alone again in that small strange isolated farm town.

Maybe I could get a job as a deputy county attorney, I thought, but the county attorney said he had a good young man coming, one who was undoubtedly a veteran and who had been in a fraternity and who had not failed the bar. Anna and I already had our second child by now, this darling daughter Kerry. I can see her baby eyes, her baby face, round like her mother's, and the life in her eyes out of the best parts of the universe, innocent and alive. I decided to run for the office of county attorney myself. No other choice. Knocked on every goddamned door in the county, and went out on the reservation and talked to the Indians, all of them, and I was elected. I appointed my own deputy, a new partner, Frank P. Hill, ten years older, maybe an older brother for me, a kind man. And it was Spence & Hill for ten years, and as I said, I never lost a criminal case, and was elected again in elections which were hotly contested in both the primary and general. I ran as a Republican, and after my second four-year term was over, having been a young Tom Dewey myself and cleaned up the county, run out the whores and closed down the gambling, shut the bars that sold liquor to kids, well, it was only natural that I should run for Congress. Wyoming needed to be heard in Congress, I said.

I announced on the same day as Teddy Kennedy announced for the Senate. He was only thirty, and I was thirty-three, and there was a picture in the paper of him smiling, standing in front of a microphone with his wife Joan, he in Boston, and me in Riverton, Wyoming. My

announcement started like something out of Lincoln:
"When a young man contemplates his destiny, he must
discover first the path on which his state and nation proceed, for on such a path he and his children must also
follow, and as I did so I beheld the frightful spectacle of a
runaway nation tumbling uncontrollably down a pre-
greased road to socialism, and as the monster hurtled by,
it squashed each individual that stood in its path," and
the announcement went on, for Christ's sake, and this
time it sounded like FDR. "It's to this task that I resolve
to lend my total vigor, and it will be in the furtherance of
that task that I will search tirelessly for those who will
join me. I will seek the people in every farm and ranch, in
every mine and oil patch, in the sheep wagon, in the cow
camps and roadstops—and together the people of our
state will be heard and our force felt in Washington," I
said. Nobody gave a damn.

Again I knocked on all the doors I could find in the
state, as I had when I had run for county attorney. Door-
to-door campaign. I could outwork any man, especially
William Henry Harrison III, my opponent, who was old,
with that grand old name. The people would know—they
would see me, and they would know they needed to be
heard in Congress, and I talked to the housewives, caught
with curlers in their hair, plain and unpowdered and pale
with kids hanging at their legs, and the soap operas weeping away through piles of dishes and diapers, and I caught
them at the door for just a fleeting moment and said, "I'll
represent you. We need a good man who will speak up
for the people in Congress. You've met me now, and
please don't forget me on election day. Please don't forget me. I'll represent you the very best I can."

And they said back, "No. No. Of course we won't forget you. We won't forget you, and it was sure good
meetin' ya."

"Thanks. Thanks a lot." And I went to the next door,
and at Sundance, Wyoming, I knocked on every door,
every damn door, talked to the people—Gerry Spence
for Congress. Let's be heard in Washington, and then I
took my own telephone poll to see how I'd done. There

would be a surprise on election morning, no doubt. My opponent could not live on the sound of his name alone. Picked numbers from the phone booth at random for my poll.

"Hello."

"Hello. We are conducting a poll. Your number was picked at random. Could you help us?"

"I suppose. What's it about?"

"Well, in the coming election for Congress, who do you favor? William Henry Harrison or Gerry Spence?"

"Gerry who?"

"Gerry Spence."

"Oh, never heard of him."

"Oh," I said. "Well, who do you favor?"

"Harrison's been a pretty good man, I guess."

"Thank you."

Hello. We are conducting a poll. Spence? Never heard of him.

The fuckers didn't want to be heard in Congress. They had nothing to say in Washington anyway, but on election night the first precinct in was Bill, Wyoming, with its three votes, and it was two for Spence and one for William Henry Harrison, and that precinct and a few others maybe, I can't remember any others, were all the precincts I carried in the state. It was a resounding mandate from the voters for Gerry Spence never to get involved in politics again. It was humiliating. I was wounded. Sick. I wanted to run away. I went home to my little family, to Kip, Kerry, Kent, and Katy, and that good woman who worked so hard for me in the campaign, and I hurt too badly to go back to the same old chair in the same little office with my partner, Frank Hill. But I was trapped. There was no other place to go. I opened up an office across the street and I took any case, all the cases, any trial, all trials, and I won. I got good, I admit, and soon I was this big-time lawyer in little old Riverton, Wyoming —trapped there. I was trapped there for fifteen years and I became an expert not only at trying cases, but at drinking whiskey, and with the women, I thought. To hell with it.

Sometimes I stepped into the middle of an early summer morning in Riverton, Wyoming—before the town's people had seen it, like a child who steals into his mother's bed at the first light of dawn. Riverton was my place, my mother-place, and sometimes I could still feel the warmth of my mother and smell her special smell, different from the smell of all others, and in the sweet light of the morning she had slept softly, barely breathing —was she dead? I listened carefully, wet my finger and put it close to her nostrils. Ah, yes, thank you, dear God, she was alive, and I was not alone with her dead in this bed. At that sweet moment she belonged to me and not to father, or little brother, or to whimpering children at Sunday school, or to anyone else but me.

"You surprised me," she had said awakening suddenly, and then she gave me a half hug and a little pecky kiss and she was up and gone, and I was a little boy alone in her bed, warm and smothered in her smells like a baby kangaroo, I thought. I am a baby kangaroo.

And sometimes in the early morning in Riverton in the summer I would put back the top of my new bright plum Oldsmobile convertible—let in the early Riverton sun, as yellow as joy, and drive to the edge of the town, down Riverview Road into the country. I saw the wild sunflowers growing at the road's edge, which were gaudy, too bright a yellow for the plain green countryside in the early morning, and along the road the wild sunflowers were as pure a yellow as the sound of the morning killdeer peeping and protesting with its yellow song out in the field of second-hatched dandelions, which were coming ahead of the hay.

I would set up my easel and paint the sunflowers, thinking of Van Gogh. All great artists must paint sunflowers, I thought, and besides I felt a certain kinship with Van Gogh—of spastic souls, of wretched, smashing strokes in the early morning light. I saw crows crossing the road to peck at the old hide of a prairie dog, lately flattened by some fat tire. I saw the crows of Van Gogh flying over yellow grain—the goddamn crows, and then I left with the sunflower painting wet, smelling of turpentine, just as the first heat of day set in. They were the long lonely years in Riverton after I ran for Congress, and the people said no, and there was no place else to go. They were the empty years before Imaging Crow, before I had gone off to Bethel, Maine, to fight the witches and the demons who rose out of the rotted flesh of my mother, and after I painted the sunflowers on one of those early summer days, I drove back through the main street of Riverton where the people hardly noticed me, with the easel sticking up out of the back seat, with the painting sitting there, too, for everyone to see, but no one saw, because nothing much interested the townspeople.

They were opening the little doors of their shops and sweeping the sidewalks, and they were religiously washing the windows in anticipation of the first morning's customers. It was the shopkeepers' morning liturgy, and walking by with a long, slick step was this shopkeeper's wife I knew, walking in a light bright yellow cotton thing of a dress with the hemline almost to the fine bottom line of her buttocks. It was the style in those days. I had never talked with her much. Whenever I talked to her at different times, she would giggle and then look away, and then she'd catch me suddenly—catch me looking down at her, down past her front and her flat belly, to her thighs, which were always tight, or tightening, and then she would say by her look that she had caught me and turn away again, saying something that was unrelated. I could never remember. She had yellow hair.

About a year before she'd delivered certain photographs to my office showing her husband and some huge-busted woman, both naked, both smiling an insipid smile into the camera. She said she had come to talk about a divorce and asked me about her rights, but when I began to ponder the answers she giggled again, and finally I resolved in my own mind that what she really wanted was for me to see the photographs. I was very professional about it. I opened up a file for her and put the pictures in my floor safe in the office.

"Who took the pictures?" I asked.

"I don't know," she said. "He gave them to me," "he" being her husband, and she giggled again.

I pulled the new plum convertible over next to the curb where she was walking.

"How about a lift, beautiful?" I said.

"I'm almost there, silly," she said, and giggled. "I can walk fifty feet more."

"You need a ride," I said. "Come over here and get in this car," and then she obeyed and with an exaggerated swing of her hips she got into the front seat.

"All right, then, where are we going?" She giggled, and when I looked at her she turned away.

"We're going to make love out in this broad daylight—in this good sunshine." I gestured to the world with both hands.

"Oh, how you talk." She giggled once more. I pulled her over close to me by a warm brown leg, and the townspeople on the street saw nothing, saw only their own feet walk by, never looked up, and I drove back into the countryside with the painting and the easel still in the back seat, out into the beginning heat of the morning and past the sunflowers beginning to droop and the fields of wilting morning dandelions.

"I have to open the shop," she finally protested. I slammed on the brakes, which left a straight skid on the hot pavement until the convertible came to a stop. Across the way was a farmhouse with squawking chickens running loose in the front yard, running by the noisy farm children, one boy and one girl, who played in an old tire swing next to the corrals. A lazy black Angus bull switched his tail from side to side against the flies, and a startled collie pup began yapping, and the chickens ran faster and squawked even louder. It was a place smelling of breeding and blooming, with purple lilacs, half-past blossom, at the farmer's front door, and the farmer's wife came out in an old faded dress and stared over at us, openmouthed, fat in the middle and string-haired. Behind the farmhouse a little way the farmer stood on steady legs spread out like country stumps, covered in bib overalls, no shirt, and he leaned on his irrigation shovel and stared and squinted his eyes hard at us to make out what we were doing, and two crows flew by, two crows over the yellow fields, squawking. I kissed the woman in the front seat of the convertible and then while they stared, I drove off through high willows to a place I knew under the cottonwoods which towered along the old Wind River, and I heard the early summer flood waters drumming up against the riverbanks in good rhythm. Good rhythm.

Afterward I felt guilty.

I sold the painting of the sunflowers, or gave it away, I can't remember now—it makes no difference—to my wife's friend, and it was after that that I met Imaging Crow, and I would not fall in love, of course, and the records showed that Joe Esquibel was insane, schizophrenic, and Imaging Crow and I had run off together for brief times in April, and Joe Esquibel and Imaging Crow and I were all hallucinating in April. When I came back to Riverton from Bethel, Maine, I burned the mother-painting I had left in my studio, face to the wall, and later I knew I had to leave Anna Wilson Spence and those four children.

I was in love with Imaging Crow.

In May of 1968, Dr. Jack Tedro examined Joe again to determine his sanity. No one had examined me. Imaging had only touched me softly, gently.

"Who is your father?" the doctor had asked Joe Esquibel.

"Can't remember," Joe said. He was wide-eyed still, blank-faced. His face was puffy, the color of cream sauce.

"Your mother?"

"She is good to me." Flatly—he spoke with flat affect, the doctor said.

"Married?"

"No."

"Children?"

"Yes."

"What kind of work do you do?"

"Don't do no work."

"What kind of work in the past?"

"Didn't work."

"How did you get by?"

"Mother gave me money," the way someone would say that is a table or my feet are on the floor.

"Where did you get the scar over your left eye?"

"Don't know."

"Why are you in this hospital?"

"Don't know. Them guys say I shot a girl. Never did. Them white guys is lyin'. Never been in no trouble." He was flat as a board.

"Hear any voices talking to you?" There was a long pause.

Finally he said, "Just my mother."

"What does your mother say to you?"

"She is saying to get up out of bed and do what them guys tell you to do so them guys will like you and be nice to you."

"Does she say anything else?"

"No."

"Dreams?"

"Sometimes."

"What?"

"Me and my brother Timato. Them guys is gonna kill us. Them guys is after us. We are runnin'."

The doctor said he was not as hostile as he was on the last exam, but he was hallucinating more, still had a puzzled look on his face. The doctor's diagnostic impression: psychotic (schizophrenia). The doctor had never touched him, not even gently. Never. He only examined a subject.

The attendants at the Wyoming State Hospital were mostly young men from Evanston who needed work. They authored the nurses' notes, which were their observations of the subject. Tried to write in a professional way. Appetite good, the attendant wrote. Personal grooming very good. Still isn't associating. Spends all of his time watching TV. Polite. Helps older patients. Does good job. Has a cut on the side of his left wrist. Said he did it on a can in the kitchen. Was to have a spinal tap today. Stated, "Shit, I don't want another needle stuck up my back." Cooperative. The records showed that in April while I was writing poems to Imaging they had x-rayed Joe's skull, given him an EEG, which is a brain wave test, tapped his spine, and that afterward he had had serious resulting headaches, which went on for days. Got so bad that he threw up, the records said. The attendants said Joe used a lot of swear words when he discussed the headaches. They would not write the words down. Joe stated that the white pill (aspirin) didn't help. The records went on with more observation of the subject, shift on shift, day on day, and for months. They did not reveal that anyone loved Joe Esquibel. They showed only that each week he was visited by his mother or his sister Elma, and her husband, Frank Fisher.

By June of the second year the record said he was out playing baseball—had good manners, but when he asked someone to do something he expected him to drop what he was doing and to do as he asked. Worked on the farm at the hospital. Liked to work on the farm. Dr. Jack Tedro tested him again and found him to be more friendly, more responsive, but he didn't remember murdering his wife. Vaguely remembered her at all. Still psychotic in June. On Compazine—30 mg, b.i.d., and Kemadrin, 5 mg.

In July Dr. Karn diagnosed Joe—295.95, schizophrenia, and also 310.90, borderline mentally retarded, with an I.Q. of 79, handy labels out of the Psychiatric Handbook, but the labels did not help Joe Esquibel. It is a lonely business, psychiatry. Labels leave psychiatrists lonely.

The attendants' records reported that Joe Esquibel was seen with a woman. Didn't say who. It was July 1968, and Joe Esquibel seemed happy. Has a pink card, the notes said, which gave him certain privileges off the grounds of the hospital. Attended Catholic Mass. Left the hall unattended, on his own, and ran errands for the attendants. Another note said, went over to Campbell Hall to help put the other patients to bed. Was on medication. Worked in the greenhouse. Picked up his own medication at the pharmacy. Started basic education classes. Did not share his feelings. His real feelings and problems he kept to himself. Given pass to visit sister in Salt Lake City. Was interested and involved with a female patient. Seemed better. Pleasant. Clean. Was pleased about his family's reaction to the changes in him. Said he felt he had changed a lot. Talked about his own feelings and problems. Seen with female patient.

Love doesn't cure insanity. Love is just another form of insanity. I had left an old insanity behind for this new one.

"Are you in love with her?" Anna asked.

"Yes. I am in love with her. I am leaving." Anna looked sick. Her face was pasty, the bright freckles were gone now, and her eyes were pained and pale and dry. I wanted to run away from the horrid thing I had done to this good woman. I can't remember much of it now, but I remember that I'd finally left my home and my children and Anna who cried, and we'd cried together, and I'd also screamed out irrational agonies at her, and she could only scream back, like pangs of thunder booming senselessly in the night and echoing back again from twenty miles away.

Sometimes in the morning there was laughter in my new insanity, and Imaging and I ran naked hand in hand across a green summer meadow in the mountains or hid in the trunk of my new Cadillac, and made love in the parking lot. And I painted paintings without demons, painted Imaging Crow nude, surrounded by a flock of descending crows, and we promised not to make promises to each other, and out of this love came the great pain of becoming a breaker of promises. But I was not a breaker of promises. I had not broken promises to Anna. This Anna was a different woman, I said, and I was a different man from when I made those promises. We were only children then. We looked a little the same now, not much, had the same names, and our lives were strung together with a mutual history and our genes had mixed together and there were those four babies, but we were not the same people and, therefore, different people could not be held accountable for promises they had not made. I was not a breaker of promises, I cried. I couldn't bear it.

Oh, God, I loved this woman Imaging. Look at her, and I was trapped again. How could I leave Anna? Yet I tried. In desperation I moved into a little house across town and insanely painted insane figures on the walls, and I painted breasts of all sizes, mothers' breasts and the pointed breasts of maidens and the hanging breasts of unknown women. I'd decorated the place with a yellow porch swing hung from the ceiling and a round table with a red doughnut-shaped cushion, which Imaging had also made along with various other brightly colored pillows, and once my children had come to my house and had met her there for the first time, and they wanted to know what her name was, and not wanting to say, she called herself "Pillow." "My name is Pillow," she smiled. And the children liked Imaging, but the children didn't know what to do with their crazy father, and when I cried at night alone I put my arms around myself, and I said I was my own mother and I would love myself. But I had trouble loving that man, that breaker of promises, that marriage-breaker, that breaker of hearts, a man who broke a decent woman and left four innocent babes, and I lay there at night dying of guilt. Then Imaging would save me in the morning, would come to me and look at me lovingly, and I knew she loved me, and I felt alive, and I was well again for a little while.

On December 7, 1968, Joe Esquibel was found in Nick's Bar in downtown Evanston with a former female patient drinking beer. He was returned to Johnson Hall, given a red card, which meant he was required to stay behind the locked doors of a locked hall, and on February 2, 1969, Dr. Karn proclaimed that Joe Esquibel was sane. It was not, once a skitz always a skitz. It was that Joe was now sane and well again. They had cured him, and consequently he should be tried for murder. Dr. Karn wrote: "The diagnosis of schizophrenia is to be dropped at this time because it is not clinically discerned," which means he looked and acted sane. He should hereafter be diagnosed as 310.90, borderline mental retardation.

Eighteen days later, on February 20, 1969, Owen Kennedy found evidence in the Minnesota Multaphasic Personality Inventory (MMPI) that there was evidence of both paranoia and schizophrenia. Joe was improved but still psychotic. Undoubtedly Owen Kennedy had not yet read the orders of Dr. Karn that the diagnosis of schizophrenia was to be dropped. And on April 26 of the same year Dr. Max Cutler, the clinical psychologist, said that the MMPI showed Joe to be grossly psychotic still, with extreme thought disorders. "Sexual anxiety and conflict are extreme. This is evident everywhere one looks, particularly on the human figure drawings where he became so involved with the crotch area of the male figure that he placed a huge black spot right at the junction of the legs in the groin. Paranoid tendencies are still evident . . . He is washed out emotionally . . . There can be little doubt that he is capable of explosive loss of emotional control . . . Much anxiety centers around the female card on the Rorschach, and he was finally unable to cope with it at all and rejected it, his only failure on the test. Whether this is a function of his tendency to identify with his mother is difficult to say, but there can be little doubt that he is intensely conflicted in the sexual area . . . He completes sentences as follows: *My greatest fear is:* 'life.' *My mind is:* 'not too good' . . . Mr. Esquibel appears to be functioning primarily as a passive-aggressive, passive-dependent character disorder at this time, as noted dependency persists. When asked what kind of an animal he would choose to be if turned into one, he said, 'a horse or a dog because people treat horses and dogs pretty good.' Although he is functioning as a passive-dependent personality which would be subsumed under passive-aggressive personality 301.81 . . . he also could be classified under schizophrenia, residual Type 295.6 as no longer manifesting psychosis after suffering a psychotic, schizophrenic episode. He can function outside the hospital," the doctor reported, and the diagnosis of schizophrenia was dropped. Dr. Karn's orders. Insanity is a label. It is also an order.

Dr. Charles J. Katz, associate superintendent at the hospital reported, "It was the consensus of the staff that the patient can become a productive member of his community and this should be encouraged, fostered and continued. A letter will be written to the court outlining our evaluations and recommendations." This meant Joe Esquibel was ready to be tried for murder, and gassed—that's how I read it.

On July 14, 1969, Dr. Karn wrote a letter to Judge Reuel Armstrong, who was the resident judge at Rawlins after the death of Judge Stanton. Dr. Karn cited "unique problems" and "unprecedented occurrences" with Joe. It was the first time Dr. Karn could remember, he said, that a subject who was sane when they had examined him at the hospital later became insane before his trial. Dr. Karn said there was no doubt that Joe Esquibel was neither medically or legally insane at the time he killed his wife—*totally sane then*—but he was insane when he was returned to the hospital on December 31, 1966. Then he said, "We are pleased, Your Honor, to state that we have fulfilled the letter and intent of the late Judge Stanton's order in that Dr. Charles J. Katz, Associate Superintendent, in his most recent evaluation of Mr. Esquibel found him restored to mental health. My recommendations are that Mr. Esquibel now be returned to the court for legal disposition, and that this disposition would include the adjudication of Mr. Esquibel as now sane, competent and triable." They locked him in Johnson Hall and waited for the sheriff to pick him up.

It was January of 1969 when Imaging got her divorce and the custody of her two little boys, Brents and Christopher. I can't remember much about that either, but she assured me it had nothing to do with me. No guilt, please. Let me do what I must do. It's true that I love you. It's true that I fell in love with you and I never intended to. It's true I broke my promise to you, and fell in love with you, and although it is wrong to break promises, it is not wrong to love. But as for me, I couldn't stand the pain of it, of children asking why I didn't come home, frightened little children hanging onto Anna, and in March of 1969, I moved back with Anna Spence. Imaging knew I was going. We held onto each other that one last time, and we cried until we could cry no more, and then silently I got up in the dark and left my darling Imaging.

I decided instead of leaving my family I would become a judge. I would straighten out my life, give up my wild ways. I would regain my sanity, go into judicial monk-hood, and live out my life in service to mankind. But the good people of Riverton, Wyoming, would not hear of it. Spence a judge? The son-of-a bitch is nothing but the local stud—got no morals—no business being a judge, that's for sure. Crooked bastard, too, I hear. Sued Emmy Lewis' husband. Damned near broke 'em. I couldn't vote for the bastard if he was the last man alive. Write the governor. Campaign. Call old Stan. I know Stan. Good governor. Good old boy. Won't appoint a lousy shyster like that to the judgeship. Of course, if you're needin' a lawyer, you'd be better off with him fer ya rather than against ya. But a judge? That's somethin' else again. Drinks like a goddamned fish. Does crazy things, too. Ever see his crazy paintings? The man's nuts, I tell ya. I'll tell ya, he's plumb nuts. Got a blue-eyed Indian girl friend. Jesus Christ. A fuckin' squaw man. Don't know how his wife and kids put up with him all this time. Run off and left them for that fuckin' little Indian, and he's got tits painted all over the friggin' walls of that house he rents. Damned near destroyed it I hear, and I hear he come to the door once when the Jehovah Witnesses knocked, stuck his head out and asked them what they wanted, and they said they come to talk to him about God. Then he opened up the door and was standin' there plumb naked and said that he *was* God, and that ran 'em off, scared 'em half to death.

Yeah, I know. A guy come to his office one time and he was sittin' out in that patio of his in back of his office there in the broad daylight stark naked like ya said, dicta-tin' a letter on his dictating machine. Craziest bastard this

town has ever had. I seen him once on top a the roof
drinkin' whiskey with that Indian woman in the broad
daylight. . . . Pretty bitch. Gotta give 'em credit for
that. Little thing with long braids and a cute ass, and she
can wiggle it. And the two of 'em was up there on the top
of the roof waving at the cars as they went by, half drunk
in the middle of the mornin', for Christ's sake. Great
judge he'd make. Probably smokes dope, too. Probably a
commie. Acts like a commie. Write the governor. Letter
campaign. Telephone campaign.

The governor said it didn't make any difference, that
the bar associations of both counties in the district had
endorsed me. He knew they just wanted to get rid of me
—better have Spence as a judge than as an opponent the
governor said the bar had reasoned. Get rid of the bastard. Put him up on the bench. But no, the governor
couldn't do that. He never got such an organized protest
from one small town in his life. Never heard of any such
protest before. No, he couldn't appoint me as a judge.
Gerry, we're great friends, and all, and I helped you in
your campaign for Congress. You remember that. But no.
You'd be no use to the people.

Then I realized that I was no longer trapped in Riverton, Wyoming. I had been thrown out of the trap. I
rented an old auto parts store downtown, hauled everything there that Anna and I owned, everything, paintings,
furniture, keepsakes, my guns, our dishes, all our earthly
possessions, even Imaging's pillows, and we sold everything at a sale called "Spence's Last Remark." We sold
our house and the tiny ranch called Hidden Valley on the
reservation up high in the mountains where I had written
great poems and made paintings of my ghosts and demons, and where I had irrigated the summer meadows
and drunk manhattans with old Indian John, old as the
mountains, and I sold my office building and left Cleo
and I moved my family to Mill Valley, California, moved
out of that place of insanity and ordered a new life for me
and for them. It was springtime in 1969, and I thought I
was still insane, still hallucinating in April, but whether I
was or not made no difference now.

I decided to enroll in San Francisco State for a Masters in Art. They liked the slides I sent of my paintings, the crazy birds, the purple robin, the tumbling figures in space, the insane images. I would give my life to the young people of the world. I was forty. I knew about life, didn't I? I had experienced it and I would teach young men and women about living by painting, but I was in love with Imaging. I was dying. I got a call from John Ackerman. "Imaging is drinking too much, Gerry."

"Oh, God," I said. "How is she?"

"She looks like she's dying."

"Oh, God, I can't stand it," I said. "What'll I do?"

"I don't know," John said. "Are you gonna cross the bridge?"

"What bridge?"

"The one that's got the sign over it, 'Don't Cross This Bridge Until You Get Here.' Are you there yet?"

"I talk to her every day," I said. "I tell her to believe in us, to keep the faith, to believe it will be okay."

"I think she's going crazy. She doesn't cry any more. Just drinks."

"She's on her spot."

"What spot?" John asked.

"I tell her every day on the phone, 'Don't get off that spot—that black spot right there, the one I want you to stay on—to wait for me on.' I'm going to get out of this— gonna get out. I gotta get out of this, John. Tell her to stay on her spot and I'll come get her."

"When?" John asked.

"I don't know," I said weakly. "I don't know when I can get out."

I hired a psychiatrist in San Francisco, across the bridge from Mill Valley, a pleasant man, seemed lonely— recovering from a heart attack of his own. "Why do psychiatrists have heart attacks?" I asked.

"You didn't come here to talk about me," he said in a kindly way.

"May I hire you to do a job?" I asked. "You know— like a client hires me to do a job for him."

"Maybe," he said. "What job?"

"I want you to help me get out of my marriage. Help me break my promises."

"Okay," he said. I came to see him twice a week. Anna thought I needed counseling, to help me come to my senses—to see the light of day. She was patient and supportive as I talked to the psychiatrist. But I can't remember now what I said to him. I remember he said very little to me, listened, asked questions now and then, didn't take notes, didn't seem sleepy, didn't say he cared about me, seemed strong and distant like a man on a mountain, like a man alone. And I was alone too, talking, and I think I talked of the double-bind—double-bind, the trap I couldn't get out of. If I left Anna and the children, I was wrong. And I couldn't stand the pain of my guilt. And if I left Imaging, I was wrong, and I would die and wither away and my soul would bounce out one day, shriveled and shrunken and brown like a dried-up old carbuncle. That would be the end of me. I wrote long letters to my brother, Tom, who was teaching art in a little college in the Appalachian Mountains, and he wrote back saying that to get out of the double-bind one needed only to make a move. It didn't make any difference what the move was. What was important was to make a move.

Then one day I rushed to my car with a frenzy and drove back to Wyoming. I left the wife of my childhood, and my children, and the art school, and the psychiatrist who had done his job. I had grown a beard. It was gray and scraggly and my eyes were wild, some said. And I drove into Casper, Wyoming, wearing a pair of white pants and barefooted, and I remember Imaging running to me, and we held onto each other and I promised myself, I did not promise her, but only myself, that I would never let her go again. It was July 1969.

I started into practice in Casper, Wyoming, but this time with my old friend Robert R. Rose, and I began trying cases and I lost three in a row. I was no trial lawyer any more. I must have lost something along the way. I didn't know what it was, didn't care really because I had Imaging. I lived in a little apartment alone, and Imaging came to see me and she cooked for me sometimes and we were together, almost always, and we would always be together.

In October I divorced Anna Wilson Spence. I got on the witness stand in front of Judge Reuel Armstrong, of Rawlins, Wyoming. Can't remember what I said, only the weeping. It was known as a default divorce, that is to say, we had finally agreed upon it, Anna and I, her lawyer and mine, Bob Rose—there was a settlement. She should have it all, I insisted—all of it—but no, that was insane Bob Rose said. What we had gathered together should be divided equally and I should support the children. Judge Reuel Armstrong granted the divorce. I would never make promises again—never marry again. Never. "No," Imaging said. We'll never get married. We've had enough of marriage, Imaging said, so we bought a beautiful old house together in the tree section of Casper, Wyoming, but we would never get married. That was a promise.

On October 19, 1969, Oscar Hall filed a motion in Judge Reuel Armstrong's court to discharge Joe Esquibel from the hospital as sane, and to cause his return to the county jail to await trial. They did more testing and wrote more reports. Dr. Max Cutler said Joe had a performance I.Q. now of 123 and an overall I.Q. of 98—dead normal. Joe was bitter about being locked up, and he told Dr. Cutler, "It don't help a guy, either, being locked up again, over just a little drinkin' downtown after he's been in an open ward for more than a year. I get kinda depressed." He seemed hostile, the doctor reported, and on the MMPI his psychotic scales were slightly more elevated than previously. He was more paranoid, the doctor said, but he was labeled passive-aggressive, not insane, and borderline mentally retarded.

Dr. Katz reinforced the above findings saying that although Joe had not adjusted at a mature level, he has no illusions and hallucinations and is at least "capable of assimilating data which could help him on a purely survival level." He was not insane.

On October 30, 1969, Judge T. C. Daniels of Casper, obliged the hospital and, without any jurisdiction, without a hearing, without notice to us, without notice even to Judge Reuel Armstrong, who did have jurisdiction, signed an ex-party order to have Joe delivered to the sheriff, and on November 5, 1969, the order was carried out.

A few weeks after my divorce from Anna, on November 18, 1969, I married Imaging. But now that I was divorced I was a different man, wasn't I? I couldn't bear living a day longer without somehow defining my relationship to Imaging for the whole world. Even swans have a mating ceremony, even hummingbirds, I think, and so we stood under the trees at Lake Tahoe, Nevada, and we repeated a ceremony of our own to each other which we had written without any promises in it to keep. I was a breaker of promises.

Then we moved into that beautiful old home on Eleventh and Durbin streets, which we bought together, and on November 20, 1969, Judge Armstrong assigned the Esquibel case to Judge Robert Forrister of Casper, Wyoming, because he, Judge Armstrong, knew Mona Lee Murphy, the mother of Sharon Esquibel. They were old friends, and he had known Sharon, too, and, therefore, he said he was disqualified, and Judge Forrister, who knew no one involved in the case, would take over. The first time I learned that Joe Esquibel was in the county jail was when Raymond Whitaker called me.

"Joe is in jail, Gerald," he said. "Tried to kill himself."

"What do you mean?" I asked back on the phone.

"Gerald, he slashed his wrists, slashed his chest with a razor blade. Don't know how the hell he got a razor blade . . ."

"What's he doing in jail? I thought he was in the state hospital. They can't send him to jail. He's been adjudicated insane. That stands! It's never been changed by the court. Can't be changed without another jury trial."

"Of course, Gerald," Raymond Whitaker said.

"Well, we'll haul their asses up," I said.

"Yeah," Raymond said. "But we've got to figure out in whose court. Judge Daniels signed the order putting him in jail without a hearing, and Judge Armstrong had jurisdiction. Judge Forrister got an assignment from Judge Armstrong. This is the first time in the annals of Anglo-Saxon jurisprudence that a murder has been committed in Carbon County, the defendant incarcerated in Sweetwater County, and two judges from Natrona County have taken jurisdiction. We'll file a writ of *habeas corpus.*"

"Yeah," I said. "Exactly. A writ of *habeas corpus.*" And then Raymond argued before Judge Forrister very sternly. The order of Judge Daniels was a nullity—no jurisdiction. Judge Daniels was as foreign to the proceeding as the King of Siam. There had never been a trial as to Joe's sanity since the last jury found him insane, and Dr. Karn had no right to upset a jury's finding. Dr. Karn was no jury. There had to be a trial. *"Habeas corpus* is the mother writ of the law," Raymond said. It tested the right of the sheriff of Sweetwater County to hold Joe Esquibel in the county jail, and there was no right. Judge Forrister agreed, and on February 5, 1970, he signed an order sending Joe Esquibel back to the state hospital. On February 6, 1970, a Dr. Gordon H. Scharman, staff physician, wrote a note saying Joe's diagnosis was to be deferred. On March 12, 1970, Dr. Karn also wrote a note saying that a physical examination revealed a tumor mass or traumatic deformity at the level of the third rib anteriorly just lateral to the sternum, otherwise a healthy male. They never chased the tumor or the so-called traumatic deformity further. Dr. Karn also deferred his diagnosis.

On February 20, 1970, Dr. Cutler, the psychologist, tested Joe again—overall I.Q. this day was 81—barely dull normal. This is a "startling change," he said. "The human drawings are the smallest he has yet produced and he is more psychotic on the MMPI, going over the scale in the schizophrenia factor, and very nearly on the paranoid . . . he completes phrases as follows: *I like:* 'my son.' *My happiest time is:* 'when I see my mother.' *I want to know:* 'when I can go home.' *I suffer:* 'when I don't see my mother.' *My greatest worry is:* 'my son.' *I am best when:* 'I see my family.' *I wish:* 'I could go home.' " Dr. Cutler said, "I am very strongly inclined to the opin-

ion that we are seeing increased paranoia and increasing
schizophrenia. He is less likely to be able to aid in his
own defense than six months ago . . . He seems to be
deteriorating. *He is not bright enough to distort the tests in
a consistent fashion.* On the Rorschach he sees 'the hide
of a skin—it's torn up, you know.' I can only assume he is
actually deteriorating," Dr. Cutler reported. Dr. William
D. Pace on the same day said he had seen Joe Esquibel in
the company of some other patients. Joe was laughing,
and when Joe saw that Dr. Pace was observing him, he
stopped laughing. He diagnosed Joe as 1) borderline intelligence, 2) malingering. Faking, Dr. Pace reported. He
can stand trial, Pace said.

In April 1970, Dr. Karn was still ordering the diagnosis
deferred. Then Joe slipped away again—downtown just
to have a beer, he said. They found him with a former
female mental patient and then Dr. Cutler tested him
once more. This last time he was no longer schizophrenic
—all right again. The human figure drawings were large
once more. Although he was anxious, he was not psychotic. Everybody now agreed. And in August 1970, even
Dr. Cutler said Joe had not proceeded into psychosis as
he thought, and he was again ready to stand trial. At the
staff meeting in September of 1970 following Joe's elopement to the downtown bar with this woman the staff
voted him sane.

The hospital was impatient to get Joe out of there. Dr.
Pace reported Joe was a leader among the patients, and
put him on a red card—locked up in Johnson Hall again.
Nobody knew why, but Dr. Pace said in March of 1971
that Joe was responsible for "many total patient problems." Pace diagnosed him sane—301.80. Passive-aggressive. The hospital wrote Oscar Hall and the judge. There
were many telephone calls. They wanted Joe Esquibel
out of the hospital, but in May of 1971 Joe was still
locked up in Johnson Hall.

In a feminine hand, someone wrote a letter for Joe to
Raymond Whitaker. "I have been confined here . . . no
treatment. I have only been permitted to go to the hall
for government meetings and to work. They are putting

pressure on all of us . . . The patients are depressed. Dr. Pace won't tell me why I am on a red card. Won't talk to me . . . Good friends of mine which are the aides here say Dr. Pace is doing this deliberately to me . . . he won't let my son visit me . . . and he will only let two people at a time from my family visit. Since February 1970 I have not received any medication whatsoever . . . he changed all the rules. They are so restrictive patients are escaping in masse." And Joe was calling me as well on the telephone to get him out of this crazy place.

"Want to go to jail again, Joe?"

"It's hell here, Mr. Spence. This is jail. It's worse than jail."

"You'll go crazy in jail, Joe," I reminded him. His voice was clear and plaintive. "I'd rather be crazy in prison than here," he said.

"You'll get depressed again. Well, we'll file a motion—motion to dismiss the case, Joe. They haven't given you a speedy trial," I said.

"Please, Mr. Spence. Please do somethin'."

We filed the motion. The court personnel talked. The people talked. Silly lawyers, they said. They should give up, for Christ's sake, those shysters—abusing the system, claiming he's insane. Put him in the state hospital, and then when the state doesn't try him those shysters say he hasn't had a speedy trial. Esquibel's a killer. Deserves to be killed himself. That's justice. Did you ever represent a man you knew was guilty, Mr. Spence? Of course. We are all guilty. Why do you cause so much trouble for the system? It's lawyers like you that hurt all of us. The system wasn't meant to be abused like that. It's meant to serve the innocent not the guilty. There is no question here. Eight solid citizens witnessed the shooting. If the system can't deliver justice here it can't operate at all. You lawyers are obstructionists. Justice would work better without a bunch a lawyers. I'd drop the pill on the bastard. No problem at all. Give me the pill and a little pan of acid and I'll give you justice. Speedy justice. What is justice? Justice is watching that bastard choke to death on the gas. You can't go around killing your wife. This son-of-a-bitch causes more trouble than a whole jail full of them pukes. Can't turn your head on him. He'll kill you. Vicious bastard, some said.

Judge Forrister overruled our Motion to Dismiss, of course, but he set the case for jury trial on June 23, 1971. The jury would again determine if Joe Esquibel could stand trial, but there were conflicts in the lawyers' schedules, and the court had to reset the case, and the summer passed.

26

THE TRIAL of Joe Esquibel was finally set for September 27, 1971, in Casper, Wyoming. I knew they'd get us this time.

They've had him all these years, and Dr. Tedro was writing new reports saying that he had reviewed the records from Joe's first day at the hospital, and "Joe Esquibel probably was not insane at the time of the alleged crime, and that all his amnesia may very well have been feigned from the beginning," and he said Joe probably never hallucinated. "At the time of my second and third interviews with Joe Esquibel . . . my interpretation of his inappropriate affect was not accurate. It was feigned behavior, designed to hoodwink the examiner into believing he was psychotic when he actually wasn't." Tedro was willing to state that he was wrong when he previously found that Joe was insane. Now he said Joe faked it all.

"They really want to get Joe Esquibel out of that hospital," I said to Raymond.

"He's causing them trouble, Gerald," Raymond said.

"He's just standing up for his rights, and fighting for some helpless crazy little people up there—that's all," I said.

"That's enough," Raymond said. "Who is this Tedro?"

"A forensic psychiatrist. Forensic psychiatry—the art of convincing juries the defendant is sane and should go to the gas chamber, that's what forensic psychiatry is,

Raymond. They say this Dr. Pace, who is in charge of these cases now, kicks every defendant out as sane and triable. He has a little song and dance he gives to the juries. Thinks he is doing society a great favor flushing the criminals out of the hospital like fresh turds. Pulls the chains. Out they go." I was angry, afraid first and then angry. "What are we gonna do?"

"Well, Gerald . . ."

"Raymond, how could a borderline retardee fool every doctor in the hospital, not once but dozens of times—not one day but for every day for five years? That's ridiculous."

"Well, who says a borderline retardee isn't smarter than those doctors?" Raymond asked.

"What are we gonna do?"

"Give another great final argument, Gerald."

When I am afraid I attack. When a lion is afraid he does the same. Every beast has its way. The rabbit runs looking for a hole, and the turtle hides in its own shell, but it's the same animal emotion, fear—my friend, fear. But I prepared for the attack first. I called my old friend Phil McAuley at the Casper *Star Tribune,* Wyoming's largest newspaper. Get me a photographer, Phil, secret story, big story. Sure, Gerry. Then I went to Judge Forrister for an order authorizing me to inspect and photograph the Wyoming State Hospital for the purpose of gathering evidence.

"What are you looking for?" he asked.

"How do I know?"

"Well, what kind of things are you looking for?"

Judge Forrister was a small man with much handsome black hair, which he kept slicked neatly, and a well-sculptured young-looking face. He smiled when he talked out of a long habit of trying to be pleasant, and his eyes twinkled mirthfully, too, even when he spoke of things that were unhappy. It was his way.

"I have heard rumors that the place is like a snake pit," I said. "Filed an affidavit to that effect in support of my motion here. They say the patients are held like animals.

I want to swoop down like an avenging angel, ha, ha, with the cameras flashing."

"Should I hold a hearing?" he asked, smiling, with happy eyes.

"No."

"No hearing? It was you who last told me how vital a hearing is to the system. To be heard is the 'life blood of freedom,' is how I think you put it. It was a wonderful quotation. I wrote it down," Judge Forrister said. "I was duly impressed."

"I can't get the evidence if the hospital knows about my coming first. They'll have it all tidied up by the time I get there. It's your discretion. Judicial discretion is the cornerstone of justice," I said.

"That's a very impressive quote, too," His Honor said, reading the affidavit carefully. "I shall make a note of that as well." An attorney needs to be aware of exactly the right time to push the papers over to the judge for signing, like when to close the sale on a bouquet of sweetpeas, or a used car—not to oversell, but when there is that sense that the parties have come together, well, that's the time, and I smiled back at His Honor and pushed the order over to him for signing, and he smiled back and with a judicial flourish of the pen the order was signed. I chartered a single-engine Cessna, and the photographer, a congenial fellow from the *Star Tribune* named Chuck Morrison, and I bopped and bounced and dipped over the prairies, and over the mountains, and finally down into the town of Evanston where my old friend Vince Vehar met us at the Evanston airstrip in a little valley with a creek running by. Vince brought the sheriff, as I asked, because the sheriff would swoop down with us, serve the papers, and then we'd run through the buildings, photographing, like wild bulls in the halls, and no one would be able to stop us. We would look at the records and talk with the patients as we chose, and gather up the evidence. I followed the sheriff into Dr. Karn's office and the sheriff handed him the court's order. He seemed unperturbed. He smoked his pipe, tapped it out casually, laid it down, and said his "hellos," agreeably, and smiled at the sheriff, and at me, and he smiled at Chuck Morrison.

"Have a seat, Mr. Spence," he said. "Let's talk about this a little bit."

"Oh no. In the next thirty seconds we're going to take a look at this place the way it is."

"Well," he said. "It'll be the same sixty seconds from now. What are you looking for?"

"We're just looking," I said. "Come on," I said to the photographer. "Let's go. I want to take a look at Sublette first."

"Very well," Dr. Karn said. "I'll send someone along with you."

"That won't be necessary," I said.

"Yes, it will. Someone has to let you in. The hall is locked," Dr. Karn smiled back.

"Oh," I said. "Well, let's go!"

"Let's see . . ." The doctor picked up his pipe again and he reached over for his tobacco pouch as well. He began to load the pipe with tobacco.

"You!" I hollered to a man walking by the office with keys dangling from his belt. "You have a key to Sublette?" The man looked startled. "Yes," he said. "Come with me," I said. The man hesitated. "Tell him to come with us," I said to Dr. Karn.

"You may go with the gentlemen," Dr. Karn said. "If there is anything else I can do, come back and ask. I'll be only too glad to assist you."

We walked fast. Speed is the secret to the panzer attack, I thought. "When I point, you shoot," I said to the photographer. The man with the keys opened up Sublette, and the smell of the place came rushing out. I could smell the misery. It was in the stale air, heavy, as if men could not walk through it.

"Where's Joe Esquibel?" I asked the first attendant we came to.

"Not here," he said, surprise registered on his face. "Who are you?"

"Court order," I said. The man looked frightened and then he began to look angry. I pointed at the man. The photographer shot. Flash. The man backed away. Golden Gate . . . listen. The screams. The incessant screaming of Jason. "There," I said to the attendant. "Open the gate." He shook his keys until he found the right one, and we pushed through, and there was Jason, naked, screaming on the hard wet cement floor. It was a scream from neither man nor beast, a terrible noise out of Jason's protruding belly, fat from squatting all those years in an eight-by-eight cage. Even his blackness had faded. His eyes were not human eyes. They were dull, and untamed, looking and not recognizing, and he shook the bars as we passed and screamed again and the shivers went up my spine. I pointed at Jason and the camera flashed. Hideous. And next to Jason was a little child. He was sobbing. Ten, maybe twelve. Blond.

Sobbing.

He reached a hand out of the cage for me to take. He looked in my eyes. I touched the boy and he grabbed my fingers and held on.

"Unteachable," the man said. "Autistic, they call it," but when I touched the boy he stopped his sobbing. "Should have give the kid another lobotomy a long time ago," the attendant apologized. The boy gripped my fingers as if he were hanging onto them for his life. I pointed at the child with my free hand. The photographer's camera flashed.

"Lobotomy?" I asked.

"Yeah. They stick them needles up there through the eye socket or something, behind the eyeball, and then they punch holes in the brain up front. Call it a frontal lobotomy. They already give him one. Usually quiets 'em right down. Didn't work on this kid though."

"Oh," I said. The boy held onto me.

"Name's Billy," he said.

"Hi, Billy," I said. And he held onto my fingers and looked into my eyes like any lonely little boy. He was a naked boy in a bare cement cage.

"Why is he naked?"

"Tears his clothes off," the orderly said. "But you get used to it," he said cheerfully. Billy wouldn't let loose. He held onto my fingers as if there were nothing but space below him.

"Let him loose, Billy," the man said, and started over for the boy, but I said no, and I stood there for a little while and let Billy hold on. Let him have me. Things wouldn't be different in sixty seconds, as Karn said. And then finally I slid my fingers free of Billy with the other hand and I could hear him sobbing again behind me. Autistic. Some say that a sensitive, thinking, feeling, fully aware child is trapped inside the autistic child, trapped like we all are trapped, but unable to speak from inside the trap and crying to get out, to be recognized and to be loved. Trapped.

"Jesus Christ!" I said to the photographer. "Let's get the hell out of here." They shut the Golden Gate behind us. Joe had been here. Some patients were reaching their hands through the bars as we walked by, like chimps in a zoo wanting candy, peanuts, maybe, waiting to be touched. Cigarettes. They begged for cigarettes, and then an attendant handed them something through the bars out of a sack, and I pointed, and the photographer flashed his camera.

There was a sense of permanency here. Nothing changed. Hopelessness seemed permanent, and the screaming of the creatures without interruption was the permanent sound of the place, and the cream-colored paint peeled from the ceilings, eternally peeling, and there were no calendars, no clocks on the walls, and the sun rose and set, and the place looked the same because after sunset the lights remained on through the whole of the night, and when the sun rose the lights burned on all day, and there were the listless monotonous motions of men, which were like the mindless rhythmless heaving of matter, moving, expanding, and coming back again. In eternity there is nowhere to go, and so the empty faces came back again unchanged, looking like flat rocks from the creek bottom, hardened and immobile, and they moved slowly in the creek bottom, and they were the undulating dead, and but for the crying out and a quiet mumbling in the corner they did not even exist.

"What's the point?" the photographer finally said.

"The point is that they claim Joe Esquibel is now sane again. But Joe wasn't sane when he came to the hospital the last time," I said. "The jury found that he was insane."

"Yes, but was the jury right?" the photographer asked.

"Dr. Karn even admitted that the jury was right—that he was insane when the hospital got him back."

"Oh?"

"And then they brought him over here to this place where he's been more or less, for the last couple of years. When I saw him the last time he was comatose. Looked like a log. Didn't even know me."

"Yeah?" the photographer said patiently.

"Now you tell me how the hell anybody who was kept in this hell hole can regain his sanity. Look at these people! That's the point. If they dumped an insane man in here it would be like trying to grow daisies in the dark, like trying to whisper the rosary at a rock concert, like trying . . ."

"I get the point," the photographer said.

"See that?" I pointed to a bent-up tin dishpan just outside the cage of a patient. It still had food in it, and some was spilled on the floor. "What's that?" I asked the aide.

"Oh, you can't feed them crazy ones with a plate—feed 'em in that pan. Have to shove it in on the floor like that. Them crazies bent the pan up and throwed it around."

I pointed, and the photographer snapped the photo.

"Where's Joe Esquibel?" I finally said to the attendant who had been with us all along.

"I'll show ya," he said, and then we walked through the Golden Gate and we were out of Sublette Hall and magically we were on the other side of the Golden Gate in Johnson Hall, in the same building. I had seen Joe Esquibel here back in early '68. He had been in Johnson Hall this last time for fifteen months under the orders of Dr. Pace. Red card. Locked hall. The place was filled with the smell of old cigarette smoke. The insane smoke, puffing, expressionless, walking, and standing, swaying as they stand, and there stood Joe Esquibel, alone at the side, silently.

"Hey, Joe," the aide hollered. Joe spun around, looking surprised at first, and then he stood ready as we approached him. I saw no recognition on his face.

"Got a visitor for you, Joe," the attendant said.

"How ya doin', Joe?" I asked. I held out my hand and he took it, and his hands were still soft, and then suddenly I could tell he knew me.

"I gotta get out of here, Mr. Spence. I don't like that Dr. Pace," he said as if we had been speaking to each other for an hour.

"Who's he?"

"He's in charge of us guys. He don' like me. I tol' him, 'I don't like you, Dr. Pace,' I tol' him. He took my card away for no reason. I don't do nothin'. Used to could go to town. Used to have a job at the café washin' dishes. Come back here at night. Worked there all day. Could go anywheres I wanted. Took my card away. Put me here."

"How long you been here, Joe?"

"Don' know. Long time."

"Well, maybe I can do somethin' about it."

"Makes me depressed sometimes. Wish you could get my card back for me," he said. "That Pace, he changes all the rules. The people are depressed. How come I'm here, Mr. Spence? I never done nothin'.'"

"Well, maybe you misbehaved. Maybe you went off drinking downtown or something with a girl friend. I heard about that."

"That was a long time ago. I never done nothin' to nobody. Some of the other guys is just walkin' aroun'—go downtown all the time, and a couple of 'em is waitin' for trial like me. Them white guys murder people and they are just walkin' aroun' but they stick me in here. I never done nothin',' he said. "You got to get me out of here, Mr. Spence."

"Well, we're gonna have another trial, Joe. If we win I can get you a new card—maybe a white card so you can walk around outside and go places like you used to." He didn't say anything. Maybe he didn't believe it either.

"Are you crazy, Joe?" I asked quietly.

"No," he said matter-of-factly.

"Are you okay now, Joe?"

"Yeah," he said. "Yeah, but you gotta get me out of here 'cuz I go crazy in here."

"Well, you know, they want to send you back to jail and try you for murder, and that scares me a little. I don't want 'em to try you for murder. A fella could lose that case. If they ever get you to court on a murder charge, the doctors are going to testify you were sane when you shot Sharon, and Hall will ask the jury to send you to the gas chamber. You're at least alive here. If we win this case, I'll make 'em put you on a good card, Joe—send you to a good hall—and get treatment for you and everything. . . . Well," I said to Joe. "What time is it?"

"I donno."

"We go to trial Monday. Do you know what day this is?"

"No." His expression was pained and he had a tired look in his eye like the eye of an old draft horse who had been in harness too long and pulled too many heavy loads.

"Joe, it'll be better. See you in court," I said cheerily. I shook his wet limp hand, and left him looking after me. I wanted to say something more, but what else could I say? I got out of there.

"Take us to the records room," I said to the attendant, and we followed him and when we got there I Xeroxed all of the records that were handed to us—a thick file of papers, which was all that remained of this man's life in that hospital. Then we walked over to Dr. Karn's office once more and the secretary let me in. The doctor was still at his desk, still puffing his pipe, and he got up and shook my hand as if he were seeing me for the first time and motioned me to a chair.

I sat down. "Do me a favor," I said.

"Sure," he said.

"Examine Joe Esquibel for me."

"Sure will," he said. "Glad to."

"No, do it right now."

"Right now?" he asked. "That's a little out of the ordinary. We have procedures."

"Yeah, I know. But I just saw him. Give him a psychiatric examination now. I'll wait."

Dr. Karn shrugged his shoulders and picked up the phone. "Bring Joe Esquibel over here for me, will you please?" He hung up the phone and smiled. I sat back down in the outer office and thumbed through the Bible-thick file of records we had copied. They were mostly of the daily observations from each attendant on each shift. What the attendant saw of Joe and wanted to write he wrote down. What the attendant didn't see or didn't wish to write was forever lost, and the accumulation became Joe Esquibel, but they were notes written mostly by those young men, some nearly illiterate, their spelling and writing crude as they attempted to create a professional-sounding record. I thumbed through the nurses' notes as I waited for Dr. Karn to complete his examination.

3-29-69—Had visitor. Couldn't find Joe. Later said he had been at the greenhouse but we looked for him there, too. He had been seen driving around with another patient in her car.

4-7-69—Talks to aides. Very pleasant. Jolly person.

6-7-69—A female patient called Joe. When asked who was calling she hung up. Patient's former girl friend is known to be in town.

6-27-69—The staff decided the court should be notified of his progress—able to function in the community—ready for trial.

7-21-69—Joe riding around with a friend instead of working downtown at the café. It appears that Joe might be taking advantage of his card privilege.

7-24-69—New card given to Joe. May not have employment outside of the hospital.

8-17-698—Apparently Joe is overriding his privileges. Was seen driving a car on the grounds this afternoon. Perhaps this should be discussed at inservice meeting. Raymond Lavato says he has seen Joe driving the car on other occasions.

8-26-69—Spends considerable time outdoors visiting with female patients. Pleasant, friendly, cooperative.

9-19-69—Transferred to Johnson Hall. *Red card.*

9-23-69—Joe called attorney Whitaker. Told his attorney he was picked up Friday about 4:00 P.M. and brought by security to Johnson Hall, and he doesn't get to leave the hall and it is making him depressed.

9-26-69—Transferred to Laramie Hall. Pink card.

10-1-69—Joe was not on the hall at 8:00 P.M. We sent patients out to look for him. When we found him he said he didn't know he didn't have a green card.

10-20-69—Charged with drinking downtown—elopement—denies it.

10-20-69—Joe transferred to Johnson Hall again by security, for closer observation—red card—locked hall.

11-5-69—Sent to Green River jail to await trial.

Joe was in Green River when he slashed his wrists and his chest and it was then that we had filed our writ of *habeas corpus,* and he had been returned by order of Judge Forrister to the hospital again to await a jury trial on the question of his sanity. Then the nurse's notes continued.

2-6-70—Received back in Sheridan Hall (an unlocked hall). Says he cut his wrists but doesn't remember doing it.

2-11-70—Seen by Dr. Karn. Transferred to Johnson Hall—red card (no reasons stated).

From February 11, 1970, until his trial Joe remained in Johnson Hall. An attendant by the name of O'Brien reported almost every day that the patient, Joe Esquibel, wouldn't even ask for a better card, that he wouldn't go to the cafeteria, or accompany the other patients for their weekly workout in the gym—wouldn't leave the ward.

On May 4, 1970, the nurse's notes report that Joe said, "He is ashamed to have an attendant take him everywhere," and, therefore, he won't apply for the next card upward. Offers no help to anyone, and when asked to help bring breakfast up one morning he said, "Go to hell —I don't have to do a fucking thing on this hall but eat and sleep."

During this time Joe had been calling me. "Mr. Spence, you gotta get me out of here. They got me here on this red card and they won't let me go out, and it is driving me crazy, and I ain't goin' out with any aides walking around after me because it makes me ashamed." I told him I would write Dr. Karn a letter.

On June 27, 1970, the nurse's notes said Joe followed Dr. Pace into the office of Johnson Hall without permission, and he started expressing his opinions, and was hostile and wouldn't leave the office when told. I wrote Dr. Karn a letter, and on June 28, 1970, the nurse's notes said Joe was on a yellow card and should be held under close observation. Still confined in Johnson Hall. The next day the notes said he wouldn't get up when asked. The day after that he was in a scuffle with another patient, who threw a book at him. Bad mistake for the patient, but Joe only took him to the floor and held him there until the attendants came. A few days later he backhanded the same patient for being smart with him the notes said, and the next day he was on a red card, again, and refused once more to ask for a yellow card. "I won't get into trouble if I stay on a red card, so I'll just sit here, playing cards and watching television," the notes quoted Joe as saying. About a month later, on September 12, 1970, Dr. Pace saw Joe again, but he was still on a red card. Still wouldn't go to the gym. On September 24, 1970, the staff found him competent to stand trial. On January 1, 1971, a couple of girls called Joe, the records said, and Dr. Pace was notified of the calls but wouldn't let the staff put the calls through to Joe. On the same day, another patient hit Joe in the face. Joe fought back and the fight was finally broken up and the patient was hurt. How seriously the record didn't say. On February 23, 1971, Joe was still red-carded and still refused to leave the hall. O'Brien was the attendant who wrote the notes, week after week. The patient refused to ask for a yellow card, he said, and still refused to go to gym. Other attendants made no such observations of him. Maybe it was because they worked on a different shift with different problems.

On April 24, 1971, it was noted that other patients

came to Joe with their problems, and then two days later O'Brien wrote that the patient was bossy, always suggesting things to the attendants, and that he considered himself to be the "authority figure of the hall." O'Brien said, "The patient is always right and never wrong in his own eyes, but few see him like this." On May 21, 1971, O'Brien was still reporting that Joe Esquibel would make no request for a yellow card, but I can remember this high pleading voice during this time. "You've gotta get me out of here, Mr. Spence. Them guys won't let me out. I never done nothin'. Don' cause no trouble. I'm goin' crazy in here. They won't even let me go to gym. They take everybody else but they don' take me."

On June 7, 1971, it was noted that Joe had gone to the laboratory and donated a pint of blood for another patient. A month later an attendant recorded that Joe had asked another patient to change his dirty shirt. The patient hit Joe in the mouth and Joe struck him back. The other patient's eye was swollen and black. On June 20, 1971, the record said, "On the surface the patient appears to be satisfied with being here, comfortable in his role of 'boss of the hall,' " and on the following day O'Brien wrote "the patient's association with other patients is good, but very poor with staff members. Continues to be on a red card. Remains on the hall. Doesn't wish to venture off the hall—this is by the patient's own request." The record revealed little treatment. He was merely being housed again. I saw it as a tactic on the part of the hospital to get rid of this problem Joe Esquibel one way or another.

But the hospital probably saw it another way. They would argue, we gave this subject his privileges, let him go downtown, let him work, and he seemed happy enough and he had been with this female ex-patient, and he got well and could stand trial. The hospital did the right thing by Joe Esquibel, and when he was cured, the hospital simply sent him off to the sheriff to await trial, and the thanks the hospital got was his slitting his wrists, slashing his chest, and the lawyers claiming he was crazy again so they could stall things further, and then the court sent him back to the hospital again. So why shouldn't he be locked in Johnson Hall? Let him listen to the screaming of Jason. Let him cry to his attorneys, beg them to get him out. Put a little pressure on the lawyers. There's more than one way to skin a cat.

As early as October 25, 1969, Dr. Cutler examined Joe, and said in his report, "I still don't know why he is in the locked ward at this time, and Joe submits that he doesn't know either . . ." Well, I thought I had this all figured out. I stuck the nurses' notes and the other records in my briefcase and waited for Dr. Karn to finish his examination of Joe. In a few minutes the door to the doctor's office opened. He couldn't have been in there for more than fifteen or twenty minutes. Then Joe came walking out, nodded to me, and I nodded back, and then Dr. Karn motioned me to come in.

"How is he, Doctor?"

"He's a surprise to me, Mr. Spence," Dr. Karn said. "I think he's still sick. I don't believe he ought to go to trial."

"Well, if that's the case, all you have to do is write a little note to that effect, we'll get Joe out of Johnson Hall and into a decent spot, and we'll forget this whole mess again for a while."

"I guess I can't do that, Mr. Spence."

"Why not?"

"Well, Dr. Pace believes that Joe is sane. He thinks Joe is a malingerer. I don't happen to subscribe to that theory. I believe he's really sick. But I have to support my staff people, don't I?"

"For Christ's sake, you're the boss here, aren't you?"

"That's true, but then if a man goes against his staff, he can't have any organization at all—can he?"

"But, Jesus Christ, Doctor, we're dealing with a man's life!"

"I don't run this institution for a single man. I try to run this institution for the people of the state of Wyoming," he said very quietly as he pumped on his pipe.

"I'll subpoena your ass, then," I said in sudden exasperations. "You can tell the jury you think he's sick and your staff doesn't. How will that look?"

"Well, Mr. Spence, you can do as you choose. I have an obligation to tell the jury the truth as I see it. But I don't wish to countermand the position of my staff."

"Come on, Doctor," I said. "What you're really doing is having it both ways. You can't lose, can you? The position of the hospital is that he's sane, and the position of the hospital superintendent is that he's insane. Ain't that nice?"

"Well, Mr. Spence, nice or not, I've stated my position." And that was it. Chuck Morrison, the photographer, and I flew back to Casper and the next morning there was a picture of Jason's cage on the front page of the Casper *Star Tribune*. It was clear that a naked figure was sitting in the cage. Phil McAuley, the editor, asked me to write a letter concerning my visit to Evanston and McAuley would publish it. It read, "Sublette, behind the 'Golden Gate,' is simply a jail and not a very modern one either. It is grim and bare to the cement floor. The 'dry side' is a facility without running water or toilets. Prisoners have no shoes. Some of them are naked. The mattresses are without covers and the cells cannot be more than 8' square . . . According to Dr. Fairchild, Sublette Hall has been used as a place of punishment, and it even houses juveniles.

"In the Esquibel case, the records show that Joe Esquibel was incarcerated in the Johnson-Sublette area for about 15 months, over the protests of his attorneys. No one was able to explain to us why. He received very little treatment and it was my feeling he was simply 'the forgotten man.' There were others awaiting trials on charges of first degree murder who were given ground privileges, or even the privilege of going into the town of Evanston to work. All were Caucasian. Whether Joe Esquibel's nationality (Mexican-American) has any bearing on his treatment, (or lack of) is something I cannot verify.

"There is a tragic need for the legislature to appropriate sufficient monies for a humane and adequate place to deal with the problem patient. *But money isn't everything.*

There is a need for the attitude of the hospital to change
. . . in the over 40 cases which have been reviewed by
the hospital this year, there has not been a single case in
which the patient has been found 'not triable by reason of
insanity' . . . Some have been actually found to be suffering from psychosis (insanity) and yet the people raising this defense have been systematically returned for
trial."

I called for the governor of the state, Stan Hathaway,
to appoint a board of professionals and lay persons who
cared about people, to make recommendations to the
governor and to the legislature to correct the problem. I
sent a copy of my letter to the governor and the governor
lost no time in making his own release to the paper saying, "We asked for 1.2 million dollars for a new psychiatric center in the last legislature and we'll be back to try
again . . . the maximum security area is bad, but the
staff is good. When you work in a bad facility, you can't
do a good job." The article ended with a quote by the
paper from Dr. Fairchild, who said the maximum security
area was the worst she had seen after visiting twenty-five
other similar institutions.

Then Governor Hathaway wrote a letter to me. He
said he didn't agree with some of my conclusions. He
wrote, "There are some patients confined to the deten-
tion center who have severe problems that cannot be
dealt with in any normal fashion. For example, there are
a couple of patients who are seriously retarded and who
pose a constant threat to themselves and others. If they
are dressed, they tear off their clothing immediately and
stuff it into the commode. [No commode on the dry side.]
They throw their own dung at the attendants and do not
respond to any psychiatric treatment." He denied there
was any discrimination and gave Dr. Karn "major credit
for the improvements that have been made from the time
that he started when most patients were virtually confined in dungeons and chains." He said he didn't intend
to appoint an investigative committee because he
thought it might take on the aspects of a kangaroo court
and do more harm than good. He concluded by saying, "I

hope we never again see photographs of retarded people in the nude in the newspaper. I believe this to be inhumane and perhaps a violation of the constitutional rights of the individuals who do not know how to intelligently give their consent."

And, of course, I couldn't let the governor have the last say, and I wrote him back telling him that his letter grieved me. I said I understood that politically he needed to defend his institution but I knew him as a good and caring human being, and his assumption that an investigating committee would be a kangaroo court presupposed that he would be unable to find any honorable persons in this state to make non-political and honest recommendations. The institution could defend itself, but there were innocent people who couldn't defend themselves; one of these, whose picture was in the paper, could communicate only by throwing his dung—which might be the only way he could communicate effectively. I said I doubted a 1.2-million-dollar psychiatric center would cure the problem, and then I wrote, "You mentioned the last time you were in the office you had always wanted to try a case against me. Well, Stan, I don't share that desire. To quote the bard of the current generation, Bob Dylan, 'All I Want Is To Be Friends With You,' and I want you to *hear me,* and I want you to give me an opportunity to be useful to you and to the people of the state who I know you also love. You can't dismiss me with a two-page letter like the one you wrote to me, my friend. Love, Gerry." But he did dismiss me with the letter, and the next legislature provided the funds for a new psychiatric center. I thought they should have called it Esquibel Hall.

27

ON SEPTEMBER 27, 1971, we chose an all-white jury in Casper, Wyoming, to decide whether Joe Esquibel was still insane. For me insanity was no longer a matter of the magic of medicine. All Dr. Karn had to do to save us all from the agony of another trial was to simply exercise his administrative authority in Joe's favor, to order the diagnosis of insanity. He had ordered diagnoses before. He himself had found that Joe was a schizophrenic, and once a skitz, always a skitz, you know. But now, to take care of his damned administration problems we would have to try the case. We were being used, the jury, and the court, to get Karn off the hook with Dr. Pace and his other personnel. He could blame it on the jury. Or maybe he'd decided to punish us for having made our little raid on the hospital the week before.

Again I came to court early, about seven-thirty in the morning, to claim the same table closest to the jury. Pretty soon Raymond Whitaker came in cheerily, waltzed up to me and tossed his hat at the hat tree. Without saying good morning or anything else to him I said, "You know, Raymond, the fuckers are getting even with us."

"You're sounding pretty paranoid, Gerald, my friend, for someone who claims to be sane himself," he said.

"Well, I am paranoid, and I never claimed to be sane."

"Insanity?" he asked. "What's insanity?" And he looked bull-dog serious asking the same old question again.

"Insanity is a doctrine, like any religion—and it's always changing," I said. "You can't ever keep track of what's sin and you can't keep up with what's sane either. One day it's sin and the next day it isn't. One day it's sane and the next day it isn't. They even have different schools of psychiatrists and they can't agree either, kinda like the Methodists and the Catholics, for Christ's sake, Raymond," I said. "Insanity is a religion."

"No, insanity is politics," Raymond said. "Insanity is how a bunch of politicians down at the legislature in Cheyenne define it." Then John Ackerman came in. I nodded and he walked over and started to listen, also with a serious look on his face.

I said, "That's right. Insanity is just a label that men put on other men, a label you write out of the Psychiatric Handbook, if you please. Here, you are a 295.99, skitz. Let me pin you. Let me make you mine," I said sweetly. Then John Hursh came in and sat his briefcase down and said hello, and he looked serious, and Raymond and I nodded to him, but hardly anything more, and after a while the courtroom began to fill up with the prospective jurors, twelve of whom again would decide the issue of Joe's sanity, and while we talked, we knew that Joe must be sitting out in the same little anteroom waiting for us, and we talked on because it was easier to talk than to go face the man again.

"Well," Raymond said, as if to end the discussion. "It is simply a question of who's being judged."

"What do you mean?" I asked.

"Well, do you think the hospital would have any trouble in ordering a diagnosis of schizophrenia if Joe were the son of the chairman of the Appropriations Committee in the legislature? What is insanity? Insanity is a tool —used by the power structure for its own ends, and, therefore, Joe Esquibel will never be found insane, because it is not in the best interests of the power structure to deal out its compassion to mere Mexicans. Compassion belongs to the wealthy. Compassion belongs to the chairman of the Appropriations Committee. Insanity is a device for the rich to exercise power over the poor. It is an economic concept, my friend Gerald, and not a medical diagnosis at all. Remember, only the rich have psychiatrists."

The four of us huddled around our counsel table. I sat on top of the table. We didn't want to think about Joe Esquibel. We didn't want the trial to start.

"Well, that's true," I said, "but insanity is also for bureaucrats. Now if there were a whole bunch of empty beds in the state hospital, and the hospital were about to lose half its budget for want of patients, and if they hadn't filled up the goddamned place with alcoholics already and turned it into an alcoholic rehab center, which is all right with me, don't misunderstand me, but if they were needing patients, I can assure you that they would find Joe Esquibel insane and keep him—fill a bed. Insanity is a bureaucratic device to keep the kingdom of the petty bureaucrats intact."

"Nothing has changed, Spence," Whitaker shouted.

"Nothing ever changes."

"Shhhhh," I cautioned. "The jury will hear you."

Whitaker said, "I got a letter back in 1967 just after the jury sent Joe back to the hospital the first time. Here," he said, reaching for his briefcase, rummaging around in a file, and then coming up with a document on the state hospital's letterhead. "I've been carrying this damn thing around in this file for a long time." He handed the letter to me. It was addressed to Raymond B. Whitaker and said that like letters had been sent to other members of the trial bar. The letter bore the date of February 6, 1967. It was from Dr. Karn. It said, "I am writing to request your understanding and cooperation in a matter which seriously concerns the administration of the Wyoming State Hospital." It dealt with the financial difficulties of the hospital . . . strained funds . . . "You can be of significant help to us in the following ways." And after mentioning several ways, it said, "I realize it is a touchy point to request attorneys to use the conventional 'insanity plea' more sparingly, but the evaluations of these subjects costs the Wyoming State Hospital between $500 and $600 per person. In my eight years' experience at the hospital, only one subject in over 400 such persons has ever been officially adjudicated 'Not Guilty By Reason Of Insanity.' "

"One out of four hundred?" I shouted to Whitaker.

"Shhh, the jury will hear you," Raymond said.

"One out of four hundred? That's ridiculous. That's bullshit."

"Insanity is bullshit," Raymond hollered.

"Shhh," I said. "Insanity is real enough to the person who suffers from it, and to the victims of the insane, and it's insane to tell us that only one out of four hundred persons who claim to be insane actually is. Psychiatrists are mostly sick anyway, trying to cure themselves. Everybody knows psychiatrists are insane," I said. And I felt insane sitting on top of the counsel table pontificating about insanity with the room almost full with prospective jurors, with the court personnel bustling busily about their business, and the noise in the room swelling and fading and swelling again with loud talking and laughter. It was insane-sounding. I should go find Joe and talk with him. I could feel the tension in my belly again. Fear. It always came. I could never escape the frightened boy and become the brave man. It was easier to talk, to argue, to rave away the time, and then pretty soon a deputy came over to the table and politely said that Joe was out in the little anteroom, and did we want to see him, and we all got up and followed the deputy out, but Raymond kept talking while we walked.

"Insanity, Gerald, my boy, is just a pure device of the law made for lawyers like us. That's all it is—a device for us, Gerald, to use as we choose, or abuse." He laughed at his own rhymes.

"To use as we choose or abuse," I mocked, and we were finally in the little room, and Joe was sitting there still cuffed to another deputy. We walked in and they unlocked him. Both deputies left, but Joe didn't seem to notice. He wore the same J. C. Penney business suit as before. Black shoes. White socks and white shirt. His hair was freshly cut. Crew cut still, and he had gained weight from having been locked up in Johnson Hall all of those months without any exercise. He looked older, slack-faced, had the expression of a blackjack dealer at about 6 A.M. in Reno.

"How ya doing, Joe?" I asked.

"Okay," he said.

"How ya feeling?"

"Okay," he said. "Them guys is gonna get me."

"Who, Joe?"

"Dr. Pace and them guys. He don' like me."

"I'll fix Pace for you, Joe. Don't worry. I want you to look at your shoes again like you did the last time. Can you do that?"

"Yeah," he said.

"Show me." He put his head down and locked his eyes to his laces. "Don't look up ever, Joe, understand? If you ever look up it'll all be over."

"Yeah," he said, with his head still down.

"Now don't worry, Joe. Just sit there and relax. Don't move. Listen to what's going on. But don't move. Don't look up. I'll get Pace for you. He ain't gonna get ya—I'll guarantee you that."

Then we picked a jury, as before. I got people who had lived and suffered some, who had grown, from their own suffering. People don't grow much from joy. People grow out of pain and sorrow, and fear and loneliness and from guilt. I wanted people on the jury who were afraid like I was, who didn't want to judge their fellow man, because there are two kinds of people in this world—those who want to judge others because they've been harshly judged, and those who do not want to judge others because they have also been harshly judged. I chose the jury. It was my jury, and then Oscar Hall began speaking to my jury, giving them about the same opening statement he had before. Then I got up to make my opening and I talked about how this man Joe Esquibel was a flower which had bloomed out of mad seeds, seeds spawned by society's abuse of an innocent child. I said this was a madman grown out of poverty, out of the despise of a community against a poor Mexican family—that insanity is a disease of the soul, a disease planted and

grown there out of ugly words that say, "You are only a
Mexican, a spick. You are worthless."

I spoke of the innocent child whose only wrong was to
be born in Rawlins, Wyoming, on the wrong side of the
tracks. "Insanity," I said, "is the fruit of hate and the
product of injustice. Even a little child knows when he is
innocent, and the innocent cannot bear to be punished
and the unjust punishment of the innocent steals away
the sanity of human beings," I said, and Joe Esquibel was
insane and he could not be tried, and I said it was the
duty of the state to prove that Joe was sane beyond a
reasonable doubt. "How can they expect you to know," I
asked, "when they do not know?" Then I said it would
not be justice to put an insane man on trial for his very
life if he could not help his own attorneys in his own
defense. The law protects against such injustice. The law
will require that he be sent back to the state hospital and
that he be given humane treatment. He didn't get humane treatment before. He has never been treated as a
human being should be treated by other humans. "By
your verdict you can decree it. By your verdict you can
demand it, demand it!" I pounded my fist on the podium
and then I looked the jurors square in the eyes.

Ken Keldsen, Oscar Hall's deputy, called Dr. Pace as
the state's first witness. Among his long list of qualifications was his experience of recently evaluating sixty-five
men who claimed they were unable to stand trial because
they were insane. Among them was Joe Esquibel, he said,
and while he was trying to make up his mind about Joe he
had come to some conclusions as to why Joe just sat there
in his office blankly, answering Pace's questions in mono-
syllables, and saying he didn't remember—didn't even
remember dates like his own birthday, and claiming he
couldn't remember how far he'd gone in school, and saying he didn't even remember who his father was, and
saying that he'd never been married, and such things.
While he'd been trying to conclude why Joe Esquibel
would give such answers, he'd seen Joe with some other
patients laughing and playing around, being bright and
happy, but when Joe looked up and saw Dr. Pace, he quit

talking, and then suddenly Pace knew. Joe was malingering. He'd always been malingering. He was faking his illness. The doctor said he had just attended a seminar at the University of Southern California Medical School and had been introduced to a new test which could be used by psychiatrists to determine the triability of an accused, and he had given Joe Esquibel the test.

"And what was the result of your testing, Doctor?" Ken Keldsen asked.

"Just a minute, please," I said. And then I turned to the court. "May I *voir dire?*"

Yes, the court said. I began. I approached the doctor. "Tell me about the test, Doctor. How does it work?"

"Well," he said, "there are a series of questions which are asked of the subject, and the psychiatrist rates the subject's answers as to his incapacity to aid in his own defense. His incapacity is either severe, moderate, or mild, or none at all."

"I see you have some notes here, Doctor. May I see them?" The doctor looked up to the judge for protection. But Judge Forrister looked down at some papers on his desk, and I reached out and took the notes from the doctor's hand. "You rated Joe Esquibel as having only a mild incapacity to relate to his attorney?"

"Yes."

"You don't know how Joe Esquibel relates to me, do you, Doctor?"

"What?" the doctor asked, surprised.

"Which attorney were you having him relate to as you rated him?"

"No particular attorney."

"Well, for you to score his ability to relate to his attorney, don't you need to know which attorney he was relating to?"

"No."

"Aren't attorneys different from each other—and don't we all relate to some people better than others?"

"Yes."

"Did you pretend to be his attorney in order to test him?"

"No."

"Do you know what an attorney defending Joe Esquibel needs to know in order to defend Joe?"

"Well, you would want to know what happened at the time of the shooting."

"What if Joe said he didn't remember? Would that be an impairment? Would that hurt his ability to relate to his attorney?"

"I don't know. That's in another category," the doctor said.

"Well, Doctor, answer my question, please. Would it impair Joe if he couldn't remember?"

"Well, if he truly couldn't remember there would be some degree of impairment, I guess."

"Would you want to know his mental state at the time of the shooting?"

"Yes."

"Does the mental state of Joe Esquibel show here on this record? Did you ask him his mental state at the time of the killing?"

"Yes."

"What did he say?"

"He said, 'I don't remember.' "

"Now the next number in the test, Doctor, seems to be called 'Planning Legal Strategy.' Did you ask him any questions about that?"

"Yes, I did." I looked at Dr. Pace's notes. There was nothing noted on that topic.

"Nothing in your notes on that, is there?"

"No."

"Before you would know whether he could aid in planning his legal strategy you would need to know something yourself about legal strategy in a first degree murder case, isn't that true?"

"Oh, I think the pleas he might enter would be 'not guilty,' 'not guilty by reason of insanity,' or 'guilty.' These are the three possibilities."

"Well, that isn't a legal strategy. That's just entering pleas. What kind of strategy would be available to Joe Esquibel in your opinion?"

"Oh, for instance, if he were offered a lesser charge would he be able to deal with his attorney on that basis?"

I saw the doctor had written no notes on that either. "Did you ask him what he might do if he were offered a lesser charge?"

"Yes, I did."

"That doesn't appear on your notes, does it, Doctor? What did you do, just record on your notes what you wanted to record, or did you really try to make a *complete* record?" The doctor didn't answer. "What other legal strategy is there?"

"I don't know frankly," Dr. Pace said in an angry voice.

"And the next category is the defendant's understanding of the 'role of the defense counsel,' isn't it?"

"Yes."

"What sort of things would you expect from defense counsel in a trial, Doctor?"

"Judgment," he said.

"What else?"

"Skill." He began to frown.

"What else?"

"Honesty would be one." He seemed exasperated.

"Would you expect him to fight strongly for your case?"

"I would expect him to do his best."

"Would you expect him to care about you?"

"That would be another quality," he said begrudgingly.

"Did you ask that of Joe Esquibel?" I could see his notes were still blank in this category.

His face was red. Now it was growing scarlet, and there was a nasty tone to his voice. "No, I didn't."

"Thank you, sir. One of the questions you were to ask Joe Esquibel is, 'Will he be able to tell his lawyer everything pertinent?' Did you ask Joe what 'pertinent' meant?"

"Joe knew what 'pertinent' meant."

"Yes," I said. "Of course, and now the test asks whether or not the defendant could 'understand court procedures.' " There was nothing in Pace's notes about that either, and to the question, "What would you do if false testimony were given against you?" Joe had answered, "Guess do nothing," and the doctor had rated him only mildly impaired with the answer. When the doctor asked him if he had any specific handicaps, like problems with hearing, Joe had said, "I hated white people. I thought they were out to get me. I do not feel that way now."

I turned to Dr. Pace. "When you asked Joe, 'Do you hear anything—any voices which say they will get you?' didn't Joe say, 'I hear voices and have dreams about people going to do things to me.' Didn't he tell you that?"

"Yes," Dr. Pace said.

"And if he heard voices, Doctor, as late as last month, what kind of insanity would that be compatible with? Give us the name of the mental disease."

"If he heard voices?" the doctor asked as if he were terribly irritated.

"Don't look at the county attorney. Look at me and answer the question!" I said in a strong voice.

"I *am* looking at you," he shouted, his face as red as a beet.

"All right, answer my question, then."

"Schizophrenia."

"Are you aware of the fact that since 1968 Joe Esquibel has been diagnosed repeatedly as schizophrenic?"

"Yes, I am aware of that."

"But you don't believe your fellow doctors either, do you?"

"I think that was an incorrect diagnosis."

"Did you ask the defendant whether or not he got despondent in jail?"

"Yes. He said he felt okay while he was in jail."

"If Mr. Esquibel were trying to fake mental illness, wouldn't you expect him to say that he felt terrible when he was in jail or that he felt despondent?"

"That would be one thing he might say," the doctor said, and looked over at Hall again.

"Isn't it true that you would more often see somebody who was faking it try to tell you how *sick* he was instead of telling you how *well* he was?"

"That's correct."

"If somebody inappropriately thinks somebody is trying to do something to him, you might call that paranoid behavior, isn't that true?"

"Yes, that's true."

"Well, Doctor, what happens if the psychiatrist is paranoid? What happens if the examiner himself believes that a mentally defective man is trying to hoodwink him? What is the result then?"

"I don't think that situation exists, Mr. Spence," he said disgustedly.

"I didn't ask you whether it existed. I asked you what would happen under such a circumstance."

"First, I would object to the statement that he is mentally defective and that he tried to hoodwink me."

"Doctor, would you like me to have the question read back to you so that you can remember it and answer it?" I said very politely.

"Yes, would you repeat it?"

" 'What happens if the *examiner* is *paranoid* and he believes that a poor mentally defective Mexican is trying to hoodwink him?' "

"Are you saying that I am *paranoid?*" The doctor was shouting again.

"I am just asking questions. It seems like a simple question, Doctor. Are you having difficulty with it?"

"I am trying to *think* how to go about answering it."

"Then let me withdraw the question and give you a simpler one. What happens in any examination if the examiner himself is paranoid or has paranoid tendencies?"

"I think the validity of the examination would be less than it should be."

"Is it possible for people to be paranoid on some subjects and not on others?"

"Yes, that is correct."

"All right. Let's take these sixty-five persons you used this test on. How many did you find sane?"

"I can't answer that without going over the cases."

"Isn't it true that out of the sixty-five reports you made

you didn't find a single one insane—you found them *all triable*, all sane?" The doctor didn't answer. "I have the reports, you know, Doctor." I held them up for him to see, and now he began to look very serious.

"I see," he said quietly.

"I have subpoenaed all of your reports from the hospital, Doctor, so please be careful with your answer, but be accurate."

"I can't answer the question," he said.

"Well, don't you remember at all? Was there one person out of the sixty-five who claimed they were insane who you in fact did find insane?"

"I can't recall any," Dr. Pace said.

"I have no further questions, Your Honor," I said to the judge. "I object to the introduction of any testimony by Dr. Pace. There is no sufficient foundation for his test, Your Honor," I said.

But before the court ruled, Oscar Hall was on his feet.

"Well, Your Honor, may we call Dr. Karn?"

"Of course," His Honor said, and Pace stepped down from the stand, walking out of the pit to safer places. Oscar must know what Dr. Karn's testimony would be. Maybe he thought it would be better for the state to put on Karn's testimony rather than for me to call him as my witness, or had Karn changed his mind? Dr. Karn sat down in the witness chair easily and looked up at Oscar Hall with a quiet smile on his face, and then he looked over with a little smile to the jury.

"Doctor, based upon your contact with Joe Esquibel and also upon the observations and examinations made by you last Friday, September 24, do you have an opinion based upon reasonable medical certainty as to the capacity of Joe Esquibel to stand trial at this time?"

"I believe I do, yes," Dr. Karn said.

"Would you tell the jury what that opinion is?"

"I am not convinced that he is fully capable of standing trial."

"Do you entertain a reasonable doubt, at this time, in this courtroom, that Joe Esquibel is not triable or capable of standing trial?"

"Yes, sir."

"Your witness, Mr. Spence."

What the hell did he do that for? He gave me the case —conceded it, right there with Karn. Did it himself!

"No questions," I said, matter-of-factly.

"The state rests," Oscar Hall said. Old Oscar would probably explain it by saying, "Well, if the truth is against us we just as well face it. Never believed in hiding the truth." Or maybe they hoped to end it all right there before our witnesses testified and the press got ahold of it. I doubt that Oscar gave a shit.

They gave up. Maybe the jury wouldn't trust the state. Looked too suspicious. Looked too easy. Maybe the jury wouldn't believe Karn. Be careful. Don't take anything for granted. We'd better proceed as if it were our burden to prove Joe's insane, even though the burden was on the state, not us. Take no chances. I called Imogene Fairchild. We had found her in Iowa and brought her to Casper. She gave her background and then testified that shortly after Joe had returned to Evanston in late 1966 she had seen him at the state hospital. She gave a stern look to the jury, answered preliminary questions, and began her testimony by saying, "I said to Dr. Karn, 'Did you testify that that guy was *not* psychotic?' and he said that he had, and I said I would certainly have to disagree. When I saw Joe he was sitting in a chair staring straight ahead; he did not respond to any questions. I asked Dr. Karn what he intended to do, and he said he intended to put Joe back in Sublette, which is the maximum security ward, which is more like a cellblock. I said, 'Well, if you testified that he was *not* psychotic, why did you feel it necessary to put him back in maximum security, because in fact you are confirming Mr. Spence's position that he is psychotic. Why don't we try to activate treatment?' He was not transferred out of Sublette until early March."

I showed her the pictures we had taken. She identified them, one at a time, the pictures of the Golden Gate and behind Golden Gate where the cells were stark, bare, and dreary.

"Are you saying that every person who is sent by the district court for observation is put behind these bars?"

"Yes. Not only that, anybody, even if he comes to the hospital voluntarily or by a physician's admission, if he acts out in any way, such as trying to leave the hospital, or even asking to leave, he may, at Dr. Karn's discretion, be placed behind these bars, even if he has committed no criminal act at all." During the time she was there she said she was not allowed to have anything to do with the patients who were there for observation by court order.

"Patients are not allowed to shower themselves. There is a squawk box in the office that is turned on all the time to overhear any conversations from the patients who are not aware that the squawk box is in the office."

"Could you, as a psychiatrist, make accurate, valid appraisals of a patient maintained under such circumstances?"

"No, I couldn't and I don't know how anyone else could."

I showed her the picture of Jason we had taken and asked her if she recognized him. She recognized him. He had been incarcerated there for how long she didn't know, as long as anybody could remember. "He's always in the nude," she said. For a brief time she had an opportunity to work with Jason and she gave him a bucket and told him he had to clean the walls. She said he was mentally retarded but that didn't provide any excuse to treat him like an animal. "He responds to work and to treatment. He tears his clothes off. But again," she said very plainly, "if I were backed into a corner I'm not sure how I would react. I might throw my tray at you, which is one of the things he has been accused of doing. He is animal-like because that is the way he is treated. He spends a good deal of time doing nothing but yelling, hour after hour, so just eight hours of it alone would be very disquieting to other patients in the hall."

"When Joe Esquibel was on that floor would he be within hearing distance, day and night, of the screams of Jason?"

"If he were in Johnson, yes, and surely when he was in Sublette."

"What effect would such circumstances have, in your opinion, on the accuracy of any test made on Joe Esquibel?"

"Well, it would be difficult to concentrate with that kind of noise going on."

"Is that the kind of atmosphere for the treatment of sick people?"

"Not in my opinion, no, sir." She described how the patients on the dry side had to be taken from their cubicle to the toilet by a guard. Patients went barefoot on the cement floor. It was cold and sometimes the wind whistled through. Portions of Sublette and Johnson Halls were shown in the pictures and identified by Dr. Fairchild. They were shabby places, dingy, forgotten rooms with forgotten people in them.

"Now the records show that Joe was in Sublette and Johnson Halls for more than fifteen straight months. What effect would that have on Joe's sanity?"

"Well, if you weren't crazy when you went in, you would be when you left there," she said. Every eye in the courtroom was on her.

Then I took the welfare records that had been introduced in the last trial, and I read from the record page after page of Joe's history, of his life as a child, of his degradation and poverty and abuse, and I asked the question: "Now taking into account this social background of Joe Esquibel, what effect, if any, would confinement of the kind Joe has experienced at the Wyoming State Hospital have on his mental health?"

"Well, as I said before, if this man weren't psychotic when he came to the hospital, he would be when he left. I examined him as late as this morning. He admitted to me that as recently as three months ago he was hearing voices. I saw him when he was psychotic during 1966 and 1967 and I've had no contact with him after June of 1968. But I did a thorough mental examination on Joe this morning, and he does not know where he is and he doesn't know the date or the time of day. He doesn't know who I am. I asked him if he knew why he was here and his response was, 'Those people keep talking all the time, but they never explain nothin' to me.' I explained the situation to him but he didn't understand. I asked him about the voices because I wanted to see if he was still going in and out of those psychotic episodes as he was during the time I had him as a patient. Psychosis can come and go. He is one of those psychotics whose thought processes are working one time and not working the next, and so it is entirely possible that he was psychotic at the time of the alleged murder."

"Dr. Pace stated that Joe Esquibel was malingering—faking—trying to hoodwink people into believing he was psychotic. What is your impression?"

"I think it would be impossible to carry out such a hoodwinking for this long of a time. That's not possible." And then she said, "Joe's underlying psychosis would cause a spotty memory. However, most epileptics don't remember what happened prior to their seizures, nor the seizure itself. Brain damage also affects memory."

She told the jury that Joe's defect in smelling could be related to brain damage. She said the fact that Joe went into a kind of thrashing immediately after the shooting was consistent with what she called the "fugue" state in epilepsy. What Sheriff Willis described, thrashing around on the floor, his weakness, talking to himself, his inability to walk to the car, and later being helped there and thrashing around in the front seat, all of that was consistent with an epileptic seizure, she said, and if he were suffering from epilepsy he would probably not recall the shooting. His attempt at suicide at Green River was consistent with schizophrenia. She said that if he were placed in jail he would grow psychotic again very soon.

"Do you think Joe Esquibel was faking—malingering?"

"Not in the least, no, sir," Dr. Fairchild said.

"Doctor, if you had seen a patient in your office for a mental status examination who had a bad memory and seemed not very open in his answers and later on you saw him on the street laughing in the presence of other people, would that cause you to conclude that the patient had been malingering or lying to you?"

"No. I would have to know what the circumstances were. Maybe somebody had just told a joke. That, per se, would not make me think anything one way or the other."

On cross-examination Oscar Hall had Dr. Fairchild admit that it was easy for a person who was pretending to be sick to say, "I don't remember," and she admitted that she had found no organic basis for his hallucinations. Oscar asked her if hallucinations couldn't in fact be feigned, to which she replied, "When I asked Joe this morning about the nature of his hallucinations he said there were good voices and bad ones, and the ones he heard most recently were bad. He thinks something terrible is going to happen to his mother or brother, somebody is going to do something to them and that he can't help it, and then he burst into tears. I let him cry for a little while. Finally I asked, 'Could I ask you why you are crying?' And he said, 'I am thinking of the people who are still in Johnson Hall.' Later he said he wanted to be a barber—wanted to be with his son and his mother in Salt Lake City, and he doesn't know why he is here," she said. "He's not able to communicate with his attorney. He doesn't understand the nature of the proceedings that are brought against him." Then she had to admit that people have epilepsy and still have an adequate memory and that blood in the spinal fluid doesn't necessarily mean brain damage.

Finally Oscar said, "Then the difference between you and other professional people at the hospital is merely one of philosophy or opinion."

And she said, "That's right."

And he said, "I have one last question, Dr. Fairchild. You were, in fact, discharged from the Wyoming State Hospital, is that not correct?"

She said, "That is *not* correct, I resigned and the governor has a copy of my letter. I resigned because I disagreed strongly with the way Dr. Karn treated the patients and the staff."

There was a recess. I wandered out into the hall and there was Oscar at the drinking fountain. I sauntered up to him. "Well, Oscar, how's it goin'?" He looked up at me with a disgusted look. "Dammit," he said with fire in his eye. "Why didn't Karn tell me he was going to testify like that. I could have saved us a trial."

"I don't know, Oscar."

"Well, Gerry, why didn't you tell me?"

"Oh, Oscar," I said. "You and I both know you had to try this case. Otherwise everybody from Judge Armstrong on down would be on your ass, including Pace and all the others up at the state hospital. You didn't have any choice," I said.

"I guess that's right," Oscar said, "but Karn could have told me how he was going to testify. I didn't find out till this morning what he was going to say. Then I figured it'd be better for me to call him. Made me look like a damn dummy."

"I'm going to go in there and ask the court to dismiss this case, Oscar. There isn't enough evidence to go to the jury on the question of Joe's sanity. Why don't you join me? We'll both ask the court to dismiss it and then nobody loses."

"Well, goddamn it, I might. I've had it with the state hospital," Oscar said. "Jesus Christ, you can't ever tell what's goin' on up there. I ought to move to have the case dismissed. I just ought to." Oscar thought a minute and then he said it again. "Yeah, I ought to join you to have the judge dismiss this goddamned case." Then he started back into the courtroom. "But I'm going to put Karn back on the stand and ask him a question or two first. I want the record to show I didn't know how he was goin' to testify till just before he took the stand this morning."

And then Oscar did call Dr. Karn back to the stand and Karn had to admit he had only told Oscar about his testimony that very morning. "Why didn't you tell me before?" Oscar asked.

"I didn't know I was going to be called upon to testify to that," Dr. Karn said very calmly, and then on cross-examination I asked a few last questions of the doctor myself.

"You are still of the same opinion as before, Doctor?"

"Yes."

"You testified to the best of your skill, honesty, and belief, haven't you?"

"Yes."

"You have done so for the benefit of the *truth* of this case?"

"Yes."

"That's good enough for me. Thank you," I said. I didn't ask the doctor to restate his opinion. I didn't want to give Oscar the chance to fiddle around with the doctor again—might not get answers as good the next time around. A fellow needs to know when to quit. And then Oscar made one last blast. "But that knowledge came to me this morning for the first time, in this building, isn't that true?"

Dr. Karn said, "Yes, that is true."

I moved Judge Forrister to dismiss Oscar's petition and to return Joe Esquibel to Evanston, Wyoming. There was no dispute of fact for the jury to decide. Then Oscar said, "I join Mr. Spence in his motion that the case be dismissed," and there was nothing left for Judge Forrister to do or to decide.

The judge turned to the jury and explained to them that they wouldn't have to decide the case. Some looked disappointed, and when the jury had left, I gave a little nudge to Joe. "It's okay now, Joe." And his head came up and he blinked his eyes and looked around the courtroom again. Then he looked up at me.

"Well, we won, Joe," I said. He nodded his head as if he understood.

"Can you get me out of Johnson Hall, Mr. Spence?"

"You bet, Joe," I said. "We'll get you out of there."

It had been another victory without winning, and then in a few minutes it was hard to feel the victory as I watched the sheriff haul my client off to those dark places again. God rue the day we took this damned case to show off our so-called beauty and to screw the system for fun, just for fun. I watched Joe walk through the courtroom door with the two deputies. They would lock him in the county jail, and later they would haul him on that long trip back to the hospital in that faraway desolate place called Evanston.

"Well, there he goes again, Raymond," I said.

"Yeah," Raymond said. He rubbed his chin and looked at the empty door for a long time.

"What I'd like to know now is whether Joe Esquibel really is insane."

"What is insanity?" Whitaker asked again.

"We've been through that one before," I said as I picked up my briefcase.

"Joe has sat in this courtroom for over twenty days now, in two trials, and he never once raised his head or made a mistake. Not once. If the legal test for insanity means anything—that he can follow the instructions of his attorneys and aid in his own defense—well, I guess I'd have to vote for Joe being sane."

"Well," I said, "for a man to sit for twenty days with his eyes locked on his feet—sit on a hard oak chair with a blank stare on his face listening to them tell how he killed his wife and all about his hideous childhood—to never react, not to move once, never to look up—well, he must be endowed with the mysterious superhuman powers of the madman."

28

AFTER THE JURY left and after they took Joe away, Imaging came up to the counsel table to get me. "Come on home, darling," she said, and then she held out her hand and I took it and it was good to follow my love to a warm, safe place, to that old house at Eleventh and Durbin. People said the house was haunted with the ghost of old Walter, who had previously lived there. Old Walter liked good whiskey, they said, and sometimes at night we thought we could hear him rummaging around looking for a drink in the cupboards, and we would hold onto each other and laugh. We liked Walter. He was a part of the family now, and Imaging and I were in love, and love made us safe.

When we had gone up to Lake Tahoe to be married we checked into the Sahara Hotel on her former husband's birthday.

"Oh, Lord," Imaging had said. "I'm feeling strange, really strange."

"Well, I'm too tired to get married, myself," I said.

"I'm too tired, too," she said. And she looked sad, like she was going to cry, so I put my arm around her and squeezed her. "Let's just go to bed and we'll get married in the morning," I said, and Imaging still looked sad, and then I said, "I promise you, babe, I ain't gonna run away. I'll marry you in the mornin'." Then Imaging laughed and said, "That's what they all say. We'll go to bed tonight and get married in the morning," and we both laughed, and in the morning we got married, vowed our non-promises to each other under the trees, and then we drove to San Francisco, called up my kids, Kerry, Kent, and Katy. They came over to the Jack Tarr Hotel. Kip was off on his own, eighteen and tough. I felt happy, like a gas-filled balloon. "Well, we have a surprise for you kids," we said when they got there.

Kerry was seventeen, beautiful with skin like a prize peach, auburn hair and blue eyes, tall like her mother, and she was the spokesman. "We know what the surprise is," Kerry said. "We know!" She giggled, and the other two kids were giggling, and Kent, fifteen, had his hands in his pockets and was swaying back and forth with a big grin and little Katy, eight, and blond as young cornsilk, had a big grin on her face, too, and was stamping her feet, wanting to say it.

"What?" I said. "What is the surprise, then, if you guys know so much?"

"We know. We know you and Pillow got married." It suddenly came bursting out of Kent.

"How do you know?" I asked with a serious look on my face.

"You did. You did. Didn't you?" Kent said.

"You did, didn't you?" Katy said. "Daddy, you did, didn't you?"

And I said, "How do you kids know all of these things?" and then Kerry said, "Kids just know things—just know. You don't have to tell us anything." And they seemed happy. And when I said, "Yes, we did. You're right, we did," they squealed with joy and hugged us and we all hugged each other together into a big bunch and we held onto each other as one happy family, and we all went together on our honeymoon—to Zim's and the zoo.

"Let's celebrate our new lives together," I said. "To Zim's—to Zim's for the wedding toast," hot fudge sundaes, no champagne, quit drinking, gave it up because we needed clear heads to get through this new life right. Too many people invested too much pain in this marriage, we said, and we needed to be sober, to be able to work through all the problems, and it was all over for the booze. Good-bye Cabin Still. I miss you, have to admit that. "And so here's to all of us," I said, raising up a big glob of ice cream with the hot fudge drooling down.

"And here's to you," Kent said. "And here's to you," little Katy said. Imaging was laughing, saying she never thought she would ever have a wedding party in such a place as this with all the plastic and those gaudy colors, and the bright lights, and we laughed some more and kissed a lot and said we didn't care because what was important were the people in this place, and the hot fudge sundaes, of course, I said. A toast:

> "It is the people in the places
> With chocolate on their faces."

We laughed some more and then off to the zoo, and we watched the female black panther pester her mate lying sleepily in the sun, pawing him, lightly, and he ignored her, and then she pawed him again, and he ignored her, and then she kept after him, pestering, and finally he gave out a terrifying roar and batted the old lady halfway across the cage.

"Good thing to watch animals," I said to Imaging. "Learn a lot from animals."

"She was just wanting a little attention, darling," Imaging said. "She was lonely."

"He just wanted to be left alone—to live his rich inner life," I said. "A man needs to be left alone sometimes."

"Yes," she said with a little mock smile. "Women need to be left alone, too, and don't get any idea about batting me around." She flexed her biceps, and then we hugged each other and hugged the children some more and we were happily looking down at the gorillas in their gorilla pit. Wonderful honeymoon—one family of primates looking down at another in a pit, and I thought that was the way it was outside these cages, too. Later we went sailing, rented a boat and crew at the dock where there was a crazy parrot.

"Hello," I said to the parrot.

"Hello," the parrot said.

"Hello," I said to the parrot.

"Hello," the parrot said back again.

"Hello," I said to the parrot.

"Hello, hello, hello, hello, hello, hello, hello," the crazy parrot said, and it was so ridiculous we couldn't help but go into hysterics, and after we had finished sailing we hugged each other one last time, said our good-byes, and the children promised to come to Wyoming in the summertime. And then I wept.

In Casper sometimes we woke up to a heavy wind lashing at the morning and the trees, and the trees moaned and the tall spruces in the front yard creaked and complained like old men who no longer want to do their work, and the awning flapped away over the windows, and the old house was full of strange noises as if the wind had wakened Walter to a panic. The newspaper was at the front door and I got coffee for Imaging and me, and crawled back into bed with the paper and Imaging, and we talked.

"Is it right to do this? I mean, Imaging, is it all right for us to be so happy and to have hurt all these innocent people—just for us? Isn't that selfish? How far can a man go for his own happiness?" And Imaging said she felt guilty, too, sometimes, and it wasn't that he had been a bad husband or a bad man or a drunk or that he hadn't supported his family. He was guiltless. She was the bad one and she felt guilty, too, but all she could do was believe in how she felt about us. She knew that that was real.

"You have to know what is real and then believe in it," she said.

"Well, yes, because that is the test of insanity. If one doesn't know what is real, then one is insane, they say."

"Yes," she said. "And if I am crazy it is only over you. We have to have faith in us. If we're going to believe in someone we should believe in ourselves," she said. "Love is real." I felt it, and it was real. I could feel it all the way through me and out into some great connection with the universe. It had filled up the empty places in me and grown around my hollow ribs and imbedded itself, warm and strong around my heart, and I felt like a new man was growing there. I had killed the old Gerry Spence, the old arrogant bitter bastard, that killer who killed in the courtroom for fun. I killed him one day when I met a poor man I had beaten in a trial a few days before—convinced a jury again this man hadn't been hurt. Pleased my insurance company all to hell once more. They would have paid him a piddling sum, happily, because our client had been drunk and run the intersection and smashed into his car and left him crippled. But I didn't want to pay anything. Just wanted to win. It was another good cross-examination that destroyed the man. He had fought back in the wrong way as witnesses will, and I had learned how to deal with that and the jury didn't believe he'd been injured.

Several days after the verdict I saw him at Safeway going through the checkout line. Imaging and I were there hand in hand, happy, and there was that poor man struggling away with his groceries. I helped him to his car, and I put my arm on his shoulder and I said, "Sorry it turned out this way." He looked at me with kind eyes. It is a great power—to love one's enemies. And the old man smiled at me and said, "You were just doing your job, Mr. Spence."

The next morning in bed having coffee with Imaging I said, "Is that my job? Is this what my life is all about? My grandparents struggled so hard in those old poor barren places, and the best product of their life's labor were my parents, and my parents have struggled and yearned for my success, and my poor mother—and I am their product. I am the product of all of those generations." I was giving a speech and Imaging was listening intently. Sometimes I gave speeches because I am a speechmaker. "Is this my job, really? To cheat little helpless people out of their just dues for the profit of some damned insurance company?" I looked over at Imaging as I spoke and she looked like someone who was hearing the truth. I could see the truth mirrored on her face. "Is this what I'm supposed to do with my life, honey?" I whispered now.

But Imaging only whispered back, "You know what you are supposed to do with your life."

"Yes," I said. And I knew that I should go out and kill all the pigs, like Grandpa Pfleeger. He knew, and when he finally got the word it was against the Bible to eat pork he killed them all, no hesitation, hauled them all off and dumped them. And that was it for Grandpa Pfleeger because he knew what was right for him, and I decided to kill my own pigs. I went to the office that same morning and I dictated a letter to my secretary, Dee Kleppinger, Dee Dee I called her, one for each of my insurance company clients, a letter saying the company would have to find somebody else to represent them, and I sent their files back. Dee Dee looked at me like I'd lost it. I wasn't going to represent insurance companies or banks or corporations against little people any more. I killed the pigs.

And I killed the old Gerry Spence who propositioned all the townspeople's wives and drank all the whiskey, or all of it he could get. "I think I've been killing him, honey," I said to Imaging one morning in bed. "I think it's been a kind of suicide. I think I wanted to kill all of Gerry Spence except the one little seed-place in his soul which I kept alive for you." I had shed everything—the wife of my childhood and my darling children—and I had sold the office. I had abandoned my practice of fifteen years and I abandoned the town of Riverton as well, and my friends there and my enemies, too, left them all as if it were a kind of suicide.

When I made speeches like that usually Imaging didn't answer and only listened. I made speeches with this woman in my arms.

"I killed my old self," I said.

"Maybe you didn't like yourself, Adam," she said.

"Well, maybe that's the way of life. Life grows out of death, and there is a new season every spring, and new flowers bloom out of the dust of their ancestors." She listened to my poetry. "I think when a man doesn't like himself he goes insane. A man has to like himself and that's what falling in love is—when you showed me what I could love in me, and then I loved you back for showing me. Love cures insanity," I said.

"You weren't insane, Adam," she said. "You were just unhappy."

"Pain causes insanity too," I said.

"I don't know," Imaging said, and then she snuggled her head down under my naked arm and it seemed like it didn't matter.

In the summer that followed, in accordance with the divorce decree, Kerry and Kent and Katy came to visit. Sometimes Kip stopped by in his wanderings. Anna tried to abide by the decree, to be right about it all. She vowed that no matter how she felt about me she would not turn the children against their father, but she was hurt, and sometimes she raged over the telephone at me, and I couldn't stand it, and I raged back. I tried to remember that anger was a secondary emotion. It didn't do me any good to remember it. Anger replaces something else—hurt. "She is hurt, Adam," Imaging said. "She feels rejected and you feel guilty. And you both hurt and it is easier for both of you to be angry than it is to just hurt."

"I know," I hollered out to the wall across the bedroom, but I couldn't feel her hurt. I could only feel my guilt.

"Goddamn it! How can I do this, Imaging! I have killed her, too," I said one morning in bed. "I killed Anna just as sure as Joe Esquibel killed his wife. I could just as well have put a bullet between her eyes. And I killed my mother, too."

"How can you say that?" she said with horror in her voice. "You didn't kill anybody."

"I killed my mother and I killed my wife and then I killed me. I have killed my children. You are living with a killer."

"It's guilt, Adam." She snuggled closer to me and I knew she loved me even though I felt unlovable. "If you weren't a good man," she said, "you wouldn't care. And if you weren't a good man, you couldn't feel pain, nor love. I couldn't love a man who didn't care," she said.

"God, Imaging," I whispered. "Do you realize I was all

Anna had? I was her whole life. She hung onto me because I was all she had. She gave everything she had to me. Then I left her," and now I was choking with sobs. "What have I done? Oh, God, what have I done?" Imaging didn't answer. She just held me and after a while I felt better. Finally I said, "Joe Esquibel was at least kind. He shot his wife clean and straight, one shot, between the eyes, but me—what I did to Anna, left her alone, afraid. Abandoned her. She doesn't have anybody to hang onto like this."

"I know," Imaging said.

"She is stronger than I. Braver," I said. "I wish she would find someone to make her feel like you make me feel."

"I know," Imaging said.

And after a while I seemed better again, and Imaging seemed better, too. We weeded out the garden every morning. It was our time together. We were growing new people, we thought. And although that mammoth guilt set in at times, and forced me down into bad dark places, I knew I was right with Imaging, and that she trusted our love, believed in it, and believed it was real. And once in a while Imaging and I would celebrate and have a hot fudge sundae.

In the summer of 1970 we took the kids, all but Kip, to Europe. Late honeymoon we said. "Great honeymoon, honey," I said to Imaging. "Whoever heard of taking the kids, especially two teenagers, on a honeymoon?"

"It will be good for all of us to be together. You need to be with your children more," Imaging said. We fantasized how it would be tripping through Europe together, this new little family, having fun and laughing, but the two oldest ones drove me crazy—like trying to manage a couple of spastic chimpanzees, I thought. When I looked up Kerry was gone, and when I found her she was out chasing some Frenchman someplace, and she got involved with this smooth swivel-hipped officer on our cruise ship to Greece. I couldn't keep track of either of them. Sometimes they were gone together and sometimes separately in opposite directions. It was like trying to chase duck feathers in the wind, and when I got them together I wished I hadn't. They fought with me and argued and hollered. We had been a hollering family. Anna had hollered at the kids. The kids had hollered back and I had hollered at all of them, but all that was supposed to be over with now. It was maddening. Goddamned kids didn't want to see the Louvre. The Sistine Chapel was bullshit, they thought, and then some Italian patted Kerry and Imaging on the ass, and I was going to fight, and Kent went off with Kerry someplace on a Greek island where our ship stopped and was late and the goddamned ship was going to leave without them, and part of me said I didn't give a good goddamn and part of me was frantic.

In Paris we rented a car to tour the French countryside, and one morning I woke up realizing I was nothing but a fucking travel agent for a zoo. Get the car, get the baggage, get the kids, get the itinerary, Daddy, when are we going to eat, Daddy, I gotta pee, and stop fighting in the back seat. We were charging through Paris traffic in some silly French car that looked like a half-squashed doodle bug, and you had to really charge, blind charge in that traffic or they'd run over you. Everybody in the car was screaming and the sweat was running down my face and my heart was beating and the crazy goddamned Frenchmen were driving in every direction honking horns, and the brakes on ten thousand of the bastards' cars were screeching all at once, and I prayed to God to get me out of that place. I would have jumped out of the car with my family, left it in the middle of the street and run, except they would have run us down and we were safer in the car, but not much, and then finally, only through a miracle, we were out of Paris and driving down a quiet country road and everybody in the car was quiet, exhausted, maybe. Kent and Kerry were probably hung over. Kerry was sitting in the front seat next to me with Katy, and Kent and Imaging were in the back, and we had been driving along silently for a while. It was peaceful for once and I looked in the back seat to see what was wrong, and there was Imaging crying softly to herself.

"God, what's the matter, honey?" I asked.

"I don't know," she said.

"You do, honey," I said. "What's the matter!"

"I left my kids at home and you have yours . . ."

"Well, honey, Chris was too little and we couldn't bring Brents and leave Chris at home without him, don't you remember?"

"I know," she said. "But I miss them, and I'm afraid they're worrying about me." She had left them with their father, who was responsible and who loved the children and would take care of them.

"And . . ." And then she started to sob again and I drove on. And I asked her what else was the matter. "What else?" And she said she was tired, and I said yes, but there was something else. Then she finally said, "I don't know where I belong in this new family. I mean I am stuck back here in the back seat like another one of the kids—am I your wife or what?"

"God!" I said. I stopped the car. "Kerry, you get in the back. Imaging, you get up here with me. This is where you belong, next to me. You are the queen." And then later we had laughed about it, and I said we were all like a bunch of goddamned jackdaws—we had to establish the goddamned hierarchy.

In the French countryside outside an old castle, we watched a crow crying crazily, circling its young, which had flown from the nest. "Look at the crow, Kerry," I said.

"Yeah, I see it, Daddy," she said.

"Do you know what's the matter with the father crow, Kerry?"

"How do you know it's a father crow, Daddy?" Kerry asked.

"Take my word for something, Kerry, for Christ's sake! It's a father crow! And the crow is having trouble. Its baby has flown from the nest, and the baby can't fly very well yet, and it's helpless there on the ground. You can see that. Anything can get the baby—cat will probably get it. And the baby can't fly back into its safe nest."

"Yes, Daddy," Kerry said, but she wasn't impressed.

Later on she would fly from her nest, move out of her mother's house, and quit high school before she graduated. She came to live with us for a little while in Casper, and then she flew from that nest, too, taking her own apartment and working as an aide in an old folks' home. She ran around with a lot of damned hippies, and I raged about it and hollered. God I was afraid for her, and I forgot that anger was a secondary emotion, but I couldn't help it. I was only a father. I raised all kinds of hell until I literally drove her out of town. She said she had to live her own life. And I said she couldn't live her own life, that she was too young and vulnerable and that the young crow couldn't fly very well yet, and that there was nothing more stupid than a young crow. Just gawk and squawk and the cats get 'em. But I couldn't get her back in the nest, and I couldn't save her, and all I could do was to squawk myself. Just squawk.

"I am a terrible father," I said to Imaging one morning in bed. "Neither of these children would have acted this way if I had been a good father. Look at 'em. Kip has gone off with a bunch of hippies to pick strawberries some goddamned place, and I've lost him. Now I've lost Kerry, too, and I'm gonna lose the others. There's nothing I can do. It is karma. It is karma-kickback. What goes around, comes around, or whatever it is that they say. Anyway I'm getting it all back."

"You are a good father. Good fathers care, and they anguish a lot like you do. It is the poor father who doesn't give a damn," she said. But what she said didn't make any difference in the way I felt about my fatherhood, and then before the whole matter had even begun to get resolved Anna moved to Jackson, Wyoming, and brought Kent and Katy with her. She put them in school there, and that made me feel guilty because I knew she was alone and maybe feeling afraid, and that she hadn't been able to settle her life in California and to find any satisfaction for herself there. I knew she must be hurting and looking for a way to get through her life and as I watched her suffer, I suffered with her. But I had to let her be—to cut the ties, and I was helpless to do anything but watch her struggle. I was only this father crow living with Imaging Crow, and then before the winter was over Kent came to live with us and that hurt Anna more. Now all she had left was little Katy. Kent said he left because he couldn't stand it in high school in Jackson, Wyoming, with those red-necked goat-ropers, as he called them. He said, "Jesus, Dad. This kid came to school with peace signs bleached out on his jeans with Clorox or something—like it was something new. I got through all that crap two years ago in the peace marches in San Francisco." And now he had fought his way out of the nest of his mother and into ours, and later he and I had fought, father against son—the mouthiest little bastard I had ever met in my life—in my whole life, I told Imaging. Had to have the last word no matter what. Came by it naturally, Imaging said. Well, yes, I said, but there's got to be respect here.

"He's angry," Imaging said. "Remember, you left his mother. Hurt him. Kerry is angry, too."

"It's that Oedipus thing—son against father," I said. "He'll probably kill me, too."

"No, it's just the way of boys. It's healthy," Imaging said.

"It is not healthy," I said. We were drinking our coffee in bed again and talking and we were each other's therapist. "He is going to kill me, one way or the other, and I can't stand that screaming—I get no peace."

"Well, Kent and I get along fine when you're not here," she said.

"Fine," I said. "I'll leave you with 'em," I hollered.

"No," she said. "I'm going with you." And then we laughed and held onto each other under the morning covers and once in a while we heard that Kip was someplace doing something or other with his hippie friends and I knew there was nothing I could do about him, either. "Let him be, let him be. He'll come back. Remember how you were?" Imaging said. "He'll be all right. So will Kerry. You have to trust your children. You have to learn to trust, Adam."

"Well, one thing I'll tell you for sure," I said to Imaging. "We're going to get this fucking hierarchy straight-ened out in this family once and for all." That morning I met Kent down in the kitchen, and he had dumped some kind of a verbal barrage on me, and I was dripping mad from it. I stopped in front of him and I said, "Now listen, Kent, in this little kingdom of ours, do you know who the king is?" I looked him coldly in the eye like my father used to look at me at those times. It didn't faze him a bit.

"Yeah," he said. "But . . ."

"Never mind having the last word . . ."

"Well," he interrupted me. "You may be the king . . ."

"Now, just stop. Stop just once, please, so we can get this simple little thing figured out as to what's what and who's who in my house . . ."

"Well," he interrupted again. "So it's gonna be the 'You're in my house stuff' . . . Well . . ."

"Goddamn it," I interrupted again. "Stop a minute!"

"It ain't fair at all. You're supposed to be . . ."

"Goddamn it, it isn't a matter of what's fair and what isn't!" I said.

"Well, if you're the king, kings are supposed to be fair. And as for her . . ." He was referring to Imaging, and there was that sarcastic teenage sound in his voice and he had started to bob his head fast up and down and then he began to shake it sideways with a sneer on his face. "As for her . . ." He was six feet tall, this kid, and I gave him just a little punch, just right, in the belly, like a man knows how to do, and he went to the floor like he had been hit in the back of the head with an ax. Imaging came rushing in.

"You didn't need to hit him!" Imaging cried, rushing up to poor Kent, who was gasping for breath. I was stand-ing over him like Tarzan.

"Don't you ever refer to Imaging as 'her' in that tone of voice," I said. "Do you understand? Imaging is the queen here," I hollered, and Kent made more of it than it had ever been or could ever be. He doubled up and gasped and rolled on the floor, making all kinds of horri-

ble noises and commotion. You would have thought I'd
maimed him permanently.

"What did you do to him?" Imaging screamed, and she
got down next to Kent on the floor, and he just rolled and
gagged and gasped all the more. I was ashamed. Later I
held him on my lap like a little boy, that big six-foot-tall
kid. But he didn't call Imaging "her" anymore. "If you're
going to call her 'her,' say it with a capital *H*," I said.
"Her name is 'Her' with a capital *H*," and we both
laughed, but Kent still had to have the last word finally. It
came out like breathing for him. And finally he said it was
the high school at Casper he couldn't stand, and he went
back to his mother, who had moved to Mill Valley again.

Then one day Bob Ranck, a friend of mine, who was
then the county attorney at Jackson, Wyoming, called me
to say that Kerry was sleeping in her car in the cold in the
middle of the winter there, no place to go, no job—just a
vagrant. What did I want him to do? Should he have her
picked up? He could put her in jail so I could come get
her and get a little control over her again. But no, Imaging and I thought. We were just the mother and father
crows—we had to let the baby go, let the baby face her
own dangers, and all we could do was to squawk. And
later on Kerry joined a bunch of other crazy kids, and
they lived in some kind of a damned commune in a cabin
snowed in in the winter, and it was all very exciting for
her, but I couldn't bear it, couldn't even think of it.

"How can she do that to me, Imaging?" I asked. "How
can she run off like that and waste her life?"

"She's not doing it to you, darling," Imaging said.
"She's doing it for herself."

"She's destroying herself."

"No, she isn't. You're forgetting about what you did
when you were her age. Don't you remember?" I remembered the whorehouses, the whiskey, the adventure, and
my poor mother—I remembered my poor mother and
her suffering, and then my heart filled full of guilt again,
and I knew I had killed my mother, and then Imaging and
I had to go through that whole thing once more—that I
hadn't killed her, that it just felt that way, and that some-

times you had to trust your head, and what I felt about
my mother were feelings, all right, but the feelings didn't
tell the truth. I wasn't guilty!

"But why did my mother do it?" I kept asking.

"She did it for her own reasons. Maybe it was the
menopause, remember? Women do strange things in the
menopause sometimes, and she'd been up at fourteen
thousand feet, and had just come down after three years
at that elevation and that does something to a person,"
Imaging said. And we'd go over it and over it until I
thought surely I'd worn it out, worn it away, that I understood it perfectly, and then something would happen and
it would all come flooding in on me again as new and
dark and ugly and as painful as if I had never dealt with it
before, and I had to fight through the whole damned
mess again for the answers. Imaging was patient.

Then one day Anna moved from Mill Valley to Casper,
Wyoming, for Christ's sake. Bought a house down the
street from us, for Jesus H. Christ's sake, and now the
whole goddamned outfit was there, Imaging and me, and
the kids, both sets of them, and Imaging's former husband, and Anna, and all the dogs and every goddamned
body and everything! Anna phoned to say she was moving to Casper, had friends there, she said. Could she store
some of her things in our garage? God Almighty, it
wasn't that I was such a dirty stingy bastard, too cheap to
let her store things in the garage, but I had to say, no—
cut the ties, cut the . . . I couldn't explain it. I dreamed
she filled the garage full of her things and one of the
things was a coffin, and I dreamed I opened the coffin up
and it was full of California oranges, whatever the hell
that meant. It was crazy.

"Imaging, I'm goin' crazy," I said. "I'm havin' crazy
dreams, about coffins with oranges in them, and about
people in coffins who I don't know, who I can't identify."
I thought a minute. "Yes, I can identify her. It's my
mother, and she's in a coffin, and she's dead, but she
doesn't know that she's dead, and she doesn't want to be
left alone in the coffin in the funeral home, and she
doesn't know that we are going to bury her. She's abso-

lutely dead. All the blood has been drained out of her veins, and her veins are full of formaldehyde, and she's perfectly embalmed, but she doesn't know it, doesn't believe it, can't understand it, and won't accept it, and she won't quit talking to me. And I dreamed other people were also dead and talking out of their coffins and wouldn't stop talking. Can't stop anybody from talking. One of my children was in the coffin. It was Kip. He was dead in the coffin and talking to me, and didn't want me to bury him either."

"I know," Imaging said. "But you're *not* crazy." And when we were close the crazy feeling went away, and sometimes we held onto each other like children in a strange dark forest, and later on it was Imaging who was fighting her own battle—her mother was dying of cancer. Our arms protected each other from everything in those days, from the cold staring critical world, from the demons within and without, and from our children, whom we loved, and now her mother was in the hospital. And in the mornings in those days Imaging and I healed ourselves and each other.

"You have to finish up your business with your mother," I said.

"Why?" she asked. "She'll be all right. She'll get well. I know it."

"No," I said. "She won't be all right. She's dying, darling," I said. And then Imaging and I cried together until she finally admitted she knew her mother was dying, really knew it, and she also said she knew she did have to finish up her business with her mother before she died. I hadn't done that with mine so that here we were still trying to finish up my old business with my mother after twenty years, twenty years of being haunted, of her following me, whispering to me, and I was still trying to hush her. "Imaging," I said, "you have to finish up your business with your mother."

Then she thought about it for a while and she asked, "What business?" trying to think of what it might be.

"Well, how do you feel about her? She left your father one day—just walked out on him."

"It was what she had to do. And I loved my father, and it hurt him, and she was hurt. I loved her, too. But she was crazy, Adam. They put her in a mental hospital. Schizophrenic. She got violent. Once she was violent with Brents and me when Brents was little, but she was clever and charming, and she charmed her way right out of the mental hospital, and then she divorced my father and pretty soon she seemed all right again," she said.

And it wasn't once a schitz, always a schitz. It was that Imaging's mother had learned to love herself, and she had gotten well, and her love had cured her insanity. But Imaging needed to be with her mother now that she was dying.

One morning Imaging left for Washington, D.C., where her mother was in the hospital. The surgeons had cut off one of her breasts a couple of years before, but the surgery hadn't stopped the cancer's spread. Now the woman was sedated and in the last stages of the disease. She looked dead when I got to Washington later on to be with Imaging—looked gray and in pain, but even near death her face was still beautiful, finely chiseled and delicate, and her gray skin was almost transparent. She was a brave and beautiful woman dying under white sheets in a dim hospital room. I was glad I'd met her when she was happy and well, a bright woman, a marine biologist, who worked at the Smithsonian where Imaging's father also worked as a curator.

Now Imaging sat with her mother and sewed together little doll clothes for Katy's dolls, and when her mother had brief periods of lucidity she saw her darling daughter sitting there sewing, the sewing she had taught her, and that made her mother happy. She wanted to know, was Imaging happy? Yes, Imaging was happy. Was Imaging's former husband happy? Yes, he had remarried now. A fine woman—beautiful, tall, blond—and she was good to him. And he was happy. And that made a peaceful look come on her mother's face. And were the children happy —were all of them all right? Yes. But Imaging had to let Brents go to his father. It had been a terrible struggle for Brents because he was only twelve, but he felt guilty about having left his father, Imaging said, and Brents had been grieving over his father. He couldn't understand why she had left him. Imaging told her mother she'd had to let him go, else he would have grieved more and grown up to hate her, and that would have hurt Brents worse. It's all right, Mother, that I let him go to his father. His father needs him, and I haven't lost him, Mother. I'll never lose him. And when the time comes, he'll come home again. He's all right, Mother, and it's hurt me, but I'm all right, too, and his father is all right, and his father is happy. His father and Adam are friendly, and his father and Christopher see each other, and the children from both families get along with each other and they are all, all right. And Pete, Imaging's brother, and Magie, his wife, and Sissy and Hans, their kids—they are all happy and all right.

Her mother seemed at peace being with Imaging when she died, knowing that her children were happy, and that her grandchildren were safe and happy, and that finished up Imaging's business with her mother, she said. When her mother died she felt perfectly loved, Imaging said. I was with Imaging when they buried her mother, and then we came home together to Casper, and one morning Imaging told me of her dreams of her mother. She woke up suddenly as if her mother were there, and during the day sometimes she said she heard her mother calling out her name, calling, calling, and I told Imaging that we all hear our mothers calling us.

Joe Esquibel began phoning me again in the early part of 1972. We had been successful in getting him into a different hall after the trial, and he was receiving better treatment than before, had a job at the laundry in the hospital and lived in an open ward. He had the free run of the place, he said, and they weren't giving him any trouble. He felt good, but he needed out—needed out. "I need out, Mr. Spence, please."

"I got good news for you, Joe," I told him one afternoon when he had called again. "I'm going to come on down and see you. We'll talk about it together." Then I drove to Evanston and through the town and up the hill to the hospital. He did look good. Looked alert and bright and he actually smiled at me. First time I can remember Joe Esquibel ever having smiled at me. He was handsome.

"How come you're so happy, Joe? Never seen you so happy." He was actually bouncing down the hall and I had to walk fast to keep up with him. You could see the reflection of our feet coming down on the shiny waxed floors of the place. "What's it all about, Joe?"

"I don't know," he said as if he was embarrassed.

"Tell your old pal."

"I got me a girl."

"That's great, Joe," I said. "Every fellow ought to have a girl friend. Are you in love?"

"I don't know." He looked down and grinned.

"Yes, sure you do. You're in love, aren't you?"

"Well, Mr. Spence," he said, changing the subject, walking even faster, "let me show you aroun' this place." I followed him. "Let me introduce you to my friends. I got friends here, Mr. Spence. They like me. These people all like me," he said excitedly. I followed him up to a skinny little old man. "Now this here is George. Now, George, this is Mr. Spence. I been telling ya about Mr. Spence. He's the lawyer. Ya know, the lawyer—big-time lawyer." He gave me a little elbow in the ribs. "Now George has had trouble at home—with his wife. He's an alcoholic, ain't ya, George?" And George nodded obediently and grinned back. "Now, some guys tried ta push George aroun', but I kicked the shit out of 'em for you, didn't I, George?" And George nodded and grinned again. And then we moved on to the next man, who popped out of the next doorway to face us as if we were a couple of inspecting generals. "Now this here is Peter J. O'Hara. He's a lawyer, like you." O'Hara was a gray-haired man, twenty years older than I. I wondered how an old lawyer could get in such trouble and end up in a place like this. "You remember me telling you about Mr. Spence? Well, this is him," Joe said proudly. "Everybody knows about you, Mr. Spence," Joe said. "Now, O'Hara is in here for beating up his wife. Got crazy one day. But she drove him crazy, didn't she?" Joe looked at the man after having stated his case.

"Yes," the man said. "I suppose so. Nice to meet you, Mr. Spence. Nice of you to come." We moved on down the hall.

"These people trust me. I take care of 'em. Nobody fucks with my friends," Joe said seriously. "I feel sorry for these people," he said in a high easy voice. "They are so lonely. Nobody comes and sees O'Hara. Only got a wife. No kids. And he beat her up. She's divorcing him and O'Hara is alone and is scared. My mother and sister, they come see me every week. But nobody sees him. I wish I could help them people. I try to help. Nobody fucks with 'em, though. Not even the aides. Grabbed that one aide, one time. Never hit him, or nothing, but he knew. He was the tough aide that everybody was scared of, but he didn't scare me none," Joe said proudly. "I am a friend of all the poor people," he went on, as if he were no longer one of them. "I talk to 'em. I understand 'em. I don' even get mad anymore if they say bad things to me. Sometimes they say things and don' even know what they are sayin'. They can't help it. Been hurt too bad. Ain't responsible." We walked on down the hall. I couldn't believe this was Joe Esquibel. He was a different man, one I had never met before. "My girl friend, she helps me a lot. She makes the difference to me. I'd still be crazy if it wasn't for her. I ain't crazy no more, but I gotta get out of here. Sane man can't stay here. What's the surprise you was telling me about?" he asked.

"Well, Joe," I said. "The U.S. Supreme Court wrote a decision the other day in a case called *Furman v. Georgia.*"

"Oh?"

"And it says that the death penalty statute in Georgia is unconstitutional."

"Oh. Well, this ain't Georgia," Joe said.

I said, "The Wyoming death penalty statute is unconstitutional, too. It's like the one in Georgia. I mean, they can't kill you in Wyoming now until they pass a new death penalty statute. They're going to have to close up the old gas chamber for a while," I said. "Is that good news?"

"I ain't a-scared a the gas chamber," Joe said matter-of-factly. "Lots worse things can happen than dyin' in the gas chamber—like staying here forever. I'd rather be in the pen than here. I gotta get out," he said.

"Well, remember, you go crazy when you're locked up. Don't forget that." I followed him into a large area and we sat down in some chairs over in a corner. Looked like the lobby in an old hotel out of the late twenties. A few people were walking around quietly. The people seemed peaceful, nothing going on, and as I sat down I thought of poor Jason.

"This isn't like over at Sublette, is it?"

"That was something else, Mr. Spence. I go crazy even thinking about it. I wouldn't go over there any more. They'd have to kill me first," he said.

"Can you stand to go to the penitentiary if we lose?" I asked him, and I put my hand down on his and looked into his eyes, and they were as alive as I have seen eyes, and I thought I could see clear back into the core of the man.

"I ain't a-scared no more. They can't scare me no more. I'm through being scared. Scared makes you crazy," he said.

"What does your girl friend think about this?" I asked.

"We want me to be free," he said. "We want to have a life together. We want to make it, Mr. Spence. We want to gamble it all. We're gonna lay it all on the line, Mr. Spence. I gotta get free. And I'm okay. Gotta take the chance."

"Okay," I said. What else could I say? "Okay."

"We could have kids . . ."

"Okay," I said.

"And I could get me a good job with my brother-in-law on the railroad. He's a machinist, and . . ."

"Okay."

"And I could help my mother, you know, and . . ."

"Okay, Joe. And how are you getting along with your mother?"

"Okay. She comes all the time."

"Having any more dreams?"

"A few. But they ain't crazy dreams."

"What are they?"

"About my mother and things," he said, like it was nothing.

"What?"

"Oh, nothing, you know. I dream about them white guys yet," and then he looked over to the window and gazed off to the distant mountains.

"What is it you dream about those white guys, Joe?"

"Oh, you know, like when I was a kid and I seen them with my mother and all, and I want to kill them white guys for hurtin' my mother, and then my mother leaves, and I'm a little kid, and I'm crying and sometimes I wake up crying at night."

"We all dream about our mothers, Joe."

"I know," he said.

29

ON MAY 17, 1972, Paul Saxon, M.D., clinical director of the Wyoming State Hospital wrote me, and everybody else in the Esquibel case, claiming Joe Esquibel was again sane and ready to stand trial. He said, "In many ways his functioning is better than it has been since 1966." Although the tests pointed up some residual anger against his mother Joe denied any such anger, and seemed to "go overboard to show his concern for his family. I saw Joe yesterday," Dr. Saxon wrote. "He is eager to get back into court and have his case resolved, and I feel he is capable of handling this bit of pressure at the moment."

I called Saxon for a little bargaining. I wasn't interested in dragging Joe back into court to then have the state's psychiatrists get up on the stand and tell the jury that Joe was perfectly sane when he shot his wife. I said, "Well, I'm not ever going to take Joe into court so a jury can kill him. You'll have to keep him at the hospital till hell freezes over. But if you fellows would tell me you think he was insane when he pulled that trigger, well, that might be something different again," and Saxon said he just didn't know for sure, but it looked to him like we might have a good case for insanity at the time of the shooting, taking all of the records and all of their experiences with Joe into account. Then I said I wanted to talk to Dr. Karn.

Karn was an enigma to me, like trying to understand

what makes a cutthroat trout bite. Done a lot of fishin'
but I can't tell you much about why trout bite. I called
Karn and he said, Well, in good conscience, he couldn't
testify that Joe was insane at the time he shot Sharon. "I
can't," he insisted. "Can't say either way."

"Well, if I can't get somebody to testify he was insane I
got no defense, and I'll play tiddledywinks with you guys
for the rest of your life and his. He'll have a beard to his
toes before they take Joe out of your hospital. I'll make it
my life's work, but if I could get somebody on my side, I
could get him out of your hair."

"I feel immobilized by this thing, Gerry," Karn said.
"Feel sorry for the guy—but I'm back on dead center. I
don't know."

"Well, who asked you to *know?* Nobody knows anything in the law. Experts only have opinions in court. I
don't know who my parents are for sure, but there's a
whole body of evidence from which I can draw valid conclusions and arrive at an opinion." What was I saying all
that for, for Christ's sake? He knew the difference between fact and opinion as well as I.

"I don't know how I could, in good conscience, say he
was insane at the time—just couldn't," Karn said again.

"Well, you already admitted you were wrong about Joe
once—got up there on the stand and swore Joe was sane
back in '66, and then you testified at the second trial
you'd been wrong, said he was still insane then. How in
the love of hell can you, in good conscience, come to any
other conclusion but that he was insane when he shot
Sharon?"

He said nothing back.

"And besides, you've got a new staff—not a single
member of your staff was with you back in '66." I said
that just in case he was worried about another administrative problem like last time. He said nothing. "And just
between us girls"—I put on the finishing touches to the
argument—"you'd be doing old Oscar Hall a hell of a
favor—take a heavy burden off his shoulders."

"Well, maybe Joe could plead guilty to second degree

murder. I hear Oscar has offered you second degree," Karn said. And then I started hollering.

"What kind of a goddamned idea is that? You know that if he's insane, he's not guilty of murder and all. That's askin' an innocent man to plead guilty to save his life. And Oscar never offered us a damn thing," I shouted. Karn was silent again. Then I began again, quiet and sweet. "The real problem here is a social problem, isn't it, Bill?" Get down to it, call him Bill, not doctor, get personal, get to the nubbins of this thing. "It's like, 'What am I going to do with this Joe Esquibel, and how am I, Bill Karn, as superintendent of this hospital, going to make everybody happy?' "

"I make a lot of people unhappy. I just gotta be square with myself—satisfy me, and I don't have an opinion." There we were back to that conscience thing again, but I ignored it. I said when we went to court he'd be a lot better off on my side of the case, and he said, well, if he took my side of the case it would make him turn around 180 degrees from where he was originally, and besides Dr. Pace and Dr. Tedro would be against him, and he didn't like being on this hot seat. "I'd feel dishonest to myself, mainly, if I went any other way." Then he must have sat back and looked up at the ceiling—I could see him in my mind's eye. He'd be puffing his pipe and talking calmly. Then he said, "But the guy has suffered enough. Seems like Oscar Hall is the one who could solve this damn thing. He could just plain drop it after all these years," Karn said. Here was the solution—pass it on to Oscar Hall.

"Well, Joe can't cop a plea and go to prison. He goes crazy in prison. You know that. Goddamn it, you've said that yourself."

"I don't think he should go to the pen. The guy's had enough. We've all had enough," Karn said with the slight sound of suffering in his voice.

"Well, talk to Hall," I said.

"Okay," Karn said, "but Oscar isn't too happy with me. Thinks I let him down in the last trial. But hell, Gerry," he said, and it sounded like we were friends trying to solve a problem. "There's certain things you can do and certain things you can't, and Joe's getting edgy—he's volatile, nothing serious yet, but he's edgy."

"Tell Joe I called," I said.

"Glad to," he said back, but that hadn't ended the conversation. We talked about just letting Joe out—letting him go on leave to his brother-in-law, Frank Fisher, in Salt Lake—out of sight, out of mind. Or maybe Joe could plead to second degree, get a ten-year sentence, have all his time at the hospital apply as "good time" and let him go on parole. That seemed reasonable. Or maybe, and Karn kept bringing it up, maybe Oscar ought to just dismiss the case. Joe had suffered enough, he kept saying, and I thought he meant it. He'd call Oscar and call me back.

In a couple of weeks Dr. Karn did call me back—he'd talked to Ken Keldsen, the deputy, not Oscar Hall, who had been out of town. There'd be no deals for the murdering bastard at all, Keldsen told him. It was first degree murder. That was it. Period.

I said, "Does that change your attitude, Bill? Does that help your conscience?"

"Well," he said, "I'd like to get the thing over with . . ." and then he got to talking real fast, and the words just came rolling out, so mumbly I couldn't get most of them, but I heard something about "irresistible impulse."

"What are you saying?" I interrupted him.

"Well," Bill Karn said, slowing down a little, "I don't think he could have prevented doing what he did at the time he did it. He was the classic 'policeman at the elbow' case. He would have shot Sharon even if there were a policeman there, no matter what the consequences, and under the Durham test, which asks, 'Was the act the *product* of mental illness,' well, he certainly fits that, too. And under the M'Naghten's Rule—'Did he know the difference between right and wrong?'—well, it's so inflexible, unless I would do to that test what I haven't done to it so far—bend it so far out of shape it doesn't make sense—"

"And what was his mental illness under the Durham test?" I asked.

"Schizophrenia. In retrospect, it could actually be acute schizophrenia." Then he paused a minute and he asked, "Is Dr. Fairchild going to be at the trial?"

"I expect her," I said.

"Well, if we're going to take this particular route it would be well if we both say the same thing."

"Yeah," I said. "Now suppose you happened to be standing by Joe just before he pulled the trigger, and you said, 'Joe, Joe, don't you know this is wrong?' like in the M'Naghten's Rule, you know, 'Did he know the difference between right or wrong?' what would Joe have said?" I asked.

"Well, I think he would have been so preoccupied in his state of mind that he would have shot her anyway—never would have heard me."

"Will Tedro agree with you?" I asked.

"Don't think so. He's ready to say Joe was malingering, going to say he shot his wife because he wanted to."

I said, "That begs the question. Insane people have wants. You have a whole hospital of insane people wanting to do things. Jason wants to throw his dung. Doesn't mean a damn thing, does it?"

"Not really," Karn said.

But Tedro was Karn's consultant. Lived in Salt Lake City, out of the jurisdiction of the state court, and I doubted that Tedro would want to come into Wyoming voluntarily now and testify to a position which contradicted the man who hired him in case after good case. Dr. Pace? Well, maybe he had had enough of me. Oscar Hall was the sole remaining problem.

So if Dr. Karn was going to testify that Joe was insane at the time maybe I could get old Oscar to let loose of the case—maybe he'd just say, "Well, all right. It's been a good fight. You got me, Gerry. You got my witnesses, and I got no place to go. I'll work something out with you." Maybe he'd say I could plead Joe guilty to manslaughter, and we'd put him on parole, give him good time for the six years he spent in Evanston, and let the state keep control of him for a while, and then everybody would be satisfied. Surely Oscar would see it that way. No other choice.

I wrote Oscar telling him that Dr. Karn was going to testify that Joe was legally insane at the time of the killings. "I therefore request you advise me at the earliest moment as to how you wish to proceed and when. If you need to discuss the matter with me by telephone, I will be at my office on Monday, June 12." Let old Oscar stew in his own juices for a while—Karn was going to testify Joe was insane when he shot Sharon—Oscar would talk to the other doctors at the hospital, do his hollering, and finally when he saw we had him cornered, he'd call me up and make a deal. I'd probably hear from him on Monday, all right. Looked like we were about at the end of this long road. Joe would be free, and so would I, thank God. Everybody could be free, Karn, the hospital, even old Oscar, and Joe could live his good life with this woman he'd found, his love, whoever she was, and they could have their babies, and he could go to work on the railroad and raise his family, and help his mother . . . it was only my dreaming. I heard nothing from Oscar.

Then one Sunday in July Oscar and his wife dropped by to visit with Imaging and me at our little ranch out on the reservation, on the "North Fork," as we called it, the North Fork of the Little Wind River, where we built a wonderful home on an island, our hideaway in the quaking aspens. There was a porch out over the creek, and the little ranch had a hundred cows or so and less than a thousand acres, and Oscar and I sat on the porch and listened to the creek speak to us in its universal language, which every man understands. We talked, but not about the Esquibel case. He came by to share his grief with me. He'd lost his son in a drowning accident, and it had almost killed Oscar. I could see that—feel it—and we grieved together there on the porch. Oscar needed to talk to his old friend, Gerry Spence. Sometimes a man's foes are his best friends. It is a strange phenomenon, the closeness that grows out of the gut-fighting between two old warriors in the pit.

"Friendship is sharing," I mused to Oscar as I listened to the creek run by. And we both stared down into the water, and I watched the ripples, and although each ripple held its place in the creek, each ripple was always different in the same place, and sounded different, too, if a man put his ear to it. "Maybe friendship is the most important thing a man has," I finally said.

"Yeah," Oscar said.

"It's a strange thing, Oscar, how a couple a fellas can grow close out of fighting."

"Yeah," Oscar said, still looking down at the clear water going by, and I knew Oscar was hearing the talk of the creek, which was saying something soothing to him. A creek could speak to Oscar at a time like this better than a man.

But I said, "Well, Oscar, what we share in the courtroom is our fear, and our struggle. We both know we put it all in as straight and true as we can, and it's respect, isn't it? A man has respect for a good opponent, and he cares about him."

"That's right, Gerry," he said. "We do our best." And Oscar was fixed on the ripples of the creek that passed under the chokecherry bush. Across the creek the thrushes were singing happy songs in the aspens, oblivious to the grief of my friend, and the flickers were making early summer noises, claiming their territory, and across the creek farther on you could see the Wind River Mountains, with the snow still on the top of Horse Ridge, and beyond them it seemed like eternity. Oscar looked across the creek. There were tears in his eyes, and I wished I could take away his pain. What can a man say to another man who has lost his son?

"I wish I could take away your pain, Oscar," was all I could say, "or even take a little bit of it from you." And he nodded because he knew if he talked he would cry and men don't want to cry in front of each other.

I waited a couple of weeks and then I wrote Oscar another letter. Since Dr. Karn would testify that Joe was insane at the time of the killing, well, shouldn't Oscar just plain dismiss the case? Would he please call me? And then on August 8, 1972, Oscar finally wrote his letter back. Formal as hell. "This will acknowledge your recent letter written prior to my family tragedy with reference to Joe Esquibel. Since our last personal conference I submitted to major surgery in Denver and have just returned to the office. Please excuse the belated reply. I suggest a jury trial be set as soon as possible. This is assuming that the plea of triability is withdrawn." The old bastard wouldn't give up, goddamn it! He was as stubborn as hell and the letter said he wanted to try the case in Sweetwater County—down in Green River, for Christ's sake. Well, that's where the case was venued all right, as they say, that's where Judge Stanton had moved the case those many years ago and jurisdiction in the murder case was still in Sweetwater County, I guess. But maybe I could trade off our plea of "Not triable by reason of present insanity" for something. We were going to give that up anyway and go for broke—freedom for Joe, once and for all—put it all on the line, and so I said to Oscar on the phone one day, "Well, Oscar, I'll waive the 'not triable plea,' admit he's sane now and can be tried—if you'll just agree to try this case in Casper so we can at least sleep at home at night during the damned trial." He said, "Okay. I don't want to try it in Green River anyway." The old bastard wouldn't give me an inch.

The time dragged on for Joe Esquibel and he kept calling, "Get me out," and I kept saying, "Well, Joe, I'm trying to put the heat on him to dismiss. I don't want to take the chance of putting you in front of a jury if I don't have to. They might send you to the penitentiary for life, for twenty years, or even one year—it's all the same. I know I can make that hard-headed bastard see the light if I keep at 'em. I just know I can. His witnesses are gone. He has to give up," I told Joe.

Then I filed a Motion to Dismiss. It said that since there was no competent evidence in the possession of the state that Joe was sane at the time of the shooting, and since the state had to prove his sanity beyond a reasonable doubt, the court should dismiss this case. All responsible psychiatrists at the hospital agreed that Joe

Esquibel was insane at the time of the shooting. There-fore, there being no evidence to the contrary, the court should dismiss the action.

The months dragged on and finally Judge Forrister ruled. He thought there was *some* evidence of sanity, all right. Some. And then Oscar bowed his neck some more. He was going to try Joe for murder. I let time pass hoping that the state hospital's pressure on Oscar Hall to help them get rid of Joe might soften him but the passing months rendered no change in Oscar. Time was like mere wind against granite. Finally on May 18, 1973, Judge For-rister set the case for trial in Casper at ten in the morning on September 24, 1973. I wrote Joe a letter.

"It looks like this long wait has come to an end. You have been a good and patient man. Be good and patient another few months and we will have it licked—I hope. I believe your chances for a good result in this case are excellent. Sincerely." It's called reassurance. Doctors' pa-tients need it, and lawyers' clients need it also. We all need it. I got mine from Imaging.

I wasn't going to give up on Oscar. I started a tele-phone campaign. "Oscar," I called. "How come you're so damned stubborn? You know you haven't got a case. Be reasonable, man!"

"Well, Gerry, I gotta try the case."

"Why, Oscar, why?"

"You never lived in Rawlins, Wyoming, or you'd know. You don't know how hard it is to be a prosecutor down here."

"How're you gonna try this case with both Karn and Saxon as my witnesses?"

"I'd rather you'd have them than me. A jury doesn't believe those damned psychiatrists. Who in the hell's gonna believe Karn?"

"He's a good witness."

"You can have him," Oscar said, and we talked awhile more and hung up. Then on another day after Joe would call me, I'd call Oscar again. "Oscar, for Christ's sake," I said. "I just got a call from Joe. He's depressed. He's suffered enough. It's been so damned long and he's still stuck there in that hospital. Justice is justice. You know in your own heart he wasn't sane at the time. He was crazy as hell. You know that in your heart," I said.

"I don't know anything about this case, Gerry. The longer I'm involved in it the less I know about it. Craziest damned case I ever saw. But I'll tell you one thing," Oscar said, sounding like Moses again. "If I agreed to dismiss that case, the people of Rawlins would tar and feather me—'Turned a murderer loose—a goddamned Mexican murderer,' they'd say. 'You turned a goddamned Mexican murderer loose on us.'"

"What if you lose the trial? What if the jury turns him loose? They'll say, 'That's a hell of a prosecutor that can't even win a case where the killing was in cold blood in front of eight eyewitnesses and a deputy sheriff with his gun drawn.'"

"Well, the jury has to take some of the blame, too, if I lose. At least I didn't turn him loose. The jury turned him loose." And we talked some more but we got no place— no progress. Like talking to the goddamned Russians. And then I'd call him again.

"Oscar. Joe is going crazy. We'll never get this case over with. He ought to be set free. Dr. Karn says he'll revert back to a psychotic state if he's ever locked up again. We'll lose everything we've gained in all these years of treatment."

"I could never explain that to the people of Rawlins," Oscar said in his deep godly voice. "You don't know 'em, Gerry."

"How about going to 'em with a deal? We'll plead him guilty to manslaughter. You agree to a parole. State can have a little control over him then—keep the state's hands on old Joe so that nobody can claim he was turned loose on the street." There—I'd finally given Oscar the bottom line of my proposition. He'd see the logic of it. It took the risk out of a risky case for both of us.

"I'll let you know," he said. "Gotta talk to some people." And when I hadn't heard from him for weeks I called him up again.

"Oscar. Haven't heard from you for quite a spell. What's up in the Esquibel case?"

"Nothin'."

"Can we make a deal on old Joe?"

"I don't know, Gerry. It's a hard one. I talked to Mona Lee Murphy. She doesn't want me to make any deals. Wants the goddamned case prosecuted."

"How the hell can she have anything to say about this case? You don't represent her."

"Well, she's got the kids. Those Esquibel kids. She's got some rights, don't you think? A mother's got some rights."

"What kind of rights do you think she has? You represent the state of Wyoming, not her. She has no right to dictate justice here."

"She's entitled to some justice, Gerry. She's the victim."

"I don't know whether she's the victim or not. I think Sharon was the victim. Maybe the kids were the victims. But I don't know about Mona Lee Murphy. Anyway, why don't you ask her what she would think if you tried it and the jury turned him loose on the Rawlins streets again. Then it would be her fault that Joe was out on the street without any parole or any supervision or any damned thing. How would she feel about that?"

"She doesn't understand. She's just a mother. Mothers don't understand a damned thing. Joe killed her daughter right in front of her. That's all she understands. She wants him in the gas chamber."

"It's a little late for that. *Furman v. Georgia*, you know."

"Well, I don't know, Gerry. That's the way it is."

"You gonna let Mona Lee Murphy run your goddamned office?"

"She isn't running my office, Gerry. But I gotta listen to her. These are the people I live with. They're my neighbors. They elect me. I'm a public servant, if you know what I mean. You were a prosecutor once, Gerry, and I gotta talk to Ken Keldsen, my deputy—respect his judgment, you know," and that was it. He wouldn't budge. Like talking to a damned rock, that Oscar Hall. And when the trial was only about two weeks away, they sent Joe Esquibel to Casper—just turned him out of the hospital on what they called a "furlough." He would stay with some friends in town. That's how sane he was, they said, absolutely trustworthy, and I was getting desperate. It's not that I don't trust my own skills, or the jury—but I could lose the case. A fella can lose any case. You can be the most beautiful lawyer in the history of the world and lose a case. As a matter of fact, the more beautiful you get, the easier it usually is to lose, and I don't care how clear the evidence is, and I don't care if the evidence is stacked a hundred to one in your favor, you can still lose. And our case wasn't all good. I could hear the jury say, "Well, the damned shrinks never have been right yet. Why should they be right now?" The jury could say, "And a guy can't go around killin' a woman—cold blood, and then claim he's insane and bring in them shrinks to vouch for him. That's just so much bullshit. Gotta stop all that bullshit, all that killin'. It ain't safe to live here no more," the jury could say. And I was afraid. It's like going up to the damned crap table at Las Vegas and laying down the life of a man as the stake and then rolling the dice. Good crap shooter, that Spence, I thought, but it's crap shooting nonetheless. But Joe wanted to take his chance at being free, and I wanted him to be free without taking any chance.

"Well, Oscar, how are you doing with Ken Keldsen and Mona Lee Murphy and all the rest?" I asked on the telephone another day when the trial was just about on us, and I was working night and day getting ready.

"Not doin' so good, Gerry. But if Esquibel will plead guilty to second degree murder, and if Judge Forrister wants to parole him, well that's all right with me. The judge can parole if he wants, but I'm not making any recommendations. I'm not gonna go back home and have the people back there shove this case up my ass. Forrister is the judge. He's the one who's supposed to sentence people. Let him be the judge."

"Couldn't you give a little encouragement to Judge Forrister?"

"Well, hell, Gerry. Judge Armstrong is my judge here in Rawlins. You know that."

"Yeah, I know him. He's a friend of mine. Good man."

"Judge Armstrong and Mona Lee Murphy are friends, too, and he knew Sharon before she was shot, and he wants Esquibel brought to trial. He knows what we all know—that he's nothin' but a damned troublemaker, damned stud, got half the little girls in Rawlins pregnant. Turn him loose and it'll start all over again, and if he gets crossways with somebody he kills them. Armstrong says I better do my job, so I'd better do my job."

"It's none of Armstrong's damned business," I said.

"He thinks it is."

"You know it isn't. He sent the case over to Judge Forrister because he was disqualified. He's out of it!"

"He's still a citizen of Rawlins, isn't he, Gerry? And I gotta practice in his court for a long time to come. This is just one case. I work with Judge Armstrong every day."

"Goddamn it, everybody wants their pound of flesh—Mona Lee Murphy and I suppose the whole damned welfare office wants his ass, too!"

"You finally got it figured out, Gerry."

"Jesus," I said. "What shall we do?"

"Well, let's see what happens," Oscar said. "Maybe Judge Forrister will take the rap himself and parole him. He doesn't get elected over here in Rawlins. He could afford to help us a little bit. He can tell 'em all to go to hell over here," Oscar said. "Why don't you call Judge Forrister up and see what you can work out, but I won't say a damned thing one way or the other."

And so I called Judge Forrister. "I'm calling you, Judge, with Oscar Hall's permission," I said.

"And how are you today, Counselor?" he said in a melodious voice, like almost out of the opera. He was a reasonable man. I knew I could get the case settled. He knew Joe had been imprisoned in a place worse than any prison and that we'd already been through two trials. He himself had presided over the last trial. I told the judge that Dr. Karn had now taken the position that Joe was insane at the time of the shooting and that Joe had been on many furloughs from the hospital to go to Salt Lake to see his sister Elma, and his brother-in-law, Frank, described how Joe had grown, had become a sort of god-father to the helpless in the wards, and how he took care of people up there and had learned to love them. He was a changed man who cared about people now, I said, and I knew I had touched the judge. "And the bottom line, Judge Forrister, is that I'd like you to parole him, let us plead him and parole him. He's been there a long time. Suffered enough. Dr. Karn says if he goes to prison he'll go insane again, and I believe it." I did. Joe went bananas every time he was locked up, and the only way to cure him was to unlock him.

"What we do is play a filthy game." I went on with my argument to Judge Forrister. "Joe's punishment, if he loses to a jury, is not just to go to the penitentiary. His punishment is insanity because he gets psychotic every time he's locked up. So if he loses, when you sentence him to the penitentiary, you sentence him to a very cruel and unusual punishment—a sentence of psychosis."

"That's an interesting theory, Mr. Spence," the judge said. "Certainly is an interesting theory." He always enunciated well. "Now, how does Mr. Hall see this?"

"Well, Oscar says whatever you do is all right. Can't make any recommendation himself one way or the other. Lives up there, you know."

"Well," the judge said. "But you see, Mr. Spence, I am just the judge. I have no responsibility for the prosecution of this case. That rests with the state, with Mr. Hall, the county attorney."

"Yes, of course, Your Honor," I said.

"The prosecutorial responsibility belongs to him," the judge went on in slow, well-spoken words. "The exercise of prosecutorial discretion is always his discretion—not mine. I will not attempt to exercise it for him. When Mr. Hall is ready to perform his function, I will perform mine."

But I argued that nobody in Casper gave a damn about

poor Joe Esquibel anyway. Couldn't the judge please help us with our problem? Couldn't he please understand the pressure that was on old Oscar? But no. The judge was just as stubborn as Oscar was, I thought. When Oscar did his job the judge would do his. Finally I called Oscar back. "Oscar, come on over here. Let's go talk to the judge in person together."

"Okay," he said. Oscar drove over from Rawlins the next day and we got all settled down in Judge Forrister's chambers and Oscar and I were sitting there like friends, and we both smiled at the judge and he smiled back, and I knew, finally, that it would be all right. No one in Casper, Wyoming, cared in the slightest about this artless killing by this unknown Mexican seven years before. The people in Casper had their own problems and couldn't care less. But judges are responsible to a system, and the system needs them to care, to worry, and good judges do care what the people think. They serve the people. I remembered shaking ten thousand hands when I ran for Congress and I smiled until new wrinkles formed on my face, and I nodded my head in agreement until my cervical spine felt arthritic. I didn't know whether I was happy or even if I were real. I was only a politician. I didn't know what was good until I asked the people. I was plugged into their every vibration; every public whim real or imagined was my mandate, and I tested the air continually, neurotically, like a groundhog who could not see but could hear the closing hounds. I didn't recognize that people are more concerned with a Sunday football game or a beer after work than they are with what seem to be the crucial matters that keep politicians awake and twisting all night. Nobody really cares. Politicians don't know that. But more than that, judges are bound by the law.

"Well, Judge, here we are." I smiled. "We think we have an answer to the Esquibel case."

"That's fine, gentlemen, are you prepared to present it to me?"

"Yeah," I said to the judge. "Oscar and I have agreed to take a plea of manslaughter with parole. Joe is a changed man, you know, and if we put him in jail he goes insane. We'll lose seven years of hard work."

"Very well," the judge smiled back. "We'll call in the court reporter and you can dictate your agreement into the record."

"I'd like it just kinda informal," Oscar said.

"I never do anything in a criminal case without the record," Judge Forrister said.

Oscar hesitated for a long moment. Finally he said, "Well, I'll get too much heat at home. Can't live with it, Judge. They'll want my hide back there."

"I'm not going to exercise your judgment for you, Mr. Hall. You are the prosecutor in Carbon County, Wyoming, and unless you gentlemen wish to reduce your recommendations to writing in the record, we'll just have to let a jury decide it. Is there anything else, gentlemen?" He raised his eyebrows, smiled politely, and we left. We walked down the stairs together, Oscar and I.

"Oscar, what do you think?"

"To hell with it. Let the jury decide it."

"You're going to pass the buck to the jury then?" I said. "Poor jury, we're going to put Joe's life on the line, gamble his life so everybody can solve their own personal problems."

"That's what juries are for," he said, and that was that. And then I called Oscar one last time. "Oscar, I got a new idea. After all, the mess you're in is the fault of the state hospital. It isn't any fault of yours. It's the doctors at the hospital who can't make up their minds. First he's sane and then insane, and vice versa. They're the ones who change the diagnosis whenever they feel like it for whatever reason suits their fancy at the moment. Why don't you call a press conference? You can tell the press that the hospital has screwed things up so badly you have no choice but to offer a manslaughter plea with parole. Otherwise the jury would turn him loose on the streets, you could say. Ain't that a hell of an idea?"

"Well, I don't know why the judge won't take the bull by the horns. He's the judge, after all. I'm not. He sen-

tences the criminals, I don't. Judges never listen to prosecutors anyway. Do what they damned well please."

"What do you think? Shall I get the press together for
you—have a press conference?"

"I'll let you know," he said. I didn't hear from Oscar.

The trial was on us. I was up from the early hours of
the morning until late at night getting ready, and Joe was
at the office with us every day. The secretaries loved him.
It's the way he looks at you, one said. It's his animal
stature. Animal stature? What the hell is that? He's so
nice. He's just so sweet. He's the nicest, sweetest man.
We all just love him. Loovve! But Oscar didn't call back. I
called Oscar.

"Oscar. I thought you were going to call me back.
How're you doing? How's our Esquibel case?"

"Oh, I don't know, Gerry." He sounded discouraged.

"What do you think?"

"Doesn't look good, Gerry."

"You're not gonna make me try this against you again,
are you?"

"Looks like it," Oscar said.

"I don't want to try it again, Oscar. Let's settle this."

"Can't, Gerry. Mrs. Murphy wants me to try it."

"You still lettin' Mona Lee Murphy run your office?"

"Well, it isn't that."

"Jesus, Oscar!"

"Well, let's just try 'er," he said finally.

And all I could do was say, "Okay," kinda weak-like.
That's all I could say.

And now the gauntlet had been thrown down, and I
had no choice but to pick it up. Oscar and I were in the
pits again, in that place of blood and death, a place where
men die as surely as if the spear were run through their
hearts. We kill men with words now, the words of lawyers
in combat, the words of the jury in their verdicts, the
sentence of the judge—words. We wound with words in
the pit, in the courtroom, and men bleed there in their
souls, and some die there and there was no way out of
that place which was rife with the stink of death. "No way
out, Joe," I said. "We're gonna go to trial."

Joe Esquibel sat across from me in my office library in a neat baby blue sweater and a pair of slacks, and he looked like a college boy from Mexico City, or someplace.

"Where'd ya get the clothes?" I asked.

He just grinned. Pretty soon he said, "Got a friend."

"Who?"

"Girl friend," he said. "My girl." The words came out proudly.

"Well, Joe, the time has come. Let's talk about what's hard to talk about. Let's talk about Sharon."

"Well, it's easier to talk about her now, Mr. Spence. I loved her but she was runnin' around on me. I knew it. I saw her driving up and down the streets of Rawlins—she didn't know I saw her but I saw her. I can remember it. Couldn't used to remember it, but I do now."

"Yeah, good," I said, but that sounded like a motive for murder to me.

"And sometime she had the kids in the back seat and they was dirty, and she just kept drivin' around, and I'd try to stop her, and she wouldn't stop. She wanted a divorce. I didn't want her to leave me. I loved her. I loved them kids, and all," he said, looking up at the ceiling like he was thinking and feeling his way back into ancient times, and his forehead was wrinkled. "And she was driving me crazy," he said. "And she kept after me for a divorce. And I says no, and she says, 'It won't be no different after the divorce, Joe. I'll always love ya and I'll always be the same with ya. But I gotta have my freedom, and if ya love me, you'll give me my freedom.' And she kept after me, and finally she had old Bates draw up a paper where I wouldn't have to pay for them kids' support, and she kept on begging me and I signed it, and finally I let her go. Couldn't help it. Didn't have no money to fight it or nothin', and she was begging me, and finally I just let her go."

"What do you mean, you just let her go?" I asked.

"I never contested the divorce or nothin'," he said.

"Oh," I said.

"Yeah," Joe said. "And then she come to me one day

and says that the judge wouldn't give her no divorce unless I agreed to pay support for them kids. And I said, 'What about that paper?' and she said Judge Bentley wouldn't pay no attention to the paper. Bentley was the same judge as tried that rape case against me. Wouldn't go along with the paper, she said. Said I had to support them kids or he wouldn't give her no divorce. I remember all that now."

"Well, that's good," I said. "Then what happened?"

"Well, I figured that Bentley and her was after me. I figured they was gonna get me—they was gonna make me pay for them kids, and I couldn't get no jobs, and then they'd put me in jail like they did my old man. Put him in jail whenever he couldn't pay, and if they put me in jail, I'd go crazy, and maybe they'd put me in the pen, and they kill Mexicans up there in the pen," Joe said. "And I told her no I wasn't gonna sign no papers to pay for them kids. And then pretty soon she got a divorce anyway and the divorce papers read that I had to pay for them kids, and I never signed nothin' like that. They just did that to me. Lied to me and everything, and I didn't have no money to fight it."

"I see," I said, and I could see it. Sounded like he was laying out a really clean neat motive for first degree murder. I should have stopped him then and there with his story, but I had to hear the rest.

"And then she had the kids' names changed to hers— took my name off of my own kids. Took my name off of my own kids! And it drove me crazy. And I loved her, and she was leavin' me, and she was takin' my kids, and she took my name off 'em," and then he began to sob. "That's all a man's got, and my name was on my kids, and she took it off of 'em!"

I didn't say anything, just nodded so he knew I understood, and pretty soon when he had stopped sobbing he started talking again in a high tight whisper. "And I tried to see her, and she had that divorce, and she wouldn't even talk to me. She told me it was going to be the same, but it was different. She didn't tell me the truth, Mr. Spence, 'cause after the divorce it was different, and she wouldn't let me come see her, and she wouldn't let me see them kids. And I went up to her apartment, and I just walked up quiet to the door to hear if she was in there, and I could hear 'em!"

"Who?"

"I could hear her and that white guy."

"Who, Joe?"

"I could hear 'em . . . that white guy and her. I could hear 'em, you know. I could hear the sounds, ya know, like they was makin' it, and then I knocked on the door and she wouldn't open it—I can't remember much more. I seen it in my mind like when I was a kid—them white guys, and I could see 'em in the boxcar—like I seen in my dreams, and I drove around all night, I think. Can't remember. Had some beer. Can't remember no more."

"Do you remember chasing her into the welfare department?"

"No."

"Do you remember being in the welfare department?"

"No. No I don'," he said. "And that's the God's truth." And his face was as blank and flat as paper now, and almost white. "No, I don' remember none of it, Mr. Spence." And that was the story.

We spent days preparing for the trial—and nights. We talked about fear. That was the important issue left for us to deal with. He would be afraid in the courtroom. It was a fearful place and the stakes would be high, and it was all right to be afraid, but it would not be all right to let that secondary emotion, anger, take over. He must not be afraid of being afraid. If he got angry, the jury would find against him because we always destroy what we fear, and Joe's anger would make the jury afraid of him, and they would destroy him, I told him, destroy him out of their own fear. But if he could only share his fear with the jury in its pure form, and say, yes, I am afraid, yes, I'm afraid of all of you. I'm afraid you won't believe me. If he could be honest with the jury, they would be able to hear him and understand him, because the jury was afraid, too— for another reason. They were afraid they wouldn't be able to do their job right, that they couldn't find out the truth—afraid of the strange surroundings there in the courtroom and the strange proceedings and afraid of the lawyers and doctors and judges who talk in big words. They would understand Joe if he said simply that he was afraid. They would believe him because he would be speaking to them, to their own raw fear, because people believe what they have experienced themselves.

I turned Joe over to my partner, Bob Rose, for a good cross-examination, a tough, pushy, mean cross-examination, and Joe stood up to it. He was calm. I cross-examined him myself for countless hours and he never hollered back. He was gentle. He looked down just right, naturally, like a frightened man telling the truth, and finally the night before the trial I felt ready for the ordeal. But ready or not, we were going to trial in the morning.

30

IN THE MORNING Joe and I took an early walk from my office to the empty courtroom, claimed our same old table next to the jury box, and then I ran Joe through the script.

"Here's where the judge will sit. Remember the judge?" I pointed to the bench elevated a couple of feet above our heads. Judges sit in lofty places to do common things sometimes. They sit above us to look down on us so that we will respect them. I used to argue that we should respect men for what they do, not for how high they sit, but their high seat is only symbolic of the power of the judiciary. And it is a power that often confounds a good judge and makes him wonder and feel weak and wince from all that power, and a good judge isn't always sure how he should use his power. It is only the bad judge who never has any doubt, who by a mere nod of the head, or with a single word, can cause quaking in the very souls of frightened people who fight for their lives below him in the pit. It is easy to manipulate the frightened and injure the helpless.

"Judges are lonely people, Joe," I said. "I'll bet God is lonely, too, nobody to sit up there with Him and help Him make all those big decisions about so many important things, and nobody to talk to, or complain to, even if He has a bellyache. God and the judge are supposed to be wise and to love and to be just. Hell of a burden for one man to carry when he's up there sitting on that high chair all alone. Now listen, Joe. We came over here early this morning to learn what's going on in this courtroom together. You say you don't remember the judge?"

"No," he said flatly, looking out of place in that same brown business suit with the same white shirt and brown tie with the fleur-de-lis and the black shoes. But he'd lost some weight and he seemed even more handsome. Lost the baby fat around the cheeks, too, and as I looked at the man I thought it strange that his years of suffering in that strange hell hole full of raging witches and demented demons had not left him somehow marked on the outside. "Well, this judge is a decent man. He wants to do the right thing. You'll like him." I try to imagine Joe and Judge Forrister as pals, friends sharing each other's most intimate thoughts, strolling along together on a country road for a walk on a Sunday afternoon. "Now I don't want you to be afraid of the judge, understand? He's a man just like you—looks different, dresses differently, sits in a different place up there, but inside he's a little afraid too—just like you."

"How come?" Joe asked, looking puzzled.

"He's like all the rest of us—he wants to do his job right—wants to feel like there's been justice done in his courtroom, but sometimes a judge doesn't know how to get justice. Lawyers cause judges a lot of trouble, too, you know."

"Yeah?" he said, and he stood looking me in the face with his hands in his pockets.

"Yeah. Sometimes lawyers aren't prepared or don't know how to bring out the facts or how to cross-examine a witness, and sometimes they're too afraid, and the judge just has to sit up there and watch justice fail right in front of him, right in his own courtroom, and he doesn't know what to do about it, and it makes him feel sad," I said. "Sometimes he even gets angry about it."

"Oh."

"And so when you watch Judge Forrister you should watch him knowing that he's trying to do right—and that he has a little of the same fear in his belly that you have in yours this morning—and your fear is about the same thing—you both are afraid of the same thing."

"Yeah?" Joe asked.

"You're both afraid you won't get justice in this case."

"That's right," Joe said, and he smiled a little.

"Now the jury sits over there, and the jurors want the same thing as you and the judge want, and they're afraid, too. They're just ordinary people. They don't know any fancy things about law, and they haven't done this jury work before. Think how it would be for you to sit over there in the jury box in a murder case. A man killed his wife. Frightful thing. Jurors have never seen a man who killed another human being before. Scare a fella half to death just to look at such a person—and the lawyers all talkin' and squawkin' and hollerin' and making strange legal noises—and the judge lookin' down at ya so damn solemnly, talkin' legal talk too, sounds like monkey-talk, and the juror has sworn to do justice, raised his hand and took an oath that he would follow the law, and he's afraid he can't even understand what the law is, much less follow it, and he's sitting there with eleven others just like him who don't know very much either, and they're all scared and pretty confused, but they want to do the right thing. They want justice in this case, too. And so when you're feeling a little frightened down in your belly, just look over at the twelve folks on the jury and you'll know that behind their faces, which are just masks, because we all wear our own masks, don't we, Joe?—well, when you look at their faces you'll know that behind their masks they're just like you, and they want the same thing."

"Well, I never thought of that," Joe said. "I been scared of them juries—them white guys you know—I figure them white guys all hate me," he said.

"Well, you learned up at the hospital that a lot of those white guys loved you and needed you, didn't you?"

"Yeah," he said, and his face looked soft and gentle. I'd never seen it like that before.

"There won't be any Mexican-Americans on the jury, Joe. Just aren't hardly any around Casper." Joe didn't answer. "And you'll sit over there on the witness stand.

Come on, let's see how it feels." I started over to the chair, which was also elevated a little off the floor, one step up, but Joe didn't follow me.

"Come on, Joe. I want you to sit in it so you're not afraid of it—just get the feel of it a little bit. This isn't the electric chair. They don't strap a fella in this thing," I said. Joe moved with hesitancy at first and then suddenly he charged into the chair and plunked himself down.

"How's it feel?"

"Little cold," he said. "Never have liked it up here. Been here before."

"Well, you see, some people call it the 'hot seat,' but it's okay. And now I want you to look up where the judge will be. Yeah, that's right, and now over where the jury is. Yeah. Now when I say to you, 'Tell the ladies and gentlemen of the jury about this or that—whatever,' I want ya to look over at the jury, not me—at them—and give your answer to the jury. Talk to 'em. They're just folks, plain folks like you and me, and they want somebody to talk to 'em, and they'll understand ya if you look 'em in the eyes and give 'em just plain honest answers. Nothing fancy. Nothing angry. Nothing bitter or mean. Just plain decent talk—they'll be able to hear ya," I said. "And just think to yourself that they're the white folks up at the state hospital who needed you—needed your help—and these folks will need your help, too. They need you to help them understand your case."

"Okay," he said as if he understood.

"Now just sit there a minute," I said. I moved over to Oscar Hall's table. "Now this is where Oscar Hall and Ken Keldsen sit. They'll try to get you."

"Yeah," Joe said.

"They're the enemy."

"Yeah, I know."

"Now a fella can do one of a couple of things about his enemies. A fella can hate 'em. That's easy. But the jury doesn't hate Mr. Hall. He represents the people of the state. He's an elected official. They want to trust him and believe him, and they don't hate him. So if you hate him when the jury doesn't hate him we're in trouble. Understand why?"

"Yeah."

"Tell me why," I said. Joe was sitting in the witness stand still looking a little afraid.

"Well, if I get mad at them guys' friend, well, they'll be mad at me."

"Right, and the jury's going to like you, too, because you're gonna be a nice guy, and you're going to help 'em, and we all like people who help us, so if Oscar Hall is mean to you, well, that's great for us. Do you know why?"

"Yeah," Joe said again as if he was enjoying school. "Because if he gets mean with me the jury will stop liking him, and we'll win."

"Well, I'll be damned," I said in mock surprise. "I'll be damned if you aren't a better psychiatrist than old Pace himself," I laughed. And then Joe laughed a little bit, too.

"Yeah," Joe said proudly. "A guy learns quite a bit in six years up there in that hospital."

"And so it's easy. The meaner he gets the nicer you get, and the nicer he gets, then the nicer you get, too, until you're the nicest guy in the courtroom." Suddenly I walked up to Joe Esquibel and looked him in the eye and he was wondering what I was going to say, and suddenly I said it. "Do you believe in Christ?" Joe looked surprised and nodded, "Yes."

"Well, Christ said, 'Love your enemies,' didn't He?"

"Yeah."

"Well, Christ wasn't any dummy. Christ was a man just like you in a lots of ways," I said. My God, I was preaching a sermon in this empty courtroom to a Mexican killer, and my mother's face came to my mind, and I just let her stay there. I said, "Christ was poor like you, and powerless. The Romans and the old Jewish establishment held all the power in those days, and Christ was a member of a minority group and He had no political power at all and like you, my friend, Christ knew a secret—and do you want to know what His secret was?"

"Yeah," Joe said, and his eyes were bright, and he looked alive and ready.

"His secret was that there is huge power in love—
'Love your enemies,' He said. And, Joe, if you want
power in this courtroom, then love your enemy."

"Yeah," Joe said. "But they crucified Christ."

"You'll do all right," I said, and I grinned and Joe
grinned back. "They ain't gonna crucify us. Understand?" I said.

"Yeah," Joe said. And I thought he believed it. He was
ready. Pretty soon Raymond got there and then John
Ackerman, who had passed the bar and was already a
new lawyer, and the courtroom was filling up again with
prospective jurors, and in a few minutes we would begin
the selection of a jury in this case of murder.

Judge Forrister came in and everybody rose, and there
was a soft thunder as the people stood and a soft thunder
again as they sat down, and then Ken Keldsen began his
questions of the first twelve whose names had been
drawn from the same tin box by the clerk. The first lady
that Ken Keldsen spoke to looked at Keldsen seriously
through thick glasses. She said, "I have never committed
a crime," and she seemed embarrassed, "but I know that
to kill somebody you would have to be pretty close to the
edge." She looked down and fidgeted nervously with her
hands.

"And so you'd allow these personal feelings of yours to
interfere with your verdict?" Keldsen asked. He had
thick glasses of his own. "I probably would," the lady said
apologetically.

"Challenge this juror for cause," Keldsen announced
to the court. But I jumped up before the court could rule.
"May I ask a question or two, Your Honor?"

"Yes, of course," Judge Forrister said with a pleasant
smile.

"One of the court's instructions in the case will be to
the effect that if Joe was insane at the time of the shooting you must acquit him. Could you follow the law in that
regard?"

"Yes. I do feel he has to be temporarily insane to have
killed somebody—if he did," she added.

"So what you're trying to explain to us then is that

you'll make the state prove Joe Esquibel was perfectly sane at the time, isn't that true?" And she said yes, and I smiled at her, but she didn't know if she was supposed to smile back or not. "You understand there are other people in this courtroom who will argue the other side of this case from the one you and I have taken—they'll say, 'I don't think people ought to get away with murder by claiming they're insane.' "

"Yes, I know some say that."

"And so what we're really saying here is you'll go into the jury box with your own experiences and listen to the evidence and apply the court's instructions, and if the state has carried its burden, so be it, and if the state hasn't, so be it also?"

"Yes," she said. And I had saved a juror from a challenge for the moment, but Ken Keldsen questioned her further and this small woman said she was sure that this case would make a nervous wreck of her and that she didn't think she could stand being cooped up for ten days with her three kids at home, and besides she didn't believe in capital punishment, and, "I think it's wrong for one man to sit in judgment of another. Morally, I could not deliver a verdict that would involve the death penalty."

"Well," Ken Keldsen began, "this case . . ."

"Just a minute," I interrupted. "May we approach the bench, Your Honor?" The judge summoned us up. At the bench we whispered to the court and the court reporter was there, too, taking it all down for posterity and for the appeal. I looked up at the judge. "Mr. Keldsen is about to tell the jury that this isn't a death penalty case." I turned to Keldsen. "That's what you were about to say in front of this whole jury, isn't it?"

"Well . . ."

"Are you or aren't you going to seek the death penalty?"

"Well, since *Furman v. Georgia* we really can't. We're not asking for the death penalty."

I turned to the reporter. "Those are life and death words, Mr. Reporter. Do you have them down?"

"Yes," the reporter nodded.

"And now, you know and I know and His Honor knows that it is improper in a non-capital case to mention anything about penalty to the jury."

"All I wanted to do was to tell this jury that the death penalty isn't involved."

"That's no more relevant and proper to say than it is for me to discuss the other side of the penalty issue—to say to the jury, 'Could you find the defendant guilty if you knew he would have to spend the rest of his life as a madman in a horrid, cruel, dark place called the penitentiary?' "

"Gentlemen," the judge began, with his smile firmly planted, "can't we proceed without getting into the issue of penalty?"

"All right," Keldsen said. I walked back to the defense table and the court called a recess.

"What was that all about?" Raymond asked.

"Maybe we got it set up now so the jury will think this is a death penalty case," I said.

"How'd you do that?" John Ackerman asked.

"Well, lookee here." I put a smart-aleck grin on my face. "The state can't qualify the jury for the death penalty, and so they can't get jurors off who are against the death penalty because this isn't a death penalty case. So we're gonna get some jurors on this jury who wouldn't give the death penalty, right?"

"Right," Ackerman said.

"And up at the bench Keldsen agreed not to talk about the death penalty."

"Yeah," John said.

"And now the jury may go out thinking this is a death penalty case, and the people on the jury who are against the death penalty, thinking it's a death penalty case, may hang the jury, or they may even talk the rest of the jury into an acquittal."

"Yeah!" John Ackerman said.

"It's too good to last," Raymond said.

After the recess Keldsen went on with his questioning. He found a juror who had sat on a drug case. The verdict was "not guilty," and Keldsen made a note of that on his chart where he was keeping track of the jurors' answers. He found a juror who was employed at a Casper bank and when Keldsen asked the woman if there was any reason why she couldn't be fair and impartial in this case, she said, "No, not really," which meant to me, no, and yes, and I made a note on my chart. Keldsen wanted to know if any jurors or their family had epilepsy, and then he asked, "What do you think of the defense of insanity?"

"I think it is quite possible," one juror said. High school teacher. Math. I made a note. Good.

"And if the court tells you that a test for legal insanity as a defense is different from medical insanity . . ."

"Just a minute, please, Mr. Keldsen," I objected. "The court isn't going to give such an instruction. That statement is improper and counsel knows it."

"Well, gentlemen, let's stay away from the court's instructions, please," Judge Forrister said.

Keldsen knew Dr. Karn was going to say Joe was psychotic at the time he shot Sharon, and he was trying to set the jury up for his argument that would go like this: "The mere fact that Dr. Karn says Joe was psychotic, which is a medical term, hasn't anything to do with this case. Esquibel wasn't insane according to the legal test for insanity. The legal test for insanity is different from the medical definition . . ." and off he'd go. I got him stopped for a while, but you could see the state's theory building already.

Then one juror said his brother-in-law had been treated by a psychiatrist seven years before, and one poor old lady had a back injury and she said she hurt just sitting there, and the lawyers both showed their compassion and respect for the aged and the injured and agreed she could be excused, and the judge let her go. Then Keldsen began questioning a Mexican-American cement finisher with five kids who said he had trouble with the English language, but his conversation with Keldsen was clear and precise, with a little Spanish accent. He lived in the white community, worked subcontracts under white contractors, and was a member of the Casper Jaycees. I wrote "strike him" on my notebook. Wanted to be white. Then there was a special deputy sheriff, and we argued he was disqualified, and the court excused him. After a recess, Oscar Hall took over the questioning, and I wondered why, but I didn't object, and about the first thing he said was, "Now you know the state isn't asking for the death penalty here."

"Just a minute, please," I said, jumping up, but what could I do? He'd said it already, and you can't unring the bell, as they say.

"Well, Mr. Spence." His Honor looked at me, his eyebrows raised, waiting for my objection. What could I say? Should I object because Oscar Hall told the jury the truth? There were more narrow, technical grounds for an objection, but there was nothing to be gained, maybe something to be lost. Oscar beat me. I made a motion with my hand for Oscar to proceed and sat down. He asked a few more questions, just enough, I thought, so that it wasn't apparent as to why he had taken over the questioning, and then he passed the jury for cause and it was my turn to question them.

"Ladies and gentlemen," I began. "This is our client, Joe Esquibel. Come up here, Joe." Joe got up and walked to my side. He walked with a certain self-conscious dignity up to my side, and I put my arm around him. "He is a human being, like you and me. He has the same rights as we do under the Constitution, and the purpose of my questioning here this morning will be to help us decide who should sit on this jury so that Joe gets a fair trial, and so his constitutional rights are protected." And then I motioned for Joe to go sit down. "If Joe's constitutional rights are protected, you will acquit Joe Esquibel," I said. "For seven years now we have represented Joe Esquibel, Raymond Whitaker and John Ackerman and I," and I motioned to Raymond Whitaker, who stood up, too, and then to John Ackerman, who rose and gave a little bow, "and two prior juries of folks just like yourselves have each heard this evidence on two separate occasions before, and each time they have found that Joe couldn't even be tried for murder then because, on each of those two occasions he was insane. Now after almost seven years of incarceration at the state mental hospital, he has finally regained his sanity, and he must stand trial for murder, and the question you must decide in this case is this: 'Was Joe Esquibel insane also at the time he killed his wife?' " Twelve prospective jurors sat in the jury box listening to me, and they had their arms folded and their legs crossed. They weren't going to be taken in. "How many of you have ever looked at a man who is an admitted killer?" Nobody raised a hand.

"Take a look at Joe Esquibel sitting here." I walked over and put my arm on Joe's shoulder. "Look at this man," I said. He looked peaceful, humble, a little frightened, and I went on, "Are any of you so frightened of him that you couldn't try this case fairly?" Nobody answered. I stepped back and looked at Joe myself. You had to like him. A juror raised his hand. "I think it would bother me a lot. I'd hate to convict him."

"Thank you," I said. "How would you feel about letting Joe go after all of these years?"

"He looks kind of sick, and I don't know . . ." Looked sick and you can't turn a sick person loose on the streets or he'll kill again, that was the point.

"Well, sir," I said to the juror. "Well, sir, we only hold people accountable for their acts who can choose between right and wrong. Do you think that is a just rule?"

The juror began as if he were going to say something profound. "If a man is sick . . . that sickness has got to be different than ordinary sickness."

"Do you think that someone who is mentally sick should be *punished* for his sickness?"

"Well . . ."

"By that I mean, if a man had an epileptic fit, a sickness that was not his fault, and during his seizure he hurt or even killed somebody, do you think he should be put in jail or charged with murder?"

"No."

"Why not?"

"Because he didn't mean to, he couldn't help it."

"Oh," I said. "That's what the law calls 'intent.' Do you think a person should have an intent to kill before he is found guilty of murder?"

"Yes, of course."

"Yes, you are right," I said. "If that weren't true, if you didn't have to have an intent to kill before it's murder, everyone who suffers the horrid misfortune of having killed accidentally would be considered a murderer in this society, and that wouldn't be right, would it?"

"No," the juror said.

"And that means we don't punish people for murder who don't intend to do an evil act—who didn't intend to kill. Isn't that true?"

"That's right."

"Yes," I said, "and if one is so mentally sick that one doesn't know what he is doing, doesn't have an intent, doesn't know the difference between right or wrong, then do you think that that person should be punished for being sick?"

"No. But how do we know that he isn't sick now?" the juror asked.

"Dr. Karn at the state hospital has had this man under his care for over six years now—says he's all right now. Says he can stand trial. He'll be here to testify. You can hear him yourself."

"Oh," the juror said. "Well, anybody who does things like that has got to be sick, don't they?" The juror had a troubled look on his face. Several of the other jurors nodded.

"I sort of agree with you. But Mr. Hall says Joe killed with malice, with an evil intent to kill, that Joe knew what he was doing, and we say he had no intent at all, evil or otherwise, that he didn't know what he was doing because he was too sick mentally to form an intent. In the criminal law, remember, we hold people accountable for their acts only if they are sane—only if they know the difference between right and wrong—only if they have an intent. Do you think that is a fair law?"

"Yes."

"And do you believe we should be a society of law and

order?" Law and order? The defense asking law and order questions?

"Yes."

"And, Mrs. Bannister." I turned to a tall handsome black woman who was well educated and a leader in her community, one of the few blacks in Wyoming. How her name got into that jury box in the first place I'll never know, the odds being what they were, and how her name was picked out of the box as one of the first twelve, I'll never know either. "You know we have a right to expect that the law will protect us, don't you?"

"Yes," she said in a rich deep voice.

"And as a member of a minority race, you know that sometimes it is hard to get protection from the law in an all-white society, isn't that true?"

"That's true."

Now I turned to the whole panel.

"I don't think it is fair for me to ask you any questions that I wouldn't answer myself first. So I am going to do that. 'Mr. Spence, are you prejudiced against minorities?' Yes, I'd have to say. I don't know why. Don't want to be prejudiced. Try not to be—but I'd honestly have to say that I am prejudiced sometimes. Now I want to ask the same question of you," I said to the jury. "Is there anybody else here who sometimes feels prejudiced like I do?"

Several jurors timidly raised their hands.

"I do," a lady said in a quiet voice.

"Who else?" I asked. Several other hands went up. I said their names, Mrs. Russell, Mrs. Stroh. "See, I am making little notes about all of us. Mrs. Smith . . ."

Mrs. Connell said, "I'm not prejudiced according to color. It's just that some folks . . ."

"Some folks turn you off?" I interrupted.

"Yeah."

"Me, too."

"I'm not prejudiced according to race. But some people . . . it's what they do."

"Thank you," I said. "Now, Mrs. Fuhrer, and Mrs. Earp, and Mrs. Snyder and Mrs. Bauer and Mrs. Schroeder—none of you is prejudiced like I am sometimes, is that right?" They didn't answer. "Would any of you adopt a Mexican-American child?"

"I haven't, but I would," one of the women said.

"Have any of you ever known a Mexican-American well enough to touch him?" I went over and put my arm on Joe Esquibel's shoulder again. One lady said, "My contact with Mexican people has been as a teacher in Head Start."

"Has that experience helped you overcome any prejudices you might have otherwise had?"

"Guess so. They're as good and as important as others," she said.

And then an attractive woman on the front left-hand corner volunteered, "My husband is a minister, and in our church in Montana we had a representative from about every nationality there was, and we all got along very well."

"Well," I smiled. "That's nice. I remember a song in somebody's Sunday school, 'Red and yellow, black and white, all are perfect in His sight . . .'"

"Yes," she smiled back sweetly. We enjoyed it. I made a note.

"All right, do any of you folks feel there is a difference in the intelligence of the races?"

"No," somebody said. "But there is a difference in the environment."

"Yes, you will hear a good deal about that during this trial. How many of you think that differences in environment are important?" Several jurors raised their hands. I made notes.

"All right. Among those of you who aren't prejudiced, how many of you would honestly object if your daughter married a Mexican?" No response. I waited until the silence got heavy. And I looked the jurors in the eyes. Looked from eyes to eyes. "None of you would object?" I waited. "Now . . . really?" And I waited some more. Finally one of the ladies raised her hand timidly. "Thank you," I said. "That took courage. Most of us can't deal with our prejudices very well."

Another juror spoke up. "I think it depends on the boy. Is he educated? What has he done with his life? It takes an education to make a living nowadays," she said very sternly, frowning.

Mrs. Bannister said, "I would object to the marriage, not because of race but because of society—because every marriage is hard enough as it is without adding the obstacles society sets up in a mixed marriage."

"Would any of you lend money to a Mexican-American?"

"Depends on how much money," one of the young men said and he laughed, and the pretty young woman in the middle of the front row laughed. I made notes.

Another woman juror said, "I have an Eskimo baby-sitter, and I have Mexicans next door to me. Depends on who they are and what their attitude is. You can't dislike 'em just for no reason."

"Let me give you some reasons," I said. "Joe's wife, whom he killed, was white. He just shot her one morning in the presence of a whole roomful of people. Does that change any of your minds on the issue of prejudice—to just shoot a white woman?"

A juror: "Well, it doesn't make no difference if she is white or Mexican—still his wife all the same."

Then I said, "But everywhere I go I hear people imply that it's all right if a damned Mexican kills one of his own —just one less damned Mexican. But if he kills a white woman—that's something else again. What do you think of that?"

"Killing one of their own is as bad as killing one of the others, I think." And other jurors were nodding.

"Do any of you think guilty people escape the law too often by pleading insanity?" There it was. There was the question.

A juror: "I think that happens a lot."

Another juror: "Me, too."

"Who else?" I asked.

"I think it's the easiest way out," and a couple more jurors nodded in agreement.

"And so most of you think that sometimes people escape the law by pleading insanity, isn't that true?"

"You bet," the young man in front said.

Another juror: "Doesn't somebody have to prove it?"

"Yes," I said. "In this country the state has to prove its case beyond a reasonable doubt. The state must prove he was sane at the time of the killing. Do you think that's fair?"

"Yes," a juror said. "Yes," others nodded.

And I said, "Right now what I want to talk about is whether any of you, as you sit here right now, have come to the conclusion that Joe Esquibel is trying to escape a murder charge by claiming he was insane." There was no response.

"How can I defend him if his only defense is that he was insane, and we all believe that that is the defense of a guilty man trying to escape? How can I defend him?" And then there was a longer silence. And that is all I needed to say.

There are those who say I try to prejudice the jurors during jury selection, but I say I only try to prejudice them against their own prejudices. I say, if the jurors are prejudiced into believing that the defendant is innocent before they hear any evidence, then they are only delivering to the defendant that which is his natural and constitutional entitlement—the presumption of innocence, and all attorneys and all courts should encourage attorneys to prejudice juries in favor of every accused, in favor of the presumption of innocence, which is meant to shield every person accused of a crime. But juries always believe the accused to be guilty at the outset of every trial. He must be guilty, they say. The state wouldn't have charged the bugger if he wasn't guilty. Where there's smoke there's fire, ain't there? Let's see what some smart shyster's gonna come up with in this case—waste a man's time. Gotta stop this criminal element, this crime in the streets. Gotta stop 'er and start puttin' a few of them criminals away. It's the duty of the citizen.

I turned to the preacher's wife in the front row. "What's the last book you read?"

"The Answer Is God, the story of Roy Rogers and Dale Evans." Oh, God! I thought, with all due respect to Roy Rogers and Dale Evans. How could I explain this case to her? Mrs. Bannister said she had just read *Chariots of the Gods,* and she had enjoyed it. And she liked science fiction and history. Another woman said she had read *All of My Children,* a book about teenagers, and some had not read any books at all—most, in fact. I made notes.

"Who wants off the jury?" I asked. Several raised their hand. "Why?"

"I can't stand this kind of case—can't stand sitting here in judgment on another man," a frightened-looking man in the back said very softly. I made a note. Those who want to pass judgment on others too often need the power, and those who need the power ought not to be trusted with it. We should never let our judges and our politicians seek office. Too many need the power or else they wouldn't ask for it, beg for it, fight and struggle so for it, and even lie for it, and all but die for it—give it all up for it, sell it all out for it. We should draft our judges from qualified trial lawyers, and we should draft our politicians too—the way we were drafting this jury—people hauled in off the streets, from out of their homes and off their jobs who did not choose to be here—who did not ask for this power over their fellow man, who are only forced to do so as a patriotic duty in order to make the system work. You can never fully trust people who want power over others. Why do they need power?

"How many of you know a psychiatrist or a psychologist?"

"I know Dr. Browning," one of the women said.

Another juror said, "My children were tested by a psychiatrist."

Another said, "My sister had a nervous breakdown. She went to a psychiatrist."

Another said, "My sister-in-law had temper tantrums. She'd be okay a day or two and then suddenly she'd get wild-eyed. Sent her to a psychiatrist." I was making my notes. I wanted those who had experience with mental illness, who knew it was real. No person can understand what he or she has not experienced.

"Do any of you believe that if you are once mentally ill you can never get well again?" Once a skitz always a skitz.

"I would say they couldn't," the good-looking young man in the front row said.

Another: "I think mental illness is like any other illness. You can get over it, if you try."

Another: "Yes, but maybe you can get over it and then get it again like malaria comes back, or something, and what if we find he was insane and turn him loose and then he kills again?"

I said, "There's no way out for Joe, here, is there? I mean, if Joe was sane when he shot his wife, well, then he's guilty of murder. But if he wasn't sane when he shot her, you'll have to find him guilty anyway because if you don't he might go insane again and kill somebody else, and a person wouldn't want that on his conscience, would he? So, that's really the problem here, isn't it?" And there was a lot of nodding in the jury box, and a long silence in the courtroom. "Maybe I should just deliver him over to the sheriff. Nothing much we can do, is there? I mean, you have to find him guilty whether he's guilty or not, isn't that true?"

"I think he's entitled to a fair trial," one said.

"Well, okay," I said. "Let's make sure we give him a fair trial before we find him guilty of murder. That way we'll all feel better, won't we? Don't you agree that you're going to have to find Joe guilty of murder because if you don't there's the possibility he might go insane again and then kill again?"

"No," a juror in the front row said emphatically. He had been sort of quiet through all of this. "I don't think that's right," he said.

"How many of you agree with this gentleman?"

"I do," a woman said. And then a couple of other jurors nodded, too, and some looked skeptical and were wondering what was happening.

"You see," I said, "if we have to find Joe guilty whether

he was insane or not, then he's been deprived of his lawful defense. You would be finding an innocent man guilty. How many of you would like to find an innocent man guilty?" Nobody said anything. "Well, how many of you would listen to the psychiatrists who will testify in this case to find out for yourself whether Joe will likely kill again?" One or two raised their hands. Some refused to respond. "It's been seven years since Joe shot his wife. Would any of you leave room for the proposition that some people, maybe even Joe Esquibel, can be cured of their insanity in seven years?" A couple of jurors nodded. I made notes.

"What happens to Joe after this trial if he is found sane is this: He'll be ordered back to the state hospital until the state hospital certifies to Judge Forrister that Joe is a fit and proper person to release, and the judge orders his release. Would you trust His Honor's decision in that matter?" I asked.

"Yes," one said. Yes, most of the others nodded. And then I went over to Joe and put my arm around him again and I whispered in his ear. "Joe, I want you to look at each juror with me—look each one of them in the eyes. And then I'll look at you, and you nod yes. Nod yes on every one of them as we go down the line. I want these jurors to feel you personally approve of each of them, that you personally selected each of them—understand?"

"Yeah," he whispered back.

"It's because if a person accepts another person they are more likely to accept you back. Understand, Joe?"

"Yeah," he said. And then I looked at the first juror in the back row on the left-hand side, and Joe looked, too, and Joe nodded yes, and we looked at the next one, looked her in the eye, and Joe nodded yes again, and we went through all twelve of them just that way. Then I walked over to Raymond. Raymond nodded yes, and I talked to John and John nodded yes, and after all of that I said, "Your Honor, we pass this jury for cause." Next both sides, first one side and then the other, exercised what the law refers to as "peremptory challenges," which means a challenge that can be made without any cause.

Don't like the way he parts his hair. I'll challenge him.
Don't like the way the prissy little lady in the front answers my questions. Kick her off with a peremptory challenge. Each side has ten challenges, and I took off the
woman who loved Roy Rogers and Dale Evans and those
who wanted to stay on the jury, no matter what, because
they needed the power. I took off those who would not
admit their own prejudices, and those who sounded too
self-righteous and pious because those who do not understand their own weaknesses can never understand anyone
else's. I took off the one sexy cuddly young woman who
sat in front and smiled and wiggled, and I took off the
two men who paid attention to her because they were like
young bulls, and would probably fight each other for
dominance over this small herd, this jury, and I am a bull,
and so is Joe. It is hard to feel truth when the gonads are
grinding. The issue of animal sex, of this man and woman
thing, which exists in every group of people, also exists in
a jury, and the tensions cross from juror to juror and
from juror to attorney and from juror to defendant, and
they are powerful tensions, and explosive, and they are
unpredictable and uncontrollable, and I eliminated them
as well as I could with my challenges.

And I struck off the jury those who said they just
wanted to help people. Professional people-helpers
sometimes don't like people very much. What they don't
like about themselves is that they don't like people, but
when they hear themselves say they want to help people,
well, they feel better. And then they put people in prison
to help them, put them in there for their own good, these
people-helpers do. It is the father whipping the child to
help him, and the child grows up and becomes a people-
helper, too.

Oscar Hall struck Mrs. Bannister and the cement finisher, and he helped me get off the people-helpers because he believed they would actually help Joe Esquibel,
and before the day was over we had a jury, twelve good
men and women true, as they say, sworn "to truly try the
issues and to render a true verdict," whatever that is, so
help them God.

Oscar Hall stood up to make his opening statement to the jury. He brought up a few notes, and as he began, he sounded more like God than Moses this time. His voice got deeper, as if he were making proclamations, and then his voice rose, like one out of the wilderness, prophesying, and then it told of the horror of murder—of a killing in cold blood, of a killing of this poor little girl, and the need now, the crying need for justice, and already justice had been delayed too long, these seven years, but the time for justice had finally arrived. The defendant was as sane then as he is now, and the jury already knew what it needed to know about this case, nothing much more, that this man killed his wife, admitted that he killed her, this little girl, this little Sharon, and he killed her in cold blood to solve his problems as he always solved his problems, with violence. And it was finally time for justice. And then I talked to the jury for a long time, about the two previous trials and how other jurors like them had found that Joe Esquibel was insane, and now that Joe had recovered he had to stand trial for that terrible tragedy which came out of his nightmares, out of the nightmares of his insanity, and Dr. Karn, the highest official at the state hospital, the superintendent himself, would tell the jury that Joe Esquibel was insane then and that he had fully recovered his sanity. Now, after seven years of hell, it was time to set Joe Esquibel free. He had suffered enough. He was innocent under the law. He had no intent to kill. He was innocent by reason of insanity.

The state's first witness was the mother, Mona Lee Murphy.

31

MONA LEE MURPHY, the mother of Sharon, was a serious-looking woman, about fifty, I suppose, still trim, no gray in her blond hair, but with a hint of peroxide where it was a little too yellow. Her once plain face was now marked with the lines of her life, which spoke of her life, a better face now I thought, pulled tight at the cheek and loose at the jaw. She had heavy creases that marked where her young cheeks had once bloomed. There were multiple small lines at the edges of her eyes, too, and two frown wrinkles in the center of her forehead, and there were numerous parallel lines across her forehead, like the hash marks on a sergeant's arm. But her eyes were tired and she wore rimless glasses now, which sat on a straight nose that no longer looked so plain on her face. She didn't look altogether like a grandmother, and she had a certain dignity about her, almost a royal bearing, which belied the fact that she still labored loyally among the poor and the pitied in the Welfare Department of Carbon County, Wyoming. She wore a black skirt and what appeared to be an expensive raspberry-colored sweater buttoned up the front with silver buttons, and underneath she had a high-collared white blouse. She walked with a quick, straight walk to the witness chair, took one step up, and sat down, as if she had been there many times. She smiled at no one, looked at no one in particular, and although she glanced at me in the sweep of her eyes, as if I were a table lamp or something, she gave me no sign of recognition, and she looked over at the prosecutor in the same way, with an expressionless face.

I turned to Joe. The jury was looking at Joe, too. They already knew who she was. Anybody could have told. She was the mother. She was the mother sitting in the room with her child's killer. She didn't look at Joe Esquibel. One could have expected her to explode off the witness chair, to run screaming to Joe's table after all of these pent-up years and strike him, fist on fist, tiny soft fists flying at his face, or to suddenly reach into her black purse on her lap, which she held onto with both hands, pull out a small pistol, walk quickly to Joe, and before he could react, before anyone could realize what was happening, point the pistol between his eyes, as Joe had done to her daughter, and pull the trigger. She would have said that that would be justice, because there is no justice in this place of justice.

It had taken seven years to bring this man to trial, and she had lived with him every day because every day she could see the face of this man on the faces of his innocent children. She had gone into their rooms many times at night and had seen those faces framed against the white sheets, and then sometimes the face of Sharon appeared, coming magically over those baby faces, and she would catch herself, and could actually hear herself gasp, and she would grab her own throat, and then she would shake one of the children as if by waking a child she would awaken from her own nightmare, and the child would say, "What, Grandma?" and Mona Lee Murphy would lean down to the baby's face and kiss the child, tears coming to her eyes, replacing the terror, and she would whisper, "Are you all right, darling?" And the child would nod and bury her face in the pillow. But it was also during these times that certain lines had formed on Mona Lee's face that told of this woman's sorrow, and now she had tried to paint over them.

I watched the jury as Oscar Hall began to question Mona Lee Murphy, first asking her who she was and what her relationship was to Sharon Murphy, and what did she do? But the faces of the jury were mostly passive, because faces that do not have to move in speech can make better masks over the feelings the masks hide, but when the words come crying out of the mouth, the feelings form freely on the flesh of the face, and the face is easy to read. The jury's faces were locked to the face of Mona Lee Murphy, which moved only slightly as she spoke, and at first she recited the answers practically without any expression, and her answers were direct and precise: Sharon was born in 1942, graduated from high school in 1960, started dating Joe Esquibel in 1961. When Mona Lee said the word "Esquibel" her mouth moved up in a false smile, and it struggled there for a moment against her feeling for the man. She looked blindly in his direction, but she could not bring herself to look right at him, and then her face grew grotesque for that brief moment and became immobile again, and even as she began to tell the story of her daughter and Joe Esquibel the mask held firm against her feelings underneath.

"Yes," she said. She was very upset over her daughter's having dated Joe Esquibel. And she was afraid something terrible would happen to Sharon, who was only nineteen then.

"Did you voice an objection to Sharon about this?" Oscar Hall asked with his godly sounds, which were in contrast to the clear emotionless words coming from the lips of Mona Lee Murphy.

"Yes, I did. Many times," she said, as if she were merely reciting facts and figures.

"When did you first come face to face with Joe Esquibel?"

Her mask tightened and her lips narrowed for a moment, but the words sounded the same. It was in the hospital when the first baby was born. That was in January of 1963, she said. She had forgotten her own history with Joe, of the trip taking the children to the orphanage when Joe was only ten, and she had forgotten all the rest that was in the records, because to her, although Joe Esquibel existed in the business of the welfare office, he was nothing special in her heart above all the others until he became her own daughter's lover. Of course, she had cared about all of her clients, but in truth he was another faceless suffering child for whom she bore a composite pity.

She told the jury she had not gone with Sharon to the hospital when two of the children were born, and Oscar asked the questions in such a way so she didn't have to tell the jury that Sharon and Joe had not been married even by the time the third baby came. Oscar thought it was irrelevant to the state's case, no doubt, and why abuse Mrs. Murphy with the memory of such painful times in her life. She continued to recite the facts with very little passion in her voice, like a child playing a piano who had no ear for music. One could follow the tune, all right, get the drift of the music, but the sound was mostly empty. One time she said Joe had seen her driving down the street and had motioned her over. She had obliged, and then he came up to her car window and asked why Sharon had filed for a divorce against him. And Mrs. Murphy told Joe she didn't know. It was something the two of them would just have to work out, she said.

I leaned over and whispered to Joe, "Remember that?"

"No."

And then Joe Esquibel just walked away, Mrs. Murphy said. He just walked away and didn't seem angry or anything. She kept her eyes on Oscar Hall and sometimes she looked quickly at her hands to catch a moment she needed before her next answer. Now she sat with her feet crossed at the ankles, and I didn't interpret her toneless answers to mean she had any lack of feeling—to the contrary—she sifted the feeling out—held it back, and she was a very brave woman.

She said that on October 17, 1966, shortly after eight she had arrived at her office. Jean Moore, the receptionist, handed her a note with a telephone message on it. Sharon had called. It was urgent. Mona Lee Murphy had taken off her coat and the phone rang again. It was Sharon.

"Call the sheriff," Sharon had screamed. "Send the

sheriff over to the filling station. I'm over here. He's going to kill me." And Mrs. Murphy had run to the phone and called the sheriff. In a few minutes Sharon came into the welfare office with Joe chasing her and after they were inside they began arguing. Joe said, "I just wanna talk to you, Sharon. Just wanna talk. Lemme talk." Sharon said, "No," but Joe kept it up and Sharon was looking to the people in the office for protection from this man. Then Mrs. Murphy had stepped over to Joe and said, "This is a business office, Joe. Let Sharon go to work. Leave her alone. Let me go to work, too. This is a business office."

"I just wanna talk to Sharon for a minute—just a minute. Couldn't you go with us? Couldn't we go into the office?" he said. And then Mona Lee Murphy had said, "No, we're not going into anybody's office. And Sharon isn't going into anybody's office. You just leave Sharon alone and get out of here."

And Joe said, "Please, please, let me talk to you and Sharon for just a minute."

And Mrs. Murphy had said, "Well, you can come to my home after work and we'll talk about it then."

And Joe said, "Nobody'll listen to me."

"Joe, that's not true," Mrs. Murphy said. "You know that isn't true at all. I have listened to you many times," and then Luke Massingill, the director, walked in.

"Luke, this man keeps bothering us. He wants to talk to Sharon and to me and I've tried to tell him that he should leave, that this is a business office. He should leave everybody be." And then Luke Massingill took Joe by the arm gently, barely touching him, almost friendly-like, and the two of them walked outside. They talked for a little while about something and then in a few minutes they came back in and Joe started his pleading all over again.

"Please let me talk to Sharon," he said to Mrs. Murphy. "Please let me talk to the both of you, please."

And as Mona Lee Murphy's voice told the story, her voice began to gradually tighten, and her face began to match her voice, but the sounds still seemed hollow, and the combination of the empty sounds of her voice and the frozen expression on her face made me feel like I was watching someone walk on thin clear ice, which was about to break through, and underneath would be a cold bottomless pool, and at the bottom of the pool would be the single chilling cry of this mother, and I suddenly felt shivers coming over me, starting at my lower ribs, and I felt strange sitting next to this killer as he was being re-created out of the mouth of the mother seven years after the killing, out of the mouth of the mother of the dead.

Mrs. Murphy said Sharon had left the three children in the car, and they had been crying, and the little girl had finally gotten the car door open by herself, and the three children had all come running into the front door of the welfare office, to Mrs. Murphy who had seen them coming and let them in, and they had been crying so hard that they had been shushed into an office and the door closed and somebody gave them candy, but that hadn't stopped their crying. It was as if nothing would stop them, and they began to cry so violently that Mona Lee Murphy was afraid the baby would choke on the candy so she took it away and the children had followed her back out again where Joe Esquibel was. Then Mona Lee had seen the gun.

"Put that thing away, Joe," she said. "You don't want the children to see that thing." And she had turned to the screaming children, and said, "Hush. Hush. It's all right. Grandma is here. It's all right." She had gathered the children up and hugged them all together but even that hadn't stopped the screaming.

Then Mrs. Murphy heard Joe say to Sharon, "Are you going to make trouble for me?"

And Sharon had said, "Yes, you're damn right. I'll have you in jail before the night is over," and Joe still had the gun out, and Mona Lee said she had tried in every way to get him to put it away. She even shamed him.

"Aren't you a big brave coward, though, with that gun in your hand," she had said. Her voice was sarcastic. "How would you feel if your sister or your own little children came home all beaten up?" Mona Lee Murphy was speaking now of how Sharon had come home, bruised and beaten and crying. Joe didn't answer her. Then she said she had turned her head slightly to the right and she could see out the window and as she said that from the witness stand she moved her own head slightly to the right, illustrating, and she said she noticed that a car from the sheriff's office was coming and a uniformed sheriff's officer came around the corner into the building. It was then that Joe took a step forward toward her daughter. Sharon threw her hands up over her face, and Joe pulled the trigger. The voice of Mona Lee Murphy was still empty.

"Where were you?" Oscar Hall asked.

"I was standing directly behind her. The gun was pointed at Sharon's temple. After he pulled the trigger something fell to the floor, is what I remember, and then he pulled the trigger again and she fell to the floor. I can remember beating Mr. Esquibel in the face with my fists and seeing the gun laying on the floor."

"What was Mr. Esquibel's response, if any, while you were beating on him?" Oscar Hall asked.

"None whatsoever."

"Did he say anything to you?"

"No, sir."

"Did he resist you?"

"No, sir."

"Did he beat you back?"

"No, sir."

"How long did this continue?"

"I don't remember."

Then two people had taken Mona Lee Murphy to the coffee room, away from this horror, but she told Oscar Hall that Joe looked like he usually looked, nothing out of the ordinary, and he behaved calmly, she said in her own calm voice, as if she were only describing the peeling of a carrot, and as I listened, the scene Mona Lee Murphy described became like a hideous dream, with desperate people running around speaking to each other as they always did with voices that were as dead as old water and

I felt afraid, and then I knew it was my own nightmare that frightened me.

"That's all the questions I have," Oscar Hall said. Now it was my turn to examine this mother, to attack the enemy—a grieving mother, the enemy? But she was a friend of the jurors, this brave woman who had survived the questioning of Oscar Hall without a tear. The case was already in the balance. If I did nothing, we might lose the jury, but we could certainly lose them if I did the wrong thing now. The jury would never forgive me if I attacked her. There were hostile looks from some of the men as I got up to examine. Leave this mother alone. She's just taken us through the murder of her daughter, shared that horror with us, can't you understand that? Leave this brave woman be, bereaved and beautiful in this one moment, which belongs to her.

"Mrs. Murphy," I said as quietly and as gently as if I were speaking to my own grandma on her deathbed, in a reverent whisper. "Mrs. Murphy, would you like a recess? You have been on this stand for a long time."

And Mona Lee Murphy said, "All right," without a smile, with her face still frozen, and the court called a recess.

John Ackerman came up to me as soon as the jury filed out. "Jesus Christ, what are you going to do with her, Gerry?"

"Don't know," I said.

"God, be careful," he said. "Maybe you shouldn't ask her any questions. Pretty risky, I'd say."

"Yeah," I said. "You're right." Raymond Whitaker said nothing. He was an old wise artist himself and he knew that one artist does not tell his colleague how to paint a picture. "What do you say, Raymond?" I asked.

Raymond said, "You just have to call 'em like you see them, Gerry," and he walked out toward the hall to get a drink of water.

"Yeah," I said, still not knowing what I was going to do exactly. It would have been easier to sit down with no questions. All of them would have thought it wise. The jury would have respected me for it. There would be no risk in that, but no gain either, and her testimony had been devastating. Take on the other witnesses but leave this woman alone. That could be an acceptable tactic. But before I could decide what to do, Mona Lee Murphy was on the witness stand and the recess was over and I was asking her questions, carefully, gently. "We haven't met before, have we?" I asked Mrs. Murphy, who looked back at me blankly.

"No."

"This is the first opportunity I've had to meet you in these past seven years?"

"Yes."

"It's been very difficult for you." She didn't answer and looked at the purse on her lap. "We are very sorry, and I will not ask you any questions that would injure you, but I must ask you some things. It's my job. You are an important witness, do you understand?"

"Yes," she said, looking up at me. She admitted that when she learned that Joe and Sharon were going together she had tried hard to break them up—that it troubled her that her own daughter had gone off to live with some Mexican without being married and that it had embarrassed her. She tried her best to break them up, she said. I understood her feelings, I said, "And your attempt to break them up included filing a criminal charge against Joe?" I asked gently.

"Yes," she said.

"You charged them with fornication?" Again kindly and gently.

"Yes, sir."

"Sharon was let out of jail immediately, wasn't she?" I asked matter-of-factly.

"No, I believe she was there a day and a night."

"But Joe was there considerably longer than that?"

"I don't know," she said, and now her eyes were fastened hard on me.

"You didn't find out?" I said, again matter-of-factly.

"No."

"You knew the sheriff?"

"Yes."

"Knew him on a first name basis?"

"The same as I knew the sheriff before him."

"Mrs. Murphy," I said gently, "if you please, that doesn't answer my question. Did you know the sheriff on a first name basis?" I held her firmly.

"Yes, sir." She said her daughter was bright, while Joe Esquibel had a low I.Q., an I.Q. of about 65, she said the records at the welfare office showed, and she admitted that she had never once spoken to Joe Esquibel until her daughter had the first baby.

"Did it occur to you that Joe might have needed your help and advice?"

"He could have had it if he had come and asked me," she said. Now there was a hard sound in her voice and it came through on her face.

"Would that have been before or after you threw him in jail?" She didn't answer. "Did you expect him to come to you after you had thrown him in jail?"

Oscar Hall jumped to his feet. "I object to the characterization of having him 'thrown in jail.'"

"I withdraw the question," I said. Then I went on to something else. Sharon was an independent young woman, her own person. She went out of the state sometimes, and Mrs. Murphy herself said she had helped her go out of the state, to Las Vegas once, to visit an aunt and uncle, she said, and yes, that was all a part of her effort to separate the two, and when they had finally gotten married in October of 1965, she hadn't attended the wedding, and then Sharon had divorced Joe one year later.

"Joe asked Sharon why she had filed for divorce, didn't he?"

"Yes."

"He seemed very concerned?"

"Yes."

"And when he was in the welfare office he wanted to know why Sharon had divorced him, and you wouldn't talk to him, isn't that true?"

"Yes."

"And he asked you over and over?"

"Yes."

"And you also refused to let Sharon talk to him up there in the welfare office?"

"Yes."

"And Sharon was how old?"

"Twenty-four."

"And finally in desperation Joe said, 'If you will only talk to me for a moment, I will never bother you again for the rest of your life,' isn't that true?" I already knew her answer. It was in the statements of the other witnesses, which had been supplied to us by Oscar Hall under the court rules. Yes, she said, and Joe kept pleading to talk to Sharon and to Mrs. Murphy and he had kept it up for at least fifteen minutes, even suggesting that she could bring in anybody—just let him talk to Sharon and to Mrs. Murphy. "I thought it was something between my daughter and me and Mr. Esquibel and not Mr. Watkins," she said.

"You were sort of in charge there, weren't you, Mrs. Murphy?"

"No."

"The children were crying. Do you remember Sharon saying, 'I hope you hear that crying for the rest of your life'?" It was in one of the statements of the other witnesses.

"Yes," and her voice was getting harder now and her eyes were bright.

"And didn't you see a change of expression on Joe's face when Sharon said that?"

"I don't remember."

"And the children ran up to their father and threw their arms around his legs, isn't that true?"

"Could be. Didn't see it," she said. Her voice now began to sound openly hostile.

"And didn't you drag the children away from their father and take them into the office?" I asked matter-of-factly, quietly.

"I didn't drag them," she said coldly. "I brought them into my office."

"And after Joe said, 'No one will ever listen to me,' did you ask him what it was that he needed so desperately to talk about?"

"No."

"Ask him what was on his mind?"

"I just said it wasn't true that nobody would ever listen to him. I'd listened to him many times."

"And Joe also said to the other people there that nobody would ever listen to him, isn't that true?"

"Yes."

"And did one single person out of the seven or eight people who were there ask him the simple question, 'Joe, what's on your mind'?"

"No."

"And as he stood there with the gun in his hands you called him 'a big brave coward'?"

"Yes," her eyes flashing.

"And he just held the gun and kept pleading with Sharon?" I asked.

"Yes. And he kept the gun on the others to keep them away."

"And didn't you hear your daughter say, 'Go on, if you're going to kill me, do it!' "

"She threw her hands over her face the first time—then I heard the sound of something falling on the floor, and then she threw her hands back down and said, 'If you're going to shoot me, go ahead and do it.' "

"Did she laugh?"

"No."

"Are you aware that others who were there said she laughed?"

"I have read those statements myself."

"Would you deny the testimony of others who say she sort of laughed when she said that?"

"No, sir."

"That was her way, wasn't it?"

"Yes, sir. She was a happy-go-lucky girl."

"Yes. And then Joe recocked the gun and fired?"

"I didn't see him recock it."

"And your daughter fell to the floor after he pulled the trigger the second time?" I asked matter-of-factly.

"Yes."

"And as you beat on his face he said nothing."

"That's right."

"Nothing—he said nothing!"

"That's right."

"There was no response from him of any kind while you continued to beat him on the face?"

"Not that I can recall."

"Said nothing? Made no response?"

"None that I can recall."

"Did you beat as hard as you could?"

"Probably."

"Where was the gun?"

"On the floor."

"Within reach?"

"If he had bent down he might have been able to reach it."

"But he just stood there?"

"As far as I remember."

"Do you remember your saying as the sheriff walked up—just before Joe pulled the trigger—'I've got no choice'?"

"No, sir." Now I waited, giving silence to the courtroom.

Finally I said, "Now, Mrs. Murphy, these children are all with you?"

"Yes."

"They are fine young children?"

"Yes."

"You are very proud of them?"

"Very proud."

"They are bright little children?"

"Yes."

"Healthy?"

"Yes."

"Happy?"

"Yes."

"And from the day of this horrid tragedy until now they have not seen their father?"

"No. Only pictures in the paper or on TV."

"You have never taken them to Evanston?"

"No. They are afraid of him."

"You have never let them write to him?"

"They never wanted to."

"You gave them the name Murphy?"

"That's the name on their birth certificates."

"But didn't you know that when Sharon married Joe they became his legitimate children?"

"I didn't know that for a long time."

"The children live with you and feel like little Murphys?"

"Yes."

"I just want to thank you for your bravery and for being a good witness here. I hope that this is the end of this misery for you," I said.

"Thank you. I hope so, too," she said. And when she left the stand the look on her face was different, and the look on the faces of the jurors was different, too. It is the truth that awakens us from nightmares, and it was the truth that dissolved the gloomy haze of ghosts, and washed away the mystery of mothers for the moment, that wiped out the magic that shrouded the mother of the murdered, and left a woman named Mona Lee Murphy, who stepped down from the witness stand not guiltless, not different from myself, not sacred. And the jury saw her, too, and out of the cross-examination of a trial lawyer the jury knew the truth and saw a whole woman walk from the courtroom.

Then Oscar Hall called Marcella Redmond.

Marcella Redmond said she had lived in Rawlins all her thirty-one years and had known Joe. They were members of the same Latin-American club at school, and she was ready to testify that Joe was a belligerent and aggressive person even then, but I had seen it coming and stopped it before she had a chance. I interrupted her testimony and summoned Hall to the bench and argued that how Joe Esquibel acted in the Latin-American club in 1955 was too remote, and Judge Forrister sustained me.

On the morning of the shooting, Marcella Redmond was already at work in the welfare office. She heard Joe holler to Luke Massingill, "Get Marcella out front," and

then she had gone out in response, and she saw Joe there
with a gun and she saw him lunge toward Sharon and put
the gun to Sharon's head.

" 'It's now or never,' he said. 'Now or never' "—and
there was that "deadly click" she said, and Joe recocked
the gun, but Sharon turned her head so that now he put
the gun up to the side of her head. Then he pulled the
trigger and Sharon fell to the floor, and Marcella said
Mrs. Murphy began beating on Joe. A caseworker named
Ray Ring picked up a cane and started to strike Joe with
it, and Marcella Redmond had stopped him because she
didn't believe Sharon was dead. She thought she had just
fainted or something—that is until she bent over Sharon
and shook her, and that's when she said she saw the
blood.

Then the gun just sort of slid out of Joe's hand to the
floor. He didn't drop it, and when Mrs. Murphy began
beating on Joe, he raised up his hands to protect himself.
Marcella Redmond's testimony left no doubt that Joe
was sane, all right. Anybody could see that. He had sorta
dropped his arm when somebody said he shouldn't let the
children see the gun, and he was sane because when one
of the ladies suggested that the children be taken away so
they wouldn't have to see all this he had agreed, and that
was before the shooting, all right, and he was sane because when the deputy sheriff pointed his gun at Joe after
the shooting and told Joe to put his hands up, well, Joe
did, and this all showed that he had the perfect ability to
follow instructions. Then Marcella Redmond said Joe
had even tried to prevent her from calling for an ambulance—and that would be evidence of his malice. "I was
trying to call the ambulance, trying to pick up the phone,
and he had his hands covering mine to keep me from the
phone, and he was obviously aware of what he had done
because he was saying, 'Oh, Joe, look what you have
done. You have *really* done it,' or something like that,"
and what Joe said clearly implied he had thought about
killing poor Sharon, and now he had suddenly realized
that what he had plotted, what he had premeditated, had
actually come to pass. "I kept on trying to tell him to let

me have the phone," Marcella Redmond said. "But Joe kept saying those words in a calm tone of voice." Calm, collected, premeditated. "I didn't call the ambulance. He wouldn't take his hands off me, but Anna Emery had already called." She found that out later, she said.

At the recess Raymond said, "This is a tough one, Gerald. Be beautiful."

"Yeah," I said, and I began the cross-examination carefully again. "Mrs. Redmond, we've never met?"

"No."

"Someone from my office tried to talk with you so we could prepare our defense. Remember that?"

"If you're referring to the woman . . ."

"Just answer my question," I said quietly.

"I received a phone call from someone who said she was working for you."

"She said she wanted to talk to you to get the facts of the case, isn't that true?"

"Yes."

"And you told her you thought it wasn't quite 'kosher'?"

"Well . . ." she laughed. I looked over at the jury. No one laughed.

"Just answer my question, please."

"Well . . . I remember the word 'kosher,' yes," she said.

"And you refused to give her any information?"

"Yes, sir."

"Isn't it fair to say your friendship lies with Mrs. Murphy and her deceased daughter?"

"Well, let me go back . . ."

"Just please answer my questions. It's a simple question."

"Yes." And she admitted she had read her own statement a number of times over the last seven years, and the welfare office was a close, tight-knit little family.

"Now, Mrs. Redmond," I said. "You testified that the sheriff told Joe to 'put your hands up.' Is it possible that you misstated yourself?"

"No."

"But that isn't in your written statement, is it?" I handed her a copy. She took the statement and read it carefully.

"That's correct," she said.

"Do you have a clear memory now of the sheriff saying 'Put your hands up'?"

"He may not have," she said, with her voice lower now, and more serious.

"Mrs. Redmond, a man's life is at stake here and you're testifying under oath . . ."

"Well, I will have to say I don't remember."

"Now, Mrs. Redmond, Mrs. Murphy sat in this very witness chair and said Joe Esquibel did nothing to protect himself. But you have testified that Joe raised up his hands to protect himself when Mrs. Murphy beat on his face. Are you certain of that as well?"

"I am sure."

"Are you aware of any place in your statement where you said that?" I motioned for her to look at the statement again.

"You will have to understand . . ."

"Mrs. Redmond," I interrupted. She stopped cold and I caught her with my eyes and I repeated the question slowly. "Are you aware of any place in your statement where you say you saw him lift his hands to protect his face?"

"It's not in the statement," she said.

"When did you give this statement?"

"Immediately after this happened."

"Was the matter then fresh in your mind?"

"I was very shocked."

"But was it fresh in your mind?"

"Yes."

"And your memory would be clearer as to the specifics then than now, seven years later?"

"You'd think it would be, yes."

"And you've read the statement a number of times since this happened, over these seven years, and you haven't made a single correction in the statement, have you?"

"No, I have not."

She was ready now, because the cross-examination had made her ready for the jury. I would attack, easy at first.

"Now, Mrs. Redmond, you wanted the jury to believe from your testimony that Joe Esquibel wouldn't let you call an ambulance, isn't that true?"

"I don't know what I wanted the jury to believe. . . . I wanted to bring it out that Joe fought me for the phone. He was fighting me for the phone."

"You wanted the jury to believe it was his intent to keep you from calling an ambulance, didn't you?"

"That's how it seemed to me, sir."

"Well, read your statement." I motioned her to the statement again and I walked up and pointed to a place on the statement for her to begin reading. She read it very fast.

" 'I ran for the phone and was going to call an ambulance. Joe, I don't know if he was trying to keep me from calling or trying to get himself off the floor after falling there, after realizing what he had done, but I had to fight his hand off the phone to use it.' "

"Thank you," I said. And then I had her read it again to the jury, slowly.

Oscar Hall asked a few more questions of his own, and in answer to one she said she remembered seeing Mrs. Murphy beat on Joe's face for five minutes.

"Five minutes?" I asked on re-cross-examination.

"I remember Mona Lee beating on his face and chest."

"You said for five minutes!"

"It could have been for a few minutes or two seconds. It seemed like five years."

"But your testimony was *five minutes*. Was that your best estimate at the time?"

"Yes."

"Let's see how long five minutes really is," I said. "Let's look at the clock on the wall over there. All right, start now, and you tell me when five minutes have passed." Five minutes is an interminable length of time in a silent courtroom, and in the silence one could see Joe Esquibel talking to himself, and then answering, and

Mona Lee Murphy beating away on his face, with no response from him, not even a raised hand, for five minutes beaten by that small mother with little bare fists until he fell to the floor and the beating continued and the five minutes seemed to stretch out into eternity in this courtroom from which the specter of a madman began to appear.

Then after lunch, Oscar Hall called Jean Moore. Jean Moore was a prim, respectable, hard-working woman, who labored over the papers and the files in the welfare office and was a loyal employee there. As I heard her answers to Oscar Hall's questions, I thought I was listening to a woman without personal involvement. She spoke without excesses, matter-of-factly, almost without interest in her voice. She remembered small new details, like the youngest boy grabbing Joe by the leg and saying, "Daddy," and Joe having put his empty hand down to the child, and then Mrs. Murphy taking the children away to Luke Massingill's office. And she remembered Luke Massingill in the welfare office edging toward Joe along the wall, and Joe hollering, "Get back, it won't hurt me to shoot you or anyone else in this room," and she remembered that Joe demanded they bring Marcella Redmond out front from the back room. But it was all evidence elicited by Oscar Hall to show that Joe had control, knew what he was doing, all right, and that he was sane like the rest of the killers, without a defense, trying to escape by saying he was crazy, that he didn't really mean to kill.

Mrs. Moore remembered that Luke Massingill thought Mona Lee Murphy maybe ought to talk to Joe. Talk is cheap, and, after all, that's all Joe seemed to want, just to talk, but Mona Lee had said no, there wasn't going to be any talking, and then Mrs. Moore said she heard Sharon laugh, and say, "Well, Joe, if you're going to shoot me, go ahead and do it." Then Joe recocked the gun, and Sharon leaned back and turned her head to the gun. The shot rang out and Sharon fell in a heap directly in front of her mother, and Mona Lee leaped over the body of her dying daughter and began pounding Joe on the face—so hard, she said, so very, very hard that Joe had to brace himself against the door. Ray Ring ran into his office and got a cane as a weapon, but by the time Ring got back with the cane, Joe was already on the floor on his knees talking to himself, " 'Oh, Joe, you didn't do it—oh no, Joe, you didn't do it.' "

So far as Joe Esquibel was concerned, Mrs. Moore said, there must have been two people there, Joe who was talking and Joe who was talking back to himself, and on cross-examination I painted the picture for the jury with a question to Mrs. Moore.

"And even after the shooting, Sharon is on the floor bleeding, and Joe is being attacked by Mrs. Murphy with such fury that he braces himself against the attack; Ray Ring is over there with a cane about to hit him; and all the while the deputy is there with a gun pointed at Joe, and Ray Ring is screaming, 'Kill the son-of-a-bitch,' and your testimony is that Joe's eyes were calm and normal and his voice was quiet, isn't that true?"

"Yes."

Oscar sort of shrugged that off, and immediately called Ray Ring to the stand. Ring was a tall, dark, well-built man who walked to the witness chair with long, dignified strides. He sat down, and peered out over the courtroom with anticipation on his face waiting for Oscar Hall's first question. And his answers to Oscar's questions sounded as if he were reading from memory a literary creation of his own. I picked up a copy of his statement, and I was able to follow his testimony word for word there, which was five pages long. I walked up to the bench while Ring was still reciting and handed my copy of the statement to Judge Forrister, pointed to the place where Ring was in his recitation, and went back and sat down. While Ring finished, the judge followed along, word for word in the text he had memorized. When he had finished, I began my cross-examination. "You've done a good deal of writing in your time?"

"Yes."

"You wrote a five-page statement in this case at the request of the sheriff, isn't that true?"

"Yes."

"And you have a copy and the county attorney has a copy?"

"Yes."

"You had it here at the last trial?"

"Yes."

"And you've memorized it, haven't you?"

"Yes."

"It's hard to remember the details of something seven years ago, isn't it?"

"In detail, yes."

"And so as to the details in this case, it's fair to say you have testified from a memorized statement, not from your own separate present memory, isn't that true?"

"Yes, I think so," Ring answered honestly, with a certain dignity.

Then I turned to His Honor, who had Ring's statement still in his hands, and I said, "I move the court to strike all of Mr. Ring's testimony. It is not testimony of the witness from memory, but a mere recital of some memorized statement."

The court ruled: "The testimony will be stricken and the jury will be advised to disregard the entirety of Mr. Ring's testimony, the same as if it had not been given." Ring looked shocked at the judge's ruling. He had only attempted to remember the facts as he had recorded them seven years ago, and when Oscar dismissed him, he pulled himself up and walked slowly from the stand, disbelief clearly registered on his face, but Oscar seemed satisfied. The jury had heard Ring's testimony, and as they say, you can't unring the bell. But the credibility of the state's case was now at issue.

Oscar called everyone who had been at the scene of the shooting, probably afraid I would make a big issue of a missing witness or something if he didn't call them all, and the witnesses repeated the same story of the witnesses before them, but I picked at little places to emphasize my points on cross-examination. One witness said, "He was resting in the chair after the shooting," and said Mona Lee Murphy sat on top of Joe, beating on him, and still another said Joe was sitting on the floor "crying and hysterical," and pretty soon Oscar Hall had called all the witnesses and he finally announced, "The state rests."

The state rests?

He hadn't called a single psychiatrist, and it was his burden to prove Joe had been sane! He was going to let me present the doctors as my experts, and he would cross-examine them, and he would point out how one day they were yea, as to insanity, and the next day, nay, and how some of the doctors even on the same day couldn't agree with each other. He would put me in the place he had occupied in two previous trials, and he would say these experts say whatever they want whenever they want, and their testimony is just so much administrative flimflam, ladies and gentlemen, just so much psychiatric baloney. He might even be holding back his own rebuttal psychiatrist, some expert he would bring in from out of state who had reread all of Joe's records and who would put it all together for the jury as the last state's witness, and this expert would probably say that the reason nobody could keep his testimony straight was because none of them were really competent. None could see the clear signs left by this Mexican-American because he had been wiser and smarter than all of the hospital personnel put together. This so-called Mexican of low intelligence had simply outsmarted all the psychiatrists and psychologists and social workers and criminologists—outsmarted them all at the Wyoming State Hospital, and he was sane, perfectly sane now, and had been perfectly sane all these years—that he was sane when he pulled the trigger on his wife, sane when he watched her fall, evil but sane, and he would look at the jury with a commanding look on his face that told them he knew and that they had a clear job to do.

"Well, Raymond," I said at the recess. "It's our turn. It's do or die now, baby."

"Justice will prevail," Raymond said.

"Yeah, I heard that story," John Ackerman laughed out of his belly.

"Did you hear the story, Gerald?" Raymond asked.

"What story?" I said absently, getting my notes together.

"Go get Joe Medina," I said to John Ackerman. "He's up first."

"The story about the great trial lawyer," Raymond persisted. "He left the courtroom after his closing argument and the jury had retired to deliberate the case and he told his young assistant to receive the jury's verdict for him and to wire him the results of the verdict when the jury came in."

"Yeah," I said. And John was already back with Joe Medina, who followed John up to our counsel table.

"And the jury's verdict was for their client. They had won. So the young lawyer wired his boss, 'Justice prevailed.' And the boss wired back, 'Appeal.'" And Whitaker grinned his bulldog grin, but he didn't laugh, and I knew they were just trying to ease the tension. Joe Medina and I quickly reviewed his testimony.

"Well, Raymond, we've got to go ahead with the game plan. No other way to go."

"That's right," Raymond said.

I said, "I've learned something along the way. When you don't know what to do exactly because you're not smart enough to see how the whole damned thing's going to come out in the end—and it looks bad down every trail —well, you'd better do something, anything, go one direction or the other, but go! We might just as well go with our game plan and look for the fumbles."

"You got your metaphors all mixed up, Gerry," Raymond said.

"Well," I said, "nobody but you will know the difference."

The jury came back in and the court was in session again. I called Joe Medina as our first witness. He managed the Silver Spur Bar in Rawlins. He testified how some cowboys got smart with Joe once and one of them, a big bastard, picked Joe up and tossed him across the room, and another one hit Joe on the back of the head with a bowling ball from the little bowling game that they had in the bar. They took Joe to the doctor, and the doctor looked him over carefully and finally said, "My God, Joe, if you have to have any more stitches we won't have any room for 'em in your head."

And then once Medina said he and Joe had been in another bar together and a woman broke a beer bottle over Joe's head, and the woman pointed to Joe and told her boyfriend that Joe had hit her, and Joe had to fight that guy, too, Medina said. Afterward Joe had to go to the hospital and get sewn up again.

Still another time there had been "five guys looking for trouble," Joe Medina said, and Joe had been fighting with one of them and was on top of him. And then the others began kicking him in the head, and beating him over the head with beer bottles, and he had to be stitched up that night, too.

In September of 1961 Medina said he and Joe were driving around in Medina's car and that Medina pulled into a gas station, drove over four pumps—knocked them all over. After the accident, Joe got out of the car, holding onto his head, walked around a little bit, leaned over the car, and then just sort of rolled over onto the ground and lay there looking straight up, and they had to take him to the hospital. He had two fractures and suffered a concussion. He was there two weeks and three days. We exhibited the hospital records to the jury. After the accident Medina said, Joe acted strangely. He was a different guy, like he had turned in his old brain for a new one. He'd be a good guy one minute, give you the shirt off his back, and then suddenly out came his temper. Never could predict it.

I called Uncle Chris Montoya as our next witness. Uncle Chris, a pleasant man, seemed timid, was smallish, with hair as black as jet, and he was Agneda's brother. He remembered that one time there had been a birthday party for one of the little Esquibel girls, maybe Donna's party on Valentine's Day, he thought, and at this party Joe's little brother, Johnny, was reaching for a sandwich and Joe just slugged him in the face and knocked him over. Uncle Chris's voice was kind and he had a certain dignity about him. Joe knocked Johnny down for no good reason, Uncle Chris said, and he said he took Joe aside and asked him what was the matter, and then Joe just slumped to the ground himself, "and his body just sort of gave out on him as if he were fainting." Uncle Chris helped him up into a chair, and "Joe started writhing," and I emphasized the word by repeating the question and listening to the answer carefully, and I looked at the jury as the word "writhing" came out again, and Uncle Chris said, "His eyes were rolling and he was shaking all over like he was having a convulsion." And then after about five minutes it was all over, Uncle Chris said, and Joe didn't remember anything. There wasn't much cross-examination by Oscar Hall.

Then Leo Trujillo, a brown young buck, testified that Joe and he were close friends and that Joe had hit him for no reason at all, and later Joe didn't remember doing it, and Joe felt so bad about it and he insisted that Leo hit him back.

" 'Go ahead, Leo, hit me back,' Joe said. And I says, 'No,' and Joe says, 'Go ahead and hit me, Leo. Hit me good.' And I says, 'I don't want to.' And Joe says, 'Go ahead, goddamn it, and hit me,' and I says, 'No,' again. And Joe says, 'If you don't hit me back, I'll hit ya again myself,' and so I hit him a good one." The jury laughed, and I smiled, too, but it made me afraid all of a sudden. Was the jury laughing because it was just funny, a little humorous relief maybe, or did they laugh because they were happy that Joe Esquibel had finally got it?

Another time Joe and Leo were out target practicing, and Leo said Joe suddenly turned toward Leo and shot in Leo's direction and both shots went right through the side of Leo's car and Leo hollered, "Are you crazy or something, Joe?" And Joe tried to laugh it off.

Then the whole family took turns testifying, taking their oaths and taking the stand in this war in which the spoils for the victor was this alleged Mexican madman sitting at the table in his neat brown business suit, and plain brown tie.

Elma took the stand for Joe, little Elma, this wisp of a brown girl who looked like sixteen, with her hair past her

waist and with big innocent eyes, and who was too tiny to
be anybody's mother, but who was this huge mother to
her brothers and sisters. She walked shyly up to the witness stand, and I could hardly hear her answers to my
questions. Everybody strained. She said that once Joe
was hit over the head with a pipe and that whoever hit
him just dumped him, unconscious and bleeding, in front
of the Esquibel place, and Elma said he seemed different
after that. She had to watch him all the time, she said in a
high little girl's voice, and her face was like an open book.
"Sometimes they'd throw Joe at the door after he had
been drinking all night, and Joe was always blacking out,
and he'd black out after just one or two drinks, too," she
said—there was just a hint of the Spanish accent left in
her speech—"and sometimes he'd just fall over." When
Joe went back to the hospital after the first trial, "he
didn't even know me—acted like a dog crawling around.
Didn't do no good while he was locked up in Johnson
Hall and he couldn't get no fresh air," she said. "Then
Joe started to get better. The past seven years he has
grown up and has started to think of himself a little bit
and to think of others. He never used to think about
himself," Elma said. Oscar Hall didn't cross-examine
Elma much either.

Then I called Uncle Casey Gonzales. Uncle Casey was
married to Agneda's sister and he said he and Joe were
friends from the time Joe was a little boy. Uncle Casey
seemed like a good old boy, and when he took the stand
the whole courtroom sort of relaxed. He said he lived just
three houses away while Joe was growing up. "Joe was
awful young when his father was killed in that accident.
He was a nice little boy, but nobody brought him up. He
wanted to learn to work, and he was a good worker, but
he was close to his father, and after his father's death,
well, it just affected him. He was always talking about his
daddy to me." And the jury looked over at Joe and
maybe they could see him as a little boy. Every killer was
once a nice little boy. Then Uncle Casey said the Sunday
before the shooting Joe had stopped at Uncle Casey's
house but he didn't stay to talk. Usually Joe would hang

around an hour or two, but on this day Joe didn't look
well when he left, and so Uncle Casey followed him over
to Joe's house and asked him if he was all right, and Joe
said he was okay. Then Uncle Casey said, "I came back in
an hour to check him again just to be sure, and when I
got back Joe was gone. That was the last I saw of him
before the shooting."

Uncle Casey visited Joe in jail afterward and he testified, "Joe just looked up and said, 'I haven't seen you for
a long time.' He didn't remember having seen me on the
Sunday afternoon before. He didn't remember anything
about the killing," Uncle Casey said.

Eight days before the shooting Joe and Uncle Casey
had gone out deer hunting and Joe started shooting,
crazy-like, at anything he could see and he was laughing.
And then he had a blackout. It was when they were eating their lunch. Joe said he had a terrible headache and
he sort of lay down and then suddenly he sat up again,
said he felt all right and he was all right for the rest of the
afternoon. Uncle Casey said he also remembered that
Joe took along the .22 pistol that Joe had shot Sharon
with, and that sometimes the damned pistol jammed. Old
pistol, ya know. Didn't amount to much, and Oscar Hall
didn't cross-examine Uncle Casey at any length either.
What could he do with the likes of Uncle Casey, and
anyway Oscar had some expert lying in the wings. All this
testimony amounted to was the hopeless struggle of poor
people trying to save their own.

I called Dr. Farhang Soroosh, a neurosurgeon from
Casper, an Iranian with a dark face and tight wavy hair
and large soft eyes, and a heavy charming accent. Jurors
liked to listen to him. He turned to them with his shy
smile, friendly-like, not like some big-shot doctor with
long scientific words, but a man who stumbled along with
his broken English. "How you say?" he would ask, and
then the jury would help him with the word, and before
long the jury had made him their own. He was their
friend, talked to them as if they were his equals. "You
know," he would say, and they would nod their heads to
urge him on, and there was something even a little ro-

mantic about his accent. The women in the jury would lean forward to listen to the doctor. His words curled on the ends and floated across the courtroom like something out of the *Arabian Nights*.

Dr. Soroosh had examined Joe just a few days before the trial. He gave Joe a thorough neurological examination, knew his history—the accidents, the fighting, and the blows to the head. Joe, the doctor testified, had been brain-damaged by a fracture of the skull. The doctor found a 50 percent hearing loss, which came from the brain damage, and said that people with such brain damage commonly suffer from "post-traumatic epilepsy." Then Dr. Soroosh smiled at the jury, and the ladies smiled back, and the men were transfixed, hanging onto every word, trying to understand the rococo sounds, to translate them into understandable English. He said the spinal tap made at the hospital almost seven years before also indicated brain damage. It was very clear. The brain damage could cause a sort of personality change like the one described by Joe's friends and family.

I put a hypothetical question to Dr. Soroosh, the way lawyers do. The hypothetical case presented to the expert summed up the testimony of the witnesses in the Welfare Department who had seen Joe shoot Sharon—and who had seen him stand defenselessly as he was beaten to the ground by Mona Lee Murphy—how they saw him writhe—and I underlined the word with my voice in the question—and how he rolled on the floor and later kicked purposelessly at the front panel of the sheriff's car on the way to jail. "Considering the foregoing hypothetical case, do you have an opinion, based upon reasonable medical certainty, as to what caused Joe Esquibel to conduct himself in the manner described?"

"Yes, I have an opinion," Dr. Soroosh said.

"And what is your opinion?"

"I think at the time of the shooting Mr. Esquibel was in an aura of temporal lobe seizure, and that after that he went into a seizure. During the aura he was not aware of what he was doing."

"Would he know the difference between right and wrong?"

Hall objected to the question as being outside of the expertise of the witness. The court sustained the objection.

"Would he be conscious of his acts?" I asked.

"No."

"Would all his conduct then have been on a subconscious level?"

"Yes."

"Therefore, would he be consciously able to determine the difference between right and wrong?"

"No."

"Therefore, would he be able to stop doing what he had commenced to do?"

"No."

"Were his acts the result of a disease of the mind?" I kept asking the questions as fast as I could to get his answers before any further objections.

"Yes, sir, in my opinion."

And then Dr. Soroosh said that amnesia was consistent with the seizure. Joe's insistence that he couldn't remember was explainable in terms of epilepsy, and 75 to 80 percent of those suffering from post-traumatic epilepsy get well, he said, and even of this witness Oscar's cross-examination didn't amount to much. It was all coming later on with his own expert, which he was holding back. I could feel it, but there wasn't anything I could do but head right into it, so I called Agneda Esquibel.

Now Agneda was fifty, thickened by the years, her skin leather-tough, stretched over a broad face, and she had gray hair. She was less than five feet tall, and when I called her to the stand, she walked slowly forward like a small plow woman behind horses, straight in the furrow, steady but plodding. I called Uncle Casey to act as her interpreter. I knew she could speak well enough, all right, but she wanted an interpreter, she said. "I no speak English good. I no understan' good." I thought she felt better having Uncle Casey sitting beside her. I asked the questions and Uncle Casey repeated them in Spanish to

Agneda, and then they seemed to talk a little and Uncle Casey answered in English. He was a solid honest man and the jury already liked him.

"How many children do you have?" I began after she told us her name, her age, and where she lived.

"She got six kids livin'," Uncle Casey announced in English after her answer in Spanish. "She got three, four more who died." Then Uncle Casey said she married Dario twice, but they got divorced, and he said, "Agneda say that was hard on Joe." Agneda's voice was soft, and the Spanish words sounded like a special kind of music, maybe like the sounds of the creek under the porch at North Fork. She never looked at the jury, spoke with a bowed head, spoke almost in a whisper, as if she were speaking in the presence of God, saying her prayers, speaking in a holy tongue only part of which came back out of the lips of Uncle Casey.

"She say he cried a lot for his father," and then Casey said that they had sent her to the women's prison in Canyon City.

"Why were you sent to jail?" I asked.

"I don't know," Uncle Casey interpreted for her.

"Well, tell Mrs. Esquibel not to be afraid. It is important for us to know. We understand she must be ashamed."

"She say, 'Because I was a bad woman,'" and then Uncle Casey told her story as she whispered into her hands from the witness chair. After Dario left she was alone. There was nobody to help her take care of them kids and she done what she had to do to take care of them kids. They put her in jail and them kids was always hungry and never had no clothes. The gas company shut off the gas, only two beds, and some of them kids slept with her and the rest in the other bed. They couldn't go to school all the time because they didn't have no clothes, Uncle Casey said for Agneda.

She took Joe to see where his father had been killed because a boy should know them things out of respect for his father, and Joe saw the blood of his father, and at the time of the funeral Joe wouldn't let go of his father's coffin, Uncle Casey interpreted. It took a lot of people to pull him loose because she couldn't pull him away by herself.

And then pretty soon they come and put her in jail, she said, and the sheriff made her a trustee, and she cleaned his house and did his laundry and while she was in jail, this time for ten months, she saw them kids once, out there on the courthouse lawn, and they was cryin' and beggin' for her and then she moved into a house with this man who just come out of the pen. She done that so she could get a home for them kids, and Joe, he no like this guy. And then Joe got into trouble and they sent him off to Worland to the boys' reformatory, and one time this guy shot Timato, killed him, right there while Joe was just standin' there and this guy shot Joe, too, and when Joe come out of surgery, they had to keep him doped to keep him down. And then Joe got into them fights and he lost his memory and had them dizzy spells. Her voice never changed, came in the same soft sounds of the rippling water, as if all that were left out of all of those years and all of these memories were the quiet sounds of her voice speaking in Spanish in the courtroom.

Then she said that on the Sunday before the shooting Joe came to the house at three o'clock in the afternoon and Sharon came to the house with him. Sharon and Joe had gone out to buy groceries for their kids. They was divorced already, but they left the house together, and they wasn't quarreling then. Joe had his paycheck from the city, and they was gonna get food for them kids, she told Uncle Casey. And then she didn't know anything more about what Joe did that night—didn't hear him come home. But Joe got up early Monday morning, real early, she didn't know what time, but it was unusual for him to get up early like that. And then the first thing she knew Sharon was calling her on the phone asking her to come to the filling station to get Joe, that he was running into her with his car, and she had hurried right down to the station, but Joe and Sharon were gone by then. She didn't know where they had gone, and then later on Agneda's sister called her—about nine-forty in the same morning—and said Joe had killed Sharon. Her voice never changed. She talked on, and Uncle Casey interpreted her words clearly, without emotion, and the words touched me. I let the story come out without interrupting much with new questions, just let the witness paint her own picture. As I say, every artist has to paint his own painting.

They wouldn't let her in the jail for a week after the shooting, and when she finally saw Joe he was pale and looked sick and had lost weight and they wouldn't let her give him the candy and cigarettes she had brought. Had to buy them all over again in the jail commissary, and after that they took Joe to Evanston. While he was in Evanston she saw him every other week for all of those years he was there. She remembered when Joe was first there. He wouldn't talk to her. When he saw her he ran off, and when she got up to him he told her to leave, but now Joe was better. That was her whole story. That's all she knew. There wasn't nothing more to say. Oscar Hall did not cross-examine Agneda Esquibel. He was a smart lawyer.

I called Frank Bowron, Joe's attorney in the statutory rape case. He was still the tallest man in the courtroom, and his bald head still shone and he spoke in the same soft voice of a gentle intellectual. He told about the trial he had conducted for Joe, and he said that the judge had said repeatedly outside the courtroom that Joe was guilty, if not of that offense, then plenty of others, and how, about a year after the trial, Bowron talked to the foreman of the jury in Joe's rape case, who said they were sure that Bowron had been hired by the Mafia to defend Joe.

During the course of the rape trial, Bowron said Joe became aware of the fact that one of the Mexicans from Rawlins, a man by the name of Ray Sanchez, who was in the penitentiary at the time, had been murdered while he was serving out his term there. This man was the brother-in-law of Roberta Rodriguez, the girl Joe had supposedly raped, and Joe was terrified about being confined in the penitentiary, Bowron said. Joe said over and over again,

"They kill Mexicans in the pen, and if they get me in the pen they will kill me too." Two weeks before her death, Sharon had called Frank Bowron. They had talked for about half an hour. She was hysterical and it had taken some time for Bowron to calm her down, and after she was able to speak, she told Bowron she had filed for divorce, and "Joe went crazy," she said. "I'm afraid he's going to kill me." She wanted Bowron to explain to Joe what was going on because Joe did not understand. He was upset about the judge, Sharon thought, because the judge in her divorce case was the same one who sentenced Joe in the rape case. The judge wouldn't accept the agreement that she and Joe had entered into, and the judge wouldn't give Sharon a divorce without Joe's also agreeing to support the children. Joe believed that the judge wanted to fix it so he could throw Joe in jail, just like Dario, Sharon said, and Sharon said Joe believed the judge was going to find a way to put him in the penitentiary, and that he would be killed. Oscar didn't ask many questions of Bowron either.

Now it was Joe's time. Get on with it, I thought, don't hesitate, don't act like it's anything special, just an ordinary person going to the stand, saying a few words—not a man taking the stand fighting for his life, and I walked over and touched him on the shoulder and he looked up to me and nodded because he knew it was his time.

"Call Joe Esquibel," I said. Joe got up and I watched him go, like a man watches a friend walk out the door for the last time, not knowing where his friend is going, maybe into the light or maybe down into dark places. His steps to the stand were graceful. He sat down. The women liked the sight of him. You could see it in their faces. The men, well, some of them looked down, and there were two men in the front row who would not look at him—who only looked at their feet. They had their arms crossed. Maybe I had chosen the wrong people for the jury, but it wasn't me who really chose them. Oscar had taken some of our best defense jurors off with his challenges, and those who were left were men and women who were not the first choice of either side.

Maybe I should have left that preacher's wife on. And, yes, some juror would say, the one looking down right then with his arms crossed against us, yes, they put that Mexican killer on the stand—had the nerve to put him on. The son-of-a-bitch lied—couldn't believe a goddamned thing the murdering bastard said, lying on the stand is only perjury, ya know, and the son-of-a-bitch tried to lie out of it so he wouldn't get murder. Nothing else the murderin' bastard could do, but he never got me caught up in his lies. Never got me feelin' sorry fer him. I lived with my old lady all these years. We ain't had it so good all the time. Liked to kill her myself sometimes. Felt like shooting her right between the eyes a time or two myself. A man can get mad at his wife, all right, any man does, but that don't give him no excuse to kill. A man just lets the feelin' pass, cause if a man killed everybody he got mad at there wouldn't be no safe place for none of us. Gotta stop this killin'. The son-of-a-bitch shouldn't a got up there on the witness stand at all. I knowed a guy once charged with a killin' and he never took the stand, and the jury turned him loose. Leastwise he didn't get up and lie about it.

"Will you tell the jury who you are?" I asked.

"I am Joe Esquibel."

"Where do you live?"

"Rawlins—well, I live in Evanston, but I am from Rawlins."

"What hall are you living in in Evanston?"

"Lincoln Hall."

"How old are you?"

"Twenty-nine years old."

Preliminary questions. Easy. I asked them softly so that the answers would come back softly. I wanted him to get used to the seat, the surroundings.

"How long have you lived in Evanston?"

"About seven years."

"How old were you when you went there?"

"Twenty-three or twenty-two approximately."

"You have lived about a third of your life there, is that correct?"

"It's been a long time, yes, sir." He sounded stiff and tight.

"What's the matter, Joe? Are you afraid?" He didn't answer. He nodded a little and looked down at his hands.

"How long have you been afraid?"

"I don't know. I have been scared and nervous through all of this."

"Have you thought about this case for quite a while?"

"Yes, not as much as I have now though." He looked over at the jury suddenly, looked back quickly.

"Are you afraid of this jury?"

"Yes," he said.

"Why?"

"I don't know. I am just scared and nervous."

"Are you willing to testify here?"

"Yes. I will speak the truth."

"Do you understand you don't have to testify?"

"Yes, I know."

"And you understand that whatever you say the jury can use against you?"

"Yes."

"Are you willing to tell them everything you know about this case?"

"I am going to tell them what I know, yes."

"Are you afraid of Mr. Hall over there?"

"Yes."

"How about the judge?"

"Right now I am scared of everybody in here. I am even a-scared of you—everybody, I am a-scared."

"Well, I think, Joe, we can understand that. Dr. Karn is here listening to your testimony, and it is necessary for us to bring out the facts of your life since he needs this information as part of his final evaluation. Will you be willing to let us talk with you about that?"

"Yes."

"We may have to ask you some things that are very close and personal, things that we might not otherwise ask in public. Do you understand?"

"Yes."

"Do you remember that you took an oath in this case before you took the stand?"

"Yes."

"What does that mean?"

"You are supposed to tell the truth, and I will."

"And do you know what it means if you do not tell the truth?"

"Yes."

"Do you have anything you want to lie about in this case?"

"No."

Then he painted his own picture with broad simple strokes of his brush. He loved his father. Liked everything about him, didn't know why, just did, and sometimes after his father was dead, his mother was gone for days, "and we just stayed around." Sometimes Joe hesitated in the middle of his answers and his eyes were sad. Sometimes he looked at his feet and when he couldn't find an answer I didn't interrupt the silence to help him. I let him struggle alone on the witness stand.

"Are you having difficulty in answering these questions —or thinking about them?"

"Yes."

"You have never talked about this before like this, have you?"

"No."

"You haven't even talked about some of this to Dr. Karn, have you?"

"No."

"Nor to anybody else, except me, is that right?"

"Yes."

Sometimes his grandmother fed them when his mother was gone. She was poor, but they found something to eat —fried potatoes—whatever she had. And he remembered going to the Cathedral Home. Mrs. Murphy took them, and when he was fourteen he got into trouble. His mother was living with this man. "I didn't like that man," he said like a child saying it. He looked over at the jury. They had unfolded their arms and there were no more crossed legs and some leaned forward to hear his soft replies to my questions. At the boys' reformatory the older boys hit the little boys, and he had learned how to fight, and he had been afraid so long and fought so much that finally fighting got easy for him. And he told how they whipped the boys with a strap and made them pull a "John-bar," a heavy bar of some kind, sometimes for more than an hour, always in front of the other boys, and sometimes they had to pull it until they fell, exhausted. When he got out of the reformatory he collected junk and sold it to buy food for his family.

Then he told the story about Louisa and little Joe, his first son, who was still living with his mother, and when he was about sixteen he met Sharon, who was nineteen. She was working at the bank, and was rich, he thought, and she had a new car, and bought him things, and gave him money. He'd never been out with a white girl before. She had those blue eyes and blond hair and was real smart, he said. She wrote his letters for him and told him what to do and what to say, and he loved her. She was good to the rest of his family, too.

Joe and Sharon started living together in Sharon's apartment, he said, but then sometimes she got mad and told Joe to leave and then Joe would go home to his mother. Other times Sharon would leave the apartment for long periods of time and Joe didn't know where she'd gone. But after while she'd come back, and she'd pick up Joe at his mother's house again and she'd say, "Come on, I got an apartment, let's go," and Joe followed her. He didn't know why. He just did, and they would start all over again. She was a good talker. "Always talked. She never stopped talking. She knew everybody. She talked and laughed a lot. People liked her." And then after a while she would tell Joe she was tired of him, and she would take off and leave him, and so after a while Joe said he started to take off, too, whenever he felt like it, he said, and sometimes they fought about that, and he hit her. They could be eating and she would get mad and throw things at him, he said. She had a quick temper, and sometimes when he hit her she hit him back, but he never hit her with his fists—just pushed her around and slapped her sometimes, but she was tough and would try to fight back, a good fighter. That was the way it was between them. They used to fight all the time. Everybody knew that.

She got to be a secretary for an insurance company, he said, and she even went to work at the welfare office for a time as a secretary, and after that at the hospital as an aide. Sometimes Joe worked, he said, and sometimes he didn't. He found jobs where he could. Worked as a construction worker, a laborer, just anywhere doin' anything. Wasn't proud. He'd been workin' for the city for about a year at the time of her death.

Sharon handled the money, wrote the checks, and she gave him five dollars to go downtown with, and sometimes she was nice and other times not. Joe never knew how she'd be, he said, or why, and when he asked her why, she'd just say, "I'm not mad no more. I was mad yesterday, but I ain't mad no more." And then one time she said she was leaving him and never coming back, and she did leave, and Joe started going out with this other girl, this Mexican girl, and that all ended up in that statutory rape trial. He couldn't remember much about the trial now, but he remembered that Sharon was with him again and taking care of things again. She was the one who got Bowron, and she was the one who got the witnesses, and put the whole case together. Sometimes she made scenes in public. Once he was down in a bar and she came in and screamed, "Why don't you go home? You got three kids at home, you know," and he left, but he felt ashamed about her having said that to him in front of all of the people, and later on she did it again.

He never hit his kids, he said, and he thought his kids loved him. He loved them, and he hadn't seen his kids for all of these almost seven years. He wished he could. It had been so long. It made him feel real bad, but now he didn't even know what they looked like. No one had ever shown him a picture of his children. None of the children had ever written him a letter in all of those years. He thought it was better, maybe, just to "leave 'em be."

Over the years his mother or sisters had come to see

him at Evanston almost every week, and that had made him feel good, he said. A lot of people there had no one to visit them at all, ever. He thought the visits from his mother and sisters helped him get through those long years. I asked the questions in a quiet easy way, just enough of a question to let him go on.

Well, Mrs. Murphy had thrown him in jail. She had done that more than once, and Sharon had thrown him in jail, too. He didn't remember how many times, but at least four or five. Sharon would get mad and then the sheriff would tell him that Sharon had signed a complaint and they'd take him off to jail. Sometimes he was in jail for two weeks and sometimes three. He didn't remember them giving him any papers. He never had a lawyer, and he never had any trials. They just locked him up, and then one day they would turn him loose again, just like that, and he would go back home to Sharon and she would say, "See, if you don't do what I tell you I will put you in jail again." And he said he was afraid in jail, didn't like being in jail, it made him feel crazy, and that other guys who were in jail just laughed and jumped around and tore everything up, and he didn't like being there with those people. His voice got soft again and he looked down at his feet. "They would just go around laughing loud, and pushing little guys around up there in the jail, picking on them little guys," and he said he had fought with those crazy guys. He hated the jail. Couldn't stand it.

Then one day Frank MacDonald, one of the deputies, had come after Joe again, and this time Joe refused to go. He told Frank MacDonald to go ahead and shoot. And later there were times that he woke up in jail, and he didn't know how he got there. He couldn't remember the fight or whatever it was, and he couldn't believe some of the things he had heard in the courtroom about his hitting people without reason. He knew he was having blackout spells, but he didn't know what to do. Sometimes Sharon would tell him to go see a doctor. "But they didn't have them kind of doctors, you know, in Rawlins. I knew there was something wrong, but I didn't know what."

After Sharon filed for divorce, Joe lived with his mother at home, but sometimes even after the divorce Sharon would want him and she would come and get him and take him to her apartment. Sometimes he would stay there and other times he would knock on the door and she would answer and tell him, "I don't want to see you today," and that was all there was to that. Sometimes he had sex with her and slept over there, and other times not.

On the day of the "tragedy" as I called it in the court-room, he didn't remember being with Sharon at all. He said he knew she had been out with other men. He had heard that. It had always been that way. He remembered the Welfare Department asking him to come to the office and sign papers that would make the children legitimate, and he had signed the papers. "White people are strong. White people are smarter," he said. And he said he didn't know how to say it, "But that's the way it was. And Sharon was white. She was older. She was smarter."

He got his paycheck on the fifteenth of October 1966. He knew that because he got paid on the first and fifteenth of each month, but he didn't remember now anything about the fifteenth or the sixteenth, the day before the killing. He thought he remembered driving, just driving the car, and maybe he had some beer to drink, but drinking made him sick now. He had no recollection of going home on Saturday night, or of talking to Uncle Casey, or of getting up on Monday morning between four or five, or of being at Sharon's apartment on Monday morning at about one o'clock. That was in the statement of Sharon's landlord. He knew nothing about the filling station scene. "All I remember is waking up in jail."

"You have heard all of these witnesses, Joe, saying you were there. Do you believe them?"

"Yes, I believe them. I believe them, but I can't remember being there."

"Was there a time when you didn't believe all of this to be true?"

"I didn't believe them for a long time. I couldn't believe that I done that." He said they kept telling him in jail he had killed his wife, but it seemed like a nightmare to him and he thought for a while that the people at the state hospital were all insane, all of them, and that they were just telling him a lie. All he knew was that he woke up in jail. It was in the afternoon and he didn't know why he was there again. He said he started banging on the jail door to attract someone's attention. Maybe he was there for another fight, he thought. Finally some jailer told him why he was there, but he wouldn't believe him either. After about a week he saw his mother and then Uncle Casey. They were standing there, and his mother was crying and asking him, "Joe, what did you do?" And he said, "I don' know." And then they told him, and even now it was hard for him to believe.

He was in the Carbon County Jail a long time. He lost track of the days. When he went to the Carbon County Jail he weighed 210 pounds, but six months later he weighed 170 pounds. In jail there were no sheets on the bed, just a mattress, one blanket, no pillows. They were fed twice a day—for breakfast a bowl of cereal or mush, sometimes with sugar, never milk or cream. They ate in the morning about six o'clock, and the second meal came early in the afternoon, usually deer meat or antelope or beans, and there were days he got nothing to eat at all. Sometimes they would open the door and throw slices of bread in to him.

Then they took him to Evanston for eighteen days and brought him back to Rawlins again, where he remained for six months, alone in a small cell without any magazines or books to read, nothing to look at, no radio, no light in the cell except from a window that had been painted over. Once he was let out of the cell to talk to Raymond Whitaker, and Whitaker made them give him a haircut, and once his lawyer came and "raised hell" about Joe not having food, and after that things got better. Sometimes it was cold in the cell and other times it was too hot. For six months he was without shoes. He asked only for a mop to clean the cell and he got that. Once he asked if his mother could bring him a sandwich from home, something to eat, but they said no. He could buy candy bars and cigarettes from the commissary. From time to time he got sick from headaches, and he asked for aspirin, but they gave him none.

He said he had no present recollection of the first trial in this very courtroom. He didn't recall that I visited him after the first trial. They put the real sick people in the maximum security cells, he said. That's where they locked him up. And he told of the people screaming, of Jason, and the little boy, Billy, and after a while he said they took him out of the maximum security ward and he made many friends at the hospital. He said there were people there who were businessmen and doctors and lawyers, all kinds of people from all over. He said he found out that he wasn't so bad after all. That was when he started to learn. He said he was accepted then and that in the last year they were good to him. Dr. Karn was good to him and he knew Dr. Karn had been sitting through the whole trial waiting to testify for him.

"It has been quite a struggle, hasn't it, Joe?"

"Yes," he said, and I knew that's where the story should end. "That's all of my questions, Your Honor," I said. "You may question, Mr. Hall." What would happen on cross-examination? Would my hours of work preparing Joe pay off now? Remember, Joe, the meaner he gets the nicer you get, that's the rule, and when he asks you a question, don't look at me. If there are problems I will take care of you, but don't look at me. Take plenty of time. You can control the pace of his questions by taking as much time as you need to answer, but I remembered the words of Frank Bowron. "Under stress, Joe could make no decisions—tended to explode, tended to be violent." The smallest explosion, the slightest inappropriate response would end it all. I gathered my papers from the lectern and walked back to my chair. I turned to Oscar Hall. "Your witness," I said quietly again.

"I have no questions," Oscar Hall said.

32

I CALLED Dr. Karn to the stand. After seven years he was now approaching fifty, his hair graying, but he was still a nice-looking man, I thought, with a pleasant demeanor that the jury would appreciate. He walked toward the witness chair dutifully, giving the impression he didn't want trouble. He wore a dark navy blue two-piece suit and plain black shoes and his white shirt was starched and stiff. He was Joe's witness. Joe's witness—about to testify that Joe Esquibel was insane on that October morning in 1966 when he shot his wife the way some farmer slaughters a beef.

I got up to examine him. I grabbed the thick file marked "Dr. Karn." The first letter in the file was his to the court dated Christmas Eve, 1966, that same infamous letter saying Joe Esquibel was just a "malingering subject" who "bent the social and moral codes to fit his own needs." Dr. Karn found Joe Esquibel perfectly sane. There wasn't even a question of his being the victim of some irresistible impulse. He chose to shoot his wife because he wanted to. That was it—not insane. Try him—for murder.

Now Dr. Karn sat quietly, looking confident, and he was *my* witness, waiting for my first question. He was still an enigma to me. Just last January he had said, "He couldn't in good conscience," was how he put it, "testify that Joe was insane at the time of the shooting."

"I can't," he'd said. "I don't honestly know if he was insane or not. Can't say either way."

Now Karn was going to testify for us. I began my questioning of the good doctor by taking the thrust of Hall's cross-examination away from him at the outset. We would explain it all to the jury at the very beginning, why the doctor had said in the first trial that he believed that Joe was sane and now had changed his position. It was all very simple—when you do a psychological evaluation you play detective, Dr. Karn explained. You need all of the information you can get, he told the jurors. And he hadn't been provided with all of the information. The Welfare Department hadn't been open with the defense —wouldn't talk to any of my investigators. Well, they'd treated Dr. Karn the same way, he said. They hadn't provided all of the information to him either. And someone like Joe Esquibel can't tell you his history. You must depend on other sources, "collateral sources," Dr. Karn called them, and he smiled his quick little apologetic smile at the jury for having used such words. He hadn't been given the complete social records on Joe Esquibel, or the complete medical records, either, and "if the facts are incomplete, the conclusion may be wrong, too." He smiled again. He had been wrong before. Now he had all the evidence—and besides, he had almost seven years of experience evaluating Joe, and in his opinion, Joe had been insane. He was cured now, but he had been insane, insane at the time of the shooting. He had suffered from that profound mental disorder called schizophrenia, a disease principally of young adults, mainly from the time of puberty to the thirtieth year, and schizophrenia was curable now, he said, thank God. They had cured many in the state hospital, including Joe Esquibel. There were those new drugs now. "Before," he said, "schizophrenia was a one-way ticket to hell."

And what causes schizophrenia, Doctor? Well, the authorities are not in agreement. He smiled again, as if to say he was sorry about that, too, but he said that at the moment the most impressive explanation was there was a lack of "significant relationship between child and parent, an emotional trauma during childhood."

"Emotional trauma?"

"Yes," Karn said.

"Like a child walking through the snow barefoot for something to eat?" I asked.

Yes, Dr. Karn said. Like children being taken from their mother, like a child being placed in an orphanage, like a child being taken to see the blood of his father on the road and being torn from his father's coffin, like a child at fourteen seeing his brother shot dead, like a child, his head shaved because of lice, being separated from other children, like a little boy cold and hungry, without a mother, a boy being sent to a reform school and being subjected to beating, yes, yes, said the doctor, smiling, sadly, yes, those are the causes of schizophrenia.

This was a young man who lived in a state of constant anxiety, he said. Things were happening to him that he could not understand. He never knew where his next meal was coming from, the doctor said, or when his mother would return. Why he wasn't schizophrenic long before he was seen at the state hospital was a mystery, the doctor said. Maybe he was. He had never seen a case with a more adverse environment, with such total social deprivation. How could the child understand why he was being deprived of everything a child needs, particularly a child with a low I.Q.? The child must have concluded there was something wrong with him, that it was his fault his mother was gone, although he could not understand what he had done.

And M'Naghten's Rule applied, the rule that asked whether the defendant knew the difference between right and wrong, and knew the nature and consequences of his act, with the little additional helpful twist in Wyoming, "Was the act the product of an irresistible impulse?" which means would a person have committed the crime even if there had been the proverbial policeman standing at his elbow? And the newer test that asks, "Was the act a product of his mental illness?" also applied. It made no difference which test was used. One who suffers from schizophrenia meets all tests, and Joe was suffering from schizophrenia at the time of the killing.

"Do you have an opinion as to whether or not Joe Esquibel was legally insane at the time of the killing?"

"I do," Dr. Karn said solemnly.

"Is that an opinion based on reasonable medical certainty?"

"Yes."

"What is your opinion?"

"I believe he was insane at the time of the commission of the offense."

And now that I had him on the stand and he was testifying easily, and he had the jury with him, I attacked the state's case. "How do you explain, Doctor, if Joe Esquibel was suffering from a schizophrenic episode, that he was able to recognize people, to call them by name, take charge, lower the gun out of sight when the children came in, notice that somebody was absent and require her to come back? It all seems like a man who understood, who was sane."

"Such conduct is inherent in schizophrenia in the very definition of schizophrenia itself. The individual may be normal in certain ways and totally deranged in others."

"And when Joe Esquibel said, 'I have no choice—it has to be now,' what significance did that have in terms of your diagnosis?"

"From all indications that I have now, he was propelled by some force—whatever it was—and his need to talk to Sharon and her mother was very important to him. The irony was that he had many other choices besides shooting Sharon. Yet, he had no choice other than what his psychosis required him to do."

"Does that have anything to do with 'irresistible impulse'?"

"I think it was an irresistible impulse because even the physical appearance of the deputy sheriff did not stop him. As a matter of fact, it is the classic 'policeman at the elbow test.' A sheriff coming through the door would have deterred a rational person."

"How do you explain the writhing of Joe Esquibel, his kicking at the front panel of the sheriff's car?"

"Last night I thought about that," he said with a vague look in his eye. Then he looked back to the jury. "It could be an epileptic seizure triggered by the emotional trauma of the tragedy itself."

"And when Joe said, 'Joe, Joe, what have you done? Did you do it, Joe?' What was that about?"

"He was struggling with the reality of the situation. There was the acute schizophrenic episode that morning —and then there was the explosion of the gun, perhaps, or the shock of seeing his wife falling, or of seeing the blood. Whatever it was, it wakened him momentarily from the nightmare, and then he lapsed back into it."

Then Dr. Karn told us about mothers. Ah, the mothers. "His feelings of hostility toward his mother were undoubtedly expressed toward his wife," the doctor said. "Sharon was the most important person to come into his life, because she gave him the things he wanted from his mother. But Sharon rejected him. On a subconscious level, then, when he killed Sharon he also killed his mother."

When he killed his wife he killed his mother.

Oscar Hall didn't examine Dr. Karn. Instead, it was Keldsen, his deputy, who attacked now. Our case would probably stand or fall on Keldsen's cross. He stared across at Karn with a resolute look on his face, bowed his neck forward, and took the doctor on. Yes, the doctor had to admit the report he made in 1966 was certainly inconsistent with his testimony now. No, he couldn't say when he changed his mind. Yes, it was possible for one to be sane at the time of the commission of the act and insane later on. Keldsen was relentless, impelled by the natural resentment of a lawyer for a turncoat witness. An entire staff—doctors, social workers, psychologists—had concluded that Joe Esquibel was sane, wasn't that true? Yes. And Esquibel had told the doctor about his head injuries and the blackouts, and the doctor had been fully advised from the beginning that Esquibel could not remember the twenty-four hours before the killing. Wasn't that true? Yes, said Dr. Karn. And, yes, hospital psychologists had given Joe Esquibel a battery of psychological tests in 1966, which did not reveal that he was schizophrenic at all, wasn't that true, too? Yes, Dr. Karn had to further admit that that was true too—that there was no evidence in the original examination of any epilepsy and that Joe had been given no medication all of these years specific to epilepsy. Yes, the killing itself could have caused an emotional shock great enough to cause insanity as distinguished from insanity at the time of the killing. Yes, it was also possible that Joe's long confinement in the Carbon County Jail could have caused insanity after the killing as well.

And besides that, Keldsen pushed on, now gathering up a good head of steam, a schizophrenic may know the difference between right and wrong. And he may appreciate the natural consequences of his act. Yes, Karn had to admit that. And amnesia can come from the emotional trauma of having killed one's wife while one was totally sane. Amnesia could occur in the absence of epilepsy or schizophrenia. Yes, many things could cause amnesia. It was possible that Joe Esquibel, even if he were schizophrenic, was in a period of remission when he killed his wife and so he would have been totally sane and accountable for his acts. Yes, that was true.

It was the end of a good cross-examination, a good fight, but I had the last word.

"Well, you heard counsel for the state ask you whether it was possible for the amnesia in this case to have resulted merely from the emotional trauma of killing, and you said, 'Yes, it is possible.' Do you remember that testimony?"

"Yes," Dr. Karn said calmly.

"Dr. Karn, anything is *possible,* isn't it?"

"Yes, let's be fair. I said it was *possible,* but I do not think that it was probable."

"Do you think that mere emotional trauma caused the amnesia?"

"No."

"You said it was possible that confinement in jail might

cause psychosis. Do you believe that that was what actually caused Joe's psychosis in this case?"

"No," he said matter-of-factly.

"And at the time of the first trial, you testified that you had seen Joe for only an hour and a half before you testified, but now you have had seven years, is that right?"

"Yes, that's right," he said, as if the recognition of a simple fact was the final line in the case.

"Are you sure of your diagnosis now, Doctor?"

"I am far more comfortable, now," he said. He would push, so I pushed him.

"Are you *sure* of it now, Doctor?" I asked again.

"I am sure of it now," he said, and looked over to the jury with an expression on his face that asked for the jurors' acceptance of him, and the jurors looked back, and I thought they looked relieved.

I walked over to counsel table.

"Well, Raymond," I said. "That's it. How does it look?"

"Well, it looks about as good as it could ever get," Raymond said. "We couldn't hope to get it any better than this."

"Shall we rest?"

"Let's rest. Let's let 'er fly," Raymond said.

I stood up then, turned to the court, and the jury, and with a slight, very humble bow, I said, "The defense rests."

Now we were going to face a surprise witness from the state. Oscar Hall called a recess. My stomach churned. Would I be able to handle him on cross-examination? Who would he be and how impressive would he come across? And when the court was called back to order, Oscar Hall announced his next witness.

"The state recalls Marcella Redmond as a rebuttal witness." I turned to Whitaker, "What the hell does Marcella Redmond know about the price of tea in China?"

"Don't know," Whitaker said with a troubled look on his face.

But Oscar was soon qualifying her for expert testimony. As an expert in epilepsy! She had attended the Colorado Institute for Medical Assistants, for Christ's sake, and had worked at the hospital in Rawlins between 1960 and 1962 as a ward clerk, and later on for some doctors in Rawlins, as a "girl Friday." She had been in contact with patients who had had seizures, and by seizures she meant "convulsions." And in epileptic seizures there were two kinds, she volunteered authoritatively, the "grand mal" and the "petit mal."

"For Christ's sake," I whispered to Whitaker. "This has gone far enough." I asked the court for permission to approach the bench, and there, quietly at the bench out of the hearing of the jury, I objected to any testimony of Marcella Redmond on the grounds that there was no showing that she was an expert on epileptic seizures or anything else. She could not give an opinion. The court sustained the objection, and that was it—there were no other witnesses for the state—no secret expert. It was Oscar's obvious theory that the experts, all of them, the state's and therefore his, are insane, not Joe Esquibel. Everybody knew you couldn't trust psychiatrists. Why would he call a psychiatrist? Their testimony isn't worthy of belief—neither the state's nor the defendant's. The jury knew that. What just plain folks like him and the jury knew was more reliable than all the fancy talk from the psychiatrists, which had been proved untrustworthy over and over again. He wasn't going to call any damned psychiatrist in this case. And he didn't.

In the morning Judge Forrister read his instructions to the jury, which seemed full of complicated phrases of law, and the jury sat listening intently as he read on, page after page, in his pleasant voice tinged with just the right amount of authority. The jurors acted as if they understood. Some were leaning forward, but all were alert.

I could feel my fear again in the bottom of my belly. The court told the jury about the presumption of innocence, that it was the burden of the state to prove the defendant was sane at the time of the commission of the crime, and that such proof must be made beyond a reasonable doubt. And then the judge read the test for insanity carefully: The defendant must have known the difference between right and wrong, and he must have understood the nature and consequences of his act, and the defendant must not have been acting in response to an irresistible impulse. It all seemed so civilized, so dignified, the black robe, "ladies and gentlemen of the jury," and everybody being so polite to each other, but the issue was still the same. The issue is the blood of my client. They have the desire to pen him, to kill him, to stamp out his very life and bury Joe Esquibel in Rawlins, once and for all.

. I was an officer of the court in this civilized place called a court of law, and I sat quietly and calmly at the counsel table dutifully making notes with a peaceful look on my face. I recognized with gratitude the intellect that guided me, that countermanded the feelings, that logically explained to me that this fight was different, that real blood would never flow in this courtroom, that there would be no actual killing here, that that would wait for a different time and a different place, perhaps. I was grateful for a mind that told me, no, do not stand up and attack even though there was something inside of me that said, attack. Attack your enemy. It was insane watching men struggle for the life of a man with pleasant smiles on their faces and bowing to each other. It was worse than my insane dreams of the dead who did not know they were dead. The judge said, "You may make your final argument, Mr. Hall," and then Oscar Hall arose, pulled up his trousers, shuffled his papers at the podium, and began.

"The rules of the game say it is time for the summation," Oscar Hall began. "You are at liberty to disregard anything I say since what I say and what Mr. Spence says in his argument is not fact." He talked calmly, moving into his argument, thanking the jury, reminding the jury that the defendant is presumed innocent. Then he began to preach. They must "keep their heads high." They should "do their job well." "There is no greater thing than human life." But soon he would be asking them to destroy the life of Joe Esquibel by their guilty verdict.

"Someone must talk for Sharon Esquibel. That is what

it is all about. She left life young, with three little children. It was not her choice." And then he said the defendant had admitted the killing, and so the only question was whether or not he did it intentionally. Was he insane? "If I take my pen out and throw it and hit one of you on the jury, I am, under the law, presumed to have intended that, because we are all presumed to intend to do what we do." His voice rose in indignation as he argued that the defendant killed, but now wished not to be responsible for it, because the defendant—there was incredulity in his voice—claimed he did not intend to kill, that he did not remember!

The defendant remembered his childhood, his father, the blood of his father on the road—he remembered fighting—that he did not like to be in jail, the beer bottles over his head. He remembered the orphanage, the reform school for boys—he remembered being married the first time and the birth of Little Joe. He remembered his friend being killed in the penitentiary, but on October 17, 1966, he didn't remember anything! I could feel my muscles tighten in my belly but I made simple notes on a scratch pad and looked over at the jury with a bored look on my face. "He remembered to bring the gun into the welfare office! He remembered to bring the gun! He remembered to hide the gun behind his back, and he remembered how to operate the gun when it misfired, to take it down, to reload it, and to reposition it against the head of Sharon Esquibel." He told the jury that on October 17, 1966, Joe Esquibel was able to dress, to drive his car, to follow Sharon, to bump her car, to follow her into the filling station where she ran for help. "She hung onto the man in the filling station and cried, 'He's going to kill me.' What did little Sharon Esquibel experience to cause her to say that?" asked Oscar Hall, and then he reminded the jury that Joe's own friend, Joe Medina, had told of Joe's hot temper, a killer temper.

The motive? It was simple. Just shortly before Sharon Esquibel had got her divorce. That was the reason—that was the motive of a man who had married because "he didn't have nothin' and she would give him what he wanted." How was Joe that morning? As he always was, Mrs. Murphy said, and Marcella Redmond said he looked calm. And the witness, Emery, said he didn't look much different. And the others said he was calm and under control. How could the jury conclude in the face of this unrefuted testimony that Joe Esquibel was insane? Hall's voice boomed out, "Joe knew what he was doing, called people by their names, took command, logically and precisely, asked Luke Massingill, 'Are you gonna make trouble for me, Luke?' He knew exactly what he was doing. He knew it was wrong, and anticipated trouble. But Joe had a job to do, a purpose to fulfill, and so he went about his business." I wanted to jump up and attack Hall physically, but I leaned back in my chair and gazed quietly and sleepily at the ceiling.

Oscar Hall made it sound as if the defendant had undertaken the killing as methodically as a storekeeper opening up for business in the morning. It was Oscar's time. His blows were landing. "Esquibel's brain, his nerves, his muscles, they were all working; they were all doing what he was directing. He put the gun into position. That takes thought. He put it up to her head. It misfired. He knew it had misfired. He knew it had misfired! He recognized that it didn't fire! He reloaded the gun and put another shell in the chamber. Epilepsy? Skitzo? Ridiculous! We must get on with this business. He pulled the trigger and Sharon fell. And then Joe Esquibel, clearly knowing what he had done, said, 'Oh, Joe, you have done it now!' It was remorse. 'My little Sharon, who gave me everything I wanted, she is gone.' It was remorse, not insanity."

It was remorse, not insanity!

Oscar Hall's voice quieted, quieted almost to a whisper. The last finishing stroke was about to be made. "Everything you heard was the action of one person unlawfully taking the life of another. He knew what he was doing. He was there to do the job, and, ladies and gentlemen, that is what he did." Oscar Hall picked up his notes and walked confidently back to his chair. The five-minute recess that followed was too long. I had taken my notes to the lectern, and paced up and down the empty courtroom waiting for the judge and the jury and the small courtroom audience to return. The adrenaline was flowing, but I felt wounded.

Judge Forrister turned to me and said pleasantly, "Mr. Spence, you may make your final argument." I was a warrior who had been given permission by the king to fight. It is a remarkable thing, this control that has been trained into us, like wild beasts taught to do tricks for the circus. I walked slowly to the lectern, nodded to His Honor, addressed the court, turned to opposing counsel, to the man who was responsible for the blood dripping down my groin, and politely acknowledged him and his deputy. Then I spoke to the jury in an ordinary conversational voice.

"Ladies and gentlemen of the jury—" I wouldn't fail. I had a file marked final argument into which I had shoved notes throughout the trial. At five o'clock this morning when my head was clear I had reorganized the argument. It was all in front of me now. It was fear that I felt in my belly, which would drive me and impel me—but I would be all right—I wouldn't fail.

"Ladies and gentlemen of the jury, I want to just take a moment to thank you. None of us can know how it is to be a sequestered jury, to be locked up away from your families and your own lives. None of us will ever be aware of your sacrifices, or understand your contributions to this case. Your pay is meager, but your gift has been great. It is quite an extraordinary service. It really is a giving of a part of your life to somebody else." The jury was not ready for an onslaught. There is a time, like before one makes love to a woman, a wooing. A time to develop trust, an opening up, as there is in all human relationships.

"Ladies and gentlemen, this case came to Mr. Whitaker and me almost seven years ago. Joe Esquibel was a man who had obviously killed, and his killing had been witnessed by eight eyewitnesses. Joe Esquibel was a penniless Mexican youth, and unpopular with the courthouse club. We could have had a simple two- or three-day trial on the question of Joe Esquibel's guilt seven years ago without questioning his sanity at all. But, ladies and gentlemen, that alternative would have been to turn him over to the mob, who wanted him. It would have been giving in, to capitulate to the mob. We would have become part of the mob ourselves, the mob's tools.

"Now, ladies and gentlemen, the job of an attorney is not to turn guilty people loose on the street to commit further crimes. The job of a defense attorney is not to convince you of facts that don't exist, or by clever argument to change your minds, to twist the facts. The job of a defense attorney is to defend his client with integrity and with all of his ability, so that the facts speak out on behalf of his client, so that a jury may fully understand his client's position. Should an attorney do anything less he would deprive you, the jury, of a full understanding of his client's case, and thereby prevent you from making a fair decision. I am an officer of this court just as Mr. Hall is, and just as you are. I hope that you will understand that in this argument I do my duty not only to my client, but to you and to His Honor." I could feel the fury, but I could introduce my own argument now with a simple, quiet proposition.

"Ladies and gentlemen, show me a man who is quick to condemn another man, and I will show you a person who out of his own guilty heart has the need to condemn another. And show me a community, ladies and gentlemen, that has zealously and relentlessly striven to crush an illiterate Mexican boy now for over twenty-five years, and I will show you the guilt of that community out of which Joe Esquibel was spawned. I do not speak of every man, woman, and child in Rawlins, Wyoming, but of the symbolic community, the non-caring part of the community that was the courthouse club. Before this case is over, you too will have to choose whether you will become a tool, a part of that system, a member of that club, of the courthouse club which so hated Joe Esquibel.

"What caused the insanity here? I have said it was the insanity of a community itself. Was it a sane community that permitted a mother to sell herself to feed her little children? Was it a sane community that sent such a mother to prison and left her children as orphans? The children were starving, half naked, and freezing. Did a sane community interpose itself to prevent that? I say to you that the money it took the state of Wyoming to keep Mrs. Esquibel in jail at Rawlins would have provided the food for these little children and the gas heat they needed for so many years. They would rather have her labor for the sheriff than care for her children. Is that sanity?

"What kind of a woman was Mrs. Esquibel? You heard the pitiful answer to the question, 'Why were you put in jail?' 'I was a bad woman,' she said. She was, indeed, a bad woman, was she not, this mother, whose only real crime was her sordid sacrifices for her children?

"I am sickened, ladies and gentlemen. Here was a mother sufficiently trustworthy to have the free run of the sheriff's house, sufficiently trustworthy, ladies and gentlemen, to clean his house and wash his clothes, but not trustworthy enough to be with her children? We listened to the strange logic of the Welfare Department. We listened to it closely and then wondered why Joe Esquibel was insane. I say to you, ladies and gentlemen, his insanity is the product of such insanity."

I was pounding the lectern and shouting. It was my own anger being unleashed in every space in the courtroom, my courtroom! It was my time!

"Listen to this organization, this Welfare Department of the courthouse club. 'Let us take her children. We are experienced in child welfare,' they say. 'In our wisdom we will take the children from her. We will put her in jail. We will leave her six little children in the house alone, with this little mother, Elma, a twelve-year-old girl.' But when the children were taken to the orphanage, they decided in their wisdom that at twelve Elma was too old to go with them, too old to be with her brothers and sisters, too old to be with Little Joe, the only mother he had now.

"I ask you, ladies and gentlemen, who is insane and where did all of the insanity come from? We are parents, but we have all been little children. I can still feel the little child in me. As parents we respect our children, knowing that to love our children returns love, that hate returns hate, and hurt, hurt. And, ladies and gentlemen, insanity is returned with insanity.

"How could Joe's little mind have begun to understand all it was called upon to understand? Let's look at the wisdom of this Welfare Department in charge of these children, in charge of Little Joe." I could hear my voice saying to me in my ear, Gerry, be careful. Tell the truth to this jury. Do not fool or mislead the jury. This is a superior body of people. One must never lie to a jury. There are twelve of them and but one of you. They are about forty years of age and there are twelve of them—four hundred and eighty years—almost half a century years of wisdom there. Tell the truth. Tell it well.

"Let us look at the wisdom of this Welfare Department when Mrs. Esquibel was let out of jail. They gave her $141 a month to live on—for six little children, for her to pay the rent, buy the groceries, the heat, the clothing, to keep them alive, to keep them on the horrible edge between life and death. Perhaps it would have been kinder of them to let the children starve or freeze to death, because then it would have been over, once and for all. But they gave this family just enough so that they could neither perish nor live, and they sent Mrs. Esquibel away —and they brought her back with the admonition to be a good mother or they would take her children from her again. How easy it is to sit in judgment of those who are helpless and beneath us. How easy it is to tell the helpless what they should do when they can do nothing. Is there one of us here who could not predict what would happen to Mrs. Esquibel and her children?

"It is an outrage to justice, an outrage and a disgrace to our system, and it makes me ashamed. Slavery is a crime in this country. If I had come to you two weeks ago and said, 'Ladies and gentlemen of the jury, slavery is not at an end in Wyoming,' what would you have said? You would have told me I had lost my own mind. But this woman was a slave to the system! The alley cats in Rawlins, Wyoming, feeding off the garbage have a better life than this woman and her children had. She took in men to live with her so she could feed her children. You read it in the welfare records that when she was released she got into a fight with another woman over a man just out of the penitentiary, because she said, 'If I had him, he would help feed the children.'

"As if what they had done to Mrs. Esquibel was not enough, the courthouse club turned its attention then to Joe Esquibel himself, who had got into a little trouble. Your kids and mine would have been sent home to their parents with a warning. It wasn't the kind of trouble you send a boy off to Worland for, to a penitentiary for boys, but that's where they sent Joe Esquibel, and the Welfare Department watched and wrote their reports, and made their judgments in the name of the law. You don't have to go to college, or become an expert in family life, or a psychiatrist or a psychologist, or have fancy degrees, or be a high official, or write technical reports to know that this was, indeed, insanity. Out of that insanity came a predictable product, a little child who reflected his environment, a little child who did not laugh or run carefree and happy as our little children do—a little child who reflected the only thing he knew—utter, unmitigated, social insanity. It was Dr. Karn who spelled it out so clearly for you the other day when he said, 'These symptoms, this kind of environment, bring on schizophrenia.' That was no surprise to us, was it? But it was nice to know as a scientific fact just the same. And that testimony, ladies and gentlemen, is unrefuted. Unrefuted here.

"And, ladies and gentlemen, if you want to turn a little fat-cheeked, wide-eyed Mexican boy four years old into an insane person, I'll tell you how you can do it. You will take him away from his mother—he will not understand that. We will take him away from the warmth of her protection and leave him hungry and leave him cold and he will not understand what he has done to deserve that. We will let the other children laugh at him and put him in school without adequate clothes and leave him dirty and full of lice, and later on we will shave his head and throw him in jail. We will put him in a reform school and let

those boys who are almost men beat him senselessly. He
will not know why this is happening to him. Ladies and
gentlemen, you have heard it all. We will show him what
real justice is, and later on we will teach him about justice
in school, about the American flag and about how this is
the greatest country in the world, a country where all of
us are treated the same. Then we will throw this seven-
teen-year-old Mexican boy in jail and let the nineteen-
year-old white woman go free. That will show him what
the American system is, that it is fair for all, and I will tell
you what else we will do. We will take this young man and
put him in the company of a little Mexican girl, and then
when the little girl is pregnant, we will say to the little
girl, 'If you don't charge and prosecute Joe Esquibel we
won't help you and your baby.' And by all of this we will
turn this Mexican boy, ladies and gentlemen, quite easily,
surely, into a madman! It is a wonder his poor mind
didn't crack long before it did! It is quite a wonder!"

And now I was whispering. There is music to a final
argument, a cadence, a rhythm, from the staccato of word
upon word, from the sounds, from the long hesitation,
the rapid movement of new sounds across the courtroom
that turns the human voice into its own kind of music—
strong music, and soft. It is a joy to make the music, to
hear it from your own throat. It came out of a thousand
arguments I made as I drove across the prairies of Wyoming in the loneliness of my car and spoke to myself. I
said the arguments in the mirrors of a hundred lonely
hotel rooms, and I had grown to hear those sounds in the
language of the people, out of the sound of the auction-
eers in a little country auction. Listen to the auctioneer.
Listen to the music of his words and the excitement they
create. Listen to the local preacher—remove the guile
and the zealousness, but hear the excitement and rhythm
in the sounds. Then I listened to my own sounds, spoke
to myself for half a lifetime, and there were some who
would say that was insanity, that it was now an insane
man raging at the jury.

"What did the courthouse club do with Joe Esquibel—
what was left of him? Did they treat him like a human

being, or did they stuff him like a thing, into the Carbon County Jail? Joe Esquibel said, 'I thought they were going to kill me in the Rawlins jail.' He was surely dying. He lost forty pounds in solitary confinement.

"Ladies and gentlemen, you have been in confinement here yourselves for these ten days. How has it been? You had television, good food, the company of one another, the fellowship of other warm human beings who knew and understood you. Can you, from these few days, understand how solitary confinement for six months must have been? With Joe Esquibel there was a window that was painted over, a little cell, a mattress with no covers, without even a sheet—no pillows, nothing to read, nobody to talk to, and if he dared to talk to someone across the way in another cell, they put him on a diet of bread and water.

"And where was the courthouse club in the meantime? They had invaluable information that Dr. Karn said constituted 90 percent of the basis of his evaluation. The courthouse club knew that if Dr. Karn did not have that information, he could not properly do his job on behalf of Joe Esquibel. Nobody knows that better than those experts in that Welfare Department. Those are the same people who would not talk to my assistants, who would give them no information. It was the courthouse club, the sheriff, who told the young lawyers, 'We ain't gonna talk to you. We finally got that goddamned Mexican.' These are the people who stand for truth—who care about people, who serve the people; they are the ones who have come into this courtroom seven years later to tell you that Joe Esquibel was sane and that you should find him guilty.

"I have known the prosecutor, Mr. Hall, for many years. He is a fine man. He has done his job the best he can. He has had no choice but to present this case as he has presented it. Yet he is an unwitting tool of that courthouse club, and that fact comes to you clearly when he says he is speaking on behalf of Sharon Esquibel. It is not his job to speak on behalf of Sharon Esquibel. This is not a vendetta, even though the courthouse club asks you an eye for an eye and a tooth for a tooth. Ladies and gentlemen, it is Oscar Hall's job to stand for the state of Wyoming, for justice, for all of us. He represents all of the people, including Joe Esquibel.

"Now you will remember when Mr. Hall threw his pen and said he was responsible for that and used that as an example to show that Mr. Esquibel was responsible for what he did, as well. I observed throughout his argument to you he never once mentioned the law. He asked you if you would follow the law when you were chosen as jurors. But now, when the time is here for you to abide by the court's instructions, the law, he ignores it completely. May I use your instructions, Your Honor?" Judge Forrister smiled and handed me his instructions. I walked to the jury box and leaned over, displaying the instructions to the jurors so they could read them along with me.

" 'The court instructs the jury that the defendant has been charged with murder in the first degree by the state of Wyoming. The fact of such charge is no evidence whatsoever that the defendant is guilty of such crime. Instead, you are instructed that the killing in this case is admitted by the defendant, but every killing is not a crime for which a person is answerable to the law'—just like throwing a pen may not cause you to be answerable under the law. And the court's instructions continue, 'In this case, the defendant could be guilty of the homicide only if at the time of the killing the defendant was sane.' Oscar Hall is, ladies and gentlemen, responsible for throwing the pen at you only if at the time of the throwing Mr. Hall was sane. You see the judge's signature at the bottom of this instruction."

I asked the court for a recess. A juror in the back row was beginning to squirm. There is a limit to endurance, and I paced up and down the empty courtroom during the recess like a lion in a cage.

"You're doing great," Raymond said.

"You're doing just fine," John Ackerman said. "You finally got to the bridge and you're crossing it, by God," he said, and laughed. And when the jury had filed back in, it seemed like an eternity later, I began again.

"Ladies and gentlemen of the jury, Mr. Hall told you the defendant was sane because he could drive a car, speak the language, and recognize people he had known all of his life. If that were the test for sanity, we would empty all the mental hospitals, for most madmen can drive a car or shoot a gun. Why didn't Mr. Hall tell you that truth? Why did he avoid reading the law to you? And what about irresistible impulse?

"It made no difference how many people were there or who they were. It made no difference that his children were there and that a deputy was there with a gun drawn on him. The impulse to carry out the shooting, which was later commanded by Sharon herself, must have been irresistible! He could not stop it. 'I have to do it now,' he said. Remember?"

I discussed the presumption that the defendant, having once been judged insane, is presumed to have been insane at the time of killing. It was the burden of the state to prove otherwise now, to prove it beyond a reasonable doubt, and I argued that Sharon Esquibel, who had known him best, had recognized his mental illness, and that Frank Bowron had recommended to the judge as early as 1963 that Joe be sent to Evanston.

"But the courthouse club would have no part of it. They wanted him in the penitentiary. The insanity of the defendant has been admitted by every witness of the state of Wyoming, including the state's own medical examiner, Dr. Karn, by everyone except the members of that club. Dr. Karn almost made a horrible irretrievable mistake for reasons that he explained to you, a mistake based on the refusal of the Welfare Department to give him the records he needed for the proper evaluation of the defendant. And the testimony of Dr. Karn has gone on unrefuted. When Deputy County Attorney Keldsen cross-examined Dr. Karn he tried to make Dr. Karn appear a liar or an incompetent. Mr. Keldsen's argument really went like this when you get down to it: 'Dr. Karn, we of the courthouse club didn't give you the information. Dr. Karn, the information we gave you was incorrect. You, therefore, made a mistake. How can you have the courage to stand before this jury and reverse yourself after finding out about all this information we withheld from you?' That was his argument. Is it a fair argument? I saw Mr. Keldsen badger Dr. Karn mercilessly, and it was the most patent example of the unfairness of courthouse club tactics I have yet to see.

"There is no one in this case, ladies and gentlemen, except Oscar Hall and his associate, Mr. Keldsen, who denies Joe Esquibel was insane. Not one of the state's witnesses has denied it, not even the people from the courthouse club themselves, and the burden of the state is to prove the contrary beyond a reasonable doubt." I looked at Ken Keldsen. He looked knowingly back at me. We had been adversaries before, and he knew it was a battle, and we respected each other, and that when the case was over we would be friends again. But for the moment he looked tight and drawn, and I knew my opponent was feeling the blows.

"Did the state prove its case?" I continued.

"It had the awful power of the state behind it, the unlimited resources of the state to smash Joe Esquibel, the ability to secure any number of psychiatrists, to subpoena every doctor Joe had seen from the beginning of his life. They had this power, and all the state did instead was to call the members of the courthouse club, and no one else. Yet, they expect you, the jury, to join this seamy affair! Will you join them? Will you join the courthouse club?"

I am always afraid to stop arguing a case, because when I stop it will be over for us, and then the waiting will begin, and the unbearable anxiety of not knowing the verdict will set in. But the time to stop had come.

"Ladies and gentlemen, sometimes in all of the arguments, we forget what a case is really about. I would like to remind myself and you what this case is about by asking Joe to stand up here." I took Joe by his soft, sweaty hand, and led him to the jury. There we stood, two men, side by side. I put my arm over his shoulder. "You see, he is not a wild animal, something to be afraid of, a fearful, mad killer. He is not a rabid dog; he is a human being and you should not be afraid of him.

"This case is about Joe Esquibel. I want you to know he is a human being." I was speaking softly now. "He is alive. I can feel his warmth through his coat. I hope that when you go to the jury room you don't forget that. I hope you will be able to feel him, too. I hope it never slips your minds for one moment that the final fate of Joe Esquibel, a human being, rests in your hands.

"I am about to leave you now. When I sit down I will never be able to address you again as an attorney in this case. Few lawyers have had the privilege Mr. Whitaker and I have had in becoming a part of this case with you. It has been a very heavy burden for us to bear these seven years, but we have been glad to bear it. And now we put that burden on your shoulders. I know it has been a difficult case for you, too. We thank you. I hope these words of thanks don't come to you as hollow words. We are proud of our system. We are proud of you. We are proud that we have been a part of it together."

I took Joe back to his seat. And then at the jury box I concluded the argument.

"I want to leave you with a story. It is the story of a wise old sage and a smart-aleck boy. The wise old man and the boy were together one day, and the boy decided he would show up the wise old man for a fool. The boy had found a small bird. It was his plan to ask the old man what he had in his hand. The boy was sure the wise old man would say, 'You have a bird, my son.' And then the boy would ask the wise old man, 'Is the bird alive or is it dead?' If the wise old man said, 'The bird is alive,' the boy would crush the bird until it was lifeless and show him a bird quite dead. But if the old man said, 'The bird is dead,' the boy planned to open his hands and let the little bird fly away. So as planned, the boy asked the wise old man what he had in his hand, and the old man said, as expected, 'You have a bird, my son.' 'Wise old man, is the bird alive or is it dead?' the boy asked, and the old man answered, 'The bird is in your hands, my son.' Ladies and gentlemen, I give you my client, I give you Joe Esquibel. He is yours. He is in your hands." And I sat down.

Oscar Hall stood up to give his rebuttal. I could say nothing. The last beating would be laid upon my back and upon the back of Joe Esquibel and I could do or say nothing. The state always has the last word. The last word belongs to the king. Hall approached the jury quickly and told them how proud he was of these defense attorneys, the best in the state, who appeared on behalf of a Mexican lad without funds. It was all very flattering and disarming, I thought. This poor boy had these great attorneys, but why? That was the question that was raised by the flattery. And these great attorneys appeared on behalf of Joe Esquibel against old Oscar Hall, a mere country boy from Rawlins.

Yes, it was poverty, Oscar Hall said. "Yes, poverty is wrong, but that is life. We know that 'as the twig is bent, so grows the tree,' but a life is gone and the decision is for you to make, and it should not be made on sympathy." Then he attacked Dr. Karn's reversal of his opinions. That is why he had called no psychiatrists—you could see it in Dr. Karn himself. Why should he call in psychiatrists when the state's own psychiatrist was able to reverse himself so handily, so easily. A life has been taken. That was the theme. The state's witnesses had not given exact testimony, but they had done the best they could. "And I can only do the best I can," Oscar said. "And when the state's own psychiatrist contradicts himself, what can I do? You must answer to nobody. You must do the best job you can. Do the job as you see it, and if you do that, your job will be properly done," he said. The jury knew what he meant, and I knew what he meant. The state wanted Joe Esquibel. Give us Joe Esquibel.

And then the bailiff took the jury away.

I watched them march out, mostly with their heads down, thoughtful, serious. The door to the jury room closed behind them and my hell began. I vowed I would never try another case. The pain of waiting—oh, the horrible pain of waiting just a minute outweighs the joy of ever winning. The long weeks there in court, the years of vague, nagging worry, waking at night with a groan, worrying if I had failed to file a pleading or had not interviewed a witness, worrying about the eventual verdict that was now almost upon us. I thought of the days preparing for this case, days of total commitment when no one could interrupt me, no pleasures could be understood or felt, of preparing the cross-examination of every witness, of indexing every item of evidence—organizing and reorganizing, plodding and thinking and planning and striving. I thought of preparing for this combat. The energy had run high and at night my muscles had ached and my head was dull and sick. And now the jury was out on Joe Esquibel and it was out on me. It was my case. It was my life! It would be my win or my loss. If I won I would survive to be thrown into another pit in another time. If I lost, the part of me that was lost, that was killed, was lost forever, and like any fighter I would wonder if this was the time when I started my long painful trip downward, from which a trial lawyer can never return.

I could not feel for Joe Esquibel in this fog of my own feelings. Joe sat somewhere in the courtroom with his family. I looked around. He was talking to a woman. How did he survive? I did not even ask. How was he feeling? I was so full of my own fear I could not feel for him. I was too full of my own misery. And what was the jury doing? What was it saying? Who would it listen to? Did they really trust me? Did I overdo it? Did they buy Oscar Hall's country boy routine or did they see him as just a man doing his job, and me as too tough, too slick? Was I too hard on the courthouse club? Would they let Joe Esquibel go, this Mexican, after killing his white wife? What would I do if they convicted Joe? How could I face him? What would I say to him? Could I look at his poor mother?

Oh, the mother?

Could I look at the mother?

What is keeping them so long? How long will they be out? Would they have to eat lunch first? I couldn't wait for them to finish lunch and start their deliberations. It was cruel to make me wait. If they only knew how I suffered, how low my pain threshold was, if they only knew what a coward I really was, they would, from compassion, hurry their decision.

I could bear it no longer. I called a friend, Billy Asbel.

"Hey, Billy, I'm waitin' for a jury. Want ta go take a drive in the country? Let's go see if we can find us a horse to buy. Need a new horse at the ranch."

"Sure, Gerry," Billy said. We drove out into the barren countryside of Casper, Wyoming, just a couple of men, an old friend and me looking for a horse, and I thought the passing of the miles and the open spaces and the smell of the crisp winter air would soothe my soul and maybe I could escape my misery. And when I came back, maybe it would be all right. I called the Clerk of the Court from a pay phone at a roadside filling station an hour later. The jury had returned its verdict.

33

AGNEDA STOOD alone by the casket lined in baby
blue satin. The lid of the casket, also in baby blue, was
higher than her head. Her face was stony, and without
tears, and her skin looked as dry as prairie grass. She
didn't stand there long, and she said nothing. Then she
turned away and walked out, and Elma and the others
followed.

Pam, who was Joe's last woman, stayed back, and when
the others were gone the black-suited mortician gave
Pam one of his warmest smiles and walked up close to
her. He handed her a brown paper sack with some of
Joe's things in it, his wristwatch, a silver good luck piece
Pam had given him, his billfold with seven dollars and a
picture of his kids and his Social Security card.

"Thought you were the one who should have these,"
he said, and he made his eyes look kind and he gave her
another good look.

"Thanks," Pam said. "I brought along this other ring of
his," she said, handing the mortician a gold-looking ring
with a snake's head on it. "I'd rather have this on his
finger."

"No trouble," the mortician said. He picked up the
limp hand, which looked too small for the man, and
slipped the sapphire ring off and then he slid the snake's
head ring back up the same finger, and it went on too
easy, as if it were a size too large. Then the hand fell

obediently into place, and the fingers moved by themselves into their same relaxed-looking way.

"Here ya go," the mortician said, and he walked over close to Pam again, handed her the ring, and gave her another smile.

"Thanks," Pam said.

"Would you like to be alone a little while with your loved one?"

Pam stood at the casket, and she didn't cry either, until later. Then without answering the mortician, she turned and walked out of the mortuary, carrying the brown paper bag.

I didn't say much to Raymond Whitaker when he called to tell me that Joe Esquibel was dead. Maybe he thought I didn't care, but nothing came to mind to say and I felt empty, and like I said, I also felt afraid. I walked up the creek, up old North Fork, and where the tangle along the edge of the water was too thick to pass through I parted the bushes with my hands and pushed my head through first, and sometimes the spider webs between the bushes stuck to my face.

A man ought to be a willow, I thought, grow a little each year, appreciate the creek running by, the good sounds, and then be useful, fodder for the moose in the winter, but in the spring new fingers would pop out, green and tender at the ends, and the soft silver puffs that cause us to call them pussy willows would burst out all around the branches and turn magically into leaves. A man could do worse than come back in the spring as a pussy willow, I thought, trying not to think.

They shouldn't fill a man's flesh with poison when he's dead so as to hinder his return to the earth. It would be good to just be buried under a clump of willows. The place for the burying should be dug carefully; push the roots aside, gently, so as not to injure them, and don't dig the hole too deep—not six feet deep because willow roots are shallow—dig it a little past the waist of a tall man, and put him in a plain box of good pine boards, and don't worry about the knot holes, or about the moisture seeping in. Willows are mostly water, and man, too, not dust, and it is by way of water that a man can slip in fast and easy into willow roots.

They should bury a man in a soft pair of Levi's, and maybe a cotton flannel shirt, or just wrap him in an old blanket, but get him into the ground fast. And the whole family should take part if possible, like a picnic up Little Goose Canyon, weather permitting. My boys are carpenters, I thought. They could easily make the pine box, and then everybody could dig and sweat a little in the hole, and share each other's joy in helping a man who needs help in getting back to where he came from; and when the grave is filled up again, and the willow roots spread out over the pine box, nice and easy, and with love, and the good earth is packed around the roots, then the people could talk to each other, and they could be aware of their lives together, and they would know that life in the presence of death is beautiful. Maybe they would read some poetry by the man, an easy poem without sorrow, and let the sound of the words give comfort, and peace, and after the poem, if they listened, they might hear the distant song of the hermit thrush that gives a voice to the quaking aspens, and if they are silent longer there would be the song of the yellow warbler and there would also be the irreverent squawking of young magpies from the lower branches of a cottonwood tree. And when it was time to leave, the family and friends could leave together, and they would be happy knowing that next spring there would be new green willow shoots, and the branches would bloom their silver pussy buds, and in the winter there would be new fodder for the moose.

I wove my way through the thick willows out to the dusty trail, and I followed the trail upstream to the headgate in a fork of the creek where the water flowed out of the main channel into the irrigation ditch. I took off my boots and pants, and waded out into the water barefooted, and the water felt icy, melted as it was from the glacier ice above, and my feet looked white and bloodless. I shoved some more rocks up against the flow of the creek and stuffed some old burlap sacks in below the rocks, and pretty soon I had a good head of water flowing down the ditch, and then I followed the little stream down, and the year's first head of water washed out last year's collection of old leaves, and the twigs went floating by, and then I saw some moose droppings floating in the ditch, little dark gray objects smaller than a sparrow's egg, and I let the water out on the thirsty midsummer roots in the brown meadow, and I became God to the meadow grasses, and I knew that living was all right.

I wondered how Oscar Hall and I could be friends, but even now we were. He used to say, "A lawyer's duty doesn't have to interfere with his friendship, and vice versa." Old Oscar said he liked being a prosecutor. I never could understand why, but he said he felt like he was "making a contribution," that's how he put it. "Ward off the mob with law and order," he said. "If it weren't for the cold reason of the bar and the bench, well, God help us. And the prosecutor has got to stand on his own convictions and not worry about the next election," but I knew Oscar worried just like the rest of us did.

"Let's face it, Gerry," Oscar said to me one day, a couple of months after Joe died, when I was passing through Rawlins and stopped at Adam's Restaurant for a cup of coffee. "Joe lived in a jungle. He was an animal," Oscar said.

"Yeah," I said. "But this doesn't look like much of a jungle." Nothing much green growing there, I thought, just the dusty street going by the Esquibel shack, and the old shanties next door, and the muddy ruts in the springtime, and no willows, a scraggly tree here and there and a half-dead lilac bush in the front yard, the blooms gone to seed and dirt for lawns, and a piece of paper blowing by in the hot wind of a Rawlins summer.

"He lived in a jungle," Oscar said. "All he knew was how to fight. As a kid he never went to bed with a full stomach. Even a wild animal was better off than Joe Esquibel." Oscar looked off in the distance.

"Let's have one more cup of coffee before I have to go," I said to Oscar.

"Sure," he said. "We start kickin' 'em around when

they're just little boys, and we never stop kickin' 'em,"
Oscar said, raising his cup for another sip.

"That was my speech in three trials, Oscar," I said.

"Well, I know," Oscar said. "You were right. Everybody knew that—that is, so far as your thinkin' went."

"Yeah, how's that?"

"Well, a man's gotta be practical. You know that. A
man's gotta solve the present problem, and Joe was a
present problem. Troublemaker. The local Mexican stud.
The rest of the people have rights, too, ya know."

"Well . . ." I began.

"Well, let's not argue about it anymore. The case is
closed, thank God."

"Yeah," I said, and put down my empty cup. I was
feeling empty, too. I started to get up to leave, but Oscar
wanted to talk some more.

"How'd you hear about Joe's death, Gerry?" He motioned to the waitress.

"I was out on the porch where you and I talked once
about your boy's death. Remember? And Raymond
Whitaker called."

"Oh," he said, and he looked sad again, and he was
quiet for a while, and he sipped away at the hot cup.

"Raymond told me he was shot by some bartender."

"Shot in the head," Oscar said, coming back. "Shot
just like he shot Sharon."

"Yeah," I said.

"Strange irony. He got it back, the same way he gave
it."

"Yeah," I said. "You can never beat the rap on the big
one."

"What?" Oscar said.

"Oh," I said, "it's like old Tom Fagan says, 'Ya can
never beat the rap on murder one!'"

"You beat it," Oscar said. "The jury turned him loose."

"Yeah," I said. "But Joe never beat the rap. Gimme
another cup of coffee," I said to the waitress. "I told Joe
never to go back to Rawlins—never."

"He had to go back, Gerry," Oscar said. "A man's
gotta go home." I thought Oscar knew. He couldn't leave

Rawlins himself, or he didn't want to—same thing. "A man's just an animal, and every animal's got his territory," he said. "He had to go back."

I said, "He came in to see me one day after the jury found him not guilty—and after Dr. Karn told the judge he oughta be released from the hospital because he'd recovered. He came in with this Pam and he was so damn proud! 'This is my girl, Mr. Spence,' he said. This Pam didn't say anything. Good-looking woman, too. She was a bartender in Casper at the Townsend, but she acted scared or something. Didn't say anything."

"Oh," Oscar said, "when was this?"

"About a month before he was killed."

"Oh," Oscar said again.

"Joe acted like he was bringing his bride home to meet his father, and that's how I felt about Joe sometimes— like his father."

"Yeah. I can understand that," Oscar said.

"And this Pam didn't say anything at all. Sat in the far end of my office like she was tryin' to hide. Maybe she just wanted it to be Joe's moment. I don't know. Joe said she helped him get well. 'Love makes ya get well, Mr. Spence,' he told me, and he said he loved this woman. And the woman hardly smiled back when Joe said that, and she still didn't say anything at all, and he kept sayin' that if it wasn't for her he'd still be up in Evanston, and he seemed so happy. Told me how he'd sneak out with her all the time, and how he got caught and they threw him into Johnson Hall for it, and he was laughing, but I could remember how he used to cry over getting a red card. He said, 'Love causes a lot of trouble, Mr. Spence, but love can cure ya from bein' crazy.' And I said, 'Yeah, Joe. That's right. Love cured me, too.'"

"Well, his love life sure cost Carbon County a lot of money," Oscar said, being the practical prosecutor that he was.

"And anyway," I went on with my story, "Joe thought it was funny that this woman sat through his trial and nobody but the two of them knew it."

"Well," Oscar said, looking at me with a serious face. "Do you think Joe was really insane?"

"What's insanity?" I asked.

"Oh, for Christ's sake," he said. "Let's not go through that again." Then he laughed. "No," he said, "what do ya really think?"

Finally I said, "I don't know. What *is* insanity? I know one thing though."

"What's that?"

"It all came out all right, like it was supposed to under the law."

"Why?" Oscar asked, ready to argue again.

"There was a reasonable doubt, wasn't there?"

"Well, you might say that," Oscar said as if he hadn't conceded a point.

"I guess the system worked," I said.

"Maybe Joe was just too smart for all of us. Those wild animals are pretty cagey, and Joe Esquibel was just a wild animal," Oscar said.

"Maybe he was always crazy. They say the insane are pretty cagey, too, have a certain superior intelligence—one we don't understand. And I have a theory anyway," I said. "I don't think people really change very much."

Once a skitz always a skitz.

"Oh, I think we change," Oscar said. "You've changed."

"How's that?" I asked.

"I don't know. You've grown up or somethin'. Some people grow and some don't. You seem more like a person. Used to be a terrible smartass," Oscar said, and then he added quickly, "but I always did like ya."

"Thanks, Oscar," I said. "But maybe it's you who's changed."

"Nah," he said back, "I've never changed."

"Well, anyway, I kept tellin' Joe never to go back to Rawlins, but when he was in the office to see me he was so crazy-happy I don't think he really ever heard me, and I told him that more than once. And when I asked him what he'd been doin' he said nothin', that he'd just fought in some smoker—in some bar. They needed a heavy-

weight to fill the card and he took the fight on ten minutes' notice and knocked the guy out the first round.
Some white guy, Joe said, but he admitted he wasn't
working. Said he was going to be a carpet layer. And I
told him to stay out of the bars. And Joe said, 'Well, I
changed, Mr. Spence. I just have a beer or two. That's
all.' And I told him, 'Joe, you haven't changed. People
don't change the way they can tolerate booze. That's
what you used to do—have a beer or two, and Elma told
me that a beer or two would set you off and you'd lose
your memory. Might have something to do with bringing
on epilepsy,' but he wouldn't pay any attention to me. It
was like he didn't hear me at all, or if he heard me he
knew something I didn't know that he wasn't going to tell
me. I said, 'Joe, you don't change epilepsy. You don't
change all the blows you've had to the head. You can't
change any of that . . . You're who you are. You don't
change.' But he acted like he didn't hear me. He was too
happy to hear."

Oscar said, "A man only hears what he wants to hear."

"Yeah," I said. "And then I gave him a real preachin'
to. I said, 'Joe, you're in love, right?' And Joe says, 'Yes,'
and I says, 'Joe, love saved me, too. Imaging saved me
just like Pam here saved you, and Joe, maybe love does
cure insanity.' And I could tell he heard that. And then I
said, 'But if a man is saved, he's gotta change or he really
isn't saved at all.' And then I told him how Imaging and I
had quit drinkin' the day we got married and how we
hadn't had a drink since because we wanted to change,
and then I told Joe I loved him, and I wanted him to
change, too."

"Some can and some can't," Oscar said. "I don't see
how he could quit drinking with her being a bartender
and all, but one thing I can say, and that is that Joe
Esquibel never changed."

"Maybe not," I said. "Couple weeks after his death
Pam came in to see me by herself. She asked me if I
remembered her and I told her sure, she was Joe's girl
friend, and she said yeah, and she wanted me to help her
get her stuff back, and I asked her what stuff, and then

she told me that after Joe got out of Evanston she bought him a car, and a new motorcycle, and a lot of other things, but Joe's family wouldn't give 'em back to her now that he was dead. Belonged to her, she said. Not them. They didn't buy the stuff. She did, and she was mad as hell. I told her if she gave it to him then title was in his name when he died and she'd have to deal with the administrator of his estate, and then she really did get mad. She said, 'Well, I got the goddamned ring anyway. His family went together and bought him that sapphire ring when he was in the state hospital,' she said, 'and I at least got that. They were crying about him being buried with the ring on. But I got it!' she said."

"She musta made a lot of money," Oscar said.

"I don't know," I said. "She told me she gave him everything he wanted, like a little boy—gave him his toys —the car, the motorcycle. She told me, 'He didn't trust anybody. Didn't trust women, especially. So I put all the stuff in his name and I put his name on my checking account, too, so I could teach him to trust me, but I don't think he ever did.'

"She said he couldn't find a job, and he was a proud man, and felt ashamed having to live off her, and she said he almost drove her crazy. She'd be working at night and he'd stay down at the bar while she worked, and if anybody made the least little pass at her, well, he'd want to fight 'em. Watched her all the time and wanted her to stay at home, and he'd keep watching her. He damn near drove her crazy. Wouldn't let her out of his sight."

"Oh," Oscar said. "Sounds familiar."

"She said he was jealous as hell."

"Yeah, that sounds right," Oscar said.

"And she said one time he saw a white guy touch her on the shoulder and the guy hardly did anything more than that, and Joe went wild, and got mean, and they fought—she actually physically fought with him and he beat her up. Blacked both her eyes once and bruised her all over."

"He was like that," Oscar said. "He was an animal. He never changed."

I said, "I'll bet I could tell you the whole story without even hearing any more. She said she kicked him out more than once, and then she said he would come back and beg her and plead and whine like a little pup."

"He was a little pup inside that got kicked around a lot," Oscar said again. "You can't change the little pup in a man."

"She said Joe was an animal, more animal than man, but down inside he was warm and honest and real. That's what Sharon used to say about him, too. He treated her like he treated Sharon," I said.

"Maybe she treated him like Sharon treated him, too," Oscar said.

I said, "Well, he tried. But he couldn't change."

"Maybe he didn't want to change," Oscar said.

"She told me that one time he took a fourteen-year-old girl with him. 'He warned me!' she admitted. She said Joe told her if she kicked him out he'd have to go to another woman."

"History repeating itself," Oscar said. The wheel turning over and over.

"She said, 'Jesus, a fourteen-year old! She was a little blond thing.' Pam told me the girl rode over to Rawlins with him on the back of his motorcycle. And when they got back the girl called Pam up and said she wanted to talk to her—just like that. And the girl told Pam how wonderful her fourteen years had been and how crazy Joe was about her, and how she just drove him wild. Then Pam told Joe to get his ass out and that he couldn't come back, and then he started calling her again and he'd say his brother was in trouble, or anything else to get her sympathy. Then Pam would tell him they didn't have a goddamned thing to talk about, and if he kept it up she'd call the cops, but he'd plead and beg and make promises. She said by the time he was killed she figured it was about over. 'I loved him,' she told me, 'and I felt sorry for him. He needed me. I was smarter than he was. But sometimes I wondered. Maybe he was smarter than I thought.'"

"Did she tell you whether he ever talked about his killing Sharon?" Oscar asked.

"She said he never talked about it. She said she didn't think he remembered anything. One of the patients at Evanston told her Joe had an airlock around that part of his life and didn't remember anything. She said sometimes she thought he was crazy and sometimes not. Depended. But he was crazy jealous. She could say that much."

"Well, that doesn't meet the test for insanity," Oscar said.

"Yeah, but we've already argued that for seven years, Oscar. This Pam told me she thought if she had stayed with him much longer he would have killed her for sure. She said she'd kicked him out and one night she decided to go out and get drunk. She said he followed her everywhere she went. She and a girl friend were going to go to the Cozy Club—place down on the Sand Bar."

"Yeah, I heard of it," Oscar said.

"And she said she got to the parking lot and he drove up behind her, and she ran back to her car and locked the door. She said she didn't think he'd do anything to her with her girl friend there."

"Why not?" Oscar said. "He killed Sharon in front of eight eyewitnesses."

"Well, he didn't bother her that night. He changed that much. But she said if they'd gone on much longer he probably would have done her in."

"People like that don't change," Oscar said.

"Well, I grant you that you can't change all the pictures a person sees in his mind's eye like seeing the same home movie over and over," I said.

The white asses, pounding.

"Well, I gotta go, Oscar. Come see me sometime." My cup was empty again.

"Yeah," Oscar said. "Been nice. I'm prosecuting the guy that shot Joe."

"Yeah, I know," I said. "Good luck." I meant it. Now I wanted justice.

A couple of months later I saw Pam again. I was over

in the Townsend Coffee Shop having coffee when she came in. She walked up to my booth and sat down.

"I haven't got my car and motorcycle back yet. But I got a lawyer workin' on it," she said.

"Well, good luck," I said. Pam wanted justice, she said. "The trial on that white guy that killed Joe is coming up."

"Yeah, I know," I said. She looked better than the last time, and she blew smoke toward the ceiling and sucked on the cigarette like the two of them belonged together.

"The white guy killed Joe in front of a lot of people, ya know—down there at the VFW Club in Rawlins. Place was full a Mexicans. That white guy, name's Joe Roach. Didn't have any business goin' over there in the first place."

"I know," I said.

"He heard Joe was looking for him, so he went lookin' for Joe, is how I got it."

"That's a little crazy, I'd say, knowin' Joe."

"Well, after he shot Joe his lawyer pleaded him not guilty by reason of insanity."

"You gotta be kiddin'," I said.

"No, that's what his lawyer did, all right. Hired old Bob Bates to defend him. Gonna go to trial first of the month."

"For Christ's sake. Bates?"

"Yeah, Bates," she said. The wheel kept turning. "You know this guy Roach killed Joe's cousin—Floyd Montoya —Christmas night in '73. Fight about some girl or something. The jury let Roach off of that one. Self-defense. Joe couldn't forget it. Floyd was like a brother to Joe, he kept telling me, and sometimes when Joe had a beer or two he'd get mixed up and call Floyd Montoya, Timato, and he'd get to crying, and then he'd say he was gonna get Joe Roach for killing his brother. Joe told everybody he was gonna get Roach. County hired a bodyguard for Roach for a while he was so scared. But Roach got to drinkin' that night and decided to go lookin' for Joe himself. I tried to keep Joe from goin' over to Rawlins, but I couldn't. He went over there all the time."

"How come Roach shot Floyd Montoya?"

"I don't know," she said. "Roach managed the Silver Spur Bar. Floyd beat on him once before, I think, and there was some girl there. They said Floyd was bothering the girl, but Roach was afraid, so he got the gun. It was closin' time. Floyd was walkin' after Roach—right on top the bar, and Roach fired two warnin' shots, but Floyd kept on comin'. He shot Floyd in the heart is how I got it. But this Roach is big, bigger'n you—weighed 250 pounds, they say. Never saw him myself, and Floyd was just an average-sized kid. Joe said that Roach gettin' off with self-defense was bullshit. Said them white guys always got off with self-defense in Rawlins for killin' Mexicans, and he just kept tellin' everybody he was gonna get Roach for killin' Floyd, but Roach got Joe first," she said, and looked down at her hands and the tears started to come to her eyes. "I really loved him, I guess," she said. "Can't get over 'em."

"How did it happen?" I asked, not really wanting to know.

"I wasn't there," she said, lighting up another cigarette. "But the guy over there was." She pointed to Orville, who was sitting in another booth across the room. He was also smoking a cigarette. "Ya could ask him." She started to weep quietly, and Orville was looking over at us, and then she looked up and saw him and motioned him over. "This is Mr. Spence, Joe's lawyer. He wants to know what happened." Orville was a skinny, nondescript fellow with a lot of hair. Looked like a sixties' hippie. His eyes were vacant. "Orville saw Joe killed," she said again. "Go ahead and tell 'em, Orville."

"You tell 'em. I already tol' you once," Orville said, and then he grinned at me like he was apologizing, and he started right in without any more prompting. The both of them sat there looking almost like twins if you saw them from a distance, both with long straight hair and both of them puffing away, and the smoke coming up like the booth was on fire.

"Well, I seen the son-of-a-bitch shoot old Joe," he said the way a good storyteller begins. "Seen 'em shoot 'em plain as I'm lookin' at ya." He sucked on his cigarette again and watched the smoke go up, and then he flicked the ash and looked over at me.

"Want a cup a coffee?" I asked.

"Yeah," he said. He was warming up, and Pam was still crying softly into her lap. The old green plastic seats in the booth were sticky, and there were adhesive tape patches here and there covering up past cuts in the upholstery. I looked at Pam. Pam's upper body shook with her silent sobs. "We was at the dance and we was all standin' out on the porch lookin' at Joe's motorcycle and coolin' off, me and Joe and some others, and there was this kid by the name a Charlie standin' out there, too, and he was 'bout to leave. Christ, it was quarter ta three in the mornin', and this kid did leave, I guess, and he meets old Joe Roach comin'. And the kid tol' old Roach he better not go up there, on account a Joe Esquibel was there, but that didn't seem to make no difference to 'em." Orville looked over at Pam, who had quit crying now. "Jesus Christ," he said. "Imagine the guy goin' right on up there with Joe Esquibel standin' there. I wouldn't get near old Joe if he was lookin' for me, but the guy had a gun in his pocket, and a gun is brave, and he come on up to old Joe." Orville kept looking at Pam, who was wiping her eyes and blowing her nose into a paper napkin, and he gave her a weak little smile. Then he put a serious look back on his face and went on.

"Old Joe seen 'em comin', and he locks his eyes on 'em and he never said a fuckin' word to me or nobody else. Just got his eyes locked on 'em and he hands his drink to this other kid who was standing there, and Joe still don't say nothin', and about that time Roach got up to where Joe was standin'. And old Joe just takes one step forward and lets fly with a right up alongside a Roach's head, and his knees buckle, and then I heard this little pop, kinda like a little firecracker, and I could see a gun in Roach's hand. Then Joe grabs Roach an' the two of 'em falls backwards with Roach underneath, and Joe is holding onto Roach, and then I hear another little pop. That was the second one," Orville said. "And they fell onta the front end of a 1959 Chev sittin' there, and about that time

I seen the gun comin' up again to Joe's head for the third shot. Third time's the charm," Orville said, and smiled again, and then he looked over at Pam, realizing he shouldn't have said that, and he got serious. "I seen the gun coming up to Joe's temple, and I says, 'Oh, shit,' and I drops my glass and I leaps through the air when I heard the third shot go off, and Joe just falls to the ground on one side of the car, and old Roach falls off the hood a the Chev on the other side, and Roach was laying there on the ground panting, exhausted like, and I grabbed the pistol off of 'em and I turned it on 'em and that's when old Roach kept sayin', 'No. No.' He could see I was gonna shoot 'em. I pulled the trigger and nothin' happened. Just went click-like. I figured the gun was empty, and that's why it didn't go off, but the police told me later there was three shots in it, and the one in the chamber misfired.

"I went over and picked up old Joe's head and held his head on my lap and I was feelin' for a pulse in his neck. And I held him till the ambulance come. He was alive before they put 'em in the ambulance." Orville looked around to see if anybody was listening. "Then them Mexicans started kickin' old Roach, and they kicked him, and they just kept kickin' 'em. Most of 'em were friends a Joe's like me, and they just kept on a-kickin' like they been needin' ta kick somebody for a hundred years, and they kicked until old Roach's pants were down below his ass, and it looked like his head was kicked in on the side and ol' Roach's eyes were popping out, and they kicked at him like he was a damn soggy sack a ol' potatoes, and they kicked till they was all kicked out, and he wasn't nothin' but two hundred fifty pounds a blubber. Ya could hear them kicks. I quit lookin'. Made me sick. But ya could still hear 'em. Thud. Thud," he said. And I could hear the dying flesh giving back its own thick sounds. "Gimme 'nother cup a coffee," Orville said, like he needed the stimulus. "I seen the hole in Joe's head and it looked like his brains was oozin' out."

Pam was crying again, but Orville didn't see it. "When they put him in the ambulance old Joe was staring up at me, and he had that shit-eatin' grin on his face. His heart stopped and I gave him mouth to mouth, and I beat on his chest but he was dead. D.O.A.," he said, like he was used to the lingo of the police. "Patched him up pretty good." Orville looked over at Pam with a guilty look.

"Did you tell the police that Joe hit Roach first?"

"Hell, no," he said. "Why should I? The sucker pled not guilty by reason of insanity. 'Magine that!" he said. "Claims he can't remember nothin'."

"Jesus Christ," I whispered to myself. Full turn of the wheel.

"Course, he probably can't 'member with all the kickin' he got. Lucky ta be alive I'd say. In the hospital hell of a long time. All kinds of internal injuries and damage to his head and everythin' else," he said.

"Well, you oughta tell the police or the county attorney what you saw."

"I ain't tellin' 'em nothin'," Orville said, looking over at Pam as if he were being a true friend. "Nothin'! The son-of-a-bitch can fry for all I care. Hope he does."

"But, Orville," I said, thinking out loud, "he might have a defense of self-defense. Under the law . . ."

"Fuck the law, Spence," he said. "Pardon me. But that's how I feel about 'er. I ain't talkin'."

Then Orville leaned forward, trying to protect Pam from what he was going to say. He whispered, "He had that same shit-eatin' grin on his face at the funeral. They must not a been able to get it off."

But Pam had heard, and it was then that Pam first told me about the funeral, and the casket lined in baby blue satin, which was too small, and the old man's suit and all the rest.

I didn't know what to do with the facts Orville gave me. He might be able to provide Joe Roach with a defense all right—self-defense, a toe-hold to freedom for the man. But I didn't know what I should do. I was angry at Roach. And then as I was leaving, Pam reached into her purse and handed me a piece of paper. It was a Xerox copy of a poem in Joe's handwriting. I thanked her and put it in my pocket.

I didn't want the facts Orville gave me. Wished I'd never heard them. I wanted justice. I wanted Joe Roach convicted.

In the morning I talked to Imaging in bed during coffee, but I didn't want to talk about what Orville told me. Instead I picked up the copy of Joe's poem Pam had given me. I read it to Imaging.

TWENTY-SEVENTH BIRTHDAY

Having just gone through the year myself
I know that twenty-seven can be hard.
But there are Sunday breakfasts
And April fields
And blue on blue
And green growing things to change that all.

I know that spring is hard
Because you wait for summer.
And fall is the hardest of them all
Because you must not be alone
When winter comes.

I know love is worth the time
It takes to find.
Think of that
When all the world seems made
Of walk-up rooms
And hands in empty pockets.

I know your smile
And it is much too warm to waste
On people in the street
Though smiles are plentiful.
I know that if you keep the empty heart
Alive a little longer
Love will come.
It always does.
Maybe just at the last moment.
But it will come.

You must believe that
Or else
There isn't any reason to be twenty-seven.

"It's beautiful," Imaging said. "That's a wonderful poem. I hardly believe that's Joe's poem, though. My God. That's somethin' else," she said. "There's your crazy person. There's your demented Mexican."

"It was in his address book, in his own handwriting," I said. "I don't think he wrote it either. Probably copied it some place, but Pam said he did—said he wrote it about his own twenty-seventh birthday. Here." I handed the poem to Imaging. It was written in the hand of a man not used to writing, in careful straight letters. Then I told Imaging about what Orville said. "Honey, the guy told me that whole story in confidence," I said. "It could save old Roach."

"Well," Imaging said. "A confidence is a confidence. You have to respect that."

"I know," I said. "But he didn't speak to me as his lawyer. I wasn't representing him. There was no confidential relationship between us."

"Well, maybe not legally—is that what you mean?"

"Yeah," I said.

"Well, but Orville didn't know that. He wouldn't have told you if he thought you were going to tell anybody else. He trusted you."

"I know," I said. "And I think Roach deserves being convicted. He killed Joe—went lookin' for him—had the gun. He knew what he was doin'. Damn it. It isn't right."

"Maybe you know now how Mrs. Murphy felt and all the rest of 'em, too."

"Well, yeah, I suppose so," I said. "And I feel used— like I've been wasted. I spent seven years of my life workin' to save ol' Joe."

"I know, honey," she said, and she sounded like she understood me. "But now you know how Mrs. Murphy felt. She spent a lifetime raising Sharon. It's all such a terrible waste. And it doesn't look like the wasting is over yet." Imaging was thinking about the trial of Joe Roach.

"Well, I hope they get 'em," I said, "and they will if Orville doesn't tell his story."

"Are you just going to let it happen?" Imaging asked.

"Well, I ought to." Imaging didn't say anything, and then she got out of bed to get me another cup of coffee. I yelled to her as she left the bedroom, "What about justice? What about justice, goddamn it!" And then Imaging came back with two fresh cups of coffee.

"What's justice?" she said, and then she answered her own question. "Justice depends on whose ox is being gored."

"Yeah," I said. "But Roach shouldn't get away with it. That's two he's killed. Both Mexicans. Justice is justice," I said, as if everybody should know what it means, as if it defined itself.

"Well," she said. "Don't you believe in the jury system? Don't you think you ought to leave it to a jury?"

"I guess," I said. The hostile Casper wind was blowing already, and the old spruce trees in the front yard moved with the wind and were creaking and groaning. That's all they did, creak and groan. The trees had lived longer than I had, and seen more Casper winds than I'd seen, and all they did was creak and groan. But someday the wind would fell the trees.

"The wind in the trees and the trees in the wind are justice," I said.

"What do you mean? That doesn't make sense," Imaging said. She was a practical woman.

"I guess not," I said.

"And how can a jury decide the man's case if it doesn't have all the facts? You always say, 'Tell it all to the jury. Tell the truth to the jury. Trust the jury.' Remember?" she asked, and she looked at me with love in her eyes.

"Yeah," I said.

"Justice isn't what any one person wants. Justice is what a jury says after it has all the facts. I've heard that speech from you a lota times," Imaging said. "It's the system."

"Yeah, the system," I said.

"And how would you like it if the jury convicted Roach

without knowing all the facts? How would you feel?" I looked at her. She was picking at her long eyelashes like she does when she is thinking hard, and I didn't want to think about Joe Roach anymore. I felt the springtime inside of me, like a man should feel sometimes when he's close to the woman he loves, and I saw the sagebrush buttercup that comes popping up in early April and affirms that beneath the old rotten layers of winter snow there is new good life. I loved her.

"I love you," I said. And she reached over in her gentle way, and touched me, and then she said, "Well, we have to do the right thing." And then I kissed her on the cheek, and then lightly on the ear, and on the cheek lightly again. And then I kissed her on the temple. "We're lucky to have each other." Then I kissed her just above her upper lip, and we held onto each other for a long time and I could feel her warmth coming through and the winter snows melted and left a field of bright-colored spring flowers, the dark pink of the wild geraniums, and the tall light blue lupine, foxglove, some called it, and the darker blue bluebells, and the deep blue crocus, and the yellow bells, too, and winter was gone in Little Goose Canyon.

"I gotta call Oscar, and tell him, and I better call Bob Bates, too," I said, and as I held onto Imaging, I knew that Joe was right, that love does cure insanity, and I knew that Oscar was right, too, that some can change, and some can't, and as I held onto Imaging, and she held me back, I realized that my demons were gone, as if they had melted away with old snows, and I also knew that Joe Esquibel had finally been released of his demons, too.

I reached over to the telephone next to the bed and called Oscar Hall.

"Well, Gerry, I don't believe it," Oscar said. That was a cold-blooded murder if I ever heard of one. It wasn't self-defense. That's for damn sure. Won't be justice for him to get off with self-defense.

"Well, Oscar, the wheel made a full turn."

"What's that?" Oscar asked.

"Nothin'," I said.

"Wish we could get this thing buried once and for all," Oscar said. "I'm gettin' tired of this case. I wasn't put on this earth just to prosecute the Joe Esquibel cases. Oughta bury this goddamned case once and for all." Imaging moved closer to me and laid her head down on my shoulder. "But Joe Esquibel was buried the day he was born," Oscar said.

And later I called Bob Bates, too, told him what Orville said. The judge postponed the trial, and the flowers of spring seeded in the late summer, and then one day after Imaging and I sat in the quaking aspens at the ranch listening quietly to the song of the hermit thrush, I got a call from Raymond Whitaker. He wanted to know what I was doing.

"Listening to the birds with Imaging," I said. "I'm writing a poem . . ."

"I know," he interrupted. "Someday you'll be a great poet."

I waited for him to tell me why he'd called, and finally I heard him clear his throat, and I knew he was ready to tell me. "Did you hear what happened in the Joe Roach case?"

"No," I said. "What happened?"

"Well, the jury turned him loose. Self-defense, Gerald," he said. "Self-defense," and I heard a little sardonic laugh, but I wasn't sure it was Raymond Whitaker who was laughing.

Epilogue

THE SURVIVING members of the Esquibel family have taken solid places in the community, as is surely their right. Agneda, sixty, is a custodian at Rawlins High School—cleans the same halls Sharon used to walk as a bright, bouncy girl. Agneda says, "Maybe it is jus' old age creepin' up on me, but it is hard to go to work sometimes. I feel it in my bones." She's been there four years, and in two more years she can retire—Social Security. She rents a small house from Uncle Casey near the place where the Esquibel children were raised. Carpet on the floors—TV, nice furniture, and she keeps it clean as a whistle. The old shack is gone now—torn down—just a vacant lot next to where Uncle Casey has his home, and Uncle Casey owns the lot. Agneda says she sold it to get money to help Joe all those years.

Agneda owns a camper-trailer and a pickup truck to pull it. That is what she likes to do in the summertime, she says, to go camping. "I like to take Donna," Agneda's middle girl, "and her baby, and Johnny," her youngest son, "and Johnny's two kids and Lorinde, his wife—like ta take 'em all campin' in them mountains," she said, looking off to the distance toward Saratoga. Donna and her baby live with Agneda.

Johnny, the youngest Esquibel boy, is an operator at the Sinclair Refinery out of Rawlins a little way. Johnny and Lorinde own their own new house in a new part of Rawlins, south of the tracks, about a quarter of a mile from the old Esquibel place. Johnny is a damn good man, solid citizen, they say.

And Elma and her husband, Frank Fisher, still live in Salt Lake. They own their own home, too, and have two girls, nineteen and twenty-two, one a switchboard supervisor at the YWCA, and the other is in beauty school. Frank has eighteen years' seniority at the Union Pacific as a pipe fitter foreman.

JoAnn, Agneda's youngest, will soon graduate from the Salt Lake City Police Academy. Elma said, "We are all so proud of her. We never thought any of us would get to be somethin' like that," and then Elma said to me, "And when you come to Salt Lake, you'll come over to our house and I will cook you Mexican food," and I said I would come, and Elma said, "I can cook Mexican food almost as good as Mama, and you will come, won't you?" And I promised I would come.

Joe's son, Little Joe they call him, looks just like Joe, is at Draper, Utah, in the Utah State Prison—armed robbery, which he says he didn't do. Elma says he didn't do it either. "He was framed," Elma said. She said they had the witnesses to prove he didn't do it. "I had them witnesses," she said. And Agneda said Little Joe had changed. "He's changed, Mr. Spence. Little Joe, he say, 'Grandma, when I get out I'm gonna come home and take care a you.'"

And I said, "Agneda, do you believe him?"

And she said, "Yeah." And then Agneda's face got soft as any grandma's face, as soft as her voice, and she said, "Yeah, I believe him, Mr. Spence."

Gerry Spence, America's greatest trial lawyer, has never avoided tough cases or difficult issues. No comments and opinions of any attorney in America are more respected than those of Gerry Spence.

But here, off-camera, uncensored and with his passions on fire, he exposes a frightening inventory of government misconduct as he discovered it in his defense of white separatist Randy Weaver, and he tells us the lessons we may learn from that tragic case. Spence exposes the biased court system, the new corporate and governmental tyranny, and the hidden role of the censored media, as well as foreseeing the gravest threat to a free America—our apathy and our fear.

FROM FREEDOM TO SLAVERY

GERRY SPENCE